# Between past and fu

## the Roma of Central and Eastern Europe

# Between past and future

## the Roma of Central and Eastern Europe

edited by

WILL GUY

UNIVERSITY OF HERTFORDSHIRE PRESS

First published in 2001 in Great Britain by
University of Hertfordshire Press
Learning and Information Services
College Lane, Hatfield
Hertfordshire, AL10 9AB

A catalogue record for this book is available from the British Library.

ISBN 1 902806 07 7 paperback
ISBN 1 902806 17 4 casebound

Design by Geoff Green, at Geoff Green Book Design, Cambridge CB4 5RA.
Cover design by John Robertshaw, Harpenden AL5 2TB
Printed in Great Britain by J. W. Arrowsmith Ltd., Bristol BS3 2NT

*Cover: Young Roma, East Slovakia, 1971*
This image was the cover picture of Race Today, March 1972. This issue included an
article by Davidová and Guy, which quoted internal Czechoslovak government
documents admitting that restrictions on the freedom of movement of Roma were
unconstitutional and that local authorities were breaching ministry directives in refusing
to register Roma migrant workers as permanent residents. Similar local authority practice
was reported in the 1990s in both the Czech Republic and Slovakia
Photographer: Eva Davidová

*Inset (upper):* Hristo Kyuchukov, IRU Secretary General-elect, moderates the election
proceedings, Fifth World Romani Congress, Prague, July 2000. Security guard (left) of
Radio Free Europe, which provided the congress venue. Photographer: Will Guy.
*Inset (lower):* Emil Ščuka, IRU President-elect, addresses the Fifth World Romani Congress,
Prague, July 2000. Photograph: ERRC

*Back cover: Will Guy at roundtable on Romani migration*, Prague, November 2000. Photographer:
Dagmar Havranková, Institute of Ethnology, Academy of Sciences of the Czech Republic.

*Frontispiece: Last Roma in Pejá, Kosovo.*
Here Roma were driven out and their homes set on fire by former neighbours
– ethnic Albanians. Photographer: Rolf Bauerdick

# Contents

# Foreword

*Ian Hancock*

In the 1780s, a group of Romani musicians arrived in Vienna, the capital of the Austro-Hungarian Empire, but were stopped by a soldier who demanded: 'How in God's name did you dare to come here? You know that Gypsies aren't allowed to frequent this place!' They replied: 'But we aren't Gypsies! The King has made *'Uj Magyar'* (New Hungarians) of us now!' (Anon. 1787). At the same time that Romanies had been stripped of their identity in this way in Austro-Hungary, they were likewise being turned into *'Nuevos Castilianos'* (New Castilians) in Spain, following a royal decree of 1783. Indeed, over a century earlier, King Philip IV of Spain had declared that there was no such thing as Gypsies because there existed no country of that name. In the twentieth century, on the other hand, the Nazis saw us very much to be a real people and, as such, a threat to their own 'racial purity' – to the extent of attempting to exterminate not only those identified as Romani but even those who resembled Romanies.

Romani identity, indeed the very right to exist at all, has been in the hands of non-Romanies at so many times and in so many places. Thirty years ago, Cohn articulated this when he wrote that 'the Gypsies persist because they, or groups like them, are needed in our culture' (Cohn 1973: 61). Notwithstanding this need, ignorance about Romanies is still widespread and profound. Despite the massive amount of literature that exists on our people (the Romani Archives contains tens of thousands of books, articles and documents on the topic, and the libraries in Liverpool, Boston, Leeds, Moscow, Paris and Vienna similarly contain extensive collections), and while the Indian origins of our language and culture became public knowledge well over two hundred years ago, enquiries such as the following continue to be made. As recently as April 2001, the Archives was asked: 'I was wondering if you had any information about Roma, and how to become one. Any information would be appreciated' (Romani Archives 2001).

The first section of this collection of essays is entitled 'A truly European people', and the question of identity is addressed in the first contribution.

Can a people be 'truly European' if Europeans don't recognise them as such? Are Romanies in the Americas – amounting to perhaps a third of the entire world Romani population – also 'true Europeans' despite where they live? What does 'European' mean? It is not an ethnicity or a race; one doesn't need to have a country to qualify; but it is geographical, and it is a state of mind. As the single largest transterritorial ethnic minority in Europe, and as a population which has only really existed west of India, the claim to being 'truly European' has some merit, but we have a considerable way to go before this status becomes more than just something idealised on paper. My own research is also leading towards some revisions in the matter of identity. While the Indian roots are both demonstrable and undeniable, there is reason to believe that our Romani language, and a good part of our core culture, only crystallised once the migration westwards had reached Anatolia, which it seems to have done in less than fifty years after leaving India. There, in Anatolia, influence from Greek and (subsequently) other Balkan languages helped shape the Romani language. It is also apparent that our ancestors were not a single, pre-existing population in India, but were assembled from various linguistic groups which only came together outside of India proper – a pattern which has continued to perpetuate itself. From this perspective, Romani identity is a western phenomenon, albeit one with early and significant Asian roots. Yet this is important to know about, for it gives us a history and a legitimacy as a people.

Perhaps because some Romani representatives have voiced a desire to return to the pre-1989 Communist period – a matter of obvious concern to the democratic West – to the time when there was a measure of protection from anti-gypsyism and more employment, and perhaps because of the horror stories reaching the rest of the world of the terrible violence now being directed at the Romani minorities, the past decade has seen a radical change in the quantity and quality of publications dealing with Romanies and a sharp increase in the awareness of the Romani presence in Central and Eastern Europe. In our language, this part of the continent is known as *'Kali Oropa'* (Black Europe), as opposed to the name for Western Europe, *'Parni Oropa'* (White Europe), clear reflection of the fact that the East is where the greatest concentration of Romanies is to be found. With the re-emergence of ethnic nationalism – suppressed but not eradicated during the four decades of Communism – and the resulting claims for nation states, Romanies have become the ultimate intruders and a prime target for ethnic cleansing. Romanies have been denied the right to be anywhere because, as King Philip said, we weren't a people since we didn't have a country.

These developments have presented a dilemma of gigantic proportions. Here are several million people, located throughout every country in Europe and in some places constituting ten per cent or more of the population – but at the same time a people alienated for centuries for a complex variety of reasons, some internal (such as culture and language) and some external (such as governmental legislation). Yet, for the most part, these people everywhere occupy the lowest position in terms of education, employment, housing and health care. Attempts to deny us our identity haven't worked. Attempts to isolate or physically remove us haven't worked. Attempts to exterminate us haven't worked. The only solution, then, must be to reach a compromise between the Romani and the non-Romani populations, and to learn to co-exist. There is no conceivable alternative.

I have written many times, and repeat yet again, that a proper understanding of the contemporary situation of Romanies can only be reached in the context of history; to know why present-day conditions exist, they must be acknowledged as being at the end of the centuries-old continuum of the Romani experience following their initial westward migration. The social and historical factors that have brought Romanies in Europe to the appalling situation they face today must be properly understood before that situation can be addressed and confronted. This anthology of essays, written by some of the leading researchers in the field, is the latest – and in my opinion quite the most thorough – in a small but growing number of modern works that are attempting to do that.

*Between Past and Future* will serve as a work of reference for the policy-making as well as the academic specialist for years to come. It presents a variety of opinions and interpretations that, together, bring the reality of the Romani situation into sharp focus, and will serve as a basic educational tool for Romanies as well as non-Romanies – for certainly both must know more. With the other titles available from the University of Hertfordshire Press, it adds to a growing number of publications on Romani issues essential to any serious Romani library.

Ian Hancock
*Romani Archives and Documentation Center*
*April 2001*

## References

Anon. (1787) News item, *Magyar Kurir* no. 3,781, Budapest.
Cohn, W. (1983) *The Gypsies*, Reading: Addison-Wesley Publishing Co.
Romani Archives (2001) E-mail enquiry, *The Romani Archives*, 2 April.

# Acknowledgements

*Will Guy*

Countless people have been involved with this volume in various ways. Although conceived only two and a half years ago, the book draws on years of collective experience and demanding research. For some contributors this extends to a lifetime's work. Along with my fellow authors, I wish to thank all those who have given information, assistance, encouragement and sustenance. Foremost are our Romani friends, whose tolerance, good humour and resilience despite often difficult circumstances are a constant source of inspiration. This help is especially appreciated since the field of Romani Studies is usually undervalued and marginalised in the academic world – as indeed are the people we seek to celebrate and defend in the real world.

Twenty people are listed as contributors but to their number should be added the publisher, Bill Forster, who fully shares the passion and commitment of his authors and who has done so much to draw the Romani people to the attention of a wider audience. The labour involved in editing such a large collection would not have been possible without his eager participation and unflagging help.

On a personal level I should like to thank those who have encouraged me both in my initial Romani studies and more recently. These include my close friend and co-researcher, Eva Davidová, as well as Mick Lineton and Michael Banton, while Thomas Acton, Angus Fraser, Ian Hancock, Donald Kenrick, Judith Okely, Grattan Puxon and Michael Stewart have long been a valued resource. I am grateful to all the contributors for their patience and positive support and in addition to Bella Edgington, Laura Laubeová and Peter Vermeersch for their help. I owe a particular debt to Martin Kovats, whose reassurance, insights and critical scrutiny have been invaluable. For the striking images I have to thank all those who generously responded to our appeal and whose names appear beside their photographs.

Friends in the Czech Republic and Slovakia are numerous and include Eva Davidová and Jan Kočnar, Jan and Betka Harničar, Mary and Nigel Hawker, Pavla and Radim Rybka, Otilie Starostová, and Ludvík and Milena

Šereda, who have all provided generous hospitality and convivial company. My thanks and apologies to the many others I have been unable to mention by name.

Finally, and especially strongly felt, I must thank my children, their partners and my grandchildren, as well as my wider family and friends from whom, even if physically present, I have been almost completely absent 'in a bubble' for at least the past six months. Most of all I am deeply grateful to Jackie West who has been unfailingly supportive.

Will Guy
*April 2001*

# Introduction

*Will Guy*

T he appearance of this book is prompted by concern for the Romani
people of Central and Eastern Europe whose long history of tribulation
shows little sign of ending. The contributors from various countries are a
group of leading non-Roma and Roma researchers with active and continuing involvement in the events they write about – often over a period of many
years. Their main aim is to present – for non-Roma and Roma alike – a
stimulating collection of rich resources and at times provocative views for
policy makers, administrators, journalists, politicians, researchers and the
general public in the hope that this will inform debates about this complex
and emotive area. Ultimately this might help lead to more pragmatic and
realistic policies to aid the integration of the Roma – the largest, poorest and
most marginalised minority in Europe.

At the heart of the collection, comprising Part Two, is the first comprehensive account of the Fifth World Romani Congress, held in Prague in the
summer of 2000, which was probably the most significant event in Romani
politics since the ending of Communist rule. Preceding this, chapters in Part
One address thematic issues from a theoretical perspective although solidly
based on factual evidence, while the country-by-country chapters in Part
Three provide accounts of the differentiated experience of particular states –
so necessary in counteracting the practice of vague generalisation about 'the
Roma'. This final section should demonstrate conclusively the wide diversity
of circumstances – not just between countries but within them – and if the
collection achieves no more than making people aware of this variety and its
significance, it will have provided an invaluable service. In the process Part
Three makes a broad geographical sweep from north to south, ending in the
Balkans where Roma have been longest established in Europe.

The title of the book attempts to express something of the agonising disorientation that has overwhelmed the Roma of Central and Eastern Europe
since they emerged little more than a decade ago from virtual obscurity into a
new, harsh world and the glare of the international media. Formerly regarded
as an obscure and mysterious people, the preserve of a handful of folklorists

and scholars, their plight now commands the attention of feature writers, human rights groups, national governments and international organisations. The situation and treatment of Roma have even become key conditions for the eventual entry of their home countries into a European Union intent on expanding eastwards.

For all this new interest, the estimated five million Roma of Central and Eastern Europe still represent the overwhelming bulk of the continent's largest and most excluded minority. They are present in every country yet remain on the margins of society without a nation state to defend them as they suffer the sharp pain of racist assaults and the more grinding pressures of material deprivation and daily humiliation. Some experienced worse as the former Yugoslavia disintegrated amidst bloodshed. Many Roma, crushed in these ways and seeing little prospect of improvement either for themselves or their children, migrated westwards. Whether driven by ethnic cleansing or attracted by tales of freer and more tolerant Western societies, they travelled in the hope of a sympathetic reception. However, the Western states, which had earlier condemned the human rights abuses perpetrated against Roma, were quick to brand the very same victims as 'economic migrants' and send the refugees home when confronted with them on their doorsteps as asylum seekers. Chapter six of this book analyses the hypocrisy at the heart of discourses about migrants and citizenship.

In the process of ejecting the refugees both politicians and media have often reverted to hostile stereotypes, not entirely from malice and political expediency but also from ignorance, for in truth little has been known in the West about these new arrivals. When a European expert's report on Roma laboured under the delusion that this desperate flight was some resurgence of ancestral nomadism, how were others in the West to know that the vast majority of Roma refugees had been settled for centuries and were no more 'nomads' than they were themselves?

A significant problem in resolving the predicament of Roma is indeed one of ignorance about these people but the remedy cannot be dispensed in the form of a simple story. For the Roma, flung in a diaspora across Europe and beyond, always had to adapt to a wide range of local conditions in order to survive in the role of subordinate outsiders. Consequently they have become a richly diverse or even multicultural people – pursuing different occupations, speaking a mixture of languages and playing every kind of wonderful music imaginable.

The varying situations in which they lived gave rise to a plethora of identities, which are reflected in the different group and sub-group names they have adopted over time. This re-creation of identities is an on-going process as is made evident from the second chapter of this book, which provides an illuminating historical and ethnographic background for what follows. Following current usage this collection has mostly adopted the umbrella name 'Roma' to try to encompass this diversity but, as used nowadays, this term carries the implication of a political project. By no means would all those written about accept this name and likewise some contributors adopt other formulations. With hindsight 'Romani people' (or peoples) would perhaps have been preferable.

However, this difficulty over a generic name does highlight one of the main dangers of the increasing volume of formal reports on the Roma, for bureaucratic pressures encourage officials to oversimplify the complexities of Romani identity and experience by homogenising them. In this way misconceptions like 'nomadic refugees' arise – perhaps with disastrous results for all concerned. This book should prove a salutary corrective to such conceptual short-cuts with its thorough and patient research. The need is only too evident as chapter five on the emergence of European Roma policy reveals an apparent and disturbing deterioration in comprehension in expert European reports that should be informing and guiding policy-making rather than spreading mystification. The fear is that generalised policies might be devised which could prove inappropriate and damaging in particular circumstances. Here the case is strongly argued for a country-specific approach, grounded in experience.

A central focus of this collection is the bitter experience of Roma in the years following the ending of Communist rule. The initial promise of democratic freedoms and the satisfaction at the long-awaited recognition of their ethnic identity soon turned sour. Instead, they were left exposed – to the ruthless logic of a fledgling market economy in which they were made redundant, to the moral vacuum of a legal interregnum in which they were left defenceless against an upsurge of murderous racism and to democratically-elected governments which were uninterested in a constituency without electoral power. Not everywhere were conditions so extreme and some Roma took advantage of increased freedom of travel and entrepreneurial activity to prosper. How these years were differentially experienced throughout the region is explored and analysed, country-by-country, in chapters nine to eighteen of Part Three.

Although it might seem otherwise from media reports only a small proportion of Roma have fled the hostile conditions of the new post-Communist world. The great majority stayed at home and some of these organised politically to resist the forces that were threatening their communities. This mobilisation occurred at local, national and international level and also among those who migrated. The theoretical context and potential aims of such activity are examined in a chapter three by two leading contributors to a continuing debate.

At the same time pro-Roma non-governmental organisations attracted recruits from the majority society and offered support to Roma, often gaining funding from international charities and later from the EU, through programmes like PHARE. Roma, too, created their own organisations, including Romani women's groups. Human rights NGOs drew attention to violations of basic freedoms, while others promoted social, educational and cultural activities. However, the growth of what amounted to an NGO sector, including both Roma and non-Roma, with disparate access to funding and often with better-paid jobs than were available locally, created its own problems as is discussed in chapter seven.

The struggle to win adequate Roma representation in the national parliaments of Central and Eastern Europe during the 1990s was largely unsuccessful, apart from a few initial gains. However this failure was mitigated to some extent by the growing political influence of Romani activists at supranational level. Foremost among Roma organisations attempting to gather support across national boundaries was the International Romani Union, arising from the first World Romani Congress in 1971, which by 1979 had already achieved some recognition by the United Nations. The Fifth World Romani Congress, held in Prague in the summer of 2000, came at a crucial time in the development of Roma politics and was marked by the claim for full yet non-territorial nationhood for the Romani people. In view of its importance a complete section of the book (chapter eight) is devoted to a full and unique account of this historic congress, containing vivid ethnographic narrative as well as analysis, by two of the participants – one of whom had also been present at that very first congress. However, before engaging in politics many Roma had turned to the organised religion of the region where they lived, both as a solace and also as a means of seeking at least partial integration in wider society. More recently the Pentecostal church has attracted growing support as is attested in chapters fifteen and sixteen. This phenomenon is also present among Roma in Western Europe.

Although attention in this collection is primarily concentrated on the post-Communist period it is important to appreciate that a vital and unifying feature of the experience of Roma discussed here is that they have emerged from over forty years of Communist rule. Most researchers and activists are in agreement that on balance, in spite of many disadvantages, this period was more beneficial for Roma than either what preceded it or came after. In the same way that the incredible diversity of the Romani people is often oversimplified out of all recognition, so too is the crucial period of state socialism.

Communism is often seen as a colossal steamroller crushing Romani identity ruthlessly and yet, paradoxically and also grudgingly, it is admitted to have somehow improved the situation of most Roma. Most frequently it is blamed by successor regimes for almost all the current problems experienced by Roma, much as the Communist ideologues before them blamed everything on 'previous social orders'. Yet, examined in more detail, the monolithic face of Roma policy under Communism fragments in multiple ways. For not only did states within the region pursue different and even contradictory nationwide policies at various times but there are usually significant disparities between how these policies were articulated, at state and ministerial level, and how they were implemented – or circumvented – at local level.

Given the broad acceptance that the economic and social circumstances of Roma did markedly improve during the decades of state socialism, it is therefore important to re-examine the lessons of those years. This should be undertaken in a far more discerning and scholarly way than simply to dismiss all Communist policy as deformity of democracy. This decisive experience needs to be recaptured and re-evaluated if we, Roma included, are to make progress in devising practical ways of enabling Roma and non-Roma to live together as equals. This is all the more essential given the subsequent dismal record in this field of the professed liberal democracies of the region.

For this reason, therefore, chapters one and four in Part One critically examine policy practice in the post-Communist and Communist periods, probing a number of troubling and still unresolved issues. Both here and elsewhere divergent evaluations of the Communist period by contributors provide much useful material for further, much-needed discussion. Meanwhile country chapters in Part Three do not limit themselves to the relatively short period following the revolutions of 1989-91. They also look back, not just to the important years under Communist Party rule, but still beyond to the underlying historical experience that moulded both Roma consciousness and that of their more powerful gadje (non-Roma) neighbours.

This collection is driven by a spirit of urgency that is evident in the desire to place this considerable body of evidence before others as soon as possible. Although contributors may share similar opinions on some topics, they undoubtedly diverge on others – and of course take individual responsibility for their own published views. However, rather than thrash out such disagreements in private or refine their academic positions over time, participants in this project are eager to present their ideas as contributions to a continuing public debate in the belief that the start of the new millennium will be a decisive period for Roma.

Negotiations over the approaching enlargement of the European Union offer a rare opportunity and unique 'window' when political interest has focused on what is usually a neglected backwater in the scheme of what is regarded as important on the world stage. If this moment is allowed to slip the consequences could indeed be critical and lead to a new and even darker period in the already grim history of the Romani people. In the view of two of the most perceptive Romani intellectuals:

> There is no question that the Roma of the end of the twentieth century and the beginning of the twenty-first are in the most uncertain period of their European history.
>
> (Andrzej Mirga and Nicolae Gheorghe 1997)

# PART ONE

# 'A truly European people': Themes and issues

## CHAPTER ONE

# Romani identity and post-Communist policy

*Will Guy*

*We don't have to worry about the government; they're fine.*
*But public opinion – that's the problem.*
(Emil Ščuka [Czech Roma leader] 1997)[1]

**T**he following frank assessment summarised the shared bewilderment of participants at a 1992 meeting of government officials from Central and Eastern Europe (CEE) with Roma leaders when confronted with the scale of the problems facing them.

> [T]he contentiousness that was so often evident [at the meeting] came to seem not so much a conflict between two clearly identifiable 'sides' [government officials and Roma leaders] as a reflection of a collective inability to grapple with a set of social problems so complex and contradictory as to defy any foreseeable prospect of solution.

(PER 1992: 1)

A decade later it is still doubtful whether any real progress has been made in improving the situation of the region's Roma. This is in spite of a steep escalation of interest on the part of Western governments, the European Union (EU) and supranational organisations, prompted partly by recurring reports of human rights violations but more acutely by highly publicised waves of Roma refugees seeking asylum in the West.

The exodus of refugees reached its peak precisely at the point when the EU had begun entry negotiations with neighbouring countries to the East. These formerly Communist states are home to the bulk of the continent's Roma population and their incorporation into the EU carries the potential of further westward migration of Roma – but this time as EU citizens with rights to freedom of movement.

Although Roma asylum seekers are almost universally dismissed by Western governments as economic migrants, research studies reveal that their predominant motivations stem from the sharp deterioration in their social relations with other groups within society. In a review of such studies Matras lists specific reasons,[2] amounting to a '[l]ack of confidence in the social structure and institutions of their countries ... and a consequent loose attachment to those countries' (Matras 2000: 35–9). In other words recent intensification in their social exclusion has unsurprisingly led to correspondingly weaker identification of Roma with homelands that reject them.

The long-established deprivation and exclusion of Roma from mainstream society over their many years of residence in CEE countries is still very evident and is well documented, as is the way Roma are often regarded in CEE countries as pariahs or even a sub-human species. Opinion polls regularly report that significant proportions of the general public support the physical segregation of Roma from 'normal' people, advocating what amounts to apartheid as a solution. Such exceptionally hostile perceptions are based on the popular belief that Roma are not just ethnically distinct from other groups but in a special category of their own. This is mirrored by the Romani view of all non-Roma as gadje.[3]

This chapter looks once more at the roots of this persisting and peculiarly denigratory view of Roma in the light of their historical experience and relates recent discussion of ethnic and social aspects of Romani identity to post-Communist policy orientation. Here it is maintained that underlying the negative stereotypes the dominant aspect of Romani identity is social rather than ethnic, in spite of the well-founded claims of Roma to be considered as ethnically distinct. If this argument is valid then the implications are profound for any attempted solution aimed at reducing the social exclusion of Roma in the region, requiring urgent prioritisation of effective, concrete measures to accelerate their social integration.

To consider identity in terms of 'ethnic' and 'social' aspects is by no means to accept a '"primordialist" theory of ethnicity' (Hobsbawm 1992: 24), where ethnicity is regarded as some immutable 'given' rather than the consequence of a social process and transactional in nature (Barth 1969). Nor is it to see these aspects as necessarily dichotomised opposites for population groups in human society have overlapping social and ethnic dimensions. However, both Communist and post-Communist policies have been articulated in these terms and can even be contrasted in this way. Whereas the Communists 'insisted that the 'Gypsy question was a social question, ... [now] ... for a series of more or less cynically calculated foreign policy objectives, official policy has been reversed and Roma issues tend to be ethnicised by the governing [post-Communist] parties' (Stewart 2001).

Indeed, policy to tackle Roma-related issues has developed in a reciprocal relationship with the shifting and growing ethnic status of Roma over past decades – from non-existent, via ethnic and national minority, to what is now affirmed as full nationhood. Romani activists have mobilised on this basis, following the familiar path of nationalism – both in the region and beyond. Meanwhile, CEE states have increasingly tended to concede such claims – perhaps in a spirit of democracy but also in the belief that acceptance costs little and might prove politically beneficial.

Therefore it is crucial, particularly now, to reflect on contemporary policy formulation and to query to what extent 'ethnicisation' is a substitute for tackling social issues. Policies on multiculturalism, minority rights and equality of opportunity are undoubtedly essential to a solution, as is effective legislation against discrimination. Yet, by themselves, these are unlikely to alter the social situation of Roma, or fundamentally change the way other people see them, if Roma remain without the employment, education and accommodation that many of them crave.[4]

## The social construction of Romani identity[5]

The continuity running through Roma experience during their long centuries as Europeans is the persecution and discrimination they have suffered. This has deeply affected not just how they are seen by others but, in a defensive reaction, their own perception of themselves (Gheorghe and Acton 1994: 20, Mirga and Gheorghe 1997: 4, PER 1992: 8). But how they were treated and viewed has never been an unvaried given and needs to be understood in the context of specific socio-economic and historical circumstances (Guy 1975: 202–3). Identity is not static but something that is constantly shaped and reconstructed.

Likewise Romani 'culture' as such, understood in a broad sense, is not a unique and isolated entity, in spite of characteristic elements, but rather arises out of and is a response to the nature of the symbiotic relationship between Roma and the wider majority communities on which they have always depended for their livelihood.[6]

> Always immersed in other cultures, Romani life has been characterised by ongoing adjustment and adaptation to a changing environment.
>
> (Mirga and Gheorghe 1997: 12)

Acton made the same point when he 'hypothesised a direct economic causal influence on some [Romani] cultural or social change', arguing that the context of the wider economy structures the ways in which Roma are able to make a living, thus exerting 'a powerful effect on every area of ... [Romani] life, including the social relations with the host community' (Acton 1974: 246–7).

In his perceptive analysis of the roots of Romani identity, Nicolae Gheorghe, a leading Roma theoretician and sociologist, recognised the significance of Roma labour power and the inter-group relations involved in its utilisation as a crucial factor in defining the nature of Romani identity. This

5

was most evident in the Romanian principalities[7] where for three centuries Roma were seen as 'an important resource which had to be put under a harsh dependency in order to be used/exploited' (Gheorghe 1997: 159). For there, until the mid nineteenth century, Roma 'were slaves in the full technical sense of the word [and] treated like chattel property in the jural codes of the Romanian principalities' and it was this enforced subordination that determined their identity. Indeed, to such an extent that 'Tsigane [Gypsy] in the Romanian language was equivalent with *rób* which might be translated as "slave"' (Gheorghe 1997: 158).

> So it was a social identity, much more than an ethnic cultural identity, marking ... an inferior social position, a legal segregation between Gypsies and non-Gypsies and between Gypsies belonging to different owners. So the fragmentation of the Gypsy population was reinforced by the legal treatment of them as property, starting from the Middle Ages.
>
> (Gheorghe 1997: 158–9)

A comparable argument was offered by Allen in suggesting that the contested concept of 'race' sprang directly from the social identity of slaves in the southern United States[8] at a point when previous white bonded labour was replaced by black slaves from Africa, whose different features made them more immediately identifiable as 'other' (Allen 1994).[9] Roma, too, were in general readily distinguishable from the surrounding population by their 'appearance, language and cultural behaviour' (Hancock 1991: 136).

Even though they were not slaves elsewhere in Central and Eastern Europe, Roma nevertheless formed a separate and pariah stratum there and were 'useful and made a contribution' to the host economies where they lived (Gheorghe 1997: 159, Hancock 1988).[10] Mirga and Gheorghe noted the contrasting situation in Western Europe and explained the difference in structural terms.[11]

> To some extent, the development of capitalism in Western Europe helped to develop modern Romani nomadism in the form of 'service nomadism'.[12] By contrast, the persistence of a feudal type of economy in Central and Eastern Europe maintained the need for a large, coerced labour force which took various forms of servitude.
>
> (Mirga and Gheorghe 1997: 5)[13]

An earlier study of Roma in the former Czechoslovakia took a similar approach and had drawn similar conclusions. It, too, suggested that '[p]robably the general differences between "Western" and "Eastern" [Roma] development are related to more fundamental modes of economic development (capitalist industrialisation/feudal ruralism) and related methods of state formation (nation states/multi-national states)' (Guy 1975: 204).

In the [economically developed] Czech lands of Bohemia and Moravia, the development pattern is similar to those of Germany, France and England, where Roma were more usually seen as useless pests by the authorities, who ignored them or legislated savagely to expel them and deter new immigration. In these areas the Roma remained largely nomadic.[14]

In [underdeveloped] Slovakia however, which until 1918 was part of the Hungarian lands, the pattern resembles those of the Danube lands and the Balkans, where Roma were often seen as useful and from their first appearance were permitted, encouraged and even forced to settle. They were also taxed by local authorities or the state. It is these countries that have the larger Roma populations.[15]

(Guy 1975: 204)

The underlying difference in determining state policy towards Roma was the structural demands of the host economies in which they lived and the extent and manner in which their labour power was required. Consequently, the development of capitalism in West, where Roma were regarded as 'unproductive vagrants', led to legislation 'to limit their numbers' or expel them, while to the contrary in the East, there were attempts to settle Roma in order to make better use of them.[16]

Thus in some countries of Eastern Europe the need for an extensive labour force led to their incorporation into the local labour market and to the eradication of Romani nomadism – that is their sedentarisation and the creation of large Romani ghettos.

(Mirga and Gheorghe 1997: 5)

At times this 'incorporation' extended to attempts at direct assimilation, as in Austria and Hungary during the latter half of the eighteenth century, but here a problem arises – for if a powerful state required assimilation for economic reasons, why did such policies fail? Evidence shows that in the Habsburg lands, the interests of the rationalising monarchs in raising taxes were in conflict with those of the local lords and communities, required to implement the policies as well as to bear the costs (Horváthová 1964: 123–4). Consequently, state decrees were frustrated at local level by administrative sabotage, a process which the central government proved powerless to prevent (Guy 1975: 209–10, Fraser 1992: 157–8).

Other countries in Central and Eastern Europe varied in their experience, but the fact that Roma were evidently needed by these economies did not protect them, anywhere in the region, from being physically separated and stigmatised. Their position as the very lowest segment of the labour force, often with specialised tasks, was maintained by means of their distinct appearance and by widespread although varying segregation – in employment, in residential location and in most other social situations. This generalised form of 'apartheid' made it possible for the pariah social identity of

7

Roma to be constantly reconfirmed and thus perpetuated.[17]

Predictably, the stereotypical identities of Roma in Western and in Central and Eastern Europe reflect their different socio-economic situations.

> [I]n the Western context 'Gypsies' means nomadic, travelling or migrant, whereas in the Central and Eastern context, the corresponding terms, 'Tsigani' or 'Cigany', imply socially subordinate, impoverished, and marginal groups.
>
> (Mirga and Gheorghe 1997: 5)

Here it is argued that formerly in Central and Eastern Europe the dominant aspects of Romani identity were not ethnic, as is generally believed, but social, and that this social identity derived from the subordinate position of Roma as workers in the wider economy. Experience in Habsburg times suggests that government attempts to mediate social relationships between Roma and majority populations may be frustrated by conflict between the needs of the state and perceived local interests. In such a contest the apparent power of central government may prove insufficient to counteract local resistance.

While these views are based on interpretation of remote historical circumstances, it is remarkable that similar patterns are evident throughout the more recent decades of Communist rule and help explain the mixed experience of Roma during this influential period and beyond.

## Official perspectives of Romani identity: Ethnic to social group and back again

Seismic shifts in Romani experience have always been closely linked with major changes on a broader stage.[18] During the modernising twentieth century the pace of change quickened, producing three such shifts – the Second World War, the long period of Communist rule and the decade or more of 'transition' to liberal democracy and a market economy. All of these involved very differing official perspectives of Romani identity and consequent treatment of them in Central and Eastern Europe.

The creation of new, supposed nation states from the ruins of the Habsburg, Ottoman and Russian empires after the First World War did not fundamentally change the situation or perception of Roma, in spite of their formal recognition as national minorities in several countries.[19] However, the view of them as primarily an ethnic group was taken to its extreme with tragic consequences during the Second World War. The systematic attempt to purge conquered territories of what Nazi pseudo-science classified as racial and social undesirables was an echo of Western European state policy towards Roma four centuries earlier and led to the death of up to half a million of the region's Roma, alongside Jews and other 'misfits'. Because of their obsession with racial purity, the Nazis prioritised the ethnic identity of Roma as an alien people over their social identity as 'asocials', although they were

8

regarded as undesirable on both counts. The blood groups and skull structures of Roma were examined in an attempt to disprove their Aryan origins (Kenrick and Puxon 1972: 60). Should any Roma be inclined to forget their fate in the Holocaust they are still reminded by non-Roma neighbours of what might yet lie in store.[20]

The darkness of attempted extermination was immediately followed by what many Roma hailed as the 'dawn' – a complete reversal of their fortunes (Lacková 2000: i). In the wake of liberation by the Red Army from Nazi occupation and de facto acceptance by the West of Soviet hegemony over the whole region, a new approach towards Roma gradually emerged in the second major shift in which they were defined as a social as opposed to an ethnic group.[21]

In spite of the theoretical trappings of Marxism-Leninism, this policy resembled that of the Habsburg monarchs two centuries earlier in attempting to assimilate Roma in order to turn them into productive workers. Their experience under Communist rule confirmed once more that the pivot on which their treatment turns is the extent to which Roma are regarded as potential labour power.

The situation of Roma improved not least because an expanding economy replaced the widespread economic depression of the 1930s. During the Communist period the overall structure of the economies of CEE countries shifted decisively in a way that benefited Roma by opening to them new opportunities that had never existed before. The programme of rapid industrialisation at the heart of the Soviet-inspired command economies required an almost unlimited supply of unskilled manual labour to fuel it.[22] Formerly the lowest stratum of backward rural economies, Roma were now in demand as shock-workers in the unrelenting drive to 'build Socialism'. Instead of subsisting as pariahs, eking a precarious living as a dispensable pool of casual labour, they were now full citizens, at least formally, with the potential of entering the mainstream labour force at equal wages to their non-Roma fellow workers. This changed situation affected all Roma, though to very differing degrees, but was most pronounced in former Czechoslovakia, as the most economically developed state in the region. Yet, by a cruel irony, the same political and economic forces that initially offered them hope also trapped them and eventually led to their downfall.

It is often argued that Communism forcibly proletarianised Roma and deprived many artisans of their independence as small-scale producers, by banning their trades as 'parasitic' as well as de-skilling them as craftworkers (PER 1992: 8).[23] Here two points need to be made. Firstly, what are regarded as 'traditional' Roma occupations, the provision of various wares and services, were usually insecure and marginal to the broader economy and were increasingly made redundant by the spread of factory-made goods and mass entertainment, just as had happened in the West. The extent to which such occupations lingered was determined by the pace of general economic change (Mróz 2001). Secondly, even those previously enjoying relative prosperity were nevertheless dependent, often as deferential subordinates in local patron-client relationships. The highly unequal position of Roma, whether as providers of craftwork, services or more general labour, was reflected in the common practice of payment in kind, generally by food, rather than in cash (Hübschmannová 1998: 260).

The point about the unviability of former crafts and services, in the eyes of Roma themselves, is illustrated by events in Czechoslovakia in the early 1970s. When Roma were permitted to form the state socialist equivalent of workers' co-operatives, very few Roma turned to craftwork. Instead, the vast majority opted to set up heavy labouring gangs as a far more profitable way of making a living (Guy 1977: 495–6, Davidová 1995: 206–7).

Critics of Communist policy are sometimes tempted to contrast this period with a rosy picture of the inter-war era as 'live and let live' (Ulč 1969: 429). While accepting that at this time 'trades with the highest prestige among Roma – horse-trading, music and smithing – were also valued by the host populations' (PER 1992: 8), it should not be forgotten that for the majority of Roma the 1920s and 1930s were years of deprivation and discrimination. The reality of the former social situation of Roma is best illustrated in a 1930s pogrom in East Slovakia, where villagers burned down the nearby Roma settlement. This was not for the usual reason – in retaliation for crop thefts – but simply because Roma musicians had declined to provide a band for the local Slovak firemen's ball. Here, skilled and 'valued' musicians had to be reminded forcefully of their lowly place in society and punished as 'uppity niggers' for their presumption (Kollárová 1992: 64).

Those who appeared least likely to benefit from the economic and political transformation of CEE countries under Communism were the relatively small numbers of nomads. However, some managed to maintain an advantageous economic niche in more rural economies and even prospered in the early years of Communism – such as horse-dealers in Poland. Later, when their travelling was abruptly terminated following the wave of legislation in the late 1950s, many eventually turned to other means of livelihood – mainly dealing in valuables or goods in short supply (Mróz 2001).

In the experience of most Roma, however, the Communist era was a period of increasing 'proletarianisation' and in spite of continuing discrimination they were able to benefit from regular wages to improve their social situation, by building new and better houses and sending their children to school. For the first time in history[24] larger numbers of Roma had the opportunity to achieve some sort of limited integration into wider society, although not without costs, even for those who experienced the greatest advances in their standard of living.

As the majority of Roma became employed, to some degree families also became socially and economically secure. The result was the creation of a Romani proletariat as a distinct segment of the 'working class'.

(Mirga and Gheorghe 1997: 6)

Both encouraged and coerced by the Communist Party, a few Roma took the bold step of pushing for further education and qualifications, at least for their children, which eventually resulted in the growth of an influential Roma intelligentsia. While relatively tiny this is significantly larger than any equivalent stratum among Roma in the West and from its ranks was to emerge a new type of Roma leadership (Gheorghe 1997: 157–8).[25]

However, as in Habsburg times, the price to be paid for admittance to full citizenship in state socialist society was often the enforced abandonment of Romani identity, although by less drastic means. Marxist-Leninist theorists argued that Roma did not even represent an ethnic group[26] but to some extent the prevalent classification of them as a social group reflected a more generalised attempt to curtail any expression of ethnic minority identity within Communist states.[27, 28] All aspects of their culture, without exception, were regarded negatively as relics from the past and as obstacles to their successful integration into wider society. As a result, many of those who took advantage of opportunities for social mobility sought to disguise their origins. During that period 'their main strategy was of masking themselves, being assimilated as Romanians or Czechs or whatever. They hardly spoke the Gypsy language' (Gheorghe 1997: 158). The rationale for assimilation penetrated the self-perceptions of Roma, compounding the psychological damage caused by long-term discrimination, for it strengthened feelings of inferiority and self-hatred (Guy 1975: 223–4, PER 1992: 8).

Although official exhortations were issued that Roma should be embraced as fellow workers and citizens, quite contrary messages were conveyed in practice. These alleged that Romani culture was entirely worthless, having been destroyed beyond redemption by previous social orders. Such accounts only served to reinforce continuing popular beliefs that Roma were less than human. Gadje memories of wretched and impoverished Roma were deep rooted, particularly in the countryside, and examples could always be found to confirm negative stereotypes. Local officials shared the views of their non-Roma constituents and connived with them to maintain barriers against social integration, especially in perpetuating residential and educational segregation (Mirga and Gheorghe 1997: 6). In Czechoslovakia, an ambitious, nation-wide programme to speed up Roma assimilation by dispersing them among non-Roma was frustrated by local authority opposition and had to be abandoned (Guy 1975: 219–20). While some frank internal documents mentioned prejudice and discrimination against Roma, these were exceptional and no anti-racist campaigns were undertaken. Like other crimes such as prostitution, drug addiction and grand larceny, racial discrimination simply could not be admitted to exist in states that aspired to be a socialist paradise.

The main policy approaches applied to Roma were contradictory and ultimately self-defeating. While Communist rule had the effect of strengthening the social identity of Roma through their increased integration into the general labour force, it simultaneously endeavoured to destroy their ethnic identity by denying its existence in the vain hope that Roma would somehow dissolve into wider society. Unrealisable, coercive assimilation policies made social integration of Roma all the more difficult.

However, in the last few years of Communist rule, there were signs of an apparent relaxation in the official view of Romani ethnic identity as first Yugoslavia recognised Roma as a national minority and then Hungary, in 1986, acknowledged them as a cultural group. Even in the hard-line Czechoslovak regime federal ministry officials moved some way towards the Hungarian position in the late 1980s.

In the Hungarian case at least, there are grounds for suspecting that this change in direction was not motivated entirely by altruism. Roma were hardly a high priority at the best of times and in a troubled period of economic stagnation public resentment at substantial state funding for this despised people would have been even stronger. A pragmatic assessment indicated that the massive resources required to achieve the previous policy goal of socio-economic equalisation for Roma would be unavailable for the foreseeable future (Kovats 2001b).

Rather than hailing the Hungarian decision as unequivocally liberal, it could also be seen as cynical acceptance by the state that material equalisation for Roma was unrealisable; in its place a far cheaper alternative was 'the promotion of "difference"' (Kovats 2001b). Hitherto, Communist rule had meant some strengthening of Romani social identity at the expense of their ethnic identity. From this point onwards the emphasis was soon to be completely reversed.

By this shift the Communist regime in Hungary pioneered what was to become the most common approach adopted by successor post-Communist governments during the 1990s, not only in Hungary but throughout the region. Acknowledging the ethnic identity of Roma carried few risks and would incur only minor costs, while effective social integration would require levels of funding commensurate with a major development programme, as well as active legal and administrative intervention. Instead of work opportunities, decent housing and adequate laws to safeguard them against discrimination, Roma could be offered the peripheral trappings of nationhood.

12

## Post-Communist developments – the 'ethnicisation' of policy

The outcomes for Roma of the regime change in individual CEE countries are chronicled at length throughout this volume. In summary, while the moribund assimilation policies of the Communists lapsed, they were replaced by pandemic unemployment and destitution, verbal and physical racist attacks sometimes escalating to murders and pogroms, increasing segregation in education and housing, and widespread health problems aggravated by poverty.[29] In January 2000 the head of the Council of Europe Specialist Group on Roma, Geraldine Verspaget, declared that Roma were now worse off than under Communist rule.

> More Roma – compared with the period before – are without a job, also compared with other parts of the population. More Roma lack education. Many more Roma children, compared with the situation ten years ago, do not go to school. You can compare also the human rights situation with ten years ago. There are many more racist attacks on Roma.
>
> (Verspaget quoted Hill 2000)

A main reason why Roma fared better during the Communist period than afterwards is very clear. Command economies needed unskilled Roma workers; emerging market economies did not. As a result of their usefulness Roma achieved some sort of legitimacy, albeit limited, within state socialist society. Not that this prevented Communist regimes infringing on Roma human rights whenever it was expedient. Nevertheless, Roma did move towards integration and equalisation without provoking a public backlash, partly because they were often seen to be improving their situation by their own labours, partly because any resentment was mostly held in check by the universally repressive atmosphere of Communist rule. As might be expected, centuries of deeply entrenched popular hostility would inevitably take time to dissipate but whenever Roma built new houses with their savings or occasionally qualified as lawyers or doctors their negative stereotype was challenged rather than confirmed.

After 1989 post-Communist economic restructuring, involving the closure of outdated smokestack industries and privatisation of collective farms, soon turned what had been substantial Roma employment levels into almost universal unemployment.[30] Not all such industrial and agricultural workers were shed but Roma were the first to be made redundant and the last to be hired to fill any vacancies, often as a direct effect of institutional discrimination. Such an eventuality had not been unforeseen. The 1979 report of the Czechoslovak dissident group Charter 77 had correctly predicted, a decade before the fall of Communism, that any structural switch to a more developed economy would leave the massive numbers of unskilled Roma labourers superfluous to modern requirements (Guy 1998: 57–8, 2001). And that is precisely what happened. In contrast, a small minority of Roma, such as those who had previously turned to dealing, were able to take advantage of new freedoms to expand into car-dealing, restaurant ownership and other entrepreneurial activities.

As employment levels plummeted, Roma were driven to subsist on whatever state benefits that existed, although many were deemed ineligible, and on child benefits for their families. Many sought work in the black economy at subsistence wages. At the same time crime rates among Roma appeared to rise. These developments were widely reported and when the initial euphoria of revolution swiftly dissipated as economic and political difficulties multiplied, such media coverage fuelled mounting resentment against Roma.[31] This helps explain popular indifference to and tacit approval of the terrifying upsurge of murderous assaults and even pogroms against Roma.[32] In place of reluctant acknowledgement as fellow-workers, Roma were now viewed unequivocally as a drain on limited state resources at a time of acute uncertainty.[33] Consequently, the Roma found themselves cast in their familiar role of scapegoats as structural changes intensified their predicament as 'the poorest, most disadvantaged and despised of all East Europeans' (Barany 1994: 246).[34]

According to the newly adopted ideology of the free market, at least in the variant embraced by most successor regimes in the former Communist CEE countries, it was not the function of government to intervene in order to provide employment (Galbraith 1990). Not that Roma were ever likely to have been a high priority in any job creation schemes as national unemployment rates rose sharply throughout most of the region. Yet, while governments stood aside as the fragile social status of Roma was devastated, there was willingness to offer instead acknowledgement of their ethnic identity. Accordingly, in most CEE states Roma were granted their democratic right to be recognised as an ethnic or national minority. On this basis state support was provided to encourage Romani culture including language.[35] One consequence of this change in status was the inclusion of Roma as a separate category in the national census though, for understandable reasons, most were too wary to identify themselves as such.[36] To be seen as ethnically distinct had its disadvantages, particularly at a time when instability and uncertainty had stimulated nationalist feelings throughout the region (Miroslav Hroch quoted Hobsbawm 1992: 25). Ethnic cleansing took various forms and directly affected Roma, most brutally in the former Yugoslavia but also where new citizenship laws were used in an attempt to expel them as in the Czech Republic, Latvia and Estonia.[37]

During the first half of the 1990s government action to redress the harsh impact of market economy-driven conditions on Roma was negligible and the wry assessment of the situation in Bulgaria was equally valid elsewhere.

In general the Gypsy policy of state institutions and local authorities since 1989 can be summed up as abdication of real political action and, instead, imitation of activity, although the forms taken by this approach differ over the years.

(Marushiakova and Popov 2001b)

Although critical reminders were issued to CEE governments about their inactivity in a series of condemnatory human rights reports, both from domestic non-governmental organisations (NGOs) and supranational organisations, it was not until the second half of the 1990s that the whole matter assumed far greater urgency. Impending negotiations on EU entry would involve periodic reviews of the situation of minorities, including Roma. Meanwhile, the whole issue was thrown into embarrassingly sharp focus by the growing haemorrhage of Roma refugees to the West.

## The involvement of Europe

The European Parliament had recommended that EU member governments should co-ordinate approaches towards their Roma (Gypsy) populations as early as March 1984 (Liégeois and Gheorghe 1995: 22) but policy interest intensified after 1989 with the prospect of European enlargement. The relevant conditions for applicant countries were specified in what are referred to as the Copenhagen Criteria (1993) and the somewhat later *Framework Convention for the Protection of National Minorities* (Council of Europe 1994). The Copenhagen Criteria required candidates for membership to have achieved 'stability of institutions guaranteeing democracy, the rule of law, human rights and respect for minorities' and 'a functioning market economy' (European Commission 1999: 3). The Framework Convention was even more explicit in its demand for 'full and effective equality' for minorities – not just in terms of respecting cultural aspects but also material conditions – requiring that:

[t]he parties undertake to adopt, where necessary, adequate measures in order to promote, in all areas of economic, social, political and cultural life, full and effective equality between persons belonging to a national minority and those belonging to the majority[38]

(Council of Europe 1994, Article 4 §2)

Subsequently a 1997 overview of prospects for enlargement (*Agenda 2000*) reported that in general the integration of minorities was satisfactory 'except for the situation of the Roma minority in a number of applicant[s] [countries], which gives cause for concern'. Those named were 'Bulgaria, the Czech Republic, Hungary, Poland, Romania, and Slovakia', where Roma were reported as suffering 'discrimination and social hardship' (European Commission 1997, 1999: 3).

Two years later in October 1999 the second in a series of Regular Reports on applicants by the European Commission was even more outspoken in its criticism of the slow rate of progress, concluding that:

> deep-rooted prejudice in many of the candidate countries continues to result in discrimination against the Roma in social and economic life. There has been an increasing incidence of racially-motivated violence against the Roma which has not received the unequivocal response from the authorities which it demands. Roma communities suffer unemployment, slum-like living conditions, poor health and education and increasing dependence on social welfare (where it exists). Roma children are segregated in some school systems and many are street children. While there have been encouraging developments in some of the candidate countries with the adoption ... [of] specific programmes aimed at improving the situation of the Roma, a concerted effort is still required to ensure that these programmes are actually implemented.
>
> (European Commission 1999: 4)

Although this was nowhere stated explicitly, refusal to allow one or more of the CEE candidates entry to the EU appeared a distinct possibility in view of the poor progress reported in improving the situation of their Roma citizens. Nevertheless, in this context certain worrying inter-linked questions linger unanswered:

- Desired goals have been defined, but it has never been spelt out how they are to be achieved. It remains problematic, therefore, whether they are realistic and attainable in practice and, if so, over what time-scale.
- It is unclear to what extent candidate states are expected to have complied with the entrance requirements at the point of EU entry.
- If stated goals have not been achieved at the point of entry, will successful entrants, as new EU members, continue to be bound by the requirements that Roma attain freedom from discrimination and socio-economic equalisation?

In their analysis of the application of the Copenhagen Criteria and Framework Convention to CEE candidates with large Roma populations, researchers concluded that these states lacked the resources to achieve socio-economic equalisation of Roma with non-Roma (Braham and Braham 2000: 107).[39] In their view:

> the resolution of the socio-economic disadvantage of the Roma [needs] ... massive long-term funding which, unavailable within candidate states, will be required from the international community, particularly the EC.
>
> (Braham and Braham 2000: 112)

The Brahams were equally sceptical about whether the human rights criterion, including protection from discrimination, could be satisfied quickly, suggesting a time-scale of 'ten years or more, if not a full generation'

(Braham and Braham 2000: 108).[40] In the light of the slow progress reported by the European Commission it would seem that such caution is fully justified and that therefore 'it is unlikely that ... [this] Copenhagen Criterion ... can be fulfilled other than in merely formal terms in the forseeable future, and *certainly not by the time of accession*' (Braham and Braham 2000: 108, emphasis added). The same is equally true of socio-economic equalisation, as spelt out in the Framework Convention, when the state with probably the most developed economy in the region, the Czech Republic, is proposing a time-scale of twenty years (Czech Government 2000).

Since, as seems almost certain, the entry requirements can at best be only partially satisfied for front-runners by the projected entry date – currently around 2005 – what might be the probable implications?

On the one hand, the European Commission has produced critical reports about the situation of Roma and issued warnings like those of the EU chief negotiator on enlargement, Eneko Landaburu, that 'the EU body of rules must not only be adopted by candidates but also seriously applied in real situations' (O'Rourke 2000). On the other hand, EU officials have periodically sent contradictory messages, reassuring candidates that failure to meet the entry criteria, in relation to Roma, should not result in rejection of their applications.

Only a few days before Slovak entry talks began, Jan Marinus Wiersma, official correspondent for the European Parliament's Foreign Committee, played down the issue of human rights when, 'as have other EU officials before him, [he] reiterated the Union's view that the Romanies' problems in Slovakia were economic rather than ethnic. ... "This problem can't be solved in one year," he said' (Domanovsky 2000). The same stance has been evident in the practice of EU governments in rejecting asylum claims of Roma refugees 'from countries like Slovakia and Bulgaria ... because there are no political problems there which would justify this' (Belgian Prime Minister, Guy Verhofstadt, 20 September 1999, quoted Cahn and Vermeersch 2000: 73). Meanwhile, an influential MEP, representing the European Parliament at a 1999 PER-sponsored roundtable on 'state policies towards the Romani communities in the candidate countries to the EU', declared that neither should failure to improve the material conditions of Roma debar applicants from entry:

> [T]he demand is not that all social and economic problems be solved, but that civil and politic rights be achieved. For example, Greece was not necessarily up to standards in the social and economic fields, but in terms of political criteria, it was acceptable for accession.
>
> (PER 1999a: 4)

If EU opinion was confused this was no thanks to an increasing tendency in international reports – including those by EU-supported specialists – to oversimplify, homogenise or ignore the complexity of Roma communities and the issues arising from this diversity (Kovats 2001a). The assertion by Geraldine Verspaget for the Council of Europe's European Committee on Migration that Roma refugees were 'merely a return to the normal mobility of Gypsies' (Verspaget 1995: 13) was so misconceived that it amounted to misinformation (Kovats 2001a).[41] Likewise the cursory treatment of Roma unemployment in three paragraphs in the 175-page report by the High Commissioner on National Minorities (van der Stoel 2000) hardly reflected the vital importance of this issue.[42]

The contradictory positions of EU representatives about the necessary extent of compliance with EU requirements on minority rights for accession are less surprising when it is recognised that they reflect a deep ambivalence on this subject within the Community. EU inconsistency in demanding that CEE applicants respect the rights of their minorities, while remaining virtually silent about those of existing members, has been noted by various scholars (e.g. Amato and Batt 1998). Indeed, because of the conflicting approaches and strongly held views of existing member states, 'the EU has traditionally been reluctant to apply the language of minority rights in its internal agenda' (Vermeersch 2000: 2).[43] While CEE countries were being urged to comply with Framework requirements as a condition of accession, only nine of the fifteen EU members had ratified the Framework Convention by late 2000. This contradiction led the Brahams to fear the removal of Roma minority rights from CEE agendas following their accession.

> [A]s the current members are not bound by the Framework Convention, there will be little reason for the new members to remain so, unless the EU is to be a club with double standards.
>
> (Braham and Braham 2000: 112)

Consequently, there is deep irony in the situation where the supposedly 'liberal "civic nations"' of the West are giving lessons on minority rights to the 'illiberal "ethnic nations"' of the East (Kymlicka 2000: 185). Kürti identifies this 'remaking of European boundaries as an ideological separation of the backward East from the rest' and 'akin to the orientalising project known from colonialism … lending credence to … expansionism' (Kürti 1997: 31). Kymlicka dismisses the contrast between East and West in terms of respect for minority rights as '[t]he myth of ethnocultural neutrality'.

> Virtually all liberal democracies have, at one point or another, attempted to diffuse a single societal culture, namely that of the dominant majority. …
>
> To pursue this aim, liberal democracies have been selectively repressive of ethnocultural diversity, particularly of minority nationalisms, rather than neutral.
>
> (Kymlicka 2000: 185)

Kymlicka reinforces the point with Eriksen's remark that 'majorities and dominant peoples are no less "ethnic" than minorities' (Eriksen 1993: 4).

It is unclear where this hypocrisy, equally evident in Western discourses surrounding Roma refugees,[44] leaves the question of EU entry for CEE candidates. Even if little more than token compliance on Roma integration and minority rights has been achieved by the time of accession, no doubt other factors will be taken into consideration – political and economic factors which may well have overriding importance when set against the condition of an impoverished and powerless minority.

## Ethnogenesis

All previous attempts by the countries of the region to devise policies aimed at managing their Roma populations had been without any participation by Roma themselves. This was not because Roma had not tried to make their voices heard. Indeed, long before the Communist regimes of CEE countries had launched their assaults on the validity of Roma ethnicity, activists had attempted to strengthen Romani ethnic identity by a process of political mobilisation.[45]

Influenced by contemporary nationalist movements of the ethnic majorities amongst whom Roma lived, Romani activism was evident during the late nineteenth and early twentieth centuries, particularly in the long-settled communities of CEE countries. Roma conferences were reported in Germany (1872), Hungary (1879), Bulgaria (1906) and Romania (1934) (Acton 1974: 101, Hancock 1991: 139–40).[46] That such conferences voiced modern demands is evident from the 1906 Bulgarian petition, sent to the national parliament, which demanded equal rights for Roma. A further surge occurred after the Second World War, and Roma eventually attained very limited and sporadic political representation in both Communist and post-Communist periods, although they began to receive international recognition as a group in their own right only in the last quarter of the twentieth century.

In the late 1950s and early 1960s, when assimilationist pressures on Roma in the East were at their strongest, the impetus in building broader Roma organisations passed to the West, but under the leadership of Roma activists who had moved to France from Romania, Poland and Hungary. This new dynamism inspired the foundation of other unprecedented organisations in the West, such as the Gypsy Council in Britain and Nordic Rom Council in Sweden and eventually led to the landmark first World Romani Congress, held in London in 1971 and attended by delegates from fourteen countries. The name Roma was preferred to variants of pejorative terms such as Gypsies, *Zigeuner*, etc., research commissions were established and in confirmation of the overtly nationalist agenda, a flag and anthem were adopted (Liégeois 1994: 258). This was to be the first stage in the long campaign for international recognition of the Romani people.

The second congress, held in Geneva in 1978, established the International Romani Union (IRU), a working committee to carry out agreed policies between congresses, and the following year this organisation was granted observer status at the NGO office of the United Nations (Liégeois 1994: 258). But it was not until after the fall of Communism in 1989 and the fourth congress, held the following year in Warsaw, that Roma began to win wider recognition from international bodies. This started in 1990 with the adoption by participating states in the CSCE Conference on the Human Dimension in Copenhagen of a document in which Roma were included as a national minority.[47] Three years later the Parliamentary Assembly of the Council of Europe adopted a recommendation which emphasised that 'as one of the very few non-territorial minorities in Europe, Gypsies need special protection' and the same year the UN upgraded the consultative status of the IRU (Liégeois and Gheorghe 1995: 23–25).

Roma of Central and Eastern European origin made an important contribution to all of these developments, not only those who had moved to the West but also Roma still living under Communist rule. Some activists derived their power base, as formerly, from extended family structures but during the Communist period this pattern began to alter as a tiny and varied Roma élite emerged in CEE countries. Mirga and Gheorghe characterised this élite as a 'thin strata of Romani intellectuals, party activists, and a middle class, a by-product of the state's coercive educational measures' (Mirga and Gheorghe 1997: 3, 6).[48] This 'small Gypsy bourgeoisie ..., educated and articulate,' corresponded to the segment of society which had led the nineteenth-century nationalist movements of the region (Gheorghe 1997: 157, Hobsbawm 1977: 106–7). However, they were also the product of state socialist education and political culture and fears have been expressed that a 'democratic deficit' not only permeated the original statutes of the IRU but has continued to influence the practice of office-holders to this day (Acton and Klímová 2001).

Gheorghe and Acton (1992) compared recent Roma mobilisation to earlier regional nationalist movements. However, there were also significant differences, not least that of time-scale, for Roma were 'among the last groups in Europe to discover the potential and power of ethnonationalism and to struggle for a political space of their own' (Mirga and Gheorghe 1997: 3). Also, because of the dispersed distribution of Roma – between and within the countries they inhabited – the Zionist goal of the creation of a Romani nation state was far more unrealistic than for their non-Roma predecessors.[49] Partly for this reason Gheorghe argued that the understandable adoption of the eastern European model of nationalism was unhelpful for Roma activists. Likewise, the demand for national minority status for Roma carried an implicit acknowledgement of the legitimacy of claims to 'ownership' of their states by ethnic majorities (Gheorghe 1997: 160).[50] In the meantime, following Liégeois (1976), it was proposed that Roma might be legally acknowledged 'as a transnational or non-territorial minority', a concept without 'secessionist implications' (Gheorghe 1997: 161, Mirga and Gheorghe 1997: 16).

Although Roma activism did not aim at the creation of a nation state, it adopted similar strategies for ethnic mobilisation to those of previous nationalist movements in the region. Within the empires of which they were subjects, embryonic nations had consisted largely of 'subordinate peasant people in a hierarchical society'. Low social rank was their predominant identity and consequently the first stage of 'national revival' was the promotion of an alternative ethnic identity, based on 'the oral culture ... the customs and ways of life of "the folk" – the common people' (Gheorge and Acton 2001, Hobsbawm 1977: 112, 107). Gheorghe termed this shift 'ethnogenesis' and saw this as a widespread regional phenomenon also experienced by Romanians, for whereas Romanian is now regarded as a nationality, 'the *rumain* during earlier historical eras just meant a peasant in an enserfed position' (Gheorghe 1997: 159).

This experience was comparable, though not equivalent, to that of Roma currently seeking to escape from their overwhelming and highly stigmatised social identity. The difference for Roma was that, as a result of their diaspora through Europe and beyond, they formed what could be termed an 'archipelago' of communities, characterised by 'multiculturality and multi-territoriality' (Gheorghe and Acton 2001). Nevertheless, in spite of this diversity, ethnogenesis is a relevant project for Roma, being a process – at least in one sense – whereby:

> a social group, previously occupying a despised and inferior position, mov[es] ...
> from this position to some kind of respectability with a sort of equality with
> other social groups in the hierarchy of social stratification on the basis of a
> revised perception of their identity.
>
> (Gheorghe 1997: 158)

However, the problem remains how the process of ethnogenesis, 'by which a social identity is transformed into a cultural, ethnic identity', can result in meaningful social equality for Roma with others. Led by an emerging bourgeoisie, a key element of the standard nationalist project to achieve a nation state was to secure access to and control of the economy of the territory bounded by that state. For many, therefore, their new ethnic identity was far more than an assertion of cultural values but an important bridgehead on the road to improved employment possibilities and upward social mobility. In this light, the traditional path of advancement for Roma appeared unachievable and therefore new conceptual and political strategies were required.

The concept of 'transnational or non-territorial minority' and the claim by the Fifth World Romani Congress for recognition of Roma as 'a full nation without territory' represent variants of such a fresh approach.[51] By raising the ethnic status of Roma from minority to nation, with its own parliament, the IRU aims to increase its power of leverage with both national governments and supranational bodies such as the UN and especially the EU (Acton and Klímová 2001).[52] The hope is that this strategy will lead to increased funding to improve the material conditions of Roma, thus strengthening their social identity. Such resources would come not only from agreements with national governments, following the German Sinti model, but also from the EU and other international bodies and not least in the form of Holocaust reparations. More radically, in the context of an expanding and changing, multiethnic Europe, some believe the role of Roma activism is to spearhead the deconstruction of the idea of majority nations and, perhaps in consequence, 'nothing less than the abolition of the nation-state' (Gheorghe and Acton 2001).

## Conclusion

The search for a solution is now a desperate race against time and against ever mounting odds. The situation is not helped by the fact that central features of the two defining tenets of the post-Communist order – liberal democracy and a market economy – perversely constitute a hindrance. And, while national governments in the region belatedly introduce multicultural education policies and anti-discriminatory legislation in order to comply with EU entry requirements, it remains to be seen how effectively these can be enforced on the ground.

Governments of the region are faced with the same problem that confronted both Communist and, before them, Habsburg planners – how to ensure that legislation and directives are implemented at local level. Here central authority directly confronts local 'democracy', that is lower-level power structures where minor officials both share and act on the deeply entrenched views of their constituents to the detriment of those without an effective voice. While the democratic credentials of post-Communist CEE governments might be superior to those of their predecessors, in important respects their actual predicament is far worse than that of Communist regimes. Not only must they abide by democratic constraints in seeking to enforce their will[53] but they have lost the precious advantage and key to a solution that the Communists failed to utilise sufficiently.

For, by their widespread loss of legal employment Roma have also been deprived of whatever improvements in social identity and limited popular legitimacy they had been grudgingly accorded in state socialist society. Instead of making a recognised livelihood as formerly, impoverished Roma now subsist on insecure, short-term payments in the black economy or remain inactive in their urban slums or rural hovels by day. Some may be driven to pilfer or steal crops from the peasants' fields at night – just as they had done during the depression of the 1930s, provoking pogroms in reprisal (Scheffel 1999: 45). In this way many Roma are forced daily to confirm their negative stereotype in local eyes as work-shy, scrounging thieves, while those who behave quite differently are nevertheless branded with the same image. All the time the task of central governments in counteracting this denigratory labelling process with carefully-crafted schemes for multicultural education becomes all the harder. Likewise, assurances that anti-discriminatory legislation will be enforced nation-wide become ever more implausible.

Nor are there realistic prospects that the developing market economies of candidate states are likely to change in a way that might offer large-scale employment prospects to those who, through no fault of their own, are increasingly becoming an unskilled, uneducated and unemployed lumpenproletariat. Over a decade has been lost already and, even by the most optimistic projections and assuming massive successes in education measures, it will take at least another decade before skilled Roma emerge to join the workforce in any numbers. Certain retraining and work-creation schemes are currently in place but not only do they tend to be small-scale but they are treated as on a par with all other types of project. Even if there were to be an assisted upsurge of entrepreneurial activity among Roma, this would be unlikely to reduce significantly the vast numbers of unemployed.

Since the link between Roma employment and their identity within society has remained unappreciated, its crucial importance is neglected. Instead, Roma are acknowledged as a special group in ethnic terms, whether as a national or supranational minority or nation, and projects are devised to support aspects of their culture. In spite of the undeniable importance of these initiatives it is doubtful whether elevating Romani ethnic status, in itself, can translate into real improvement in how Roma are regarded by others.[54]

It remains to be seen whether the EU and other supranational institutions will demand real compliance with entry criteria as regards Roma or will tacitly accept that the costs of achieving socio-economic equalisation and the problems of enforcing the removal of discrimination are insuperable in the short term. Following this logic, all that can be realistically required of applicants is a show of good will in the form of legislation which, while enhancing the formal rights and status of Roma, leaves their material prospects fundamentally unchanged and therefore their dominant social identity. Mirga and Gheorghe depicted the consequences:

> Because of the underdevelopment and marginality of the Romani community, the growing unemployment ... and the demographic growth of the Romani community (already it is the largest single minority in Europe), there is a danger of it evolving into an ethno-class or underclass, and thus further perpetuate its

marginality in society. Such a development could lead to deadly conflicts with the majority society.

(Mirga and Gheorghe 1997: 24–5)

Such a prospect leaves the ever-growing Roma population without hope of a viable future in their home countries. How do human beings react to such a predicament? Despair in their own and children's future was a major motivating factor in the departure of Roma asylum seekers in the late 1990s and it is certain that others would try to follow the same path. For the majority remaining, mostly trapped in their rural and urban ghettos, the future would appear bleak and the conditions conducive to increased tensions. The relatively minor skirmishing of today between Roma and gadje could escalate, as Mirga and Gheorghe warned, into explosions with unpredictable and terrifying consequences, not just for Roma but for individual nations, casting a stain over the whole European project.

The challenge, therefore, facing all those involved – Roma organisations, national governments, supranational institutions and concerned researchers alike – is how to resolve a set of apparently irreconcilable contradictions to enable Europe's largest and most deprived minority to escape this bleak scenario. Until recently it was confidently believed that such developments were unthinkable in a modernising Europe, but the traumatic experience of Bosnia and Kosovo in the 1990s suggests that the Holocaust was far from an isolated, freak aberration as had been imagined.

An alternative to the desolate doomsday scenario is offered by positive examples of the successful resolution of inter-ethnic tensions both in Australia, with the successful reversal of the previous 'White Australia' policy, and Canada, with the virtual disappearance of prejudice between English and French-speaking communities (Kymlicka 2000: 203, 207). Moving testament was offered by a Canadian delegate to the Fifth World Romani Congress that such supposedly intractable problems as the widespread failure of Roma children in school are more the product of majority society institutions than 'Romani culture'. Karolina Bánomová, a Romani refugee from the Czech Republic, contrasted the dismal record of Roma children in her homeland with their educational success in Canada. However, similar successes – especially in education and employment – need to be achieved, and swiftly, within the heartlands of Central and Eastern Europe.

There is always hope that education programmes might change attitudes, that proven projects will be replicated and that the energy of dedicated individuals can transform hostile social relationships. But it is sobering to consider the recent comment on the progress towards EU entry of one of the most prosperous applicant countries, which also appears the most active in taking measures to integrate its Roma population:

Estimated Roma employment remains very high at 70–90 per cent. Health and housing conditions are much worse in the Roma communities than amongst the local population. Attitudes at local level are largely unaltered ...

(European Commission 2000: 26)

## References

Acton, T. (1974) *Gypsy Politics and Social Change*, London: Routledge and Kegan Paul.

Acton, T. and Klímová, I. (2001) 'The International Romani Union – An East European answer to West European questions? Shifts in the focus of World Romani Congresses, 1971–2000', in W. Guy (ed.) (2001).

Allen, T. W. (1994) *The Invention of the White Race: Racial Oppression and Social Control*, I, London: Verso.

Amato, G. and Batt, J. (1998) *Minority Rights and EU Enlargement to the East*, RSC Policy Paper 98/5, Florence: European University Institute.

Bancroft, A. (1999) '"Gypsies to the camps!": Exclusion and marginalisation of Roma in the Czech Republic', *Sociological Research Online* 4, 3: 1–16.

Barany, Z. D. (1994) 'Nobody's children: the resurgence of nationalism and the status of Gypsies in post-Communist Eastern Europe', in J. Serafin (ed.) *East-Central Europe in the 1990s*, Oxford: Westview Press.

Barany, Z. D. (1998) 'Ethnic mobilisation and the state: the Roma in Eastern Europe', *Ethnic and Racial Studies* 21, 2: 308–27.

Barth, F. (1969) 'Introduction', in F. Barth (ed.) *Ethnic Groups and Boundaries: The Social Organisation of Cultural Difference*, London: George, Allen and Unwin.

Bauer, O. (1924 [07]) *Die Nationalitätenfrage und die Socialdemokratie*, 2nd edn, Vienna: Volksbuchhandlung.

Braham, M. and Braham, M. (2000) 'Romani migrations and EU enlargement', *Cambridge Review of International Affairs* XIII, 2, spring-summer, 97–114.

Cahn, C. and Vermeersch, P. (2000) 'Group expulsion of Slovak Roma by the Belgian Government: a case study of the treatment of Romani refugees in western countries', *Cambridge Review of International Affairs* XIII, 2, spring-summer, 71–82.

Council of Europe (1994) *Framework Convention for the Protection of National Minorities*, Strasbourg: Council of Europe, 10 November.

Czech Government (1997) *Report on the Situation of the Romani Community in the Czech Republic,* Prague: Office of Minister without Portfolio, 29 October.

Czech Government (2000) *Conception of Government Policy towards Members of the Romani Community Designed to Facilitate their Social Integration*, Decision 599, Prague: Government of Czech Republic, approved 14 June.

Davidová, E. (1995) *Romano Drom/Cesty Romů 1945–1990* (Romani Roads), Olomouc: Univerzita Palackého.

Domanovsky, D. (2000) 'Roma flight stumps officials', *Slovak Spectator*, January 17–23.

Eriksen, T. (1993) *Ethnicity and Nationalism: Anthropological Perspectives*, London: Pluto Press.

European Commission (1997) 'Opinion on the application for membership', *Agenda*

*2000*, Brussels: European Commission, July.

European Commission (1999) *Enlargement Briefing: EU Support for Roma Communities in Central and Eastern Europe*, Brussels: European Commission, December.

European Commission (2000) *Regular Report on the Czech Republic's Progress towards Accession*, Brussels: European Commission, 8 November.

Fonseca, I. (1995) *Bury me Standing: The Gypsies and their Journey*, London: Chatto and Windus.

Fraser, A. (1992) *The Gypsies*, Oxford: Blackwell.

Galbraith, J. K. (1990) 'Why the Right is wrong', *The Guardian*, 26 January.

Gheorghe, N. (1997) 'The social construction of Romani identity', in T. Acton (ed.) *Gypsy Politics and Traveller Identity*, Hatfield: University of Hertfordshire Press, 153–63.

Gheorghe, N. and Acton, T. (1994) 'Dealing with multiculturality: minority, ethnic, national and human rights', *ODIHR Bulletin* 3, 2, winter 1994/95, Warsaw: OSCE, 18–25.

Gheorghe, N. and Acton, T. (2001) 'Citizens of the world and nowhere: Minority, ethnic and human rights for Roma during the last hurrah of the nation state', in W. Guy (ed.) (2001).

Guy, W. (1975) 'Ways of looking at Roma: the case of Czechoslovakia', in F. Rehfisch (ed.) *Gypsies, Tinkers and Other Travellers,* London: Academic Press, [reprinted in D. Tong (ed.) (1998), 13–48].

Guy, W. (1977) *The Attempt of Socialist Czechoslovakia to Assimilate its Gypsy Population*, unpublished PhD thesis, Bristol: University of Bristol.

Guy, W. (1998) 'Afterword 1996', in D. Tong (ed.) (1998).

Guy, W. (2001) 'The Czech lands and Slovakia: Another false dawn?', in W. Guy (ed.) (2001).

Guy, W. (ed.) (2001) *Between Past and Future: The Roma of Central and Eastern Europe*, Hatfield: University of Hertfordshire Press.

Hancock, I. (1988) *The Pariah Syndrome: An Account of Gypsy Slavery and Persecution*, 2nd edn, Ann Arbor: Karoma.

Hancock, I. (1991) 'The East European roots of Romani nationalism', in D. Crowe and J. Kolsti (eds) *The Gypsies of Eastern Europe*, London: M.E. Sharpe, 133–50.

Hill, D. (2000) *'East: Poor Conditions for Roma Harm all Citizens'*, reporting statement by G. Verspaget, head of the Council of Europe Specialist Group on Roma, Prague: RFE/RL, 27 January.

Hobsbawm, E. J. (1977) *The Age of Capital 1848–1875*, London: Sphere Books.

Hobsbawm, E. J. (1992) 'Who's fault-line is it anyway?', *New Statesman and Society*, 24 April.

Horváthová, E. (1964) *Cigáni na Slovensku*, Bratislava: Slovak Academy of Sciences.

Hübschmannová, M. (1998 [84]) 'Economic stratification and interaction: Roma, an ethnic jati in East Slovakia', [reprinted in D. Tong (ed.) (1998)].

Kalinin, V. and Kalinina, C. (2001) 'The Baltics, Belarus, Ukraine and Moldova: Reflections on life in the former USSR', in W. Guy (ed.) (2001).

Kenrick, D. (2001) 'Former Yugoslavia: A patchwork of destinies', in W. Guy (ed.)

*Between Past and Future: the Roma of Central and Eastern Europe*, Hatfield: University of Hertfordshire Press. (2001).

Kenrick, D. and Puxon, G. (1972*) The Destiny of Europe's Gypsies*, London: Chatto Heinemann/Sussex University Press.

Kollárová, Z, (1972) 'K vývoju rómskej society na Spiši do roku 1945', in A. B. Mann (ed.) *Neznámi Rómovia*, Bratislava: Ister Science Press.

Kovats, M. (2001a) 'The emergence of European Roma policy', in W. Guy (ed.) *Between Past and Future: the Roma of Central and Eastern Europe*, Hatfield: University of Hertfordshire Press. (2001).

Kovats, M. (2001b) 'Hungary: Politics, difference and equality', in W. Guy (ed.) *Between Past and Future: the Roma of Central and Eastern Europe*, Hatfield: University of Hertfordshire Press. (2001).

Kürti, L. (1997) 'Globalisation and the discourse of otherness in the "new" Eastern and Central Europe', in T. Modood and P. Werbner (eds) *The Politics of Multi-culturalism in the New Europe*, London: Zed Books.

Kymlicka, W. (2000) 'Nation-building and minority rights: comparing West and East', *Journal of Ethnic and Migration Studies* 26, 2:183–212, April.

Lacková, I. (1999) *A False Dawn: My Life as a Gypsy Woman in Slovakia*, Hatfield: University of Hertfordshire Press/Centre de recherches tsiganes.

Lemon, A. (2001) 'Russia: Politics of performance', in W. Guy (ed.) (2001).

Liégeois, J.-P. (1976) *Mutation Tsigane,* Paris: Presses Universitaires de France.

Liégeois, J.-P. (1994) *Roma, Gypsies, Travellers*, Strasbourg: Council of Europe Press.

Liégeois, J.-P. and Gheorghe, N. (1995) *Roma/Gypsies: A European Minority*, Minority Rights Group International Report 95/4, London: MRG.

Lovenduski, J. and Woodall, J. (1987) *Politics and Society in Eastern Europe*, Basingstoke: Macmillan.

Marushiakova, E. and Popov, V. (2001a) 'Historical and ethnographic background: Gypsies, Roma, Sinti', in W. Guy (ed.) (2001).

Marushiakova, E. and Popov, V. (2001b) 'Bulgaria: Ethnic diversity – a common struggle for equality', in W. Guy (ed.) (2001).

Matras, Y. (1998) 'Review of *The Roma in the Twenty-First Century: A Policy Paper*' (Mirga and Gheorghe 1997), *Journal of Gypsy Lore Society* V, 8, 2: 151–4.

Matras, Y. (2000) 'Romani migrations in the post-Communist era: their historical and political significance', *Cambridge Review of International Affairs* XIII, 2, spring-summer, 32–50.

Mirga, A. and Gheorghe, N. (1997) *The Roma in the Twenty-First Century: A Policy Paper*, Project on Ethnic Relations policy paper, Princeton: PER.

Mróz, L. (2001) 'Poland: The clash of tradition and modernity', in W. Guy (ed.) (2001).

Okely, J. (1983) *The Traveller-Gypsies*, Cambridge: Cambridge University Press.

O'Rourke, B. (2000) *EU: Enlargement Negotiations Adhere to Tough Criteria*, Prague: RFE/RL, 15 March.

PER (1992) *The Romanies in Central and Eastern Europe: Illusions and Reality*, Project on Ethnic Relations (PER) report on roundtable discussions in Stupava, Slovakia (April 30 – 2 May), Princeton: PER, September.

PER (1999a) *State Policies toward the Romani Communities in the Candidate Countries to the EU: Government and Romani Participation in Policy-making*, PER report on roundtable discussions in Brussels (July 26), Princeton: PER.

PER (1999b) *Roma and the Law: Demythologising Romani Stereotypes*, PER report on roundtable discussions in Paris, France (7–8 October), Princeton: PER.

Scheffel, D. Z. (1999) 'The untouchables of Svinia', *Human Organisation* 58, 1: 44–53.

Stewart, M. (2001) 'Communist Roma policy 1945–1989 as seen through the Hungarian case', in W. Guy (ed.) (2001).

Tong, D. (ed.) (1998) *Gypsies: An Interdisciplinary Reader*, New York: Garland.

Tritt, R. (1992) *Struggling for Ethnic Identity: Czechoslovakia's Endangered Gypsies*, Helsinki Watch report, New York: Human Rights Watch.

Ulč, O. (1969) 'Communist national minority policy: The case of the Gypsies in Czechoslovakia', *Soviet Studies*, April.

van der Stoel, M. (2000) *Report on the Situation of Roma and Sinti in the OSCE Area*, Office of the High Commissioner on National Minorities, Organisation for Security and Co-operation in Europe, The Hague: OSCE, March.

Vermeersch, P. (2000) 'Minority rights for the Roma and political conditionality of European Union accession: The case of Slovakia', unpublished paper for *Conference 2000: New Directions in Roma Studies*, University of Greenwich/ University of Birmingham, 28 June – 1 July.

Verspaget, G. (1995) *The Situation of Gypsies (Roma and Sinti) in Europe*, report adopted by the CDMG, Strasbourg: Council of Europe, 5 May.

## Notes

1  Personal discussion with W. Guy in office of ROI (Romani Civic Initiative), Prague, July 1997.

2  The specific reasons listed by Matras are: social conflict, ethnic tension and the failure of authorities to contain this, severe restrictions in occupation and employment, single acts of violence, the effects of war and changes in status (such as loss of citizenship) (Matras 2000: 37–9).

3  This is similar to the categorisation made by another persecuted group, the Jews, of all non-Jews as goya (gentiles).

4  Here it should be noted that among the wide diversity of people gathered under the umbrella name of Roma not all groups, or indeed individuals, find themselves in similar situations or have the same requirements and demands. This chapter does not attempt to encompass all Roma but it does claim relevance to the experience of many Roma of CEE countries, probably a significant majority.

5  Much of the argument in this section is stimulated by and is a response to the writing of the eminent Roma theorists Nicolae Gheorghe and Andrzej Mirga. It also draws on the research and insights of Thomas Acton, Ian Hancock and Martin Kovats, among others. The section heading acknowledges the contribution of a seminal article of the same name (Gheorghe 1997).

6  On this point also see Okely (1983: 33–4). However, in view of the diversity of Roma experience, it would be more accurate to talk of a constellation of Romani cultures and likewise discussion here of Romani identity refers to a cluster of varying and related identities rather than a homogenous entity (see Marushiakova and Popov 2001a).

7   The Danubian principalities of Wallachia and Moldavia (see Marushiakova and Popov 2001a).

8   Kymlicka is disappointingly unhelpful in his brief discussion of Roma where he rejects the comparison of them with African-Americans on the mistaken grounds that 'the situation of blacks is really quite different ... [since they] have always lived in settled communities' (Kymlicka 2000: 204). Although Roma are indeed different in important ways from African-Americans, and also from Jews, comparison with these two groups is often illuminating in understanding the complex relationships between Roma communities and majority society.

9   I owe this point to Martin Kovats.

10  Although Gheorghe's argument is based primarily on the experience of Romania, it is far broader in scope and seeks to suggest an explanation of relevance to other countries in Central and Eastern Europe with similar structural features. Such a general model remains an 'ideal type' and proves helpful in differing degrees in accounting for the diversity of Roma experience. It seems directly applicable not only to Romania but to former Habsburg lands (what are now Hungary, Slovakia and southern Poland). It fits, to a lesser extent, the experience of Bulgaria and the Balkans and least of all the remainder of Poland, the Baltic states and Russia.

11  The nomadic Roma of Western Europe also made largely unrecognised economic contributions to their host communities (Okely 1983: 64). Okely, too, recognised that 'modern capitalism generates nomads, it does not simply inherit them' (Okely 1983: 32).

12  Acton's term for this development was 'economic nomadism' (Acton 1974: 254, 257).

13  Gheorghe made the same point elsewhere 'contrasting the east European situation, where societies needed an intensive exploitation of labour, with what has happened in western European countries which produced the nomads, who were marginals, in contrast to the slaves [of Romania] who were incorporated in the economic division of labour and in society as such' (Gheorghe 1997: 159).

14  Until almost all perished in the Holocaust.

15  Mirga and Gheorghe also offer structural explanations of demographic and other patterns among Roma. 'The distribution of Romani populations in Europe and the variations in their social positions and the issues facing them in Central and Eastern as against Western Europe are the result of deep historical processes' (Mirga and Gheorghe 1997: 5).

16  This summary of the argument above anticipates the analysis of Mirga and Gheorghe (1997: 5), from which the quotations are taken to emphasise the similarity of approach.

17  The importance of identifiable physical differences in this process is emphasised, presumably by Gheorghe and Mirga, in a 1992 PER roundtable discussion. 'Traditionally [in Eastern Europe], the Roma were a social caste – a separate collectivity that inherited an imposed position of inferiority. ... This status was "justified" by racial characteristics' (PER 1992: 7).

18  Initial diaspora throughout Europe accompanied Ottoman invasions; widespread persecution in Western Europe coincided with attempts to regulate the landless poor; systematic assimilation in Central Europe formed part of Habsburg attempts to rationalise their Empire and liberation after three centuries of enslavement in Romania was a part of the ending of feudalism. Such concurrence is hardly surprising for, as a relatively weak and dispersed group, Roma were unlikely to have been 'sole arbiters of their fate' and consequently 'it was far more likely that their history would be more a tale of what was done to them than what they themselves had done' (Guy 1975: 203).

19  For example, Russia, Czechoslovakia and Bulgaria. However the change of regime in Russia did affect Roma more fundamentally than in other CEE countries and Soviet policy (see Lemon 2001) can be compared to some extent to that elsewhere in the region following

the Second World War.

20   Venomous cries of 'Gypsies to the gas chambers!' and the like are not uncommon (Tritt 1992: 3, Bancroft 1999: 8–9). Meanwhile non-Roma who work with Roma are struck by the never-distant fear that an overwhelming catastrophe could descend at any moment. Some Roma appear almost to have succumbed to the inevitability of such a horrific outcome as in the Roma settlement where a recent folk myth anticipates their annihilation in a bombing raid by the Slovak air force (Scheffel 1999: 47).

21   As individual chapters in this volume make clear, Communist regimes were not entirely consistent but a more or less analogous approach was pursued in Czechoslovakia, Hungary, Poland, Bulgaria and Romania, following the 1956 lead of the Soviet Union.

22   The peasantry, undergoing collectivisation to different degrees throughout the region, provided the main source of recruitment but Roma were also seen as fit for this purpose. In fact, some had already been used in similar ways in wartime labour camps. Extensive illiteracy among Roma was no handicap for those required to dig trenches or mine coal.

23   Even more bizarre is the misconceived claim that 'until the end of the Second World War Gypsies fulfilled a specific function in the rural world having a number of traditional jobs … *all of which were compatible with their nomadic lifestyle*' (Verspaget 1995: 4 quoted Kovats 2001a, emphasis added).

24   Here, however, the relative integration achieved by means of Roma quarters (*mahala*) within Ottoman society should not be forgotten (Marushiakova and Popov 2001b).

25   For the majority this course of action appeared not only painful and unrealisable but also an irrational strategy. Educational aspirations were understandably low among Roma, not just in terms of expected employment, but for more practical reasons. When premium wages were paid for manual work what was the point of forcing young children to endure a still discriminatory education system for the prospect of forfeiting higher wages while training – all for a lower income as a white-collar worker. Far better to maximise earnings, build a house and enjoy the admiration of other Roma and perhaps, in the process, prove something to the gadje as well.

26   Ethnicity was seen as dissolving as human society progressed and therefore any attempt to strengthen ethnic identity among Roma would necessarily be counter-productive (Guy 1975: 221–3). Kymlicka identifies a similar view in the West. 'For most of this [twentieth] century, ethnicity was viewed by [Western] political theorists as a marginal phenomenon that would gradually disappear with modernisation' (Kymlicka 2000: 184). It is not clear whether Kymlicka would include Marx and Engels among these Western political theorists with their somewhat earlier anticipation of the effects of globalisation in the Communist Manifesto.

27   Instead, the alternative ethos of socialist internationalism was promoted, for the Party was only too well aware from recent history of the divisive, centrifugal forces of minority nationalism in a region where 'most … states contained one or more national minority which would rather have been somewhere else' (Lovenduski and Woodall 1987: 25).

28   On rare occasions this strategy of containment escalated into forcible assimilation, as in Bulgaria in the latter half of the 1980s. Confronted with intractable economic stagnation the regime of Todor Zhivkov attempted to bolster its flagging legitimacy with the majority Bulgars by targeting the ethnic Turkish minority. The campaign to make them renounce their language and Muslim religion as well as bulgarise their names also affected Turkish-speaking, Muslim Roma groups (Marushiakova and Popov 2001b).

29   Linked to their impoverishment and poor living conditions Roma were almost certainly the most unhealthy of East Europeans, with reported TB rates two or three times than the national average in several states (van der Stoel 2000: 117–8). Even in relatively prosperous

Communist times their life expectancy was far lower than for non-Roma (Guy 2001).

30   This drastic effect was experienced most devastatingly in the key state of Czechoslovakia, as the most industrialised in the region and consequently with the greatest degree of Roma participation in the general workforce. Here, where already by the 1970s over 90 per cent of male Roma of working age were recorded as having jobs, the situation was completely reversed. Within a few years of the advent of liberal democracy Roma unemployment in the Czech Republic was officially estimated at between 70 and 90 per cent at a time when the national rate stood at only 5 per cent (Czech Government 1997: I, 17).

31   See PER (1999b) *Roma and the Law: Demythologising Romani Stereotypes.*

32   Such incidents began soon after the ending of Communist rule, with the removal of the protective shield of fear of officialdom, and were widespread throughout the region. In any case, there is evidence that law agencies sometimes participated. Far from arousing condemnation and sympathy such violence was accompanied instead by verbal attacks on Roma, in the media, by policians and in popular speech. Most alarming were the pogroms against Roma communities – a mark of the rise of fascism between the wars – that were reported from Romania, Poland and Slovakia.

33   At the same time, the few prosperous Roma businessmen and dealers were also resented since they stood accused of exploiting non-Roma at a time of economic hardship (Fonseca 1995).

34   Roma themselves attributed their loss of status to these structural changes. In a 1997 survey in the Czech Republic 90 per cent of the Romani representatives interviewed saw their 'minority's social and educational decline' as a 'very important' factor in their 'different [lowered] status in society' (Czech Government 1997: II, 2–3).

35   Only Hungary seemed to go beyond this and offer a certain amount of autonomy with the 1993 minority self-government system. However, even here the resources provided were extremely limited and insufficient to make any impact on major problems such as unemployment (Kovats 2001b).

36   See various chapters in this volume.

37   For the former Yugoslavia see Kenrick (2001) and for citizenship laws in the Baltic states see Kalinin and Kalinina (2001). The 1993 Czech Citizenship Law was deliberately aimed at 'ridding the country of unwanted workers', mainly Roma to be expelled to Slovakia (see Guy 2001).

38   Article 4 of the Framework Convention affirms commitment to equalising action in paragraph 2, while paragraph 3 declares that any such action is not itself discriminatory.

39   Furthermore, since market reforms tend to 'disenfranchise underprivileged groups such as the Roma', fulfilling the Copenhagen requirement for a market economy would actually make it harder to satisfy the criterion guaranteeing the protection of the Roma minority, particularly its right to social and economic equality (Braham and Braham 2000: 106).

40   In an uncertain economic climate any substantial attempt to achieve socio-economic improvement in the situation of Roma, vis-à-vis others, might well provoke a backlash, thus threatening fulfilment of the human rights criterion (Braham and Braham 2000: 109).

41   In contrast, Matras grasped the key point about the asylum seekers: '[T]he extraordinary feature of Romani migration is that so many Roma are prepared to take the risks of migrating *despite their lack of nomadic traditions*' (Matras 2000: 32, emphasis in original).

42   In the High Commissioner's report there was no separate section on employment but the equivalent of three pages under the subheading of discrimination (van der Stoel 2000: 31–34). Similarly, unemployment was not included as a topic in its own right but as a contributory factor in poor health conditions (van der Stoel 2000: 119–20). See Kovats (2001a) for further discussion of this report.

43  I acknowledge the insights of Peter Vermeersch in clarifying these important points.

44  CEE states are condemned for abuses of Roma human rights that occur on their territory but when the victims arrive as refugees they are immediately branded as 'economic migrants' and sent home.

45  According to fragmentary records, such efforts by Roma to achieve political aims by common action occurred throughout Europe from the fifteenth century onwards. See Hancock (1991: 139–45).

46  Hancock distinguishes such wider mobilisation from earlier negotiations with the powers of the day by those representing Roma bands for 'the activities of single individuals, speaking for their group, must be seen differently from large-scale efforts to reunite Romani populations' (Hancock 1991: 139).

47  Originally the Conference on Security and Co-operation in Europe (CSCE) this later became the Organisation for Security and Co-operation in Europe (OSCE).

48  Among the leading Czech and Slovak Roma activists of the 1960s and 1970s were a doctor (first president of the IRU), an architect, a sociologist and a lawyer.

49  This option had been suggested, most notably by Polish Roma leaders. During the 1930s various members of the Kweik family announced plans for a Romani homeland in India, South Africa and Abyssinia. A few years later the Nazis thought the death camps a more suitable destination for Roma (Hancock 1991: 142–3).

50  The alternative strategy of seeking special rights as a national minority, stressing long-term links with the host country, has been pursued with a certain amount of success since 1952 by the Association of Sinti in Germany and by later umbrella groups (Liégeois 1994: 252).

51  But here we should remember the arguments of the Austrian Social Democrat Otto Bauer who also advanced a theory of non-territorial cultural nationalism as a solution to the similar problem of the scattered distribution of ethnic groups within the multi-national Habsburg Empire (Bauer 1924).

52  Some are suspicious of reliance on spokespersons from the élite negotiating with existing powers, fearing this to be a modernised version of 'traditional' Gypsy politics and liable to result in deals between leaders to the detriment of grass-roots supporters. Nevertheless, Rudko Kawczynski (the leading figure in the Roma National Congress), has a somewhat similar 'vision of a transnational minority with special European provisions' (Matras 1998).

53  Here the Czech lands provide a salutary example demonstrating the power of local democracy for Article 8 of the Czech Constitution upholds the principle of self-government of territorial units. The Chamber of Deputies of the Czech Parliament voted to prevent the local authority constructing a wall in Ústí nad Labem to separate Roma from other inhabitants. The wall was built and subsequently dismantled after negotiation – and a government grant. However, the Constitutional Court upheld a subsequent town council complaint that by their vote the Chamber of Deputies were exceeding their authority (European Commission 2000: 26).

54  A major problem for Roma activists, in particular, is that 'stigmatising discourse' in terms of the 'Roma problem' sees problems as caused by Roma themselves, even by those in government who should best understand the plight of Roma and defend them. For example, Slovak Roma emigration was condemned by Human Rights Minister Pál Csáky as 'ethnobusiness', i.e. 'typical ... abuse of the state's welfare resources' (Vermeersch 2000: 11–12). Likewise, the head of the Inter-ministerial Roma Commission at recent Czech Academy of Sciences roundtable in Prague attributed Czech Roma emigration to manipulation by activists rather than to the underlying, desperate situation of Roma in the Czech Republic (personal observation).

## CHAPTER TWO

# Historical and ethnographic background:
## Gypsies, Roma, Sinti

*Elena Marushiakova and
Vesselin Popov*

In order to understand the historical experience as well as the ethno-social structure, ethno-cultural features and problems of the Gypsies[1] in present-day Central and Eastern European countries,[2] we have to consider the following circumstances.

Firstly, Gypsies form a specific ethnic community – an 'intergroup ethnic community' – which has no parallel among other European nations. The broader Gypsy community is divided into a widespread archipelago of separate groupings, split in various ways into metagroups, groups and subgroups, each with their own ethnic and cultural features. Sometimes these groupings are even opposed to each other and their problems are frequently completely different in nature and therefore cannot be generalised.

Secondly, the cultural and historical context of Gypsy life during past centuries and the contemporary social, economic and political situation in the different countries of the region are extremely important explanatory factors. The region has a rich and complex history and the conditions today differ markedly from one country to the next. All of these aspects continue to exert a powerful influence on Gypsy life, therefore all attempts at analysing the current situation of Gypsies must always take account of the specific experience of each country (or group of countries).

In this chapter we are able to give only a brief outline of the overall picture of Central and Eastern European Gypsies (or Roma).[3] We will try to explain both the complex subdivisions of this diverse community and their unique history which has played such an important part, not only in moulding group perceptions of their own identity but also in determining their fate. Before starting it is helpful to explain some of the difficulties – not just in the past but just as much today – in obtaining reliable data about the people we are writing about.

## Estimating population figures for Gypsies in Central and Eastern Europe

No one knows exactly how many Gypsies currently live – and used to live – in Central and Eastern Europe. There are no reliable statistical and demographic data for their distribution or their internal subdivisions, only a significant amount of imprecise and fluctuating information. Until now no model has been created which enables such data to be verified and one can only combine information from different censuses with personal observation and subject these figures to critical analysis, and even this cautious approach only provides approximations. The problem is complex and is related to questions of preferred ethnic identification (the intentionally misleading or genuine affirmation of another, non-Roma identity). Many Gypsy groups in these countries do not want to be considered as Roma, many more do not wish to declare their ethnic identity for fear of repression, while others frequently cannot understand the questionnaires; and in many cases, censuses are carried out by officials who, in dealing with Gypsies, deliberately or inadvertently alter the information they have obtained.

Consequently, we would argue that recent official statistical censuses generally record only about one third of the real number of Gypsies in each country.[4] In some instances the discrepancies can be even greater. A number of examples support this conclusion. For example, only 32,903 people declared themselves as Roma in the Czech Republic's 1991 census but experts estimated their numbers as up to ten times higher. According to data provided by the National Institute of Statistics there were 83,988 Roma living in Slovakia in 1999 in contrast to estimates by informed researchers of around 500,000. Similarly, in the 1992 Romanian census 409,723 people declared themselves as Gypsies, while others estimated their numbers as varying between 800,000 and 1,500,000 and some even thought that the total could be as high as 2,500,000. In Bulgaria 313,396 people declared themselves as Gypsies in the 1992 census but according to the unofficial census of the Ministry of the Interior their number was between 500,000 and 600,000, whilst experts estimated the true number to be from 700,000 to 800,000 and Roma leaders claimed a figure of more than a million. In the 1981 Yugoslav census 1,471 people declared themselves as Gypsies in the Republic of Montenegro, while a decade later, according to the 1991 census, not a single person claimed to be a Gypsy.

Similar examples can be cited for other Central and Eastern European countries but even without them it is evident that population statistics are unreliable with estimates varying for the number of Gypsies in each country and in the region as a whole. The minimum number for the region based on national censuses is about 1,500,000 while the maximum estimate, if one includes those of Roma leaders, is around 6,300,000.[5]

One can summarise this complex and confusing picture by stating that today, as in the past, the population of Gypsies varies considerably from country to country and the proportion they represent of the population as a whole also differs. In some countries (Bulgaria, Romania, Hungary, Slovakia and possibly the Czech Republic) they currently represent 5–10 per cent of the total population, while in others (the countries of the former Soviet Union) they constitute less than 1 per cent.

## Gypsies in the history of the region and their internal structures

The Gypsies constitute a specific ethnic community within south-eastern Europe.[6] The first evidence we have of the presence of Gypsies in Europe is on the territory of the Byzantine Empire. Large-scale settlement of Gypsies in Balkan lands can be traced to a period between the eleventh and thirteenth centuries, although some believe an earlier arrival is plausible, perhaps as far back as the ninth century. Later, numerous historical sources recorded the presence of Gypsies in Byzantium and their entry into Serbia, Bulgaria, Wallachia and Moldavia. During the fourteenth and fifteenth centuries Gypsies gradually spread to many other European countries and by the sixteenth and seventeenth centuries relatively large numbers of Gypsies were permanently settled in Central and Eastern Europe where they were influenced by the surrounding social and political environment.

The demographic pattern of Gypsies in Central and Eastern Europe shifted with each alteration in state borders which usually led to an exchange of Gypsy groups between neighbouring countries. The population balance was also affected by mass migration of Gypsies at certain periods. The most important of these migrations in modern times were:

*from the second half of the nineteenth century to the first half of twentieth*
The ending of slavery in Wallachia and Moldavia and the subsequent scattering of Gypsies all over the world – known as the 'great Kelderara invasion'.

*1960s and 1970s*
The open borders of former Yugoslavia during the period of Tito's rule which led to the 'Yugoslav wave' of Gypsy migrations, mainly heading for West Germany.

*1990 onwards*
The end of the so-called socialist period in the countries of Central and Eastern Europe and the subsequent changes leading to the most recent of Gypsy migrations – westwards. These migrants included Roma refugees from former

Yugoslavia (at first mainly from Bosnia and Herzegovina, and subsequently from Kosovo).

As well as these great migratory waves across national borders there were also cases of considerable internal migration within countries, which affected previous population balances. Following the end of the Second World War large numbers of Gypsies from eastern Poland moved to the newly acquired western territories that had formerly been part of Germany. At the same time Gypsies from East Slovakia were migrating to Czech cities, particularly the industrialised Czech border regions from which the previous German inhabitants had been expelled. Within Yugoslavia, Kosovo Gypsies settled in the more prosperous regions of Serbia, Croatia and Slovenia as early as the 1960s and 70s and this process intensified with the violent disintegration of Yugoslavia in the 1990s.

The present-day Roma of Central and Eastern Europe are extremely diverse and can be classified on the basis of certain key criteria such as their language, lifestyle, boundaries of endogamy, professional specialisation, duration of settlement in their respective countries, and so on. All these specific features strongly influence their self-consciousness and sense of identity and, taken together, provide a full picture of the current state of the wider Roma community. However, since situations change and Roma are adaptable, such a picture can be regarded as a snapshot, valid at the time it was taken but not necessarily true of the past and likely to change in future as conditions alter over generations.

Gypsies have been settled for centuries in the Balkans – specifically in the countries of former Yugoslavia, Bulgaria and Albania – and *Romanes*-speaking communities who use variants of the Balkan dialect group are the oldest Gypsy settlers in this area. Gypsies speaking *Romanes* belonging to the Old Vlax dialect group are the descendants of a substantial migratory wave from Wallachia and Moldavia, who dispersed all over the Balkan Peninsula in the seventeenth and eighteenth centuries. The area of the Balkans is also home to a relatively long-established variety of groups and metagroup communities who practice either Islam or Christianity. Some evidently converted from one religion to the other in different periods. The main difference between these communities is the distinction drawn between Muslims (*Xorax-ane Roma*) and Christians (*Dasikane Roma*), who form more or less autonomous groups within each locality. The groups are differentiated at various hierarchical levels and are often internally divided into separate subgroups.[7]

Fewer Gypsies belong to groups who mostly entered these lands at the time of the 'great Kelderara invasion' and who speak the *Romanes* of the New Vlax dialect group. Today they live primarily in Bulgaria and Serbia. This community is most commonly referred to in general terms as

*Kaldarash/Kardarasha* and in some places also as *Layesha* or *Katunari* (i.e. Nomads). A very popular self-appellation is that of *Rom Tsiganyaka* (meaning 'true Gypsies'). Within this group there are numerous subgroups and subdivisions (for example in Bulgaria: *Zlatari, Tasmanari, Zhaplesh, Dodolania, Laynesh, Nyamtsoria*), and in addition family and kinship subdivisions.

The numerous community of *Rudara/Ludara* are spread throughout the whole Balkan peninsula. They are also called *Kopanari* (cradle-makers), *Koritari* (trough-makers), *Vlasi* (Wallachians), *Karavlasi* (black Wallachians), etc. by the surrounding population. The *Rudara* have preserved a certain extent of intergroup subdivisions based on their occupations, such as *Lingurara* (spoon-makers), *Ursara* or *Mechkara* (bear-trainers), and on regional features, e.g. *Monteni, Istreni, Thracieni*, etc. Instead of *Romanes* they speak their own dialect of Romanian.

The *Rudara* are among those Balkan Gypsies, who have forgotten their mother tongue and discarded certain other ethnic and cultural traits. They are also inclined to change their ethnic allegiance and are examples of the phenomenon of 'preferred ethnic identification'. The *Rudara* often present themselves as true *Vlaxs* (old Romanians) and some are even involved in the search for a distinct identity for themselves, which is both non-Romanian and non-Romani.

Other numerous Muslim Gypsy communities are also experiencing processes of identity change. Most of them speak Turkish or are bilingual (using both Turkish and *Romanes*) and pretend to be Turks – mostly in Bulgaria and in Eastern Macedonia. In Kosovo and Western Macedonia the preferred community for self-identification is Albanian. Among others preferring Albanian identity are some of the Albanian speaking *Ashkali* in former Yugoslavia. At the same time, some Gypsies are gradually accepting the identity of the surrounding population. These developments are similar in content to those described above, although expressed in different ways, and affect those in groups referred to as *Dzhorevtsi* (mules) in Bulgaria or *Beli tsigani* (white Gypsies) in Serbia.

The search for and affirmation of a different, non-Gypsy identity has taken new forms among the *Egyupti* in Kosovo, Macedonia and Serbia, as well as the *Yevgi* in Albania, where many in both groups present themselves as Egyptians and insist on being recognised as an Egyptian minority. This tendency has also been observed recently among the *Ashkalia* in Kosovo.

In Romania,[8] too, there is a complex mosaic of Gypsy groups which up till now has not been fully researched. The main patterns in this mosaic are largely determined by the former division of Gypsies into different categories during their period of slavery in the Danubian principalities of Wallachia and Moldavia. Over time the ancestors of the *Vatrashi* category have lost their distinctive characteristics as a group and have merged into a large metagroup community where regional or occupational traits are still noticable. The

*Vatrashi* derive their name from *vatra* (fireplace in Romanian), hence settled, domestic slaves, and are also called *kherutno* (meaning those who live in houses). Most of this group speak only Romanian and many prefer to affirm a Romanian identity. Only a few of them speak *Romanes* as well.

There are many other groups in Romania that have maintained distinctive characteristics, mostly descendants of the *Leyasha* category. These used to be nomads and paid an annual tax to their patrons (the prince, boyars, or monasteries). Such groups and subgroups, which have preserved to a certain extent their own cultural and other features, include: *Kalderara, Zlatara, Kolari, Gabori, Kazandzhi, Pletoshi, Korbeni, Modorani, Tismanari, Lautari, Ursari, Spoitori* and others.[9] The Romanian speaking *Rudara* (or *Aurari)* form another large community that was also assigned a special status at the time of slavery, but only a few speak *Romanes* as well. In Dobrudzha there are Turkish- or Tatar-speaking Muslim Gypsies whose preferred identity derives from the lanuage they speak. Transylvania is the home of a significant number of *Romanes*-speaking *Rumungri* (*Roma Ungrika*), who are internally differentiated according to the region where they live, as well as Hungarian-speaking *Rumungri*, who prefer to affirm Hungarian identity.

In Central Europe the variety of Gypsy groups is smaller than in the Balkans and in Romania. In Slovakia more than two thirds of the Gypsy population have been settled for centuries, mostly *Slovenska* (Slovak) *Roma* (divided into *Servitka Roma* and *Bergitka Roma*), speaking Carpathian dialects of *Romanes*. In the south there are also *Ungrika* (Hungarian) *Roma* or *Rumungri*, who mostly speak only Hungarian, and some of whom prefer to affirm a Hungarian identity. This country is also the home to *Vlashika* or *Olah* (Wallachian) *Roma*, although their numbers are far smaller, subdivided into *Lovara, Bougeshti, Drizdari* and others. The *Vlashika Roma* are former nomads, part of a wave of Kelderara migrants, who have preserved their new Vlax dialects of *Romanes*, related to those of the *Kalderara/Kalderasha* in the Balkans. Small communities of Romanian speaking *Koritari*, who are related to *Rudara* in the Balkans and *Boyasha* in Hungary, are settled in Eastern Slovakia.

The situation in the Czech Republic mirrors the situation in Slovakia because during the Second World War the local Czech and Moravian Roma and Sinti were almost entirely annihilated in Nazi concentration camps. After the war the Czech lands were repopulated by Gypsies who came from Slovakia, primarily from the region of Eastern Slovakia. Only a few families of Czech and Moravian Gypsies survived the Holocaust and have mostly lost their *Romanes* language and elements of their ethnic culture. In spite of their small numbers the South Moravian Gypsies, who were relatively integrated and educated, provided the leadership for the Czech Roma movement of the late 1960s and early 70s.

In Hungary the overwhelming majority are the settled *Rumungri* who no longer speak *Romanes* and have lost many of their ethnic and cultural characteristics. There are also small numbers of Romani-speaking *Rumungri*, mostly in Eastern Hungary, as well as an insignificant presence of *Slovenska Roma*. Even fewer are the *Vlashika Roma* or *Olah* Gypsies, subdivided into *Lovari, Kelderari, Churari, Drizari, Posotari, Kherara, Cherhara, Khangliari, Tsolari, Mashari, Bugara* and others. Hungary is also home to a community of Romanian speaking *Boyasha*, corresponding to the *Rudara* in the Balkans, subdivided into *Ardelan, Muntian, Titian,* etc. amongst some of whom a Roma identity is developing.

Poland is a country with a relatively small Gypsy population. In the regions which used to be parts of the former Russian Empire live the *Polska* (Polish) *Roma*, former nomads who are now scattered all over Poland. Their community also includes the group referred to as *Xaladitka (*or *Ruska) Roma*, living near the borders of the former Soviet Union, as well as the related *Sasitka* (German) *Roma*, located near the former Prussian border. *Bergitka Roma*, who have been settled for centuries, live along the Polish-Slovak border, and groups related to them live on the other side of the border. In addition some *Kelderara* and *Lovara* are scattered throughout the country. In recent years many Romanian Roma travelled to Poland, mostly from Transylvania, and nowadays these are often more numerous than the local Roma.

The European countries of the former Soviet Union are populated predominantly by related Gypsy communities. Divisions are not clear cut and are often a consequence of their historical experience. The largest community is the Orthodox *Xaladitka* or *Ruska* (Russian) *Roma*, subdivided on the basis of the territory they inhabit into *Veshitka, Smolyaki, Piterska Roma, Bobri, Uraltsi* and *Toboliaki*, etc. Closely related to them are the *Polska Roma* (also called *Xaladitka Roma*) in Lithuania, and *Litovska* (Lithuanian) *Roma* in Lithuania and Belarus, with various subdivisions such as *Beni, Fandari, Lipentsi, Pintchuki* and others, most of whom are Catholics. They are also related to the *Lotfika* (Latvian) *Roma* (sometimes also called *Tchuxni,* i.e. Finns) living in Latvia, Lithuania and Estonia and territorially subdivided into *Kurzemnyeki, Vidzemnyeki* and *Laloro* (Estonian Gypsies) etc., who are Lutherans.

The second largest Gypsy grouping in terms of numbers is the community referred to as Ukrainian Roma but who call themselves *Servi/Servuria*. Their dialect is defined by some linguists as proto-Vlax. These Gypsies settled in eastern Ukraine and the southern parts of Russia as early as the middle of the sixteenth century after migrating from Wallachia and Moldavia. Nowadays they are scattered all over Russia. In addition a considerable number of *Vlaxs/Vlaxuria* live in the Ukraine. Their *Romanes* belongs to the old Vlax dialect group since they arrived as part of a later wave of migration from the Danubian principalities. Smaller communities, such as *Plashchuni* in southern Russia, *Chukunari* in Moldova and others, also came from these principalities at different times.

Gypsy communities speaking *Romanes* belonging to the Balkan dialect groups are relatively numerous in this region. They migrated from the Balkan peninsula in the eighteenth century and include the *Ursara* (*Richinara*) in Moldova and south Ukraine with two subgroups – the *Bessarabyania* and *Prutyania*. Related to them linguistically are the *Kirimitika/Kirimlitka* (Crimean) *Roma* who inhabit the Crimea, southern Ukraine, southern Russia and the area of the northern Caucasus. These have a number of subdivisions – *Kirlides, Chornomorludes, Orudes, Kubanludes,* etc.

As a result of the 'great Kelderara invasion' there are a few groups in Russia who speak the new Vlax dialects of *Romanes*. These groups are referred to as *Moldovanskie tsigane* (Moldovan Gypsies) (*Kishinyovtsi*) in southern Ukraine and southern Russia. These *Kalderara* communities, subdivided into *Vungri, Serbiaia, Bugari, Moldovaia, Dobrozhaia, Grekuria,* etc., and *Lovara,* subdivided into *Ungri, Prayzura* etc., who arrived in Russia mainly by way of the territories of the Austro-Hungarian Empire, are scattered in small family and kinship groups throughout the former Soviet Union.

The *Servitka Roma* and *Rumungri* are long settled in the Transcarpathian Ukraine and some of these *Rumungri* are Hungarian speaking. There are also Romanian-speaking Gypsies, such as *Besarabi, Lingurara* and others, living in Moldova, the Ukraine and Russia, who travelled there at various times from the territory of present day Romania.

As well as the *Sinti,* from the subdivisions of *Prayzi, Poyaki* and *Esterxaria,* there are other non-Roma Gypsies living in the European countries of the former Soviet Union. Armenian-speaking *Bosha* as well as individual families of Asian Gypsies, *Karachi* from Azerbaidjan, can now be seen – mainly in the larger cities.

These complex, internal subdivisions among the Gypsies of the region help to explain seemingly contradictory and paradoxical facts about the situation of present-day Roma. Some of these subgroups, such as the *Rumungri* in Central Europe, have lost their language, their distinctive ethnic culture and to a great extent even their Roma identity and nowadays many of them are poor and socially marginalised. Meanwhile, other subgroups have managed to preserve much of their *Romanes* language and traditional ethnic culture, including the internal self-government institutions such as the public tribunals or assemblies – the *Kris* of the *Olah* Gypsies in Central Europe, the *Meshariava* of the *Kardarasha* in Bulgaria and the *Sendo/Syondo* of the *Ruska/Polska Roma*. Even within the same country the varied experience of separate groups is inevitably reflected in their contrasting ways of life and social standing. For example, the *Bergitka Roma* in southern Poland mainly live in segregated villages and have acute social and economic problems, while in the rest of the country other Roma are scattered among the surrounding population, are considered wealthy and their problems are of an entirely different nature. Likewise, in some Bulgarian cities there are 'Gypsy ghettos' where Roma live on the brink of human existence, while only a few kilometres away, in some villages and small towns, the largest house belongs to a Roma family who are the richest people in the neighbourhood.

Differences in attitudes to self-ascription have already been noted in connection with preferred ethnic identification at censuses and on other less formal occasions. This sense of identity within a particular group or sub-group[10] is evidently influenced by the long-established, if changing, patterns of internal subdivision among Gypsies. At the same time, and in parallel with this sense of identity derived from their group or subgroup, most Gypsies in Central and Eastern Europe have added a qualitatively different, new level to the complex structure of their communal identity. This is the feeling of belonging to the state in each respective country where they live. Examples of this feeling are adherence to the now superseded ideas of Yugoslavism, Czechoslovakism or even the united nations of the Soviet Union, the so-called 'Soviet nation'. The presence of such a level in their identity structure as a result of their developed sense of civic awareness seems somewhat puzzling when compared with the Gypsies in Western Europe and the United States. However, this becomes more explicable in the light of their fluctuating historical experience including the effects of varied policies aimed at regulating them. Equally important is their sustained participation in the social life of the countries and regions where they have been settled for many years – often centuries – which, in turn, has affected their relations with the surrounding population as well as the internal development of their ethnic community.

## Policies towards Gypsies: alternative models

The ethnic and cultural characteristics of the Gypsy communities of the region, as well as the underlying attitudes of the authorities and surrounding population towards them, were formed and moulded within the particular structures of the states where Gypsies lived after their arrival in Europe. Initially this was the Byzantine Empire, then afterwards – for those who remained on the Balkan peninsula – its successor, the Ottoman Empire. Later the Austro-Hungarian Empire and Russian Empire became the home to Gypsies who continued their migration. For those living in the Danubian principalities of Wallachia and Moldavia[11] their status was especially sharply defined. The situation of the Gypsies in these historical states and political formations is particularly important since it sheds light on the origin of their distinctive status and subsequent inequalities in Central and Eastern Europe states which later emerged from the ruins of these empires.

41

There is a wealth of historical information about the Gypsy presence in Balkan lands during the period of the Ottoman Empire. In the fourteenth century many Gypsies came to the Balkans with the Ottomans, either serving the army in various ways or simply as camp followers. Thereafter, the civil status of Gypsies in the Ottoman Empire is somewhat complex since they occupied a unique position in the overall social and administrative organisation of the Empire. Despite the classification of subjects into two main categories, the faithful as opposed to the gentiles, Gypsies had their own, specific dual status outside these two categories. Gypsies were classified on the basis of their ethnicity, an anomaly for the Ottoman Empire, with no clear distinction between Muslim and Christian Gypsies as regards tax and social status. On the whole, Gypsies shared the subordinate position of the local non-Gypsy population. The only exceptions were that Muslim Gypsies and those who worked for the army enjoyed some minor privileges.

In spite of their relative subordination many Gypsies preserved ethnic and cultural characteristics such as a nomadic lifestyle and some traditional occupations. Yet at the same time, many others began to establish themselves in towns and villages and by the fifteenth century there were settled Gypsies in the Balkans who made a living as agricultural labourers in villages and as unskilled workers, petty craftsmen or service providers in towns. Meanwhile, a new type of semi-nomadic lifestyle emerged, where some Gypsies took shelter in a permanent dwelling during the winter but travelled locally in other seasons. Nowadays, however, many Roma in the Balkans still live in urban quarters or neighbourhoods, inhabited predominantly by members of their own ethnic group. This originated as an early pattern of settlement during the Ottoman Empire and created a specific Balkan Roma ethnic culture.

Elsewhere the Gypsy groups living in the Austro-Hungarian Empire felt the effects of the period of Enlightenment when, under its powerful influence, the first systematic attempts were made to integrate them into wider society. The main aim of state policy at that time was to transform Gypsies from a largely nomadic people with no civil status into settled, tax-paying subjects of the Empire. Imperial decrees issued by Maria Theresa in 1761 and 1767 and by her son, Joseph II, in 1783 were particularly significant as landmarks in the so-called 'new policy' towards Gypsies.[12] In this transformation process Gypsies were to abandon their nomadic way of life for a permanently settled one as agricultural workers or craftsmen. To achieve the goal of full integration they were no longer allowed to speak their language, were obliged to dress like peasants and were even issued with replacement, non-Gypsy names. In return, they were granted rights and corresponding responsibilities before the law, including the duty to pay taxes. Special efforts were made to capture the younger generation. Gypsy children were separated from their parents at the age of four, forbidden contact with them and brought up in peasant families. Meanwhile, state and religious education were made compulsory for

42

Gypsy children and after the age of ten they were required to learn useful trades. The ultimate aim of this comprehensive series of measures was the annihilation of a distinct Gypsy community as such and the complete assimilation of all Gypsies.

However, the final outcome of this policy differed considerably from that intended and the consequences are now evident in the countries which later emerged from the Empire. These included the establishment of segregated Gypsy settlements (called *kolonia* in Hungary, *osada* in Slovakia and Poland and *tabor* in Transcarpathian Ukraine) some distance from villages and towns as well as the loss of their language and fundamental ethnic and cultural characteristics for most Gypsies in Hungary and some in the present-day Slovak and Czech Republics.

The situation of Gypsies in the Russian Empire was quite different. There, they were not usually the targets of special attention and mostly stayed beyond the reach of state politics, except for some inconsistent attempts in the eighteenth and nineteenth centuries to apply Austro-Hungarian legislation to Gypsies. These measures included a ban on nomadic life, compulsory settlement in villages, denial of entry to larger cities, etc. However, these attempts invariably failed. For example, the ban on nomadic life turned out to be inapplicable in the vast territories of the Russian Empire and plans to build special Gypsy villages in Bessarabia were unsuccessful. Consequently the authorities soon abandoned any further attempts to regulate Gypsies. The lack of a consistent policy towards Gypsies and the relatively small number of them in comparison with the total population largely explain how these Gypsies managed to preserve their community identity and ethnic culture. Until the end of the Russian Empire most Gypsies lived as nomads or semi-nomads, scattered all over the vast territory of the empire, with the exception of Gypsy musicians in large towns and the settled Gypsies in certain regions such as the Crimea and Bessarabia.

The experience of Gypsies was altogether different in the territory of much of present-day Romania for soon after settling in the Danubian principalities of Wallachia and Moldavia they were enslaved. Gypsy slaves were divided into several categories: slaves of the crown, of the monasteries and of the boyars, as well as the above mentioned distinction into *Vatrashi* or domestic slaves (mostly of boyars or monasteries) and *Layashi* (mostly slaves of the crown). The latter were nomads who were exempted from compulsory settlement on payment of an annual tribute and were permitted to continue travelling while pursuing their traditional occupations. Gypsy groups of this type remained predisposed to nomadism and so have been one source of migratory waves until modern times. Many Gypsies from the principalities emigrated to the Ottoman Empire as early as the seventeenth and eighteenth centuries. Later, what is known as the 'great Kelderara invasion' began as a result of social and economic changes in this region and peaked after the abolition of Gypsy slavery in Wallachia and Moldavia in the aftermath of the Crimean War. These new waves of Gypsy groups moving westwards across Europe in the second half of the nineteenth century changed the previous ethnic balance within the wider Gypsy community throughout Central and Eastern Europe.

The extended account given above has outlined the main patterns of development among the varied Gypsy groups of Central and Eastern Europe set in their specific historical contexts. This background is crucial in explaining both the formation of different patterns and the resulting attitudes of non-Gypsy macro-society, including the adoption of particular state policies, towards this whole community. In the process several basic policy models have been identified, which are still very relevant in seeking to understand the contemporary situation. These models are of the Ottoman Empire (applied on the territory of the present-day Bulgaria, Macedonia, Albania, Serbia and Montenegro, Bosnia and Herzegovina), the Austro-Hungarian Empire (Czech Republic, Slovakia and Hungary, as well as parts of Romania and Poland), the Russian Empire (Russia, Ukraine, Belarus, the Baltic countries and parts of Poland) and finally the unique case of the Danube Principalities (Wallachia and Moldavia in Romania), where Gypsies were enslaved, not regarded as human beings but bought and sold as property.

The three main models[13] can be characterised in the following way as regards the general treatment of Gypsies and ultimate policy aims:

1. Ottoman Empire: civil status of Gypsies preserved but lower than that of non-Gypsies. Policy aim: maintenance of status quo – but free option of voluntary assimilation.
2. Austro-Hungarian Empire: state control over lives of Gypsies, paternalistic role of state in deciding Gypsies' 'best interests', deliberate policy of 'civilising' a 'primitive' people. Policy aim: enforced total assimilation.
3. Russian Empire: on the whole, non-interference in the internal life of Gypsies. Policy aim: sporadic attempts at integration but lack of any consistent policy.

However, these models are clearly only generalised 'ideal types', which actually occur in different variants specific to the individual countries of Central and Eastern Europe. This is especially true of those countries (such as Croatia) or regions (such as Transcarpathian Ukraine) which, due to changes in state borders, were included in different cultural and political regions at different historical periods. Romania, whose present-day territory includes not only the former principalities of Wallachia and Moldavia but also parts of all the three great empires (Transylvania, Dobrudzha and Bukovina) is another specific case.

These basic models exerted considerable influence on state policies adopted by the new ethno-national states that emerged in the nineteenth and twentieth centuries in Central and Eastern Europe. There Gypsies were viewed through the nationalistic lens of the dominant ethnic group in each new 'nation state' of the region and consequently were considered a minor problem compared to the realisation of major 'national goals'. That is to say the governments of these countries did not regard a 'Gypsy policy' as a priority and any such policy was always secondary to more important national interests, e.g. other minorities which were of more immediate concern for various reasons. To give a few examples – in Bulgaria the determining factor in Gypsy policy has always been the prevalent attitude towards the Turkish minority; in Slovakia by the attitude towards the Hungarian minority; in Hungary by the attitude towards the Hungarian minorities outside of Hungary, etc.

In Central and Eastern Europe two fundamental patterns in the relationship between the non-Gypsy population (and its corresponding state) and Gypsies can be distinguished:

1.  *'Traditional' pattern (typical for the pre-industrial age)*
    This pattern is manifested differently in particular cultural and historical regions. According to this model the Gypsies, although categorised as 'alien' and regarded as having a 'detached' status in relation to mainstream society,[14] are nevertheless seen as an inseparable part of society and of the common cultural environment, with their own place in it. However, they are not perceived as an integral (let alone equal) part of the wider macro-society. They are not seen as having any particular problems, since 'they know their place' and do not aspire to change it. This largely explains why Gypsies today constitute a relatively high proportion of the population in a number of countries or regions, especially in the Balkans (including Wallachia and Moldavia) where pre-industrial patterns and social structures are relatively better preserved than, for example, in the West. This helps account for the much lower numbers of their brothers and sisters in Western Europe.

2.  *'National' pattern (first appeared during the Enlightenment)*
    This pattern gradually became dominant in the era of modern nation states – including the so-called 'socialist era'. During this period attitudes towards Gypsies are determined by the requirements of the ethnonational state, which considers them self-evidently as an actual or more commonly potential threat. This is the origin of the general view of them as second-rate humans, whose only positive future is to be initially 'integrated' (i.e. annihilated as a distinct community) and finally – assimilated completely. (In certain historical periods this takes the more extreme form of being seen as sub-human and the 'destiny' proposed is physical extermination.)

45

In fact, whatever the pattern of relationship, Gypsies are influenced by processes of change in wider macro-society and endeavour to improve their social status as well as seeking ways for their total emancipation as communities, especially during the past century within their respective ethno-national states. These Gypsy responses provoke counter-responses, in various forms, of society and state institutions. Such processes are still continuing, especially in those countries or regions of Central and Eastern Europe where the processes of national (and respectively state) development are far from being completed.

During the past decade the development of the countries in the region and the 'Gypsy policies' of their governments have been influenced by the shadow of the previous political order, to be more specific the 'socialist era'. The policies of the state socialist countries towards Gypsies were largely similar and relatively co-ordinated. The best example of this is the enforced settlement of nomadic Gypsies. In 1956 the Soviet Union issued a decree banning nomadism and shortly afterwards, in 1958-9, this action was repeated in Hungary, Czechoslovakia, Bulgaria and Poland.[15] This process of compulsory sedentarisation took place a little later, in the 1960s and 70s, in Romania, Yugoslavia and Albania because of their special circumstances and history. The implementation of the decree took a different form in each country where it was imposed. For example, in Czechoslovakia the authorities made the nomads cease travelling in the place they were when the decree was enacted, and the local authorities then determined where and how they were to settle, while in Bulgaria the Gypsies were moving from place to place in search of suitable villages until the end of the 1970s.

In state socialist countries Gypsies were not granted an equivalent status to that of other minorities. On the basis of Marxist-Leninist theory regarding the hierarchical development of human societies – tribe, nationality, nation – Gypsies were thought to be a community still insufficiently developed to be considered as a nationality, let alone a nation. Moreover, since they lacked a territory, they were regarded as at best an ethnic group and were thus deprived of the rights of minorities recognised as nationalities or nations.

After the Second World War and the assumption of power by the Communist Party there was a short initial period when the state encouraged the Gypsy ethnic community and the development of its culture in all state socialist countries. These few relaxed years were soon followed by prohibitions and restrictions that were relatively severe in some countries (Romania, Bulgaria), while in others (the Soviet Union, Yugoslavia, Hungary) the ostentatious presentation of selected aspects of Gypsy culture still continued, mostly limited to folklore performances of music and dance. Such policy inconsistencies persisted, both between and within state socialist countries. Occasionally the creation of 'Gypsy cultural and educational organisations' was encouraged, only for them to be dissolved later and their organisers

46

frequently persecuted. Meanwhile, hostility to any manifestations of Gypsy ethnicity or culture, condemned as undesirable relics of previous social orders, was gradually mounting throughout the region. Another cause of alarm was the rate of natural increase among Gypsies. Because of their large numbers in most countries, with the exception of Russia and Poland, Gypsies were regarded as a demographic threat. They were a population with a young age structure and high birth rate, giving them the potential to destroy the ethnic balance where they lived and in places even outnumber the surrounding population.

The general aim of Communist policy was to make Gypsies equal citizens of their countries but successful equalisation was understood to mean the complete assimilation of Gypsies, so that they would swiftly vanish as a distinct community. In each country of the region this assimilation attempt had specific forms of implementation. Traditions inherited from earlier periods resulted in subtle nuances in the policy of 'enforced assimilation' in each region and subsequently affected the present-day status of Roma in these countries. In the countries of former Austro-Hungary, Gypsies were regarded first and foremost as a social problem and state policy assumed a mainly paternalistic nature, while in other countries Gypsy-related problems were seen as primarily ethnic in character, with an added touch of religion in the Balkans.

After the 1989–90 regime changes in Central and Eastern Europe the policy[16] of each state towards Gypsies – increasingly referred to as Roma – remained mostly within the established parameters of the corresponding cultural and historical region. Indeed, changes in the ideological foundations of such policies (e.g. the replacement of the concept of socialist internationalism by that of civil society) did not bring about any tangible changes in the attitude of wider macro-society towards the Gypsies or in the main thrust of state policy towards them. In this respect the centuries-old historical patterns of attitude towards Gypsies (both of the society and the state) turned out to be extremely durable without any real hope of change in the foreseeable future.

## Development trends in the Roma community

The Roma in Central and Eastern Europe should not be regarded simply as the passive object of experiments in social engineering throughout different historical periods. They live within broader macro-society and are affected by its many varied influences (economic, political, ideological, etc.), which have had a marked impact on the development of their community. This development is uneven, multi-directional, sometimes even contradictory, but nevertheless three principal interrelated and interacting trends are discernible.

### Development within the community

Internal change is an intrinsic characteristic of community development. The Roma community, like any other community, is not static either in terms of its ethno-social structure or features. Developments within the community bring about continual fundamental changes in its overall structure – divisions within subgroups are established from which new Roma groups are created, while at the same time internal group distinctions dissolve and previously separate groups merge creating different hierarchical levels of metagroup unity. After the break-up of the old empires and the emergence of new states in Central and Eastern Europe this kind of development in the Roma community is now largely confined within state boundaries. Consequently this leads to the appearance of a new level of Romani identity, as mentioned above – a feeling of belonging to particular states.

### Development of the community as citizens of the state

Greater participation in mainstream society is a relatively new phenomenon, typical of the new era, which first appeared at the end of the nineteenth and during the first half of the twentieth centuries. These processes were particularly influenced by the 'socialist era', and it would not be too far-fetched to say that this period was a key factor in the development of the wider Roma community in the countries of Central and Eastern Europe. State socialist policy initiatives, which stimulated and supported the development of the Roma as a community, were mostly limited in duration and contradictory when implemented. These innovative schemes rapidly gave way to the old-established, national patterns of attitudes towards Gypsies. Nevertheless, the effect of such policies in combination with the overall social and political context, was to create and guarantee the existence of a number of opportunities for the relatively equal participation of Roma in social life and the growth of their civil awareness. The end results of these processes for the Roma of Central and Eastern Europe are markedly different from the fate of their brothers and sisters all over the world. In this region there are now many thousands of relatively well-educated Roma, some with prestigious jobs – teachers, medical doctors, lawyers, military officers, journalists, artists, scientists and so on. In this way a new type of Roma élite was created, with new qualities and values, and very different from the traditional Roma élite. Nowadays both types of élite exist alongside each other. The members of this new Roma élite, including their children, are now an important factor in the overall community development of Roma. However, the emergence of this group is not entirely unproblematic and its members should not be considered as the only and necessarily leading representatives of their community.

## Development within global Roma nationalism

Roma nationalism, as a twentieth century phenomenon, is the most recent development trend in the Roma community. Even since the birth and the first steps of the organised Romani movement, representatives of the Roma community from Central and Eastern Europe (or emigrants from this region) have been both its moving and leading force. A central feature of this fresh trend in community development is the construction of a new national ideology. In the process a series of surrounding ideas and tasks is vigorously promoted. Some of the most important are: the use of the general name 'Roma' for all Gypsy subdivisions, an aspiration to union of all Roma, a denial of the right of existence to Roma with a preferred or new, non-Roma identity, changing dimensions in the Roma – gadje dichotomy involving political confrontation (either genuine or pretended), a fresh approach to Roma history strongly emphasising the Holocaust and the standardisation of the *Romanes* language. These developments have attracted a very thin layer of educated Roma, termed 'international Roma' or 'professional Roma'. Amongst their number some are even now endeavouring to rediscover their forgotten Romani ancestors (possibly imaginary). These individuals are not bound to a specific country but to an international institution or non-governmental organisation and have worked at a global level (often without the support of the Roma in their own country).

At present the future development of this third major trend in Central and Eastern Europe is unclear. Many factors are influential – such as the influx of new ideas after the collapse of the Communist regimes, the critical experience of transition in the countries of the region, the rise of nationalism and consequent inter-ethnic tensions, the enlargement of the European Union, the interest in Roma displayed by the human rights movement and its powerful lobby within international institutions, the rapidly developing 'Gypsy industry' of the non-governmental sector and many more besides. Because of the complexity of these processes, it is impossible to predict what might be the outcome of this embryonic global nationalism but there is no doubt that its relative importance in the overall development of the community will continue to grow for the foreseeable future. However, in spite of the many imponderables, Roma nationalism will be unable to develop at all without the active participation of Roma from Central and Eastern Europe. Their presence, in terms of their numbers and abilities, will be the decisive factor in its progress.

These three main trends in Roma community development constantly intertwine and in this way draw strength from each other. In this escalating process members of the new Roma élite in Central and Eastern Europe occupy a key position. A product of state socialist policy, they have made a significant contribution to the growth and promotion of global Roma nationalism, as was demonstrated at the most recent World Congress of the International Romani Union in Prague where Roma from this region played a dominant part. Meanwhile, the expansion of Roma nationalism on a global scale and the effective lobbying of international and human rights organisations have given Roma self-confidence and validated their ambition for participation by Roma, in their own right, in political life. Indeed, such involvement has increased in recent years in many of the countries of Central and Eastern Europe. At the same time representatives of the 'traditional' élite of the Roma community (mainly the *Kalderasha* and other related groups) are becoming more active in the Roma movement at both a national and international level. All these developments are also affected by many external factors operating at quite different levels. These range from the specific situations in the various countries of Central and Eastern Europe, the common procedures for the enlargement of the European Union and the effects of world globalisation. At this stage, therefore, it is difficult to predict how this whole issue might appear in the near or more distant future.

## References

Bartosz, A. (1994) *Nie bój się cygana* (Don't be afraid of the Gypsy), Zglobice: Asterias.

Bari, K. (1999) *Gypsy folklore Hungary – Romania* I – X, (CD collections), Budapest: VTCD.

Bodi, Zs. (ed.) (1997) 'Studies about Boyash Gypsies in Hungary', *Studies in Roma (Gypsy) Ethnography* 6, Budapest: Magyar Neprajzi Tarsasag.

Chelcea, I. (1944) 'Ţigani din România', *Monografie etnografică*, Bucharest: Editura Institului Central de Statistica.

Cherenkov, L. N. (1986) 'Nekotorie problemi etnograficheskogo izuchenia tsigan SSSR' (Some problems in the ethnographic survey of Gypsies in the USSR), *Malie i dispersnie etnicheskie grupi v evropejskoy chasti SSSR*, Moscow: Nauka, 5–15.

Crowe, D. A. (1995) *History of the Gypsies in Eastern Europe and Russia.* New York: St. Martin's Press.

Crowe, D. and Kolsti, J. (eds) (1991) *The Gypsies of Eastern Europe*, New York/London: M. E. Sharpe.

Davidová, E. (1995) *Romano Drom/Cesty Romů 1945–1990* (Romani Roads), Olomouc: Univerzita Palackého.

Demeter, N. (1984) 'Etnonimia tsigan evropeiaskoi chasti SSSR' (The system of ethnonyms of Gypsies in the European part of the USSR), *Etnicheskaia onomastika*, Moscow: Nauka, 28–35.

Demeter, N. (1996) *Tsygane – mifi i realnosti* (The Gypsies – myths and reality), Moscow: RAN.

Druts, E. and Gessler, A. (1990) *Tsigane: Ocherki* (The Gypsies: essays), Moscow: Sovetskij pisatel.

Durić, R. (1983) *Seoba Roma krugovi pakla i venac srece* (Circle of Hell and wreath of luck), Belgrade: Biblioteka Publicistika.

Erdős, K. (1958) 'A classification of Gypsies in Hungary', *Acta Ethnographica* VI, 449–57.

Ficowski, J. (1986) *Cyganie na polskich drogach* (Gypsies on Polish roads), Kraków/Wroclaw: Wydawnictwo Literackie.

Fraser, A. (1992) *The Gypsies*, Oxford: Blackwell.

Gheorghe, N. *et al.* (1997) *The Situation of the Roma and Sinti in Central and Eastern Europe*, Study for European Commission, unpublished.

Gjorgjeviç, T. R. (1903–1906) 'Die Zigeuner in Serbien' (The Gypsies in Serbia), *Ethnologischen Forschungen* I-II, Budapest.

Hancock, I. (1987) *The Pariah Syndrome: an Account of Gypsy Slavery and Persecution*, Michigan: Caroma.

Hancock, I. (1995) *A grammar of Vlax Romani*, Columbus: Slavica Publishers.

Horváthová, E. (1964) *Cigáni na Slovensku* (The Gypsies in Slovakia), Bratislava: SAV.

Hübschmannová, M. (1993) *Šaj pes dovakeras/Můžeme se domluvit* (We can come to an understanding), Olomouc: Univerzita Palackého.

Jurová, A. (1993) *Vývoj rómskej problematiky na Slovensku po roku 1945* (The development of the Roma question in Slovakia after 1945', Spoločenskovedný ústav SAV v Košiciach, Bratislava: Goldpress Publishers.

Kalinin, V. (2000) 'Peculiarities in the functioning of the Baltic Romani dialects under the conditions of biligualism and monolingualism in Eastern Europe', paper presented at *Fifth Romani Linguistic Conference*, Bankya.

Kogalnitchan, M. de (1840) *Skizze einer Geschichte der Zigeuner ihrer Sitten und ihrer Sprache nebst einem kleinem Wörterbuche dieser Sprache, von Michael von Kogalnitchan. Aus dem französischen übersetzt und mit Anmerkungen und Zusatzen begleitet von Fr. Casca*, Stuttgart.

Kovats, M. (1977) 'The good, the bad and the ugly: three faces of 'dialogue' – the development of Roma politics in Hungary', *Contemporary Politics* 3, 1: 55–71.

Liégeois, J.-P. (1994) *Roma, Gypsies, Travellers*, Strasbourg: Council of Europe Press.

Liégeois J.-P. and Gheorghe, N. (1995) *Roma/Gypsies: a European Minority*, London: Minority Rights Group.

Marushiakova, E. and Popov, V. (1997) *Gypsies (Roma) in Bulgaria*, Frankfurt am Main, etc.: Peter Lang Verlag.

Miklosich, F. (1872–1880) *Über Mundarten und die Wanderungen der Zigeuner Europas*, I-XII, Wien.

Mirga, A. and Gheorge, N. (1997) *The Roma in the Twenty-First Century: a Policy Paper*, Princeton: Project on Ethnic Relations (PER).

Mirga, A. and Mróz, L. (1994) *Cyganie: Odmieność i nietolerancja* (Gypsies: difference and intolerance), Warsaw: Wydawnictwo Naukowe PWN.

Popp-Serboianu, C. J. (1930) *Les Tsiganes: Histoire – Ethnographie – Linguistique – Grammaire – Dictionnaire,* Paris: Payot.

Potra, Gh. (1939) *Contributioni la istoricul Tiganilor din România.* (A Contribution to the history of Gypsies in Romania), Bucharest.

Remmel, F. (1993) *Die Roma Rumäniens: Volk ohne Hinterland*, Vienna: Picus.

Szabo, G. (1991) *Die Roma in Ungarn: Ein Betrag zur Sozialgeschichte einer Minderheit in Ost- und Mitteleuropa,* Frankfurt am Main: Peter Lang Verlag.

Soulis, G. C. (1961) 'The Gypsies in the Byzantine Empire and the Balkans in the late Middle Age', *Dumbarton Oaks Papers* 15: 143–165.

Sturkelj, P. (1980) *Romi na Slovenskem* (Roma in Slovenia), Ljubljana: Cankareva zalozba.

Vukanovic, T. (1983) *Romi (Tsigani) Jugoslavii* (Roma (Gypsies) in Yugoslavia), Vranie: Nova Yugoslavia.

Zemon, R. (ed.) (1996) *Zbornik na trudovi za etnogenezata na egiptanite vo Makedonia* (Collection studies on the ethnogenesis of the Egyptians in Macedonia), Skopje: Logos-í.

## Notes

1   Before the changes in 1989–90, the name 'Roma' was used most commonly as an endonyme (an internal community self-appellation) in the countries of Central and Eastern Europe (except for former Yugoslavia) when the Gypsies spoke *Romanes* (the Gypsy language). This name was not widely popular and did not have an official status. In order to be faithful to the historical principle we use the word Roma only for the period after 1989. In all other instances we use the term 'Gypsies'. We think that 'Gypsies' is wider in scope than 'Roma' and we also use it to include the Gypsy communities who are not Roma or who are considered to be 'Gypsies' by the surrounding population but do not wish to be considered as such.

2   The term 'Central and Eastern Europe', as used in that region, refers to the countries from the former 'socialist block', i.e. the Czech Republic, Slovakia, Poland, Hungary, Romania, Bulgaria, Albania, as well as the new states which have emerged from former Yugoslavia (Serbia and Montenegro, Macedonia, Bosnia and Herzegovina, Croatia, Slovenia). It also includes the European part of the former Soviet Union, i.e. Russia, the Ukraine, Moldova, Belarus and the Baltic states of Lithuania, Latvia and Estonia.

3   Since the Sinti in this region are nowadays very low in numbers, with only a few families in Russia, Poland, Hungary, the Czech Republic, Slovakia and Slovenia, we will speak mostly about Roma without needing to make a special distinction between them and other Gypsies.

4   The 1995 estimates accepted by European institutions reflect expert opinion rather than unreliable census data. For these figures, see Liégeois and Gheorghe (1995: 7).

5   According to the 1995 estimates accepted by the EU the maximum number for the region is 6,199,000 (Liégeois and Gheorghe 1995: 7) which is only slightly less than our figure.

6   South eastern Europe includes the previously Communist-ruled countries of former Yugoslavia, Albania and Bulgaria.

7   Examples of such subdivisions, differentiated at various levels on the basis of specific features, in the countries of former Yugoslavia are the following: Arli, Gurbeti, Dzhambazi, Bugurdzhi, Muhadzhiri, Madzhupi, Gabeli, Chergara, Khanyari, Tamari, Romtsi (Shiyatsi), Slovenska Roma, etc. There is corresponding differentiation between groups in Bulgaria, namely: Dzhambazia, Kalaydzhia, Chilingiri, Koshnicharia, Burgudzhia, Futadzhia, Fichiria, Drindari, Vlaxoria (Vlaxichki, Laxo), etc., while in Albania can be found: Kaburdzhi, Mechkara, Kurtofi, Chergara, Bamile, etc.

8   Consisting of the principalities of Wallachia and Moldavia and later also the annexed

territories of Transylvania, Banat, Maramuresh and Dobrudzha.

9 The *Ursari* and *Spoitori* are linguistically closer to the Balkan dialect group.

10 This is not to suggest that all members of a specific group or subgroup necessarily share the same sense of identity. Within a single group individuals may well, and often do, pursue contrasting strategies involving differences in preferred ethnic identification. For example, attempts at 'passing' by individuals of non-Roma appearance as members of the majority community.

11 The status of the principalities of Wallachia and Moldavia within the Ottoman Empire was nominally that of vassals but in practice they were relatively autonomous.

12 In fact, the very name 'Gypsies' was forbidden and replaced with the terms 'new peasants', and 'new Hungarians' on Hungarian territory which at the time included Slovakia.

13 The treatment of Gypsies during the Nazi period could be regarded as an extreme variant of the Danube Principalities model in that in some countries Gypsies were sent to forced labour camps. It is also worth remembering that a contemporary populist solution to the 'Gypsy problem' is to segregate them in special work camps – or worse.

14 As determined by the dominant world-view of the period.

15 In Poland the process of settling nomads was prolonged and a new law for compulsory sedentarisation was passed in 1964.

16 In referring to the 'policies' of these new, post-Communist regimes it should be noted that in some cases a more accurate description would be the lack or pretence of a policy.

## CHAPTER THREE

# Citizens of the world and nowhere:
## Minority, ethnic and human rights for Roma during the last hurrah of the nation-state

*Nicolae Gheorghe and Thomas Acton*

N o one presents a greater challenge to the 'classic' situation in social and cultural policy of equating one people with one culture than the Roma, or Gypsies. For many other groups in Europe, during the last 200 years in European political history, we have witnessed the process of nation-building and the formation of national states. 'Culture' played an important role in this process, since in Eastern and Central Europe cultural nationalism was (and still is) a driving force in the formation and legitimisation of nation-states which have a tendency to become ethnic states, that is states which 'belong' to an ethnic majority.

The idea of state unity is put into practice, among other means, through a policy of cultural unity and cultural homogenisation, frequently imposed by hegemonic political élites on subordinate social groups which are depicted as culturally peripheral and socially marginal. By a process of homogenisation, the local and regional cultures are brought into a 'national culture' which traces its symbolic boundaries in contrast and in sometimes violent competition with 'aliens' and 'strangers' from both within and outside the geographical boundaries. Language, religion, folklore and traditions become the epitomes of this national culture. The peasant communities frequently offer a reservoir of rituals and artefacts which are skilfully processed by an urban intellectual élite produced by the national schools and employed by the expanding state bureaucracies.

This process of state- and nation-building and consolidation via cultural artefacts has its own rituals, frequently sponsored by the state machinery. We are exposed to folk shows, festivals and exhibitions. The contemporary media of mass communication and culture lend this process more penetration and glamour. Traditions are invented and the peasants become French, Germans, Romanians, Slovaks, etc.

Those peoples and groups who are less successful in creating their own nation-states and who are incorporated into the nation-states of other peoples become 'ethnic' or 'national minorities'. They strive for more group rights or the defence of basic freedoms and human rights in terms of their distinctive cultural traits, which then become 'ethnic cultures'. They use similar means (i.e. folklore, festivals, schools and publications in their own language) to affirm and preserve their specific cultures, competing with the dominant nation for the resources provided by the state.

The smaller or even less successful ethnic groups follow or simply imitate the more numerous and successful corporate groups in creating a cultural niche for themselves within the framework of the dominant nation and their state. Local and regional groups such as the *Vlachs* of the Balkans, or the plethora of ethnic groups in the former republics of the ex-Soviet Union provide present-day illustrations of a process which has been repeatedly re-enacted in modern history, only with different actors.

The world's Romani population is increasingly becoming part of a process of political mobilisation, manifest throughout Europe. Cultural affirmation is a component of such a process. We can identify among Romani communities in various countries the indicators (or symptoms) of the cultural mobilisation which preceded and accompanied the process of nation- and state-building described above. An emerging Gypsy political élite has now been for twenty years engaged in a type of self-rallying process. Here and there are cultural festivals, publications in and about the Romani language, readings in Gypsy folklore, textbooks for Romani children in schools and advertising of Gypsy groups and events.

In this chapter we will provide the conceptual background of the strategies used by Roma (Gypsy) associations in different countries to promote the Gypsies' interests in social and political contexts marked by ambiguities of attitude if not by overt group conflict. The main point of our argument is that Romani history and present-day social realities are unusual and diverse cases, in respect of the historic patterns which shaped the cultural nationalism and the tools of cultural policy currently used both by the administrators of the nation-states and by the active élite of various national minorities.

While East European administrators tend to look for the 'uniqueness' and the unity of a people's culture as a prerequisite for promoting distinct cultural entities and a distinct cultural policy within territorially confined administrative units, the Romani people is presenting itself as a huge diaspora embracing five continents, sharing the citizenship of a multitude of states, while lacking a territory of its own. The Gypsy 'archipelago' is formed by a mosaic of various groups speaking both different dialects of Romani as an oral language and a variety of languages of the surrounding societies. The Romani and associated other Gypsy communities share a number of religions and church affiliations; they maintain cultural boundaries not only between themselves and the surrounding environment, but also between various Romani groups themselves.

*Multiculturality* might be an appropriate concept to describe the basic reality of the Gypsy people. While multiculturality could form the basis of an enlightened policy in specific local communities where several ethnic and cultural groups interact and co-exist, it is still difficult to imagine how multiculturality and multi-territoriality could become the basis for the cultural affirmation and development of people, or at least of communities, which strive to identify themselves in respect of other groups in terms of unity and specificity.

The historic diversity and multiculturality of Gypsy groups impose serious constraints upon the formalisation or codification of Romani culture for the purposes of teaching and propagating it, and for putting it on an equal footing with other group or ethnic-minority cultures, not to mention better established 'national cultures'.

What, then, has determined the choice of strategy for Romani people as they face an intensification, even a globalisation of oppression against them? Since we first addressed this issue (Acton and Gheorghe 1992) it has become clear that the epidemic of localised violence against Roma in Central and Eastern Europe was not a temporary by-product of the fall of Communism, but a deep-seated structural feature of the transplanting of laissez-faire nationalism to the role of ruling ideology in those countries. Numerous publications of human rights organisations, above all the tireless European Roma Rights Center (ERRC) in Budapest, give details which show that the twenty-odd racist killings and 400 house-burnings we recorded for 1990–1 were but the swallows of the high summer of murder and mayhem that the 1990s became (Angelova 2000, Cahn 2000) and that have been officially noted by the Organisation for Security and Co-operation in Europe (van der Stoel 2000: 31–42).

The involvement of the latter is symptomatic of the fact that there has also been substantial organisation, both by Roma and by humanitarian sympathisers to support the rights of Roma, and that this has been recognised at both governmental and inter-governmental level. The co-option of able members of minorities by the former Communist regimes had enabled a cadre of Roma activists and intellectuals to gain an education. Part of this cadre now came forward to campaign for their own people facing the problems of 'transition'. They have been greeted by the authorities with small grants and fine anti-racist words. These have not stemmed either the crisis of poverty for Romani workers, who lost their jobs after the fall of Communism and were pushed to the bottom of a new dog-eat-dog economy, or the vicious stereotyping of Roma as parasites not just by skinheads but by other ordinary workers, who have equally suffered as private affluence for the newly rich (including just a very few Roma) is observed from surroundings of increasing public squalor. Roma cannot win against these stereotypes: if they are poor, they are scroungers; if they are rich, they must be thieves; and if they are professionals or intellectuals – what a terrible chip they seem to have on their shoulders – so uncharacteristically bitter that they surely cannot be real happy-go-lucky Gypsies! And emigration continues to mount.

Nonetheless, in seeking legitimacy for their struggle Roma politicians have no choice but to lock onto the same concepts of human rights and anti-racism that operate in international organisations and relations between existing states. But within the set of these concepts, there are some surprisingly sharp choices, as between 'civil rights', 'human rights' and 'the rights of indigenous peoples' which lead to different strategies. Since most states present themselves as nation-states, it is not surprising that the idea of presenting Roma as a 'political nation' has gained some currency (Acton and Klimová 2001). The problem is, however, the nation-states create their structure of rights mainly for their own 'citizens' that is, members of their own 'nation'. The ideology of citizenship as presented in the rhetoric of politicians like Tony Blair, is one of inclusion but the reality of actual laws of citizenship is one of exclusion of asylum-seekers, immigrants, noisy neighbours and Travellers. So, even those who call themselves Romani nationalists had no choice but to organise transnationally, to appeal to international organisations.

This new strategy was set with the revitalisation of the International Romani Union (IRU) after the fourth World Romani Congress, held in 1990 in Warsaw, which despite its organisational haphazardness, legitimised a negotiating team which notched up a number of diplomatic triumphs. Most notably this organisation was recognised by the Pope at an audience with around sixty Roma and others after an international symposium at Ostia, near Rome. In his speech (Wojtyla 1991), the Pope made an unprecedentedly specific endorsement of the International Romani Union and its officers, who were praised by name, and of its participation in forming European Union anti-racist policy. He also made a frankly sociological analysis, reflecting discussions held earlier the same week between his officials and Romani academics and activists, which still encapsulates the hopes and perils of the Romani struggle:

> Your history has been marked by marginalisation and by episodes of discrimination or even violence. But we have now reached a moment in history which, even if some of its aspects are complex and contradictory, presents as never before certain hopeful possibilities. The fall of barriers which seemed till very recently inviolable offers the possibility of a new dialogue between peoples and nations. Minorities are seeking to be recognised as such, with the freedom of their own responsible self-determination and the desire to participate in the destiny of humanity as a whole.
>
> In this revitalised scenario of hopes and plans, you are also invited to contribute to the building of a more fraternal world of an authentic 'common

home' for us all. You constitute a minority which knows no territorial limits and which has repudiated armed struggle as a means of coercion; a minority paradigmatic in its transnational dimensions, which brings together in a single community people dispersed around the world and diverse in race, language and religion.

(Wojtyla 1991)

This goes beyond support for the specific struggle of Roma to a search for a more general framework for the reconciliation of particularist and universalist aspirations. Within this framework, Roma are cast as some ultimate ideal type of minority, implying that if their legitimate rights can be secured, then so surely can those of any other minority. And in justification of the Pope's appropriation of the terminology of the globalisation debate to describe Roma as a 'transnational minority', Romani activists (Rome Conference 1991) claimed that their strategy had already by 1991 created a firm international legal basis for their action through:

(a)  Resolution No. 21 adopted by the 43rd session (August 1991) of the UN Submission for Prevention of Discrimination and Protection of Minorities
(b)  Article 40 of the Concluding Document of the Copenhagen Meeting (June 1990) of the Conference on the Human Dimension of the Conference on Security and Co-operation in Europe (CSCE, now the OSCE)
(c)  the recommendation concerning the solution to the particular problems of Romanies, included in the report of the CSCE Expert Meeting on National Minorities (July 1991)

The most recent OSCE report (van der Stoel 2000:165–175) lists these and later OSCE and Council of Europe texts, culminating in Policy Recommendation no.3 (1998) of the European Commission against Racism and Intolerance, *Combating Racism and Intolerance against Roma/Gypsies*.

## But who are the Roma/Gypsies?

The most intractable problem in drafting these statements of goodwill always seems to be the deciding what word to use as the name of the minority. Not all those politically defined as Roma call themselves by this name; and some of those who do not, such as the German *Sinte*, outraged by what they perceive as claims of superior authenticity by *Vlach Roma*, even repudiate the appellation Roma.

The unity of ethnic struggles is always illusory; but to the participants the task of creating, strengthening and maintaining that unity often seems the prime task. We continue to argue that this strategy, adopted by ethnic militants, is not necessarily either irrational or self-deceiving. If, however, any strategy of ethnic unity is to assist in combating the oppression of an ethnic minority, its militants must be clear about possible sources of disunity. They must also be clear about the way common expectations of ethnic unity have been socially constructed within the framework of various racist discourses created during the decomposition of the Byzantine, Ottoman, West European and Soviet empires.

The illusion of ethnic unity is created by the existence of a common threat – racism. The most far-reaching example in many West European societies is that of anti-Black racism. This has called into existence a Black identity used by militants to embrace groups of startlingly diverse culture, language and physical appearance. But, in so far as these groups share a common experience of discrimination based on dominant ethnic groups' perception of them as non-white, and in so far as culture is experientially determined, that common identity will become an increasing reality. Hancock (2000a), as a Creole linguist of Romani ethnicity, has recently shown how parallels of oppression may lead to parallels of linguistic and cultural development.

This is not to say that racism or Black or Romani identity are the same in different countries. Africans settled in Moscow, London and New York might come to find the others' experience foreign to each of them. But ideas of anti-racism which started in North America have nonetheless been transplanted to Europe, where along with nationalism, Zionism and the ethnic communalism of former Ottoman and Communist lands, they provide the reservoir of concepts from which legitimisations are constructed within ethnic politics.

The need for this chapter arises because the words we borrow to describe Romani struggles already carry with them a pseudo-ontology, pre-suppositions about reality which determine strategy. Both anti-Gypsy racisms and Romani anti-racisms (or Romani nationalisms, or Romani communalisms, not to prejudge terminology) are as diverse as Black anti-racisms and anti-Black racisms. On the face of it, this may make the determination of Romani intellectuals in many countries to construct a common Romani political struggle quite remarkable; but despite the sneers and scepticism of some non-Romani social scientists (criticised by Acton, 1993), Romani activists are subject to the same political logic as other ethnic activists.

The interests which activists from different Romani groups seek to promote by the rhetoric of unity come from different historical experiences, a diversity which goes right back to the earliest periods of migration from Northern India. Recent linguistic arguments suggest that the Romani language and identity derives from a relatively late twelfth century emigration, distinct from the earlier eighth century migration which created the Dom or Nawar and similar groups of the Middle East (Hancock 2000b). It is possible, however, that members of the latter group were the first Gypsy/Indian presence in Greece, but were lumped together by Greeks and

Turks with later Romani entrants. To this day in the Balkans, as in the rest of Europe, there are groups considered by non-Gypsies as Gypsy, on the basis of appearance and lifestyle, but who start their account of their own ethnicity by asserting that, whatever else, they are not Roma.

It is now argued by Hancock (2000b) that the political heart of both Domari and Romani emigrations was probably an army recruiting members and camp followers from a wide spectrum of North Indian society which, by playing an independent military role in the Middle East, assured a continuing cultural identity to its former members. But these armies were treading a path already established by Indian commercial nomads dealing in metalwork, transport and entertainment, and included many from these communities both as soldiers and camp followers, and facilitated the passage of others. In the wake of eventual military defeat these communities may have been drawn together by their common Indian-ness outside India, by their ability to communicate in the Prakritic *koïné* or *lingua franca* (or series of mutually intelligible *lingua francas*) which became the languages we know today as Domari and Romani.

After the reduction by the Ottomans in 1361 of the last Armenian principalities with whom Roma had allied, the large communities in Anatolia and the Balkans began to assume their present shape; rather smaller groups fled Muslim domination to Northern and Western Europe. Much modern historiography tends to represent the European reception of Gypsies as generally hostile from the beginning, but this is misleading. It is true there are examples of bad community relations, slave status and accusations of spying prior to 1530, but these cannot be compared with the sustained genocidal persecution and enslavement over the next century or so (Acton 1981, Gheorghe 1983).

This persecution cannot be explained by any special characteristics of the Romani community, as Gadjo historians claim: if the genocides were really the result of Gypsies being thieves, why did they not start a century earlier? The stereotypes of thieving and fecklessness are the *consequences*, the post-hoc legitimations, of genocide and enslavement, not their *causes*. The decomposition of Catholic feudalism into the West European nation-states, and the beginning in them of agricultural capitalism, together with the redefinition of the Muslim-Christian border, with Romania and Serbia as buffer zones ruled indirectly within the Ottoman Empire, led to general phenomena of inflation, unemployment and xenophobia. These led to religious and ethnic scapegoating against Jews and Africans as well as Gypsies; and in the West Gypsies also suffered scapegoating as 'vagrants'.

Although it was only the most extreme instance of a general phenomenon, this sixteenth century Gypsy holocaust changed the situation of Romani people everywhere and created the new groups and modes of co-existence which lasted until the new holocaust of the twentieth century. Between 1600 and 1800 there was almost no international migration of Roma except in the wake of European colonialism. Large sedentary slave or underclass communities and smaller nomadic groups lived in the Balkans (and in Spain); in the West each sixteenth century political unit created a local ethnic group combining Romani and local commercial nomads; in Poland and the Baltic and in core areas of the Ottoman Empire Roma had a less invidious position as primarily taxable communities.

The content of traditional stereotypes differs between Eastern and Western Europe, though both are overlain with nineteenth century romantic racism. In south-eastern Europe the Gypsy was seen as a slave, someone shiftless, ignorant and stupid, an image quite similar to that created by American anti-Black racism. The north-western European stereotype was more like a down-market version of anti-Semitism in which the Gypsy was seen as a cunning fox, but, unlike Jews, illiterate.

We should add that there are also substantial differences of social organisation between western commercial nomadic groups and eastern sedentary groups. An un-nuanced differentiation might paint the western nomadic groups as anarchic societies, regulating relations between close-kin groups by the process of feuding, and practising marriage by elopement; the eastern, primarily sedentary groups would be portrayed as possessing an embryonic state either in the form of groups of elders or in the form of the consensual *kris* tribunal, which regulates justice, including disputes over arranged marriages (Acton *et al.* 1997).

In practice, of course, actual Romani groups may be somewhere between these ideal types of regulation and anarchy. Furthermore, the return of international migration in the nineteenth century means that over the past century Romani groups with very different culture, dialect, economy and social organisation may co-exist with little contact within the same physical territory.

## And which Gadje are defining the 'Roma/Gypsy' minority?

Very different Romani groups, therefore, exist in different political systems. Since the way the group is defined in each system in academic and policy literature relates to policy justifications, these groups are usually (with exceptions we note below) attached to a conceptual category from the discourse of ethnic/national/anti-racist politics. These conflicts overlap and sometimes conflict. For example, 'nationality', 'national minority' and 'ethnic group' are concepts which Stalin (1942), codifying the residues of Tsarist and Ottoman practice, defined as exclusive categories, and which remain almost as facts of nature in the East. In the West, however, these terms are used much more randomly, almost as synonymous alternatives. They compete with other terms such as 'linguistic minority', 'race' and 'racial minority', and, in the lands where West European colonialism permanently dispossessed previous residents, the 'indigenous and tribal peoples' mentioned by the International Labour Organisation Conventions (nos. 107 and 169).

Within these categories, in particular political-cultural or academic contexts, there may be various sub-species, such as *Deutsche Volksgruppe* or *Österreichische Volksgruppe*. Such groups, whose labels indicate some state recognition of historically-rooted local minority rights, may be contrasted to others, such as 'migrants', 'immigrants', 'refugees', 'displaced persons', 'stateless persons' and so forth, perceived as not thus historically-rooted.

Whenever Gypsy groups are considered by governments as belonging to any of these categories, however, they are being classed within universal human types demarcated by the processes of cultural differentiation which exist throughout the human race. This must be contrasted, however, with another set of concepts which governments use precisely to deny that Gypsies belong to universal categories. For Gypsy groups these are labels like 'Travellers', '*Migranti e Itineranti*', '*Woonwagenbewoner*', '*Resende*', '*Voyageurs*', '*Population Nomades*' '*personnes sans domicile fixe*', 'vulnerable groups', 'a-socials', 'criminal tribes'.

Social scientists may want to place all these labels in a single universal category like 'pariah' or 'under-class', but for governments a major function of such labels is precisely to say that their problem is unique, something that foreign do-gooders know nothing about. These groups are designated as defined by a localised deviant lifestyle, and therefore not ethnic, or possessing any ethnic (in the West) or national minority (in the old Communist East) rights.

Resisting such assimilatory pressure has meant that it is important for Gypsy groups who say they are not Roma to establish that they are ethnic minorities in their own right, whether they are *Sinte* in Central Europe, Irish Travellers, *Beash* in Romania or *Yifti* in the Balkans. Paradoxically, all five World Romani Congresses since 1971 have both solicited and welcomed the participation of such groups, as if asserting that the supposed natural fact of ethnicity is more important than its particularity.

Historical deconstruction reveals to us, however, that ethnic status is more a consequence of policy than a determinant of it. Acton (1995) carried out comparative field and archive research on Romani groups and the *Seui-seung-yahn* fishing and canal-boat dwelling population of Guangdung, China. When he tried to ask Chinese officials in 1980 about this comparison, he was invariably rebuffed by the assertion that the two situations were completely different, because Gypsies *are* an ethnic minority and *Seui-seung-yahn* are not. In fact, however, during the entire Qing and Kuomintang periods, both academic and policy discourse had treated the boat-dwellers as a non-Han Chinese minority, a position only reversed by official research in the

1950s. In contrast, over the same period Gypsy groups had often moved from not being treated as an ethnic group, perhaps not even as 'true Romanies', to being brought within the discourse of 'Race Relations'. In both cases official beliefs about the groups' primordial status had completely reversed themselves, in opposite directions, within the space of about thirty years, at the end of which time officials appeared genuinely ignorant that their predecessors had ever believed differently.

The problem for campaigners, however, is that one may have an analysis that deconstructs concepts like 'race' and 'nation' as malign fictions, socially constructed within the ideologies of 'racism' and 'nationalism'. But if one is campaigning within the framework of laws about 'Race Relations' or 'National Minorities', one has no option but to claim racial or national status. Like much other anti-racist activity aimed at making an impact on racist practices, that of Romani activists often has to make *ad hoc* arguments in terms that capture the immediate attention of powerful persons and exploit their ideological contradictions. It is hardly surprising that most anti-racist rhetoric borrows the conceptual apparatus of racism, seeking to discredit the content of particular racisms, rather than to undermine racism in general. Most ethnic struggles have too much to gain in the short term from their own racisms.

The contradictions which arise from this practice are particularly apparent with Roma. Unlike the common situation of ethnic minorities who are more or less confined to certain territories or regions, Romani communities are dispersed both within and across the boundaries of countries, states and continents in a world-wide diaspora. Specific concepts may be theoretically and politically meaningful in some countries, but meaningless or even misleading for Romani communities in other countries. A specific concept of minority rights may be applicable, even essential, to some particular Romani ethnic groups existing in many countries (cf. Gheorghe 1997) and yet be irrelevant to describing the situation or informing the strategy of other Gypsy groups – even in the same countries.

For instance, the demand of large populations of sedentary Roma in Eastern Europe for recognition as 'national minorities' is shaped not only by post-Stalinist definitions of the latter, but also by historical traditions of cultural nationalism and by the political rhetoric forged in the building of conflicting national states in that particular geopolitical space. Such influences can even be shown in the strategies for creating a literary language, as Friedman (2000) has shown, particularly in relation to Jusuf Shaip's (1980) *Romani Grammatika*, which followed techniques earlier used in the construction of literary Macedonian (Friedman 1985).

This East European concept of 'national minority' cannot easily be appropriated for ethnically similar groups in the West. Could we, for example, imagine one of the more widespread (and more anthropologically documented) groups, the *Kalderash* Roma in New York, Buenos Aires, Balham and Paris, getting together with their relatives in Moscow and the Balkans in a common political action based on their claims as a 'national minority'? If that seems improbable, could we imagine the *Kalderash* or other presently mobile or nomadic groups in the West finding the concept of a 'tribal people', as defined in international law, useful for seeking legal recognition and protection of their distinct cultural identity? Adopting such a label would enable them to network into the political alliances of 'indigenous peoples'. But such an identification would probably be profoundly unacceptable to organisations of Hungarian Romani musicians, or to the developing Central and Eastern European Romani intelligentsia in general.

The difference of interest between long-established communities and more recent migrants recurs throughout the Romani world. In the 1990s Romani refugees in Germany seeking a *Bleibenrecht* had to identify themselves as 'stateless' in order to benefit from the provisions of the 1951 Geneva Convention. Given the reappearance of fascist movements calling for genocide or expulsion in the East, the identification of Romani people as a 'stateless minority' became instrumental for refugees in Germany and some other countries. From the beginning, however, such a strategy was already in conflict with the demand of *Sinte* Gypsies (represented by the *Zentralrat Deutscher Sinti und Roma*) seeking constitutional rights as a *Deutsche Volksgruppe*. Conflicts like these have appeared ever since the renewed international migration of Roma in the nineteenth century and have been exported to the Americas, and even Australia.

We have only begun to explore the diversity of the cultural traditions, class position and interests of Romani groups within specific and also highly variable national and regional contexts, with correspondingly variable approaches to minority rights issues. This variety is not an unfathomable mystery or an impenetrable puzzle, as some traditional social anthropologists who have studied only one Romani group would have us believe, but it is very complex.

## Locating East European Romani politics in an international spectrum

Despite the variety of culture and interest, noted by every sympathetic observer from the Pope down, and even though the content of rejecting stereotypes varies, the brute fact of virulent and persistent rejection has drawn together politically-minded Romani individuals. They stand together against English politicians who, despite never having met a Gypsy, believe Gypsies somehow do not deserve the protection of the Race Relations Act. Likewise they stand together against Romanian politicians who, despite Indian diplomatic intervention in the last decades acknowledging India as the putative country of origin, do not accept Roma as a national or historic minority. Romani politicians assert an ethnic solidarity, expressing the feeling that they belong to the same and distinct people, who share common and enduring cultural traits, similar patterns of interaction with multicultural environments, and common problems resulting from widespread prejudice, ethnic hostility, racial hatred and violence.

Nonetheless, only some of the themes that have engaged the World Romani Congress affect East European Romani politics. One, at least – the defence of a nomadic lifestyle which is the crucial issue for most Gypsy organisations in north-western Europe – is explicitly repudiated by many Central and Eastern European politicians. Many East European Romani politicians in Communist times were engaged in just the same kind of state promotion of sedentarisation that West European Romani leaders were resisting by fighting for camping sites.

At the same time the struggles for cultural and linguistic rights (at least at the folkloric level), which were the most permissible form of group self-promotion in many former Communist countries, were little more than a pleasant but irrelevant dream to most West European Romani leaders, for whom the language issue had little salience.

Equally, the emergence of the asylum-seekers from Eastern Europe has divided the movement. Some Romani people in Western Europe have reacted in the traditional way, resenting immigrants as endangering their positions. The majority, however, have been radicalised during the last decade by pictures of Romanian orphans, and under the growing influence of the Pentecostal churches, have begun to give money towards their relief, a movement towards institutionalised charity which is a radical change in itself. So the majority of Western Romani organisations, both political and religious, have done whatever they can to support asylum-seekers – and are sometimes disappointed to find that some Romani leaders in Eastern Europe tend to regard the asylum-seekers as those who have run away from the struggle against the growing racist violence and discrimination in Eastern Europe.

## Developing theories of human rights

The organisations and campaigns created in these struggles always exist in dialogue or interaction with state authorities and practices, even if this sometimes seems a dialogue of the deaf as far as the state is concerned. Romani organisations respond to policy categories already adopted by the state. The September 1991 Rome Conference statement – of the working groups of academics and International Romani Union presidium members – attempted to square the circle of this diversity by saying:

All Romani political strategies have to combine:

(a) a human rights approach
(b) a minority rights approach
(c) a social movement and community development approach.

While closely inter-related, each of these approaches entails distinct goals, techniques of action and different networks of alliances which may be promoted jointly or severally by governmental agencies, NGOs and by Roma communities and associations.

(Rome Conference 1991: 40)

In fact, if we look more closely, we may see that the second and third of these approaches are often in conflict, while the first may be a kind of synthetic construct used (at least by those Romani activists at the Rome conference) to reconcile rather different struggles. We shall argue that, more than the manipulation of concepts, the adoption of a human rights approach is essential to provide moral legitimacy for sustainable Romani political action, and to allow political solidarity or unity that is not in itself oppressive of Romani diversity.

The social/community development approach, corresponding to 'assimilation' or 'integration' strategies within British 'race' relations, tends to see Gypsy communities as 'backward' or 'underdeveloped' compared with majority communities, and therefore in need of special help. In some contexts, such as that of India, where such special help might consist of building new wells or clinics in a Ghor Gypsy village, one can see how the patronising ideological baggage of such an approach might be presently irrelevant to the villages, though Ruhela's (1968) account of a failure of sedentarisation policy with *Gaduliya Lohars* shows that ethnocentric assumptions can mislead policymakers as much in India as in Europe.

As some European policy-makers came to see the disadvantages of Romani communities as intolerable, they too say the problem is one of civilising a community 'scarcely advanced beyond the stone age' (Hampshire County Council 1962). Caravan sites were seen as transitional arrangements into housing. Special educational provision, although sometimes made to avoid bringing Gypsy children into classes alongside non-Gypsy children whose parents would object, was seen as adapting Gypsy children into school.

It is easy to mock the paternalist racism of such an approach; perhaps too easy to forget that even patronising officials, creating segregated and substandard provision for Gypsies, could be marginalised and insulted by colleagues for providing anything for Gypsies at all. They would have to fight for such policies against the traditional policies of leaving a Gypsy village or ghetto to stagnate in muddy quagmires without electricity or clean water, or simply evicting Gypsies altogether in the West. It is easy to criticise Romani organisations who accepted subsidised folklore programmes in place of civil rights, or accepted bleak caravan sites next to sewage farms in the 1960s and 1970s, if one forgets the realities of forced assimilation, sedentarisation or continual eviction, compared with which any recognition of rights at all for Roma constituted an advance.

Indeed, while Romani activists might now wish to assert there is no specifically Romani problem of poverty, ill-health or housing, it still remains the case that for many Roma their problems of low income, poor health and housing are more politically salient than formal issues of equality or non-discrimination. Thus, although a minority rights approach is more favoured now, it has never entirely been able to subsume the struggles in which Romani activists have been engaged (Gheorghe 1997).

A minority rights approach, as defined in the Rome statement, may appear rather confusing in British 'race' relations terms, because it includes both the account called 'multi-cultural' in Britain (or 'inter-cultural' in European Union terminology) and that called 'anti-racism'. That is to say it can vary from simply bringing a little Romani cultural material or books with positive images of Gypsies into schools, to analysis of the way non-Gypsy racism, rather than some imagined Romani psychopathology or 'backwardness', has led to the sustained disadvantage of the Gypsy community.

Given the fierceness of the anti-racist critique of multiculturalism in Britain (Brandt 2000), it may surprise some that only rarely does this debate break out in Romani politics and studies. The reason is that, given the pervasiveness and respectability of anti-Gypsy racism, (as compared with anti-Black racism or anti-Semitism), a certain solidarity is essential among all those who wish to affirm Romani/Gypsy/Traveller groups' own cultural identity, with associated rights to education, use of Romani dialects and collective public and political representation. That is to say there are too few who wish to deny that total assimilation into the host culture is the price Gypsies should pay to avoid discrimination, for them to fall out too often among themselves.

The problem is that any argument based upon ethnic particularism may be turned back to limit and control the ethnic group in question. In writing this we do not mean in any way to endorse the common racist complaint that any action against racial discrimination constitutes an unfair privileging of ethnic minorities. Rather, we mean to suggest that as long as state action to help end discrimination against Gypsies is organised as a form of counter- or positive discrimination aimed at a particular community, rather than individuals with specific needs and rights, then it is bound to give state agencies more power to define and control those communities.

It was never the point of Indian Reservations to give power or independence to Native Americans. We should not be surprised that official Gypsy caravan sites in Western Europe have multiplied the dependence on state benefits of their residents. A kind of social inadequacy is built into the official perception of Gypsy particularism, so that Romani individuals who might be businessmen, students or professionals are seen as 'not really Gypsies'. A policy in the West of tolerating nomadism is seen as an exception just for Gypsies and in practice means segregated caravan sites. To criticise this is not to deny the rights of individuals to live near others of their own ethnicity, or to choose their own neighbours. One does not need to have a policy of rigidly ethnically segregated housing to achieve such freedoms, however, and such a policy is not, in fact, one of respect for anyone's cultural identity or autonomy. It would, for example, put wholly unjustifiable obstacles in the way of inter-group marriage. In short, defending caravan-dwelling, or nomadism, as an ethnic Romani privilege, is a political blind alley. The right to lead an economically viable nomadic lifestyle, conducted without invading the rights of others, is either a human right, or no right at all.

Does this mean we are saying there is no morally legitimate specific ethnic Romani politics? Far from it. The economic history which has made nomadism a cultural motif for Romani people in north-western Europe is one that gives them a special interest in its defence, and perhaps should oblige Eastern European Roma to understand a little more, if they wish solidarity from Western Europe. The demand for resources to promote Romani culture and identity remains. But the political defence of the Romani language, say, cannot be on the grounds that it is a peculiarly beautiful language (however much we may believe that), but must be on the grounds that everyone has the right to have their mother tongue respected. Everyone has a right to their own cultural identity and to be protected against racism; in short, ethnic rights are morally defensible only as a sub-class of human rights. When Roma fight for theirs, they are also fighting for the future of humanity. A new holocaust would not merely be a disaster for Roma; it would taint, contaminate or destroy all the hope we now have of building a new Europe.

The advocates of the nation-state and the new right in Eastern Europe are charging national minorities with disloyalty; against Roma and the remaining Jewish communities they are reviving the charge of 'cosmopolitanism'. Perhaps Zionism can be seen partly as the ultimate riposte to the charge of 'cosmopolitanism'; certainly the Zionist state may claim to be one of the most anti-cosmopolitan of political entities, a kind of *reductio ad absurdum* of nation-state ideology. There were in the 1960s Romani nationalists who took Zionism as a model, such as Vaida Voevod (Acton 1993: 234), but they have had little influence, for whoever is going to provide the territory or the political will to create Romanestan as a second Israel?

Romani activists are stuck with their cosmopolitanism; they cannot cop out from it with an imitation Zionism or any other kind of ethnic particularism. In fact, while Jews can still imagine that they have learnt from the Holocaust that only having a place of their own can protect them from a repetition, for Roma the lesson is the opposite. For them the twentieth century

Holocaust abolished the protection of the *mehalla*, the ghetto, the segregated pariah nomadism, and the other sanctuaries that emerged as refuges after the holocaust of the sixteenth century.

There is no substitute for having human rights everywhere; this is the logic of seeking to define Roma as a transnational rather than a national minority. It is not so much that the rights of ethnic minorities must be protected, as that ethnic majorities must be in themselves deconstructed. The foundation of global human law must shift from the self-contradictory illusion of national self-determination to a new bedrock of individual human self-determination. The unfolding agenda of Gypsy activism may be nothing less than the abolition of the nation-state. The mere existence of such an agenda has profound implications for any sociology of group conflicts.

## References

Acton, T. A. (1981) *Gypsies,* London: Macdonald.

Acton, T. A. (1993) 'Myth and counter-myth: a response to Jiří Lípa and Werner Cohn', *Nationalities Papers* XXI, 2: 273–81.

Acton, T. A. (1995) 'La construzione sociale dell'identità etnica di gruppi di commercianti nomadi', in L. Piasere (ed.) *Comunità Girovaghe, Comunita Zingare,* Naples: Liguori.

Acton, T. A. and Gheorghe, N. (1992) 'Minority, ethnic, national and human rights: varieties of strategy and interest in Romani (Gypsy) politics in different countries as a case study in the sociology of group conflict', in M. Reidy and S. Udodesku (eds) *A Call for a New Community: Racism and Ethnic Conflicts in the Countries around the Baltic States,* Geneva: World Council of Churches, 29–36.

Acton, T. A. and Klímová, I. (1992) 'The International Romani Union: An East European answer to West European questions?', in W. Guy (ed.) *Between Past and Future: the Roma in Central and Eastern Europe,* Hatfield: University of Hertfordshire Press.

Acton, T. A., Caffrey, S. and Mundy, G. (1997) 'Theorizing Gypsy law', *American Journal of Comparative Law* 45, 2: 237–49.

Angelova, K. (2000) 'Bulgaria's problem is not 'Gypsization' but the abuse with people's prejudices', *Obektiv,* Newsletter of the Bulgarian Helsinki Committee, January-April, 21.

Brandt, G. (2000) 'British youth Caribbean creole: the politics of resistance', in T. A. Acton and D. Morgan *Language, Blacks and Gypsies – Languages without a Written Tradition and their Role in Education,* London: Whiting and Birch, 227–36.

Cahn, C. (2000) 'Unhousing Roma', *Roma Rights,* Journal of the European Roma Rights Center, 2: 4.

Friedman, V. A. (1985) 'Problems in the codification of a standard literary language', in J. Grumet (ed.) *Papers from the Fourth and Fifth Annual Meetings of the Gypsy Lore Society North American Chapter,* New York: Gypsy Lore Society.

Friedman, V. A. (2000) 'Historical, nationalistic and linguistic considerations in the formation of literary languages: past and current problems in the Balkan states', in T. A. Acton and D. Morgan *Language, Blacks and Gypsies – Languages without a Written Tradition and their Role in Education*, London: Whiting and Birch, 37–51.

Gheorghe, N. (1983) 'The origin of Roma slavery in the Romanian Principalities', *Roma* 7, 1: 12–27.

Gheorghe, N. (1997) 'The social construction of Romani identity', in T. A. Acton (ed.) *Gypsy Politics and Traveller Identity*, Hatfield: University of Hertfordshire Press.

Hampshire County Council (1962) *Rehabilitation of Gypsies in Hampshire – A Report by the County Welfare Officer*, Winchester: Hampshire County Council.

Hancock, I. F. (2000a) 'Standardisation and ethnic defence in emergent non-literate societies: the Gypsy and Caribbean cases', in T. A. Acton and D. Morgan (eds) *Language Blacks and Gypsies – Languages without a Written Tradition and their Role in Education*, London: Whiting and Birch, 9–23.

Hancock, I. F. (2000b) 'The emergence of Romani as a koïné outside of India' in T. A. Acton (ed.) *Scholarship and the Gypsy Struggle*, Hatfield: University of Hertfordshire Press, 1–13.

Rome Conference (1991) 'Est e Ouest a confronto – sulle politiche regionali e locali versi i Rom', *Lacio Drom,* Rivesta Bimestrale di studi zingari 27, 6.

Ruhela, S. P. (1968) *The Gaduliya Lohars of Rajasthan: A Study in the Sociology of Nomadism*, New Delhi: Impex India.

Shaip, J. and Kepeski, K. (1980) *Romani Grammatika*, Skopje: Nashe Kniga.

Stalin, J. V. (1942) 'On the nationality question', repr. in J. V. Stalin (1970) *Selected Writings*, New York: Greenwood.

van der Stoel, M. (2000) *Report on the Situation of Roma and Sinti in the OSCE area*, Office of the High Commissioner on National Minorities, Organisation for Security and Co-operation in Europe, The Hague: OSCE, March.

Wojtyla, K. (Pope John Paul II) (1991) 'Di fronte alle minoranze etniche si consolodi una cultura dell'accoglienza e della solidarietà', *L'Osservatore Romano* CXXI (223), 37 September.

## CHAPTER FOUR

# Communist Roma policy 1945–89 as seen through the Hungarian case

*Michael Stewart*

This chapter presents the history of one Communist Party's engagement with a Romani population over the period of its one-party rule. I have not chosen to concentrate on this case because it is typical nor because the lessons we might draw from it are any more generally relevant than those to be found in other cases. My justification is more pragmatic: the Hungarian case is still the best documented and, in the present state of our knowledge, provides the only example from the Peoples' Democracies where we can follow the ebbs and flows of Communist politics with any reliable evidence from the late 1940s through to 1989.

That said, the reader will find in this material general patterns which will, I suspect, emerge more clearly elsewhere as scholars dig into the relevant archives and the history of Romani people in other Eastern European countries is written. The main features of this general pattern I would summarise as follows. First and foremost, Communist policy towards all minorities throughout the regions was decisively shaped by Soviet Marxist doctrine, notably Joseph Stalin's *Marxism and the National and Colonial Question*, originally published before World War I in 1913.[1] Gypsies did not fit easily into Stalin's rather mechanistic model of what constituted a nation and posed a continuous challenge to Communist theorising. Meeting this challenge was made more difficult by the very rigidity of classification within which the Communist Party theoreticians worked. The effects of this intellectual rigor mortis were reinforced by centralised, Party control of all decision making which prevented any form of spontaneous self-expression by Roma and Gypsies. Nor should the role of the police and interior ministry, with their inevitable tendency at that time to view all social problems as threats to 'national/party' security, be underestimated. As a result of the combination of these factors, across the Peoples' Democracies one finds that an explicitly assimilationist Gypsy policy was introduced at the end of the 1950s and beginning of the 1960s. These policies were organised around the notion that Gypsies are a 'social and not an ethnic' layer who needed to be drawn into the proletariat. Finally, in this list of similarities, it seems likely that in each country the Party had to respond to counter-tendencies emerging among Romani groups and persons who sought some form of public expression of their own self-understandings.[2]

Beyond these intra-Communist similarities, there were also, as shall become apparent, ways in which the language of social difference – developed for talking about Gypsies and non-Gypsies in Hungary – was continuous with equally pernicious discourses familiar from the western part of the continent.

## Hungary in the aftermath of war

In August 1947, in the last free elections held in Hungary for forty-one years, the Hungarian Workers (aka Communist) Party (HWP) offered the Hungarian electorate a choice. They could revert to a time when their country was known as 'the land of three million beggars', to a quasi-feudal world in which superiors were sycophantically addressed as *úrám-bátyám* ('my master-uncle'), and when the only routes to advancement in public life were through patronage and corruption, or they could turn and embrace a new future, build a modern industrial society, a social order without injustice and outrageous social inequality.

This vision of a revolutionary transformation within arm's reach was, at best, utopian. The Communists claimed they could construct a post-capitalist regime out of a society that hardly knew what capitalism was, that a people who had no experience of even the 'formal' equality of the capitalist contract, would within a matter of years be able to experience full-blown Communist egalitarianism.[3] Moreover the Communists knew they had to achieve this in a landscape more apocalyptic than any in the capitalist sphere. There were the ravages of war. After six months of fighting on Hungarian soil nearly three-quarters of the livestock had been destroyed and one-fifth of all agricultural wealth. Likewise, the road and rail infrastructure had been reduced to ruins, and this was on top of the earlier dislocation resulting from the subordination of the economy to the needs of the German war machine (Berend and Ránki 1985: 180–3). And then there were the less tangible depredations of the preceding half century – the sixty year-long depression during which Hungary had lost millions of its population in emigration to the other side of the Atlantic and was forced to restructure its economy and infrastructure after the massive loss of territory in 1919. But Hungary's historic underdevelopment did nothing to temper the HWP's certainty in its ability to turn the world around. Just as their Party model in the Soviet Union had produced, in a mere twenty years, a country capable of resisting the mightiest war machine on the continent, so, they were convinced, similar miracles could be achieved in a generation in Central Europe.

Just like the other Eastern European Communist Parties, the Hungarian had been raised in the shadow of its big brother, the Communist Party of the Soviet Union (CPSU). Many of its leading cadres had fled to and then had been trained in Moscow during the 1920s and 1930s. When, after a decade or more of absence they returned to their homeland, they brought with them an unwavering admiration for Stalin's achievement, a rigidity of mind inculcated by his regime in Moscow and a war psychosis in which any line of thought not based on a Soviet model could be seen as a betrayal of 'Uncle Joe' to the capitalists beating at the door to be let in (Berend and Ránki 1985: 196). Their guiding theory, their 'Marxism', had been forged in double quarantine. The intellectual atmosphere of pre-war and wartime Moscow was firmly sealed from external contamination.[4] Moreover many Communists, believing themselves to be the bearers of an objective, scientific discourse, deliberately cut themselves off from alternative, potentially 'polluting' intellectual currents. Secondly, outlawed since the fall of Béla Kun's short-lived 'Soviet Republic' of 1919, the Communists had had little direct engagement with the people whose interests they claimed to represent. Thus, when they took power in 1948 they brought with them a social model forged not from direct experience of local conditions but at a distance, in hushed conversations in bugged Moscow flats.

Isolated, dogmatic, purist and dictatorial it may have been, but the Hungarian Workers' Party was not inefficient. It was typical that in the pell-mell of land reform, nationalisations, cataclysmic inflation and political chaos, it should have found space to begin some kind of debate on Gypsy policy. Though this never got further than the theoretical journal of the Party and, like all other political formations operating after the war, it made no mention of Gypsy issues in its electoral or other manifestos, alone of all the parties that sought the support of the poorer members of Hungarian society in the two elections after the liberation, the Communist Party at least considered whether to address the Gypsies as a distinct group with their own interests (Kálmán 1946).

No doubt, the concern of the HWP with the Gypsy question reflected in part the genuine affinity of interest some party members felt with the poor and their desire to set right the persecutions of the pre-war and Nazi years. As a later commentator noted, the resolution of the Gypsy question was obviously a necessary part of the 'perspective of a model state proclaiming central planning, the rapid arrival of general welfare, the rectification of historical wrongs and the possibility of eliminating social antagonisms' (Báthory 1988: 615).

At the same time, it is telling that the one article in the Party journal argued in brief for the introduction of Soviet policy to Hungary, though it seems this was based on a fundamental misunderstanding of the situation in the Soviet Union (Sághy 1999). Because of the existence of a Romani theatre in Moscow, Kálmán seems to have formed the opinion that in the Soviet Union at that time there were 'developed cultural institutions and literature' of Soviet Gypsies. In Eastern Europe such an institution as an ethnic theatre could only have existed for an officially recognised 'national minority' and so Kálmán seems to have assumed this was how the Gypsies were classified in the Soviet Union. This led him to argue that although the majority of Gypsies had assimilated into Hungarian society through involvement in the labour market, 'for an objective observer there can be no question that the problem of the unassimilated Gypsies is a question of a "national minority" (*nemzetiség*). We are, after all, talking about a social layer which economically, socially and in part linguistically constitutes an independent group'.[5] In reality, the status of national minority had been withdrawn from the Gypsies in the Soviet Union in 1936 along with the associated schools, newspapers and even independent collective farms and workshop co-operatives. The Theatre was simply a rather small hangover of this Bolshevik legacy.[6]

Though Kálmán's may have been a mere personal opinion of a leftist intellectual,[7] his claim, that in the postwar elections the Gypsies 'recognised that it is the Communists who stand up most consistently to overcome social injustices and for the rights of the oppressed [and i]n the elections for Parliament their majority lined up behind the Communist Party', may have carried some weight with more senior officials. Certainly, on the ground the Communists were able to draw on considerable good will from Gypsies. It was the Red Army which had saved the lives of many thousands of them by bringing an end to the Nazi deportations that had begun in Hungary during the summer of 1944, and which had seen through the introduction of a new constitution in which all racial distinction was forbidden. As their *de facto* saviours, the Communists could draw on an enviable political capital. Even forty years later, older Gypsies would talk to me as if the Communist regime still protected them from the wilder elements among the Magyars.[8]

And yet for an outsider it is hard to avoid the conclusion that early HWP interest in the Gypsies was cynical and manipulative. Whenever something of import was at stake, as in the land reform of 1945, the Gypsies were simply forgotten. While other landless labourers, who were reticent about demanding land, were encouraged nonetheless by agitators to make a claim, the Gypsies – one-third of whom had been landless agricultural labourers before World War II – were ignored (Csalog 1984: 50).

The strangest aspect of this is the way in which the persecution of Gypsies by the inter-war regimes and then the deportation of many thousands of Hungarian Gypsies to the German slave labour and death camps was simply forgotten by the Communists, who had so readily taken on the mantle of 'liberators' just a few months back. Despite the promise to offer Gypsies a new place in society, no acknowledgement was made of the events of 1944–5 in which Hungarians and Hungarian troops and police had played a role. No reparations were paid and no memorials were established until the mid-1980s. That period was simply to be swept under the carpet, hardly a good basis on which to establish a wholly new relationship between majority and minority.

A few years later, however, when facing peasant refusal to collectivise the land, the Communists needed other rural people with nothing to lose to form co-operative farms, and they turned to the Gypsies. Writing about the early 1950s a Hungarian dissident sociologist wrote:

> In Ocsárd (Southern Hungary) the Party's propaganda had had such an effect that many Gypsies had joined the Party and as party members agitated amongst the peasants for them to join the collective farm. They attempted with words that had been put in their mouths to raise the sense of responsibility towards collective property among those [peasants] who were formal Co-operative members but who worked exclusively among their own vines and around their own homes. One can imagine the kind of hatred towards the Gypsies thus awakened among the peasants. When later the economic position of the Co-operative improved and peasants joined or became active within it, they drove the Gypsies out straight away.
>
> (Havas 1982)

And just as Gypsies had occasionally been used in the distant past by the authorities when taking anti-peasant actions, they were used to collect agricultural produce for the forced deliveries of the early 1950s.[9]

At the same time, at a central level, harsher weapons were being forged in the Interior Ministry under whose control came the police and security organs. In the pre-Communist past, since at least the 1880s, these had been at the forefront of what they saw as 'the fight against the Gypsy menace'. There had, of course, been a partial personnel exchange since the war, but institutional reflexes die hard. In 1954, in the wake of the introduction of 'identity books' for the whole population (a kind of internal passport with details of residence, employment, children, marital status, etc.), the police took the opportunity to give Gypsies special black books reserved for 'untrustworthy' (*megbízhatatlan*) citizens. By September 1962 an internal report by the Criminal Department of the Interior ministry was able to report that 'the substitution of black identity books, which mark the Gypsies out (sic!) (*megkülönböztetését szolgáló*), has now taken place across the country'.[10] Other, non-police sources were less sanguine about this achievement. An earlier report by the County of Pest in 1957, said that 'the nomadic Gypsies are offended by the actions of the interior ministry's agents who are proceeding to swap the red identity books for black ones, and feel that this is a form of racial discrimination' (Sághy 1999: 18). The practice seems to have stopped around 1963, but the separate treatment of so-called 'Gypsy crime' by 'specialised' police detachments continued throughout the state socialist period.[11]

However, such heavy-handed and openly repressive responses to the

'Gypsy question' never accounted for the whole picture. In 1948 a Welfare Ministry official proposed the development of a new social policy aimed at Gypsies, and although the initiative floundered on opposition from the Interior Ministry, the fact it occurred at all demonstrates the existence of an alternative to what were known as 'administrative measures' (Sághy 1999: 17). The most dramatic example of such a differing approach comes from the support that a Romani woman, Mária László, received in establishing the Hungarian Gypsy Cultural Association (HGCA) (*Magyar Cigányok Művelődési Szövetség*) in 1957. This was the first ever national organisation of Hungarian Gypsies and despite its short-lived existence remained an inspiration to the generation of activists who emerged thirty years later during the twilight years of state socialism. Thanks to the diligence of a Hungarian journalist, Erna Sághy, we now have a much fuller picture of the background to this initiative (Sághy 1999).

Mária László was the Romani-speaking[12] daughter of a Gypsy musician from the village of Pánd. The fact that she had grown up speaking Romani is in itself rather striking, as only a few so-called 'musician Gypsy' communities had retained their own language in Hungary by this time. In all likelihood this profoundly shaped her political horizon. In the 1930s, as a journalist, she had fallen foul of the authorities when she had protested against anti-Gypsy discrimination. She had been arrested and sacked from her job in 1937 and then kept under surveillance.

After the war she rose to seniority within the Budapest Social Democratic Party which 'merged' with the Communists in 1948. In August 1954 she wrote to the Budapest Party committee asking for the creation of a specialist committee to address the problems of Gypsies. Eighteen months later she approached the Council of Ministers, 'with the request that you bring into existence an organisation for the Gypsy fraction of our people, like those that exist for other national minorities, which would deal with economic, political and cultural issues' (Sághy 1999: 21). She went on to complain that the Romani language was not allowed in official communications, there were no Romani newspapers or schools and Gypsies suffered from continuing discrimination. Attached to this request were two other documents, one from her own community requesting that the Gypsy children be allowed into school and the other, signed by famous Gypsy musicians, requesting the creation of a national Gypsy association.

This was an extraordinary and daring request and one which, in the aftermath of the 1956 uprising amidst official fears that the Gypsies had played a disproportionate role in the 'counter-revolution', bore fruit in an organisation whose founding documents defined it as 'in part a state institution, in part a mass organisation of Gypsies for the resolution of their own problems'.[13] To understand the significance of this achievement, it is necessary to know a little about how Communist nationality politics functioned.

## Autonomy, national minorities and 'the leading role of the Party'

Unless one has lived in the old Eastern Europe, or in similar societies led by an explicit ideological credo, it is hard to imagine the ways in which the 'bottom-up' processes of public and political life were constrained, as if by a straight-jacket. If the political leadership had simply forbidden all political and civic activity on the part of ordinary citizens and explicitly decreed that there was no freedom of assembly or speech, perspectives might have been relatively predictable and transparent. Instead, socialist citizens were caught in Escher-like landscapes, offering impossible – if tempting – visions of 'socialist freedom', to persons such as Mária László. On paper socialist citizens had most of the rights of their western counterparts – including those of association. But these rights were counterbalanced by what might be termed rights of the whole society. The supreme 'social right' was to advance towards 'socialism', embodied in and guaranteed by what was known as 'the leading role of the Party'. That is to say the Communist Party as 'bearer of the historical mission of the working class' was empowered to legitimise or delegitimise any and all social initiatives in terms of whether they saw these as advancing or hindering the cause of the 'people'. To establish an organisation, it was first necessary to find a law that enabled such an institution to come into being or to find an acknowledged, theoretical status within Marxist Leninism, which would explain the necessity of this particular initiative. Even then it was possible to fall foul of the authorities.[14]

As has often been remarked, the Marxist Leninism of Eastern Europe had theoretical difficulties with the idea that people have national affiliations. Indeed it had been constitutionally incapable of deciding whether 'national sentiment' was, as Ernest Gellner (1983) put it, misdirected class sentiment or the illusory/ideological product of class society. Either way, although one might tolerate it as one does an immature child, national attachments were something to be grown out of. The first two decades after the Communist take-over in Eastern Europe were also a time when all forms of national and ethnic self-expression were discouraged as symptoms of a regressive concern with particularity and difference, as opposed to the forward-looking spirit of socialist internationalism. The fact that few of the states in the region were genuine nation-states and all were based on fragile coalitions of different ethnic groups meant that the expression of national sentiment was the road to war and disaster and was thus in a sense taboo.

Other factors played a role in this antipathy to nationalist expression. The Hungarian, as other regimes, was still committed to the modernisation of society through mobilising the greatest possible unity of the population. Unity was to be achieved via homogenisation of the population, an early version of what Ceauşescu notoriously later named 'systematisation'.[15] The resulting cohesive social whole could then be directed by all-knowing governmental agencies to the co-ordinated achievement of centrally defined goals, the output targets and projected house-construction of the five-year plans and so on. In this historic struggle against the legacy of centuries of backwardness and underdevelopment, unity was all. Economic, social, cultural and especially political variation between social groups, far from providing a source of dynamism, appeared to threaten conflict and division. Moreover, as Andras Kálmán had noted back in 1946 in the Party journal, the risk with giving the Gypsies their autonomy was that they were likely to 'understand freedom in an anarchistic fashion' (Kálmán 1946).

For these reasons a group of Gypsies in 1956 could not simply form an association to protect and advance their interests. In order to gain a public voice they had first to explain why they, as Gypsies, should be granted this privilege and gain the backing of the Party. Only if they passed this test could they hope to form themselves into a constitutionally legitimate institution. No detailed records have been found as yet of the discussions that were held around László's proposal. Certainly, some senior Party members would have been involved in discussing the possibility of a national organisation potentially regrouping so many citizens. László seems to have seized the opportunity presented by the establishment of a new Department for National Minorities within the Ministry of Culture in the summer of 1957 and pushed through a compromise resolution allowing herself and a few colleagues to begin to operate from within the ministry. Although László clearly had her supporters within the Culture Ministry, not everyone in the now renamed, Hungarian Socialist Workers' Party can have been happy since two senior members of the Ministry of Labour, György Bán and Géza Pogány, were meanwhile set to work to produce a 'scientific' report on the nature and possible resolution of the 'Gypsy question'.[16]

Quite what the relationship was between these two initiatives we may never know. It is striking, however, that only a few days before the officials completed their report and without any top-level Party decision being taken, a junior officer in the Ministry of Culture held a press conference announcing the formation of the HGCA on the basis of a decision at a meeting of deputy ministers.[17] It may be that László and her supporters suspected that the report being produced by the Ministry of Labour might not be wholly supportive of their initiative or that they could feel the wind of tolerance, which had blown since the 1956 uprising, beginning to wane. The manner of the Association's foundation is indicative of the challenges being faced. On the one hand the name of the Association was modelled on the names of the organs of other officially recognised 'national minorities', the Romanians, Germans and Slovaks. To the attentive observer this would have suggested that the Gypsies were on the way to a very major change in status and gaining the rights to social and cultural autonomy of a 'national minority'. On the other hand, the fact that the decision to launch such a potentially powerful organisation was announced at a press conference by a deputy in the Ministry of Culture, without any preceding 'high-level' Party decision, might have indicated to the reader of the Party's runes that a profound change in Gypsy fortunes was still only a possibility.[18] When Bán and Pogány did publish their study while they called for the formation of an organisation to deal with the 'Gypsy question', they noted that 'according to newspaper reports' such a body 'seems' to have been formed. Maybe Bán and Pogány were just out of the loop, but it may have been that they were trying to make a – typically indirect – point about what would be read as a 'dangerous lack of co-ordination' in this sphere.

In their own discussion Bán and Pogány offered no definitive statement on the kind of self-organisation appropriate for the Gypsies and seemed willing to contemplate certain 'messy' solutions. They were clear about the formal qualifications in Marxist-Leninist terms for a people to assert 'nationality status'. A common language, a common territory, an economic life in common and a common mentality were the accepted criteria; Gypsies had neither a land nor an economy in common.[19] It was also unclear whether Gypsies formed a united social group since in language and other terms there were major differences between distinct Gypsy populations, even within Hungary's borders. On the other hand, since they also differed linguistically from the Hungarians and appeared to have a different mentality, they could not be part of the Hungarian nation. Moreover, Bán and Pogány pointed out, though the concept of a 'nation' might be clearly defined in Marxist Leninist thought, the notion of 'national minority has never been clarified' (Bán and Pogány 1957: 12). They noted that its definition in common speech was somewhat contradictory since it referred to people who had had a nation state but was nevertheless widely applied to the Ukrainians who had never had such. So, in answering their question 'just how can we consider the Gypsies?' Bán and Pogány fell back on a different evolutionary discourse and recommended treating Gypsies as a post-tribal population among whom social classes had come into being but which still had not reached the stage of being able to form an autonomous nation-state. Citing the examples of the Mongols and the Kyrgyz in the Soviet Union, they argued that nation-states can be formed from such populations under socialist conditions. However, and here the old Communist prejudice against the Gypsy life-style came back into play, in the end they asserted that Gypsy society is 'stagnating or possibly developing backwards' and was therefore most unlikely to have the 'state-forming capacity' of these other 'progressive' nations.[20]

Bán and Pogány were possibly doing little more here than articulating Party common sense, of which Mária László would have been acutely aware.[21] Certainly, the HGCA seems to have shied away from formally demanding national minority status if only because aware of its fragile position in Hungarian national politics. For instance, in a plan of action written at the end of 1957, László announced that they would create a Romani-Hungarian dictionary, but she stressed it was not for use in schools (which would be the automatic right of a 'national minority'), only in 'scientific institutions'. She also made the decision not to turn the HGCA into a membership organisation (like those of the other national minorities) with local bodies – clearly this would have been a step too far.

Within these constraints, László did manage to operate rather effectively for a short period, providing political support and economic and administrative help to the few Gypsy steel-working co-operatives and similar ventures, some of which like the nail-making co-operative in a village north of Budapest continued right through to the end of the 1980s. But it was her very success in fighting for Gypsy rights, in turning the HGCA into a representative of the Gypsies' interests (*erdékvédelmi szervezet*) that resulted in her greatest problems. Two actions in particular may have been decisive. In late 1957 and early 1958 there was an official re-examination of all 'self-employment and tradesperson' permits and the HGCA received an increasing number of complaints from Gypsies who now lost these. Mária László was active in pursuit of her supplicants' claims. And then, from the spring of 1958, the HGCA archives reveal an increasing number of complaints about Gypsies being interned in the area around the community of Tokol for 'crimes' like 'drunkenness', 'horse-dealing', 'begging' and 'avoiding work'. László penned a sharp letter of complaint to the Chief Prosecutor (Sághy 1999: 25–6). Within weeks László Farkas, the head of the Department of National Minorities, 'discovered' that Mária László had in her youth in the early 1940s belonged to a 'fascist organisation' (in reality the University and High School Students' National Service organisation) and she was relieved of her position. From then on the affairs of the HGCA were kept under Farkas' control through two of his protégés, Sándor Vendégh and Mrs Lajos Marosán.

It was Sándor Vendégh who produced the decisive public shift in the debate on a Gypsy policy in early 1960 when, in another Communist journal *Tajékoztató* (Information), he published an article criticising the work of previous years through the device of a sharp critique of Bán and Pogány's work and in the process re-emphasising the old Communist hostility to the non-proletarian 'Gypsy way of life'.[22] Vendégh attacked the Ministry of Labour officials for a crude moulding (*sablonos*) of Marxist principles to the case in hand and suggested that their nice distinctions were 'based on philosophical principles not on the realities of life and thus put the Gypsies outside of any nation (or society)'. In his dismissive use of the term 'philosophical' Vendégh was of course referring to Marx' image of philosophy as an activity divorced from real life, from practical engagement with the world. Bán and Pogány, it was therefore implied, were engaged in an idealist, not a Marxist pursuit.

Instead, Vendégh argued, looked at 'materially', the Gypsies were more or less assimilated members of the Hungarian population and in so far as they were not fully assimilated, this was only due to their 'old, primitive life-style' (Vendégh 1960).

Vendégh continued:

[T]here are some theoretical questions which have to be cleared up in order to set out our tasks. Above all else we have to mention those harmful tendencies which obstruct work among the Gypsy population. It is not rare that we find notions that the Gypsy question is a 'national minority' question and that one should sharpen the Gypsies sense of being a 'nation' or 'national minority'.

(Vendégh 1960)

Picking up the distinction Bán and Pogány had made between 'progressive' and 'reactionary' nations and nationalisms the author went on to explain:

[T]he question of the national minorities, like all other social phenomena, does not exist of itself and it is necessary to examine in the case of each national movement whether it aids the socialist cause or not. Thus the national question, just like the Gypsy question, has to be subordinated to the socialist cause. The separation of the Gypsies, their segregation, would not help social progress, on the contrary it would push them away from those social and cultural transformations occurring in our society. The Gypsies only constitute a separate group from the point of view of ethnology, forming to some extent an ethnographic group, which is however gradually dissolving into our Hungarian nation.

(Vendégh 1960)

So, the best that could be done would be to assimilate the Gypsies as soon as possible to the Magyar working class.

In this volte-face, away from any recognition of Gypsy 'cultural specificity', the Party received support from two other sources. First, there had been changes in official attitudes in the Soviet Union after the 'discovery' in the 1952 census that there were 'still' 33,000 'nomadic' Gypsies living freely in the USSR. In 1956 Gypsy nomadism was formally banned and all Gypsies ordered into regular waged employment. Some 10,000 Gypsies were moved to Siberia.[23]

Second, and more importantly, the Party also received crucial support from the only ethnographer of Gypsies working in Hungary at that time, Kamill Erdős. Erdős' attitude was always complex and, to my mind, contradictory but in the end he resigned himself to the full-scale assimilation of all Gypsies into the socialist order. To that end he proposed a two-headed policy: firstly, campaigning against Hungarian prejudice by explanation of the 'real' condition of Gypsies and publication of their cultural treasure (songs, stories etc.); secondly, at the same time conducting the fiercest campaign to free Gypsies from the effects of the past.[24] Trying to encourage use of Romani in

81

schools, for instance, was 'utopian' and wrong-headed because 'it would prevent the progress of the Gypsies, because it would lead to a harmful separation of them [from others], and it would encourage the conservation of an anachronistic life-style whose time has passed' (Erdős 1960: 130).[25]

When Bán and Pogány had carried out their initial enquiry into the status of Gypsies they had noted that 'in determining the constitutional status of Gypsies it would be useful to know what the Gypsies themselves think'. They themselves had gone out of Budapest to survey the situation and had met and talked to at least one (sic!) Gypsy but had then relied on an early (1957) summary of Erdős on the classification of Gypsies by language and what he called 'tribe'.[26] They had left the final 'scientific' classification unresolved. In his 1957 study, however, Erdős had not posed the question of whether Gypsies saw themselves as a nation. Instead, in 1960, Erdős provided the Party with the answer it wanted to hear: 'the essence of the Gypsy question is that there is no Gypsy question – the Gypsies want to assimilate into the Hungarian population!' (1960: 190). Having opened his paper with a slogan, he tried to make it more precise, 'the Gypsies want to dissolve into the Hungarian population, they want to become Hungarian citizens with full rights' (1960: 192). In talking thus Erdős was moving among slippery categories as he must have known. I, for instance, well remember a Gypsy man telling me proudly that in twenty years time there would be no *Cigány* left at all. A week earlier he had complained bitterly that the *gazo*s so look down on the Rom that they won't teach their children in Romani at school. On the first occasion this man was talking of rights in the formal legal sphere, on the second about his basic self-understanding and desire to transmit this to his children.

So, the sole Hungarian intellectual who knew Gypsies well and had carried out research among them came down on the side of a powerful assimilationist programme. Once Erdős had fielded his contributions the game was more or less over: no one was going to give Gypsies themselves a second chance and there was no one else left on the touch line to suggest an alternative.

## The Gypsies as a 'social problem'

In the founding statement of the HGCA it had been said that 'the Gypsies' problems had to be solved by the Gypsies themselves, with the help of state organs'.[27] The HGCA, apart from providing a legal forum for Hungarian Gypsies, above all had offered them a status and rights as Gypsies. The effect of Vendégh's and Erdős' contributions to the debate was to reverse this situation. From now on even a mild degree of political and social autonomy as members of an 'ethnic group' would be the last things to be granted to the Gypsies. But if the politics of 1957–60 had been rejected, a new policy was needed, one directed by non-Gypsies even if aimed at Gypsies. Fifteen

months later, on 20 June 1961, the Political Committee adopted the assimilationist policy which, in one form or another, dominated 'Gypsy policy' until
the late 1980s.[28]

A number of features stand out about this decision. Most importantly,
the Gypsy problem was defined as being a social, not an ethnic or national,
problem. In a phrase that was to shape the next twenty-five years of Gypsy
politics the Political Committee stated 'in our policies towards the Gypsy
population we must start from the principle that despite certain ethnographic
specificities they do not form a "national minority". In the resolution of their
problems we must take into account their specific *social* situation' (Mezey
1986: 242, my emphasis). The way of life of the Gypsies was not so much a
culture with a certain autonomy from economic and social conditions, it was
a direct reflection of their lumpen social situation. Thus there were three
groups of Gypsies defined by their position in the 'mode of production' and
consequent general proximity to Magyar culture (Mezey 1986: 240).

Following on from this, the nature of the Gypsies' way of life had its
roots in their historical position in feudal, then capitalist society. While they
had performed useful social functions in the distant past 'in capitalist society
the Gypsy population was excluded; a mutual lack of trust and the deep rift
of prejudice arose between the Gypsy and non-Gypsy population' (Mezey
1986: 240). Their old skills had become redundant and as a result their way
of life now was characterised by scavenging, begging, hustling, dealing and
general laziness. In the face of what seemed no more than a 'survival' of a
defunct way of life the Party set itself the task of ending the conditions which
had reproduced the Gypsy way of life and thereby their existence as a separate population. The mere existence of three different 'groups' of Gypsies was
self-evident proof that the inexorable process of assimilation was taking place
anyway. The role of the Party was simply to speed this up.

Acceleration of the inevitable course of history was to be achieved by a
combination of campaigns. Establishing the discipline of regular labour, the
civilising effects of decent housing and educational achievement would work
together and as each improved, so Gypsies would become barely distinguishable from other members of Hungarian society. There was an almost mechan-
ical logic to their theory as if (Gypsy) x (socialist wage-labour + housing +
education) = (Hungarian worker) + (Gypsy folklore).[29]

Perhaps the most important feature of the party decision was the unrealistic nature of its assumptions even in its own terms. The Party had decided
that Gypsy self-classification would be irrelevant in determining their
response to the assimilation programme. Theoretically speaking, it is conceivable that giving work and better housing to a people wholly excluded from
society, integrating them into a 'society' from which they had no contact,
would change their whole way of thinking. But what the Party failed to see
was that all Gypsies were already intimately integrated into Hungarian

society, had constant contact with Magyars for whom they worked, had often had jobs in socialist industry and yet had maintained their distinct identity.[30]

In a sense then, the policy agreed in 1961 was impossible to implement. Completely denying the Gypsies any contributory role, the Party line would constantly have to be adapted to the unpredictable ways in which Gypsies themselves responded to official regulation. Moreover, by greatly downplaying the importance of Magyar prejudice the policy effectively opened the door to the implicit incorporation of all the worst aspects of anti-Gypsy sentiment as it was applied in practice. All the more so as, in so far as large numbers of Hungarians came into more intensive contact with Gypsies in their places of residence, education and work, new tensions and hostilities emerged between the two 'groups'.

The theoretical difficulties the Party ran into were a harbinger of later difficulties in implementing the policy. Every five years, towards the end of one five year plan, but in time to prepare the next one, committees of the Party carried out assessments of the preceding period and set goals for the next one. These were *de facto* occasions for small shifts in policy to be registered, if not formally acknowledged. In 1974 a number of factors conspired to bring unbearable pressure on a policy that had been held to without wavering since 1961. A sociological report, commissioned by the Agitation and Propaganda Committee of the HSWP and finally published in 1972 after attempts to suppress it had failed, had not only revealed that Gypsy poverty was a pressing reality in 'late socialist' Hungary, but had gone on to urge the formation of Gypsy cultural associations to help Gypsies find their own cultural resources. At the same time, and here thanks almost entirely to Communist policies, increasing numbers of young Gypsies had received higher education and some of them were pressing to be allowed to 'work for their own people'. Finally, the anti-nationalist sentiment of the 1960s had begun to pass. Thus it was in 1974 that the Agitation and Propaganda Committee (one rung below the Political Committee) introduced the term 'a social layer with its own characteristics' (*sajátos népréteg*) to describe the Gypsies. Fearful that this might introduce confusion, the report rejected the sociologists' demands for independent Gypsy cultural institutions as a form of 'left-wing communism' of the post–1968 Western sort! Again the Party may have taken succour from the various publications of a team who claimed Erdős' intellectual heritage, an amateur linguist and ethnographer, Józef Vekerdi, and his collaborator, György Mészáros, who together and severally published a string of works in official journals 'proving' that everyone, the Gypsies included, would be better off once the Gypsies no longer existed. Their amateurish accounts of Romani linguistics pandered to the folk notion that this language was little better than a slang made up of bits and pieces from various halting points along the Gypsies' 'route towards Europe' – as opposed to an (ideological) notion of pure and more or less stable real/civilised languages (like

Hungarian). With this kind of material being published, the idea that Gypsies were cultural ciphers continued to shape public policy.[31] Ironically, sympathetic Marxist writings, which one-sidedly stressed the role of capitalism in crushing the 'ancient' 'folk-culture' of Gypsies as the most oppressed landless people, may have given further credence to this view (e.g. Tomka 1984).

It was characteristic of socialist societies, that it was not until official Communist theory on the national question *in general* had been given a theoretic kick into the present, that movement was possible on the Gypsy front. In 1976 a book by the Russian ethnologist Juri Bromlej, *Ethnos and Ethnology*, was published in Hungarian. For the first time in Eastern European official Marxism theoretical legitimacy was accorded to a concept of what one might wish to call 'cultural identity'. At the same time a new book by a leading Hungarian Party theoretician, Herczeg, explained the official policy towards the recognised 'national minorities'. Herczeg noted that in everyday Hungarian one word was used to describe both the processes of assimilation and of integration (*beilleszkedés*, literally 'fitting in'). Herczeg suggested that 'assimilation' (*asszimiláció*), in the sense of the complete social, economic and cultural merging of one group with another so that the assimilated group lost all sense of ethnic identity, be distinguished from integration (*beilleszkedés*), in which the 'level of civilisation' and life-style of a people might approximate its host population while the group retained its distinct ethnic identity.[32]

The groundwork having been done on the relatively safe terrain of the acknowledged national minorities, it was possible for others to use the chance presented by Bromlej and Herczeg to open the first crack in the Gypsy policy. Thus three years after the Agitation and Propaganda Committee discussed the Gypsy question, the Minister of Culture issued new guidelines on the interpretation of the term 'assimilation'.[33] These suggested that for the Gypsies there might be an alternative to straightforward assimilation. They could now be accepted as an 'ethnos' even if they did not have the capacity (as yet) to form a 'national minority' and, as a group with an 'ethnos', they could claim the right to 'integrate' and yet not 'assimilate'. In his guidelines the minister distinguished 'direct' and 'indirect' '*beilleszkedés*' of Gypsies along the lines Herczeg had followed in separating assimilation from integration. He noted that where there was a Romani speaking population 'on occasions this will mean the use of the Gypsy language in cultural work; support for the valuable elements in Gypsy culture; and, as a stepping stone, support for homogeneous Gypsy cultural associations'.[34] This step was a significant one for Gypsy intellectuals as it gave them a legal space to continue cultural activities among their people, which had in any case begun spontaneously at this time (Mezey 1986).

So, sixteen years after having been closed, the gates to Gypsy self-expression had once again been opened. Two years later, in 1979, the Political Committee of the HSWP accorded the Gypsies the status of an 'ethnic group'. This status had no direct legal implications but reinforced the ideological-cum-moral stance adopted in 1977 and bore fruit as state policies liberalised into the 1980s. In 1984 the Agitation and Propaganda Committee admitted that 'in Hungary Gypsies make up the numerically largest ethnic group with its own culture and traditions ... their number is larger than that of all the other national minorities put together' (Mezey 1986). From now on the Party's goals for Gypsies were either the wholesale adoption of Magyar culture or integration while maintaining 'traditional culture', which was no longer held to be the reflection of social backwardness and 'lumpenisation'.

As a direct result of this decision the space for independent Gypsy activity increased: 'reading camps' were led each year by Romani and other Gypsy intellectuals for Gypsy children; cultural clubs operated with public funds in several rural and urban centres; in 1985 an advisory body of centrally selected but locally based ('trustworthy') Gypsies was set up to deal with social and political concerns; in the following year plans were laid for the foundation of a Gypsy Cultural Association and in January 1987 a partially bi-lingual monthly Romani/Gypsy newspaper (*Romano Nyevipe/Cigány Újság*) appeared on the newstands.

On the other hand, as János Báthory pointed out, the 1984 decision avoided taking a clear attitude to the previous policy formulation. It hints that those who think about Gypsies as a 'national minority' are not actually committing a political sin but refused to say so outright and above all did not renounce the earlier rejection of all forms of Gypsy 'nationalism'. It thus left Gypsy politics exactly where the rest of Hungarian social and economic policy lay in the last years of Communist rule: balancing between two stools with the now tottering élite always capable of shifting its weight from side to side when the pressure to come down on one became too great.

## Conclusion

It has become fashionable to argue in Western countries, which never suffered one-party rule, that the Communist period in Eastern Europe 'had its good sides', its winners as well as losers. In a sense this is true of any regime: think of the German autobahns. But the argument goes further in the case of the Gypsies. Many believe that because their position has by and large (though not universally[35]) worsened since 1989, Communism was for them 'a good thing'. In reality this is no more true for them than for the other poor of Eastern Europe. Indeed, crucial aspects of official policy towards Gypsies have left a damaging legacy of forty years of social mis-management. To give a few examples: the terms of reference within which 'the Hungarian question' (how can one construct a democratic, relatively stable state within the borders maintained as 'the Hungarian nation state') came to be constructed as (amongst other things) a 'Gypsy question' (it had once been a 'Jewish question'); the creation of phantasmagorical 'socialist' jobs for the Gypsies which disappeared as soon as consumers had any choice over what they purchased; the creation of what were referred to locally as new urban ghettos under the title of 'ending of Gypsy residential isolation' while in reality destroying one of the few parts of their lives over which the Gypsies had some control … I could go on.

But more than that, ten years after the fall of Communism in Hungary, the legacy of Communist policy debates from the 1950s and early 1960s can still be felt. In those discussions a theoretical distinction was made that seems very alien to modern sociology but which continues as common sense in the region, a contrast between groups that have 'social' characteristics and those that have an 'ethnic' character. 'Social' groups might be defined by professional, possible 'chosen' specialisation, but not necessarily formally, thus including, for example, beggars. 'Ethnic groups', by contrast, were in some sense 'naturally occurring phenomena' the product of an 'ethnic identity' that, it was taken for granted was one of those things 'everyone has'. Whereas anthropologists or sociologists treat the sense of 'ethnic' identification with others, of belonging to an 'ethnic group' as a contingent function of particular, modern social, economic and political relations, as a way of talking about these conditions, in Hungary (as in much of the rest of Europe today), ethnicity was (re-)inscribed by Communist discourse into the nature of things.

As long as the Hungarian Socialist Workers' Party and its satellite organs like the Patriotic People's Front insisted that the 'Gypsy question' was a social question, the effect of exploitation, historical misfortune, alienation and the like, Romani activists and their supporters could chant the opposite tune: the Roma were an ethnic group with a right to public representation and acknowledgement as such. Once this was acknowledged, they implied, then the problems of Roma/non-Roma relations could be dealt with.

Now that, for a series of more or less cynically calculated foreign policy objectives,[36] official policy has been reversed and Roma issues tend to be ethnicised by the governing parties, so Romani politics has seen some interesting reversals. In a telling case in 1998, Romani activists and their non-Romani collaborators successfully resisted the relocation of some very poor, rent-defaulting Gypsy families from the prosperous western Hungarian town of Székesfehérvár to a poor satellite village. They did this not by accusing their opponents of 'ethnic discrimination' or 'racialism', as they were urged to do by international NGOs and their employees based in Budapest. Instead they argued that this was a bad social policy for dealing with poor, long-term unemployed people, whose chances for improvement would be finally cut off by removal to a sink-village (Ladányi 1998). By arguing thus, the Romani leaders and their allies created a broad-based campaign that appealed to a widely shared sense of 'correct behaviour' by public institutions and refused to engage with the 'evictors' on their level, leaving the latter exposed as the only ones on the political scene playing 'the race card'.

The general point is, surely, that the political language which opposes in some fundamental way 'social' and 'ethnic' is always a dangerous and confusing language, giving the impression – which suits the nationalists only too well – that the word 'culture' describes closed, internally coherent systems rather than a general human ability to create, negotiate and disagree over the meaning of particular acts and institutions.[37] Describing those patterns of difference as 'ethnic' or 'social' has been and remains but one of the (cultural) means of (political) struggle between people in Hungary as in the rest of Europe.

### References

Bán, Gy. and Pogány, G. (1957) *A magyarországi Cigányság helyzetéről* (On the situation of Hungarian Gypsies), stencilled text, Budapest: Munkaügyi Minisztérium.

Bán, Gy. and Pogány, G. (1958) 'A magyarországi Cigányság foglalkoztatási problémai', (Employment problems of the Hungarian Gypsy population), *Munkügyi Szemle 5.*

Báthory, J. (1983) 'A "Cigánykerdés"' (The 'Gypsy question'), in L. Szego (ed.) *Cigányok, honnét jöttek, merre tartanak?* (Gypsies: from where, where to?), Budapest: Kozmosz, 8–24.

Báthory, J. (1988) 'A Cigányság a politika tükrében' (Gypsy issues as reflected in state politics), *Világosság 8–9.*

Beck, S. (1993) 'Racism and the formation of a Romani ethnic leader', in G. Marcus (ed.) *Perilous States: Conversations on Culture, Politics and Nation,* Chicago: University of Chicago Press.

Berend, I. and Ránki, Gy. (1985) *The Hungarian Economy in the Twentieth Century,* London: Croom Helm.

Bromlej, J. (1980) *Etnosz és néprajz* (Ethnos and ethnology), Budapest: Gondolat.

Csalog, Zs. (1984) 'Jegyzetek a Cigányság támogatásának kerdéséről' (Notes on the question of support for the Gypsy population), *Szociálpolitikai Értésitő 2.*

Erdős, K. (1960) 'A magyarországi Cigánykerdés' (The Hungarian Gypsy question), published as 'La Question Tsigane en Hongrie', *Études Tsiganes.*

Gellner, E. (1983) *Nationalism,* Oxford: Blackwell.

Guy, W. (1975a) 'Ways of looking at Roma: the case of Czechoslovakia', in F. Rehfisch (ed.) *Gypsies, Tinkers and other Travellers,* London: Academic, 201–29.

Guy, W. (1975b) Historical text (no pagination), in J. Koudelka *Gypsies,* New York: Aperture.

Guy, W. (1977) *The Attempt of Socialist Czechoslovakia to Assimilate its Gypsy Population,* unpublished PhD thesis, Bristol: University of Bristol.

Hajnal, L. E. (1999) 'Nagyvarosi Cigányok az uj gazdasagi kornyezetben', *Regio* 10, 1: 84–102.

Havas, G. (1982) 'A Baranya megyei Teknövájó Cigányok' (Baranya County troughmaking Gypsies), in M. Andor (ed) *Cigányvizsgálatok* (Gypsy investigations),

Budapest: Művelődéskutató Intézet, 61–140.

Hazafias Népfront (1978) *A Cigányság a felemelkedés útján* (Gypsies on the road of progress), Budapest: Hazafias Népfront.

Herczeg, F. (1976) *A MSZMP nemzetiségi politikája* (The national minorities policy of the Hungarian Socialist Workers' Party), Budapest: Kossuth.

Kálmán, A. (1946) 'A Magyar Cigányok problémaja' (The problem of Hungarian Gypsies), *Tarsadalmi Szemle*, 8–9: 656–8.

Kaminski, I.-M. (1980) *The State of Ambiguity: Studies of Gypsy Refugees*, Gothenburg: University of Gothenburg.

Kemény, I. (1999) 'A magyarországi Cigányság szerkezete a nyelvi valtozások tükrében', *Regio* 10, 1: 3–15.

Ladányi, J. (1998) 'A székesfehérvári gettóúgy üzenetei' (Report on the Székesfehérvár Ghetto), in Kurtán Sándor *et al.* (szerk.): Magyarországi politikai évkönyve 1997-ről. Budapest: Demokrácia Kutatások Magyar Központja Alapitvány, 313–21.

Ladányi, J. (no date) *Jegyzetek a Székesfehérvári kilakaltatási ügyéről* (notes on the case of the Székesfehérvár evictions), manuscript in possession of author.

Lemon, A. (2000) *Between Two Fires: Gypsy Performance and Romani Memory from Pushkin to Post-socialism*, Durham: Duke University Press.

Lemon, A. (2001) 'Russia: Politics of peformance', in W. Guy (ed.) *Between Past and Future: the Roma of Central and Eastern Europe*, Hatfield: University of Hertfordshire Press.

Lukács, Gy. (1983) *Record of a Life: An Autobiographical Sketch*, ed. I. Eörsi, trans. R. Livingstone, London: Verso.

Mezey, B. (1986) *A magyarországi Cigánykerdés dokumentumokban, 1422–1985* (The Hungarian Gypsy question as seen in documents), Budapest: Kossuth.

Moldova, Gy. (1986) *Bűn az Élet* (Life is a crime), Budapest: Magveto.

Sághy, E. (1999) 'Cigánypolitika Magyarországon 1945–1964' (Gypsy policies in Hungary 1945–1964), *Regio* 10, 1: 16–35.

Schiffer, J. and Dobos, J. (1963) 'A Cigány lakossággal kapcsolatos problémák a Szovjetunióban', *Belügyi Szemle* 3.

Stewart, M. (1997) *The Time of the Gypsies*, Co. Boulder: Westview.

Stalin, J. (1936) *Marxism and the National and Colonial Question*, first publ. 1913, London: Lawrence and Wishart.

Tomka, M. (1984) 'The Gypsy craftsmen of Europe', *Unesco Courier*, (Special Issue on 'The Gypsies'), 15–17 October.

Taylor, C. (1994) 'The politics of recognition', in A. Gutman (ed.) *Multiculturalism*, Princeton NJ: Princeton University Press.

Turner, T. (1994) 'What multiculturalists should know about culture that anthropologists know', in D. Goldberg (ed.) *Multiculturalism: a Critical Reader*, Oxford: Blackwell.

Vendégh, S. (1960) 'A magyarországi Cigánylakosság között végzendő munka időszerű feladatai', *Tájékoztató* 2: 38–55.

## Notes

1 The number of Roma in the Soviet Union (far less than 1 per cent of the total population) meant that Gypsy policies never occupied centre stage for the CPSU. In Eastern Europe, with the exception of Poland, where most Gypsies had died during the Nazi occupation, Gypsies represented up to 5 per cent or more of the population, and were often the largest if not the most politically important minority (that latter role being taken, for instance, by Hungarians in Slovakia and Romania, Slovaks in the Czech lands etc.).

2 See Kaminski (1981) and Beck (1993) for lesser known aspects of the Czechoslovak and Romanian cases.

3 In the year before the war broke out 42 per cent of Hungary's population had still been involved in agriculture.

4 The leading Hungarian Communist, György Lukács, described how he only just saved his life by throwing his bag of 'illicit' books into a river in 1940 a few hours before his flat was searched by the GPU (Lukács 1983).

5 The analysis of 'the Hungarian Gypsy problem' in the Party's theoretical journal went on to argue that 'those town musicians and village craftspeople, travelling salespeople and agricultural workers who essentially differ neither culturally (*lelkileg*) nor in their life style from the mass of the population and are already progressing to assimilation, require no special programme of their own' (Kálmán 1946).

6 See Lemon (2000 and 2001) for an accurate account of *Teatr Romen*.

7 This is Sághy's position (1999).

8 In 1985 an old man told me 'so many of the Magyars were *Nyílás* (Hungarian fascists) ... take my neighbour, he won't even talk to the Gypsies. If people like him had power what would happen to us now?'

9 Guy describes how Jan Zapolsky crushed the peasants' revolt of 1514 in Northern Hungary and Slovakia using Gypsy mercenaries and how Gypsies were used as executioners (1975a: 208).

10 Jelentés a cigánylakosság helyzetének megjávitásáről szóló párthatározat rendőri vonálon történt végrehajtásáról. Belügyminisztérium, Bűnügyi Osztály, Bp. 1962. szeptember 19. Found in Új Magyar Levéltár, XIX–1–4–g. 46. d., cited in Sághy (1999: 18).

11 See, for example, the account of the work of one Budapest Police captain (Moldova 1986).

12 Carpathian dialect.

13 This appeared in a tightly restricted document, *Dokumentumok a 'Magyarországi Cigányok Kulturális Szövetsége 1957–1961' életéből*. Only 100 copies were published, in stenciled format, by the Népművelési Intézet in 1986.

14 The organisers of folk dance clubs in the state-controlled Culture Houses in the early 1970s soon found themselves under suspicion of fomenting nationalism and were called in by the police to help in the deciphering of the coded anti-socialist doctrines in seventeenth century folk songs (personal communication, János Báthory).

15 Guy points out how the repression of Gypsy autonomy and the definition of an assimilationist policy in Czechoslovakia in the late 1950s was closely related to the attempt to suppress Slovakian nationalism, a nationalism which had contributed to the disintegration of Czechoslovakia in 1938 (1977: 153–5).

16 Thirty five years after it was written this report displays a remarkable freshness and willingness to engage with the world as it was, to admit areas of uncertainty. This is also the single official Hungarian document on Gypsies in forty years not to be weighed down by the tired, leaden formulations of Party-speak. Equally, of all the documents circulated by the Party, theirs was the most forthright about Gypsy conditions and the cause of these. For example,

the authors mention (and condemn) 'the practice inherited from the Horthy days' of paying Gypsies less than Hungarians as well as the systematic social and residential discrimination against Gypsies. They point out that the provision of alternative incomes for Gypsies by socialist factories would not always prove popular with the peasants who would thereby lose a cheap supply of labour. Again, when it came to dealing with official prejudice, Bán and Pogány stated 'forceful and unmistakable steps' must be taken, 'not only as a last measure against officers of the state abusing their power' (Bán and Pogány 1957: 26).

17  This meeting took place on 23 September 1957, see Népművelési Intézet, *Dokumentumok a 'Magyarországi Cigányok Kulturális Szövetsége 1957–1961' életéből (1986)*.

18  Again, the rather positive report of the launch in the Communist party's daily paper might be read as evidence of some substantial support from 'on high' (*Népszabadság*, 5 November 1957).

19  These categories were derived, of course, from Stalin (1913). Though when later the Socialist Republic of Macedonia granted Gypsies 'national minority' status they were given this on the basis that they were living 'outside their original nation-state', i.e. India.

20  These were in any case odd terms since the classic distinction was between reactionary and progressive *nationalisms*. National movements could be led in one or another way, but nations in and of themselves were neither one nor the other. Bán and Pogány thus performed something of a sleight of hand here, one they passed on to their critic, Sándor Vendégh (see below).

21  A few years later two Interior Ministry officials summarised Soviet thinking thus: 'The Gypsies do not constitute an independent nation or national minority, but rather a people – such an underdeveloped section of the population – which is being integrated into society slowly and with difficulty thanks to its past, its lifestyle and its customs' (Schiffer and Dobos, 1963).

22  A shortened version of Bán and Pogány's ministry paper had appeared for the general public in *Munkaügyi Szemle*, 1958/5.

23  Possibly in response to this change in Soviet policy both Czechoslovakia and Poland had begun to consider the development of Gypsy policies at roughly the same time as Hungary and along similar lines (Bán and Pogány: 5–8). Guy cites a Czechoslovak Party theorist who declared that, since Gypsies lacked the defining characteristics of a nation, Party policy should be to 'consciously accelerate the naturally continuing assimilation process' (1975a: 222). In the case of the small *Vlach* minority, estimated at around 6,000, this process was 'accelerated' by a 1958 law banning nomadism, under which the wheels were ripped from Gypsies' wagons and their animals were sold or killed (1975b). At the same time stricter control was exercised over the far larger sedentary majority by including over 20,000 of them, quite illegitimately, on a nomads' register. Those recorded in this way 'were to be refused employment in any place other than where they were registered, unless by mutual agreement between local authorities' (Guy 1975a: 214–5).

24  When one reads Erdős having to defend his folklore publication proposal from the charge of nationalism – 'this isn't nationalism, rather appropriate use of the dialectic. Because what is seen as nationalism among the Gypsies is often for "the white people" not seen as such' (1960: 190) – one realises how repressive the atmosphere had become by this time.

25  Erdős took the suppression of all actual forms of Gypsy culture so far that he suggested banning all new Gypsy folklore troupes as "inappropriate and unnecessary" (1960: 192). If Gypsies were to be involved in folklore 'our aim is that the Gypsies should observe the Hungarians, learn from them the rules of socialist life together' (1960: 193).

26  Sághy (1999: 19) is therefore wrong to say that they had merely collated reports from local councils, though this they did too.

27 Népművelési Intézet házinyomdában készült *Dokumentumok a 'Magyarországi Cigányok Kulturális Szövetsége 1957–1961' életéből.*

28 Guy describes how after the formation of Czech and Slovak Gypsy Associations during 1968, their room for manoeuvre was gradually restricted until they were (illegally) disbanded in 1973, much to the dismay of the Gypsy activists who had led them, formerly with the Party's approval (Guy 1975b).

29 See Stewart (1997) for a more sustained examination of both the theory behind this policy and its actual implementation and effects.

30 It is extraordinary to find today that a leading sociologist writes that 'leaving the settlements [in the 1960s] made meeting with the Hungarian majority an everyday matter...' (Kemény, 1999: 11), as if this had not been characteristic already for centuries.

31 See, for example, Hazafias Népfront (1978). There it is stated, 'the expressive and conceptual abilities of Gypsy children (and later adults) who have grown up on a settlement always remain more or less reduced'. This fact was explained by Gypsy history since 'it is understandable that in the mode of thought of "gathering" tribes living from day to day and thus unfamiliar with regular productive work or social organisation, noticing the precise logical and causal relations among phenomena did not occupy a central place'.

32 Party tolerance of such publications giving legitimacy to expressions of national sentiment may have had much to do with the worsening position of the Hungarian 'national minorities' in Slovakia and especially in Romania.

33 Kulturális Minisztérium, 18336/1977. The minister involved was Imre Pozsgay, who twelve years later played a central role in the surrender of power by the Communists. His liberal policy in 1977 came however with a warning that 'one must carry out continuous clarificatory work among a smaller group of intellectuals who support a Gypsy romanticism and also separatist efforts – thus misinterpreting the Gypsies' interests' (18336/1977: I.2). What counted as 'Gypsy romanticism' was always open to local interpretation.

34 Kulturális Minisztérium, 18336/1977: I.4.b.

35 See Hajnal's studies of Budapest trader Roma since 1990 (e.g. 1999).

36 Oriented on the one hand to Romania and Slovakia where there are significant *Hungarian* minorities and on the other hand to the EU and World Bank which express increasing concern about the position of the Romani minority.

37 Contrast for instance Turner (1994) and Taylor (1994).

## CHAPTER FIVE

# The emergence of European Roma policy

*Martin Kovats*

Over the last decade the Roma[1] have become a subject attracting increasing political attention. The fundamental reason for this has been the effects of post-Communist 'transition' on the countries of Central and Eastern Europe (CEE) and the Balkans, where the vast majority of the continent's Roma live. The end of the Cold War has allowed for the combination of issues raised by the circumstances of Roma in former Eastern Europe with those affecting Gypsies, Sinti, Travellers, etc. in the West to promote the idea of a trans-European Roma/Gypsy diaspora. This synthesis mirrors the wider process of European integration and the difficulties experienced by Roma/Gypsies (in respect of policy) within (nation) states appear to support the existential claims of supra-national European institutions to provide a superior form of governance within the framework of creating a common European 'home'. However, the symbolic significance of the emerging pan-European Roma policy paradigm[2] should not distract attention from the practical challenges confronting European institutions. These include the effects of economic and political transition on the large and growing Roma populations in post-Communist states and their consequences for economic development, political stability and social cohesion in the region. The circumstances of CEE and Balkan Roma directly impact on Western states, most notably in the form of Roma asylum seekers/migrants, but also more broadly within the context of closer co-operation between the different parts of the Continent.

While the Roma issue is a new one at the European level, Roma policy has long antecedents at state (and local) level, especially in transition countries. Novelty means that it is too early to evaluate conclusively the effectiveness of deepening European institutional engagement with the subject. Nevertheless, given the extent of the challenges raised by the circumstances of Roma/Gypsy people, this paper seeks to provide an indication of the main trends in European activities, through examining the conceptual documents of European institutions that underpin their initiatives. This analysis reveals potentially serious problems in how European institutions understand a subject area (Roma/Gypsy people and their circumstances) characterised by considerable diversity. It identifies a distinct tendency to cope with the plethora of data by presenting an increasingly inaccurate and homogenised picture of Roma/Gypsy people and their (policy-related) circumstances and to dislocate Roma/Gypsy issues from wider social, political, economic and cultural contexts.

The rapid pace of change and increase in attention by authorities claiming to support and protect Roma/Gypsy people and their culture and identity appears a progressive departure from the crude intervention or hostile neglect characteristic of national policies in recent decades. However, politics is about the pursuit of interests and any particular subject can be viewed by different political actors in a variety of incompatible, complementary or antagonistic ways. As a medium for bargaining (largely over resources and political attention), the outcome of any political process reflects the relative power of the contending interests (as well as unanticipated factors). This is particularly clear in respect of Communist policy towards Roma which sought assimilation through material equality, but which led to the unintended strengthening of Roma identity, while leaving Roma vulnerable to the economic and social restructuring of the post-Communist period. In itself, the 'Europeanisation' of Roma policy only raises the stakes, so the question of its quality is a matter of profound importance to all concerned.

To give some indication of the scale of this 'newly discovered', Europe-wide policy issue and in particular the differing situations in former Eastern and Western Europe, the table below gives estimates, published in 1995, of the Roma/Gypsy populations for selected European countries. It also shows the proportion these people form of the total population. However, it should be noted that these statistics are all calculated differently and that figures on Roma/Gypsies are notoriously subjective and unreliable. Nevertheless, these are the figures accepted by European institutions and on which their Roma-related activities are based.

## The Roma/Gypsy related activities of European institutions

Before 1990, European institutions had not been particularly involved with Roma and/or Gypsies. A number of questions were asked in the European Parliament during the 1970s, but in the following decade a process was begun that led to the commissioning of research into educational provision for Gypsy/Traveller children in member states of the European Community.[3] The Council of Europe's activities were even more limited, focusing on resolutions encouraging the greater inclusion of Gypsies and nomads within mainstream administrative systems, especially education and social security.[4]

**Figure I. Estimated absolute and relative size of Roma/Gypsy populations – selected countries**

| Eastern Europe | | | | Western Europe | | | |
|---|---|---|---|---|---|---|---|
| Country | Estimated Roma/Gypsy pop. (max.)[a] | Total Pop[b] (million) | % of Total pop | Country/Region | Estimated Roma/Gypsy pop. (max.)[a] | Total Pop[b] (million) | % of Total pop |
| Albania | 100,000 | 3.5 | 2.9 | Benelux[c] | 55,000 | 26.5 | 0.2 |
| Bulgaria | 800,000 | 7.8 | 10.3 | France | 340,000 | 59.3 | 0.6 |
| Czech Rep | 300,000 | 10.3 | 2.9 | Germany | 130,000 | 82.8 | 0.2 |
| Hungary | 600,000 | 10.1 | 5.9 | Greece | 200,000 | 10.6 | 1.9 |
| Slovakia | 520,000 | 5.4 | 9.6 | Scandinavia[d] | 32,000 | 23.8 | 0.2 |
| FRY[e] | 450,000 | 10.7 | 4.2 | Spain | 800,000 | 40.0 | 2.0 |
| Romania | 2,500,000 | 22.4 | 11.2 | UK | 120,000 | 59.5 | 0.2 |
| Total | 5,270,000 | 170.2 | 3.1 | Total | 1,670,000 | 302.5 | 0.6 |

Key:

a In fact a band is given for the estimated Roma population for each country, e.g. Albania 90,000–100,000, etc. However, only the upper figure for each band is given in this table. Source: Liégeois and Gheorghe (1995: 7).

b Source: CIA Fact Book (2000).

c Belgium, Holland and Luxembourg.

d Denmark, Finland, Norway and Sweden.

e Former Republic of Yugoslavia.

The Conference on Security and Co-operation in Europe (CSCE, later OSCE)[5] did not engage with Gypsies as they were not perceived as representing a security issue.

## European Union

Since the end of the Cold War there has been a dramatic and ongoing expansion in the Roma/Gypsy related activities of European institutions. As a forum for promoting the interests of member states, the European Union (EU) has been involved in addressing the issue of the growing number of Roma asylum seekers in Western European states. As well as continuing to support educational initiatives for Travellers, the process of European integration has meant that the EU has become involved in Roma-related initiatives in post-Communist countries, most notably through the PHARE programme and within accession negotiations with prospective new members.[6]

## Council of Europe

In January 1993 the Parliamentary Assembly of the Council of Europe accepted the report *On Gypsies in Europe* (Verspaget 1993) which led to the passage of Resolution 1203 that declared Gypsies to be 'a true European minority'. A further report in 1995 (Verspaget 1995) prompted the establishment of the Specialist Group on Roma/Gypsies which has produced reports and guidelines covering a variety of policy areas.[7] The Group's pivotal role in the development of European Roma policy was demonstrated in 1999 when the EU adopted *Guiding principles for improving the situation of Roma*, drawn up by the Specialist Group (van der Stoel 2000: 7). Roma/Gypsy-related initiatives have also been taken by the Council's Congress of Local and Regional Authorities, European Youth Centre and European Committee on Equality between Men and Women. The Council of Europe has also indirectly influenced the development of Roma policy through its initiatives in the field of minority and linguistic rights (Council of Europe 1998: 11-15).

## OSCE

Within the OSCE, Roma/Gypsies are incorporated within the framework of the Human Dimension.[8] Roma were explicitly included in the Paris Charter for a New Europe (Minority Rights Group 1995) and, since the creation of this post in 1993, the High Commissioner on National Minorities has produced two reports specifically on Roma in Europe. In 1995 the Contact Point on Roma and Sinti Issues was set up within the Office of Democratic Institutions and Human Rights (ODIHR) and three years later in 1998 the Contact Point's mandate was extended to oversee, co-ordinate and advise on legislative and policy developments affecting Roma (and Sinti) both at the European and state levels.[9]

## The conceptual framework underpinning the activities of the OSCE and the Council of Europe

Though new for European institutions, Roma/ Gypsies is not a new policy area but one that has presented challenges to governments of many different forms. These problems have consistently been found difficult to address effectively, often producing results considerably divergent from the stated policy aims. In order to assess the effectiveness of the remarkable quantitative expansion in Roma-related activities, it is also necessary to examine qualitative aspects of deepening European engagement with the issue. This paper analyses the contents of three main documents which outline how the OSCE and the Council of Europe perceive the European Roma policy paradigm. These are the two reports by the High Commissioner on National Minorities (HCNM), published in 1993 and 2000, and the 1995 report *On Gypsies in Europe*, written by Geraldine Verspaget for the Council of Europe's Committee on Migration and which led to the creation of the Specialist Group.

## Understanding the issue

'Roma' is a broad concept covering a wide variety of different people (as indicated in endnote 1). While it is possible, for a variety of purposes, to consider all Roma people as essentially similar, this tendency has to be consciously resisted in relation to the practical impact of public policies on real people.[10] Clearly many policy considerations must differ in respect of individuals and families from clan-based itinerant communities and those of people 'settled' in camps or other confined areas on the periphery of cities,[11] as well as in relation to large urban Roma populations[12] and those living in small rural communities.[13] In general, Roma/Gypsies can be found in a range of social circumstances and at many points along a spectrum from close integration with, through to extreme isolation from, mainstream society. There is a great deal of difference in the lives of Roma people across the different regions of Europe, as well as between countries and even within countries. Contemporary diversity reflects the different historical experiences of Roma populations and of the environments in which they live.

One of the problems for those involved in trying to conceptualise the Roma is the lack of any single tangible thing that is common to all within the diaspora. The most commonly cited thread is the Sanskrit-based language *Romanes* which linguists argue indicates a common origin of Romani people. Whatever the language does indicate, *Romanes* today is spoken by only around 2.5 million of the putative 8-10 million-strong European Romani diaspora and 'there are between 50-100 dialects. Romani dialects are not mutually comprehensible except at very basic levels, such as words relating to food and family' (Kenrick 2000: 2). The limited range and fragmentation of *Romanes* does not disprove the claim that contemporary Roma/Gypsies have a common (Indian) origin, but is an important factor to be considered by policy makers. This is especially the case in the field of education but, more broadly, in interpreting the relationship between Roma/Gypsy people and their home state and society.

The existence of extensive diversity is noted by both of the HCNM's Roma reports as well in Verspaget's 1995 document. However, noting the obvious is a long way from fully appreciating the entire range of differences within such an extensive group. Furthermore, it is only very recently that Roma people have contributed to the public discourse about themselves. It is this lack of public voice that has left a gulf allowing the extensive accumulation of negative stereotypes that have grown up around Roma/Gypsies. Extensive diversity among Roma combined with a lack of accountability for commentators means that just about any statement can be made about Roma which, though probably true for someone somewhere, must inevitably prove misleading unless placed in its proper context. European institutions face a considerable intellectual challenge and the extent to which the Council of

Europe and the OSCE have risen to this challenge is reflected in the three documents discussed below which, in effect, are the first to conceptualise the Roma as a pan-European policy area.

*First Report of the High Commissioner on National Minorities*
  *(van der Stoel 1993)*

While noting the 'centuries-long process' of migration that brought Roma 'to Byzantium approximately a thousand years ago' (1993: 3), the HCNM's 1993 report emphasises that today Roma 'comprise an extremely heterogeneous set of communities that are perhaps best understood in their own specific circumstances' (1993: 3) and whose relations with state and society 'have been complex and varied' (1993: 4). This characterisation of the objects of policy, Roma, reflects the explicit aim of the report to be 'thematic' rather than 'quantitative' and supports the assertion that 'the present day problems of the Roma [in transition countries] must be understood in the context of the overall situation of the region which can broadly be characterised in terms of major political and economic transformations'(1993: 5).

In placing the Roma issue firmly in the contemporary political context of transition, the report focuses on the most acute conditions within Europe where 'material hardship associated with economic recession ... as well as greater government austerity throughout the CSCE region, have hit the vast majority of the Roma particularly hard' (1993: 6). This allows for the wider appreciation of the political and economic forces conditioning contemporary events (and thus affecting any political engagement with the Roma issue). The emphasis on material hardship is also significant both in regard to the actual problems of widespread unemployment and poverty amongst Roma, as well as in recognising the relationship between low incomes and health, education and housing problems (policy areas). Identifying the political context and complexity of Roma as a subject, the report concludes that 'the problems of Roma generally require measures within each participating state to address the situation of Roma' and that policies should be based on 'objective analysis of community need', but should be sufficiently sensitive that 'intra-community tensions [Roma/non-Roma] are not exacerbated by (the appearance of) unfavourable treatment for one group over others' (1993: 12).

*Second Report of the High Commissioner on National Minorities*
  *(van der Stoel 2000)*

The substantial second HCNM report with its 175 pages reflects the proliferation of data in the intervening period.[14] It explores four themes: discrimination and racial violence, education, living conditions and political participation. Each is examined through a review of relevant international agreements and a variety of illustrative examples. In the foreword the HCNM notes that since the 1993 report the situation of many other groups had improved in CEE 'but by contrast Roma and Sinti were generally left outside the scope and beyond the reach of progressive developments'. Yet in spite of this important observation, the 2000 report represents a profound change from 1993 in taking the discussion of Roma out of the wider political and economic context and increasingly defining the issue in 'cultural' terms as essentially one of discrimination (the attitude and behaviour of non-Roma to Roma).[15]

The disconnection from the wider transition context (which is hardly mentioned) combined with the non-systematic collection of examples from different countries means the report does not discriminate between situations of differing political importance (urgency). Unemployment amongst Roma, which by 2000 was becoming an acute crisis throughout the region with rates reported of 60, 70, 80 and 90 per cent,[16]merits only six paragraphs. There it is noted that the gross disparities between Roma and average unemployment in many CEE states 'are not solely the function of discrimination, but ... [their] impact is substantial' (2000: 32).[17]

The reluctance to examine economic aspects of the Roma as a policy subject means that, not only does the report leave out any discussion of labour market developments or changes in welfare entitlements which have affected Roma populations in recent years, but it also fails to appreciate the fundamental interconnection between poverty and problems in other policy areas such as health, education and housing. Thus, although the report notes that 'the relationship between poverty and [ill] health is well established', its only recommendations are to counter discrimination and to conduct health surveys (2000: 116-27). In relation to education the report notes that some countries registered 'marked improvements in the attendance and achievements of Romani students' over substantial periods (2000: 65), but fails to point out that it was under Communist rule that those 'substantial gains' were achieved despite unreconstructed attitudes and largely due to material improvement in Roma incomes and living conditions.

One effect of this de-contextualisation of Roma is to encourage the wholly erroneous idea that 'industrialisation' is to blame for the extensive contemporary impoverishment of most Roma in CEE since it 'radically diminish[ed] their prospects for surviving through traditional trades that sustained Roma for centuries' (2000: 33). While such an idea might be of relevance to some Roma/Gypsy people, it fails to address the real causes of most Roma unemployment and undermines the chances of developing appropriate policies where there is evidently considerable need. Other policy areas including education, health, housing and policing are discussed in greater detail. Despite the wide range of examples given, the lack of analysis of what all these different data mean continually reinforces the simplistic assertion that the problem is fundamentally one of prejudice because 'discrimination is a defining feature of the Romani experience' (2000: 23). Though racist attitudes are clearly a very important aspect of matters concerning Roma, their role needs to be understood *alongside* rather than instead of the many other important factors determining the situation of Roma people today.

*The 1995 Report for the Council of Europe (Verspaget 1995)*
The clearest example of the above noted tendency to simplify the conception both of who Roma/Gypsy people are and the nature of their circumstances is the tendentious 1995 report of Geraldine Verspaget for the Council of Europe's European Committee on Migration (CDMG).[18] The report asserts that 'the people known as gypsies ... came from northern India seven centuries ago in a long march ... Their language is Romani' (1995: 1) and has more to do with a desire to homogenise Roma/Gypsies than with any known scholarship. Despite the claim that 'the history of the Gypsies is one of discrimination, exclusion and persecution' (1995: 1), the report goes on to explain that 'the foremost reason [for high Roma unemployment] is the result of changes ... in the last fifty years obliging Roma to abandon their traditional modes of subsistence', and that 'until the end of the Second World War Gypsies fulfilled a specific function in the rural world having a number of traditional jobs ... all of which were compatible with their nomadic lifestyle' (1995: 4).[19]

The report asserts that the differences between the Roma/Gypsies of Eastern and Western Europe are 'because of communism' (1995: 2), and specifically because of Roma policy during this period. What appeared 'generous measures soon turned into a policy of forced assimilation of the Roma populations through banning nomadism in most countries of the region with the resulting destruction of traditional Roma society' (1995: 3).[20] The report is so confident in its homogenous and conservative conception of Roma that it even criticises television for creating 'an identity crisis and a profound sense of rootlessness', especially amongst young Roma (1995: 5). The essentialisation of Roma is completed with the claim that 'in the Gypsy idea of society the individual exists and is defined only in relation to the group' (1995: 6) (something which, if true, would have alarming implications for the role of Roma politics in democratic societies).

The desire to simplify the diversity of the Roma/Gypsy diaspora draws attention to the related tendency to simplify the circumstances of Roma people in relation to policy. One example is the issue of Roma asylum seekers. Instead of this phenomenon being perceived as a symptom of significant structural problems that need to be addressed, the 1995 report argues that 'the increase in mobility since 1990 must not conjure up pictures of a "tidal wave" of Gypsies sweeping over the West, it is merely a return to the normal mobility of Gypsies' (1995: 13). Perceiving the asylum issue as essentially one of (Roma) culture undermines understanding of the actual causes of this ongoing movement of people, as well as the chances of developing effective and necessary policies in response.[21]

Despite noting that 'the fate of Gypsies is usually decided at the local level' (1995: 7), the homogenous image presented in the report gives a false sense of comparison both of needs/circumstances and of political urgency. The report notes high rates of Roma unemployment in Romania, Bulgaria and Northern Ireland (i.e. Travellers) (1995: 4), though it is clear that the causes, consequences, challenges and political significance of situations involving hundreds of thousands of settled Roma in the difficult economic environment of Central and Eastern Europe are fundamentally different from those affecting a few hundred itinerants in a wealthy Western state.

## Implementing Policy

The previous section noted the trend for European institutions' conception of Roma as a policy issue to downplay the broader social, economic and political contexts. It was also noted that this approach creates significant problems for policy makers in identifying needs, as well as the limitations on and opportunities for policy in any given situation. In particular, misunderstanding/misrepresenting the importance of economic factors has meant that European institutions are not able to assess the full extent of their financial commitments in this area and have become largely dependent on two methods for translating their will into practice: making recommendations and promoting Roma representation. The following sections examine the limitations of these two policy tools.

### Recommendations

The HCNM's 2000 report concludes with forty-eight recommendations covering each of its four themes. Just under half of these (twenty-two) advocate changes in law or practices to address discrimination and a further seventeen relate to Roma representation (almost half of which refer specifically to the work of the OSCE's Contact Point) (2000: 160-4). Only four recommendations make any mention of the need to increase resources allocated to Roma-related initiatives. The 'Guiding Principles', produced by the Council of Europe's Specialist Group on Roma/Gypsies (adopted by the European Union in 1999) are even more extensive, covering a wide range of areas including the structure of government through to the 'international mobility of Roma in Europe'. Of the seventy-five recommendations, thirty deal specifically with anti-discrimination legislation and practice, eighteen with Roma participation and nine directly involve resource allocation. In contrast to the HCNM report, the 'Guiding Principles' contain sixteen recommendations under the heading 'Unemployment and Economic Problems Faced by Roma' which focus on training, the need for anti-discrimination legislation and to 'encourage' Roma recruitment in the public sector, as well as advocating subsistence agricultural programmes and easier access to loans and micro-credit.

Such recommendations can provide a useful guide to national and local governments, and their endorsement by European institutions can help increase the authority of those wishing to develop and implement policies in accordance with them. However, they are also inevitably vague and thus require interpretation if they are to be applied in practice. This is an important consideration in respect of Roma policy and it is a weakness of the evolving activities of European institutions that they are not informed by the experiences of previous policy makers, in particular, Communist regimes. Despite the centralised structures of the one-party states, politburos were not able to realise their policies, largely due to the resistance of local authorities (a similar difficulty was also encountered by Maria-Theresa and Joseph II in the eighteenth century).[22] The involvement of European institutions adds an additional (and more remote) level to the policy pyramid and so it is reasonable to question the extent to which they will be able to influence practice by ensuring consensus of interpretation at both the national and local levels.

Most of these recommendations are normative statements of the obvious and contribute nothing to intellectual debate[23] and some are even contradictory.[24] However, their fundamental weakness lies in the conception developed by European institutions (as a result of simplifying the Roma and their circumstances) that the issue is essentially a technical rather than a political one. While no national government wishes to have a 'Roma problem', the last ten years have shown that states are not clear as to how to address the actual conditions in their own countries.[25] Governments are compelled to work within significant political and financial constraints and the extent to which these impact on Roma policy has led to the extensive problems which exist today and that have inspired European institutions to get ever more deeply involved with the subject. Lack of clarity over precisely what role European institutions should and could play in respect of Roma policy means that current recommendations serve only to re-state existing ideas rather than addressing the political and financial obstacles to the development and implementation of effective policies within individual countries, where knowledge of local conditions is best.

*Roma politics*

The implicit solution to the problem of interpretation lies in the role of Roma representation within the policy process. In the HCNM's 1993 report Roma input was considered of practical importance as 'identifying and addressing their own needs is a prerequisite for the effective implementation of policies'. Furthermore, this input was firmly linked to economic improvement as 'with greater inputs in efforts to improve their material condition, Roma will also be better able to demonstrate their commitment to and participation in society-at-large' (1993: 7). The 1995 Verspaget report examined the subject of Roma political activity in greater detail noting that Roma have 'been remote from decision-making processes, which is one of the reasons why many proposed solutions have been unsuitable' and that 'states have accepted that viable solutions need to be worked out with the Gypsies themselves' (1995: 7, 3). The report also touched upon the idea of Roma representation being an end in itself. The claim of 'national or ethnic minority' status was seen as compatible with integration, as an expression of 'their [Roma] standing as part of society' through asserting 'a distinctive culture worthy of respect'. By the time of the second HCNM report it had become an 'essential principle' that Roma be 'centrally involved in developing, implementing and evaluating policies and programmes' (2000: 5–6). The section discussing 'Political Participation' began with the ambiguous assertion that 'Roma face special challenges in their efforts to participate in the fundamental promise of democracy – the right to self-government' (2000: 128).

The recognition that Roma policy cannot proceed without the agreement of the subjects of policy (Roma people) represents a fundamental historical change. The need to encourage Roma representation has been recognised at both European and state level, as well as in the work of NGOs. While the active participation of Roma people in the discussion, development and implementation of policy is both desirable and inevitable, it is also questionable whether it is wise for European institutions to promote an ethnicity-based politics.[26] Seeing Roma as representing a fundamentally technical (rather than a political) issue fosters the belief that the training and promotion of Roma representatives should provide 'responsible' partners for government and other institutions in the common task of resolving problems. In fact, Roma simply represent yet another lobby competing for attention and resources from authorities together with a wide variety of other (often more experienced, popular and better resourced) interests. The success of the relationship between Roma and authorities depends not on the ability of Roma themselves but on the wider political and economic environment.

The problem of the past was that policies were inappropriate and so did not achieve their aim (which has led to the difficulties which policy makers are confronted with today). This problem can still occur, even with Roma representation, if authorities are not able or willing to develop the programmes and initiatives that Roma need and want. The main innovation of Roma politics is that the policy must develop in public. How Roma politics evolves depends on the extent to which it is capable of securing benefits for its constituency and on how other political forces react to its demands. Therefore, rather than producing technocratic 'advisers', Roma representation actually creates an additional political condition requiring policy to be developed in accordance with actual needs (expressed in political demands). In other words, Roma politics means the success or failure of European engagement must produce either positive or negative political consequences.

Given the diversity and distribution of the notional Roma/Gypsy diaspora, the conditions in which Roma/Gypsy people live and the novelty of Roma politics, it is not surprising that there is no reliable European-level representation of Roma/Gypsy people. The 'representation' of Roma within European institutions (such as in the Contact Point and the Specialist Group) is by appointment rather than election or delegation. The main contender to speak for Roma/Gypsy people at the international level is the International Romani Union (IRU). In July 2000 the IRU held its fifth World Congress in Prague (part-financed by the Czech Government and the OSCE), which illustrated the expansion of interest in Roma issues since its last congress in 1990.[27] Seeking to address its lack of representativeness, the IRU's new President, Dr Emil Ščuka, announced the creation of a Parliament, though no account was given about how an electorate could be identified or mobilised.[28]

The difficulties confronting national Roma populations in creating an effective political lobby means that Roma politics itself is very unlikely to produce overwhelming political problems. The far more considerable threat to the peaceful development of policy lies in the potential opposition that might be generated towards perceived 'favouritism' towards Roma (as noted by the HCNM in his 1993 report, see above). The symbolic relationship between 'Roma' and 'Europe' cuts both ways. The activities of European institutions must fail to achieve their stated aims if they have the effect of allowing nationalist Eurosceptics to play the populist 'race card' by portraying 'Europe' as interfering with their country's national identity. The key to the success of the inevitable and deepening European institutional engagement with the Roma issues in CEE and the Balkans is to provide sufficient inducements to encourage domestic élites and public opinion to accept the wide variety of changes necessary to ensure equality of opportunity.

## The future of European Roma policy

The problems identified above can only partly be accounted for by the inexperience of European institutions in dealing with the Roma issue. There is considerable historical and contemporary literature about Roma in many states that does not inform the knowledge base for policy at the European level. Through their burgeoning Roma-related activities European institutions are confronted with a (potentially) colossal volume of data. The conceptual documents of the OSCE and the Council of Europe display the tendency to simplify and generalise highly varied and complex issues. Rather than representing innovation, 'Europe' appears to be making the same mistake as previous policy makers who historically struggled to develop policies in accordance with the diversity and complexity of national Roma populations.

The de-contextualisation of Roma fosters the mistaken perception that the Roma issue represents a series of technical challenges that can be addressed by legal reform and the spread of good practice, rather than one requiring the substantial re-allocation of resources and considerable political sensitivity and skill. The choice facing European institutions is whether or not their expanding activities will be effective, based on full and accurate understanding of the subject.

To address the limitations on policy created by diversity and distance, consideration needs to be given to precisely what role European institutions can play within the Roma policy paradigm, especially their relationship with national governments and policy. It needs to be accepted that the Roma issue (including increased Roma political activity) is not going to disappear in the foreseeable future. The current period is very important not only because of the way the issue evolves in the future will be conditioned by steps taken now (particularly the framework constructed for policy and the identification of the aims of policy) but also because the Roma issue is increasingly part of important decisions, most notably, the enlargement of the European Union. As part of institutions without the budget or authority to promote policies toward Roma, based on ideas of social and economic development, it is reasonable to question whether bodies, such as the Specialist Group and Contact Point, attempting to address only part of the issue (such as legal reform), may actually prove dysfunctional. This is all the more likely if their initiatives are not supported by programmes designed to overcome wide-scale poverty that are sufficiently focused and of the required scale.

## National focus

A pre-condition for successful European engagement with the Roma (especially in the politically sensitive conditions of the CEE region and the Balkans) is accurate understanding of actual conditions as well as identification of the opportunities for and limitations on policy. These can vary extensively between even neighbouring states where different historical experiences have created different circumstances for Roma minorities. For example, in Hungary over three-quarters of Roma speak only Hungarian, whilst in Romania many different dialects of Romani are spoken as a mother tongue, as well as mainstream languages (Romanian and Hungarian) and dialects of these (Beash). Different Roma populations have different experiences of settlement and industrialisation (rural Slovak Roma and urban Czech Roma, itinerant Roma of the former Yugoslavia and those with many years experience of being *gastarbeiter* abroad). The economic and social structures of countries differ meaning opportunities for policies vary, such as between areas of economic growth and decline. The political traditions and cultures of countries also vary and have a considerable impact on policy developments.

For example, Hungary is keen to promote minority rights as this helps its wider programme of re-uniting with Magyars abroad, whilst the Czech and Slovak Republics are new nation-states (for Czechs and Slovaks) created by separating from the other 'nation',[29] whilst the Romanian state prefers to play down ethnic difference due to fear of fragmentation.

The nature of political relationships also supports European Roma policy focusing on states. Each national government faces particular challenges and has to contend with the political and financial limitations on its activities specific to that state. Furthermore, significant European involvement can take place only through structures within individual countries and controlled by national politicians. This is recognised in the state-by-state approach of the EU in respect of Roma policy in candidate countries within accession negotiations. European activities need to recognise (in addition to meeting the needs and winning the approval of Roma people themselves) that their success depends largely on the degree to which they are supported by national and local élites (representing the wider society). This means they must be perceived (domestically) as according with the needs of the country rather than as a threat to the stability and coherence of society. While there is certainly a transnational dimension to Roma issues (such as linguistic and cultural Roma communities living across national borders)[30] these should not obscure the fact that integration (and thus the reduction of economic, social and political tensions) can only occur through the implementation of policies which enable Roma people to enjoy genuine equality of opportunity with their neighbours in their local home environment.

## *Resource allocation*

The fundamental weakness of the evolving European conception of the Roma as a policy issue is the superficial diagnosis of the problem as being essentially 'cultural', a question of discrimination against Roma people. While it is true that post-Communist societies were isolated from the anti-racist discourse which emerged in Western Europe after World War Two, it is also true that this discourse has not resolved considerable social problems of Western Gypsies and Travellers.[31] It also needs to be recognised that inclusive, anti-racist/equal opportunities policies were developed in the West at a time of economic expansion and sought to increase the productivity of immigrant labour by improving housing, health and educational opportunities and removing obstacles to promotion in the workplace.[32] Roma policy is developing amidst fundamentally different conditions characterised by lack of demand for (un(der)skilled) labour. Part of the problem is that anti-Roma racism is poorly understood and that the long and often difficult history of Roma means that prejudices are deeply rooted in mainstream cultures (both in the East and the West). Furthermore, many aspects of the current situation, such as high unemployment, welfare dependency, poor housing and health, etc. appear to be deepening antipathy towards Roma.

The promotion of anti-racism is very important but, to be successful, a variety of other policy tools need to be employed to achieve this goal. The fact that European institutions are getting ever more deeply involved with the Roma (in post-Communist states) demonstrates that national governments are not coping well with the multiplicity of challenges represented by the Roma issue. Governments are not able to make sufficient resources available to address needs (not just Roma impoverishment but reform of educational and legal systems, infrastructure development, etc.). Their activities can be characterised more as crisis management because it has proved politically impossible to allocate scarce public resources for Roma-related initiatives at the scale required. Fear of over-extending financial commitments means that expectations are kept low. However, the emergence of Roma politics (combined with, amongst other factors, political pressure from abroad) means that such an approach is unsustainable in the medium-term.

Clearly European institutions, especially the EU, have a crucial role to play in breaking the political impasse in individual states. Due to the need to maintain as wide a political and social consensus as possible during the difficult task of addressing Roma issues, it is unlikely that a political approach that seeks to support one faction amongst domestic élites over another can facilitate the successful implementation of policy.[33] Europe needs to overcome the widespread view that Roma represent a domestic political problem, and to win the support of élites and societies by making a Roma minority an asset to a country through making new resources available. If national politicians and interests felt less threatened that Roma policy would deprive them of resources, it would be politically easier for governments to win support for effective anti-discrimination legislation. Without establishing sufficient confidence that the Roma issue can be addressed to the benefit of society as a whole, it is unrealistic to expect politicians to take the risk of courting unpopularity (and to undermine their own bases of support) by challenging deeply entrenched attitudes and demanding considerable reform in public services and administrative systems.

Unfortunately, the conception of the issue emerging at the European level not only fails to recognise the necessity of Europe playing such a role, but actually reduces awareness of the financial dimension to policy by failing to analyse the political context and downplaying the fundamental need to raise the incomes of Roma people. After a decade of work, neither the OSCE nor the Council of Europe have come up with any figures as to how much it would cost to achieve any particular policy aim, neither have they identified any mechanism by which states could negotiate over resources with European institutions.[34] This leaves European institutions without any idea of the scale of resources which are required and thus of the financial impact Roma policy is likely to have on their own budgets (long-term planning is effectively precluded). Currently the PHARE programme is the main channel of resources between Europe and CEE states in respect of Roma. However, the sums transferred so far are very small (20m ECU (17mUSD) over six years) spread over half a dozen countries. Though no official estimates have been made, it is likely that the costs of significantly reducing CEE Roma poverty (thus enabling Roma people to make the same choices about their lives as other citizens) will amount to around 1-1.5bn ECU, spread over a number of years.[35] Though this represents a dramatic increase on current expenditure, the sum is equivalent to the budget of the PHARE programme for only one year. Money is not the solution to the Roma issue, but it is a pre-condition for effective policies. In addition to allocating resources, it is also vitally important that mechanisms are put in place to ensure that they are used effectively and take into account the need for transparency and accountability created by the emergence of Roma politics and the fact that Roma policy is a public issue.

### *Approaches to European Roma policy*

The long-term challenges presented by the Roma issue and the ongoing process of European integration mean that deepening engagement of European institutions is inevitable and of increasing importance. A new area of 'European' policy and politics has been created. To ensure that European Roma policy is effective and successful it is necessary to establish the most appropriate structure for its development, which gives the greatest chances of maximising understanding of the issues involved and of adopting the best policy tools. The weaknesses of the present structure indicate how future policy can be better guided at a time when the Roma issue requires increasing political attention. As the circumstances of the vast majority of Roma in transition states continues to deteriorate, governments and societies (including Roma people) face a growing number of serious problems including migration/asylum, social division and political polarisation, strengthening (Eurosceptic) nationalism, economic stagnation/underdevelopment, infrastructure decay and decline in public services. The experience of the last decade is that the economic and political costs of addressing these matters continues to rise the longer substantive, targeted intervention is delayed. Failure to tackle the root causes of the ongoing disintegration of Roma from mainstream economy and society means that national and international authorities face the mounting costs of managing its symptoms.

At present there are two distinct approaches towards Roma at the European level. On the one hand there are the institutions with a pan-European membership (Council of Europe, OSCE) within both of which are specific offices claiming a role in constructing a framework for policy encompassing the whole Roma/Gypsy diaspora (Specialist Group on Roma/Gypsies, Contact Point for Roma and Sinti Issues). The broad boundaries to their work mean there is a danger of resources being wasted through replication. However, the main problem is their inability to develop an objective overview of the subject. Indeed, when confronted with the growing volume of data about Roma, the later conceptual documents of these institutions demonstrate a pronounced tendency to ignore difficult issues and to develop an increasingly superficial and misleading picture of Roma and their circumstances. The result of this has been the promotion of a simplistic, ineffectual framework for policy and their failure to identify the political and financial obstacles to and implications of engagement with the issue. Without the introduction of proper methods of political and scholarly accountability, the enormous potential within the Roma issue means that these offices can, for a considerable time to come, continue to produce work which further misleads decision makers (and the wider public) and confuses what is already a complicated and contentious subject.

An alternative approach is that of the European Union which, especially in relation to the candidate countries with the most politically significant Roma populations, considers Roma policy on state-by-state basis.[36] Given the problems involved in analysing the considerable (and rapidly increasing) data in respect of Roma (necessary for identifying needs and factors conditioning policy options) the latter would appear to present a better framework for European policy makers. The EU approach is specifically linked to working through structures within individual states and so is more likely to identify the opportunities for and limitations on policy in specific countries, vital for ensuring the necessary local consensus required for any substantial initiative in countries with large Roma populations. The EU's engagement with the most politically significant aspect of the Roma issue (transition states) is sited within a wider political process (enlargement negotiations) and thus includes a substantial element of political accountability. Finally, the EU (through the PHARE programme and other budgets supporting initiatives in respect of Roma/Gypsies in member states) has the financial capacity to mobilise resources (as well as to develop effective methods of financial accountability) of sufficient scale to ensure that policy achieves its stated aims.

## Conclusion

The long history of state-Roma relations throughout Europe indicates that the failure of European institutions to comprehend accurately the subject area is likely to lead to the development of ineffective policies. In addition, the scale of objective need, the symbolic importance of the subject and the acute political sensitivity (in many countries) of the Roma as a political question (including the emergence of Roma political activity) mean that policy failure is likely to have profound political consequences for all involved. It is already possible to identify the limitations and contradictions of current European Roma policy. Based on the limited (and inaccurate) definition of the problem as fundamentally one of 'culture' (discrimination), European institutions promote the homogenisation of policies across countries based on the re-statement of existing (and ineffectual) practice, in the form of guidelines and recommendations which have no intrinsic authority. European Roma policy is also based on the promotion of Roma representation, but without the awareness that strengthened Roma political activity can only exacerbate the contradictions and limitations of inappropriate policy initiatives.

The growing tendency to view the Roma issue isolated from the wider political, economic, social and cultural context means that European institutions have failed to appreciate that the role of European policy in this area must be to overcome the political and financial obstacles to effective policies within national politics, especially in transition states. Instead of seeking to develop structures and programmes for the central administration of a notional group spread across a large number of countries, European institutions need to appreciate their own limitations and to concentrate on contributing something new to break the political impasse on the subject manifest in many states. While political support is important, the need to establish and maintain consensus within states (initially amongst élites and, more generally, the wider public) limits the utility of punitive sanctions. Europe needs to raise expectations that serious problems can be addressed effectively and this requires making new resources available, as well as ensuring that these are used efficiently and with appropriate methods of public accountability. This can be done either through expanding the PHARE programme or by establishing a parallel initiative.

Only 'Europe' has the authority and the resources to provide the framework for addressing the multifarious policy problems affecting Roma/Gypsy people across the Continent. However, for Europe to play its role effectively its institutions need to be realistic about their own competence and recognise that the complexities involved require the channelling of policy initiatives through state-level structures. To be successful, European initiatives need to address the most fundamental and acute problem of widespread Roma poverty, especially amongst Roma formerly integrated within and subsequently discarded from the mainstream labour force. Raising the incomes of Roma people will reduce pressure on policy makers as Roma become better able to make the same choices as other citizens. Furthermore, by providing national governments with the resources to address problems of material hardship and infrastructure decline, Europe is far more likely to persuade local élites to support effective anti-discrimination measures and to reform administrative structures.

European institutions need to be guided by the awareness that the sensitivity of the Roma issue in many CEE and Balkan states means that their inevitably deeper engagement may backfire spectacularly if they fail to develop desired and appropriate policies based on a full understanding of local conditions. Conversely, the rewards for successful engagement are considerable in respect of facilitating social cohesion, economic development and democratic stabilisation. The Roma question (in a wide variety of different forms) has been confounding policy makers for centuries. European institutions have a truly historic role to play in finally overcoming one of bleaker aspects of European history. It would be more than a shame for them to fail to rise to the challenge.

## References

Acton, T. and Klímová, I. (2001) 'The International Romani Union: an East European answer to West European questions?', in W. Guy (ed.) *Between Past and Future: the Roma in Central and Eastern Europe*, Hatfield: University of Hertfordshire Press.

Barany, Z. (1995) 'Roma in Macedonia: ethnic politics and the marginal condition in a Balkan state', *Nationalities Papers* 18, 3.

Council of Europe (1998) *Activities of the Council of Europe Concerning Roma/Gypsies and Travellers*, MG-S-Rom (98)13, Strasbourg: Council of Europe.

Crowe, D. (1999) 'The Gypsies of Romania since 1990', *Nationalities Papers* 27, 1: 57–67.

Czech Government (1997) *Report on the Situation of the Romani Community in the Czech Republic*, Prague: Office of Minister without Portfolio, 29 October.

Danbakli, M. (ed) (1994) *On Gypsies: Texts Issued by International Institutions*, Interface Collection, Toulouse: CRDP.

European Commission (1999) *EU Support for Roma Communities in Central and Eastern Europe: Enlargement Briefing*, Brussels: EC, December.

Gheorghe, N. and Acton, T. (1994/95), 'Dealing with multiculturality: minority, ethnic, national and human rights', *OSCE/ODHIR Bulletin* 3, 2, winter.

Guy, W. (1975a) 'Ways of looking at Roma: the case of Czechoslovakia', in F. Rehfisch (ed.) *Gypsies, Tinkers and other Travellers*, London: Academic, 201–29.

Guy, W. (1975b) Historical text (no pagination), in J. Koudelka *Gypsies*, New York: Aperture.

Guy, W. 'Recent Roma migration to the United Kingdom', paper delivered to Czech Academy of Sciences roundtable, *Roma Migration in Europe: Trends*, Prague: Czech Academy of Sciences, Institute of Ethnology, 24–25 November.

Havas, G., Kertesi, G., and Kemény, I. (1995) 'The statistics of deprivation – the Roma in Hungary', *The Hungarian Quarterly* 36, 3: 67–80.

Kenrick, D. (2000) 'Inflections in flux', *Transitions Online*, April.

Kovats, M. (1996) 'The Roma and the minority self-government system in Hungary', *Immigrants and Minorities* 15, 1: 42–58, March.

Kovats, M. (2001) 'Hungary: Politics, difference and equality', in W. Guy (ed.) *Between Past and Future: the Roma in Central and Eastern Europe*, Hatfield: University of Hertfordshire Press.

Lemon, A. (1996) 'No land, no contracts for Romani workers', *Transition* 28: 28–31, June.

Liégeois, J.-P. (1994) *Roma, Gypsies, Travellers*, Strasbourg: Council of Europe Press.

Liégeois, J.-P. (1998) *School Provision for Ethnic Minorities: The Gypsy Paradigm*, Hatfield: University of Hertfordshire Press.

Liégeois J.-P. and Gheorghe, N. (1995) *Roma/Gypsies: a European Minority*, London: Minority Rights Group.

Marushiakova, E. and Popov, V. (2001a), 'Historical and ethnographic background: Gypsies, Roma, Sinti', in W. Guy (ed.) *Between Past and Future: the Roma in Central and Eastern Europe*, Hatfield: University of Hertfordshire Press.

Marushiakova, E. and Popov, V. (2001b), 'Bulgaria: Ethnic diversity – a common struggle for equality', in W. Guy (ed.) *Between Past and Future: the Roma in Central and Eastern Europe*, Hatfield: University of Hertfordshire Press.

Matras, Y. (2000) 'Romani migrations in the post-Communist era', *Cambridge Review of International Affairs* XIII, 2: 32–50.

Minority Rights Group (1995) *Minority Rights in Europe*, London: Minority Rights Group.

Mirga, A. and Gheorghe, N. (1997), *The Roma in the Twenty-First Century: A Policy Paper*, Project on Ethnic Relations (PER), Princeton: PER.

Muller, E. (1998) 'Affirmative action – the legitimate road to remedy the poor standard of Roma education', in M. Gedlu (ed.) *The Roma and Europe*, Prague: Institute for International Relations, 82-7.

Office of the Prime Minister (1997) *Report on the Situation of National and Ethnic Minorities Living in the Republic of Hungary*, Report no. J/3670, Budapest: Office of the Prime Minister.

PER (1992)*The Romanies in Central and Eastern Europe: Illusions and Reality*, Project on Ethnic Relations (PER), Princeton: PER, September.

Rican, P. (1998) 'The integration of Roma in Czech society', in M. Gedlu (ed.) *The Roma and Europe*, Prague: Institute for International Relations, 35–45.

Szilagyi, Zs. and Heizer, A. (1996) *Report on the Situation of the Gypsy Community in Hungary*, Budapest: Office of the Prime Minister.

van der Stoel, M. (1993) *Report on the Situation of Roma and Sinti in the CSCE Area*, Conference on Security and Co-operation in Europe, Office of the High Commissioner on National Minorities, The Hague: CSCE.

van der Stoel, M. (2000) *Report on the Situation of Roma and Sinti in the OSCE Area*, Organisation for Security and Co-operation in Europe, Office of the High Commissioner on National Minorities, The Hague: OSCE, March.

Vašečka, M. (1999) 'Roma', in G. Mesežnikov, M. Ivantsyn and T. Nicholson (eds) *Slovakia 1998–1999: A Global Report on the State of Society*, Bratislava: Institute for Public Affairs.

Verspaget, G. (1993) *On Gypsies in Europe*, Council of Europe Parliamentary Assembly,

ADOC6733, 1403–7/1/93–4–E, Strasbourg: Council of Europe, 7 January.

Verspaget, G. (1995) *The Situation of Gypsies (Roma and Sinti) in Europe*, report adopted by the CDMG, Strasbourg: Council of Europe, 5 May.

## Notes

1 'Roma' is the term increasingly applied in academic and political discourse to a collection of communities that, both historically and today, have been known by a huge range of not necessarily exclusive names and which refer to a variety of different characteristics such as presumed origin (Gypsy), occupation (Lovari, Rudari), physical appearance (Kalo), lifestyle (travellers), culture (Romungre) or language (Beash). The word 'Roma' comes from the language *Romanes* and has been most commonly applied to populations from Eastern Europe where most *Romanes* speakers live. The current promotion of a pan-European (global) identity requires the establishment of a (single) inclusive term, though the persistence of names such as Cigany, Gypsy, Sinti etc. illustrates the incompleteness of this process. This paper examines the attempt by European institutions a construct a policy framework encompassing the whole of this notional Roma, Gypsy, Sinti (etc.) diaspora in Europe. It uses the term 'Roma/Gypsies' when referring to all the communities concerned and 'Roma' when discussing only those in post-Communist states, as well as to describe the broad approach of European institutions. This is the arbitrary choice of the author and, though possibly confusing, is done to allow the problem of nomenclature to illustrate Roma/Gypsy diversity which has fundamental implications for the emerging pan-European Roma policy paradigm. See, for example, Liégeois (1994: 36-8), Marushiakova and Popov (2001a), Gheorghe and Acton (1994/95), Mirga and Gheorghe (1997).

2 This paradigm was first formulated by Jean-Pierre Liégeois (Liégeois 1994).

3 In 1984 the European Parliament accepted the report *On the Situation of Gypsies in the Community*. The Resolution was passed within days of another, *On Education for Children whose Parents have no Fixed Abode*, on 16 March 1984. The two issues were immediately combined with the European Commission requesting an overview of school provision for Roma/Gypsy children in member states. This report, *School Provision for Gypsy and Traveller Children*, was completed in 1986 but extended in 1989 to take account of the new member states of Spain and Portugal. An immediate consequence of the report was Resolution 89/C 153/02 *On School Provision for Gypsy and Traveller Children* of the Council of (Education) Ministers). The Resolution noted low levels of school attendance (30–40 per cent) and very high rates of illiteracy (50-90 per cent) amongst Gypsies and Travellers in the Community and promoted a variety of initiatives to be taken by member states as well as committing Community-level institutions to support change through co-ordinating information and institutional activities. See, Liégeois (1998) and Vayassade, M-C. (1984) *European Working Documents, 1983–4*, Document 1-1544/83, PE 79.328/fin.

4 In 1969 the Council of Europe's Parliamentary Assembly approved Recommendation 563 *On the Situation of Gypsies and other Travellers in Europe*. The concern of the Assembly was primarily directed at the issue of nomadism, in particular how to ensure that travelling people were not disadvantaged in their access to rights and services provided by mainstream institutions, especially education and social security. In 1975 Gypsies were specifically referred to in Committee of Ministers Resolution (75)13 *On the Social Situation of Nomads in Europe* but were not included, eight years later, in Recommendation R(83)1 *On Stateless Nomads and Nomads of Undetermined Nationality*. For fuller details, see Danbakli (1994: 101–7).

5  Renamed the Organisation for Security and Co-operation in Europe (OSCE) in January 1995.

6  European Commission (1999; for details on individual countries see, regular reports on progress towards accession by candidate countries (4 November 1998, 13 October 2000, 8 November 2000).

7  *Economic and Employment Problems faced by Roma Gypsies in Europe*, MG-S-ROM (99), 5 August 1999; Recommendation No. R (2000) 4 of the Committee of Ministers to member states *On the Education of Roma/Gypsy children*, 3 February 2000; Memorandum prepared by the Secretariat on the *Problems facing Roma/Gypsies in the field of Housing*, MG-S-Roma (2000), 3 March 2000.

8  Roma were discussed in the Human Dimension meetings in Copenhagen (1990), Moscow (1991), Helsinki (1992), Warsaw (1994) and Vienna (1999).

9  Decision of the 1998 OSCE Oslo Ministerial Council on the *Enhancement of the OSCE's Operational Capabilities Regarding Roma and Sinti Issues*.

10  It is characteristic of the current state of knowledge about Roma/Gypsies that, despite the growing number of materials produced claiming to show that Roma/Gypsies represent a coherent ethnic identity and culture and/or suffer ubiquitous discrimination and marginalisation, no comprehensive sociological survey has been carried out to identify fundamental aspects of their living conditions. Only a few partial surveys have been carried out in individual countries such as in Hungary (Havas *et al.* 1995: 67–80) and in the Czech Republic (Czech Government 1997).

11  Itinerant communities (usually representing only a minority within national Roma/Gypsy populations) can be found in many countries including the UK and Ireland, in Scandinavia, as well as in parts of the former Soviet Union and in the former Yugoslavia. Especially in countries of southern Europe (Italy, Greece and Spain), many Roma/Gypsies live in large camps, shanty-towns or areas allocated for their settlement.

12  In addition to large historical urban communities (such as in Bulgaria or Macedonia), there are an increasing number of cities with large and growing Roma neighbourhoods such as the 8th District in Budapest.

13  Over half of Roma/Gypsies live in rural areas, often in places of limited economic development. Roma/Gypsies might live in or near to villages, be recent arrivals or long-term residents and there appears to be a growing tendency for the recreation of entirely isolated 'settlements' in some CEE states, reversing the progress made during the slum clearance programmes of the Communist period.

14  The 1990s saw a dramatic increase in data (in English) focusing on human rights' abuses against Roma people. The emerging literature produced by Roma people and organisations themselves has rarely influenced policy, even at the national level.

15  The Report begins: 'The extraordinary complexity of challenges confronting Romani communities is manifest, as the range of issues in this report attests. By equal measure, the rich diversity among Roma within the OSCE makes all but a few general conclusions inappropriate. One, however, is plainly warranted: *discrimination and exclusion are fundamental features of the Roma experience*' (van der Stoel 2000: 1, my italics).

16  See, for Czech Republic, Rican (1998: 5–45) and Muller (1998: 82–7); for Hungary, Office of the Prime Minister (1997: 27) and for Macedonia, Barany (1995: 519).

17  It is widely recognised that a large part of Roma unemployment is structural, caused by the lack of availability of suitable work (Szilagyi and Heizer 1996: 14, Lemon 1996: 28–31).

18  Though not explicitly stated in 1995, Ms Verspaget's ideological position was clearly expressed in her 1993 report, *On Gypsies in Europe*, which proposed 'to replace the socioeconomic image of gypsies by a cultural definition' and which led to the declaration in

114

Recommendation 1203 of the Council of Europe's Parliamentary Assembly that Gypsies represent a 'true European minority'. Following the 1995 report the Council of Europe set up the Specialist Group on Roma/Gypsies which, since its creation in 1996, has been chaired by Ms Verspaget.

19   Many Roma communities have been settled for centuries, reflecting the considerable historical differences in patterns of social and economic development across Europe. By virtue of their greater numbers and local factors, Roma in CEE and the Balkans have historically played a larger (and more varied) role in the division of labour than the smaller number of persistently persecuted itinerants in many Western countries.

20   This is wholly erroneous and conflicts with all serious scholarship. Only a very small proportion of Roma were affected by the Communist bans on nomadism. Assimilation was explicitly linked to considerable activity designed to improve living conditions and employment opportunities for Roma people. In contrast, the post-Communist period is characterised by the promotion of Roma culture and identity and the dramatic decline in the living conditions and employment opportunities of Roma people. Contemporary policy makers need to strike a balance between these two extremes, but they can only do this if they are aware that the question exists.

21   See Matras (2000) and Guy (2000) for alternative views of Roma migration.

22   For the resistance to national plans at local level during the time of the Habsburgs, see Guy (1975a: 209–10 and 1975b) and for similar successful frustration of Communist plans by local authorities, see Guy (1975a: 219–20 and 1975b).

23   Example of recommendations include: 'Equal possibilities for Roma to participate in the political system ... should be encouraged'; 'Educational policies should incorporate measures for adult and vocational education'; 'In no case should new citizenship laws be drafted ... in such a way as to discriminate against legitimate claimants for citizenship'; 'Governments should take steps to ensure equal access of Roma to public health care', etc. (van der Stoel 2000).

24   For example: 'Governments must ensure that Roma are not victims of discrimination in respect of housing', yet 'governments should also endeavour to legalise the legal status of Roma who now live in circumstances of unsettled legality', i.e. authorities should allow Roma to continue to live in accommodation considered unacceptable for the rest of society.

25   As noted by the OSCE High Commissioner of National Minorities (van der Stoel 2000: Foreword) and by the growing number of national case studies of Roma policy e.g. Kovats (2001), Vašečka (1999), Crowe (1999), Marushiakova and Popov (2001b), PER (1992).

26   Questions of national identity vary throughout Europe and so ethnic politics is perceived differently across countries and regions. In CEE and the Balkans there is a strong affinity between national identity and political power resulting from the late creation (still ongoing) of numerous small states from within multinational empires (as distinct from expanded centralised states, such as France and the UK, or states constructed from the unification of smaller units, such as Germany and Italy).

27   For the fifth World Romani Congress, held in Prague 24–28 July 2000, see Acton and Klímová (2001); Connolly, K. (2000) 'Europe's Gypsies lobby for nation status', *The Guardian*, 28 July; Younge, G. (2000) 'A nation is born', *The Guardian*, 31 July.

28   A problem of ethnifying political boundaries has been demonstrated in Hungary where, based on universal franchise, less than a quarter of voters for Gypsy Minority Self-Governments are themselves Roma (Kovats 1996: 42–58).

29   Appreciation of the wider (political/cultural) context to the Roma issue helps understand why the Czech Republic, generally considered the most liberal and economically successful of the post-Communist states, produced a citizenship law which was widely perceived as

labelling Roma as alien and where television channels have broadcast programmes encouraging Roma to migrate to other countries.

30 Another consideration is the effect the political conditions of one national Roma population may have on the politics of a Roma minority in another country, thus on the domestic politics of another state. Given the novelty of Roma politics this is not a serious prospect in the near future, but may prove a source of tension between states if a transnational Roma politics is promoted and developed, especially if it is isolated from mainstream national political forces.

31 The multiple and manifest problems in respect of the social status and living conditions of Gypsies, Travellers, etc. in the EU reflects decades of neglect. There is no tried-and-tested 'model' which can be adopted by candidate countries where many indicators for their Roma citizens are better.

32 These are the same as the motivations behind Communist integration/assimilation policy towards their large Roma minorities.

33 This does not mean that the statements and activities of racist politicians and parties should not be condemned, but that European institutions must seek to provide sufficient benefits to mainstream political forces to enable them to work together to marginalise extremists within their own countries.

34 In March 1999 (revised in August) the Specialist Group on Roma/Gypsies produced its report on Economic and Employment Problems Faced by Roma/Gypsies in Europe (MG-S-ROM (99)5 rev). The report contains no attempt to identify the costs of any particular initiative or of engagement in any policy area, neither does it call for cost assessments to be made.

35 The low costs in the countries and regions where most Roma live mean that targeted development can support many more people than in the West and would stimulate local and national economies. Resources could be transferred either by expanding the PHARE programme or through a separate initiative, a mini Marshall plan. This raises the important question about the ethics of channelling such investment upon an ethnic basis which this paper does not have space to discuss.

36 Recently the EU has moved towards the totalising approach adopted by the OSCE and the Council of Europe. In November 1999 the Commission adopted the 'Guiding principles for Roma policy in Candidate Countries' and in June 2000 the EU presidency organised a conference on Roma in Lisbon. This greater co-ordination of 'European' Roma policy illustrates the importance of ensuring that the policy paradigm is well understood (see Enlargement Strategy Paper – Regular Reports from the Commission on Progress towards Accession by each of the candidate countries, 8 November 2000).

## CHAPTER SIX

# Roma refugees: the EU dimension[1]

*M í ť a   C a s t l e - K a n ě r o v á*

The European Union (EU) faces a crisis of migration as part of an unre-solved conflict between its requirement for the free movement of labour on the one hand and its desire to prevent unwanted movement of other cate-gories of migrants from outside the EU on the other. It is the 'other cate-gories of migrants' which cause concern; they are ill-defined and subject to increasingly strict controls. The policy process devoted to restricting the flow of unwelcome non-EU migrants into the EU rests on a combination of assumptions and bare statistical facts. The danger is that such policies will be devoid of an understanding of the real life experiences and the needs of those seeking to migrate (Bloch and Levy 1999). For a number of reasons explored below, migration has now become highly politicised, where a new 'trade off between humanitarian obligations and the national need for *realpolitik*' is being made (Brochmann 1999a: 298). This also leads to a significant shift away from a former view of 'courageous refugees', who were instrumental in breaking down the old Communist regimes (Thränhardt 1999: 29), to perceiv-ing certain types of subsequent migration as a threat or simply an anomaly.

The dividing line between economic migrants and refugees, which was never easy to define, is getting murkier and the attempted process of harmon-ising immigration and asylum policies in the EU is nowhere near to providing a more accurate or just redefinition. Since commercial trade is visibly intensi-fying, free movement of capital and goods is with us, and growing global eco-nomic interdependence cannot be avoided. Consequently tighter immigration requirements do not sit easily with current trends (Thränhardt 1992).

One of the main aims of this chapter is to seek clarification on what hap-pens to those who fall outside the accepted classical categories of migrants and among such problematic groups are the Roma of the former Communist-ruled states of Eastern Europe. Nowadays the Roma, who have been subject to forced migration in Europe since the sixteenth century, are on the move once more. To classify them simply as economic migrants would be a gross distortion but they are not accepted as refugees either. Why is it that they are perceived as undesirable, and why has the EU so far failed to find an answer to the harsh treatment they receive in their countries of origin, as well as in the countries that are their destination when they attempt to migrate?

This chapter will attempt to provide some background to a debate on what happens to non-standard refugees in pre-accession, pre-enlargement Europe. Here it can be argued that as a perplexing anomaly the Roma provide a true test case. They are significant for other reasons too as was demonstrated by the 1997 'crisis', when Roma refugees from the Czech Republic arrived in the UK. This event not only caused diplomatic panic in both countries, but is also widely assumed to have been instrumental in the re-drafting of the UK's stricter immigration legislation and its early application.

However, enlargement of the EU and the process of Europeanisation produce their own difficulties. The EU is not equipped to deal with the migration of Roma for they neither correspond to any standard categorisation of refugees nor fit into the programmes of repatriation that were set in motion after the war in ex-Yugoslavia. Nor are they compatible with the EU's more ambitious policies aimed at combating social deprivation and social exclusion. This is because all such policies deal with either workers or citizens of Europe. The tragedy of the Roma is that they are neither, that is in a full sense, in terms of access to rights. Formally, they are both but all their experiences speak of systemic exclusion and marginalisation in social, economic and political spheres of life wherever they have settled. Consequently the questions why the Roma have become the new migrating population and what lies behind their tragic fate form the focal point of the debate about the 'shifting boundaries' between citizens and outsiders in the EU (Levy 1999b).

The Roma population of former Eastern Europe is at the cutting edge of what is often termed the democratic deficit of Europe. They are the Achilles' heel of EU immigration policies and their arrival in the EU as asylum seekers from a variety of accession countries has thrown up a number of questions that challenge the EU's own future. Immigration and immigration control has become an area of high politics (Brochmann and Hammar 1999). At a time when Roma asylum seekers from Romania were making UK headlines the Conservative leader, William Hague, declared that asylum issues should become 'one of the key battlegrounds in the next election' (*The Guardian*, 31 January 2000). At the same time the message from the Labour government's Home Office was that the UK could not afford to have its immigration laws 'invaded' (Barbara Roche, *Channel 4 News*, 24 January 2000). This view was swiftly echoed by the shadow Home Secretary's call to 'toughen up' procedures by automatically detaining any refugees with a 'bogus claim', and returning them to their country of origin as quickly as possible (*The Guardian*, 28 January 2000). In such media debates, particularly involving politicians, continuing uncertainties about the impact of open borders often lead to a poorly defined contrast between 'genuine' and 'manifestly unfounded' claims for asylum.

## Changing patterns in asylum and immigration policies

At present, recognition of refugees under the 1951 Geneva Convention is falling, reportedly to below 10 per cent of those who apply under that Convention (Levy 1999a: 17). The whole approach to refugees has clearly changed, from the right to flee, to the right to enter, with the emphasis on entry restriction. The historical background to this change was undoubtedly the break-up of the old Soviet empire and subsequently the wars in Yugoslavia. As long ago as the 1980s a US Senator, Alan Simpson, noted: 'We must distinguish between the right to leave the USSR, and the right to enter the US. They are not the same thing' (Briggs 1992: 148). EU immigration policy followed this lead.

It has been observed that current fears of 'uncontrolled' migration from beyond the EU's own doorstep encourage new developments in immigration procedures. Asylum policies are now separated from wider immigration policies (Selm-Thorburn 1998: 627), with migration flows being split up into those accepted for permanent settlement and others destined to return (Brochmann 1999a: 303). In addition policies of temporary protection, external controls, etc. are adopted.

Roma asylum seekers from former Eastern Europe are clearly not the only target of such policies. However, they are now a significant migratory population throughout the EU, whose status, claims, and identity remain extremely hazy – precisely because little has been done to enable them to find their own identity, let alone their own citizenship rights, in the old as much as in the new Europe.

However, if the enlarged EU is to become a 'common European home' and to play a role in promoting, encouraging and deepening the democratic process, then the question of Roma migrants has to be addressed. For Roma are the forgotten ethnic minority of Europe, who suffer open discrimination in their countries of origin as well as in the countries where they seek asylum. They are also the largest European minority without a state to represent their interests. Of the estimated 8.5 million Roma in Europe, 70 per cent live in former Eastern Europe (Liégeois and Gheorghe 1995: 7). The EU could easily lose its way in its attempt to give a lead to the accession countries about the nature of democracy.

This challenge arises at a time when the EU is addressing issues of wider global significance, that is growing global economic integration which will inevitably bring increased rates of mobility and migration. The principle of the free movement of goods, capital and labour brought new, unforeseen consequences. The Maastricht Treaty of 1992, whilst allowing the free movement of labour of EU nationals within the EU, triggered the current dilemma of how to differentiate between the EU citizens and non-citizens without violating the long-established tradition of humanitarian treatment for those who enter EU territory (Bourdouvalis 1997). However, the testimony of many Roma asylum seekers reveals abuses of human rights by various immigration regimes. The Schengen Accord, which came into effect in March 1995, sought a solution to the new division of Europe by removing EU internal border controls and replacing them by external controls for third country nationals, prior to their entry into the EU. Such moves have achieved two things: firstly, they have strengthened the role and importance of supranational bodies, to the dismay of some individual member states and, secondly, they have assigned to accession countries the role of the new buffer zone states.

Although there was a change in Europe from unilateral measures to restrict immigration to more integrated policies in the 1970s, nevertheless immigration policies still reflect predominantly national self-interest (Briggs 1992) and according to most accounts are not delivering the efficiency that had been expected. The process of harmonisation may be formally agreed, but there is a noticeable lack of mutual trust among member states about each other's policies (Guild 1996). The continued desire to protect one's own borders generates unworkable bureaucratic solutions and, what is more, reveals the absence of control mechanisms involving the international judiciary and parliamentary institutions. The resulting confused mixture of national, supranational and international co-operation (or lack of it) lies at the heart of the much-cited democratic deficit (Guild 1996).

This chapter focuses on Roma refugees from former Eastern Europe in order to assess some of the EU's internal policies on integration and migration. Firstly, it looks at the question of accession, then moves on to examine the issue of Roma refugees and European citizenship and finally appraises the effectiveness of the EU's protective immigration policies.

## Roma and the accession process

The expected accession into the EU at some future date of some or all of the formerly Communist-ruled Eastern European countries means that the EU is in a strong position to exert a positive influence on them, even though there is no longer a clearly agreed timetable or preferred ranking for candidates. The twin criteria for accession have been and remain – a viable market economy and political democratisation. Whilst some progress has undoubtedly been made, the unresolved issues around free movement of labour from countries with weaker economies has introduced a new dimension to EU foreign policy. Currently, the states of former Eastern Europe are being financially assisted to become the new buffer zone states, which process and return migrants deemed to be asylum applicants with unfounded claims (Levy 1999b). This is consistent with the previous 'externalisation' of EU immigration control, but introduces a moral obligation on accession countries that has no precedent in international relations. The new 'gate keepers' are therefore likely to adopt the criteria of 'genuine' and 'unfounded' migrants that the EU imposes. 'The complex treaty system, linking the EU and the intermediary states in East Central Europe, shields the West from inflows from the east and the south, making countries like Poland and the Czech Republic agents of the EU countries' control system' (Thränhardt 1999: 47).

The accession process is thus clouded with issues that do not belong there. It is now evident that the problems associated with migration are not going to be resolved by shifting the external borders, or at least not resolved by proper humanitarian and democratic means. The damaging impact of the new obligations imposed on some accession countries, however, lies in the extension of the logic of economic threat, and the rigidity resulting from placing a demarcation line between the political and economic aspects of the process of social change. This has a knock-on effect on the treatment of the accession countries' own populations.

The market competition introduced to the post-Communist states brought with it extremes of poverty and affluence, as well as marginalisation of those unable to compete. The Roma population on the whole can be included in the category of the most completely marginalised. Because of their current visible and severe economic deprivation, their migration from their home countries in former Eastern Europe to the EU is readily perceived as merely a form of economic migration. However, such oversimplification has harmful consequences. It fits an argument that Roma are only seeking to better themselves, and therefore their claims to a right to asylum are false. Their situation is not helped by official refusal in their homelands to acknowledge that Roma, as an ethnic group, have suffered discrimination, especially in the Czech Republic where the argument is twisted to present Roma mainly as a 'social problem'. These countries are slow in giving Roma more than empty formal recognition. Instead, they are still largely defined, in practice, in terms of a social group that lacks adaptability. 'Once defined as a social group and [a] "problem", it legitimated intrusive state intervention to deal with the group' (Winstanley-Torode 1998: 14).

Consequently both sides, the EU and the former countries of Eastern Europe, find it more convenient to label Roma as economic migrants. In the Czech Republic, the Ministry of Foreign Affairs insists that continuing Roma migration to the UK is a well-rehearsed, even organised pattern of economic migration. One statement from this Ministry, issued in advance of the European Commission's regular report on accession countries in November 2000, objected to the continued attention paid by Western media to discrimination against Roma which, according to the Ministry, mistakenly reduces the whole question to human rights' issues (Ministry of Foreign Affairs 2000). Although there is acceptance of de facto discrimination, the Czech Republic objects to being accused of systematic discrimination. This position dovetails with the EU's non-acceptance of the asylum claims of Roma migrants.

The matter becomes more serious when we consider the EU's own double standards – on the one hand, criticising the poor human rights' record of accession countries but, on the other, willingly agreeing that the Roma question is primarily a social and economic issue. Is it the case that higher standards of human rights are expected of the accession countries – but only on paper? All sides seem to be playing the same game. The reluctance on the part of the accession countries to admit the existence of institutionalised racism while accepting the economic explanation of Roma migration is for them a surer way of gaining entrance to the EU. On a recent visit to the Czech Republic the EU Commissioner, C. Verheugen, stated in an interview that the poor situation of Roma in the Czech Republic was not unique to Eastern Europe. 'It is a social issue, not a question of racism,' he said, adding that in this respect there was little difference between the countries of the East and Europe (*Lidové Noviny*, 11 December 1999). Meanwhile, the Czech Ministry of Foreign Affairs develops this position further by declaring its intention to take action to 'Europeanise' the Roma issue. As a result of focusing increasingly on the international dimensions of the whole question it appears that no one is willing to take any direct responsibility. The 'common European home' seems to be deliberately developing blind spots in its landscape.

The concerted effort to prevent the Roma from 'invading' Europe has kept the debate locked in an unproductive and misleading scenario, primarily of economic deprivation. In the process this has also disappointed those who could be expected to benefit from accession to the EU. Undoubtedly, the Roma are economically the weakest amongst the populations of Central and Eastern Europe but this should not deter us from seeking an explanation why they are in that position. In any case, 'having an economic motive for fleeing one's country does not [need to] discredit one's claim to be a genuine refugee' (Winstanley-Torode 1998: 25). Therefore to regard migration for economic motives as the polar opposite of flight from persecution is to set up a false dichotomy. The historic lesson of mass migrations in the past is that emigration is primarily a statement about the countries from which migrants leave.

In this context, the personal accounts of Roma families who came to the UK from the Czech Republic since 1997, and earlier, clearly reveal the primary reasons for leaving their country. These were their fears of an insecure future for their children, followed by fears for their own safety, as well as a loss of faith in the institutions of their homeland (Trojanová 1999). This account is supplemented by a survey among those who sought asylum in EU countries and subsequently returned to the Czech Republic. This survey confirmed the earlier findings that the reasons for Roma emigration from the Czech Republic were: high and long-term unemployment, poor housing conditions, fears for their own safety and for the future of their children and the rising cost of living (Gabal 2000).

The economic explanation is therefore present, but on its own is inadequate, and is not borne out by research among migrants of other nationalities. According to Nigel Harris, countless studies have shown that 'it is not the poor who migrate, particularly internationally, where the costs and risks are high' (Harris 1995: 190). Harris argues that most poor countries produce few, if any migrants. 'Income differences – if people know about them – may heighten their willingness to move but they are far from being an effective cause' (Harris 1995: 191). Others confirm that migration is never motivated by a single reason, and that economic and political causes are always intermingled (Brocker and Havinga 1997). In any case, it appears that asylum seekers in EU countries face an unpromising future since further research indicates that 'unemployment among refugees remains extremely high even after several years of settlement' (Duke *et al.* 1999). Nevertheless, in contrast, the survey among Czech Roma refugees who had returned home reported that the more tolerant atmosphere in the multi-ethnic EU countries was regarded as a positive part of their experience of migration (Gabal 2000).

Perhaps the plight of the Roma could lead to a more serious reassessment of the currently inflexible theoretical framework in which EU policies have currently become trapped. In practice it is impossible to create 'zero immigration regimes', because 'free markets, globalisation and economic and refugee diasporas' generate continued population movement (Levy 1999a: 13). Growing world economic integration will only increase rates of mobility (Harris 1995). Here it should be noted that in the past phenomena such as mobility have always been regarded positively, and have been to a very significant extent the driving force of European and American economic industrial development.

In this chapter it is suggested that the EU would stand a far better chance of arriving at a fuller and more comprehensive understanding of asylum seeking by Roma if it were to adopt a different perspective from its current negative stance of explaining this migration wholly in terms of economic motivation. Copious, well-documented evidence from the Refugee Council in the UK, the UNHCR and other international organisations has demonstrated that the Roma are suffering discrimination. Terms like 'velvet ethnic cleansing' have been used to denote the willingness of officials in East Central Europe to rid themselves of their Roma (Levy 1999b). Are we then so surprised that Roma choose to leave voluntarily? One of the most important ways forward in this apparent impasse, therefore, is to appreciate that Roma migration to the EU is not motivated by economic 'greed', nor is it an individualistic solution by a few families tempted by the vision of a prosperous future for themselves. Unless we recognise that Roma migration from their homelands in former Eastern Europe is a collective expression of grief, anxiety and fear, then there will be no change, and indeed very little future for real democracy in Europe.

It has been noted that the EU has not done enough to move this debate forward. The High Commissioner on National Minorities, for example, is not directly involved in issues of citizenship concerning the Roma population, although the denial of Czech citizenship to Roma, following the break up of Czechoslovakia in 1993, was directly discriminatory. It may be suggested that influential bodies in the EU do not use their powers sufficiently to alter the situation. The mandate of the High Commissioner, for example, is to de-escalate potential tensions by promoting dialogue and by giving an 'early warning' (O'Leary and Tiilikainen 1998). However, in the case of the unresolved citizenship of Czech and Slovak Roma, this meant that the High Commissioner did not act since there was no danger of an inter-ethnic crisis between the majority populations of the two successor countries (the Czech and Slovak Republics). The Council of Europe, too, missed its opportunity to examine whether the Czech citizenship law was discriminatory when the Czech Republic applied for admission to the Council (O'Leary and Tiilikainen 1998).

Another aspect of the eastward extension of EU borders has been the associated increase in the 'number of bilateral agreements concluded between individual countries' (Lahav 1998: 684).

In November 1994, Germany and the Czech Republic signed a treaty designed to speed the return of undocumented migrants. Under the agreement, the Czech Republic would readmit individuals who crossed illegally into Germany from Czech territory. Germany, in return, was to provide the Czech Republic with DM 60 million during 1995–1997 to help finance tighter border controls.

(Lahav 1998: 684)

Similarly, Poland 'had to assure The Netherlands in 1990 of a guarantee of barriers against anticipated illegal Soviet emigrants' (Thränhardt 1992: 68).

The more recent crisis resulting from the continuing migration of Czech Roma to the UK might have led to the imposition of visa restrictions for all Czech citizens, but instead has produced some informal agreements between the two countries that render the refugee dimension invisible. Meanwhile Slovak Roma have virtually stopped coming to the UK after visa requirements were introduced in 1998.

The whole question of accession appears to be riddled with problems where the Roma are concerned and consequently it must be asked whose interests are really served by refusing to examine the situation with a critical eye?

Since Communism made the Roma invisible as an ethnic group and as a result they went unrepresented, now seems the appropriate time to make open disclosure of both past and present abuses of democracy. The EU could be the appropriate vehicle for such a project, but so far this has not occurred. Currently some small steps are being taken to help the countries of Central and Eastern Europe find their own way of dealing with the Roma issue, some money is being spent and projects initiated. Yet, even well-intentioned projects seem to succumb to pressures to curb migration, as the treatment of refugees in the EU remains predominantly an issue of control.

In the early 1970s, the coming into force of the 1971 Immigration Act in 1973 stopped primary immigration to the UK from the ex-colonies. Also, around that time, populist proposals were made to return ethnic minorities to their original homes. At present, as in those days, there is only a short step from immigration control to 'induced repatriation' (Sivanandan 1978). Roma refugees are now facing similar treatment. A project carried out by the International Organisation for Migration (IOM) has been designed to help reintegrate failed Roma asylum seekers into their countries of origin. Here the question should be asked whether return and repatriation is the same as reintegration. The answer to this is clearly a straight no, but the EU has no alternative strategy for dealing with the unwanted migrants. Admittedly, integrating the Roma ethnic minority and developing social tolerance towards them on a Europe-wide scale should be long-term goals. However, the pursuit of self-interest by most EU governments pushes such a prospect further into the distant future.

As already stated, the accession process itself is plagued by protectionism, with '[s]ome Western governments ... willing to increase certain types of international assistance [only] if they expect that this will help in reducing emigration pressures' (Brochmann 1999b: 4).

## Roma refugees and European citizenship

As described in the previous section, the countries of Central and Eastern Europe have been failing their Roma populations and therefore emigration to the EU may in some respects have served them as some kind of solution. Now the onus is on the EU with its proclaimed long history of multiculturalism, traditions of pluralism, and accumulated experience in implementing equal rights and equal opportunities policies. The questions raised at this point are how well developed is the notion of European citizenship, and what would such citizenship mean specifically for the Roma migrant population – as well as for the estimated 12–13 million third country nationals already permanently resident in the EU? (Hansen 1998: 751).

Some writers pose the question whether or not Europe is a paradox as the ultimate experiment in political pluralism. Can there be a clear sense of rights in such a diverse political environment? Can Raymond Aron's dilemma of human rights not being the same as citizenship rights be squared? (Lehning and Weale 1997). How is it possible to assess what the phrase the 'ever closer union' might mean? So far, what seems to be happening is that more liberal and inclusive policies (like freedom of movement and access to rights to social provisions) for EU citizens are accompanied by more restrictive and exclusionary policies towards third country nationals, that is non-EU citizens (Faist 1997). The sharing of the same rights between EU nationals (current and future) 'is one of the most contentious items in the enlargement negotiations' (Philip 1994: 169). Most commentators in this debate agree that the EU, as yet, does not offer a meaningful concept of citizenship (Kolb 1999), and that citizenship rights are both 'being developed and restricted as part of [the process] of integration' (Philip 1994: 187). Most of this development occurs on an ad hoc basis and as will be explored in the following section, harmonisation of policies does not seem to offer greater clarity or efficiency. In fact, Europeanisation of policies has been identified as a path towards greater restrictions, at least in the area of rights and migration (Thränhardt 1992). Indeed, 'one of the paradoxes is that the move towards European unity and greater internationalism of the Europeans has strengthened Eurocentrism' (Cesarani and Fulbrook 1996: 3).

There is no doubt that '[s]ocial rights were historically developed in order to mitigate the most negative effects of early capitalism' (Bussemaker 1999: 2), thus social rights are an 'important basis for democratic rights' and 'provide an important legitimising potential' (Kolb 1999: 168). Although there has never been a full guarantee that the most needy will benefit, the EU prides itself that 'social cohesion and equality is at the core of (its) redistributive social policy' (Kolb 1999: 176).

Whilst this is not the appropriate place to present a full account of the historical development of EU legislation, it should be noted that the Maastricht Treaty of 1992 introduced the notion of European citizenship with the definition of certain political rights. The intention, as Kolb argued, was to narrow the gap between the citizens of Europe and European integration (Kolb 1999). What is significant at this juncture and for our discussion is that the EU has not come up with a satisfactory proposal or policy for citizenship rights in a 'wider', enlarged Europe. Exclusionary practices operate and appear to continue to operate, whilst the world of ideas that we live in increasingly operates on the basis of a 'homogenised value system', and 'a diffusion of [Western] values' outwards (Hoffman-Nowotny in Thränhardt 1992: 109). From this, one could deduce that the world is split between practice and intention, between ideas and reality, between what is visible and what less visible. This is very confusing for those who do not share European culture. And it is even more confusing for those who are also without a home – the refugees and migrants who seek understanding and want to make sense of their already disturbed lives.

The political direction that the EU is taking is not dissimilar to the treatment of social rights in the UK. The tendency is to define citizens as customers. What follows is that social rights and even political rights are being offered as 'goods' to citizens. 'The EU [, too,] offers a list of new 'goods' to

[its] citizens' (Kolb 1999: 179). Kolb argued that this is because the EU's sense of a community is still feeble and the political future of an integrated community remains obscure. Thus, a focus on the consumer and the status of the consumer is supposed to bring some clarity and efficiency, at least for the time being (Kolb 1999: 179).

The Roma then are the path-breakers in this new Europe. They are the ones who, denied access to some of the rights of citizenship (in the sense of not being treated equally), are left to 'shop around' for what is being offered under the entitlement to these 'goods'. They are the ones who seek protection and rights but are being allowed only selected social benefits for which they are then heavily criticised. The reality for them is reduced to benefits, not social rights, and even those are granted on a temporary basis.

There are isolated voices that point out that the practice of exclusion negates the intended creation of an integrated market and, furthermore, 'the exclusiveness of European citizenship could have serious future implications for civic cohesiveness and public order' (Sorensen 1996: 168). One way of dealing with those regarded as posing a threat to public order is to render them powerless, or unwanted, or both. The Roma refugees fit both those categories perfectly. They are subject to the control of immigration procedures that are based on the public perception of 'immigrants' being synonymous with 'unwanted' (Brochmann 1999a: 318).

So far, the 'regulation of immigration [in Europe] assumes that the norm is either a citizen or a foreigner, and the distinction is clear-cut. The citizens have rights, and foreigners not. Transition from foreigner to citizen … [remains] difficult.' (Harris 1995: 221). However, developing citizenship and the protection of citizens' rights cannot operate in a closed-off intellectual and cultural climate. Ultimately, the future of Europe will be impoverished if the retrenchment of rights continues for those deemed to be unwanted. Citizenship can only flourish in a diverse and pluralistic environment.

The fear of open borders, migration through war, and enlargement continues to generate restrictive policies and practices. As Kostakopoulou argued: 'Although "bringing Europe closer to its citizens" was a salient agenda item of the intergovernmental conference, … the Amsterdam Treaty consolidated the restrictive conception of citizenship institutionalised by the Treaty on European Union. The new Treaty did not extend the personal scope of Union citizenship to long-term resident third country nationals. Nor did it introduce any significant changes …' (Kostakopoulou 1998: 648).

One of the outcomes of this lack of institutional change is continued retrenchment of rights for asylum seekers and other categories of non-EU nationals (Guiraudon 1998: 657). Likewise it is clear that the Maastricht Treaty 'continues marginalisation of those who are not citizens' (Weil 1998: 51).

However, if the weak continue to be undermined by these processes, conversely the strong are provided with greatly increased powers. While refugees have been subjected to ever more repressive procedures '[a]t the same time, intergovernmental frameworks of co-operation such as Schengen, TREVI and Dublin have fostered the creation of networks of civil servants and police officials whose dealings are secretive and are not the object of judicial, or legislative supervision' (Guiraudon 1998: 670). This secretive co-operation, the often missing transparency, the speed with which many asylum cases are dealt with, the discretion bestowed on immigration officials, all add up to deep-seated feelings of insecurity experienced by asylum applicants. Such a state of affairs does not foster trust and confidence among asylum seekers. Moreover, it fails to help them to orient themselves or to discover what their rights and entitlements might be. As one bad practice follows another, one set of secretive practices another, the inevitable consequence is that many economic migrants 'make false claims for asylum' (van Selm-Thornburn 1998: 627) and so many refugees are falsely branded as economic migrants. This is precisely the situation that harmonisation of immigration policies aimed to avoid, and that a truly inclusive concept of citizenship rights could have resolved. Regrettably the EU seems to have fallen victim to its own over-bureaucratised and rigidly administrative approach to social rights and immigration.

One can therefore conclude that neither Roma refugees nor migration in general constitute the main danger for Europe.

## The effectiveness of the EU's restrictive immigration policies

'Unwanted' non-EU migrants are dealt with by the immigration policies of EU member states by isolating them. The shift from internal to external controls through the introduction of 'Schengenland' reinforced that isolation. The 1990s marked 'a major shift in immigration control from apprehension after crossing to deterrence before entry', and the Schengen Agreement permitted screening of potential entrants even before arrival. Externalisation therefore meant 'preventing the movement of people at the source' (Lahav 1998: 683). Nevertheless, these new procedures have not been successful with Roma migrants, raising the question whether EU policies are inefficient and if so, why?

There is no doubt that the Bosnian crisis introduced a shift in refugee policies from the 'realm of human rights' to the realm of 'border control' and led to the introduction of temporary protection (Brochmann 1999a: 312). In response to this acute emergency '[t]he majority of Western European countries discarded their normal practice of considering each case individually, and introduced temporary protection on a collective basis' (Brochmann 1999a: 312). However, it has been argued that restrictive policies generally 'keep the immigrant population in a temporary status and provide the state with legal capacity to reduce their numbers by enforcing remigration' (Brochmann 1999b: 11).

It is argued in this section that the arrival of Roma refugees provided the EU with an incentive to strengthen its protective policies and invest in repatriation. In this way migration issues have become further politicised, and the concept of temporary protection signals a blank refusal to face up to and deal with modern diasporas. The Roma are more isolated than most ethnic minorities, partly because the general public knows little about them – though this widespread ignorance is usually replaced by popular prejudice, and partly because they lack recognised international support networks. Consequently they are the most obvious target for pre-emptive measures.

The provision of temporary status and the adoption of a strategy of temporary protection for them overlooks the fact that this is exactly how the Roma have been treated in their countries of origin until now and how they have experienced their situation – vulnerable and unwanted. The frequently repeated argument that they have no grounds for fearing persecution in their homelands because these countries are now considered sufficiently democratic and pluralistic by the EU, means that the EU is free to continue protecting itself. It could also be argued that the temporary protection option provides space for non-legally binding procedures, or indeed is a form by which EU states can avoid responsibilities (Levy 1999b: 212).

The restrictive controls go unchallenged at the European level, as do the double standards in the observation of human rights in EU member countries. Meanwhile the development of EU policies towards third country nationals continues to deny them rights. 'Guidelines are provided to member states on how to apply various concepts and mechanisms but the discourse is exclusively an interstate one.' ... '[U]nder these measure no rights accrue to individuals' (Guild 1998: 623).

What then can the EU offer? It was expected that harmonisation would produce guidance and at least some degree of efficiency. The conclusion is that we might be getting neither.

The Maastrich Treaty of 1992 'transformed work on asylum and immigration matters from informal co-operation to formal inter-governmental co-operation' (van Selm-Thorburn 1998: 629), whilst the Amsterdam Treaty moved these issues further up the scale, from inter-governmental to supranational – a move from the so-called Third Pillar to the First. The lack of trust and the unresolved complexities of matching national interests with supranational requirements, the fact that there still remain substantial differences in applying common rules, and the ultimate fear of federalism seem to undermine seriously the goals of harmonisation and efficiency. Though the expectation is that there will be uniform interpretation of the 'communitarian' legislation 'concerning asylum and immigration, the potential for jurisdiction and effective power [at the Community level] is still limited' (Levy 1999a: 41).

The current grey zone of supranational decision-making on immigration and asylum prevents an effective overview with common principles of justice being applied. It has been noted by researchers that there is an increase in 'trans-national' bureaucratic policy making, 'whereby the [c]entral policies are increasingly formulated outside the domestic political process, and indeed outside the bounds of even international or supranational legal accountability' (Cornelius *et al.* 1994: 51). However, such tendencies are matched in the opposite direction at national level. The new procedures give rise to 'evasion of judicial control by national governments' (Baldwin-Edwards and Schain 1994: 4).

In addition to selective and restrictive immigration policies, we are also witnessing privatisation in immigration regulation – a further removal from democratic control. 'These shifts in implementation to private, local or international arrangements reflect less an abdication of state sovereignty, than an experiment in which national states involve agents as part of rational attempts to diminish the costs of migration' (Lahav 1998: 690). Thus considerations of cost override human rights, and we are back to the concept of customer rather than citizen. If we add negative images of 'foreign invasions' and the caustic play on words of Czech Roma in the UK as 'giro cheques' (where their state citizenship is identified with the form in which their UK social benefit is paid), then immigration controls seem appropriate, 'natural', and sensible (Cornelius *et al.* 1994).

What are we left with? We are left with ad hoc and unsatisfactory protectionism where the rights of the 'undesirable' refugees remain undefended. The arrival of the Roma in EU countries in 1997 was the first trial of the Dublin Convention, testing the effectiveness of harmonised mechanisms of deportation. That, one could conclude, has been the only 'achievement' of the EU's policies so far.

One last argument seems to present itself in this context, especially as it was argued at the very beginning that one of the EU's key dilemmas is how to encourage free movement of labour whilst controlling other forms of migration. It has been noted by Thränhardt that regulation of migration follows a certain pattern, whereby inclusion takes place along lines of wealth. There is greater political and economic 'openness between rich countries from which migration is not expected' (Thränhardt 1992: 68). However, there is no escaping the fact that 'free economics' operates with a highly controlled flow of labour (Briggs 1992: 26), so in the end there is no such thing as free movement. This could come as a shock, but as the same author argues, mass migration would 'cause rapid equalisation of per capita income', and thus 'threaten the [economic] "achievements" of the developed [affluent] world'

(Briggs 1992: 26). Thus, many of the policies that have been reviewed here are predicated on the contradictory requirements of market economies themselves. It is time that it is recognised that immigration policies only reflect these contradictions.

## Conclusion

The numbers of asylum seekers are now decreasing and the Roma refugees from the former Communist countries of Eastern Europe are being sent back to their countries of origin. However, no meaningful steps have been taken to alleviate their plight or resolve their predicament. They are returning because of the tightening of asylum procedures and the restrictive administrative changes in the EU. But they will not stay put for long. Roma refugees know when retrenchment means unfair exclusion and recognise that the self-protective shield put into place in many of the EU countries cannot remain unchallenged. Their comprehension of their own situation is far deeper than we are prepared to accept. The migration of Roma from this region is a collective expression that will not go away. Roma will knock at our European consciousness, and ask awkward questions about human rights and about investment in human capital, and the like. They will not disappear just because the EU has, for the time being, abandoned the people of Europe 'in an orgy of national discretion' (Guild 1998: 625).

Where do we go from now? The development of democracies in post-Communist countries is part of our problem. We are no longer separated by an ideological and political wall called the 'Iron Curtain'. We are in it all together. If we make a mess of this process of democratisation, we shall reap the consequences. The indication is that if we do not accept responsibility for Roma refugees arriving in the EU, as well as addressing their discrimination in their countries of origin, the deficiencies of our short-sightedness will pursue us for generations to come.

## References

Baldwin-Edwards, M. and Schain, M. A. (eds) (1994) *The Politics of Immigration in Western Europe*, Ilford: Frank Cass.

Bloch, A. and Levy, C. (eds) (1999) *Refugees, Citizenship and Social Policy in Europe*, London: Macmillan.

Bourdouvalis, C. (1997) 'The EU and immigration problems: small steps and possible solutions', in E. M. Ucarer and D. J. Puchala (eds) *Immigration into Western Societies: Problems and Policies*, London: Pinter.

Briggs, V. M. jr (1992) *Mass Immigration and the National Interest*, Armonk, New York: M. E. Sharpe.

Brochmann, G. (1999a) 'Controlling immigration in Europe', in G. Brochmann and

T. Hammar (eds) *Mechanisms of Immigration Control*, Oxford/New York: Berg, 297–334.

Brochmann, G. (1999b) 'The mechanisms of control', in G. Brochmann and T. Hammar (eds) *Mechanisms of Immigration Control*, Oxford/New York: Berg, 1–27.

Brochmann, G. and Hammar, T. (eds) (1999) *Mechanisms of Immigration Control*, Oxford/New York: Berg.

Brocker, A. and Havinga, T. (1997) *Asylum Migration to the EU: Patterns of Origin and Destination*, Nijmegen: Institute for the Sociology of Law.

Bussemaker, J. (ed.) (1999) *Citizenship and Welfare Reform in Europe*, London: Routledge.

Cesarani, D. and Fulbrook, M. (eds) (1996) *Citizenship, Nationality and Migration in Europe*, London: Routledge.

Cornelius, W. A., Martin, P. L. and Hollifield, J. F. (eds) (1994) *Controlling Immigration: A Global Perspective*, Stanford: Stanford University Press.

Duke, K., Sales, R. and Gregory, J. (1999) 'Refugee resettlement in Europe', in A. Bloch and C. Levy (eds) *Refugees, Citizenship and Social Policy in Europe*, London: Macmillan.

Faist, T. (1997) 'Immigration, citizenship and nationalism', in M. Roche and R. van Berkel (eds) *European Citizenship and Social Exclusion*, Aldershot: Ashgate.

Gabal, I. (2000) *Analysis of the Migration Climate and Migration Tendencies to Western European Countries in Romany Communities in Selected Cities in the Czech Republic*, research report for International Organisation for Migration (IOM) Prague, Prague: Gabal Analysis and Consulting, May.

Guild, E. (1998) 'Competence, discretion and third country nationals: the European Union's legal struggle with migration', *Journal of Ethnic and Migration Studies*, special issue, 24, 4: 613–25.

Guild, E. (ed.) (1996) *The Developing Immigration and Asylum Policies in the EU*, The Hague: Kluwer Law International.

Guiraudon, V. (1998) 'Third country nationals and European law: obstacles to rights' expansion', *Journal of Ethnic and Migration Studies*, special issue, 24, 4: 657–74.

Hansen, R. (1998) 'A European citizenship or a Europe of citizens? Third country nationals in the EU', *Journal of Ethnic and Migration Studies*, special issue, 24, 4: 751–68.

Harris, N. (1995) *The New Untouchables: Immigration and the New World Worker*, London: Tauris.

Kolb, A.-K. (1999) 'European social rights: towards national welfare states', in J. Bussemaker (ed.) *Citizenship and Welfare State Reform in Europe*, London: Routledge.

Kostakopoulou, T. (1998) 'European citizenship and immigration after Amsterdam: openings, silences, paradoxes', *Journal of Ethnic and Migration Studies*, special issue, 24, 4: 639–56.

Lahav, G. (1998) 'Immigration and the state: the devolution and privatisation of immigration control in the EU', *Journal of Ethnic and Migration Studies*, special issue, 24, 4: 675–94.

Lehning, P. B. and Weale, A. (eds) (1997) *Citizenship, Democracy and Justice in the New Europe*, London: Routledge.

Levy, C. (1999a) 'European asylum and refugee policy after the Treaty of Amsterdam', in A. Bloch and C. Levy (eds) *Refugees, Citizenship and Social Policy in Europe*, London: Macmillan, 12–50.

Levy, C. (1999b) 'Asylum seekers, refugees and the future of citizenship in the EU', in A. Bloch and C. Levy (eds) *Refugees, Citizenship and Social Policy in Europe*, London: Macmillan, 211–31.

Liégeois J.-P. and Gheorghe, N. (1995) *Roma/Gypsies: a European Minority*, London: Minority Rights Group.

Ministry of Foreign Affairs (2000) *Koncepce ministerstva zahraničních věcí ve vztahu k romské problematice* (The Conception of the Ministry of Foreign Affairs in Relation to the Roma Question), Prague: Ministerstvo zahraničních věcí, October.

O'Leary, S. and Tiilikainen, T. (eds) (1998) *Citizenship and Nationality Status in the New Europe*, Institute for Public Policy Research, London: IPPR/Sweet and Maxwell.

Philip, A. B. (1994) 'European Union immigration policy: phantom, fantasy or fact', in M. Baldwin-Edwards and M. A. Schain (eds) *The Politics of Immigration in Western Europe*, Ilford: Frank Cass.

Selm-Thornburn, J. van (1998) 'Asylum in the Amsterdam treaty: a harmonious future', *Journal of Ethnic and Migration Studies*, special issue, 24, 4: 627–38.

Sivanandan, A. (1978) *From Immigration to Induced Repatriation*, Race and Class Pamphlet, 5.

Sorensen, J. M. (1996) *The Exclusive European Citizenship: the Case for Refugees and Immigrants in the European Union*, Aldershot: Avebury.

Thränhardt, D. (ed.) (1992) *Europe: A New Immigration Continent*, Munster and Hamburg: Lit. Verlag.

Thränhardt, D. (1999) 'Germany's immigration policies and politics', in G. Brochmann and T. Hammar, (eds) *Mechanisms of Immigration Control*, Oxford/New York: Berg, 29–57.

Trojanová, B. (1999) *Vypovědi romských žadatelů o azyl ve Velké Británii* (Testimony of Roma asylum seekers in the UK), unpublished report.

Weil, P. (1998) 'The transformation of immigration policies: immigration control and nationality laws in Europe', European Forum, *European University Institute (EUI) Working Papers* 5, San Domenico: EUF.

Winstanley-Torode, N. (1998) *The Gypsy Invasion: from State Persecution to Media Denigration?* MA dissertation, University of Sussex.

## Notes

1   With acknowledgements to the Royal Institute of International Affairs for enabling me to take up this research.

## CHAPTER SEVEN

# In the name of the Roma?
# The role of private foundations and NGOs

*Nidhi Trehan*

Let us think and debate, but not without involving the Romany in the dialogue.
When it concerns them, we shouldn't ask ourselves if we like them or not ...
What can we, the majority, do for them, in our own enlightened self-interest?

(Bíró 1995)[1]

This chapter offers neither a comprehensive description nor an analysis of non-governmental organisations (NGOs) whose work affects Romani communities living in the Central and East European region. Instead, it seeks to explore ethical issues and patterns of development surrounding these NGOs, including intermediary organisations.[2] Exhaustive country-specific coverage of this issue is not possible here, instead phenomena common to the NGO sector are examined focusing on development and civil rights issues in the region. These include the formalisation of intermediary organisations, emerging hierarchies of resources, and relatively weak or embryonic grass-roots support.

Throughout history, diverse movements for justice such as those led by the African National Congress (prior to its establishment as a political party), the Congress of Racial Equality (USA), or the Roma National Congress (Europe) have generally been characterised by the existence of grass-roots constituencies rooted in historically oppressed communities. For a number of reasons some of the most high-profile NGOs whose work primarily focuses on Romani communities in the region lack grass-roots constituencies, being founded and funded by NGO representatives and private foundations intent upon being partners in the movement for the achievement of rights and dignity for Roma. In the place of a grass-roots constituency for these NGOs, we see the emergence of élite constituencies, that is, among national and international policy-makers, academics, and coalitions of liberal and progressive activists. Meanwhile, Romani NGOs (with or without grass-roots constituencies) find themselves adapting their agendas to the priorities of these high-profile partners, even though they may have decidedly different priorities.

A typology of Romani NGOs in the region posited by Bársony and Daróczi (1999) suggests that the most important formations (in no particular order of significance) are: local or national cultural organisations and clubs; civil rights organisations, political and human rights organisations; national umbrella organisations representing Romani political interests; 'showcase' Romani organisations (created and financed by the state); groups organised on the basis of kin links, representing various interests (including economic) and formations with religious orientations.

Although these NGOs may have strong constituencies, Central and Eastern Europe as a whole lacks the kind of NGOs popular in established Western democracies which are based on fee-based membership and/or individual donations collected during fund-raising campaigns (e.g. Natural Resources Defence Council in the United States), and which are supported by domestic corporations.

Therefore, the critical resources at the disposal of international private foundations and their key beneficiaries make it even more valuable to explore their influence in the arenas of national and international policy-making and representation vis-à-vis Roma.[3]

## Overview: the establishment of a third sector

Listening to supposedly knowledgeable people talking about civil society at conferences and other fora, it is easy to fall into the trap of thinking that civil society is a level playing field and the new salvation for development ... Civil society is a messy arena of competing claims and interests between groups that do not necessarily like each other.

(Fowler 1997)

One of the most active participants on the stage of 'transition' from Communist rule to post-Communist rule in Central and Eastern Europe has been the third sector, primarily comprising public interest foundations and non-governmental organisations. In a region continuing to experience swift economic, political and social changes, these non-governmental actors have been able to assert their role in the development of state-independent civil society.[4]

In a parallel development, Romani populations in the region have been plunged into a crisis of deepening poverty and greater socio-economic marginalisation coupled with increasing antipathy and violence from the side of the majority. In the past ten years, Romani communities have faced government policies which, among others, can be characterised as patronising (making decisions for the Romani communities), co-opting (creating decision-making structures that institutionally marginalise them) and hostile (claiming that Roma are responsible for the discrimination and exclusion they face). The earlier success and mood of optimism among Romani members within national parliaments – such as Anna Koptová and Ondřej Giňa (Czechoslovakia), and Antonia Hága, Aladár Horváth and Támás Péli (Hungary) – has now been replaced by a growing cynicism with national electoral politics since the mid-1990s. Romani candidates are no longer on most party tickets and Roma are generally not sought out for votes.[5] As a result, the NGO sector, through which Roma have the possibility to become active agents in shaping policy affecting their communities, as well as influencing the state, has taken on an even more critical role.[6]

To get a handle on the unique frame of reference when viewing the Romani-related NGO sector in the region, discarding assumptions about the 'voluntary sector' or the 'non-profit sector' as known in Western democracies is advised. Advocates for the Roma in Europe have likened the state of many Romani communities to those in the so-called 'Third World'. Extrapolating from this, I take the logical step of likening many Romani advocates and intellectuals to Third World actors within civil society in terms of their power(less) position globally. Their common struggle as double minorities in the region (social reformers *and* Roma) takes place on several fronts simultaneously – not only against the state but now, increasingly, against structures which inhibit Romani participation in the achievement of their own emancipation, including those *within* civil society.[7]

## The state and the third sector: Structures of dependence for Roma

Liberal-leaning intellectuals in the early days of the transition extolled the virtues of a strong civil society and its potential for 'democratising' the region (Forbrig 1999). Many were anti-Communist dissidents, who had risked unpopularity under totalitarian regimes and had participated tirelessly in early 'democratisation'[8] movements in Central and Eastern Europe; others were returning *émigrés* intent on participating in the post-Communist transition.

They believed that the vacuum left by a shrinking state sector could be filled by a dynamic third sector, and that issues of justice should be taken up on behalf of Roma to serve the larger interest of eradicating racism and social exclusion in their societies. Despite their progressive views about justice for minorities, most of these well-meaning intellectuals knew little about the day-to-day problems Romani people faced. Just as Romani leaders and politicians have been dependent on state structures for financial support (historically, and now in post-Communist times), so too Romani actors within the NGO sector have become dependent on major philanthropic donors for continuing their work. Given the fact that most NGOs working in this field are not sustainable without foreign assistance (access to funding from domestic private sources has thus far been limited), and membership-funded organisations are almost non-existent, the majority of projects have been necessarily donor-driven.[9] Donor dependency seems to have the effect of undermining the independence of local NGOs and initiatives.

With respect to Hungary, Wizner (1999) and others have pointed out the symbiotic elements of the state-third sector relationship where private foundations have been significant not only for their support of government-wary NGOs, but also because of their growing influence on state policy itself. As the state has retrenched its activities since the late 1980s, responsibilities in the economic, social, and cultural sphere have been passed on to the private or non-governmental sectors. Furthermore, in many countries of the region, the state itself has established public foundations to support programmes similar to those of NGOs in various fields. State policies in the fields of culture, education and the rights of minorities are increasingly being affected by the activities of foundations, though the influence is mutual, as the functioning of foundations and NGOs also depends on the policies of the state to a large extent.[10] In addition, there is a real danger of the state absolving itself from some of its duties towards its Romani citizenry. For example, this can be seen at the local level in Hungary with the minority self-government system (Kovats 2001). Up till now the state has not been effectively held accountable to its Romani citizens, therefore NGOs have had to struggle to remind the state of its obligations.

## Limitations of the third sector

However much their work was perceived as an unquestionable 'good' by early NGO entrepreneurs,[11] it appears implausible that it could ever replace the work of a democratically functioning state. Even if we do not subscribe to the notion that the post-Communist state continues to have social policy obligations towards its citizens, we can still see the limitations of third sector work in supporting Romani communities in the region. Both Pinnock (1999) and Wizner (1999) pinpoint several reasons for this. Firstly, NGO entrepreneurs and donors often subscribe to naïve ideological agendas based on popular concepts, for example, 'empowerment', 'human rights' or 'sustainability', without connecting them to the real needs of local communities. Secondly, NGOs ultimately cannot be held accountable to citizens as can the state, since only the state has the power to legislate socio-economic policies. Thirdly, NGOs generally do not possess the large-scale institutional resources that are at the disposal of the state. Essentially, NGOs are free agents operating on a voluntary basis, having neither the need nor the responsibility to ameliorate the deep socio-economic problems that Roma face.[12] Moreover, as the boards of these organisations tend to function in a *laissez-faire* manner, and most of the board members are from outside the local Romani community and/or hail from Western countries, the perspectives of Roma, and thereby the needs of the communities in question, undergo gradual marginalisation.

In 1995, three respected social scientists warned against two trends in the NGO sector vis-à-vis Romani issues in Hungary. They argued against 'rigid ethnic coupling' (e.g. 'Romani-specific' programmes), as this ultimately results in further segregation of Roma from the majority society, and also the top-down structure of most organisations, whereby 'grants and subsidies are swallowed up at the upper levels, and the effect of the organisations' work remains unnoticeable in the communities living in the direst circumstances' (Havas, Kertesi and Kemény 1995). The observations above point to the practical limitations of the liberal theorists' *pro-voluntas* perspectives.

International human rights lawyer Chidi Odinkalu of the London-based Interrights notes that a number of NGOs financed directly by Western donors do not enjoy grass-roots constituency support (as perhaps smaller NGOs do). Thus, they are not required to be accountable to any constituency, apart from a limited number of donors, who often subscribe to agendas that may or may not reflect the most critical needs of the communities in question.[13] In a striking parallel to intermediary organisations working in the field of Romani issues, this same lawyer comments on the work of African NGOs:

> Most human rights organisations are modelled after Northern watchdog organisations, located in an urban area, run by a core management without a membership base (unlike Amnesty International), and dependent solely on overseas funding. The most successful of these organisations only manage to achieve the equivalent status of a public policy think-tank, a research institute, or a specialised publishing house. With a media-driven visibility and a lifestyle to match, the leaders of these initiatives ... progressively grow distant from a life of struggle.
>
> (Odinkalu 1999)

This polemic raises serious ethical as well as empirical questions. Who are Romani and non-Romani NGOs ultimately responsible to: their donors, the Romani communities they seek to assist, and/or the general public? Who decides and who should decide within the NGO sector what are the priorities for the development and emancipation of Roma?

## The emergence of an 'ethno-business'

In the early days of post-Communism, some NGO entrepreneurs in the region believed that recruitment efforts were necessary to attract people to the field of development and human rights. The object was to enhance professionalism in the field, and offering generous salaries was seen as an effective way to achieve this.[14] One result has been that the salary of a young NGO worker in the region, especially those NGOs sponsored directly by international private foundations, is several times that which some local profession-als earn.[15] By the mid-1990s this had the twin effects of attracting into the NGO sector a large number of people who otherwise would have joined the private or state sector (including academic work) and also of making NGO work a professional field with 'career potential'. This is in sharp contrast to the relatively low-paid jobs within the voluntary sector in Western democra-cies where, for instance, many government employees earn as much, if not more, than those employed in the non-profit sector. The generous influx of money into the region through the auspices of the Western private founda-tions has led to an adjoining phenomenon, that many Romani intellectuals cynically refer to as the 'ethno-business' or 'Gypsy industry'.[16] This has also led to a rise in tensions rooted in the pay differentials between local Romani NGOs and the intermediary NGOs, between Romani and non-Romani employees, and between foreign and native workers. This is in step with Fowler's observation that in the short-term strengthening civil society tends to increase social tensions, rather than to curb them, since more actors are able to stake their claim to public resources and policies, hierarchical though the sector may be (Fowler 1997).

Pinnock (1999, 1998: 7–8) posits that the complex of NGO projects related to Roma has become part of a survival strategy within the Romani communities, and perhaps another way of strengthening their prospects for the future by offering spaces of resistance to non-Romani notions of 'integra-tion'. Though they are the exception, a cadre of younger, professionally educated and trained Romani advocates were able to garner places in top policy-making institutions. In a larger sense, they have been able to leapfrog over veterans of Romani emancipation, as donors and intermediary organisa-tions favour younger, degree-holding, English-speaking Roma to act as interlocutors in their work over the traditional Romani leadership (in both urban and rural areas).

However, despite the opportunities afforded by work in the third sector for Roma, the 'ethno-business' could have lasting negative consequences for the current and future generations of NGO activists if cynicism is allowed to set in. The values traditionally associated with voluntary sector and public interest work such as altruism, community service, alliance-building and co-operation, etc. face the danger of being diluted or marginalised by new emphases on technocratic ability (of mainly non-Roma) and tokenism (of Roma). Work in the development and human rights sector may become 'just another job' and technocratic work may well take priority over service to the community.

As they get larger, NGOs are looking more like businesses themselves. In the past, such groups sought no profits, paid low wages – or none at all – and employed idealists. Now a whole class of them, even if not directly backed by businesses, have taken on corporate trappings. Known collectively as BINGOs, these groups manage funds and employ staff which a medium-sized company would envy. Like corporations, they attend conferences endlessly. Fund-raisers and senior staff at such NGOs earn wages comparable to the private sector.

(The Economist 2000: 25–27)

These phenomena may simply be a function of increasing institutionalisation or formalisation of the NGOs themselves. Or perhaps the larger issues surrounding economic globalisation and corporatist thinking have permeated the vulnerable third sector of the region.[17] The task of scholars is to uncover the antecedents and raise the hard questions arising from these developments.[18] The task of NGO advocates, both Romani and non-Romani, may well be to strengthen moral and ethical leadership in the field.

## The non-Roma/Roma divide: Separate access, separate agendas?

Although clear-cut boundaries cannot be drawn between the work of Romani-led NGOs and other NGOs in the field, the hierarchical structure currently in place ensures that Romani NGOs receive a relatively modest share of the funding pie compared with those intermediary NGOs usually directed by non-Roma. Naturally, when access to material resources is limited, decision-making power is also constrained for Romani-led NGOs.[19]

One source of this differential access to funding is that donor agencies themselves harbour popular (mis)conceptions about Roma. They believe that Roma make difficult 'partners' for projects because of internal political imbroglios and the assumed low level of professionalism among Romani-led NGOs. This leads to heavier investments in NGOs led by non-Roma who are perceived as more impartial and professional. Consequently such practice has a tendency to reinforce prevailing anti-Romani stereotypes in wider society, and perpetuate the limited and inferior access that Romani-led initiatives have to the more established philanthropic organisations. Moreover, it ignores the internal political divisions among non-Romani advocates working in the sector, as well as allegations of lack of professionalism within high-profile organisations.[20]

NGOs in the 'Romani sector' also have divergent philosophies and work cultures which tend to reflect the varying agendas of their founders and supporters. There are those who make up an intrinsic part of the movement for the rights of Roma like the Fund for Hope and Understanding, based in the Czech town of Rokycany, or the Romani Foundation for Civil Rights in Hungary, while there are others working towards the ideal of instilling rule-of-law practices in the region, such as the Legal Defence Bureau for National and Ethnic Minorities (NEKI) of the Otherness Foundation. Then there are the notable differences in the scope of these organisations – comprising local, domestic, and international groups. Although local NGOs are considered to be the most effective, because they presumably use the bulk of their money directly for services, thereby building up community interests and stakes, long-term strategic thinking tends to be neglected, and in many cases is not feasible given the 'crisis management' style of work. Fortunately, there are NGOs bucking this trend by combining both the grass-roots development aspects of local NGOs with the long-term strategic policy planning of national and international players in the field.[21]

The observations above point to structural barriers that Romani participants encounter in NGO sector work. Many non-Romani lawyers, advocates, and educators from the region were trained in Western Europe or the United States, enabling them to gain a command of the English language and the language of civil society, thereby giving them an upper hand in the competition for the best jobs within the field. Perhaps most critically, it is the non-Romani participants who have the contacts within the international philanthropic networks. In other words, access to the best technocratic and non-technocratic posts are restricted to those few Roma who can enter these networks and abide by the (unwritten) rules of the game. This is a phenomenon similar to what is termed the 'glass ceiling' in the United States. However, this is not a surprising development – the practice of excluding particular minority groups from various fields of work continues to be the norm globally. Even within the third sector, where emphasis is placed on concepts of inclusion and transparency, Romani candidates as outsiders to these networks, can be passed over easily.[22]

### Advocacy: a forum for common interests?

Despite the number of conflicts endemic to the field, there are a number of common interests that NGOs and activists tend to gather around. One is attacking racism within the government and society at large. When ministers of state make outrageous public statements or Roma once again become victims of racist violence, NGOs and activists take leadership roles in condemning these attacks. Naturally, this is an important function they perform, and it is at these moments, that the 'partnership' roles of non-Romani NGOs and actors are best manifested.[23]

Those NGOs subscribing to the agenda of 'Romani rights' have in many cases revealed to Europe its own deep anti-Gypsyism. In the recent past, NGOs active on the international scene such as the European Roma Rights Center (ERRC) and the Roma National Congress as well as numerous local and domestic NGOs have worked to increase awareness of issues faced by Romani communities in international forums.[24] Problems of systemic discrimination in the educational system, access to housing and employment are just some of the areas in which national and international Romani rights

NGOs are making significant headway. One of the results of this has been that visible progress (if only in legislation) on the 'integration' of Roma has become a near prerequisite for European Union accession. As David Chirico notes this is despite the fact that '... most states within the EU have very bad records of discrimination against Roma, including France and Italy, where there have been murders recently of Roma' (BBC 2000).

## The European dimension

As a result of the early work of many NGOs in publicising rights violations against Roma, the European Union has adopted specific criteria with respect to Romani integration in accession countries. Independent experts argue that post-Communist countries have adopted changes (some claim merely cosmetic) to their legal and judicial structure in an attempt to make themselves more palatable to Europe and enhance their chances of speedy EU accession.[25] According to this thesis, governments working to foster social integration of Roma are motivated less by ethical principles such as justice and equality of opportunity, than by the Machiavellian motivation of gaining entrance into the élite club.[26] Evidence does suggest that much of the pressure derives from the European integration agenda, as well as from supranational organisations such as the Council of Europe and the Organisation for Security and Co-operation in Europe (OSCE).

Most of the applicant states in post-Communist Europe with significant numbers of Romani citizens are now designing policies to meet the specific criteria of the European Union. As a result, a new niche has developed – that of PHARE-LIEN mediator. NGOs such as NROS (Civil Society Development Foundation) in the Czech Republic and Partners Hungary Foundation and *Autonómia Alapitvany* in Hungary act to implement various projects sponsored by the EU's PHARE programme, which has been described thus:

> Whereas the original objective was to promote democracy in the candidate countries through NGO funding, all funding now has to be seen in the context of the Commission's agenda for the accession.
>
> (Pinnock 1999: 198)

Apart from their strong impact via grant-making and various development projects, NGOs, both Romani and non-Romani, have generated various discourses at national and European levels (related to ethnicity, development, human rights, poverty, etc.) which has affected the policy-making process surrounding Romani communities. A plethora of literature on Roma has resulted from the concern and strong intellectual influences of global, predominantly Western actors such as the International Helsinki Federation, Project on Ethnic Relations, Open Society Institute and its affiliates, and from press-monitoring organisations such as the Roma Press Centre (Hungary), as well as from the commissioning of reports on Roma by governments, supra-national agencies (World Bank, etc.) and NGOs. Indeed, many mainstream human rights bodies did not concern themselves with Romani issues until such actors began to raise their voices internationally.[27] Paradoxically, the bulk of this discourse does not directly touch most Roma themselves, but rather a narrow group of actors on the national or international stage. This is not a wholly negative development, as many Roma have recognised the need to form alliances with non-Romani progressives at this point.

However, the fact that most Roma themselves are marginalised from much of this intellectual wealth is troubling. This goes back to the question of the development of history and of the image(s) of peoples. As noted Romani scholar Ian Hancock has emphasised on numerous occasions, if Romani people themselves do not control their own representation (history, image, etc.), they will continue to be at the mercy of outsiders, their generosity notwithstanding. This development will be reversed only when Romani social reformers assert their claims more vociferously in national and international arenas, thereby influencing policy and pushing political will. In Europe today, Dr Nicolae Gheorghe (OSCE Roma/Sinti Advisor) and Angéla Kóczé (Education Director of the ERRC and independent representative from Hungary to the Council of Europe's Specialist Group on Roma/Sinti) exemplify this possibility.

## Roads to self-determination

At times, activities within the third sector successfully support the Romani movement for emancipation and at other times, they tend to be complicit in 'social control' (a term commonly used to apply to mechanisms of the state). Indeed, many similarities can be perceived between the state sector and the NGO sector – both lead to reciprocal patron–client relationships by offering sources of income and survival for the participants, thereby creating loyal constituencies in support of largely ideological agendas. Thus, the simplistic notion of NGOs as vehicles of 'democratisation' needs to be re-evaluated, and perhaps, reformulated.

My object in this chapter is not to paint a uniformly negative picture of the NGO sector vis-à-vis Roma, but merely to point out some structural paradoxes and weaknesses. In large part, these can be ameliorated by making high-profile NGOs more accountable in particular to their Romani benefici-aries and the general public, as well as more transparent in the workings of their programmes. Meanwhile, local NGOs, community centres, and ghetto-based organisations (financed by larger philanthropic bodies) continue to provide one of the most important elements of grass-roots development or civil rights work – hope.

## Conclusion: monitoring the 'monitors'

As a recent World Bank report noted: 'Despite the eruption of activity ... very few initiatives have been evaluated or monitored' (Ringold 2000: 35). Does this suggest that the third sector has become a space of co-option and social control of the Roma in Central and Eastern Europe? To investigate this question, independent journalists and scholars need to assess the work of the sector vis-à-vis the diverse Romani communities in the region.

Independent committees, with strong Romani representation, and in particular Roma who are knowledgeable about the situation of their communities at the local level need to be formed to assess the impact of their work. If there is no real choice in the Romani community, dignity will only be a far-off goal. As Nobel Laureate Wole Soyinka (2000) noted recently, human dignity is never achieved without volition. If an element of choice is missing from Romani projects in the third sector, such as equal access to decision-making bodies for Roma themselves, than perhaps this would have the effect of undermining the long-term goal of Romani liberation and self-sufficiency.[28]

Few NGOs in the region conduct adequate needs assessment among the Romani communities: it might well be that people would prefer to have clean drinking water before they become connected to the Internet. It might be that money spent on publications for an international audience could be better used to create sustainable vocational programmes for Roma of working age. These are all a question of priorities and both long-term and short-term development strategies need to be devised within Romani communities themselves. Ultimately, Roma asserting their own voice will be the primary factor for bringing about positive changes in society.

Perhaps what is suggested here may sound like heresy to some in the 'field' but, after careful reflection, one old conclusion tends to resurface: that the ultimate goal of a successful NGO is self-dissolution, or as another observer has noted:

> As NGOs become steadily more powerful on the world scene, the best antidote to hubris, and to institutionalisation, would be this: disband when the job is done. The chief aim of NGOs should be their own abolition.
>
> (The Economist 1999)

## Appendix
### Timeline of NGOs working on Romani issues (1970–2000)

*1970s and 1980s*
Possibilities for quasi-civil society formations in various countries, including Hungary, Czechoslovakia, Poland, and Yugoslavia. Roma participate in the

*Charta 77* movement in the Czech Republic, and similarly throughout the region in diverse progressive organisations.

*1989–1993*

Throughout the CEE region, states are in decline, with shrinking budgets, period of increasing unemployment and political uncertainty. The first domestic NGOs are created by former dissidents and intellectuals. Intellectuals/activists (primarily non–Roma) develop contacts with foreign donors, preparing the ground for a third sector, a sector whose putative purpose is to enhance the empowerment of Roma.

*1993–7*

Founding of numerous NGOs and associations by Romani activists in the field of culture, education, politics, sport and increasingly, human rights. General optimism in the non-governmental sector, more philanthropic as well as governmental bodies support human rights and 'democratisation' issues in the region. NGO actors evolve into credible sites of human rights policy-making on Roma, both domestically and internationally.

*1997–2000*

Increasing institutionalisation of NGOs, professional human rights and development 'technocrats' begin to emerge. Rising cynicism among Romani intellectuals about the third sector, emergence of the 'Gypsy industry' (state and third sector), phenomenon of 'Romanisation' of programmes, whereby special projects begin to focus on the Romani community. 'Ethno-business' in full bloom. European Union integration fuels further Romani projects and policies on Roma in the region.

## References

Autonómia Foundation (1990) *Annual Report*, Budapest: Autonómia Foundation.

Bársony, J. and Daróczi, Á. (1999) *Romany Culture Center*, paper commissioned by the Open Society Institute, Budapest, unpublished.

Bartal, A. (1999) *Nonprofit Alapismeretek Kézikönyve* (Handbook on the Fundamentals of Nonprofits), Budapest: Ligatura.

BBC (2000) *Roma: The Outsiders of Europe*, electronically retrieved on 25 August, http://www.bbc.co.uk/worldservice/europe/neweurope

Bíró, A. (1995) 'The prince, the merchant, the citizen ... and the Romany', *Magyar Hirlap* (Hungarian daily), 30 May.

Cox, R.W. (1999) 'Civil society at the turn of the millennium: prospects for an alternative world order', *Review of International Studies* 25, 1: 7.

The Economist (1999) 'NGOs: sins of the secular missionaries' *The Economist* 354: 25–27, 29 January.

Erlanger, S. (2000) 'Czech Gypsies knock harder on the closed doors', *New York Times*, 12 May.

Forbrig, J. (1999) *Post-Communist Civil Society: Associative Life and Political Culture in East Central Europe*, European University Institute, May, unpublished.

Fowler, A. (1997) *Striking a Balance: a Guide to Enhancing the Effectiveness of NGOs in International Development*, London: Earthscan.

Havas, G., Kertesi G., and Kemény, I. (1995) 'The statistics of deprivation – the Roma in Hungary', *The Hungarian Quarterly* 36, 3: 67–80, summer.

Kawczynski, R. (1997) 'The politics of Romani politics', *Transitions* 4(4), September.

Kovats, M. (2001) 'Hungary: Politics, difference and equality', in W. Guy (ed.) *Between Past and Future: the Roma in Central and Eastern Europe*, Hatfield: University of Hertfordshire Press.

Lukács, R. G. (2000) 'The Roma Nonprofit – Nonprofit Roma', in Horváth, Landau, and Szalai (eds) *A cigánynak születni* (To be born a Gypsy), Budapest: Új Mandátum.

Marushiakova, E. and Popov, V. (2001) 'Bulgaria: Ethnic diversity – a common struggle for equality', in W. Guy (ed.) *Between Past and Future: the Roma in Central and Eastern Europe*, Hatfield: University of Hertfordshire Press.

Odinkalu, C. A. (1999) 'Why Africans don't use human rights language', *Human Rights Dialogue* 2, Carnegie Council on Ethics and International Affairs.

Phralipe (1998) *Phralipe* (Brotherhood), 9 January (special English-language version).

Pinnock, K. (1998) 'Social exclusion and strategies of inclusion: Romani NGOs in Bulgaria', paper presented at *Seminar on New Directions in Romani Studies*, University of Greenwich, 11 June.

Pinnock, K. (1999) *'Social Exclusion' and Resistance: A Study of Gypsies and the Non-Governmental Sector in Bulgaria 1989–1997*, PhD thesis, University of Wolverhampton, April.

Ringold, D. (2000) *Roma and the Transition in Central and Eastern Europe: Trends and Challenges*, Washington D.C.: The World Bank.

Rosenberg, T. (1992) 'From dissidents to MTV democrats', *Harper's Magazine*, September.

Samuels, D. (1995) 'At play in the fields of oppression', *Harper's Magazine* 290: 47–55, May.

Soyinka, W. (2000) 'Democracy and human dignity', *On Human Dignity* conference, keynote address, Budapest: Central European University and Hungarian Academy of Sciences, 23 June.

Trehan, N. (1999) 'The vicissitudes of Romani rights – racism, legal reform and popular discontent', paper presented at *Socio-Legal Studies Association Conference*, Loughborough University, February, unpublished.

United Nations (2000) 'NGOs decry conditions of Roma in many countries', UN Committee on the Elimination of Racial Discrimination, 57th Session, *UN Press Release*, 15 August.

Wizner, B. (1999) *The Development of the Romany National Movement in Hungary*, MA thesis, Central European University, 82–90.

# Notes

1   In 1995, Mr. András Bíró and the Hungarian Foundation for Self-Reliance *(Autonómia Foundation)*, founded in 1990, were awarded the *Right Livelihood Prize* (also known as the 'Alternative Nobel Prize') for civil-society work and income-generation projects among rural Romani communities in Hungary.

2   'Intermediary' organisations generally work at the national and/or regional level, such as the *Autonómia Foundation* (a PHARE implementing agency) and the European Roma Rights Center (ERRC) (main donor: Open Society Institute) in Hungary, and CEGA (Creating Effective Grass Roots Alternatives) in Bulgaria. Much of my own research on the NGO sector is corroborated in the findings of Katherine Pinnock's doctoral thesis (1999).

3   Major Western sponsors of NGO work affecting the Romani communities of the region include the Open Society Institute and the National Soros Foundations, Ford Foundation, Charles Mott Foundation, German Marshall Fund, Rockefeller Brothers Fund, Mellon Foundation, NOVIB (a Dutch foundation), various individual governments (e.g. USAID/USIS or the British 'Know How Fund'), the European Union (especially the PHARE programme), and more recently, the World Bank. In August 2000, a number of US-based philanthropic giants agreed to merge their activities into a 'Trust for Civil Society in Central and Eastern Europe' with a budget goal of $75 million to be spent over a period of ten years. It is too early to predict how this development will affect Romani NGOs – whether this consolidation of funds will lead to deepening problems of access by Roma themselves or whether it will open up new opportunities for a diverse set of actors.

4   The term 'transition' does not adequately describe what has happened in the region; moreover, transitions take place in all societies at all times, ranging from the imperceptible to the dramatic. The third sector is also known as the non-profit sector or in Western democracies, the voluntary sector. In Hungary alone, there are well over 60,000 registered NGOs or independent associations, including those funded by the state at present. On their history and development, see Bartal (1999) and for an insider's case study, see Lukács (2000). Various governmental and non-governmental foundations created to strengthen civil society have been active supporters of numerous Romani organisations and thus contribute to the design of policies affecting Roma. Work in the third sector has become a significant source of employment and career development in the region.

5   However, it is important to note two concurrent trends a) local level political activity appears to be increasing in the region as Roma are beginning to successfully contest local council seats and b) there appears to be the formation of parties in Bulgaria, Slovakia, and Romania which represent primarily Romani constituencies. In Hungary, the minority self-government system enables a modicum of Romani representation at the local level.

6   Many former parliamentarians (Roma or non-Roma) in the region representing Romani interests are now working in the NGO sector. Indeed, ever since the 'transition' began, there has been a 'revolving door' phenomenon, whereby the state and the NGO sector serve as alternative and/or parallel spaces of activity and employment for non-Romani and Romani intellectuals. For example, Ferenc Kőszeg, director of the Hungarian Helsinki Committee, was also a Member of Parliament with the Alliance of Free Democrats (SZDSZ) party from 1990–1998. Martin Palouš, the current Deputy Foreign Minister for the Czech Republic, was a long-time Helsinki dissident, and Dr Dimitrina Petrova, director of the ERRC, was a Bulgarian Member of Parliament in the early 1990s.

7   The term 'civil society' is not a synonym for the non-profit sector. It broadly encompasses political parties, labour unions, workers co-operatives, business associations, membership-serving organisations and religious bodies among others. Dr Nicolae Gheorghe, Aladár

Horváth, Rudko Kawczyinski, Angéla Kóczé and Blanka Kozma are a few among many Romani intellectuals in the region who believe that the hierarchical structure of the NGO sector today inhibits Romani participants from key sites of decision-making. Certainly, the burden that most Romani intellectuals carry in their attempt to represent themselves, their families, their communities, indeed, their whole people (if this is even conceivable, let alone possible), is tremendous. See R. Kawczynski, 'The Politics of Romani Politics', *Transitions*, September 1997. Mr. Kawczynski was at that time director of the Regional Roma Participation Program within the Open Society Institute-Budapest, as well as on the board of directors of the ERRC.

8　An ill-defined notion which, for the most part, has been promoted by the United States government and private Western donors, and which is closely connected to the attempt to build an independent civil society in post-Communist Europe. For an unabashed look at the power machinations behind 'democracy-building' programmes, read David Samuels' report (1995).

9　The lack of voluntary membership of these organisations was explained away in the early days of post-Communism by the 'legitimate suspicion against voluntary action, as during forty years [under Communism] there was the practice of compulsory 'volunteering', and membership fees were deducted from salaries' (Autonómia Foundation 1990). Nevertheless, Romani organisations in the region were active from the 1960s onwards, providing real possibilities for self-organisation and ethnic expression albeit with attached political limitations.

10　For instance, although the George Soros Foundation has been in operation in Hungary since 1984, it was not until 1993, on the heels of the passage of the Law on National and Ethnic Minorities in Hungary, that one of the largest non-governmental Romani programmes in the region, the Soros Roma Programme, was launched (Wizner 1999: 84).

11　I use the term 'NGO entrepreneur' as an adaptation of sociologist Howard Becker's concept of moral entrepreneur.

12　Wizner (1999) suggests that a general social programme to integrate economically disadvantaged people, including the Romani poor, would be far preferable to the current Romani-specific trend in NGO projects and government programmes. Interestingly, this is similar to policies attempted by the Kádárist regime before they acknowledged Romani *ethnicity* during late socialism. Indeed, quite a number of Romani leaders are wary of the long-term effects of Romani-specific projects at the societal level, which they believe reinforces the implication that they are not part of the body politic.

13　Though a number of NGOs in the field have Romani board members, in many cases they are usually hand-picked by donors and directors. In the case of the ERRC, the founding charter mandates that at least three board members be Romani. The legal advisory board of the ERRC currently has only one Romani member (from Spain).

14　According to Savelina Danova, former co-director of Human Rights Project (Bulgaria), currently a member of the Board of the HRP. She now believes that Roma themselves face problems of access to resources within the NGO sector (personal interview, August 2000).

15　For example, in Hungary, a teacher employed by the state earns on average $150/month; a full-time Hungarian NGO worker based in Budapest can earn over $350/month. The salaries within some international NGOs in the region are proportionally higher (taking into account the cost of living) than those working in New York or London in similar positions.

16　Monika Horáková, the only Romani Czech MP at the time, claimed that 'there is too much paternalism ... with too many Czechs who speak no Romani making a living by helping a people they do not understand, while Gypsies themselves go jobless' (Erlanger 2000).

The 'Gypsy industry' is not solely a third sector phenomenon, it also encompasses the growing number of Romani-related offices and programmes from culture to education to minority rights in the state sector as well. Indeed, the EU PHARE programmes in the region have funding earmarked for the 'development of civil society', which includes many Romani-related projects.

17    Political scientist Richard Cox (1999: 7) notes: 'Corporatism left those who are relatively powerless in society out of account; but being powerless and unorganised they could hardly be considered part of civil society'.

18    Pinnock (1999: 206) laments: 'The problems inherent in the sector such as: its ambiguous relationship to the government and business sectors; its insecure place within the socio-economic order; and the implications of cultural colonisation, are removed from the equation or dealt with only via superficial measures'.

19    A simple comparison of the annual budgets of intermediary NGOs with community-based Romani NGOs reveals that the former have far more resources than the latter. Intermediary organisations tend to have projects that are national or regional in scope, and this is cited as one explanation for the differences in funding levels.

20    Several directors of high-profile organisations in the region have been dismissed in the past, amidst accusations of poor management and/or improper personal gain.

21    The Human Rights Project (Sofia), founded in 1992, was one of the first organisations in the region to monitor systematically human rights violations and defend the rights of Roma. It currently has an active network of Roma and non-Roma working throughout Bulgaria, and has begun engaging in national advocacy work through its on-going campaign – For Equal Participation of Roma in the Public Life of Bulgaria. This resulted in the April 1999 agreement between Bulgarian Romani organisations and the government for a Framework Programme for Equal Integration of Roma in Bulgarian society, which apparently has yet to be implemented (Marushiakova and Popov 2001).

22    Though this is now changing, see Trehan (1999).

23    One example of this partnership was the public demonstration and advocacy work surrounding the Székesfehérvár 'ghetto affair' led by the Romani Civil Rights Foundation (Hungary). See *Phralipe* (1998) (special English-language version sponsored by the ERRC). The actions eventually led to cancellation of a 're-housing' programme that would have effectively ghettoised Romani families in barrack-style containers.

24    Both the ERRC and the RNC are openly critical of governments in Europe. Many domestic NGOs are blocked from doing the same as they obtain funds from the state, concurrent with their official NGO status.

25    Among others, Dr Martin Kovats of the University of Birmingham and Mrs Eva Órsós, current co-chair of the ERRC.

26    In a revealing quote from 1992, the then prime minister of Hungary, Viktor Orbán, commenting on the role of veteran dissidents, stated: 'For years, the dissidents based their politics on morality, not the political game. That is the nature of the underground ... they are clever and have good ideas, but they are not pragmatic' (Rosenberg, 1992).

27    See UN Press Release, 'NGOs decry conditions of Roma in many countries' (United Nations 2000). This document details the NGO testimonies before the Committee on the Elimination of Racial Discrimination (CERD) within the United Nations.

28    One third-sector consultant who has worked on USAID projects in the past, Carrie Greunloh, suggests that capacity-building should be one of the key priorities of NGO work globally.

Elena Marushiakova

Communist regimes were often ambivalent about Romani culture, which survived nevertheless. Musicians and dancers at opening of opening of a photo exhibition by US anthropologist, Elsie Dunin, devoted to *Xederlezi* (St George's Day). This saint's day, 6 May, is celebrated by Roma throughout the Balkans as the main Romani festival. Skopje, May 1998.

Elena Marushiakova

Roma also 'live within broader macro-society'. Contestant in Romani beauty competition 'Mis Shuzhi chaj' (beautiful girl). Skopje, 2000.

'In Central and Eastern Europe there are now many thousands of relatively well-educated Roma'. Young girls participating in Romani summer school, Vlasina, Yugoslavia 2000.

Roma activists in front of the offices of Roma NGO *Romano Ilo* (Romani heart) in Shuto Orizari, Macedonia, May 1998. Shuto Orizari (or 'Shutka' as it is popularly known) is probably the largest sizeable town in Europe with a Roma majority.

Founding congress of Union of Balkan *Egyupti* (Egyptians). Chair of Union, Rubin Zemon (centre), is from Macedonia. Ohrid, Macedonia, 1998.

Traditional and modern Roma leaders – the Kalderasha Vassil Stanev (Popusha) from Bulgaria (right) and Jorge Bernal (Lolo) from Argentina. Sofia 2000.

Romani mother and child from Romania. Evening bath before going to sleep. Casilino 700 Romani refugee camp, Rome, June 1999. The camp was the largest Romani refugee camp in Western Europe with 1,600 inhabitants. It was demolished by the city authorities in August and September 2000 (Kate Carlisle).

'Roma migration ... a collective expression of grief, anxiety and fear.' Yassenia, holding her baby girl, escaped from Sarajevo during the war. She is married with two children and her husband resells second-hand items in the markets of Rome. 'I miss my father, who returned to Sarajevo, and want to go back so he can get to know my youngest child.' Casilino 700 Romani refugee camp, Rome, December 1999.

Gheorghe, playing his violin, with his wife Maria. They live in barracks in the Romanian section of the refugee camp. Casilino 700 Romani refugee camp, Rome, 1999.

'Bemba-Fathi', husband and wife used to live in Sarajevo with their six children, where he collected scrap metal to sell to foundries. They escaped from Bosnia during the war and fled to Italy and are two of the best Romani dancers. 'We are a couple united by our love of dancing especially to Gypsy music. It was my greatest pleasure to play the guitar and sing to Emir Kusturica, [the Bosnian film-director], when he visited the refugee camp.' Casilino 700 Romani refugee camp, Rome, 1999.

# PART TWO

# The Fifth World Romani Congress and the IRU

# The International Romani Union: An East European answer to West European questions?

## Shifts in the focus of World Romani Congresses 1971–2000

*Thomas Acton and Ilona Klímová*

T he Fifth World Romani Congress was held in Prague between 24–28 July 2000, following earlier congresses held in 1971, 1978, 1981 and 1990. It was organised by the International Romani Union (IRU) which was founded in 1977 after the organisers of the first London congress failed to organise a second. This chapter examines how far the organisers placed this congress in legitimate succession to earlier congresses, and how far they have moved an originally West European organisation to an East European agenda. It will argue that through their 'political nation' strategy, its leaders are seeking a role for the IRU analogous to that of the Palestine Liberation Organisation (PLO) before the peace settlement with Israel. New statutes were prepared, and eventually declared adopted, which embodied this aspiration and were looked at by a working party. Unfortunately, though much longer, they displayed exactly the same incoherence and democratic deficit as the previous statutes (Acton 1981), but created many more organs of the IRU.

The IRU officers summoned the congress at a few weeks notice in case others might try to organise a fifth congress. The Czech Roma-dominated leadership wished to take advantage of the Czech government's need for Romani approval of its improvements in the area of human rights – a requirement for EU accession. The leadership also wanted to gain legitimacy in order to be able to administer money arising from Holocaust restitution processes. The organisers listed the Open Society Foundation (Soros) as the primary sponsor as well as various supporters including the Czech government's Inter-Ministerial Commission for Roma Affairs, the World Bank, the Organisation for Security and Co-operation in Europe – Office for Democratic Institutions and Human Rights (OSCE-ODIHR), the Norwegian Ministry of Foreign Affairs, the US Embassy in Prague, and Romani individuals. The Czech government facilitated and publicly supported the congress.

The great majority of the 122 delegates were Roma and voted in the elections for the presidency. Between seventy and eighty consistently voted according to the advice of the Ščuka–Stankiewicz IRU leadership, while another thirty or so constituted a democratic faction centred on the Nordic Romani Union members. The size of 'national' delegations did not correspond to the numbers advertised in advance. Nominations were accepted only immediately before the election, which made for a very lengthy process. In contested elections, Emil Ščuka won the presidency, Hristo Kyuchukov the secretary generalship, while – after a re-run ballot – four vice-presidents were elected: Viktor Famulson, Nadezda Demeter, Stahiro Stankiewicz and Florin Cioaba. A treasurer, Zlatko Mladenov and a parliament, with somewhere between thirty-two and thirty-seven members, were also elected. This parliament elected the presidium and court of justice on the last day, held in Štiřín Castle near Prague.[1] During the congress rapporteurs from working groups produced reports reflecting the draft programme of the IRU rather than the discussions that took place. The language group declared the success of the writing system adopted at the Fourth Congress and the migration group the need for a 'stabilisation policy'. There were also group reports on Holocaust restitution issues, Kosovo, education and culture, media, international politics, and economic and social issues.

The historical context is examined below.

## The First World Romani Congress and the founding of the IRU

The First World Romani Congress (WRC) was held in 1971 in London, formally organised by the Comité International Rom (CIR). This organisation had been founded in Paris in 1965 and its president was Vanko Rouda (Puxon 1971). At least six persons who had been present at some of the 1971 congress (T. Acton, R. Bielenberg, J. Cibula, E. Davidová, V. de Gila Kochanowski and W. Guy) were also present at the gathering in 2000.

Unfortunately, the historical background circulated before the Fifth Congress about the First Congress was inaccurate, claiming that the IRU had been founded in 1971 in London with Dr Jan Cibula as its president. The new statutes were even drafted as if claiming to be an update of statutes adopted in London. In fact, in 1971 there were people from fourteen different countries present (not twenty-one, as claimed in 2000). At that time no statutes were adopted, but instead the CIR was delegated to write some before the next congress (Kenrick 1971, Puxon 2000).

The president actually elected was Slobodan Berberski of Yugoslavia, while Jan Cibula was appointed representative of the WRC to the UN Human Rights commission in Geneva. Further congresses were promised for Paris in 1973 and Belgrade in 1975.

Participants at first World Romani Congress, held in London 1971, sing newly adopted anthem *Gel'em, gel'em* (We travelled on) with words by Jarko Jovanović (white coat). Jan Cibula (far left) later became first president of the International Romani Union and Grattan Puxon (far right) played a key role in setting up the second congress. Walsall, 1971. Behind (l to r) are Ladislav Demeter, Vanko Rouda and Juan de Dios Ramirez.

Romani Gypsy National Day, London, 8 April 2001. Jan Cibula (centre), the first president of the International Romani Union and now MP for Switzerland in the IRU Roma Parliament, returned to London to participate in a demonstration in Parliament Square celebrating Romani Gypsy National Day and the thirtieth anniversary of the first World Romani Congress. He is flanked by Charles Smith of the English Gypsy Council (right) and Veerendra Rishi, who continues the link with India pioneered by his father, W. R. Rishi, chronicler of earlier World Romani Congresses. *Uśtiben* means 'rising' or 'awakening'.

Sadly, Slobodan Berberski died, and the Paris-based CIT proved unable to organise a further congress or to prepare statutes as planned. Grattan Puxon, the secretary general, moved to Yugoslavia and together with Yugoslav Roma and with the co-operation of Dr Jan Cibula, A. Facuna and S. Holomek from the former Czechoslovakia, and others, planned to bypass the CIT to hold a new congress. To this end they founded the IRU in 1977 (*not* in 1971).

## The Second and Third World Romani Congresses

The opportunity to hold a further congress arose from a campaign which had been brewing in Switzerland since an earlier scandal there. In 1972 the Schukernak Reinhardt Jazz Quintet, contracted to play on Swiss Radio, were turned back at the border because they were Gypsies to the fury of the radio editor who had hired them (Rinderknecht *et al.* 1973: 131). The editor, Karl Rinderknecht, then worked with M. Maximoff and J. Cibula to build international support and they ultimately secured the backing of the World Council of Churches to hold the Second World Romani Congress in Geneva. It was this congress that elected Dr Jan Cibula, already president of the new IRU, as the second president of the congress and adopted the statutes of the IRU as its own (Puxon 1979). The statutes of the IRU had been hastily drawn up by the Czechoslovak members, and registered with the UN just a few weeks before the Second World Romani Congress in a document reported in its entirety by Rishi (1980). These statutes were vague, and were implemented by the officers in a profoundly 'democratic centralist' way, like most quasi-governmental Communist front organisations in Eastern Europe at the time, with local representatives being selected by the central officers (Acton 1981). No other form of a non-governmental organisation (NGO) could have functioned in Eastern Europe at that period, and it was hoped that the understanding and common purpose among the leaders would overcome the fact that the statutes provided no clear way of determining the majority in case of a split. This was the system which functioned between 1979 and 1981 (Puxon 1980).

The first two congresses were made possible because of strong motivation on the part of the local organisers to secure an advantage from hosting the congress. In the First Congress this was to gain international attention for the British Gypsy struggle; in the Second Congress it was the World Council of Churches' determination to eradicate Swiss racial discrimination. Appreciating the local motivation of the hosts is equally crucial for understanding the next three Romani congresses.

The Third World Romani Congress at Göttingen 1981 was designed to consolidate the advancing organisation of the Verband Deutscher Sinte und Roma (VDSR), led by Romani Rose. It succeeded in this aim, leading to sustained German government funding of the welfare programmes of the German organisation. This in turn consolidated support for the VDSR among its mainly Sinte constituency. The German organisation, however, then cut loose from the IRU for the following three main reasons:

*(a) The IRU Constitution*

The IRU constitution remained that of a Communist front. Also it was increasingly difficult for the VDSR to adapt to the chaotic and undemocratic administration of the Eastern European leadership following the election of two Yugoslavs to the IRU's highest posts, Sait Balić as president and Rajko Djurić as secretary general (Rishi 1982).

*(b) Roma and Sinte identity*

At first the Sinte politicians, like other Romani people who do not use the term 'Rom/Roma' as the proper name of their ethnic group, accepted the inclusive political use of 'Rom/Roma' to cover all Gypsies. But they came to see this usage as meaning, patronisingly, 'We, the true Roma, will allow you to rejoin our majority group and recover your authentic culture'. In reaction they began to insist on their own Sinte identity.

*(c) Clash of interest between German Sinte and immigrant Roma*

The majority of the Sinte, as German citizens, were concerned first to protect their own interests, which were seen to clash with the interests of immigrant Roma in Germany who supported the IRU. It is interesting, however, that when organisations representing immigrant Roma emerged at a later date, these also tried to reconcile the interests of Sinte and Roma. Consequently they affiliated to the Roma National Congress (RNC) led by Rudko Kawczynski, the most important immigrant Romani politician in Germany, and shared the scepticism of the Sinte organisation towards the IRU.

## The Fourth World Romani Congress

Both the main factions in German Romani politics went their own way, and the separation between them and the otherwise Yugoslav leadership of the IRU led to another lengthy period in which no one proved able to organise a congress. The third president, Sait Balić, summed up the situation in a rueful speech at the Fourth Congress: 'I have to ask myself why I was not able to organise at international level as I had been able to so successfully, first in Niš, then in Serbia, and then in Yugoslavia?' The answer, essentially, was lack of resources.

The resources to organise the Fourth World Romani Congress, held in Warsaw in 1990, came from a host with a rather different motivation from that of the previous three, the *Romani Baxht* foundation co-ordinated by Marcel Courtiade. This was concerned not with a particular national struggle, but with the struggle to create a Romani literature; it was truly a congress of the intellectuals, and its most important act was to adopt a morphophonemic alphabet devised by Courtiade in consultation with others. Eminently rational in principle, this alphabet has yet to achieve widespread correct usage, except in publications edited by Courtiade himself. As is explained below, these include the statutes written for the Fifth Congress. The Fourth Congress was largely financed by publishing and other interests who supported the developing Romani cultural work. Consequently resources were provided for the adoption of an alphabet, but not to assure a functioning secretariat between congresses. Seeing this, some of the prominent personalities at the Fourth Congress refused to accept IRU posts, notably Rudko Kawczynski and Dr Agnés Daroczi. The latter, the leading Hungarian Lovari Roma intellectual, resisted very strong pressure from those urging her to become secretary general. In consequence the previous, and not notably successful, secretary general, Dr Rajko Djurić, became the fourth president, while the relatively unknown Czech Rom lawyer, Dr Emil Ščuka, became the secretary general (Rishi 1991).

## Problems in the IRU

Almost completely lacking resources, especially after Djurić became a refugee from Belgrade to Berlin, the two main office holders were barely able to deal with their correspondence, let alone organise a further congress. Djurić's high-handed actions also alienated other members of the presidium, most notably Ian Hancock who had been elected representative to the UN at the 1990 congress. Acting entirely on his own initiative Djurić tried to replace Hancock by a gadjo (non-Rom), Paulo Pietrosanti an Italian Radical politician. Incidentally, Pietrosanti, now blind, was very much in evidence at the Fifth Congress, where he was elected to the presidium. At the Fifth Congress, Ščuka blamed most of his own inaction during the previous ten years on the dictatorial actions of Djurić.

The IRU continued to achieve some diplomatic triumphs, in terms of establishing relations with the EU, UN, and OSCE (formerly CSCE) – mainly through the actions of Nicolae Gheorghe, Ian Hancock and Marcel Courtiade. Already by 1994, however, the inaction of the IRU and the lack of support it commanded, together with the voices of critics like Kawczynski (1997) and Daroczi, had made it an embarrassingly incompetent negotiating partner for international organisations. For some purposes, however, a more inclusive body was created as a negotiating partner for the OSCE – the Standing Conference of Romani Organisations, which included the RNC and other organisations (Acton 1998: 14).

At this stage it seemed of little importance that the rump IRU was one faction among many. A new Romani politics was being created in the Western world which had been given a shot in the arm by a new wave of migrants from the East, the *asilante*, the asylum-seekers (Mirga and Gheorge 1997, Matras 1998). Roma in the West were shocked by what Eastern Roma had been forced to endure, and then again by the racist rejectionism of their own states. Canadian Romani politics virtually started from scratch over this issue as comfortable, invisible Romani intellectuals were driven by their conscience into taking a stand, guided by the veteran Romani activist Ronald Lee (Sijercic and Lee 1999, Lee 2000), who seems in retrospect to have been in training for this moment during his entire life. In West Germany the RNC was bitterly critical of IRU inaction and took the lead on this issue. At this point, especially after the split with Hancock, the IRU might have faded into historical irrelevance, as had the CIR before it. Why did this not happen?

## Holocaust restitution issues

The immediate answer would appear to be that fresh and important incentives and responsibilities emerged in the form of funds discovered to be in Swiss banks which had supposedly been deposited there before 1945, either by Roma, Sinte and Jews who had died or by Nazis who had stolen assets from Roma, Sinte and Jews and had then had perished.

The demand for collective reparations had been on the World Romani Congress agenda since 1971 and the pioneering documentation of Kenrick and Puxon (1972) but no sufficiently representative and responsible Romani institution had ever established sufficient legitimacy to be able to put forward a convincing claim to them. The Swiss money, however, would have to be supervised by someone, and the IRU was still the most international body in existence. And should the IRU succeed in managing the Swiss money with credibility, further collective reparations from Germany might well be within reach. Suddenly the question of who would continue to administer the IRU became an important question once more, and the leadership a prize to be grasped. However, to pursue and strengthen the claim for reparations it was evidently necessary to seek a broader base of support for the IRU.

This was undoubtedly a factor in the call for a further congress but at the same time tensions between key figures within the movement posed worrying threats for future unity. The leadership had begun to work with a US lawyer, Barry Fisher, with considerable local and international experience of Romani issues but who had unfortunately clashed with Ian Hancock on various issues. Meanwhile, the actions of Djurić had been erratic for some time and in July 1999 he relinquished the presidency to Viktor Famulson, one of the vice-presidents. An announcement was then made that there would be a fifth World Romani Congress at The Hague in April 2000 and Famulson tried to persuade Hancock to return to the IRU. However, when Emil Ščuka visited America and met him there was no meeting of minds – perhaps because by this time Hancock and other Roma aligned with him in North America were demanding that an accommodation be reached with the RNC. In consequence Hancock's split from the IRU became definitive, at least for the time being, and was possibly also linked to a misreading by Šcuka of correspondence between the UN and Hancock.

In this atmosphere of growing dissent it was the hope of the English Gypsy Council, and perhaps of activists in other countries too, that the proposed congress would be the occasion when these disputes could be resolved. Since almost a year's advance notice had been given, the congress appeared to be the opportunity for a looser, more federal and democratic constitution to be adopted and a new leadership elected with a clear mandate. Indeed, had a congress occurred in The Hague, this might well have happened. However, the prospect of such an outcome may be why the small group by this time running the IRU, and determined to go on running it, never organised the April congress that they had announced.

### The Gypsy Council initiative

It was at this point that the English Gypsy Council for Education, Culture, Welfare and Civil Rights, chaired by Charles Smith, began to question its alliance to the IRU. It had been recently re-joined by Grattan Puxon, who had organised the first two congresses but more recently had been living quietly in England. Within the Council the belief strengthened that, just as the CIR had been by-passed in 1977–8 to make the Second Congress happen, so the IRU might have to be circumvented in 2000 to bring about a Fifth Congress. From February 2000 the Gypsy Council put forward a modest plan, couched as an offer to the IRU – and other bodies – to hold a congress in Greenwich in April 2001. This proposal, unlike the previous ones, was not based on finding an overall sponsor, but rather on making each delegation pay its way, or find its own sponsors. It was argued that without an overall sponsor the congress could genuinely build an alliance of those organisations which had some substance, rather than a talking-shop of intellectuals who would go anywhere if their airfare was paid.

The reactions to this proposal were instructive. Some, reliving the battles of twenty years earlier, simply saw it as an attempt at manipulation by the gadjo Grattan Puxon, although this view was largely undermined by the clear commitment of the Gypsy Council in its own right to the proposal. Others were very supportive. In fact, Rajko Djurić wrote personally from hospital in Berlin to encourage Puxon. When Thomas Acton presented the idea informally in February 2000 at a conference in Berlin, he too was offered support by S. Palison and S. Stankewicz, who also wrote an encouraging letter to Puxon. W. R. Rishi, the veteran Director of the Indian Institute of Romani Studies, sent his son, V. Rishi, to help. When the Gypsy Council held a planning meeting in Greenwich to enable IRU members (both Rom and Romanichal, asylum-seekers and locals) to inspect the university and town hall premises that would be available, veteran journalist and broadcaster Dragoljub Acković even flew from Belgrade to take part and report back to colleagues in the Balkans whether the idea was viable.

However, those actually in day-to-day control of the IRU saw the proposal not as an offer of help, but as a threat. Shortly after the Gypsy Council had circulated notes from its successful planning meeting a leading Polish Romani intellectual, Andrzej Mirga,[2] told Ian Hancock in a telephone conversation that he had been told by Emil Ščuka that there was no chance whatever of the Fifth World Romani Congress being allowed to happen in England.

## Planning the Fifth Congress

With the help of the OSCE and perhaps other sponsors, a presidium meeting was called in Oslo by Ščuka and Famulson on Famulson's home ground. This was a more formal meeting than was customary for the presidium, and its proceedings, including a resolution on Kosovo, were duly recorded. Presidium members present included those who had been elected in 1990 (though not all of these were invited) and others who had been co-opted using a variety of ad hoc procedures during the previous ten years.

The meeting listened to the proposal from England but decided not to accept it. Instead, the secretary general Dr Emil Ščuka produced an exciting new proposal. The very next month, June, the Czech government was prepared to make available its sumptuous guesthouse at the castle of Štiřín near Prague for the next World Romani Congress. Despite the short notice, the presidium members responded with approval. In fact, the original June date proved too soon for arrangements to be made but by mid-June the eventual date had been finalised.

At this meeting the presidium was challenged by Nicolae Gheorghe to present more concrete policy positions. In his view every participating organisation needed to define its policies and to debate them with others. Failure to do so would mean the collapse of the credibility of the whole IRU. Gheorghe offered this advice not in the role of former officer of the IRU, but as an international civil servant. He explained that in his new post with OSCE, won in open competition with sixty-two other candidates, he was required to be neutral and helpful to both the IRU and the RNC.

Some presidium members were still apprehensive that the proposed arrangements might put the IRU too much into the pocket of the Czech government. These fears were voiced particularly by the acting president Viktor Famulson, who came under great pressure from other member organisations of the Nordic Romani Union as well as from young Roma intellectuals, who challenged him at a conference in Athens. At a subsequent meeting organised by the Nordic Romani Union in Malmö, he issued a joint statement with Rudko Kawczynski of the Roma National Congress (RNC) denouncing the proposed Fifth World Romani Congress as a stratagem.

The response was strong pressure from other IRU officers, especially Stankiewicz and Ščuka, urging that even if Famulson and Stefan Palison opposed the congress, they should come to Prague to put their point of view in person. Rajko Djurić, too, lent his support to this position. During these weeks Djurić had made a partial recovery from his illness and indicated his preparedness to preside at the congress and pass on the torch if Famulson was unwilling. In the event, Famulson attended as part of a strong block of delegations from associations which were part of the Nordic Romani Union, including a number of delegates more closely associated with the RNC than the IRU. This provided the main bloc of votes – some twenty to thirty – independent of those supporting the platform.

At this point it is important to query the interests of the Czech government in the matter which, in turn, are closely linked to the interests of Western governments, especially those of EU countries.

## The Czech government, the EU and asylum-seekers

Although Roma had been involved in the Velvet Revolution that liberated Czechoslovakia from Communism, they had been neglected after the Velvet Divorce which led to separate Czech and Slovak Republics. As almost all of the former Roma inhabitants of the Czech lands had been killed by the Nazis during the war, most Roma now living in the Czech Republic were descended from Slovak Roma, and many of these had become effectively stateless during the break-up of Czechoslovakia. But, whether stateless or not, all Roma in the Czech Republic had been subjected to violence and discrimination since the fall of Communism. As elsewhere in the region this situation was a result of the inability, or unwillingness, of weak successor regimes to suppress racism and exclusionary nationalism. In despair Czech Roma had begun to seek asylum in the West, following the path beaten since 1991 by Roma from Poland and the territories of former Yugoslavia. This emigration had peaked in 1997–8 and had led to the imposition of visa restrictions by Canada and a similar threat from the UK to the acute embarrassment of the Czech Republic, eager to present itself as a liberal and democratic candidate for entry to the EU.

The official response of almost all Western governments had been to assert that the Roma asylum-seekers were 'really' economic migrants[3] but that improvement in human rights provisions in the East was necessary to remove any justification for Roma flight to the West[4] and also as a condition for membership of the European Union, so that entry would not be accompanied by mass migration of Roma westwards.

The interests of the Czech government were stated quite openly during the congress and at the subsequent seminar by the Deputy Foreign Minister, Martin Palouš, and also by the representative of the European Union. Palouš frankly criticised the policy of the previous government, in which he played no part, and talked of a new approach of legal safeguards and a programme of projects designed to 'integrate' Roma into Czech society. However, a disturbing aspect of the official Czech position was the insistence that the main difficulty was one of 'communication'. Similarly, although Palouš insisted that the Czech government was not seeking to evade its own responsibilities, the eagerness to 'Europeanise' the problem related directly to the question of the future entry of the Czech Republic to the EU[5].

Of the front-runners among candidate countries, the relatively prosperous Czech Republic has the largest actual and potential number of Roma migrants and yet Roma form only a small part of the total population. In comparison, Hungary has produced fewer migrants, Slovakia is a somewhat less eligible candidate, while Poland has a much smaller Romani population than any of these. For these reasons, therefore, the Czech Republic appears an ideal country in which to test the policy of 'stabilising' the Romani masses.

## Who gets what from the Fifth World Romani Congress?

It is now possible to list the interests driving the Fifth World Romani Congress:

- the *Czech Government's* need of substantial international Romani support to legitimate its claim to be improving Romani rights, and its urgent priority to prevent Roma by humane means from emigrating, in order to win Western European approval and gain EU membership
- the *Czech Romani organisations'* wish to create a solid Romani welfare bureaucracy in the Czech Republic, similar perhaps to the one established by Romani Rose and the *Verband Deutscher Sinti und Roma* in Germany
- the *IRU leadership's* desire to create a legitimate and permanent financial administration which could administer Swiss bank repayments, potential German collective reparations, and perhaps other subsidies
- *Europe-wide organisations',* including the EU, requirement for a credible and representative Romani negotiating partner.

None of the above are unworthy aspirations or goals in themselves. In fact, to be achieved effectively, and legitimately, they require the interested parties to meet the aspirations of the others involved. That is to say, the attainment of these aims depends on the creation of a genuinely democratic association.

Such an association would enable the Romani organisations, which have grown up around the world in the last forty years, to associate and make a genuine contribution (or at least do no harm) to the welfare of ordinary Romani populations – both in the Czech Republic and in other countries. But how far did the Fifth World Romani Congress achieve these ends?

## The Fifth World Romani Congress
## Prague, 24–8 July 2001

This detailed first hand account of the congress is intended to give a vivid picture of the manner in which business was conducted and decisions reached at a time of transition for the Roma of the former Communist states of Central and Eastern Europe who remain predominant in the running of the International Romani Union.

### *Arrival and accreditation*

Although the congress had been represented as taking place in the sumptuous castle of Štiřín, delegates and guests arrived on Monday 24 July to find that only presidium members and VIPs were actually invited there. The majority of the poorer and less influential East European delegates had been relegated to the Hotel Volha, a student hostel miles away in the weed-belt, a bus-ride beyond the metro system.

In the event, most delegates never saw Štiřín. It was used to accommodate only the high ranking officials and host the parliament on the last day. The major meetings of the congress were held at the former Czechoslovak Parliament building, now occupied by Radio Free Europe/Radio Liberty – a bastion of American values in Central Europe and beyond. Whether the geographical disorientation and the separation of leaders from followers in delegations was a deliberate tactic, or merely fortuitous, must remain a matter for speculation.

On Tuesday 25 July delegates and guests were bussed to the Radio Liberty Hall and entered through an airport-style security check. Long queues resulted on the first day which gave delegates an opportunity to chat informally, including the following sharp exchange about the possible motivation of the Czech government and its role in sponsoring the congress. Martin Palouš, Czech Deputy Foreign Minister, approached Thomas Acton to criticise his report of a festival and seminar (held in Prague a few weeks earlier) as destructive. As a result he had made a complaint to the organisers. He further accused Acton of saying that the IRU officers had used KGB methods to retain control, and of mistakenly claiming that the Czech government was financing the congress. Acton denied mentioning the KGB but argued that the clear implication of the IRU presidium meeting in Oslo and of Palouš' own speech to the Khamorro Festival was that the Czech government was under-writing the congress, and indeed using this as evidence of its new-found commitment to Romani human rights. Palouš responded that the Czech government's financial contribution was small, and much less than that of the Soros foundation and the Project on Ethnic Relations (PER). However, he declined to give any figures. Indeed, although a budget for the congress expenditure was published, no figures were given for the income provided by any of the sponsors.

Practice had varied in the selection of delegations. After the Oslo presidium meeting a list had been issued, arbitrarily assigning countries a given number of delegates. In a few countries well-established organisations were allowed to choose their own representatives but a great many delegates also received personal invitations. The total number of delegates appears to have been 122, since this was the maximum number of votes cast in any subsequent ballot. However, 156 delegates had been envisaged in the Oslo list, although many of the countries originally included appeared to have sent no delegations. Among the accredited delegates from other countries the English delegation recognised at least three gadje.

Of all the delegates who attended, the IRU leadership appeared to have the dependable support of between seventy and eighty votes – shown at its most compliant when some fifty delegates changed their vice-presidential vote from Stankewicz to Famulson to honour an earlier agreement to give Famulson a vice-presidency.

When those queuing eventually arrived inside the hall on the Tuesday morning, the total number of persons present, including delegates, guests and press, was around 300. Of these perhaps two thirds or more were Romani, with a substantial Romani presence among the guests and the press corps, as well as a small gadjo presence among the delegates. There was simultaneous translation into Czech, Romani and English. More than 75 per cent of the speeches made were in the Romani language.

## Preliminary speeches

Prof. Georgi Demeter from Moscow, the oldest presidium member, opened the congress, calling for political self-reliance of Romani people. Martin Palouš, responding on behalf of the Czech government, admitted frankly that his country's government had been at fault in the past and that racism and violence against Roma still occurred among the Czech population. In particular he condemned the current level of segregation in Czech schools as intolerable. However, he called on critics to acknowledge small signs of improvement, and declared his government's support for the internationalisation of the Romani problem, agreeing with Tomáš Holomek's characterisation of Roma as the most European nation. He called for improved and increased Romani representation and communication between governments and Romani populations.

He was followed by Rajko Djurić, who stated that since 1933 Roma had endured three holocausts. Millions had died under the Nazis. Then they had suffered under Communism, in gulags and from programmes like the Czechoslovak sterilisation policy, and now they were suffering once more, especially in Kosovo. At the present, he continued, there was great danger of genocide or ethnic cleansing against Roma in Kosovo, but at the same time it had to be admitted that there were two or three Roma who had also to be condemned for war crimes there. Djurić used this example to make the point that Roma had responsibilities as well as rights. He maintained that Roma had to recognise their collective responsibilities in order to create the kind of organisation that governments would recognise and negotiate with. For example, the German government had given substantial funds for the welfare of Roma repatriated to Romania, but this money had to be channelled through the Romanian government and ordinary Roma had not seen any of it. In his view, an international Romani organisation, recognised as creditable and fulfilling its responsibilities, would be a far more suitable administrator of such funds.

Dr Djurić then listed the many meetings he had attended as president, from that with the Pope in 1991 to the most recent in Oslo, arguing that contrary to the view of critics, the IRU had been active throughout the past decade. Turning to current needs he believed that the IRU needed a substantial refugee programme. Asylum-seekers were victims of national divisions in both the countries they left and those to which they went. They were often kept out of school and subjected to marginalisation, criminalisation and degradation, which would have terrible consequences. It was necessary, therefore, for Roma to work with gadje in international organisations. At the moment those international organisations gave more respect to societies for animal protection than to Romani organisations. The IRU had to change this and gain the respect of the gadje.

The next speakers were Viktor Famulson and Emil Ščuka. Famulson, who had been acting president during Rajko Djurić's illness, emphasised the need to update the constitution of the IRU. He urged delegates not to let anyone 'treat them like dogs' and buy them off with tiny amounts of money. It was essential the Romani Union continued since the future of twelve million Roma not present at the congress depended upon it. For this reason delegates bore the responsibility to act with care to ensure the organisation did not founder.

Dr Emil Ščuka, like many other politicians of all ethnicities in Eastern Europe today, struck a strongly nationalist note, while remaining vague on questions of democracy. He opened by welcoming to Prague many of the founders of the IRU, including Jan Cibula, Jan Kochanowski, Stevitsa

Lyobov Demetrova, Russian Roma Union, sings Romani anthem to open Fifth World Romani Congress. Prague, July 2000.

Prof. Georgi Demeter from Moscow, oldest IRU presidium member, dances with Josie Lee, English Gypsy Council delegate. Prague, July 2000.

Nikolič and others. Reflecting on the past situation he maintained that the IRU should now no longer be considered as a mere association, but as the leadership of a nation. In the past the IRU had assembled important symbols – a set of statutes (though these had not been very workable), a name, a flag, as well as some progress towards language standardisation – but in themselves these had not been sufficient to make the Roma into a nation.

Dr Ščuka continued that gadje saw Roma as a minority group, social group or even a criminal group and was adamant that Roma should not let themselves be defined in that way by outsiders. Roma were, above all, a nation in their own right, and should be seated as a nation in organisations like the UN and UNESCO. This meant that the symbolism of the IRU had to be updated through new structures, new statutes and a new programme to be elaborated by the working groups about to start work. In his view this would gain the respect of the gadje, such as those who had come to the congress. The IRU had to adapt itself to represent all Roma, and all Roma should be able to respect its decisions. Gadje, in turn, had to do more than just offer small programmes of assistance. The World Bank and others should make the grants that were necessary to allow Roma to enter the mainstream of the economy and business.

The US and Canadian Ambassadors to the Czech Republic then made speeches vaunting their own countries' records and urging the IRU to represent Romani aspirations. The Canadian ambassador, however, warned of the difficulties faced by existing immigration policies. On the basis of self-identification, there were currently some 3,000 different ethnic groups in the world but it was not possible for all of them to describe themselves as a nation. The congress delegates, therefore, had to produce an answer to an important question: what common values bound them together, despite their diversity in different countries?

The representative from the commission of the EU in the Czech Republic spoke about the EU policy on human rights in applicant countries. This policy had been decided at a 1993 meeting in Copenhagen, where it was agreed that candidate countries should have established stable democratic institutions before they could be permitted to join the EU. Meanwhile, reports from the OSCE and elsewhere had indicated that improvements in human rights were required in the treatment of Roma to fulfil these requirements. Justifiably, Roma now expected to be consulted about the whole process of improvements and the proposed Roma parliament would facilitate such discussions.

Nicolae Gheorghe then took the floor, representing the OSCE. He reminded delegates that although he was now an impartial international official, he had previously worked hard for the IRU. In a short review of past IRU achievements he countered Roma complaints that the organisation had done nothing by asserting that Rajko Djurić's report had shown the extent of

IRU activity. Yet although there were other broad Roma organisations in existence – and here he pointed out that the OSCE was giving financial support to the RNC as well as the IRU – in his view the IRU was a vital part of the team. Looking back, the 1971 congress had been attended by relatively few people, but everything that had happened in the last thirty years had come from that small seed.

Nowadays, however, there were hundreds of Romani organisations, working in villages and towns, but often there was not a strong connection between them and the IRU, working at an international level. Although Gheorghe felt that there needed to be a clearer link between the two, he wished to offer the thought 'as a kind of provocation' that the IRU top-level work was necessary for ordinary Roma. For, without all the seminars and conferences attended by IRU representatives, Roma would not have the recognition which compelled states to create the context for local activities. For example, the IRU was currently urging that territory be set aside for the Roma displaced in Kosovo. In concluding, Gheorghe insisted that Roma had to do this work themselves; it wasn't enough just to complain to, or about, the gadje. Everyone should first criticise themselves and not just the leaders, he urged. For if the congress became just a festival of complaints, it would be a waste of all the money and energy that had been invested in it. In this respect he especially praised the efforts of Ivan Veselý, for carrying out the considerable work of organising such a major congress at very short notice when everyone had said this was impossible.

After short speeches from other ambassadors, presidium members and delegates presenting national reports, the assembly then broke up into a number of working groups.

## The working groups

A series of working parties had been scheduled on main areas of concern and a further group added on Kosovo, which was decided after the congress agenda had been printed. These comprised: Education and Culture, Standardisation of the Romani Language, Migration, Holocaust Restitution Issues, Kosovo, the Media, International Politics and Relations, Economic and Social Issues, and on the proposed new IRU Statutes and Charter. All except the last group concluded their discussions on the afternoon of Tuesday 25 May, and their reports were presented to the whole assembly throughout the following day. In the process, a number of delegates remarked that the discussion in working parties seemed to bear little relation to the reports that were subsequently given to the general assembly. Unlike the other groups the working party on the proposed new statutes and charter failed to finish its work on the Tuesday evening or even to agree to support the new charter by this time. Therefore its report was placed last on the list of summaries to be given on the Wednesday. In spite of this timetable, shortage of time necessitated some of the reports being left until the morning of Thursday 27 July.

*The Education and Culture Working Group*
The rapporteur, Nadezda Demeter, reported that one of the main conclusions of the Education and Culture Group was that more Roma should be encouraged to become teachers in order to motivate children to learn. Furthermore, an international Roma University should be established, teaching history, language and a full range of other subjects, and supported by a group of European experts to prepare its curriculum and methodology. This university should represent a European centre for Romani culture and include a Holocaust museum. In addition to this central resource it was recommended that media centres should be set up in every country, containing archives and with provision for training local police and other professionals, to help create a climate in which Roma did not feel compelled to emigrate.

This was followed by a comprehensive and extended debate, which included both critical discussion of the need for special provision for Roma and the dangers of separation, as well as reports on the work of individual organisations and countries. Supplementing accounts from various Eastern European countries, there was a report from Karolina Bánomová on the impressive educational achievements of Czech Roma refugees in Canada and interesting advocacy of the need for sport in education from Slobodan Mitrović, using the example of the Romani Olympic games he had organised in Serbia. Replying to the debate, Nadezda Demeter concluded that there should be two separate commissions, one for education and another for culture.

*The Standardisation of the Romani Language Working Group*
Most of the time in the language working group itself was apparently spent on discussing the obscure but fruitful theories of the aged Vania de Gila Kochanowski. The report given by the rapporteur, Marcel Courtiade, on the morning of 27 July, however, largely concerned the great success of the alphabet (devised by himself), which had been adopted by the Fourth World Romani Congress. Although Romani was the common language of the Roma nation which had originated in India, Courtiade insisted that standardisation of the language should not diminish respect for particular dialects. In his view, however, in order to survive in the modern world it was necessary for a language to be passed on through literature and not just through the family. Roma needed to be part of a multi-lingual society and the suggestion was made that the EU Socrates Programme should fund a seminar on making Romani a political language. Courtiade praised the UN for making Romani an official language in Kosovo, equal to Albanian and Serbian, and called for a campaign to further Romani language rights through UNESCO and to

make money available for the distribution of publications. This group concluded that English should be the second language of IRU meetings. In the plenary debate over this report fifteen or more speakers balanced concern for dialects with advocacy of standardisation.

### The Migration Working Group

Stahiro Stankiewicz reported that this working party felt that migration was a serious and widespread problem that was born of the ghettoisation of society in Central and Eastern Europe. He insisted that migration was not a solution to the problems of Roma in this region. However, the *stabilisation programme*, envisaged by the International Romani Union and promoted as an alternative to migration, would require a substantial increase of democracy in former Communist countries.

In the plenary session this report by the rapporteur was criticised as insufficient. Stefan Kuzhikov (Sweden) approached the situation from the point of view of its effects on Western rather than Eastern Europe. He reported that his organisation was trying to help asylum-seekers in Sweden but encountered great difficulties. Kuzhikov suggested that the working party report ought to contain a much stronger statement of support for asylum-seekers and proposed that the IRU should make a declaration that Roma are a European minority to send to governments.

After a number of delegates had debated this point, Nicolae Gheorghe stood to make one of the most thoughtful speeches of the congress. He sought a middle way between the blanket support for asylum-seekers being given by Western Romani organisations at the congress and the stabilisation programme being promoted by some in the East. His introductory preamble suggested that migration and travel now play a large part in the modern globalised economy and that Roma have as much right as anyone else in the modern world to aspire to and seek the most favourable environment. This was equally true for those now living in a country other than their country of birth. However, at present, he continued, rich countries were trying to close their borders, arbitrarily, to migrants from poor countries.

In this situation, Gheorghe felt, Roma had the right to be told the rules and to seek legal opportunities for migration. Moreover, they also had the right to flee from intolerable threats, although accepting this position did not mean, of course, that such threats should not be vigorously opposed in their homelands. Turning to the stabilisation programme, this could be criticised on two counts, he argued. Firstly, it might sound like a sedentarisation, or anti-nomadic programme, which both misrepresented the nature of migration from Eastern Europe *and* offended those Roma who actually are nomadic. Secondly, it did not take enough account of the interests of Roma who had a legitimate interest in migration. He suggested, therefore, that a new strategy was required to advocate the interests of Roma in a more sophisticated way, at opportunities like OSCE meetings and the 2001 World Conference against Racism in South Africa.

This was followed by some minor contributions over the issue of whether there should be a Romani passport and whether it would be anything like a diplomatic passport. An Australian delegate remarked that Australia had a zero immigration quota for Roma because quotas were given only to nation-states. Vania de Gila Kochanowski called for India, as their first country of origin, to support the migrants.

Stahiro Stankiewicz then replied to the debate with an extraordinary, all-out riposte to his critics. Although he probably had his own private doubts about the stabilisation programme, he clearly saw it as his duty to defend the line of the IRU leadership, which underpins its strategy of accommodation with Central and Eastern European governments and the European Union. He did so with not a trace of defensiveness or compromise but by a deter-mined vindication of the stabilisation programme – as in the interests of all concerned, as courageous common sense, and as Roma living up to their democratic responsibilities. Speaking without notes, he marshalled facts about different countries to support his case and mocked his opponents as unrealistic. This speech, far fuller and more persuasive than his introduction, largely carried the delegates and demonstrated the political talents of Mr Stankiewicz. Any politically active person can make a speech putting forward their own opinions, but it takes a master politician to make such a brilliant and passionate defence of the indefensible.

This debate over migration was probably the most impressive of the whole congress, a genuine clash of Titans that could bear comparison with debates in any parliamentary assembly in the world. Opposing points of view were advanced convincingly and with well-informed clarity by speakers who kept their audience riveted throughout. Whatever else may be said about this congress, this session at least showed that the Romani language and peoples are capable of the highest level of political discourse and debate.

*The Working Group on Holocaust Restitution Issues*
Rajko Djurić reported briefly on funds already repaid and criticised their administration in Germany and Sweden. Some brief discussion followed, including an account of gathering 2,400 questionnaires from Roma Holo-caust victims in the Ukraine. Barry Fisher, a lawyer from the US, then gave an account of progress in legal negotiations to set up a body that could receive and distribute funds returned in recompense by Swiss banks and others. He stated that the board of such a body should be composed of the most respected Roma, and also include some eminent gadje. This body should have the capability of authenticating the documentation of individual claimants. Some 1.25 billion US dollars had been promised in August 1998, but as yet no money had been released because of arguments over legal documents.

At this point Fisher criticised the OSCE for deciding to follow the German practice of referring to 'Roma and Sinte'. The Sinte, he said, were one of dozens of small Romani groups, who have their own name for themselves but are clearly part of the Romani nation. As such, they were not a parallel phenomenon to the Roma grouping but part of the Roma. Consequently, the Sinte should not be allowed a veto in Romani political negotiations, any more than any other small group of Roma. This confusion had simply delayed the process of getting restitution money into the hands of impoverished Holocaust survivors. However, at the insistence of the German government, agreement had been reached with lawyers representing two small Sinte groups to set up appropriate structures. Mr Fisher also reported on some cases being brought by individuals.

In the debate that followed, differing claims were put forward about numbers who had perished in the Holocaust. Delegates from Belarus reported that some Holocaust survivors had recently received 400 US dollars each while some from the Ukraine said that only a fraction of those who had applied were given the 400 dollars. Stahiro Stankewicz detailed the many problems Roma faced in completing forms and providing documentation of their claims.

### The Working Group on Kosovo

Moses Heinschenk reported the working party's recommendations about giving Roma in Kosovo access to police and other administrative offices. The attention of the congress was drawn to the statement on Kosovo made by the presidium at Oslo, which had been circulated to delegates. A Muslim Rom clergyman from Kosovo then gave details of the misery of Roma there, greatly moving the audience. The moderator of the day's proceedings on 27 July, Hristo Kyuchukov, responded by starting an impromptu collection with a 100 US dollar note. The collection immediately raised the equivalent of 82,000 Czech crowns (around £1,500) in more than a dozen currencies. It was later reported by Roman Růžička, in the Czech Romani newspaper *Romano Hangos*, that the eventual total collected was over 130,000 crowns (well over £2,000).

### The Media Working Group

Zoran Dimov reported from the working party on the media, starting with an account of three conferences which had been organised, the most recent in Budapest (1998) and Ohrid (1999). As director of a TV station in Macedonia, he made the case for a far more widespread distribution of Romani publications and wider use of Romani in broadcasting media to support the use of the Romani language in education. However, he also made the point that commercial, Romani-run media also had to appeal to gadje. Dimov followed this strategy himself, as with the documentary he had made on Kosovo.

To give Roma a higher profile in the media, he put forward a six point plan:

- creation of a Romani department in Radio Free Europe to broadcast Europe-wide in Romani
- development of Romani media where previously non-existent as an IRU priority
- broadcasting of future IRU meetings
- supply of all Roma centres with a wide range of Romani magazines, etc.
- systematic exchange of information between centres in different countries
- serious pursuit of language standardisation to facilitate the aims listed above.

Dimov urged that implementation of this action plan for the media and the development of the IRU website, giving clear information and links to other media, should be important responsibilities of the new IRU secretary general to be elected at the congress.

*The International Politics and Relations Working Group*
The actual working group on international politics and relations was attended by very few delegates (including Josef Bánom, a Czech Rom refugee in Canada, and members of the Croatian and Lithuanian delegations). However, a number of Czech Romani and other guests were present, including Ilona Klímová. At first there appeared to be no room available for the meeting and no one from the IRU taking responsibility, but the members of the group asked for help from Ivan Veselý, who then acted as rapporteur. Most of the discussion was conducted in Czech, and while the Czech-speakers were writing down their conclusions, the Lithuanian and Croatian delegates held separate discussions in their own languages, also recording their ideas. The Czech-speakers believed the IRU should monitor abuses of human rights everywhere and report them to governments and international organisations, in which Roma representation should be increased. They also favoured the creation of a non-territorial Romani state with its own government and embassies. Ivan Veselý emphasised the need for mass participation to legitimise and underpin such institutions.

However, the report of this working group was eventually presented by Nicolae Bobu, who had not been present during its discussions. He related all issues of international politics to the need to have appropriate IRU statutes in which Roma were acknowledged not as non-territorial minorities but as a single nation, even though they were not demanding territory. He suggested strengthening Articles 3, 5 and 7 to create national commissions, embassies, passports, as well as an anti-racism commission to bring cases to the International Court at The Hague. Bobu also proposed that the IRU should receive a share of the tax revenues that were collected by national governments from

Roma or alternatively should tax Roma directly.

*The Working Group on Economic and Social Issues*
The short report for this group was presented by Milan Ščuka, elder brother
of Emil, who spoke about various projects and called for the establishment of
a Romani bank. He suggested that when an IRU centre was established in
each country, a representative for economic and social affairs in each country
should liase with national ministries, and that this work could be funded by
PHARE.

## The new IRU statutes and charter[6]

This working group is given a separate section in our report and is analysed in
more detail than the others because this was where the long-term health and
welfare of the World Romani Congress as an institution in itself was to be
determined. The debate over its 'report' was the most crucial division of opinion in the entire congress. The leadership planned that the statutes contained
in the charter would be presented to the congress, having previously been ratified by a working group that had already discussed them. Unfortunately for
the organisers, the working group which selected itself was deeply suspicious
of the statutes. It was attended by fifteen to twenty persons, mostly members
of the UK and Nordic delegations, and was the only working group not to
conclude its discussions on Tuesday 25 July. When the report from this
group was presented on the afternoon of 26 July, heated debate about key
issues occupied the rest of the day and eventually culminated in an extraordinary vote by acclamation, taken by the IRU leadership as approval for the
statutes.

There were some delegates who did not understand Romani, so Thomas
Acton translated between Romani and English. One other delegate present
understood neither Romani nor English, and Normundus Rudevics, a Latvian Rom MP, translated between Romani and Russian for this delegate. The
fundamental language of debate was Romani, but most delegates referred to
the English or Russian texts since, as non-linguists, they found the Romani
text in the standardised Romani approved by the Fourth Congress extremely
hard to read. Discussion was made more complicated by the fact that versions
in different languages were not entirely consistent. Most of the delegates had
seen the statutes for the first time that morning when issued with them in their
delegate packs. However, since these had been put together rather hastily,
some delegates had not received all the documents or had multiple copies. An
assistant hurriedly made additional copies when these deficiencies were discovered.

Dr Emil Ščuka entered the room a little late and undertook to lead the
group through the statutes. The most important thing, he said, was to under-

stand the philosophy of the statutes, that the International Romani Union must represent the whole nation. The structures of an IRU were to be not those of a mere voluntary association, but those of a nation, complete with executive, legislative, judiciary and administrative organs. The legislature was in two parts – the congress itself, in which the number of delegates was proportional to the size of the Romani population in each country, and a parliament, which would have just one Romani representative of each country. The parliament would elect a presidium, which would consist of commissars running commissions on subjects like education and culture, and also a judiciary (*Kriselin*), which would sit in Stockholm. The congress itself would elect the major officers like the president, secretary general and three vice-presidents.

It was at this point that Dr Ščuka was first interrupted by delegates from the Baltic countries, who raised the point that Article 23 seemed to indicate that there was one vice-president, who should be elected by the parliament. There was then a great comparison of texts, after which Dr Ščuka agreed that while it might look like that in the Russian version, in the Romani and English version it was clear that Article 23 referred to the chair and vice-chair of the parliament itself. He explained that if reference was made to the Romani version all would be clear. Dr Ščuka's attention was then drawn to Article 62 of the Romani version, which clearly stated that the president chooses one of the vice-presidents elected by the parliament (not congress, as in the English version), in contradiction to Article 11 which said there was only one vice-president, and Article 17 which failed to list vice-presidents among officers elected by the congress (although the English version did mention this).

Dr Ščuka was temporarily silenced as he re-read the texts, unwilling to admit there might be contradictions. During this silence delegates began to raise other points, the most important of which was that it might have been preferable to distribute the draft statutes more widely before the congress, and that instead of adopting the statutes, a working party ought to be appointed to correct them. Dr Ščuka retorted angrily that the statutes had been distributed some three weeks in advance to every country and, in addition, a copy had been placed on the IRU website. Delegates replied that although the statutes had been placed briefly on the website, they had been there for only a day or two, and had then disappeared from the site more than two weeks before the congress. In any case, they added, most people did not have easy access to the Internet.

Charles Smith, chair of the English Gypsy Council, then raised certain general points about the philosophy. First of all, he noted, section one of Article 1 listed Roma, Sinte and Kale as the main group names of the Romani nation. He maintained that the name Romanichal ought also to be included, since there were at least 250,000 Romanichals on three continents, many more than the number of Sinte. Secondly, section 8 of Article 1 did not represent a modern equal opportunities policy. As well as opposing discrimination on the basis of race, sex, language and religion, it should also include disability and sexual orientation. There was some debate on these points. It was agreed that in principle the word *'ling'* in the Romani version meant 'gender role' rather than 'sex', and therefore in principle could be argued already to cover questions of sexual orientation. As to disability, there was general agreement that the statutes should oppose discrimination, but some uncertainty as to how best to render the concept 'disability' in Romani. (Neither *'fizikalne bangipe'* nor *'nasvalipe'* sounded quite right.)

Dr Ščuka tried to bring the debate back to the question of vice-presidencies. He accepted that the versions of the statutes before delegates were not wholly consistent, but said the important point was that the statutes were the symbol of the Romani nation and their spirit and intention were clear. The presidium had determined that three vice-presidents would be elected by the congress, ballot papers had been printed and nominations for three vice-presidents would indeed by sought from the congress the very next day. The correct version of the statutes would be printed in due course. He explained that the advice of eminent jurists had been sought and that there had been an enormous amount of debate over the statutes in the presidium, where all members seemed to fancy themselves as experts on constitutional law. Minor errors were not his fault or that of the presidium but mere drafting mistakes by Marcel Courtiade.

At this point there was a collective intake of breath as it was realised that Marcel Courtiade had composed not only the alphabet in which the statutes were written, but the statutes themselves. The point was not pursued however.

Sylvia Dunn, a delegate from England, suggested that instead of simply having one representative from each country (usually a man) there should be one man and one woman, to ensure gender equality. This gained some support around the table but was opposed by Charles Smith on the grounds that representatives ought to be elected on merit, irrespective of gender, and by Emil Ščuka on the grounds there would be too many representatives as a result.

Charles Smith then criticised Dr Ščuka for starting to chair the meeting without any election. Dr Ščuka accepted this point with good grace. It had not been his intention to act undemocratically, he said, merely to explain to delegates the philosophy and structure of the statutes. He was perfectly content for someone else to chair the meeting and asked Charles Smith if he would accept nomination, but the offer was declined. Eventually, Normundus Rudevics accepted nomination and was agreed as both chair and rapporteur. As chair he immediately brought the meeting to order to make a decision on the question of vice-presidents.

After a brief further discussion it was agreed it was acceptable for three vice-presidents to be elected directly by the congress, and that Article 62 should be struck out altogether. The chair then asked Dr Ščuka to continue his exposition of the statutes, and asked delegates to let him finish before raising points for debate. This proved difficult, however, as Dr Ščuka was continually interrupted with questions and these questions in turn led to general debates. Dr Ščuka appeared to become more receptive to points being made, given the more or less unanimously critical tone of delegates. He supported the Gypsy Council position that all affiliated organisations should pay subscriptions.[7] As the time scheduled for the end of the session approached Dr Ščuka had to leave the room for a while during which time Rudevics continued to chair the meeting.

The issues raised in discussion were wide-ranging. Delegates from the Baltic areas concentrated on the division of responsibilities between officers, and the commissars on the presidium, and on whether the correct list of commissions had been drawn up. The English delegates pointed out that there were fundamental problems with the voting rights and procedures outlined in the statutes. Although the parliament was elected by the congress, it appeared (Articles 7 and 13) that the parliament, in turn, selected the delegates for congress. This was rather circular and did not allow much room for the wider Romani people to exercise their will through any kind of election. A further query was why gadjo countries should be the units of representation for a Romani nation. Finally, Charles Smith predicted that trying to hold elections without any prior list of nominees and candidates would be a recipe for chaos and disorder.

When Dr Ščuka returned to the room he enquired of the chair whether the working group was now able to present a report the next day. Delegates indicated that they needed more time for discussion and suggested that the vote to adopt the statutes be postponed beyond this congress. This was unacceptable to Dr Ščuka who explained that the IRU needed to present adopted statutes to international organisations almost immediately after the congress. If the work of the group was not finished he suggested they should reconvene at 9am the next morning, and continue work in a directed way so as to have a report ready by the afternoon. This was agreed and delegates broke up in a good mood, feeling that their points were being heard. In their view the fact that little more than bread and salad was left of dinner was a price well worth paying.

Some musicians in costume were playing in the foyer and press photographers were given the opportunity to capture their romantic images. One point of improvement over the Communist period that a number of delegates remarked on approvingly was the absence of alcohol. In the bad old days manipulative Communist functionaries who ran Romani policy conferences used to set out rows of small glasses of schnapps and arrayed bottles of beer and, even if some foodstuffs were lacking or in short supply, allowed for leisurely meals to put delegates in a good mood. One can only commend the organisers for not trying on any nonsense of that kind with the rank and file delegates.

## *Formulating amendments*

The following morning revealed that both the Baltic and the English delegates had done much homework overnight, determined to not to miss the opportunity to produce a set of statutes which, even if unwieldy, were fundamentally democratic. Even before 9am the UK delegation found Mr Rudevics in the coffee room sitting at a table and surrounded by twenty to thirty Baltic and Scandinavian Roma, arguing furiously about details of the statutes. They were striving to reach a mutually acceptable formulation and it was hurriedly agreed that the English delegation would also try to do the same. However, no member of the IRU leadership materialised to join the discussions.

The UK delegation agreed to put eleven detailed amendments to the statutes. Their effect would have been to make the IRU a membership-based organisation, with a subscription proportional to local income levels, and with delegates to the congress being elected by ordinary IRU members instead of being handpicked by the IRU leadership as in the past. It was agreed that these amendments were the minimum necessary to render the charter and statutes a truthful and democratic document. But, in their view, even with these amendments the document would remain unwieldy. Ideally it needed to be both simplified and supplemented by standing orders, specifying election procedures with written nominations being submitted and publicised in advance.

By this time the first coffee break had almost ended and the stewards went around urging delegates and guests to take their places in the main hall. When the stewards' vigilance declined slightly, UK delegates approached Mr Rudevics and passed on to him their amendments. These were explained to him outside the main hall in the foyer, despite interruptions by stewards trying to make them rejoin the general assembly. Rudevics made a written note of all the points on his own copy, alongside others that had been proposed, but warned that each one would have to be decided either by the working group, or by the whole congress if no time was allowed for a further meeting.

## *The debate and the 'adoption' of the charter and statutes*

Normundus Rudevics was called upon in the late afternoon of Wednesday 27 July to present the report of the working group. The moderator of the afternoon session was Dr Rajko Djurić, the former president.

Mr Rudevics, it appeared later, had a strategy of first making a general introduction to the debate and then allowing delegates to put forward their own points of view. Finally, he intended to sum up at the end of the debate with particular textual amendments that he would present as embodying the debate. Unfortunately, he had not explained this strategy beforehand to the Western delegations, who understandably grew very concerned when he did not put forward detailed amendments in his opening speech.

Mr Rudevics opened by paying tribute to the hard work of delegates from a number of countries in the discussions about the new statutes. These formal introductory remarks served to emphasise the importance of the statutes and the enormous significance of the new constitution. He explained that previously the history of the Roma had not allowed the creation of such a system, but now it was the only way forward for the Fifth Congress. Roma faced huge problems in Central and Eastern Europe because of the lack of effective structures of representation and this was a major cause of emigration. The arrangements adopted had both to function well and have the flexibility to cover all problems that might arise.

The proposed structure was that the highest organ of the IRU would be the congress, meeting every four years, which would delegate its powers to a parliament consisting of one member from each country. This parliament would meet twice annually and elect a presidium of eight commissars, who would run commissions on matters such as relations with national governments, education and finance. All these commissions would report through the presidium to the parliament, which in turn would be accountable to the congress. The congress would directly elect the parliament, president, secretary general, treasurer and – it had been agreed! – three vice-presidents. The president would appoint a court of justice on the recommendation of the parliament. The parliament would make a programme and a budget each year. He admitted that this might not be everybody's ideal structure but declared that it was a working framework. Mr Rudevics then called for comments.

A lengthy and bitter debate followed. Western delegates pointed out, almost without exception, that there were vague, unclear and contradictory passages in the statutes. Aleko Stobin, a former IRU joint-treasurer elected in 1990, criticised the lack of clarity and haste and endorsed calls for a delay of three to six months. Viktor Famulson, the acting president, called for a clarification of responsibilities and said that it was essential that the authority of the president over the secretary general be clearly specified.

Charles Smith stated that, as an elected local councillor in his own country, he had come to realise the importance of clear, democratic procedures and pleaded with the congress to take the time to get so sensitive a matter right. He then criticised the leadership for failing to turn up at the morning session of the working group that had taken place at their suggestion. In Charles Smith's view the statutes should not just copy gadje institutions. His recommendation was that the text that had been distributed should be treated as a draft, which delegates could take away and carefully consider. He recommended that a working party should be allowed six months to get the constitution right and make sure it was one which would empower everybody, not just kings and presidents.

Florin Cioaba (Romania) and Petro Grigorichenko (Ukraine) and others argued that the statutes gave the president too much power; some even asserted it would be a dictatorship. Interspersed between the opposition speakers a succession of delegates pleaded that it was necessary to trust the old presidium and officers to have done a good job. Dr Ščuka then made a lengthy speech urging everybody to read the statutes properly before they criticised them. In all countries, he pointed out, presidents dissolve parliaments when they do not work properly and the IRU presidium had not even met for a period of three years. He assured delegates that these statutes had been six months in preparation and had been laid before the presidium in three drafts during the past three months. Dr Ščuka concluded by reiterating much of what he had said to the working group about the need for a constitution that enabled the IRU to represent the whole Romani nation. That is to say, in general, he again sought support for the charter by appealing to the rhetoric of nationalism rather than any understanding or practice of democracy.

The more the charter was supported in these broad emotional terms, however, the more speakers put down their names to counsel caution. Several asked where the money would come from in order to hold all the meetings required by the statutes. The majority of delegates and guests in the hall, who, it became apparent, wished the statutes to be passed as swiftly as possible became increasingly impatient and began to barrack opponents. These were, however, protected by the moderator of the session, Dr Rajko Djurić, who with a certain mischievous complacency insisted that everyone should have their say. He defended Dr Ščuka by asking the rhetorical question that since he knew he would not be elected president, why should he plan to make the presidency all-powerful? But, he continued, if delegates wished, it was possible to continue under the 1978 statutes while the new statutes were improved. This suggestion was immediately supported by Zoran Dimov.

After this intervention supporters of Dr Ščuka intensified their demands that the charter be approved. One stated that although he had not read the statutes himself, he trusted those who had worked hard on them for several months and condemned those who now wished to complain for not having complained before. Jan Rusenko declared that he simply could not understand how there could be opposition to the adoption of the statutes when it had been clearly explained that they were needed to give the IRU standing in negotiations with governments and international institutions about crises like that in Kosovo. How could delegates be opposing the statutes when Roma were dying in Kosovo, he exclaimed. Did they not care about these deaths?

The impartiality of Rajko Djurić so annoyed Stahiro Stankiewicz that he interrupted from the platform to remark that he did not see how a session could be moderated by someone actively opposing the motion under discussion. He then called upon Rajko Djurić to withdraw if he was unable to support the charter. Dr Djurić smiled beatifically at him and gently replied that delegates were right to examine the dangers of the statutes implying the creation of a state and continued the debate, which he was clearly enjoying. At this point Nicolae Gheorghe intervened to remark dryly that the working of the statutes was dependent on the availability of money, not on the existence of a state. The parliament needed revenues or taxes, to pay for its work and meetings and to make the presidium a real negotiating partner, representing Roma to international organisations. During these discussions a surprising number of delegates called for the creation of a Romani territory as complementary to statutes embodying the existence of Roma as a nation and one Romani lawyer suggested that Palestine be taken as a precedent. Another delegate said the presidium needed to include at least fifty members so that it should be strong, unlike the weak Roma 'national self-government' in Hungary.

After many more repetitive interventions, spiced by accusations of lying, spying and corruption, Rajko Djurić spoke once more, expressing respect for Emil Ščuka but offering his opinion that this was a matter that concerned everyone and was one for the whole Romani nation to decide. Emil Ščuka replied asking people to calm their emotions. He said the reason why there had been no congress for ten years was that there was no money, and God only knew when there would be money for the next congress. For this reason it was crucial for the statutes to be approved at this congress. He agreed with Rajko Djurić that it was important to discuss these matters and criticised those who had left the hall for refreshments instead of staying to participate in the debate. Emil Ščuka also approved the neutrality of the moderator and his willingness to hear all shades of opinion.

At around 7.30pm the Czech and Romani translators gave up. They had been working indefatigably with very little break since 9.30 in the morning – longer than they had been contracted to do. However, the debate raged on, in Romani alone, for a further hour. Some delegates, who were relying on the simultaneous translation began to drift away until the platform party ordered the doors shut with no one allowed to leave. In an attempt to wind up the proceedings one platform speaker said that he could not believe that delegates wished to miss dinner and stay there all night rather than reach a decision. All the time Normundus Rudevics, sitting in the middle of the hall, was taking careful notes. Eventually, the flow of speakers dried up and he was called upon to wind up the debate.

Normundus Rudevics made his way to the front of the hall once more and settled his sheaf of papers in front of him on the lectern. He began by repeating how important the charter and statutes were, and that they should and could be adopted by this congress, with just a few amendments that had emerged from the working group. The first of these, he said, peering at his notes, was that Article 62 should be struck out. At this point he paused and looked round at the rest of the platform party as if inviting assent but their response was simply puzzled looks. Dr Ščuka then walked over to stand beside the lectern where, to his evident dismay, he realised that Mr Rudevics's notes included a pile of such amendments. Somewhat nervously he suggested that in view of the lateness of the hour it might be as well, after all, to postpone the vote until the next day.

Such infirmity of purpose was more than Stahiro Stankiewicz could bear. Striding across the platform he seized the microphone from Dr Ščuka and declared that the question had been debated long enough and that he believed the will of the congress was clear. 'Who wants these statutes?' he called out. Most of the delegates and guests sitting in the centre raised their arms and their cards and then stood up, cheering as they did so. Stankiewicz declared that it was enough and the statutes were adopted. Probably some forty or fifty yellow delegate cards were raised, less than half of the 122 accredited delegates, but maybe a majority of those left in the hall. Perhaps this thought occurred to Emil Ščuka, for he spoke briefly in Stankiewicz's ear, and Stankiewicz then called out '*Kon na mangel?*' and looked challengingly round the hall for about three seconds. Before anyone could react Stankiewicz shouted out in triumph '*Nane!*' (there are no votes against!). Once more the supporters of the motion burst into wild cheering, surging forward to shake the hands of the platform party and forming a large crowd at the front of the hall, in the middle of which Stankiewicz and Ščuka could be observed in earnest conversation with Rudevics. Meanwhile the Scandinavian, English and other opponents of the statutes sat looking on in amazement and disgust, before drifting out to join the lengthy queues for the buffet supper. The second full day of the congress was over.

## Interludes: Speeches by Czech politicians and the presentation of 'certificates of thanks'

The debates listed above were interrupted from time to time by other events. Former Czech premier, Václav Klaus, arrived on stage to welcome Roma to this important meeting in the Czech Republic, which he said would help Roma and gadje to realise they had similar goals in today's modern, complicated world, which wished to homogenise ruthlessly everyone's identity. Neither Czechs nor Roma had an interest in losing their identity, he continued. In his view 'we' now had to listen to Roma and help them reach a higher level through education, while the whole Romani community had to work together on this, instead of everybody trying to monopolise the Romani problem. President Havel's press secretary was more restrained and less patronising, merely acknowledging the importance of the congress for improving Roma-gadje relationships and stimulating international Romani co-operation. She concluded by promising whatever help was within Havel's powers.

Some delegates and guests were presented ceremoniously with certificates of long and meritorious service in recognition of their contribution to the Romani nation in areas of education, culture and literature, politics and media. The certificates were in English with no Romani translation. Many of those honoured in this way were individuals who had been to some extent critical of the leadership. All of them were located, brought to the front of the hall and then videoed and photographed as they smilingly accepted their certificates from the IRU leadership. This will help the eventual video to show how widespread and enthusiastic was the base of support for the IRU.

## The election of officers

After the confusion during the vote on the statutes the previous evening, the organisers decided that only delegates should be allowed into the main hall in order to facilitate the elections being held that day, Thursday 27 July. Meanwhile guests were directed upstairs to observe the proceedings from a small balcony. The microphone system was switched on at 9am, although the platform was not yet ready, with the result that anybody who listened to the main channel on the translation headphones could hear the muttered discussions of the presidium members around the podium as they hurriedly tried to sort out the day's business. This caused much hilarity on the balcony, especially when the translator, already in position, began a scabrous running commentary, combined with jocular injunctions to individual English-speaking delegates whom he knew.

The presidium members agreed they were not quite ready for the elections yet, and that the remainder of the working group reports should be presented during the morning. However, no one amongst them was prepared to act as moderator, since all wished to be available for the horse-trading taking place during the morning. Casting around for someone outside their circle, who would be prepared to act as moderator for the day's session, they hit on the name of Hristo Kyuchukov. He was duly hailed from the balcony, while deeply involved in conversation with Orhan Galjus on cultural and media matters and summoned to chair the day's proceedings. Those in the balcony can testify that he was genuinely surprised and to some extent amused by this call, and not at all prepared for it. Nonetheless, he went downstairs to the platform to do his duty.

Once in position, the new moderator ruled that given the shortage of time, each of the remaining working group rapporteurs would give their report in a single speech, one after another, and that debate on them would be allowed only after all had finished. Although there were a fair number of speakers to be heard, the session finished nevertheless at around mid day. Some speakers had clearly been mandated to make certain points on behalf of their delegations and seized on what was clearly going to be the last open opportunity for speakers from the floor. Hristo Kyuchukov kept all of these speeches brief, passing notes to those who were overrunning to tell them to wind up within one minute. The assembly warmed to his style of moderation and in consequence the debate was much better humoured than on the previous day.

Hristo Kyuchukov clearly had not been groomed for great things by the leadership for he had, after all, been lodged with the rest of the rank and file delegates and visitors at the bleak Hotel Volha. Nonetheless, his impressive performance as moderator may help explain why, much later that same day, his emergence as a compromise candidate for the post of secretary general was rather more attractive than those who were still busy promoting their own candidacies.

The elections began after lunch and continued, with two short breaks, until shortly after midnight. At the outset the 122 accredited delegates wearing yellow badges were issued with a set of ten blank ballot papers, differently coloured for each post. Meanwhile, Hristo Kyuchukov continued to act as moderator for the duration of this highly eventful, marathon session.

## *Mandate, electoral and scrutiny panels*

Proceedings began with the election of three committees of three or four people each as mandate, electoral and scrutiny (or control) panels. One of these panels had the job of sifting and recording nominations, another of counting votes cast, while the third was charged with carefully watching the other two panels to ensure they did their work correctly. The rules were explained to delegates by Emil Ščuka and Sean Nazerali. In the event of no candidate gaining 50 per cent or more of the vote, there would be second, run-off ballots between the two leading contenders. Emil Ščuka explained the IRU decision not to publish lists of candidates in advance as a defence against any manipulation and to allow delegates themselves to assemble the lists of candidates. Nevertheless, throughout the elections individuals came to the microphone to complain that they did not understand the procedures, whereupon further explanations followed.

Hristo Kyuchukov called for nominations from the floor for these panels and, when these began to dry up, members of the platform party also began to pressurise individuals to accept nomination. The procedure for nomination was the same as that to be followed throughout. There was no requirement to gain the consent of the person nominated in advance – in fact, this seemed to be seen as a breach of protocol since many of those nominated made an initial show of reluctance. Indeed, in the real elections which followed, many allowed their names to go forward but then withdrew at the last moment, when the complete list of candidates was announced, making lengthy speeches to announce their reasons for retiring from the contest. This may explain why the written nominations offered in advance by the English Gypsy Council were completely disregarded by the congress secretariat. Likewise the resolutions sent in advance, and also drafted in both Romani and English, suffered an identical fate. However, Peter Mercer told the English delegation privately that the previous evenings at the castle of Štiřín were filled with furious arguments among the leadership as to who should be elected to which post.

The election of the panels, therefore, was a lengthy business but nevertheless proved a useful dry run for the more contentious elections to follow. Commission members included Emil Nikolae, Barry Fisher, Milan Smizic, Juraj Stojka, Alexander Machakov, Jazmina Lazic, Nikolai Stankov and Luminitsa Cioaba. After the commissions had been appointed, Hristo Kyuchukov announced that the mandate of the existing officers and presidium was terminated and that they should all leave the platform. Their seats were then taken by the three newly-appointed panels. All was now prepared for the new elections and Hristo Kyuchukov called for nominations for the presidency.

### *Presidential election*

For the next ten minutes delegates milled around the hall, passing nominations up to the mandate panel. Eventually the rapporteur of the panel came to the microphone and announced the nominations as: Emil Ščuka (cheers from a section of the audience), Viktor Famulson, Nadezda Demeter, Rajko Djurić and, he added hesitantly while peering at the sheet, Luminitsa Stankiewicz. After some confusion, this last name turned out to be a conflation of Luminitsa Cioaba and Stahiro Stankiewicz.

Hristo Kyuchukov then invited the nominees in turn to present themselves and their work to the delegates, and to declare whether they accepted the nomination. First in line was Viktor Famulson who modestly pointed out why he would be a good candidate. In his view the choice was between himself and Emil Ščuka. He was followed by Dr Nadezda Demeter, daughter of Prof. Georgi Demeter who had opened the proceedings. After a brief speech, in which she both talked about her work and declared the support of Russian Roma for the work of the IRU, she gracefully withdrew from the race.

The moderator then called on Emil Ščuka to come to the microphone. In fact, at the beginning of the electoral process, Emil Ščuka had gone upstairs to the balcony. There, for half an hour, he sat alone in the front row, his elbows resting on the guard rail and his hands steepled under his chin, unmoving apart from occasionally raising one saturnine eyebrow at the shenanigans in the hall below. For all the world he appeared like a hooded vulture gazing down dispassionately on the dying throes of its mortally wounded prey, waiting for it to lie still of its own accord. When he was called, there was a dramatic hush while he came downstairs and stalked from the back of the hall to the front and, in a speech much briefer than any of the other candidates, accepted nomination. He said simply that he wanted to be president, and raise the position of Roma throughout the world.

He was followed to the podium by Luminitsa Cioaba, daughter of the late 'King' Ion Cioaba. The previous day she had been dressed in full Holly-wood-style Gypsy gear, selling her poetry books lauding his memory. For this occasion she was dressed in a sweeping 1920s sky-blue dress with an outra-geously large hat in the same colour. She stayed at the microphone long enough to make clear her family's support for the IRU before also withdraw-ing from the contest. Stahiro Stankiewicz then took the opportunity to give a brief account of his life and work but indicated that the presidency was not the office for which he intended to be a candidate. Finally, Dr Rajko Djurić came to the podium and, in a rather teasing speech, confided that he had not expected to be nominated and had been thinking of withdrawing. However, since all but two of the other candidates had withdrawn he would, after all, let his name go forward as the third candidate.

The delegates were referred to their first two ballot papers – for the presi-dential election – the second in case a second round of voting should be required. Votes were then inserted into plastic ballot boxes, which had previ-ously been displayed empty and then sealed by the scrutiny panel. These boxes were then emptied and counted in full view of the hall. After a short delay the result was announced:

| Emil Ščuka | 79 |
| Viktor Famulson | 23 |
| Rajko Djurić | 20 |

There was no need for a second ballot. Cheers again greeted the winner, while Rajko Djurić seemed pleased at his surprisingly strong showing. This perhaps showed the distaste that some in what might be described as the 'democratic faction' felt for having Viktor Famulson as their standard-bearer.

### Vice-presidential election

The congress moved on promptly to the vice-presidential election. Again there was a call for nominations from the floor, a process which took some time since there were many. The final list was: Stevitsa Nikolič (although there is some doubt about whether he was properly nominated), Rajko Djurić, Viktor Famulson, Nadezda Demeter, Dragoljub Acković, Florin Cioaba, Ivan Veselý, Peter Mercer, Stefan Kuzhikov and, the chair of the scrutiny

Emil Ščuka, elected IRU secretary general at fourth World Romani Congress and president at fifth, talks to Estref Abduramanoski, president of Australian Roma Union. Prague, July 2000.

Roma delegates in discussion between congress sessions. Prague, July 2000.

panel added, Adam Stankiewicz, which once more proved to be a conflation – this time of Adam Aladev from the Ukraine and Stahiro Stankiewicz. Whether this was a genuine mistake, or whether the scrutineer was making a joke, was hard to tell. Each nominee was then called to the microphone in turn to accept or refuse nomination and introduce themselves, unless they had already done so. Nikolič, Djurić, Famulson, Cioaba, Demeter and Stankiewicz accepted. Ivan Veselý declined but asked his supporters to give their votes to Stankiewicz, raising another huge cheer from the loyalist faction. Mercer, Kuzhikov and Aladev also refused nomination, although at greater length, in contrast to Acković who declined without coming to the front to speak.

The next stage of the election was complicated by a problem over the ballot papers. At the point at which these had been printed, the former presidium had anticipated only two vice-presidents (as opposed to the one specified at the beginning of the statutes and the three that had finally been agreed). As a result delegates had two sets of two ballot papers, four in all – each individually marked and coloured, for two rounds of voting if required. After much discussion, it was agreed that the delegates should write one name each on the two first round ballots and the third name on one of the second round ballots, ignoring the fourth ballot paper.

Once more the delegates voted by placing their completed slips in the ballot boxes and a prolonged period of counting followed. Eventually, the electoral panel reported that there seemed to be irregularities in the ballot, which should therefore be re-run. Only 355 voting slips had been completed when there should have been 366 in total. More seriously, it appeared to the panel that some delegates, instead of voting for three different candidates, had voted for the same candidate three times, while others had voted for non-candidates, and some had even voted using the fourth ballot slip that should have been discarded. The panel suggested re-running the ballot, without even revealing the result of the first attempt, but this time using the voting machines still in place from the time when the building had been the Czechoslovak parliament. However, others objected that it had not been specified in advance that everyone had to use all their votes or that delegates could not vote for the same person three times. Therefore, they argued, the result should be accepted but in any case it should be made known. After more discussion the panel agreed to announce the flawed outcome, which was as follows:

| Stahiro Stankiewicz | 107 | |
| Nadezda Demeter | 74 | elected |
| Rajko Djurić | 54 | |
| Viktor Famulson | 48 | |
| Florin Cioaba | 42 | not elected |
| Stevitsa Nikolič | 15 | |

Among the anomalies there were a number of votes for non-candidates, including one for Emil Ščuka, and also for candidates who had withdrawn. For example, Dragoljub Acković received four votes and Peter Mercer three, which may indicate that some of the followers were less willing than their leaders to abide by the deals struck in Štiřín. Some proposed accepting these figures as the election result on a first-past-the-post basis. Even though it was obvious that a second ballot could well change the relative positions of candidates, there was great support for this proposal to let the apparent result stand.

This confused situation led to heated argument that lasted around two hours until dinner. Despite winning most votes Stankiewicz said that he was willing for a further ballot to be held. However, Rajko Djurić, who was clearly having a much better congress than he had ever expected, silkily spoke in favour of abiding by the result. An outraged Viktor Famulson, on the other hand, spoke furiously and passionately on the need for absolute probity in the observation of election rules and the necessity for a new ballot with clearer rules. His accusations of corruption were endorsed by Luminitsa Cioaba. Meanwhile, excited speakers queued to give their opinion on either side. Hristo Kyuchukov, as moderator, had to make sharp comments at times to keep them within bounds, asking delegates why they wanted to prolong the debate to such an extent, holding him there without food or drink or going to the toilet.

In an attempt to calm the heated atmosphere Emil Ščuka at one point called on an eminent *krisnitori*, Todor Mutti from Sweden, to review the whole proceedings. The mediator did so in flowery, oratorical Kalderash, first rehearsing his own credentials as one who had brought harmony to troubled situations many times before, and then carefully going over the cases put by each of the interested parties, urging them fervently to come together in some kind of compromise. He appeared genuinely shocked when other delegates from the floor suggested, equally passionately, that this kind of traditional mediation was not appropriate to the congress and that if the congress had adopted a charter and statutes it ought to abide by them. One speaker simply implored the leaders to come to some kind of compromise as quickly as possible, because 'the gadje are laughing at us'.

As some delegates began to lose interest, the doors were locked again to ensure maximum participation. This action caused some in the English delegation to remark that only those who had attended gadjo school had ever been required to ask permission to go to the toilet, and these had certainly never expected to do so again – as adults! It brought home to them how very gadjified many of the Eastern European delegates were, despite their ability to speak Romani. The English were also astounded by the extreme verbal fury expressed by some of the delegates during this row, which in English Romani culture would have led inevitably to fighting, but which those accustomed

194

to the culture of the *kris* clearly expected to be resolved through mediation.

The friends of Famulson made it clear that if the supposed result were upheld, they would be on their way home with the entire Scandinavian delegation. To allow space for this apparent impasse to be resolved a coffee break was announced, during which a compromise was noisily arranged and both sides agreed to support a re-run of the ballot immediately after dinner.

After this had duly taken place the result of the new vice-presidential ballot was announced. Viktor Famulson now topped the poll with seventy-eight votes, followed by Nadezda Demeter, Stahiro Stankiewicz and Florin Cioaba, all bunched together in the mid-forties, with Rajko Djurić close behind in the high thirties. The chair of the scrutiny panel announced that, strictly speaking, a further run-off ballot ought to be held to select amongst the lower three candidates, because none had 50 per cent or more of the vote. At this an audible groan rose from the diminished assembly. Faced with such a prospect it was suggested that since the second, third and fourth candidates were so close, it would be sensible to elect four vice-presidents rather than just three. This proposal was carried by a show of hands and the four new vice-presidents moved onto the platform. The only person who did not look pleased by this convenient circumvention of the statutes was Dr Rajko Djurić.

## Other posts

Many delegates were clearly hoping that this was the end of the evening as the time was approaching 10pm. But, remorselessly, the platform moved on to the election of the secretary general, calling for nominations, of which there was another long list, and then another round of acceptances and withdrawals. Those accepting nomination were Stefan Palison, Zoran Dimov and Hristo Kyuchukov. Those declining included Sean Nazerali, Florin Cioaba, Ivan Veselý, Nicolae Gheorghe, Barry Fisher, and Peter Grigorichenko.

Although some had slipped away, 117 people still remained to vote in the election for secretary general. Eventually, Hristo Kyuchukov beat Stefan Palison in the second round of voting, after Zoran Dimov's twenty-four first round votes were redistributed. Candidates for treasurer included Iulian Radulescu, Stefan Palison, Valeriu Dragoljubov, and Sali Benić, but Zlatko Mladenov from Bulgaria was elected. Thirty-seven delegates, no more than one per country, were reported as elected to the Roma parliament at around 1am, although at the time of writing only thirty-two names have been released. These published names did not include that of Vania de Gila Kochanowski, who left believing he had been elected member of the parliament for France. The provisional list of MPs in Appendix One shows that other countries notably unrepresented in the parliament include the US, Hungary, Spain, Scotland and Wales.[8]

## Wrapping it all up on the last day

On Friday 28 July, there was an explicit division of labour between the task of firming up the alliances which would run the IRU in the future, and the task of engaging in constructive dialogue with non-Romani politicians. The parliament and most of the elected officers, with the exception of Hristo Kyuchukov and Nadezda Demeter, met in a closed session at the castle of Štiřín to elect the presidium and the court of justice and to plan their work for the next four years. Meanwhile, the remainder of the delegates and guests, around a hundred or so, were bussed to the Czech Senate for a seminar on the Romani nation and the EU accession process.

The Czech government side was led by Martin Palouš, who expanded on his opening speech in the congress. The main contributions from Roma came from Hristo Kyuchukov, the new secretary general, who detailed the need for social and educational policies to combat racism, and from Nicolae Gheorghe, representing the OSCE. Gheorghe defended the legitimacy of the IRU, while at the same time asserting that its two most controversial political problems – the issue of becoming a 'political nation' and the question of the 'stabilisation policy' – required much fuller debate.

A number of Romani representatives related these debates to their own countries, some giving straightforward factual reports for which there had been no time in the congress proper, some launching fiery tirades against oppression, and some unashamedly flattering non-Romani politicians for their goodwill. The vice-president of the Czech Senate responded with a brief speech in favour of equal opportunities and multi-culturalism. The seminar was concluded by a representative of the European Union, who gave a detailed exposition of what was involved in the accession process, particularly in the field of human rights, and of what kind of budgetary help might be available from the EU to underwrite the necessary social programmes.

During the day delegates and guests were able to take a pleasant lunch in the Senate cafeteria. There was, however, no programme after the seminar. A few senior individuals took taxis to Štiřín, while the majority of delegates were left to take the bus back to the gloomy Hotel Volha. There, in the absence of dinner, they passed the hours till bedtime or their coaches back to their own countries by entertaining each other with coffee from the machine in the hotel lobby, and offering one another cigarettes. There was no dinner for them, and no closing ceremony.

## Conclusion

Within the time-scale in which it was organised, this congress was a considerable achievement. Some 300 people were brought together, including the great majority of living office-holders from previous congresses, and none of them denounced the proceedings – at least while they were present. The new administration is in clear organic succession to the organisation of previous congresses. This congress will therefore be widely recognised as the Fifth World Romani Congress.

That said, the Fifth Congress has not, in fact, overcome the underlying problems of earlier congresses. The new statutes may be far fuller than their predecessors, but they remain profoundly 'democratic centralist' in inspiration, without any genuine mechanisms of democratic accountability. To implement the proposed organisational structures – a large meeting of the parliament twice a year and other smaller meetings in the interim, will be an enormously expensive undertaking.[9] If it actually happens, effective power will be handed over to the shadowy 'sponsors' who finance the show – unless Holocaust restitution funds are appropriated for the purpose.

However, it may be worthwhile for the OSCE, the EU and the US foreign policy-oriented charitable foundations to ensure that such a body does exist to negotiate agreement by the Romani people to their policies of stabilisation and human rights. But, if not, the officers of the IRU have already demonstrated that they perceive the statutes as an impressive piece of paper to be given to their gadjo interlocutors, rather than as a set of rules which should in any way constrain their own behaviour.[10]

Like the Fourth Congress, the IRU is heavily dominated by Balkan and Baltic Roma, with little representation of or understanding of the Romani politics of large Romani communities, like those of Spain or Hungary whose dialect is no longer mainstream Romani, or of Romani communities in the West in general. Among the IRU leadership only the new secretary general, Hristo Kyuchukov, paid any attention at all to this imbalance. The concerns of this Fifth Congress are primarily East European; this is justifiable in the sense that the biggest dangers threatening the largest number of Roma are those in Central and Eastern Europe. But to mobilise the Romani community outside Eastern Europe in support of the East Europeans will take more sensitivity and understanding than was shown by most of the officers elected at this congress. However, their greatest asset in this task may be the new secretary general.

The new president, Emil Ščuka, has demonstrated much greater political skill than was evident before this year. A tough prosecution lawyer, with film-star good looks and a certain amount of charisma – at least in Prague, he never allows himself to get personally involved in shouting matches, and he has taken virtually untrammelled control of the organisation. During the past year his ambitions may have expanded from making himself the Romani Rose of the Czech Republic into making himself the Yasser Arafat of the Romani nation. Truculent enough to keep a large section of Romani opinion behind him (especially if he has financial largesse to distribute), but pliant enough to keep the international establishment talking to him, and even bankrolling him to stay in business, he may well be able to emulate Arafat and corner the market in Romani representation. The Palestine Liberation Organisation is in fact the closest model to what is now being adopted by IRU leaders as their method of intervention in international relations, except that it is not aiming at creating a territorial state.

This strategy is embodied in the *Declaration of Nation* (sic), which the president issued after the congress and which is presented as being approved by the congress on 27 July, although it is not clear to us at exactly which point of the agenda this declaration was introduced. Its draft was not included in the materials distributed to delegates before, at the start of, or throughout the congress and, as far as we are aware, its text was not publicly read out during the congress. Nevertheless, some ideas from this declaration have echoed in the various speeches Emil Ščuka made during the congress and have been widely reported in many major European newspapers both at the time of and after the congress. The declaration has since been presented as the main product of the congress, alongside the charter, and the president has approached heads of various countries, such as Václav Havel, Guiliano Amato and Vojislav Kostunica, bearing this declaration and has also distributed it during meetings of international organisations (IRU 2001: 1, para 2). The English version of the declaration is given in Appendix Three.[11]

With his newly acquired position Emil Ščuka has probably garnered enough credibility to be able to deliver the appearance of Romani support for a 'stabilisation' policy which will unblock the road to EU enlargement. How long he will be able to do this will depend crucially upon how realistic and how successful the policies for opposing racism and poverty, and promoting education prove to be.

Whether this kind of accommodation between the nation-states and the IRU will be accompanied by the taint of corrupt authoritarianism that dogs the PLO remains to be seen. An unhappy straw in the wind in this regard was the fate of Ondřej Giňa, a leading Czech Romani activist in the RNC, the IRU's main rival. During the congress it was reported that on 14 July three men had attempted to firebomb the house of a relative in which Giňa had been staying. On 17 July his office had been ransacked by 'unknown persons' and petrol poured over the premises. Furthermore on 21 July Rokycany district authorities filed tax evasion charges against Ondřej Giňa, implying fraudulent use of charitable funds. Since then, tax evasion charges have also been brought against Ondřej Giňa's son, the first Romani newscaster in the Czech Republic. The implications of these events remain to be seen.

The next year will reveal how far those seeking a broader, federal and democratic structure of international Romani representation will be able to win over the newly revivified IRU to the idea and practice of co-operation with other groups.[12]

# Appendix One
## IRU Officers elected at Fifth World Romani Congress, Prague, 24–28 July 2000

*Authors' note:*
A list of those elected to office became available some weeks after the Congress. This document is printed as distributed, without alterations (e.g. spelling etc.).

*Members of the Cabinet*

| | | |
|---|---|---|
| President | Emil Ščuka | CR |
| 1st Vice-president | Stanislaw Stankiewicz | Poland |
| Vice-president | Nadezda Demeter | Russian Federation |
| Vice-president | Viktor Famulson | Sweden |
| Vice-president | Florin Cioaba | Romania |
| Chair of the Parliament | Dragan Jevremovic | Austria |
| High commissar | Normundus Rudevic | Lithuania [a] |
| Chair of the Court of Justice | Edmund Rafael | CR |
| Secretary General | Hristo Kyuchukov | Bulgaria |
| Treasurer | Zlatko Mladenov | Bulgaria |

*Members of the Parliament* [b]

| | | |
|---|---|---|
| Chair of the Parliament | Dragan Jevremovic | Austria |
| Vice-chair of the Parliament | Emil Nicolae | Romania |
| Member | Peter Grigorichenko | Ukraine |
| Member | Gurali Mejdani | Albania |
| Member | Marni Morrow | Australia |
| Member | Oleg Alexandrovič Kozlovskij | Belarus |
| Member | Jan Rusenko | Belgium |
| Member | Salko Musić | BiH |
| Member | Sead Hasanović | Croatia |
| Member | Emil Stojka | Czech Republic |
| Member | Peter Mercer | England |
| Member | Roman Lutt | Estonia |
| Member | Pirke Novica | Germany |
| Member | Hadji Zylfi Mergja | Kosovo |
| Member | Romas Stankevičius | Lithuania |
| Member | Roman Chojnacki | Poland |
| Member | Alinda Fanny Miranda | Sweden |
| Member | Michael Mamilov | Latvia |
| Member | Jan Cibula | Switzerland |
| Member | Jožek Horváth | Slovenia |
| Member | Josef Bánom | Canada |
| Member | Josef Patkaň | Slovakia |
| Member | Raya Bielberger | Norway |
| Member | Stevica Nicolič | Holland |
| Member | Aleko Stobin | Finland |
| Member | Nailon Šarkezi | Denmark |
| Member | Martin Collins | Ireland |
| Member | Ariel Eliyahu | Israel |
| Member | Santino Spineli | Italy |

| Member | Pavel Andrejcenco | Moldavia |
| Member | Jusuf Sulejman | Macedonia |
| Member | Dragoljub Ackovič | Yugoslavia |

### Members of the Court of Justice

| **Chair of the Court of Justice** | Edmund Rafael | CR |
| **Chair of the Romani Kris** | Teodor Mutto | Denmark |
| **Member** | Josef Conti | Slovakia |
| **Member** | Vladimir Ivanovič Matvjeev | Belarus |
| **Member** | Vladas Stankievcz | Lithuania |
| **Member** | Juliano Raducano | Romania |
| **Member** | Josef Lakatoš | CR |

### Members of the Presidium

| **Commissar for Foreign Policy** | Paolo Pietrosanti | Italy |
| **Commissar for Holocaust** | Stefan Palison[c] | Sweden |
| **Commissar for Economic Issues** | Milan Ščuka | Belarus |
| **Commissar for Educational Issues** | Gejza Adam | Slovakia |
| **Commissar for Internal Affairs** | – [c] | |
| **Commissar for Financial and Budgetary Issues** | – [c] | |
| **Commissar for Human Rights** | Per Antič | Yugoslavia |
| **Commissar without Portfolio** | Aleko Bielberger | Norway |
| **Commissar for Central and Eastern Europe** | Georgij Demeter | Russian Federation |
| **Commissar for USA and Canada** | Caroline Banom | Canada |
| **Commissar for Australia and New Zealand** | Estraf Abuduramovski | Australia |
| **Commissar for Romani Language and Language Rights** | Marcel Courtiade | France |
| **Commissar for Management and Informatic Systems** | Osman Balič | Yugoslavia |
| **Commissar for Media Affairs** | Ivan Veselý | CR |

*Authors' endnotes:*

[a]    Normundus Rudevic (aka Normands Rudevic) is from Latvia, not Lithuania.

[b]    Vania de Gila Kochanowski (aka Jan Kochanowski) was under the impression that he was elected to the Parlament to represent France but has not appeared on the lists that have been made available to us.

[c]    These three functions have stayed open for election for some time after the Congress. The list of elected officials made available in November contains no names for these three functions. The choice of Stefan Palison as the Commissar for Holocaust has however been confirmed by the IRU Prague office.

# Appendix Two
## International Romani Union Charter

*Authors' note:*
This document is printed as distributed, without alterations (e.g. spelling etc.).

**PREAMBLE**
The Preamble of the IRU Charter expresses the ideals and shared goals of the Romani nation, whose representatives have united in order to create the International Romani Union.

*We, the people of the Romani Nation,* members of the Romani Union, *are determined* to protect the future Romani generations from national malice and hatred that has many times in our lives brought to the Romani people unspeakable hardships, suffering, and war genocide, and to trust once more in fundamental human rights, honor and value of human life, in existence in variety, equal rights of men and women, children and nations great and small, as well as to take part in creation of circumstances and conditions favorable to preservation of justice and honor to human being, and to abide the obligations resulting from international law treaties, support and improve the fundamental democratic principles, freedom and life standards.

*In order to achieve the goals* we are determined to pursue tolerance among ourselves, life in peace and freedom and a large family, to unite our forces to sustain and develop the Romani Nation as well as other nations and to assist in advancement of the economic and social development of all nations.

*We have decided to unite in order to achieve these goals.*

Therefore our Nation has decided through its representatives delegated to London to establish the International Romani Union.

**CHAPTER 1**
goals and principles

*Article 1*

Goals and principles of the International Romani Union defined in the Charter

1. The goal of the IRU is to be the political representation of all Roma in the world (Sinti, Lovari, Ashkari, Chorichani, Rumungre, Vlach, Manush, etc.), both our members and non-members, and always to act in the best interest of the Romani nation, in accordance with our best intentions and with full recognition of the great responsibility we are hereby taking upon ourselves.
2. To develop all favorable qualities of the Romani, their cultural traditions, customs and language.
3. To respect fundamental human rights and liberties, and in that respect obey all obligations resulting from international treaties.
4. Contribute to preservation and sustenance of world peace and safety.
5. To develop friendly relationships among nations based on respect paid to equal rights and equality of nations.

6. To cooperate in resolving of economic, social, cultural, educational, and humanitarian problems of the Romani in each of the individual countries in which they live.
7. To become the center that observes the activities of individual countries in achieving these goals.
8. To enforce and strengthen regard for human rights and fundamental liberties for all irrespective of race, sex, language or religion.

*Article 2*

The International Romani Union and its members are liable to act in accordance with the following principles:

1. The organization is based on the principle of sovereign equality of all its members.
2. All members faithfully meet their obligations they have assumed under this Charter in order to jointly secure rights and advantages resulting from the membership.
3. All members shall provide the International Romani Union with all assistance in every event undertaken in accordance with this Charter.
4. No provision contained herein gives the International Romani Union any right to interfere with affairs that are within the internal authority of individual countries.
5. The members of the International Romani Union who have breached the Moral Codex of the IRU, lost their repute, respect and authority with their Romani people in their respective countries following a verdict of the Court of Justice of the IRU lose their right to be members of the International Romani Union.
6. Members of the organization resolve all disputes and matters in accordance with the legal standards in their respective countries.

**CHAPTER II**
membership

*Article 3*

The original members of the International Romani Union are the representatives of the 21 countries present at the Founding Congress of the International Romani Union in London or who sign this Charter.

*Article 4*

Any other Romani organization from the member countries may acquire membership in the International Romani Union upon adoption of the obligations contained herein and considered by the IRU as capable and willing to meet the obligations.

*Article 5*

In addition, a member of the Romani organization whose membership has been approved by the appropriate body of the IRU becomes a member of the International

Romani Union.

*Article 6*

The appropriate body of the IRU, the Parliament, may upon recommendation of the IRU Presidium award honorary IRU membership to anyone who have to a great extent contributed to the development of the Romani culture, education, preservation of traditions, customs and enforced the prestige of the Romani nation. This membership is permanent.

*Article 7*

Acceptance of any new organization as a collective member of the International Romani Union is the result of the decision of the Parliament upon recommendation of the Presidium. Each organization which has become a collective member of the IRU, gains the right for their own members to become individual members of IRU upon their meeting the criteria outlined. Their membership in IRU is then determined and conferred by their own organization.

*Article 8*

Any member of the International Romani Union convicted by the Court of Justice may be dispossessed of the membership rights and advantages upon recommendation of the Court. Exercise of the rights may be reassigned by the Parliament upon recommendation of the Court.

*Article 9*

The Parliament may upon recommendation of the Presidium expel a member of the International Romani Union who continuously breaches the principles of this Charter.

*Article 10*

A member of the International Romani Union who has ceased to participate in the member organization in its country or has lost membership in its organization for whatever reason will be dispossessed of its member rights and advantages by the Parliament upon recommendation of the Presidium. That does not affect the membership of organization from the country in the International Romani Union. The Parliament elects a candidate recommended by the national member organization and the Presidium to the vacant position.

**CHAPTER III**
bodies

*Article 11*

1.  As the main bodies of the International Romani Union the following bodies are established:
    Congress
    Parliament

Presidium
Court of Justice
President
Vice President
General Secretary
Treasurer

2.   Assisting bodies may be established in accordance with this Charter.

*Article 12*

The International Romani Union shall not impose any limitation in respect to equal legal qualification of men and women for any office in the main and assisting bodies. Any individual over the age of 16 may become a member of the IRU. Any individual over the age of 18 may become an officer of the IRU.

**CHAPTER IV**
THE CONGRESS
composition

*Article 13*

1.   The Congress comprises of delegates of individual member organizations, honorary members and other members.
2.   Each member country is represented in the Congress by a number of delegates corresponding to the total number of Romani inhabitants of the respective countries. The exact key of definition of the number of delegates for individual countries and further selection of delegates is defined by the Parliament.

virtue and authority

*Article 14*

The Congress may act on all issues or matters that belong to within the scope of this Charter or relate to the authority and functions of bodies established under this Charter. The Congress also may assign members of the International Romani Union with tasks or present recommendations to the Parliament in all such issues and matters.

*Article 15*

1.   The Congress approves the Program and the long-term vision of the International Romani Union.
2.   The Congress makes recommendations whose aim it is to support concurrence of the Romani in individual countries in the fields of politics, economy, social affairs, culture, education, as well as facilitation of exercise of human rights and fundamental liberties for all irrespective of race, sex, language or religion.

*Article 16*

1. The Congress negotiates the annual and special reports, reports of situation of the Romani population in Europe and the world, presented by the President of the international Romani Union.
2. The Congress receives reports from other bodies of the International Romani Union and acts on them.

voting

*Article 17*

Each member of the Congress holds one vote.

2. Matters of significance are decided upon by the Congress by majority. These issues include:

adoption of the IRU Charter and its amendments;
adoption of the IRU Program;
election of IRU Parliament;
election of the IRU President.
election of the IRU Vice-President
election of the IRU General Secretary
election of the IRU Treasurer

*Article 19*

A member of the International Romani Union who is in default with payment of due IRU membership fees forfeits the voting right in the Congress if the due amount is equal to the sum of membership fees for the previous years.

administration

*Article 20*

The Congress meets once in four years at a regular meeting. In case situation requires otherwise, the President summons a special meeting of the Congress upon recommendation of the Parliament or majority of members of the International Romani Union.
*Article 21*

The Congress passes its Order of Proceedings. The Congress elects a Chairperson for each meeting.

*Article 22*

The Congress may establish assisting bodies considered necessary fort proper function of the Congress.

**Chapter V**
THE PARLIAMENT
composition

*Article 23*

1.  The Parliament is the body of representatives of the International Romani Union.
2.  Each member country of the International Romani Union has one representative (and one substitute) in the Parliament.
3.  Members of the Parliament are elected from among the delegates of the Congress for the term of four years.
4.  Members of the Parliament elect the Chairperson and Vice-Chair at the initial meeting of the Parliament.
5.  Parliamentary sessions are also attended by the Presidium members, Treasurer, President, Vice President and the Secretary General.

virtue and authority

*Article 24*

1.  In the period between two consecutive meetings of the Congress the Parliament assumes majority of its functions. The Parliament may not elect and dismiss the President of the International Romani Union.
2.  The Parliament meets at least twice a year at the spring and autumn sessions. The Parliament is summoned to meeting by the President.

*Article 25*

The Parliament deals on the Reports of the situation of Romani populations in individual countries during its sessions. At its autumn session the Parliament will discuss and approve the budget for the following calendar year.

*Article 26*

The Parliament defines the courses of domestic as well as international policy of the International Romani Union.

*Article 27*

1.  The Parliament negotiates and adopts the budget of the International Romani Union.
2.  The Parliament negotiates and adopts all financial and budgetary agreements with the IRU member organizations mentioned in the Article 4 above and reviews administration budgets of such organizations in order to issue recommendations.
3.  The Parliament specifies the amount of the annual fees of individual member organizations of the International Romani Union.

*Article 28*

1.  The Parliament elects and dismisses members of the Presidium upon recommendations of the President.
2.  The Parliament recommends to the President candidates to the Court of Justice.

*Article 29*

1. The Parliament is responsible for its actions to the Congress.
2. In case the Parliament fails to meet for a regular session without a reason, is not capable to exercise decisive powers for one year although the session has not been interrupted and the Parliament repeatedly summoned to session, the IRU President dissolves the Parliament and summons special meeting of the Congress.
3. The President may not dissolve the Parliament three month before regular session.

*Article 30*

1. In case the Parliament impeaches the Presidium as a whole the Presidium must demit within 30 days. During this period the Parliament requests the President to appoint candidates to the Presidium.

VOTING

*Article 31*

1. Each member of the Parliament holds one vote. Parliament is considered to have quorum provided more than half of its members are present.
2. Matters of significance are decided upon by the Parliament by two-thirds majority. These issues include:

   – election of Presidium members;
   – acceptance of new members to the International Romani Union;
   – definition of member rights and advantages;
   – expelling of members;
   – budgetary issues;
   – impeachment procedures towards the Presidium;
   – summoning of special Congress sessions.

administration

*Article 32*

The Parliament meets for regular sessions twice a year, in spring and autumn and whenever circumstances require a special session. Special sessions are summoned by the Parliament Chairperson upon request of the Presidium, the President or the majority of Parliament members.

*Article 33*

The Parliament adopts its Order of Proceedings.

*Article 34*

The Parliament may establish assisting bodies considered necessary fort proper function of the Congress.

*Article 35*

The seat of the Parliament is Bratislava. In the event that a member of the Parliament does not attend two consecutive sessions of the Parliament without an exceptional reason, they will be expelled due to passivity.

**CHAPTER VI**
THE PRESIDIUM
composition

*Article 36*

1. The Presidium composes of members-commissars.
   Each member of the Presidium is responsible for a specific area.
2. Administration of the separate is assigned to individual members of the Presidium by the President of the International Romani Union.
3. The President assigns the I. Vice-President with heading of the Presidium.

virtue and authority

*Article 37*

The scope of the Presidium is defined in the following areas – commissariats:

1. Foreign-policy Commissariat
2. Social and Economic Commissariat
3. Cultural and Educational Commissariat
4. Human Rights Commissariat
5. Internal Affairs Commissariat
6. Financial and Budgetary Commissariat
7. Commissariat for Central and Eastern Europe
8. Commissariat for America Asia and Australia
9. Commissariat without portfolio
10. Legal and Legislative Commissariat

*Article 38*

The Secretary General is a member of the Presidium and holds voting rights.

*Article 39*

The Presidium decides on all issues assigned by the Parliament and/or the President of the International Romani Union.

*Article 40*

1. The Presidium observes the IRU Program elaborated by the Parliament and adopted by the Congress.
2. The Presidium may elaborate studies and reports of international Romani affairs in economic, social, cultural, educational and related areas or initiate elaboration of such reports as well as make recommendations in these areas to the IRU

Parliament, the IRU President, individual countries and international organizations and institutions.

3.  The Presidium may make recommendations with the purpose to support respect for human rights and fundamental liberties to all.
4.  The Presidium may in accordance with rules defined by the Parliament summon international conferences on issues within the scope of the Presidium.
5.  The Presidium may accept measures in order to receive regular reports from IRU members and their expert committees on their actions in enforcement of recommendations of the Presidium and the Parliament, Congress and the President in affairs within the scope of the Presidium. The Presidium may issue to the Parliament its comments on these reports.
6.  The Presidium exercises in carrying out the recommendations of the Parliament functions within its scope.
7.  The Presidium may conduct services requested by the International Romani Union, its expert committees or other assisting bodies subject to approval of the Parliament.
8.  The Presidium exercises functions specified elsewhere in this Charter or assigned by the Parliament and/or President.

*Article 41*

The Presidium is responsible for its actions to the President and the Parliament.

administration

*Article 42*

1.  The Presidium is administered in such a manner as to carry out its functions continuously. In order to facilitate that each member of the Presidium is, subject to the financial means of the IRU, always present at the residence of the International Romani Union.
2.  The Presidium may summon its meetings not only in the seat of the International Romani Union but also at any other place that should most facilitate the activities of the Presidium.

*Article 43*

The Presidium may establish assisting bodies considered necessary fort proper function of the Congress.

*Article 44*

The Presidium adopts its Order of Proceedings.

*Article 45*

Each member of the International Romani Union who is not a member of the Presidium may be present at the Presidium meetings without the right to vote irrespective of the discusses issue if the Presidium certifies that the interests of the member are affected.

*Article 46*

It the Presidium discusses a matter of a special importance to a member of the IRU the Presidium calls on the member to participate in the appropriate session without right to vote.

*Article 47*

The Presidium may adopt measures to facilitate participation of representatives of expert committees as well as other assisting bodies in the sessions without voting rights as well as the Presidium members' attendance of meetings of the committees and assisting bodies.

VOTING

*Article 48*

1. Each member of the Presidium holds on vote.
2. The Presidium decides by simple majority of votes.

**CHAPTER VII**
THE COURT OF JUSTICE
composition

*Article 49*

The Court of Justice is a body of independent judges, elected irrespective of their membership in the International Romani Union form among persons of high moral merits, with natural authority and respect from the Romani.

*Article 50*

1. The Court of Justice is the main moral and checking body of the International Romani Union.
2. The seat of the Court of Justice of the International Romani Union is Stockholm.

*Article 51*

The Court of Justice comprises of seven members with no more than one representative from the same country.

*Article 52*

Members of the Court of Justice are appointed by the President upon recommendation of the Parliament.

*Article 53*

The term of the Court of Justice judges is six years. The Court of Justice elects the Chairperson on its initial session.

virtue and authority

*Article 54*

1. The scope of the Court of Justice includes supervision of all members and bodies of the international Romani Union and their observance of this Charter.
2. The Court of Justice pays special attention to observance of the Codex of the IRU by all members.
3. The Court of Justice initiates proceedings against any member who seriously breach any of the provisions of this Charter or the Moral Codex of the IRU.
4. The Court of Justice is authorized to recommend exclusion of IRU members or propose interruption of their membership or to levy other penalties in accordance with the Statute.
5. The Court of Justice of the International Romani Union may establish Senates in those country organizations that are members of the International Romani Union.

*Article 55*

The activities of the Court of Justice are governed by the Statute, subject to the approval by the Parliament.

*Article 56*

The Court of Justice adopts its Order of Proceedings.

**CHAPTER VIII**
THE PRESIDENT

*Article 57*

The President is the supreme representative of the International Romani Union in outside relations.

*Article 58*

The President is elected by the Congress by majority of votes. In the event that no candidate obtains a majority on the first ballot, the two candidates with the most votes shall face each other in a second ballot.

*Article 59*

The President of the International Romani Union must be of Romani nationality and must speak the Romani language.

*Article 60*

The President of the International Romani Union is elected for the term of four years.

*Article 61*

The President of the International Romani Union is responsible for his/her actions to the Congress. The office of the President is incompatible with the office of a Parliament member, Court of Justice member, or Presidium member.

*Article 62*

The President of the International Romani Union appoints his/her deputy – the I. Vice President from among the Vice Presidents elected by the Congress.

*Article 63*

The President as the supreme representative of the International Romani Union acts on behalf of the Union both inside and outside.

*Article 64*

The President summons the spring and autumn sessions of the Parliament.

*Article 65*

The President is authorized to dissolve the Parliament in cases specified in Articles of this Charter.

*Article 66*

The President is authorized to participate in the Parliament sessions and must be granted the right of speech upon request.

*Article 67*

The President recommends to the Parliament the members of the Presidium as well as recommends to the Parliament their dismissal.

*Article 68*

The President assigns the Presidium members with management of the Commissariats.

*Article 69*

The President entrusts the Secretary General with the administration of the Secretariat.

*Article 70*

The President assigns the I. Vice President with administration of the Presidium

*Article 71*

The President appoints upon recommendation of the Parliament the judges of the Court of Justice and is authorized to dismiss them subject to previous approval of the Parliament.

*Article 72*

The President does not have immunity from the judgements of the Court. In the event that the Court recommends to the parliament that the president be dismissed, the Parliament must call a Congress within three months, which has the final word in the dismissal. For this period of time the President is deprived of his functional and ceremonial duties and is replaced in these by the I. Vice-President.

*Article 73*

The President is the statutory body of the International Romani Union.

*Article 74*

The President appoints the representative of the International Romani Union to international organizations of the United Nations in New York and Geneva, Vienna, UNESCO in Paris and other representatives as necessary.

*Article 75*

In the event of the death or a severe illness of the President lasting more than six months, the Presidential powers are assumed by the I. Vice-President. In such case the parliament calls a special session of the Congress within three months.

**CHAPTER IX**
GENERAL SECRETARY AND SECRETARIAT
composition

*Article 76*

The General Secretary is the chief executive officer of the IRU. S/he is a statutory representative of the organization and must have signing rights on all IRU bank accounts.

*Article 77*

The Secretary General is elected by the Congress. Upon the recommendation of the President, the General Secretary can be dismissed by the Parliament.

*Article 78*

The General Secretary has the right to participate in the sessions of the Parliament and the Presidium.

*Article 79*

The Secretariat is headed by the Secretary General who is for that activity responsible to the President.

*Article 80*

The Secretariat runs in accordance with the Order of Proceedings approved by the General Secretary.

*Article 81*

The Secretariat is an assisting body of the President, the Presidium, Parliament, the Congress and other expert committees and assisting bodies.

*Article 82*

The seat of the Secretariat is Brussels. The President can establish as needed regional branches of the Secretariat.

*Article 83*

The IRU Secretariat is composed of the General Secretary and experts chosen by the General Secretary.

*Article 84*

The budgets of both secretariats are approved by the Parliament.

**CHAPTER X**
ECONOMY
*Article 85*

The main sources of income are the membership fees from the individual members, member organizations in the amounts defined by the Parliament.

*Article 86*

Other sources of income are gifts, inheritance, and donations of national and international organizations.

*Article 87*

Financial affairs are managed by the Treasurer of the organization, who is responsible for his actions to the Parliament.

*Article 88*

The Treasurer elaborates annual budgetary plans, economy reports and presents these to the Parliament for approval.

*Article 89*

The Court of Justice is charged with the inspection of the economy and utilization of resources.

*Article 90*

The Parliament may establish an expert financial committee headed by a Parliament member to secure transparency of financial affairs.

*Article 91*

The Treasurer is eligible to present annual financial report to the Parliament elaborated and audited by an international auditing firm.

*Article 92*

The Treasurer and the Secretary General are authorized to handle financial resources at bank accounts.

## CHAPTER XI
FINAL PROVISIONS

*Article 93*

Amendments of this Charter come into force and become effective for all members of the International Romani Union upon ratification by two-thirds majority of Congress delegates.

## CHAPTER XII
RATIFICATION AND SIGNING

*Article 94*

1. This Charter shall be ratified by all delegates of the 5th Congress of the IRU in Prague on July 25 to 28, 2000.
2. The ratification documents shall be archived at the seat of the International Romani Union in Brussels, at the seat of the United Nations, section ECO, in file of the International Romani Union.
3. Signatories of this Charter who sign the Charter after its becoming effective become original members of the International Romani Union as of the day of deposition of their ratification documents.

*Article 95*

This Charter, whose Romani, Russian, English, Czech, Bulgarian, Romanian, Hungarian, French, Spanish, and German texts are authentic shall remain stored in the United Nations archive as well as the IRU archive.

Their proper certified copies shall be sent by the IRU to all member organizations of the IRU. As proof of that the delegates of the 5th Congress of the IRU hereby sign this Charter.

In Prague, on the twenty-eighth of July, year two thousand.

## Appendix Three
## IRU Declaration of a Nation

*Authors' note:*
This document is printed as distributed, without alterations (e.g. spelling etc.).

### DECLARATION OF NATION

WE, THE ROMA NATION

Individuals belonging to the Roma Nation call for a representation of their Nation, which does not want to become a State. We ask for being recognized as a Nation, for the sake of Roma and of non-Roma individuals, who share the need to deal with the nowadays new challenges. We, a Nation of which over half a million persons were exterminated in a fergotten Holocaust, a Nation of individuals too often discriminated, marginalized, victim of intollerance and persecutions, we have a dream, and we are engaged in fulfilling it. We are a Nation, we share the same tradition, the same culture, the same origin, the same language; we are a Nation. We have never looked for creating a Roma State. And we do not want a State today, when the new society and the new economy are concretely and progressively crossing-over the importance and the adequacy of the State as the way how individuals organize themselves.

The will to consubstantiate the concept of a Nation and the one of a State has led and is still leading to tragedies and wars, disasters and massacres. The history of the Roma Nation cuts through such a cohincidence, which is evidently not anymore adequate to the needs of individuals. We, the Roma Nation, offer to the individuals belonging to the other Nations our adequacy to the new world.

We have a dream, the political concrete dream of the rule of law being the rule for each and everybody, in the frame and thanks to a juridical systém able to assure democracy, freedom, liberty to each and everybody, being adequate to the changing world, the changing society, the changing economy. We have a dream, the one of the rule of law being a method, and not a "value". A pragmatic, concrete, way how individuals agree on rules, institutions, juridical norms, adequate to the new needs. A transnational Nation as the Roma one needs a transnational rule of law: this is evident; we do believe that such a need is shared by any individual, independently of the Nation he or she belongs to.

We do know that a shy debate regarding the adequacy of the State to the changing needs of the global society - a global society which should not be organized exclusively from above - is involving prominent personalities in Europe and in the entire UN Community.

We are also convinced that the request itself of a representation for the Roma Nation is a great help to find an answer to the crucial question regarding the needed reforms of the existing international institutions and rules. Our dream is therefore of great actuality and it is very concrete. It is what we offer the entire world community. The

Roma Nation, each and every individual belonging to it look for and need a world where the international Charters on Human Rights are Laws, are perenptory rules, providing exigible rights. Such a will is a need for the Roma; is it so only for Roma?

We are aware that the main carachteristic of the Roma Nation, the one of being a Nation without searching for the establishment of a State, is today a great, adequate resource of freedom and legality for each individual, and of the successfull functioning for the world community.

We have a dream, and we are engaged in the implementation of it: we offer to the humanity a request, the one of having a representation as a Nation, the Nation we are. Giving an answer to such a request would let the entire humanity make a substancial step forward.

We know democracy and freedom to equal the rule of law, which can be assured only through the creation of institutions and juridical rules adequate and constantly adjusted to the necessarly changing needs of individuals.

We are to offer our culture, our tradition, the resource which is in our historic refusal of searching for a state: the most adequate resource of awareness to the nowadays world. That's why we look for a representation, and new ways of representing individuals apart from their belonging to one or to another nation. Nowadays politics is not adequate to the nowadays needs of individuals in a changing world; and to the needs of all those persons still suffering starvation and violations of their fundamental human rights. And we offer, we propose a question, while proposing and offering a path, a concrete, possible, needed path, on which to start walking together.

We, the Roma Nation, have something to share, right by asking for a representation, respect, implementation of the existing International Charter on Human Rights, so that each individual can look at them as at existing, concrete warranties for her or his today and future.

## References

Acton, T. A. (1981) 'Institutional tasks before the Third World Romani Congress', *Roma* 6, 1: 26–8.

Acton, T. A (1998) 'Comunità zingare e città', *Lacio Drom* 34, 2: 42–9.

IRU (2001) *Report of the First Session of the International Romani Union Parliament*, Prague: IRU, March.

Kawczynski, R. (1997) 'Roma-led strategies of resistance', *Transitions* 4, Changes in post-Communist societies, 4: 24–9, September.

Kenrick, D. S. (1971) 'The World Romani Congress', *Journal of the Gypsy Lore Society* III, 50, 3–4: 101–8, July-Oct.

Kenrick, D. S. and Puxon, G. (1972) *The Destiny of Europe's Gypsies,* London: Chatto Heinemann/Sussex University Press.

Lee, R. (2000) 'Post-Communist migration to Canada', *Cambridge Review of International Affairs* XIII, 2, spring/summer.

Matras, Y. (1998) 'Review of Mirga and Gheorghe (1997) The Roma in the Twenty-First Century', *Journal of the Gypsy Lore Society* V, 8, 2: 151–4.

Mirga, A. and Gheorghe, N. (1997) *The Roma in the Twenty-First Century: A Policy Paper*, Project on Ethnic Relations (PER), Princeton: PER.

Puxon, G. (1971) 'The First World Romani Congress', *Race Today*, June, 192–9.

Puxon, G. (1979) 'The Second World Romani Congress', *Roma* 4, 2–3: 31–104.

Puxon, G. (1980) 'World Romani Congress, activities of its praesidium', *Roma* 5, 2: 28–39.

Puxon, G. (2000) 'The Romani movement: rebirth and the First World Romani Congress in retrospect', in T. Acton (ed.) *Scholarship and the Gypsy Struggle*, Hatfield: University of Hertfordshire Press.

Rinderknecht, K., Barthélémy, A., Lang, F., Maximoff, M., Tillhagen C.-H., and de Vaux de Foletier, F. (1973) *Tsiganes, Nomades Mystérieux*, Lausanne: Éditions Mondo.

Rishi, W. R. (1980) 'Roma, keep united', *Roma* 5, 1: 3–19.

Rishi, W. R. (1982) 'Report of the Third World Romani Congress, Göttingen (West Germany) May 15–21, 1981', *Roma* 6, 2–3: 43–80.

Rishi, W. R. (1991) 'IV World Romani Congress, Serock, Warsaw, Poland', *Roma*, 33–4, 3–15, 61.

Sijercic, H. and Lee, R. (eds) (1999) *Kanadiake Romane Mirikle – Canadian Romani Pearls*, Toronto: Romani Community and Advocacy Centre (with the assistance of Heritage Canada).

## Notes

1   A full list of those elected to IRU posts is given in Appendix One.

2   In fact, Andrzej Mirga did not attend the congress in Prague a few months later.

3   Meanwhile many politicians in the West engaged in a vicious campaign against them, whipping up racism in the shameful pursuit of electoral advantage.

4   This policy has been pursued partly by hiring Romani student interns for various terms, such as Nicholas Gimenez, Angela Kocze, etc. and more recently Nicolae Gheorghe (as a high-powered permanent official, to write reports to inform OSCE policy), and partly through the funding of human rights litigation by US-based foundations.

5   A further, significant step was taken along this road in April 2001, when Czech Ministry of Foreign Affairs (MFA) became the first governmental institution to recognise that Roma living in Europe are a part of the Roma nation whose request for general recognition is legitimate in a *Memorandum of Understanding and Co-operation between the Ministry of Foreign Affairs of the Czech Republic and the International Romani Union*. Besides governmental recognition of Roma as a Nation, the agreement also includes acceptance of Romani representation and co-operation in creating foreign policy and in questions regarding the Romani nation in Europe and in the world. The interest of the Czech government in 'Europeanising' Romani issues echoes Article 5 of the Memorandum in which the MFA and IRU declare they 'share the conviction that the way of achieving genuine progress in resolving Romani issues on the European continent rests in the implementation of an all-European approach to this problem'. Negotiations are currently on the way to conclude similar agreements with the governments of India, Bulgaria, Slovakia, Romania, Sweden

and others. One function of the agreement is to bolster the position of the Foreign Ministry in debates over policy on Roma, against other sections of the state apparatus whose domestic policies might be thought to imperil Czech entry to the European Union. This strategy, however, is dependant on the IRU continuing to be seen as independent, and not a mere creature of Czech foreign policy; so achieving similar agreements with other governments is crucial to its success.

6   The IRU Charter, incorporating the statutes adopted at the Fifth World Romani Congress, is given in Appendix Two.

7   At the first session of the IRU parliament, held in March 2001 in Bratislava, it was agreed that the annual fees of member organisations should be set at the level of twelve times the average daily wage of an unskilled worker in the country of that organisation (IRU 2001: 2, para 4).

8   At their first meeting MPs decided that those countries not yet represented should be asked to nominate an MP for the next parliamentary session (IRU 2001: 2, para 5).

9   Eighteen of the thirty-five MPs attended the first meeting of the IRU parliament, representing eighteen states. Fifteen members of the presidium were also present (IRU 2001: 1).

10  The report of the first session of the IRU parliament announced 'a review of the statutes', to be undertaken by a committee of five whose task was 'to collect complaints and correct the statutes with the help of capable lawyers' (IRU 2001: 1, para 3).

11  The English in this version is less than perfect but since this is the actual document being distributed by the IRU, it was decided to leave it in this form rather than attempt to amend it.

12  Dragan Jevremovic, Chair of the Parliament, reported to IRU MPs that the IRU was participating with the RNC and others in a consultative group of the Contact Point for Roma and Sinti Issues (OSCE-ODIHR) to evaluate Roma projects. The IRU report of the first parliamentary session stated: 'The members of Parliament plead for a close co-operation with [the] Roma National Congress' (IRU 2001: 2, para 7).

*Phuri dai* (grand-
mother) from
Polska Roma grou
in Romani camp.
Kraków, late 1980

Early morning in
Romani camp –
Polska Roma group
Kraków, late 1980s.

Lech Mróz

Leader of Lovara group from southern Poland with his sister from Los Angeles.
Kraków, 1990s.

Lech Mróz

Mother and child - Polska
Roma, Galicyiaki (Galician)
subgroup. Kraków, late 1980s.

Roma settlement at Vel'ká Ida near Košice, East Slovakia. Visible in the background is part of the huge East Slovak Steelworks, which employed many Roma during Communist times, and now part-owned by multinational US Steel. East Slovakia, 1992.

REPUBLIKÁNI PROTI ZVÝHODŇOVÁNÍ CIKÁNŮ

'Republicans against preferential treatment for Gypsies' – election leaflet and billboard poster for ultra-right wing Republican Party, Czech Republic, 1997.

Roma settlement at Letanovce, East Slovakia. Ironically this settlement lies on the edge of an area of outstanding natural beauty – called the *Slovak Paradise*. In 2000 it was still without electricity or running water, in spite of a visit in 1990 by President Havel, who voiced his concern at the living conditions. East Slovakia, 1992.

Two of the most marginalised Romani settlements in Slovakia are located on the outskirts of the East Slovak town of Rudňany. This one occupies a derelict factory site; the other is built on a highly toxic waste tip.

In happier times: Roma relax outside village pub. East Slovakia, 1976.

Rural East Slovakia is an area of high unemployment, but overwhelmingly for Roma. Nowadays impoverished Roma living in segregated settlements are often forced to scavenge wood from the forests and steal crops from the now privatised farms, where formerly they had permanent jobs as labourers.

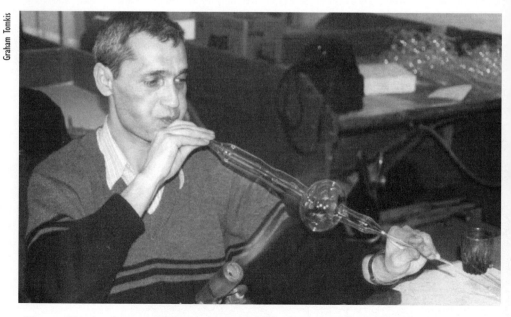

Glass-making is a long-established industry in the Czech lands and this craftsman is respected as one of the most highly skilled glass-blowers in his firm. Unlike him most Romani factory workers, whether skilled or not, lost their jobs shortly after the fall of Communism and still remain unemployed.

# PART THREE

# Diversity in Romani experience: Countries of the region

## CHAPTER NINE

# Russia: politics of performance

*Alaina Lemon*

D uring the Soviet period, Roma in Eastern Europe looked to Moscow as a cultural lodestar: in the 1920s the USSR was the first state to publish Romani texts and Moscow was home since 1931 to the Moscow Romani Theatre. Over the Soviet decades, Roma from Russia were highly visible as cultural producers, riding the wave of Russian cultural hegemony across the Soviet satellite states. Russian language films featuring Roma (*Tabor Ukhodit v Nebo, Tsygan*), though often starring non-Roma in key roles, were broadcast across the region.

Nonetheless, Romani activism in the 1970s, 80s and 90s took off not in the USSR, but elsewhere in Eastern Europe. By the late 1980s and mid 1990s, Roma in Russia generally had become economically better off than Roma in other Eastern European countries, but politically more marginal. This was the case mostly because, unlike the situation in Hungary and Czechoslovakia, where Roma worked in state enterprises after World War Two only to become massively unemployed in the late 1980s, few Soviet Roma were ever proletarianised. The fall of state socialism thus affected them less suddenly, sweepingly and uniformly.

The reasons for political marginality are more complex. While in 1990s' Hungary, the Czech Republic, Slovakia and Macedonia, some Roma sat in administrative positions, in Russia no Roma held public office, there were no Romani political parties, and cultural organisations were mainly oriented towards performance for non-Roma. Demographic factors have something to do with this difference. Roma are proportionally fewer in Russia than in Central and Eastern Europe – the 1989 Soviet census counted 153,000 Roma in Russia (though other sources estimate the real number at two or three times higher [Liégeois and Gheorghe 1995: 7]) compared with, for instance, 600,000 in much smaller Hungary. In Central and Eastern Europe, Roma are frequently the largest and most visible minority, living in compact settlements and urban ghettos, while in Russia, Roma are dispersed over vast spaces. And while Roma are actually stronger in numbers than several other non-Russian nationalities,[1] Soviet Roma lacked both the territory or the administrative structures to be make themselves heard, both in the 1920s and 30s when Soviet nationality policy was being formed, and in the 1980s and 90s, when the Soviet Union broke up along the lines of existing national republics.

Thus historical and political factors may be more significant than demographic ones. In Russia, unlike in Central and Eastern Europe, state socialism was not a post-war phenomenon – policy directed at Soviet nationalities reached an entire generation farther back, often vacillating between activism and neglect. In early Soviet decades, assimilation policy aimed at Roma was aggressive. The Bolshevik state, in contrast to the Tsarist one, stopped neither at taxation nor at regulating movement:[2] Roma were to assimilate along with all other minorities, and at the same pace. In 1925 the state classified Roma as a 'national minority', devoting special departments to Romani affairs within the National Minorities' Sector of the Ministry of Culture. (However, most other states in the Soviet bloc later denied Roma such status, Yugoslavia being the first to upgrade Roma to 'nationality' status in 1981.) There were then tentative proposals to establish a Romani Autonomous Region, to be called *Romanestan*, though these proposals came to nothing. The All-Russian Gypsy Union, established in 1925, oversaw early initiatives to distribute land and to 'liquidate illiteracy' among Gypsies.[3] Some Roma enrolled in schools that taught in Romani, while some received employment in urban collectives and co-operatives such as *Tsygpishchprom* (Gypsy Food Production) or *Tsygximprom* (Gypsy Chemical Production). But most of these initiatives were short-lived (the Gypsy Union was already closed down in 1928). The rest completely ceased to function by 1938, well before state socialism had begun to touch Romani communities farther west.[4]

Even at the height of early, 'Leninist' nationalities policy, the state never singled out Roma as its main minority target of either assimilationist restrictions or benefits to the extent that occurred in Central and Eastern Europe. But on the other hand, by the 1990s, Roma had not become the most likely scapegoats for Russian racist groups, who were as likely to persecute Africans or Armenians as Roma. Nevertheless, since the fall of the USSR in 1991 (two years after Central and Eastern Europe's 1989 revolutions), conditions for Roma in Russia changed in significant ways.

## Pre-Soviet history and Soviet policy

There were numerous shifts and inconsistencies in Soviet policy. For instance, in the 1920s, the USSR was the first state to cultivate written Romani script, based on Cyrillic, only to neglect Romani literacy by the late 1930s. Or, for example, the state nurtured a handful of Romani intellectuals and performers but forbade them to attend World Romani Union congresses until 1990. Each policy shift impacted on Romani communities in Russia in diverse ways, in part because the various states have treated Romani groups living in Russia for 500 years one way and those arrived more recently another. Indeed, many European states have dealt with Roma using a gradated social scale, preferring 'our Gypsies' to 'foreign Gypsies' (see Hübschmannová 1998[84]: 234, Guy 1998[75]).

In Russia, the mainstream media does not distinguish Romani groups (except to label them as 'settled' as opposed to 'wild') but scholars do. Russian-language sources (Ploxinskij 1890, Barranikov 1931, Demeter and Cherenkov 1987, Druts and Gessler 1991) describe three periods of Romani immigration into the Russian Empire. The first period, they write, saw Roma move from the Balkans and Wallachia into Ukraine in the mid fifteenth century, and from Poland into Belarus and the Baltic countries by around 1500. About two hundred years later, more Roma moved from Germany and Poland into the Baltic region and central Russia. Most Roma who settled in the north came to be called *Russka* or *Xeladytka* Roma; in the south, *Ukrainska* or *Servi* Roma. Other groups in the south include *Xoroxane* (Muslim Roma). A third wave in the nineteenth century included Roma from Wallachia, Moldavia and Austro-Hungarian lands – groups such as *Lovara* and *Kelderara* (together with later-arriving *Ungri* and *Machvaya* groups) labeled by scholars *Vlax* Roma. Many *Vlax* were enslaved in Wallachia and Moldavia until abolition there in the mid1800s (Fraser 1992b, Hancock 1987). Some *Vlax* were absorbed into Imperial territory starting with the annexation of Moldova in 1812, but began appearing in Ukraine and in central Russia after the abolition of slavery in Wallachian and Moldavian lands in the 1860s. A series of smaller, mainly *Vlax*, migrations continued throughout the twentieth century, clustered after the Revolution and around the two World Wars – some of these latter were repatriated to Poland in the 1950s (Kaminski 1980: 267–73). Thousands of *Vlax* were deported from Romania and Hungary after World War Two to work camps in Siberia,[5] and some *Lovara* came to Russia from Hungary after the 1956 uprising there. In the late 1970s more Roma moved into Russia, including families of *Sinte,* from Germany and non-Romani speaking *Beash* Gypsies from Moldova.

Recent ethnography (Stewart 1997) has discussed ways state policies create social distance between Roma and non-Roma. Less has been done to examine how states have influenced relations and differences among Roma – how policy affects each group differently, for instance, channeling them into certain professions or excluding them from certain places.[6] For example, starting in the late 1920s, it was mostly already settled *Russka* who worked in Soviet factories or joined collective farms.

By the early decades of the twentieth century, most *Russka* Roma had settled, though some still travelled seasonally in the summer months, renting village houses or empty city shops in the winter. At that time many of the men traded horses and did veterinary work, while women pursued petty commerce. *Russka* Roma were most famous as entertainers, though only a small minority of them were employed in this way. In 1774 Count A.G. Orlov assembled the first 'Gypsy choir' from his Romani serfs settled near Moscow (see Rom-Lebedev 1990: 45, Bobri 1961, Druts and Gessler 1991: 203).[7] Orlov's choir was liberated from serfdom in 1807, decades before general emancipation in 1861, and gained the right to settle in Moscow proper (Demeter and Cherenkov 1987: 40).

From early on, therefore, policy treated performers differently from other Roma, for whom Moscow was otherwise forbidden territory. A decree by Elizabeth in 1759 had forbidden Roma to enter the capital, St. Petersburg (German: 26), and soon after Moscow was closed to them as well (as it was to most Jews under the Pale of Settlement). Though the Soviet regime lifted this restriction in 1917, it ultimately enforced a similar zone of exclusions throughout the Soviet period, barring convicts, exiles – and most Roma. Thus, it was *Russka* performers or their descendants who, having grown up and been educated in Moscow, made up the 1920s and 30s core of intellectuals who established Romani schools, journals and the Moscow Romani Theatre.

Performers and activists included some *Servi* Roma. In southern Ukraine and occupied Moldova, as in Russia, many *Servi* were also serfs of the crown, though most had been settled even longer than most *Russka* farther north.[8] Many *Servi* were successful merchants and some settlements, often on the edges of towns and cities and dubbed 'Gypsy Burg' or 'Gypsy Street' (Barranikov 1931), had their own *Atamans* (commanders or headmen). But it was mainly in the twentieth century that *Servi* came to work as performers at the Moscow Romani Theatre.

The state institution of the Romani Theatre included very few *Vlax* Roma in its troupes. Latecomers to Russia, media and official documents dubbed them 'foreign Gypsies'. *Lovara* are especially rare on stage, only a few beginning to work as performers after the late 1970s. Among *Vlax*, *Lovara* arrived latest in Russia, at the turn of the century and just before the First World War, appearing in Moscow only in the 1920s (Demeter and Cherenkov 1987: 43). Some *Lovara* came directly from Hungary, and some fled Poland to Russia just before World War One. When *Lovara* first arrived, they sold mainly small goods; some women told fortunes and men traded horses. But in the 1930s the state classified *Lovara* trading as criminal speculation and nationalised their horses.[9] Some *Lovara* joined industrial co-operatives with other Roma but the NKVD (National Committee for Internal Affairs, replaced later by the KGB security services) shut down most of these in the 1930s, perhaps as part of the turn towards an assimilationist nationalities policy. Those *Lovara* given houses in the 1930s had to move again during World War Two evacuations and resettlements.

Older *Lovara* and other nomadic Roma recall travelling in wagons until

230

Khrushchev's 1956 decree against 'Gypsy' nomadism.[10] With a five-year labour sentence for those resisting, this was 'the only law in the history of the Soviet Union to define a crime in terms of the activity of an ethnically marked group'.[11] It was during this period (1956–8) that many *Lovara* were repatriated to Poland. After settling, *Lovara* continued to trade, making short train trips to relatives in other Russian cities to obtain goods in short supply locally.[12] This was a common Soviet strategy not peculiar to Roma, but besides trade, *Lovara* had little other livelihood and no workplace perks.

*Vlax Keldelara* were also affected by the 1956 law. They were among the first *Vlax* to arrive in Russia in the nineteenth century and because of their pleated, patterned skirts and braids, they were the most exotic to Russians who considered them to be 'real Gypsies'. Visibly less assimilated than other Roma, they were always more easily excluded from residence in major cities, under both Tsarist and Soviet regulations.[13] In central Russia their settlements dot the railways, just outside the 100-kilometre radius of Moscow or Leningrad, closer to the limits of small cities such as Tver', Penza and Tula. Kelderari men in Russia, almost without exception, work with metals and managed in the 1960s to establish stable working relations with neighbouring collective farms and industry. When they first came to Russia they repaired kettles and vessels and under late socialism they took up welding, repairing agricultural storage containers and bakery equipment, as well as dealing in scrap metal. Such enterprises remained modestly lucrative under state socialism, since Soviet industrialisation did not overwhelm small-scale repair activities to the degree that it did in the United States and Western Europe.

Certainly Soviet policy has also affected *Beash*, *Sinte* and *Xoroxane* Roma in differential ways, but more research is necessary to understand exactly how. Even cultural programs intended to unite and define Roma in many ways divided them, and the key to understanding this process is performance. Performance and policy were connected well before the Revolution – recall that the first Roma to be exempted from the Tsarist settlement regulations had been the musicians and choral singers of Orlov's Gypsy choir. Moreover, the Romani élite comprised performers and their kin and this shaped Soviet and post-Soviet perception of 'Gypsies' and how to treat them.

In addition, theatrical images reinforced policies such as forced settlement and the 'liquidation' of certain customs. The 1974 *Great Soviet Encyclopedia* explicitly asserts that the Romani Theatre was established in 1931 in order to facilitate policy, such as the Order of the Supreme Soviet of 1926 providing land to Gypsies wishing to settle. The Theatre was to 'preserve a national culture' and to 'aid the assimilation, sedentarisation, and education of nomadic peoples'. Finally, for decades, the Romani Theatre has remained the only state institution directly dealing with Roma. In the 1930s it survived even as other national theatres were closed down, after Romani journals were terminated (for not reflecting 'class struggle' between rich and poor Roma)[14] and after Romani schools were shut down.

This has been the case even though the Theatre's productions have been devoted less to Romani communities than to non-Roma audiences. After its first three years the Theatre switched from Romani-language political education to Russian-language entertainment. Still, the repertoire maintained a core of assimilation stories, stories that depicted Romani groups as divided by 'class struggle' and choosing, in the end, socialist allegiance. For instance in 1959, three years after Khruschev's 1956 decree, the Theatre premiered a play by Romani playwright Ivan Khrustaljov, a tribute to the virtues of settled life and 'Gypsy collectives' titled *Gorjachaja Krov* (Hot Blood).

Theatrical productions, along with the official press, lauded the Romani agricultural and industrial collectives of the 1920s and 30s. However, according to archival accounts, in reality most of those collectives were poorly administered.[15] Often the Ministries assigned land to Roma and sent them off with no livestock, no supplies and no instruction, only to forget them. Some Roma were thrown into collectives together with Ukrainians or Tatars, who resented the intruders (Druts and Gessler 1990: 293, *Pravda* 26 July 1932). Those few farms that did do reasonably well were staffed by local, already settled *Xeladytka* and *Servi*. For instance, a few collectives in Smolensk region and the northern Caucasus succeeded because Romani officials in the Nationalities Department of the Central Committee kept close contact with them, to ameliorate supply problems and mediate with non-Romani state bureaucrats (Druts and Gessler 1990: 288). By the late 1930s, the NKVD took over Romani collectivisation and resettlement and closed down most Romani collectives and farms.[16] Many Roma working in urban collectives were arrested well before that and others were resettled en masse to Siberia in 1937–8. Russian and Romani intellectuals did not speak publicly about these events until *glasnost*[17] was well under way. Until then, Fascist invaders were blamed and accused of having destroyed the collectives in World War Two. Indeed, in Ukraine, Belorussia and the Baltics, occupying armies had singled out Roma, throwing them into mass graves along with Jews (see Druts and Gessler 1990 and Crowe 1994).

Many Roma were not aware that Gypsies had been special targets for extermination until long after. One elderly *Xoroxane* Romani woman recounted that she had 'hidden from the fascists, because I look like a Jew' (author's interview, 1992). On the stage of the Romani Theatre, as elsewhere, memory of Nazi eugenic designs specifically on Gypsies and Jews were muted; the war was to be depicted as a tragedy for *all* the Soviet peoples.

The Romani Theatre was on tour in 1941 and when the USSR entered the war the Theatre continued its tour of free concerts to soldiers and hospital patients. It was then evacuated to Tashkent.[18] But other Roma had to make their own way to safety. Many found themselves suspect during the war and in the years leading up to it. The choirmaster at the Romani Theatre recalled resettlements of *Vlax* Roma in the years leading up to World War Two: 'They were taken away in goods wagons – not even passenger carriages. Then they were just dropped off without any supplies at all, and many died. They called it "industrial espionage" or called us "Hungarian spies". *Lovara* and *Kelderara* were the main victims' (author's interview with Vladislav Demeter, 1991). Muslim *Xoroxane* also suffered, especially those who had written 'Tatar' as their passport 'nationality' and thus were resettled along with Chechens, Ingush and other 'suspect nationalities' after the war (Druts and Gessler 1991). After World War Two many other Roma who had been removed to Siberia returned to European Russia, and while most were still excluded from settling within 100 kilometres of cities such as Moscow and Kiev, those returning to smaller cities such as Kharkov or Tula received apartments, sometimes ahead of Russian and Ukrainian majorities.

But after the 1940s the state mainly ignored issues of Romani work and education. Playwright and actor, Rom-Lebedev, wrote to Stalin before the leader's death, complaining that there had been no support for Gypsies since the end of the war and that many had returned to nomadism, especially the *Vlax* Roma and the Romani war refugees from Europe.[19] In 1953 Nikolaj Aleksandrovich Pankov, *Russka* author and translator, wrote to the Central Committee complaining that due to the war and post-war 'inertia', the state was neglecting Romani culture, especially in the provinces. Two years later he wrote again, to Khrushchev himself, on the 'situation of the disorganised wandering tribes', and urged him to take measures to settle them (Druts and Gessler 1990: 305). But settlement brought no great relief or immediate benefits for Roma. One Romani Theatre worker later recalled settlement: 'The result of the 1956 law was great hunger. Soldiers with guns rounded up all those in camps .... The Theatre received letters asking for help' (author's interview, 1991).

In the 1990s many Roma continue to view the Theatre as a mediator with the state. Of all the state programs once initiated, only the Moscow Romani Theatre remained, and Romani intellectuals spoke of it as 'the only thing the Gypsies have left'. Through the Theatre, the state had nurtured cadres of Romani élites – dynasties of performers and a handful of academics and professionals. 'The Gypsy Theatre gave birth to a national intelligentsia, whose first university it was' (Slichenko 1984).

By the late Soviet period, even though Romani literacy programmes had been terminated, by and large literacy figures for Roma in Russia exceeded those elsewhere. Although it has been argued in popular discourse that Roma have no word for 'writing' or are averse to reading and to books, this stereotype finds perhaps even less purchase in Russia than in other countries (see Hancock 1998). In Russia, *Vlax* and non-*Vlax* alike valued education and texts and did *not* speak of reading and writing as 'polluted' or 'taboo'. Those with the *propiska* (residence pass) and long-term housing sent their children to elementary school. Nowadays even Roma in isolated areas display keen interest in communication technologies and international media. In villages lacking safe drinking water or reliable heating, a cassette player or video recorder may well be found. Roma elsewhere (in the US and in Europe) are also interested in texts and technology, in gaining access to media and the Internet, but the *ways* that Roma in Russia value literacy may be a legacy of particularly Soviet modernisation. When Soviet minorities policy *did* pay attention to Roma, it seems to have focused more resources and expertise on culture and education than on other areas.

By contrast, many Central and Eastern European countries concentrated instead (and later) on proletarianising Roma into heavy industry. As a result, in Russia there are no ghetto-like neighbourhoods of Romani slums surrounding now-defunct factories. In Russia rumours do not circulate, as they do elsewhere, that 'Gypsies cannot live in civilised housing' because they would allegedly make bonfires of parquet flooring. Russian Roma were not made into an urban underclass and were never assigned substandard housing blocks. In Russia, the urban Roma were the élite cultural producers. Thus, while stereotypes do contend that the only 'authentic Gypsy' is poor and uneducated, many Roma (and some non-Roma) in Russia do not buy into this aesthetic.

## After State Socialism

In Russia, Roma played little direct role in the 1991 transfer of power. There were no Romani political parties or Romani candidates and no Romani national movements. Cultural and representational rights for Roma were not agenda-making issues as they were elsewhere. But neither did Russian nationalists make 'Gypsies' their primary foil, as did nationalists in countries farther west. Roma were one stigmatised group among many, but they were not the face of a Soviet 'underclass'.

Nevertheless, intensification of Romani political participation elsewhere in the former Soviet bloc made itself felt in Russia and Romani activists from abroad increased their contacts with Roma in Moscow. In 1990, for the first time, Soviet Roma were allowed to visit a World Romani Congress, held that year in Warsaw, and in September 1991 Moscow hosted Romani delegates at a conference on minorities sponsored by the Conference on Security and Co-operation in Europe (CSCE, later OSCE). By the mid 1990s, NGOs such as the European Romani Right Centre (ERRC) were sending investigators to Ukraine to investigate human rights abuses, and the Soros foundation maintained a branch of its Romani organisation in Moscow.

However, the post-Soviet regime change brought no policies directly intended to improve the situation of Roma, though Roma retained their status as 'national minority' from the Soviet past and the Romani Theatre continued with the same repertoire. *New* initiatives originated instead from abroad, via the United Nations or NGOs. For instance, in 1992, Unesco contributed funds to a Saturday morning class in Romani literacy for urban Romani children, where the children studied writing in Latin as well as Cyrillic characters, in order to be able to write to Roma far and wide in the diaspora. Most of this support from outside agencies and representatives was solicited not by the state but by Romani cultural producers. Most of these headed groups concentrated in Moscow, some affiliated to the Romani Theatre (such as the Moscow Children's Gypsy Choir, *Gilorri*), some connected through social ties (such as a Romani women's group organised by Ganga-Batalova). Groups active elsewhere in Russia included, most notably, Djura Maxotin's *Romanimos* in Tver', which has published Romani texts and sponsored performance groups.

Just as post-Soviet policy has not explicitly aimed to help Roma, neither does it explicitly discriminate against them. Nevertheless, policies that on the surface seem to apply to everyone, in practice are more harshly deployed against non-Russian minorities, and in some cases especially against Roma. Most significant among these is the continuance of the residence pass. Under the Soviet *propiska* system, *everyone* had to register residence with municipal authorities, and while some restrictions were nominally relaxed in the early 1990s, the *propiska* system is still in effect. It sets a limit of one registration per person, and restricts registration in cities like Moscow. People such as ex-prisoners or Roma who appeared visibly unassimilated were *de facto* denied residence within the '101st kilometre zone' of Moscow, and denied the right to travel through the city without transit visas. While many Roma do possess papers registering them somewhere in Russia, those not registered in the places they reside are denied access to local medical service, housing, schooling, and employment. The checking and exclusion of Roma and other non-Russian people has become more intense after the ending of Communist rule. Roma report being stopped frequently, sometimes as 'Gypsies', and sometimes because they are confused with other non-Russians. Beatings and fines are not uncommon (see also Human Rights Watch 1995). Nevertheless, many Roma continue to try to settle or work in or near large cities such as Moscow or St. Petersburg.

Problems with residence papers are not unique to Roma. However, Roma in Russia are much less able or willing to report such conditions to human rights NGOs. Some Roma express the view that there would be no point in complaining because 'we are [seen as] criminals' (author's interview, 1997). Local NGO workers in Moscow are inclined to describe Gypsies as a low priority and indeed most know very little about Roma. This lack of response is not limited to internal prejudice. British international workers for a religious aid organisation distributing soup to homeless Russians at a train station told this author in winter 1996 that they never gave food to 'those Gypsies' because they were 'conniving, just like Gypsies back in England'. At any rate, NGOs in Russia have not been nearly as active in challenging human rights abuses concerning Roma as they have been in other countries.

Meanwhile, the economic changes arising from the ending of Communist rule have affected Romani communities in various ways, though the predicament of most is generally more precarious than formerly. Some Roma are ambivalently nostalgic for the Soviet period, and some intellectuals emphasise benefits under state socialism, while others recall confiscation of property and money and now hope for reparations. Conversely, while some intellectuals stress the cultural destruction of the 1956 settlement policy, many nomadic Roma, though recalling cruelties of forced settlement, nevertheless said in the 1990s that they preferred living in houses.

Before 1991 many Roma (most *Lovara*, some *Russka* and *Servi*) lived a shadow life as 'speculators' in cosmetics, clothing or vodka. When restrictions on commerce were eased in the late 1980s, such people no longer faced prison sentences for 'parasitism' and could travel, for instance, to Greece or China for more lucrative goods. From the late 1980s many *Lovara*, for instance, prospered with the relaxation of border restrictions and marketing laws. By the 1990s some were living in new houses in the outlying suburbs of large cities such as Moscow, St. Petersburg and Kiev. However, as markets became deregulated, they also became increasingly competitive and Roma, who had dealt in small luxuries under *perestroika*,[20] found themselves pushed out of such local markets. Sometimes they were attracted into more dangerous ones and older Roma began to worry that their children would be drawn into the mafia and drugs trade. Meanwhile, even as they accumulated capital, relations with police and bureaucratic structures became more unsteady. Thus, merchant Roma experienced seesawing fortunes in the 1990s – building onto and renovating homes in the early 1990s only to sell and tighten their belts again by the late 1990s.

Under *perestroika*, *Kelderara* were allowed to form state-licensed co-operatives, bringing home metal canisters and parts to work on in plots between houses. When they gained enough work, they could even hire local Russian assistants. By the 1990s, those *Kelderara* who were located conveniently near surviving collective farms or industrial enterprises continued to do well, but others lost commissions as farms floundered. Their co-operatives were also vulnerable to huge new federal taxes. During transition, *Kelderari* women report increasing their petty trading and palm-reading at bazaars and train stations. At the same time more stringent residence regulations affected *Kelderara* economic activity near the big cities most of all, since their distinctive dress continued to make them easier to single out than other Roma. Though in the 1980s some had managed to rent apartments closer to Moscow city limits, in the 1990s most *Kelderari* villages remained dispersed widely throughout Russia, Ukraine and Western Siberia. Many of these villages (like some Russian villages) continued to lack basics such as running water that was safe to drink.

Other settled Roma far from the cities, such as many *Ursari*, *Vlaxi* and *Beash* Roma, live in much worse conditions, crowded into abandoned army barracks or in shacks whose floorboards open in chinks over dirt. For these Roma – and indeed, even for the better situated *Kelderara* who hold some sort of *propiska* – medical help and education are not a possibility. Acquiring health care has always been a problem for all Soviet citizens, requiring not only money but 'connections'. In the 1990s, hospitals lacked not only technology but basic sterilising and nursing supplies, food and personnel. Consequently most patients must be attended to, not by nurses but by family or friends. In the past members of the Soviet *nomenklatura*[21] were better cared for and the same is true of the newly affluent in post-Soviet society. However, most Roma lack either the money or connections to be admitted to the better hospitals and many die relatively young from viral infections, tuberculosis, diabetes and heart failure. Such conditions are even worse for Roma in rural villages as, of course, they are for all such post-Soviets.

The material conditions of urban, relatively élite Romani performers and intellectuals are obviously more comfortable. In the 1990s such people considered themselves 'assimilated' because they did not live in poverty, because they worked for wages and because they lived in urban apartments. The problems that concern urban Romani intellectuals, workers, or performers have more to do with self-esteem and anxieties about 'cultural loss', since non-Roma routinely dismiss Romani writers, scholars and performers as 'inauthentic Gypsies'.

Since the late 1980s, Romani cultural groups in other parts of the former Soviet bloc (Czech Republic, Hungary, Slovakia, Macedonia) have criticised these and other dominant images of Roma, instead offering alternative images ranging from TV documentaries about Romani Holocaust victims to translations of Shakespeare into Romani. The Moscow Romani Theatre, however, continued to stress entertaining non-Roma who are nostalgic for 'real Gypsies'. The Theatre's repertoire has changed very little, adding one new play by 1997, with a soundtrack from the Gipsy Kings – a move with cosmopolitan cool and panache but without reference to local issues.

## Conclusion

The political role of these Romani cultural producers in Russia could well become more crucial in countering popular sentiment against Roma. In the 1980s, even stereotypical reportage about Roma had always been balanced by success stories – biographies of dentists, priests, ethnographers and performers. But by the mid 1990s, the press had reverted to sensationalist accounts of pseudo-mystical, hypnotic and criminal 'Gypsy powers'. The papers printed interviews, not with Romani intellectuals, but with police chiefs, according them the authority of ethnographers. The media fretted about 'Gypsy dirt' and 'hyper-fertility'. In the 1990s such negative voices became more audible in the media and affected the ways Roma could deal with state bureaucrats, exchange partners, bosses or neighbours. In most regions of Russia, Roma and other non-Russians have borne the brunt of the envy and resentment of material inequalities that seem more visible after the end of state socialism. Amplified, and in some cases created, by the media, theories and rumours abound that Roma and other non-Russians have made use of shortages for profit, that they manipulated flows of goods through 'clan' mafia ties and so on. In the context of soaring inflation after the break-away of the Soviet Union's non-Russian republics, such accusations have influenced even those who have not personally experienced the extremes of what are to others dire new living conditions. In some towns, Russian inhabitants demanded that local authorities remove Romani populations because of their alleged market malpractice, a level of aggression never directed against Russian traders, and matched only by hostility shown towards Chechen and others from the Caucasus, labelled collectively as *chernye* (blacks).[22]

In fact, 'hatred' of Gypsies (as opposed to that expressed towards Chechens) was not a main plank in the political platform of young nationalists in Russia, as it has been in Romania or the Czech Republic, or even in Western Ukraine. Gypsies were not the only non-Russians against whom were projected anxieties about economic change. In Russia any 'black' face was suspect. In this comparative context, Gypsies were considered less well organised and less threatening than other non-Russians, such as Chechens. The press (and many ordinary post-Soviet citizens) portrayed Caucasians, Central Asians and other non-Russians as staging an 'invasion' from outlying points of the former Soviet Union, just when the republics had seceded. The phrase: 'they are turning Moscow into a little Caucasus', reverberated in headlines and in kitchen conversations. People assumed that 'blacks' were motivated to both 'invade' Moscow and to fight each other in the Caucasus, not by historical or economical forces (which Soviet and Imperial states partly determined) but by racial-psychological ones, by greed and 'hot blood'.

On the contrary, conflict between Russians and Roma took place at a local level, and was thus often overlooked both by police and local authorities (or else endorsed by them) and by international agencies.[23] Thus, Roma in Russia (and especially in Siberian Russia) may become potentially even more vulnerable to violence than they have been in Central and Eastern Europe, where Roma have greater institutional connections and more visible political lobbies to protest against violence and structural forms of discrimination. This is why representation (in both senses of the term, political and visual) is so crucial. If Roma were not scapegoats at the 1991 dissolution of the Soviet Empire, they have become perfectly situated for such a fate a decade later, as Russia deals with continuing economic stress and political conflict.

## References

Barranikov, A. P. (1931) *Tsygane SSSR*, Moscow: Tsentrizdat.

Bobri, V. (1961) 'Gypsies and Gypsy choruses of old Russia', *Journal of the Gypsy Lore Society* 3, 40, 3–4: 112–20, July-October.

Bogartyrev, O. (1996) 'Ne xodi s tolpoj tsyganok za kibitkoj kochevoj', *Moja Gazeta*, Samara, 3: 3.

Crowe, D. (1994) *A History of the Gypsies of Eastern Europe and Russia*, New York: St. Martin's Griffin.

Crowe, D. and Kolsti, J. (eds) (1991) *The Gypsies of Eastern Europe.* Armonk, NY: M. E. Sharpe.

Demeter, N. and Cherenkov, L. N. (1987) 'Tsygane v Moskve', in I. I. Krupnik (ed.) *Etnicheskie gruppy v gorodakh evropeiskoi chasti SSSR,* Moscow: USSR Academy of Sciences, 40–9.

Demeter-Charskaja, O. (1997) *Sud'ba Tsyganki*, Moscow: author's self-publication.

Druts, E. and Gessler, A. (1990) *Tsygane: ocherky* (Gypsies: Notes), Moscow: Soviet-skii Pisatel.

Druts, E. and Gessler, A. (1991) *Skazki Tsygan SSSR.* (Stories of the Gypsies of the USSR), Moscow: Nauka.

Fraser, A. (1992a) *The Gypsies*, Oxford: Blackwell.

Fraser, A. (1992b) 'The Rom Migrations', *Journal of the Gypsy Lore Society* 2, 2: 131–45.

German, A. V. (1930) *Bibliografiya o tsyganakh*, Moscow: Tsentrizday.

Goskomstat, USSR (1991) *Natsional'nyi sostav naseleniya SSSR po dannym vsesoyuznoi naseleniya 1989 g.,* Moscow: Finansy i Statistika.

Guy, W. (1998[75]) 'Ways of looking at Roma: the case of Czechoslovakia', in D. Tong (ed.), 13–68.

Hancock, I. (1987) *The Pariah Syndrome: An Account of Gypsy Slavery and Persecution*, Ann Arbor: Karoma.

Hancock, I. (1998) 'Duty and beauty, possession and truth: "lexical impoverishment" as control', in D. Tong (ed.), 115–28.

Hübschmannová, M. (1998[84]) 'Economic stratification and interaction: Roma, an ethnic jati in East Slovakia', in D. Tong (ed.), 232–67.

Human Rights Watch (1995) 'Crime or simply punishment? Racist attacks by Moscow law enforcement', *Helsinki Watch Report*, 12, September.

Humphrey, C. (1993) 'Myth-making, narratives and the dispossessed in Russia', paper read to the Society of the Anthropology of Europe, at 1993 meeting of *American Anthropological Association*, Washington, D. C.

Kaminski, I.-M. (1980) *The State of Ambiguity: Studies of Gypsy Refugees*, Gothenburg: University of Gothenburg.

Lemon, A. (1991) 'Roma (Gypsies) in the Soviet Union and the Moscow Teatr "Romen"', *Nationalities Papers* 19, 3: 359–72.

Liégeois J.-P. and Gheorghe, N. (1995) *Roma/Gypsies: a European Minority*, London: Minority Rights Group.

Lipetskaja Gazeta (1996) 'Tsygane shumnoju tolpoju' (Gypsies in a Noisy Crowd), *Lipetskaja Gazeta* 10: 7, February.

Mikeladze, N. (1991) 'Bitva nad Pskovom', *Komsomolskaja Pravda*, 17 August.

Pashkov, A. (1991) 'Vystrely v Alapaevske' (A gunshot in Alapaevsk), *Izvestija*, 29 July.

Plotnikov, S. (1991) 'S drekolom – na tsygan?', *Rossija*, 1–8 October.

Ploxinskij, M. (1890) 'Tsygane staroj malorossii', in N. A. Janchuka (ed.) *Etnograficheskoe obozrenie* 4, Moscow: Moscow University, Etnograficheskago Otdela, 95–117.

Popova, E. and Bril', M. (1932) 'Tsygane v SSSR', *Sovetskoe Stroitel'stvo* 2.

Radzinsky, S. (1945) 'A Stirring Play at the Moscow Gypsy Theatre', *Journal of the Gypsy Lore Society* 3, 24, 3–4: 120–121.

Radzinsky, S. (1947) 'Moscow's Gypsy Theatre', *JGLS* 3, 26, 3–4.

Rom-Lebedev, I. (1990) *Ot tsyganskovo xora do teatra 'Romen'*, Moscow: 'Iskusstvo' Press.

Slichenko, N. (1984) 'From campfire to footlights: Gypsies in the theatre', *Unesco Courier*, October, 26–8.

Stewart, M. (1997) *The Time of the Gypsies*, Boulder and Oxford: Westview Press.

Tong, D. (ed.) (1998) *Gypsies: An Interdisciplinary Reader,* New York: Garland.

## Notes

1    In 1989 there were officially 262,015 *tsygane* in the USSR, 152,939 in Russia (Goskomstat, USSR 1991). By contrast the 1989 census counted only 102,938 Abkhazians, who had their own autonomous republic even though a minority in it.

2    There had been Tsarist attempts at assimilationist agricultural schemes. In 1836, for instance, Tsarist ministers established, in the newly acquired Moldovan territories, settlements named *Faraonovka* (Pharoah's) and *Kair* (Cairo), the names inspired by tales that Gypsies came from Egypt (See German (1930: 29), also Druts and Gessler (1990). For a summary of these sources in English, see Crowe (1994: 151–74). Note also that similar policies were more broadly applied to Jews and others as well.

3    GARF, f. 1235, op. 15[140]. 29 December 1927.

4    For accounts see Popova and Bril' (1932), Demeter and Cherenkov (1987), Druts and Gessler (1990). See also Lemon (1991) and Crowe (1994: 174–94).

5    Sources include oral histories recounted by Roma in Europe. See 'Hitler is, Sztalin is deportalta oket' in *Amaro Drom*, a Hungarian-language journal for Roma (1991, no.7). See also 'Gypsies in New Russia', in *Moscow Tribune*, 15 May 1993.

6    Although see Guy (1998[75]: 41): 'Tribal' settlements in Slovakia . . . are far more obviously the direct product of their historical situation than an age-old Romani tradition.'

7    In Russia, most Roma were 'serfs of the crown', not enslaved as in Wallachia and Moldavia. This meant they carried a tax burden but were not necessarily bonded to an estate (though Orlov's Romani serfs seem to have been of the bonded sort).

8   Ploxinskij claims that, even in 1765, the year Romani Atamans (headmen) in Ukraine were stripped of local authority and Roma were required to register with military regiments, 'settled Gypsies were relatively not few' (1890: 99).

9   GARF f. 1235, op. 123, d. 27(3).

10  Other socialist satellite countries, such as Hungary, Czechoslovakia and Bulgaria, followed suit with parliamentary acts and decrees settling Gypsies in 1958. Poland had such a statute in 1952, issuing another in 1964.

11  Nadezhda G. Demeter, cited in a newspaper interview (*Nedelia*, 4–10 September 1989).

12  In the 1990s, a few families were rumored still to travel seasonally in Siberia (but since other Soviets often label various Central Asian refugees or other itinerants 'Gypsies' [see Humphrey 1993], journalistic sightings of 'Gypsy camps' around Soviet train stations should not be taken at face value).

13  For remarks on a roundup and resettlement of *Vlax* Roma camping 'within 45 versts of Moscow' see Gerasimov, inspector for the organization of Gypsy collectives, 8 September 1933 (report to TsIK and MOSO, in GARF fond 1235, opis 123, dela 28, 161).

14  GARF Fond 1235 Opis 123 Delo 28(4) [1933].

15  For Soviet press reports, see, for instance, *Bednota*,1928 and 1929. For archival accounts, see GARF, f. 3316, passim.

16  GARF, f. 3316, op 28, d. 794.

17  *Glasnost* (openness) was one of Gorbachev's liberalising measures during the second half of the 1980s allowing people to speak out in the hope this would accelerate reform.

18  When Moscow was evacuated, the company could not return until 1943. Most remaining Romani performers fled to Tashkent on their own. On war-time concert tours, see Rom-Lebedev (1990), and Demeter-Charskaja (1997). On the war-time and immediate post-war periods, see Radzinsky (1945 and 1947).

19  RTsXIDNI, f. 17, op. 125, d. 570.

20  *Perestroika* ([economic] restructuring) was another of Gorbachev's liberalising measures in the second half of the 1980s.

21  Trusted Party members appointed to influential positions in the administration and economy.

22  The term 'black' occupies a different place from that in American English. 'Blackness' is everywhere culturally constructed, but in Russia, 'black' (*chernyj*) refers very broadly to a whole range of people, including those whom North Americans probably would describe as 'olive-skinned', with dark eyes and hair. *Temnyj* (dark) or *smuglyj* (swarthy) may substitute as an equivalent.

23  For accounts of violence and for examples of press inciting discrimination, see Bogatyrev (1996), *Lipetskaja Gazeta* (1996), Mikeladze (1991), Pashkov (1991), Plotnikov, (1991).

## CHAPTER TEN

# The Baltic States, Belarus, Ukraine and Moldova:

## Reflections on life in the former USSR[1]

*Valdemar Kalinin and
Christine Kalinina*

T he Romani people have always excited both the interest and apprehension of others, particularly when they swept across Europe in great migratory waves. In the past decade the third such wave has put Roma into the headlines in almost every European country, including both the former Communist-ruled states of Central and Eastern Europe from which this migration originated, and the countries of the West where many Roma have recently sought asylum.

When the *first* great migration of Roma to Europe by way of Greece took place from the eleventh century onwards, they sometimes explained their wanderings with the tale that they were Christian pilgrims from Egypt, performing a religious penance. In the *second* migration, of Kalderash families who spread across the world following the abolition of Romani slavery in what is now Romania in the mid-nineteenth century, Roma arrived in their new destinations without giving any motive for their journeys – but in any case who would have been concerned about events in the far-away Danubian provinces of Wallachia and Moldavia?

As the *third* migratory wave from Central and Eastern Europe, began to arrive in the West – including North America – in the 1980s, reaching its height in the second half of the 1990s, the Romani newcomers once more offered an explanation. In the 1980s this was that they were fleeing from the persecution of the Communists, a perfectly acceptable reason to Western authorities while the Cold War continued. But after the fall of Communism, starting in 1989 in Central Europe and reaching the Soviet Union in 1991, the justification for the departure of Roma that they were still being persecuted was to prove more problematic. Those arriving in the West during the 1990s were accused of being economic migrants making false claims for asylum and the spectacle of Romanian Roma begging on the streets of Western cities did not help promote a sympathetic response. Nevertheless, it was undoubtedly deep unhappiness about their own situation in their homelands that drove Roma to leave.

This chapter mainly discusses the situation of Roma in the countries lying between present-day Russia and Poland, that is the Baltic states of Lithuania, Latvia and Estonia as well as those of Belarus, the Ukraine and Moldova. These were historically part of the Russian and Polish Empires and the memory of this is still strong in the contemporary consciousness of many Roma. For example, Roma living on the border between Belarus and Russia still remember a stone cone beyond Smolensk, now overgrown and long forgotten by the indigenous population, which used to separate the Polish and Russian Empires in the seventeenth century. All Roma who live to the East of this cone are called *Ruska* (Russian) Roma, while all living to the West of this marker are considered as *Polska* (Polish) Roma.

Apart from this historic link there is another reason for including reference to both Russia and Poland in this chapter, for there has been Roma population movement within this broad area crossing current state boundaries both before and since the break-up of the Soviet Union in 1991. Unlike Roma in Central Europe who could seek asylum in the West, these Roma could only migrate within the region during the 1990s because of continuing visa requirements.

## Roma in the pre-Soviet and Soviet periods

Eastern Europe and Russia are not usually known for sensitive handling of minorities particularly during the periods of the Russian Empire (1456–1917) and of its successor the Soviet Union (1917–91). Nevertheless, it must be acknowledged that in the countries of this broad region Roma have been treated in a more humanitarian way than in Western Europe, where far more severe measures were taken against them.

Within Russia itself many initiatives were positively philanthropic, if misguided and based on false assumptions. Such a case was the attempt by Emperor Nicholas I to settle nomadic Roma in Southern Bessarabia (present-day Moldova), following legislation enacted on 18 February 1836. Houses and 11,200 hectares of fertile land were provided for 752 nomadic Roma families in two all-Romani villages bearing the exotic names of Kair (Cairo) with 141 houses, and Pharaonovka (Pharaoh's Place) with 146 houses. After a prosperous start these villages ceased to exist in the 1880s as the Romani inhabitants of Kair burned down their houses and dispersed.

When the Bolsheviks assumed power they initially scorned their predecessors' policies towards Roma, particularly as regards these villages, and reversed the Tsarist approach. In 1925 the Soviet government recognised Roma as a national minority within the Soviet Union with the right to be educated in the Romani language. This was announced by the publication of an open letter from the Romani leaders, A. Taranov and I. Lebedev. At the same time Taranov became President of the pan-Romani Union after the first Romani Congress had taken place, although this Union lasted only until 1928. Meanwhile, urgent preparations began to establish similar unions in the Ukraine and in what is now Belarus but were successful only in the Ukraine where an all-Ukrainian Conference of Working Gypsies was held.

Like other minorities, Roma began to be involved in the process of 'building communism', through schools and colleges, collective farms and co-operatives. The peasantry was forcibly collectivised in 1931, although model Romani collective farms had already been formed in 1926–7, some based on former Jewish collective farms. Most were abandoned by the beginning of the Second World War as the Roma fled, but at least two Romani co-operative farms continued to exist, one in Aleksandrovka (near Smolensk in Russia) and another in the mountain village of Koroliovo (in the Carpathian region of the Ukraine).

The example of the Jewish minority was later used again for Roma when, during the six months from April to September in 1937, over 1,500 Romani families were transported to Siberia in a secret experiment and forcibly settled in newly prepared wooden huts in the Taiga camp. However, this attempt to found an autonomous regional 'Romanistan', following the Jewish model of Birobidzan in 1934, proved unsuccessful. Worse was to come for many Roma, particularly in the Polish and Baltic lands of the Empire, after the German invasion of Russia.

After the Second World War nomadism was finally banned in a 1956 decree that was soon to be imitated in other countries of Central and Eastern Europe. The aim was to recruit all Roma into full-time employment in standard occupations. While some groups adapted successfully to post-war conditions, such as Roma in Lithuania who traded in goods in short supply that were manufactured in 'underground' factories, others found it harder to adjust as demand ceased for some of their usual products and services. As the economy stagnated at the turn of the 1980s non-Roma were sometimes driven to enter traditional Romani occupations, undermining the confident belief of Roma that they were always shrewder and more capable than gadje (non-Roma) and were capable of anything. In some places gadje took over or made inroads into traditional Romani businesses like fortune-telling, hawking, car-dealing and horse-trading, etc.

## Roma experience of post-Communism

Roma in the successor states that emerged from the former Soviet Union feel a deep ambivalence about the demise of the previous system. On the one hand some eagerly seized the opportunity to make use of the new freedoms to pursue their entrepreneurial commercial activities that were previously illegal.

On the other hand, many take a negative view of the break-up of the former Soviet Union, just as their fellow-Roma elsewhere in former Eastern Europe see the fall of the Berlin Wall as marking a reversal in their fortunes.

In the turbulent and uncertain conditions of regime change in the early 1990s many ordinary citizens sought scapegoats for their frustrations and this followed a familiar pattern of open violence against marginal and suspect minorities such as Jews, Caucasians (particularly from Chechnya) and Roma. Many of these groups were blamed for profiting illegally at the expense of members of the majority populations who had fallen on hard times. While Chechens were accused of being involved in mafia activities (later of terrorism), the spark inciting pogroms against Roma was the visible wealth of affluent Romani traders. This resentment was expressed in everyday conversations along the lines of: 'How on earth do semi-literate people without proper qualifications, like Roma, manage to drive Mercedes and own mobile phones?' Although such views mostly surfaced only in popular speech, they were occasionally repeated in the media by TV presenters. For example, a Russian Channel Four programme, *Pogovorim na chistotu* (Let's speak plainly), discussed this topic and featured Romani groups. Non-Roma politicians were rather less inclined to make political capital from verbal attacks on Roma than in other countries of Central and Eastern Europe but occasionally this did occur.

Another section of the Romani population which took advantage of the loosening of restrictions after 1991 were activists aiming to raise the political profile of Roma, but such would-be political leaders, along with prosperous Roma businessmen and their families, soon became targets of various criminal groups that either threatened to kidnap their children or else burn down their houses unless protection money was paid. Some were driven to emigrate while those that remained were viewed with scepticism, both by the majority population and local authorities, who regarded them as a nuisance and sometimes sought to regulate and manipulate them. Not only did the authorities tend to ignore or dismiss Roma complaints about illegal acts against them but were even known to make use of anti-Roma criminal factions for their own purposes.

## Lithuania

Lithuania was the first country to break away from the USSR in 1991, and in the same year the first pogroms against Roma began. Prosperous Romani families had their property looted in the towns of Kaunas and Shyaulyai and three Roma were killed as a result of this violence, while cars were burnt or vandalised. However, when Roma applied for police protection they were told: 'Go to Russia – it will be quieter for you there'. Their pleas, that they were Lithuanian citizens and this was their motherland, were ignored.

Consequently, many Roma from Lithuania abandoned their country and went not only to Russia but also to Belarus. Many others fled to the West.

In response to these threats Roma began to organise and to seek ways of protecting themselves. Many different unions and associations sprang up and eleven were registered with the Lithuanian Department of National Minorities. The activities of these organisations were concentrated around problems such as education (Romani schools and crèches), employment (finding jobs for Roma and starting up a sawmill) and legal assistance. This last activity was particularly important since Lithuania, like other Baltic states, was extremely hostile to inhabitants from minority groups. Consequently, ethnicity (e.g. Russian, Jew or Gypsy) was still recorded in passports, even though other states of the former Soviet Union, e.g. Russia, Belarus, Ukraine and Moldova, etc had abolished this practice.

In June 1995 the Panevezis Romani Association organised the five day pan-Lithuanian Romani Conference, funded by the Soros Foundation. This included a crèche for fifteen Romani children under the supervision of two Romani teachers. Two years later, in 1997, the Department of Education agreed to open a Romani school in Porubanka, in the suburbs of Vilnius, where there is a large all-Roma settlement consisting of Lithuanian Roma and Lithuanian *Kalderari*. Although education in Romani would have been greatly helped by a standardised Romani alphabet this has yet to be agreed.

Another feature of community development among Roma throughout the region, both before but particularly after the ending of Communist rule, has been the growth in the influence of organised religion. In Lithuania one of the Romani cultural associations, led by K. Vysotskas, set out to create a Romani Christian Training Centre. I joined in the response to this initiative by visiting Lithuania in 1996 and subsequently translated the Gospel of St. Matthew into the local Romani dialect. Since then the Centre has been supplied with a considerable number of books.

The first Lithuanian Romani association was established with the assistance of Stanislaw Stankiewicz, the noted Romani activist from Poland. The Lithuanian *Kalderari* founded their own Union and set up a successful Romani music ensemble. Despite these positive community developments, the eleven Unions which had been created in Lithuania by 2000 failed to unite against non-Romani elements and criminals but instead became embroiled in mutual recriminations and disputes. Power struggles within the councils of elders, also evident in neighbouring countries, even led to the recruitment of non-Roma security guards in an attempt to control other rival factions. Through this period violent attacks against Roma intensified, which led to more Roma fleeing to the West.

## Latvia and Estonia

Latvia and Estonia were notable for their vigorous attempts at ethnic cleansing by legalistic methods. Although the strategy of refusing citizenship on the grounds of poor knowledge of the local language was directed mainly against Russian inhabitants, Roma too were victims. Only genuine Latvian and Estonian Roma were granted citizenship and many Roma in Estonia were relative newcomers since most indigenous Estonian Roma (*Laiusy* and *Laloritka*) had been exterminated by joint German-Estonian punishment squads during the war.

Latvia later proved to be the first state in the region to react positively to the new situation of Roma when, on the 6 July 1996, the Latvian government issued a statement regarding national minorities in Latvia in which Roma were specifically mentioned. In addition to this formal recognition a consultative council was established, followed by the appointment of three regional consultants, all of whom were Roma: Janis Neilands in Kurzemia, Normundus Rudievics (an engineer) in Vidzemia and Viktors Petrovs (a lawyer) in Latgalia.

Normundas Rudievics was later elected to the state parliament. He also successfully established a functioning cultural association, with four branches, offering advice to Roma at a twice-weekly surgery. One successful action by this association was in challenging the manager in the small town of Tulsa, who had barred Roma from his café and refused to serve them. A long article in the newspaper *Republic*, based on an interview with the last Rom to be refused entry, I. Dolman, eventually led to the café's licence being revoked (*Republic*, 26 July 1999). This is the only Romani association which is effective in protecting Roma, and this is entirely due to the chairman being an MP with power and influence.

In Estonia, where there are only 800 Roma, there are at present five registered organisations: three cultural societies, a Romani Pentecostal Church in Voeru and the Romani Youth Centre. The Estonian Government, in collaboration with the Finnish authorities, recently held an International Training Seminar/Conference for Roma from Estonia, Latvia and Lithuania in Tallinn on 22–24 November 2000.

## Russia and the Caucasian Republics

The new Russian Federation also experienced its share of anti-Roma pogroms in the early 1990s. In 1992–3 pogroms were recorded in Alapayevsk (in the Urals), Novosibirsk, Nievel, Ostrov, Safonovo, Yaroslavl, Tula, Samara, etc. The violence against Roma reached such a peak that special police forces were called in to protect them and many Roma fled to Belarus.

In contrast, there were positive developments at the end of the decade.

On 25 November 1999 Roma in the Russian Federation were granted national cultural autonomy, with the Romani barrister, Alexei Molchanov, as their legal representative. The main associations of the Roma in Moscow (*Romani Kher*) and St. Petersburg (*Romani Obshichina*) established branches in such regions and cities as Tula, Komi Autonomous Republic, Yekaterinburg, Samara, Astrakhan, Volgograd, Novosibirsk, Krasnodar and Voronezh. This newly-acknowledged autonomous status was marked by a large scale Romani Festival in Moscow from 31 January to 2 February 2000, organised by a *Sinti Rom*, Yanka Mauer. In November of the same year, the Council of Europe held a round table conference on Romani rights in Moscow. Similar conferences were later held in Moldova and the Ukraine.

Other Roma live to the south, beyond the borders of the Russian Federation, but far less is known about their situation. Some of these Roma have moved to European parts of the former Soviet Union, since after the ending of Communist rule many *Luli*, in particular, abandoned their homes in the Central Asian Republics and migrated westwards to Russia, Belarus and Moldova. Although it is not known exactly how many Roma inhabit Kazakhstan, there is a small Romani association of *Ruska* Roma led by Grigorii Vinogradov, while the *Luli* of Tajikistan and Uzbekistan have established their own *Luli* association under the leadership of T. Akhmetov. The Caucasus states of Georgia, Azerbaijan and Armenia are home to various Romani groups drawn from the *Ruska* Roma, *Luli*, *Bosha* (*Loma*), Crimean Roma, *Lovari*, *Kalderari*, *Karachi*, *Suzmany*, *Doma,* etc. but so far do not appear to have been able to set up any form of association or committee.

## *Ukraine, Belarus and Moldova*

One of the worst areas in the region for breaches of Romani human rights is the Ukraine. Reported incidents of violence against Roma were widespread, some implicating the police as perpetrators. This sad state of affairs was comprehensively documented in 1997 by the European Roma Rights Centre in *The Misery of Law: The Rights of Roma in the Transcarpathian Region of Ukraine* (ERRC, Country Report no. 4, April). As a result of such hostility, both in the Ukraine and in the Baltic States to the north, many families decided to leave their homes and the Romani population in neighbouring Belarus soared from 12,000 in 1986 to a staggering 29,000 in 1999. In bizarre contrast only one isolated case of violence against Roma was recorded in Belarus – in Svetlogorsk in 1993.

Fortunately, the Ukrainian Roma's internal system of legal self-regulation was still based on an appointed *starosta* (headman or mayor) for each Romani community which meant that a wise and courageous person, with the respect of the community, was usually capable of co-ordinating resistance when such attacks occurred.

Nevertheless, it took time for Roma to adapt to their new situation, and organise a network of cultural associations, centres and clubs. Significantly, in the former Soviet territories, it was only in the Ukraine that there were attempts to create a Romani political party. There are at present twelve differ- ent associations and Romani cultural centres, while in Moldova there are five registered organisations (one led by the folklorist and notable poet, Georgis Kantya) and in Belarus, two Romani cultural societies. In both the Ukraine and Moldova there is a relatively high proportion of well-educated Roma, most of whom are nowadays unemployed or work for low wages in jobs which do not utilise their qualifications.

### Poland

An example from Poland illustrates the bitter divisions that have arisen within traditional Roma communities, confronted by the new and challenging condi- tions of the post-Communist world in Central and Eastern Europe.

During August and September 1999 my Roma friends and I were shocked to watch a polemic video accusing the leader of the Polish Roma of violating the traditional Romani code of justice. This high-quality video had been pre- pared by Polish Lowland Roma and sent throughout the world to wherever Polish Roma were currently living and had a very detrimental effect – not only on Polish Roma but on Roma everywhere. To compound his apparent crime this leader (*Shero Rom*) failed to turn up at an annual meeting (*tselio*) of Polish Romani elders because he feared being denounced and vilified. Eventually, the anger and passion cooled down, and in spite of the heated controversy at this meeting the *Shero Rom* managed to retain his position as leader of the overwhelming majority of Roma in Poland. (The *Kalderari* Roma have their own council of elders, called the *Kris*.)

The institution of *Shero Rom*,[2] established by German Roma in 1925 and seen as the mainstay of the traditional juridical system, had been undermined by these events and was in danger of collapse. As a result of the *Shero Rom*'s failure to attend the annual meeting and his dismissal of his two advisers (*Yunkari*), some Polish Romani groups (*Kalishyaki, Muzynki, Jagielyanie* and some *Leshaki*) left the pan-Polish Romani Union and held their own election in Wroclaw in 1999. The *Kalishyaki* elder, Radno, at present living in the USA became the alternative *Shero Rom* for this minor group, but some of the defecting *Kalishyaki*, currently living in Sweden, rejoined the original Romani Union.

### Conclusion

The Roma of former Eastern Europe and the Soviet Union are confronted with problems of adaptation to an uncertain future. This is particularly

difficult for some members of sub-groups who are among the most conservative of peoples, in some cases even clinging to calculating in outdated monetary systems. Nor are they always the best informed of peoples and a
lingering fear of Germans can still be encountered, based on the belief that
they were not wholly defeated in the Second World War. There remain great
differences between the various Roma groups and, speaking generally, it
would seem that the Baltic Roma are at greater risk of unemployment than
Balkan and Carpathian Roma and *Kalderari* who have more skills and
experience.

Would-be modernisers in the Roma community also face problems.
Romani intellectuals are under pressure from both sides: gadje scorn them as
Gypsies, while their fellow Roma disapprove of them because they do not live
like other Roma. In fact, what might seem the road to progress presents a
dilemma, for adhering strictly to the customary Romani code rules out a
good education and becoming an intellectual. In the past, school has never
been a priority among Romani people. Many still believe that school and
education have a detrimental effect on Romani culture because they conquer
the spirit of Roma and threaten to alienate their children. In other words, in
the Romani mind there is often a negative attitude to non-Romani education
which is not viewed as an asset but as a burden. This attitude is undoubtedly a
contributory factor to poor school attendance by Romani children in both
East and West.

There are comparable problems in adapting traditional systems of self-
regulation to the modern world. Under previous internal juridical systems
what are seen as characteristic Romani volatility and emotion were channelled in accepted ways but a new system of social accountability has not yet
developed within Roma communities. Although people still come together in
social congregations, the heat of the moment takes over when it comes to
resolving important problems.

In present circumstances therefore it is only where Roma associations are
inspired by prudent and wise leaders, including Romani intellectuals, that this
typical Roma excitability will be usefully directed. Given the undeniable
importance of religion among Roma nowadays throughout the region, I
would dare to predict that the future lies in the link between church and
education. The rational perspective of atheism has always been rejected by
Roma and in their consciousness openness to God has always played a decisive role. If Roma come upon a difficulty, they always say: 'Let God's will be
done'. In the past Roma had little choice when their strategy for survival was
to resist the intrusion of the external gadjo world. However, this is no longer
viable and nowadays well-meaning, dedicated and patient volunteers drawn
from churches and elsewhere, of both Romani and non-Romani origin, are
needed to help create new ways for Roma to survive in a dramatically
changing world.

## Notes

1   This chapter is based on a lifetime's experience and the contributions of friends and colleagues in the region.

2   This system had featured prominently in the accounts of various scholars and had been praised by many as 'ideal'. It should be appreciated that the role of the *Shero Rom* is extremely difficult and complex for he has to deal with a wide variety of cases. In addition it is difficult for Romani psychology to accept that somebody who is not wealthier is placed above them. The *Shero Rom* is not supported financially by those over whom he exercises jurisdiction.

## Selected Eastern European Countries (with territory formerly in USSR)

Compiled by Valdemar Kalinin, London 20/12/2000

### Romani Community Profile

| Country | Total pop.[a] (mill.) | Romani Pop.[b] (thou) | % Roma | % Romani m.tongue | Roma leadership | Formal Romani organisations | Governmental representation[c] | Romani education initiatives |
|---|---|---|---|---|---|---|---|---|
| Russia | 146 | 307 | 0.21 | 80 | Elders' council | Cultural association/union | Romani autonomy Dept of National Minorities., | Romani groups in Moscow, Tula, Voronezh, Tver, Tatarstan |
| Poland | 38.6 | 56 | 0.14 | 92 | National Shero Rom | Cultural association | National Minorities Group representation | Romani school in Suwalki (Polish language) |
| Kazakhstan | 16.7 | 47 | 0.28 | 92 | Shero Rom in each settlement/community | Cultural association | None | |
| Belarus | 10.4 | 28[d] | 0.27 | 96 | Community council Counsellors Arbitrators | Two cultural associations | None | |
| Latvia | 2.4 | 11.5[d] | 0.48 | 96 | Romani elders' association | Five cultural associations/societies | Romani MP | Romani taught as a subject in Ventspils, Elgava, Sabile. Religious instruction |
| Lithuania | 3.6 | 4.1 | 0.11 | 99 | Romani pan-country council | 11 Romani cultural associations /societies | One advisor, Roma recognised as as Nat. minority | Romani school in Vilnius (Russian language). |
| Estonia | 1.4 | 0.8 | 0.06 | 98 | Romani elders' council | 5 regional cultural associations/societies | None | |
| Ukraine | 49.2 | 130[d] | 0.26 | 66 | Local elders' council Heads of settlements/ (W.Ukr) camps | 12 cultural unions/associations | One Romani adviser — consultant | Nurseries Religious instruction in Romani |
| Moldova | 4.4 | 22 | 0.5 | 68 | Elders' group | 5 Romani associations | Adviser in Dept. of National Minorities | Romani classes in church |

Notes:

(a) Source: CIA Factbook — estimates for July 2000.

(b) Roma population figures are mainly estimates published in regional media, based on projections from older Communist administrative records. These estimates are regarded as far more reliable than more recent census figures where Roma often preferred to declare other ethnic identities.

(c) Kalderari generally have separate arrangements (e.g. In Poland, Belarus, Lithuania, Moldova), also Lovari in Poland.

(d) These figures are far higher than those generally accepted (eg. by EU) but have appeared in local media as extrapolations from 1989 Soviet census or consequence of recent migration (Belarus).

## CHAPTER ELEVEN

# Poland: the clash of tradition and modernity

*Lech Mróz*

The dissolution of the Soviet empire and the resultant economic and political changes in the formerly Communist countries of Central and Eastern Europe were no kind of 'magical' turning point which would bring about only beneficial changes. This was as true for the Roma as for any other ethnic group in Poland. Although the countries of this European region vary considerably in terms of their cultural, religious and historical backgrounds, there were nevertheless broad similarities in domestic policies and their implementation. This is particularly true of policy towards minorities, both the action taken by the authorities and the attitudes of the majority population. But it is also important to take account of the specific characteristics of individual countries for these played a significant part in mediating the experience of the Roma.

Poland has always been more open to contacts with the Western world than other countries of the former Soviet bloc. It was, for example, easier for all citizens, including the Roma, to obtain a passport and travel abroad. Such factors should be borne in mind when trying to understand the nature of the systemic transformations in Poland after 1989 and when considering the situation of the Roma in Poland today.

One important element distinguishing pre-1989 Poland from its neighbours was its economic system. Poland had the highest proportion of private businesses, in both the manufacturing and service sectors, of all the state socialist countries. Agriculture in particular was based on the private ownership of small and medium size holdings, which explains why all farm work exploited horse power. Horses are only occasionally used in agriculture nowadays, but thirty to thirty-five years ago all the machines used for ploughing, sowing, harvesting, threshing, etc. were horse-driven. At that time trading in horses was a well-developed branch of the rural economy and every year spring and autumn markets attracted great numbers of peasants, who went there to buy or sell horses.

The Roma, too, dealt in horses. Consequently the importance of horses in farming must be taken into consideration when discussing the life and culture of Roma in Poland, since the location of these seasonal markets determined their pattern of travel and opportunities for making their living. In winter, when they were not travelling, the Roma looked for long-term acco-modation in small towns and villages, sometimes staying in farm houses whose owners they knew from their mutual business dealings.

## Historical background

By the end of the Second World War Poland was inhabited by several distinct groups of Roma. In the Carpathians and the southern region next to the mountains were numerous communities whose ancestors had arrived two hundred years earlier from Slovakia and Hungary, on the southern side of the Carpathian mountains. Their main occupation was that of blacksmith and Romani smiths manufactured all kind of tools for the shepherds, who spent the summer months with their flocks on the upper pastures. These smiths also repaired tools used in agriculture.

Since the 1870s other groups of Roma had migrated from the territories of Transylvania and Wallachia across the areas that had once been the south eastern part of Poland, but which are now part of Ukraine. These were the *Lovara* and *Kalderasha* groups. Some of them remained in eastern Poland or went on to Russia, others headed for central Poland and still further to west-ern Europe (see Ficowski 1985: 78–87, Winstedt 1912–13: 244–304).

Many small groups of Roma lived in the eastern and north-eastern parts of Poland, mostly settled in small towns. Archives confirm that they owned cottages and small plots of land but their main sources of income were from working as horse dealers, blacksmiths and in other metal-working crafts. These Roma also worked for large and middle-sized estates and on the farms of the petty gentry. One distinctive group in the small town of Smorgoń, in what was formerly north-eastern Poland but is now Belarus, trained perform-ing bears for the famous 'Smorgoń Academy'. Animal training was yet another of the traditional Romani occupations (Mróz 1992: 189–90). The latter groups identified themselves as *Polska Roma* (Polish Roma) and were also to be found in other parts of Poland. Among the *Polska Roma* two regional subgroups can be distinguished, the *Sasytka Roma* inhabiting the western and north western parts of the country and the *Xaladytka Roma*, located in the east (see Mróz 1979a: 20–26). All these acknowledged the authority of a common leader and, although differentiated because of their different social surroundings, they generally considered themselves as one group. Other groups of Roma appeared in Poland at various times but it is not now possible to ascertain their identity.

This relatively stable situation was brusquely disrupted by the outbreak of World War Two. The Roma populations in all of the countries occupied by the Nazis were affected by their savage persecution of Roma as a targeted group. Part of the Auschwitz Concentration Camp in southern Poland was the *Zigeunerlager* (Gypsy camp), to which Roma were brought from all over Europe and which became an enormous mass grave of their people (Ficowski 1985: 108–51, Mróz 1984: 5–14). In wartime Poland the Roma tried to hide in forests and were hunted like game. However, the situation of Roma in those parts of the southern mountains which were annexed by the (pro-Nazi) Slovakian puppet state was a little less extreme since the Roma population in Slovakia was very large and the relatively small numbers of additional Roma of Polish origin often escaped official attention.

## The changing situation of Roma in Poland from 1945 to 1989

Many Roma in Poland perished during the war and the number who survived is still unknown, though probably no more than 20,000 to 30,000. Before 1939 there were estimated to be twice or even three times this number.[1] The war may have completely destroyed the former position of Roma in Poland, but its immediate aftermath brought more upheaval – especially as a result of shifting state boundaries. Those Roma of former eastern Poland, who had been in hiding in forests and villages, lost their Polish citizenship when the Polish-Soviet frontier moved westwards. Fewer than one hundred Romani families arrived in Poland from the areas annexed to the Soviet Union and were resettled, together with other displaced Polish nationals who had also been inhabitants of the former eastern borderland.

Over a decade later in 1957 and 1958 some of the *Xaladytka Roma* from the area which had formerly been part of Lithuania and from Belorussia, managed to leave the Soviet Union, and come to Poland. This resettlement resulted from political changes following the the death of Stalin and the accession to power of Krushchev. These later arrivals joined their kinsfolk, who had been resettled previously, and resumed a nomadic way of life. Nomadism had been impossible during the war and afterwards in the Soviet Union. Not all these *Xaladytka Roma* were successful in moving back home and many of them still live outside Poland near the Belarus-Lithuanian border in the towns of Ejszyszki (Lithuania) and Lida (Belarus) (Mróz 1979a: 20–6).

Many factors contributed to changes in Romani culture and community relations in the period after the Second World War. Among the most significant was the fact that families became dispersed and traditional bonds of social structures were broken and some rules of *romanipen* (the fundamental norms of the Romani way of life and cultural identity) had to be suspended, particularly those concerning food taboos and the prohibition of contacts with certain categories of people. In addition some Roma leaders lost their authority.

In the immediate postwar years the new Communist authorities in Poland were preoccupied with the struggle for power and the entire apparatus of repression was engaged in this task. This explains why the Roma were left alone for a while, giving them a brief respite to recover from the shock of extermination, to restore social ties and to try and resume their former way of life. The Roma who had formerly lived a nomadic life, the *Polska Roma*, *Lovara* and *Kalderasha*, attempted to rebuild their social world in this way but small groups or single families, belonging to other subgroups, either left Poland or were assimilated into other larger groups. The settled Carpathian Roma had few opportunities for change. Their villages were within the Polish state once more and the restored state borders were strictly controlled. For these Roma it meant losing access to and breaking ties with related groups, of similar culture and language, living on the other side of the Carpathian mountains in Slovakia.

The authorities finally turned their attention to the nomadic Roma in 1952. Their need to 'subordinate' all social groups was challenged by the independent nomadic way of life with its avoidance of state control. This way of life was regarded as traditional, old-fashioned and unresponsive to new ideas of a happy society, engaged in 'building socialism'. Measures were taken to persuade Roma to settle in the underpopulated northern and western territories (which had been abandoned by many of their previous German inhabitants).[2] Such initiatives initially appeared effective, especially in the autumn, since it enabled Roma to find accommodation for the coming winter, but in the following spring the Roma would often resume their wandering.

The authorities also had another reason for turning their attention to the Roma. A 'socialist' command economy was being introduced, in which all economic activities were to be wholly subordinated to the institutions of the state and centrally controlled. Roma who made their livelihood dealing in horses and practising crafts involving farm equipment were seen as entrepreneurs and associated with the system of private land ownership. Moreover they never paid taxes. Consequently Roma were not only encouraged to settle but also persecuted and wandering groups were often driven away in order to prevent them making business contacts with peasants.

The subsistence system of the Roma allowed them to find their own economic niche – that sector of the market where they could sell their skills and which was never filled by the state economy – and it was this flexibility that made them independent. The characteristic Romani occupations turned out to be quite profitable and nomadic Roma, in particular, grew relatively rich in comparison with settled, mountain Roma and Polish peasants. Their growing prosperity was evident from their wagons. Before the war the nomadic Roma had travelled the country on simple, horse-drawn carts, much like those used by peasants, which carried people, goods and chattels. On making a halt the Roma families would put up tents. Only the few richest owned wagons with internal living accommodation and these were small and had wooden wheels. In the first years after the war these carts and wagons were much the same but in the late 1950s and early 1960s an increasing number of Roma families were able to afford large, ornamented wagons, fitted-out with living accommodation and mounted on wheels with tyres. Obviously these offered better shelter against bad weather for people and equipment and could also travel faster (Mróz 1979b: 77–94). In spite of the official attempts at compulsory settlement it seems that the late 1950s and early 1960s were, therefore, the most favourable years for the nomadic Roma.

The authorities eventually decided to impose a plan of compulsory settlement on the nomadic Roma and in 1964 the policy started to be implemented. This proved another harsh experience for this ethnic group and within a few years their nomadic Romani life had disappeared. In order to force Roma to abandon their wandering local government officials, together with the police, would forbid the Gypsy groups from making temporary halts in specified places and fine them for breaking a number of regulations – for making fires in the vicinity of a forest, for not registering their stay (which was obligatory), for not sending their children to school and for not having permanent jobs and addresses, i.e. the offence of vagrancy.[3] Sometimes wagons and horses were confiscated but the sum paid in compensation for horses only amounted to the price of slaughtering the animals. Such persistent harassment swiftly led to the settlement of most nomadic Roma.

Although Roma encampments could still be seen up to the late 1980s, for example near Warsaw or Kraków, these were in no way signs of a continuing nomadic way of life for these camps were not halts on the wanderers' way but rather seasonal meetings of lineages and extended families. Members of kin groups would come together, in rented cars and taxis, and put up tents on 'official' camp sites or meadows (usually state property), where they would spend a couple of weeks together. Men would go to market places and engage in legal and illegal business activities and about noon women would go to the town to make money by telling fortunes in the street. From time to time a new Roma family would join the camp or relatives would come to visit. Those assemblages had other important functions as well – marriages were arranged and disputes and conflicts settled.

Forced settlement did not change the life of the Carpathian Roma who had not lived a nomadic life but most Polish Roma depended on a migrant way of life for their livelihood. Horse dealing meant moving from market to market, according to a particular rhythm, and the occupations of blacksmith and coppersmith were also connected with the geography of migration. Forced settlement undermined the very foundations of their survival and contributed to breaking the economic relationships with specific regions and their inhabitants, which had been established over long periods of migration.

During the same period, other other parallel developments emerged which affected the traditional economy of Roma. The expansion of industry resulted in reduced demand for the products of Roma craftsmen – especially blacksmiths and coppersmiths. Until the 1970s and 80s coppersmiths were employed tinning copper pots used in slaughter-houses and dairies and by producers of ice cream but eventually this craft also became redundant. The only traditional occupations that remained viable were fortune-telling and playing music. Finding other sources of income became indispensable.

Polish Roma have a clear concept of *romano buĉi* (Romani work). While the duty of each man is to support his family, real 'Romani work' means the kind of work that is efficient. It allows substantial earnings to be made quickly, without taking up the whole day, leaving enough free time for a man to maintain social relations, to feast and to entertain. It is the opposite of the work of a peasant farmer, busy all day in the field and in the yard, and of the work of factory workers and clerks – all those who are bound to their work-places for long hours every day. The idea of working like this was completely alien to the Roma and settlement could not change these mental patterns. This was especially the case since most jobs were not open to them due to their lack of education. Instead, the Roma took to trading in textiles, jewellery, cars, foreign currency and antiques. Many of these businesses were illegal or, at best, semi-legal.

Apart from enforced settlement the state had little to offer the nomadic Roma. Since they had no permanent dwellings only wagons, some of them kept living in their former homes out of necessity but while wagons are a convenient place to live when migrating, they are far less suitable as permanent accomodation. Local authorities usually designated places for Roma encampment on the outskirts of towns, marginal places, often next to local slums and where outcasts lived. The situation of those Roma families who did not dispose of their wagons but continued wandering, while carrying their property on ordinary carts covered with tarpaulin roofs was equally bad. Such carts were in no way suitable for permanent dwelling, so the authorities offered the Roma 'flats' in prefabricated houses, where seasonal workers had previously been accommodated, in abandoned derelict dwellings and in places where 'problem families' lived, usually those with police records.

Such actions should not be interpreted as deliberate discrimination or intentional social marginalisation of the Roma. When enforcing settlement the authorities simply neglected to prepare any plans to enable Roma to start a new life. There were no decent flats for them, no employment and nothing that would enable them to adjust gradually to wider society and to change their previous living patterns. Where they were allocated council flats among 'ordinary people', conflicts soon appeared. The Roma often wrecked the flats they were given. Large kin groups would sit outside their blocks of flats for hours, sometimes lighting bonfires and making a lot of noise. These 'customs', appropriate to an isolated camp, were completely incompatible with the life of a housing estate. There was also another problem, deriving from cultural beliefs. Roma would only agree to live in single-storey dwellings or in top floor flats, so that they would not have any neighbours upstairs. A common taboo among nomadic Roma concerns the impurity of the lower parts of women's bodies. Therefore, by living 'under' another family, men were threatened with pollution (see Ficowski 1985: 180–1) by women in the households on the floors above.

The generation of Roma who were compelled to settle and abandon their migrations had no chance of adjusting to the new conditions and to the demands of the authorities, which were in any case impossible to fulfil. The only social group that did not reject and ostracise them were people belonging to the lowest social categories, the marginals, outcasts and lumpenproletariat. Unsurprisingly, this was where Roma found models for organising their new existence – among people without permanent jobs, who subsisted on small-scale trading, illegal dealing and crime.

In the years that followed, after the Roma had been sufficiently discouraged from resuming their travels, the authorities virtually lost interest in them. This was when Romani patterns of adjusting to their new lives were established. The Roma took to dealing in foreign currency and valuables – mainly gold, cars, antiques and carpets. Those who had relatives abroad had more opportunities for making a living by smuggling goods or selling cars stolen in Western countries.

In the 1970s the frontier separating Poland from the West was fairly strictly controlled but it was relatively easy to travel to Hungary, Bulgaria, Romania and East Germany, where goods of much better quality than those produced in Poland could be bought more cheaply. People from these countries used to travel to Poland bringing goods for sale, especially textiles and clothes. This was advantageous for the Roma and some of them eagerly took their chance. They did not go abroad to buy these commodities but exploited a situation typical of the state socialist economy. Before the arrival of a market economy shortages of goods in the shops were endemic and widespread, yet shops in big cities were usually better supplied. The Roma bought goods in demand (sometimes this was possible only by bribing shop assistants) and took them to sell in little towns and villages where attractive goods were not available. They usually played the role of foreigners from the south – Bulgarians, Hungarians and Serbs – to sustain the pretence that they were selling foreign goods, while their 'southern' appearance of swarthy skin and black hair made this subterfuge even more credible.

Meanwhile some groups of Roma had taken to music, usually playing in restaurants, and while new and better musical instruments were now available, these were also more expensive. At this time styles in popular music were changing very rapidly and traditional Romani music was becoming less and less profitable.

At the end of the 1970s more signs of the approaching economic crisis started appearing in Poland. It is in such circumstances that pogroms against the Jews and Roma usually take place. Looking at the history of Europe we can see quite clearly that every time a cataclysm, disaster or plague took place, people looked for those whom they could blame, and the Roma were usually among them. In autumn 1981 a pogrom against the Roma took place in the town of Konin (central Poland), some days later another occurred in Oświęcim (in the south) and then there was an attempted pogrom in Słupsk (northern Poland). Social tensions were palpable that year, due partly to the general and increasing impoverishment but also stimulated by the attempts of the independent trade union Solidarity to bring about political change. Disorientation and lack of a sense of security, felt by many residents of towns and villages, favoured outbursts of aggression against 'the aliens' or those who were simply defined as 'them'. These were readily distinguishable by their darker skin, but sometimes also by better cars or bigger houses. The Roma were ideal scapegoats for the Polish population. They were not employed in factories, on the railways, in agriculture, or in shops, i.e. 'normal' places of work. This led to the easy conclusion that since they were not poor, they must live on theft and robbery and state support. Such conclusions were the natural rationalisations for hostility and hatred. This was the context to the disorders of 1981.

Martial law was imposed by General Jaruzelski in December 1981, with the justification that if Poland did not put its own house in order, then the Soviet Union would – just as it had in 1968 in neighbouring Czechoslovakia. Paradoxically, this tightening of political control was actually advantageous for the Roma, particularly since the strictest constraints limiting their mobility had already been relaxed. In summer 1982 Roma encampments could be encountered in places where they had not been seen for years. There were no wagons on roads but extended families travelled by car and stopped to camp for weeks at the outskirts of towns within easy reach of the town centre. From these camps men went to do business in markets while women told fortunes to passers-by in the streets and at railway stations. The explanation of this new freedom was straightforward – the attention of the police and local administration had been completely diverted to the underground political opposition. Wholly occupied in searching for dissident political activists and seeking out their meetings the police had no interest in the Roma who were never suspected of being involved with the political opposition.

Consequently the 1980s were another relatively favourable period for the Roma. However, the previous nomadic way of life did not make its reappearance since the Roma themselves realised this was impossible. They were well aware that their traditional trades and crafts would not have provided an adequate livelihood had they returned to them. In the meantime, they had already became familiar with a settled way of life and were no longer helpless in dealing with administrative regulations and legal requirements. They became increasingly familiar with non-Roma ways of life and started sending their children to school, understanding this was their chance for social advancement. Another factor in their decision not to resume nomadism was the opportunity for a different kind of travel, due to the liberalisation of the law on obtaining passports and travelling abroad. Many Roma had relatives abroad, who had left Poland earlier, and now they could resume contact with them. New vistas were opening for the Polish Roma.

## Roma during the period of 'transition'

In the decade since the opposition assumed power in 1989, ushering in a period of turbulent political, social and economic change, there have also been some remarkable developments in the situation of the Roma. At the start the Roma themselves took no active part and contented themselves with the role of observers. However, the new opportunities for travel abroad increased further after the change of regime and one of the most important changes for the Roma has been the fact that nowadays all Polish citizens have passports and most European countries no longer require visas from them.

Another important development was that official interest focused once more on the Roma, but in a very different way from in the past. The problem of minorities and their rights came to the fore and many institutions became engaged in these issues, prompting parliamentary commissions and special commissions of the Ministry of Art and Culture and of the Ministry of Education.[4] Roma, too, were included in these debates as one of the significant minorities in Poland. As well as discussing their constitutional status these institutions established projects with the aim of providing aid to Roma and supporting them in maintaining their cultural identity. They also gave financial support for various initiatives such as periodicals, books, meetings, festivals, etc.

At the same time the Roma started founding their own formal organisations, partly because they wanted to break out of their isolation but also because such organisations could obtain government funds. While these developments encouraged many Roma to become active and participate in social events, they also made it more evident that among Roma the widespread lack of education and inability to understand more general changes might prove real obstacles to further progress. However, in order to appreciate the context in which Roma in Poland tried to respond collectively to the entirely new political, social and economic circumstances after the ending of Communist rule, it is first necessary to review their current situation in terms of their social differentiation and organisation.

At present the traditional division of the Roma population in Poland into four sub-groups – *Polska Roma*, *Kalderasha*, *Lovara* and Carpathian Roma –

has almost disappeared. As late as the 1960s these distinctions were still evident, especially the marked social distance maintained between the nomadic Roma and the settled Carpathian sub-group. The Carpathian Roma were viewed by the nomads as impure and any contact with them was regarded as polluting, thus preventing any form of social relationship between these groups, such as joint celebrations, intermarriage and dealing together, etc. This was the attitude of the nomads to another undeniably Romani community, but one which had been exposed to the influences of an alien, non-Romani culture.

Over time, Romani culture has obviously acquired many features from non-Roma society by cultural borrowing but, paradoxically, it is the settled Roma from the mountains who have preserved more archaic elements in their culture. In addition, their physical anthropological features more closely resemble those of north western India. Social and cultural boundaries between these Roma and their neighbours – Polish highlanders who were peasants and shepherds – were especially strong. The predominant feelings of these Poles towards the local Roma were scorn and dislike. Consequently, intermarriage was extremely rare, much rarer than in the case of the nomadic Roma. The *Kalderasha*, *Lovara* and *Polska Roma* justified their contempt for the mountain Roma by arguing that they ate horsemeat, a practice considered impure by all other Roma groups.

In the 1970s and 80s many Roma families left Poland and this emigration, augmented by the natural process of decline among older generations, has led to lowered numbers in the *Lovara* and *Kalderasha* groups. Once settled, different groups lived side by side, weakening the barriers that had formerly divided the *Lovara* and *Kalderasha* from the *Polska Roma*. Intermarriage became more common and these three groups are now interlinked by kinship and affinity ties. Nevertheless the previous differentiation is still present in their social memory. But the distance between them and the Carpathian Roma has proved more persistent, although the barriers are not as strong as they used to be. For example, many families of mountain Roma moved to towns where they came into contact with former nomads.

The Carpathian Roma were never an integrated society, whereas the three nomadic groups had their own strong internal organisation including their leaders. Those living in the mountains had come from Slovakia in the south, arriving not as a community but gradually in small kin groups. These Roma still live in such groups on the outskirts of villages and only two places – Szaflary and Czarna Góra – have large Roma settlements consisting of scores of households. In some cases there are sharp disputes beween Roma settlements over economic and linguistic differences or most commonly over cultural disagreements, where Roma accuse each other of not observing the rules of a Romani way of life.

After their enforced settlement the nomadic Roma occasionally formed associations. These were mainly singing and dancing ensembles, registered in order to formalise their professional activities. Since private enterprise was strongly discouraged by the regime before 1989, organising an 'artistic' group made it easier to give paid performances. Membership of such associations was strictly limited to those belonging to the same sub-group – it was not considered possible to organise an ensemble or perform together with other Roma. This precluded the possiblity of joint activity between any of the nomadic groups and the Carpathian Roma.

Given this background the Association of the Roma in Poland achieved what can be seen as a real revolution in breaking down the traditional divisions based on concepts of impurity and pollution. Until now it is the first and only organisation in which Carpathian and *Polska Roma*, as well as Roma from other groups, can meet and act together. Due to the formation of this Association the traditional leaders of the *Polska Roma* began to interact with and tolerate mountain Roma, even during unofficial meetings.

So far ten different Roma organisations have been registered, although five or six are not very active. Recently Roma organisations have become involved in compensation claims to Swiss and German foundations for wartime persecution. Others have pursued other activities: political, educational, religious and artistic. For some years annual meetings, dedicated to dance and music, have been held in Gorzów Wielkopolski. Although these are organised by the local authorities they are inspired by Edward Dębicki, the leader of one of the oldest Romani ensembles *Terno*.

The longest established Roma Association is in the town of Tarnów and its members mainly consist *Polska Roma* from south-eastern Poland. However, the most active and professional, with branches in several towns throughout Poland, is the Oświęcim Association. Its wide ranging activities include intervention in cases of discrimination, educational and unemployment research among the Roma minority, as well as making reports and collecting records about past events, usually concerning the last war. Every year a remarkable anniversary gathering is organised to commemorate the extermination of Roma in the Auschwitz *Zigeunerlager*. The Oświęcim Association is the only one with extensive documentary archives about the period of the Romani Holocaust. It participated in the publication of the two-volume book about the Roma concentration camp with records of the Roma who were imprisoned and killed there. This Association also publishes the periodical *Pheniben-Dialog*. Another Romani periodical *Rrom-po-drom* is published in Białystok in north-eastern Poland.

At present the Roma mainly inhabit large towns in central and western Poland. Only the Carpathian Roma live in villages and small towns in the mountains of southern Poland, although some Polska Roma (mostly *Xaladytka Roma*) also live in rural areas. The other groups are intermingled and dispersed, not occupying particular areas. In each of the larger towns of eastern Poland (Lublin, Rzeszów, Międzyrzec Podlaski) live groups of up to twenty Roma families. The *Kalderasha* are more numerous in northern Poland and in Silesia, i.e. south-western Poland, the *Xaladytka Roma* are confined mainly to eastern parts of Poland (Białystok, Sokółka), while *Polska Roma* are dispersed all over the country although they predominate in Łódź (central Poland).

Trade is now the main occupation of the Roma and their main source of income. They deal in gold, cars, antiques, carpets and sometimes in other goods too. Although this is a rarity nowadays, some still produce and sell frying pans – a vestige of their former traditional occupation as coppersmiths – while the few remaining blacksmiths, repairing tools and implements for local farmers, are found among the Carpathian Roma. Dealing in horses is obviously not as important as it used to be but nevertheless at annual horse markets, in Sokółka and Czarna Białostocka in the autumn and in Skarszewo (central Poland) in the spring, you can always meet the Roma. Many Roma bands play music in the streets, for example in Kraków, and often they serenade wedding groups outside registry offices, while other bands entertain diners in restaurants. At the same time a Roma middle class is gradually emerging, comprising the owners of bars, restaurants, shops and wholesale stores, etc.

The biggest social problems afflict the poverty stricken Polska Roma who live in small towns, usually on the outskirts, in areas with high crime rates. The problems of the Carpathian Roma, living in small settlements in southern Poland, are also difficult to solve. It is only in the mountains that the problem of unemployment has affected both the Roma and the non-Roma as a consequence of economic changes. In this region the settled local Roma were mainly blacksmiths but some worked as stonebreakers, wherever roads were built. The growth of factory production marginalised the craft of the blacksmith in the 1960s and 70s, while the stonebreakers had been replaced by machines even earlier. In the 1970s and 80s the usual jobs available for these Roma were as agricultural labourers on large state-owned farms and in factories in neighbouring Czechoslovakia, while some were hired by factories as homeworkers making gloves and slippers. As a result of economic transformations and the modernisation of industry most of these unskilled Roma were made redundant (Gruszczyński 1999).

In recent years altogether different groups of Roma have appeared in Poland, mostly from the Balkans and especially from Romania, who live in slum settlements on the outskirts of large towns and have little or no contact with the long-established Roma. Some of them earn their living selling leather jackets and coats brought from Romania but the vast majority beg in the streets. A few young boys play music (Polish popular tunes) in buses and trams. Hardly any of these newcomers intended to stay and settle in Poland but were sending money back to Romania to support their families. Every year hundreds of Romanian Roma are caught by border guards at the Polish-German frontier, which indicates that many of them are still trying to reach EU countries. This was a common occurrence at the beginning of the 1990s when Poland was only a transit country for them.

At present, however, some Romanian Roma families have decided to stay in Poland for longer, although they are still isolated from the Polish Roma. Since they have no professional skills and cannot speak Polish their only possible sources of income are street trading and begging. Their children know a little Polish but there is no evidence that they attend school. They are not entitled to public health care and social welfare and it is not known how many Romanian Roma babies are born in hospital maternity wards and how many in the slums. Most are probably delivered by old Roma women.

These Roma from Romania live in virtual isolation, separated both from Polish society and from the local Roma, although social organisations, social scientists and journalists take an interest in them from time to time. The authorities, however, prefer to ignore their existence; otherwise they would be required to take action to legitimise their status (at present they stay in Poland illegally and any permits they once possessed have long expired). They would also have to do something safeguard their health and education. Only when there are incidents such as fights or disturbances in the slums, or when their primitive huts catch fire, do the authorities seem to admit the existence of these Roma and eventually deport a number of families. The press response is to lament that poor people have been deported and to remind readers that back home in Romania the expelled Roma are doomed to far deeper poverty.

One of the most serious problems of Polish Roma today is education, or rather the lack of it. Poverty among the aged and unemployment are also major concerns. In the past little attention was paid to the education of Roma children. Only the settled mountain groups sent their children to school, while those in nomadic groups never obtained any formal eduction. After they had been forcibly settled nomadic Roma parents were sometimes punished for not sending their children to school but these Roma saw education as another form of repression and as a threat to their cultural and social identity. The practice of educating children seemed alien to most families and few believed that school could ensure a better future. Hardly any children who did attend school managed to complete even primary education. Usually their command of Polish was insufficient and they were not accustomed to regular systematic study. In addition there were no lessons or programmes for teaching Polish children tolerance of schoolmates from another culture and with a different appearance. Consequently Roma children were frequently discouraged from attending school by being bullied and ostracised.

With the passing of the years since settlement the nomadic Roma have obviously become more familiar with schools and the idea of education. They had been settled among non-Roma and both sets of children played together. However, this was an entirely spontaneous process since no officials have ever done anything to help either side. Ten years after the collapse of totalitarism the authorities have still virtually no idea how to educate Roma children. Some, such as those from urban, well-off families or from mixed marriages, complete full primary education and increasingly attempt secondary education, while a handful are college students or have even graduated from university.

One notable initiative is that of a parish priest near Limanowa who organises special classes in the local school for Roma children experiencing difficulties with Polish. The curriculum aims to teach the Polish language and in addition to provide professional training. This project might succeed in offering opportunities to some of the children, but on the other hand the rate of unemployment in the area is very high. Also there is inevitably a limited choice of professional courses on offer. Another drawback is that the educational background of the initiator is only theological. Roma themselves are often ambivalent about the idea of special classes for their children, since these are sometimes perceived as another way of excluding them, as a kind of ghetto. This dilemma seems a kind of vicious circle.

The Polish government accepts current international recommendations that ethnic minorities should be given every possibility for maintaining and preserving their cultural identity, i.e. their language, culture and customs. Consequently the schools children attend are meant to instruct them about their own history and culture. However, in the case of the Roma, no school has even attempted to meet this requirement since there are no suitable teachers. Even young Roma activists and social workers do not have the requisite knowledge.

The situation as regards the health service seems a little better, although problems have recently emerged. Until 1998 the Roma were entitled to public health care like all other Polish citizens. A major reform of the service, introducing many changes, began to be implemented in 1999. At the start the new procedures seemed more complicated and even now many Roma cannot understand them. It remains to be seen whether this system will prove more favourable to Polish Roma than its predecessor but it is already clear that Romanian Roma will face greater obstacles in obtaining medical aid.

Another problem concerns older and disabled Roma. Very few elderly Roma are entitled to old age pensions; only some of the Carpathian group have ever been in regular employment long enough. Some elderly Roma obtain financial aid from social welfare, although no precise overall information is available about numbers of beneficiaries since all such data is held at local government level. However, the vast majority of elderly Roma are supported by their families. Poverty is a widespread problem affecting not only the Roma but the large extended Roma families and their tradition of family solidarity usually mean that the situation is much better for them than for the elderly from peasant families.

## Conclusion

The conflict between tradition and modernity threatens the future of *romanipen*, the norms making up the very kernel of Roma identity. Younger (and even middle-aged Polish Roma), who have never known the traditional nomadic life as it was before settlement, conceive of the Romani traditions as a kind of magical formula, mysterious and impossible to understand. In their search to comprehend the real Romani rules of life they sometimes even consult ethnologists.

This clash of tradition and modernity is constantly apparent in the activities of formal Roma associations. Conflicts within them result not just from the fact that different local and clan groups are represented. The leaders of these associations try to attract respected traditional clan leaders, but at the same time seek to create an image of themselves as modern politicians. In order to win the support of the heads of clans for their organisations, they try to convince them that their activities are in full accordance with tradition and are simply a new way of obtaining money from the non-Roma. This is an ever-present cause of conflict between leaders and their organisations – balancing on the boundary of two worlds, two systems, while attempting to satisfy the modern leaders' own ambitions without antagonising traditional leaders.

Despite these endemic problems of Roma organisations they do bring the two worlds – that of the Roma and non-Roma – nearer to each other. They reveal the Roma as one of the ethnic minorities of Poland and not as some mysterious, romantic community from another sphere of existence. They help to publicise cases of racism and violence against Roma (fortunately not very frequent), which formerly used to be passed over in silence. And they make Poles aware of and accustomed to the new role of Roma associations, contributing to the growth of knowledge and education leading towards tolerance.

## References

Ficowski, J. (1965 and 1985) Cyganie na polskich drogach, Kraków: Wydawnicko literackie.

Gruszczyński, L. A. (1999) Romowie – Bezrobocie. Elementy opisu położenia społecznego Romów w Polsce, Raport z badań, unpublished report, ed. Stowarzyszenie Romów w Polsce, Katowice – Oświęcim, listopad.

Mróz, L. (1979a) 'Les Chaladytka Roma Tsiganes en Pologne', Études Tsiganes 1: 20–26.

Mróz, L. (1979b) 'Wozy cygańskie', Polska Sztuka Ludowa 2: 77–94.

Mróz, L. (1984) 'Il martirologio degli Zingari', Lacio Drom 2–3: 5–14.

Mróz, L. (1992) Geneza Cyganów i ich kultury, Warsaw.

Winstedt, E.O. (1912–13) 'The Roma Coppersmiths' invasion of 1911–1913', Journal of the Gypsy Lore Society 2, 6: 244–304.

# Notes

1    As a rule data concerning numbers of Roma are not precise. The 1931 census showed about 30,000 Roma in Poland at that time, however it is probable that not all nomadic (and perhaps not even some settled) groups were included. The 1949 census recorded 20,000, although in this case the mobility of Roma groups could also have contributed to limited reliability of the data.

2    Resolution of the Presidium of Government (no. 452/52), signed by Prime Minister Józef Cyrankiewicz.

3    Resolution of the College of the Ministry of Home Affairs (Home Office) from 5 February 1964 and of the Commission for the Co-ordination of Roma Settlement and Making Roma Productive, established in May 1964.

4    The Commission for National and Ethnic Minorities has been established at the Polish Parliament, likewise the Office for National Minorities at the Ministry of Art and Culture. These both help minorities with their organisational, legal and financial problems, prepare and print extracts of relevant legal documents, and give information about other organisations. (For example, see Biuletyn Biura do Spraw Mniejszości Narodowych, Warsaw 1994).

## CHAPTER TWELVE

# Germany and Austria:
# The 'Mauer im Kopf' or virtual wall

*Susan Tebbutt*

O ver ten years after the fall of the Berlin Wall the German-speaking world still talks about the 'Mauer im Kopf' (wall in people's minds) or virtual wall. Although the Federal Republic of Germany now stretches from Cologne to Dresden and beyond, the inhabitants of the former East and West Germany do not all feel that the opening up of the political boundaries has removed the differences between the two areas and their populations. Similarly, Austria no longer lies at the foot of the so-called 'Iron Curtain', but is equally slow to treat its Eastern neighbours as though they were in every way equals in the new Europe. In Germany today there are approximately 110,000 Sinti and Roma, in Austria some 20,000 to 30,000,[1] and just as there is still an East/West divide, so there is also a Romani/non-Romani divide.

For the Romanies[2] equality has long been denied. The indigenous population has been making the Romanies aware for centuries of their supposedly inferior status. Romanies were frequently instructed to remain outside the walls of the town at which they arrived. Legal walls were erected where no physical walls existed, and the Romanies were moved from one town to another, one region to another, one country to another. Centuries of marginalisation and discrimination culminated in the designation of *Zigeunerlager* (Gypsy camps) within the concentration camps and the genocide of over half a million European Romanies.[3]

In the post-war period this marginalisation continued. The two Germanies were founded in 1949, the Berlin Wall built in 1961. In both former Germanies, capitalist West and state socialist East, and in Austria there were two main types of Romanies. There were those forming part of the autochthonous minority group (in Germany alongside the Danes, Frisians, Sorbs and Wends, and in Austria alongside the Slovenians, Croatians, Hungarians, Czechs and Slovaks) as well as more recent arrivals of foreign nationality. Alongside the Sinti, who had first arrived in Germany and Austria in the fifteenth and sixteenth centuries, there were Roma from Central and Eastern Europe who had sought their fortunes in Germany in the mid-nineteenth century. Romanies from countries such as Yugoslavia numbered among the migrants who came to West Germany as *Gastarbeiter* (literally 'guest-workers') in the 1960s and 70s. The Warsaw Pact countries were in theory favourably disposed to each other, yet in practice there was relatively little internal movement of population between these countries, and few Hungarian or Polish Romanies migrated to East Germany.[4]

To what extent has the situation of the Romanies changed after the fall of Communism? The most obvious impact is to be seen in the arrival of Romanies from former Eastern Europe in the free market economies of Western Europe, seeking refuge from persecution and/or poverty. Although the German Democratic Republic (GDR) obviously had close links to fellow Communist states, Austria also had historical connections to many former state socialist countries, particularly Hungary. I would therefore like to compare the situation in the new Federal Republic of Germany[5] and Austria and explore the hypothesis that perceptions of the Romanies and the walls erected in the minds of the people have played a more important role than the presence or removal of physical walls or frontiers affecting the two countries.

## Borders, walls and the Romanies prior to 1945

There tend to be clusters of Romanies near borders between countries or regions, such as the Franco-German border in Baden-Württemberg or the Austria/Hungary border in Burgenland. This geographical distribution reflects the vulnerability of this ethnic group to discrimination and persecution. From their first arrival in Germany in the fifteenth century at Hildesheim, the Sinti were viewed with suspicion and seen as a threat. They were banned from staying within the city walls and were moved on to other towns and regions.[6]

City walls played both a physical and a psychological role in Austria too. Romanies first arrived in Burgenland in the sixteenth and seventeenth centuries as musicians and weapon-makers with the Turkish army. When the Turkish troops left, the Romanies remained. Maria Theresa and later Joseph II attempted to settle them in or near villages but this was opposed by the lords of the manor and local communities. In the nineteenth century *Lovara* Romanies from Romania entered Austria from Hungary and from the area which today is the Czech Republic and Slovakia.

There are parallels to be drawn between the history of the Romanies and the Jews in terms of their treatment by the majority society.[7] In both cases it sufficed to be identified as a member of the group to risk imprisonment, deportation or an untimely death by hanging, drawing and quartering. Hundreds of decrees relating to Romanies outlined the various forms state-legitimised persecution could take, from edicts banning them from practising their trade within the city walls, deportation to other countries such as South

America or Finland, and penalties imposed for being found speaking the Romani language. Children were taken away from their parents and put into Christian foster-homes[8], families resettled in special colonies for Gypsies such as that in Friedrichslohra.

These and similar political decisions were backed up by bureaucratic and administrative measures. From 1899 onwards central offices were set up in Munich, Berlin and Vienna to combat the so-called 'Gypsy menace', to record, register and by implication control all the activities (criminal or otherwise) of the Romanies. The systematic registering and monitoring reached its zenith in the Nazi period, when data on anthropometric measurements, finger-printing and genealogical records facilitated the rapid identification and location of Romani individuals and families. From 1928, for example, a *Zigeunerkarthotek* (Gypsy archive) was set up in Eisenstadt which contained information on some 8,000 Romanies. Robert Ritter, director of the Racial Hygiene and Demographic Biology Research Unit, established in 1936 in Berlin, sought to enforce the perceived demarcation lines between Aryans and Romanies, conducting experiments with the aim of proving the supposed genetic inferiority of the Romanies. Once these alleged boundaries distinguishing the Romani and Aryan populations were established, measures were introduced which radically altered the lives of the Romanies living in Germany and Austria, most of whom were engaged in traditional pursuits such as coppersmithing, basket making, dealing in carpets or horses or making music. Most still lived separate from the majority population, some in houses, some in vans, and many (such as the *Lovara* Romanies in Austria) were still moving around doing seasonal work.

After 1938 and the annexation of Austria the Romanies no longer had the right to vote and were forbidden from travelling. Their children were banned from attending school on the grounds that they would adversely affect the progress of other children.[9] Like Jews, they had to wear a badge identifying themselves, and were increasingly segregated and subject to curfews.

It was not only at government level that the discrimination was enforced. In many cities such as Düsseldorf, Cologne, Gelsenkirchen and Frankfurt the municipal authorities set up camps into which the Romanies were herded, in which the hygiene and living conditions were appalling.[10] Romanies were also employed as slave labour in factories.

Such infringements of civil liberties were only the beginning. Despite the pseudo-scientific basis of the theories relating to racial purity which underpinned the discrimination, the whole process facilitated and precipitated the rounding up and deportation of the great majority of Romanies in Germany and Austria to concentration and annihilation camps.[11] Once in the concentration camps the letter Z (for *Zigeuner* [Gypsy]) together with a number were tattooed into the arms of all who entered the gates, even the smallest children, such as the orphans from the St Josefspflege in Baden-Württemberg.[12] Both male and female Romanies were sent for compulsory sterilisation[13] and used as human guinea pigs for questionable medical experiments such as those designed to test virus resistance or the potential for surviving on sea-water alone. Thousands were gassed or died of starvation, illness, under-nourishment or the consequences of that medical experimentation. Despite the fact that the genocide of the Romanies is rarely covered in histories of the period, only some 10 per cent survived to tell their tale.[14]

After centuries of discrimination and marginalisation did the collapse of the Hitler regime then mean the dawn of a new era for the Romanies? How did the future look for those Romanies who survived?

## Remapping post-war Germany and Austria

In 1945 the political boundaries were redrawn. The general declaration of human rights of the United Nations in 1948 reflected a global awareness of the equality of all before the law and the need to respect the rights of the individual, but this was not a binding legal document. Out of the original four occupied zones in Germany there emerged two new states in 1949, the Federal Republic of Germany, with occupying forces from France, Great Britain and the US, and the German Democratic Republic, with occupying forces from the Soviet Union. Despite this new start and the new map of Europe, it can be argued that discrimination against Romanies continued in both East and West Germany, particularly in the spheres of politics, housing and education.

New policies were supposedly in place after 1945. The Nuremberg trials dealt with major perpetrators of atrocities but left many structures and individuals in West Germany free to continue along racist lines.[15] Sybil Milton highlights the fact that major researchers such as Ritter, Ehrhardt and Justin pursued their careers unhampered. The Berlin Wall, designed to be an 'anti-fascist protective wall', was erected in 1961 to stop the flood of East Germans defecting to the West. Yet despite the strong commitment to anti-fascism and the extensive de-Nazification processes, the GDR was still a breeding ground for stereotypes and prejudices as far as perceptions of the Gypsies were concerned. Neither the two Germanies nor Austria had seen fit to acknowledge their complicity in the murder of the Romanies, and it was only in the 1980s that the West German government acknowledged for the first time in an official speech that the Romanies had suffered in the Holocaust. In the late 1980s more and more people from Eastern Europe managed to make their way, either legally or via the so-called 'green' border with Hungary, into Austria and Germany. With tight border controls there were few migrants in the GDR from the Eastern European states, unlike the situation in West Germany, where there were many Yugoslavs, Romanians, Poles and Hungarians seeking employment. Given a choice, most Europeans preferred to go to the free-market economy of the FRG rather than to what were perceived as the restrictions of the state socialist GDR.

If maps were to be drawn up representing the distribution of German and Austrian Sinti and Roma within towns, how would they be configured? Despite the apparent desire of the majority of Romanies to lead sedentary lives and blend in with the Germans or Austrians, the Romanies, like the members of other ethnic minority groups such as the Turks or Poles, tended to gravitate towards the edges of towns and run-down estates and often ended up in homes with no electricity, running water or sewerage.[16] A demographic distribution map would differentiate further between the Eastern European Romanies, who migrated to these countries from the 1960s onwards, and those who had lived there for decades if not centuries. As had happened in the case of other marginalised groups, such as the Jews, a hierarchy was emerging, in which the more established Romanies were beginning to feel threatened by the presence of the poorer Roma from Eastern Europe. In the view of the longer resident Sinti and Roma in Germany and Austria the new-comers were sending out messages to the general public which were contrary to the new image they wished to promote.

Housing was not the only area in which the Romanies faced discrimination. Most Romanies were working alongside Germans and Austrians as scrap-merchants, musicians or casual labourers. Still frequently stigmatised as lazy and work-shy, they remained part of the lowest social class, particularly since few Romanies completed the regular compulsory schooling. Yet Hundsalz (1982) concluded that, although Romani children were not achieving educationally as well as non-Romanies, there was, on balance, a closer correlation between poverty and other forms of social deprivation than with membership of a particular ethnic group. There was a strong case for setting up a much stronger support mechanism to help young Romanies complete their education successfully. However, projects such as the work done by the charitable *Lindenstiftung* to promote the greater integration of Romani children living on a difficult estate on the outskirts of Ravensburg, are still an exception rather than the rule.[17]

It was against this background of political, social, housing and educational discrimination in West Germany and Austria that the Romani civil rights movement gained ground. Its mission was, as it were, to produce new maps, to establish the Romanies as an ethnic group with rights. From practical dealings with problems relating to housing, and the battle for compensation for suffering under the Nazis, to the setting up of regional groups to help both indigenous and foreign Romanies, to the widening of the movement into an international organisation, Romani activists pressed for recognition of their ethnic minority status and the concomitant rights and entitlements.[18] Meanwhile, in the German Democratic Republic, the country supposedly governed by the people for the people, the Romanies remained a marginalised group, both in terms of numerical strength and their ability to mobilise support. Gilsenbach estimates that the number of Sinti in the GDR in the first years after the war was never more than some 600. In the national memorial centres in the former concentration camps on GDR territory there was only one instance of the persecution of the Sinti being highlighted, and that was in the museum at Buchenwald where a display board was introduced with the topic of 'Gypsy prisoners' in 1985 (Gilsenbach 1993: 276–80). There was little room for the Romanies within the tightly controlled socialist state in which conformity to norms was itself the norm, whether this compliance was expressed in the world of work, music, sport or industry.

Part of the impetus of the Romani civil rights movement was devoted to the pioneering promotion of their own culture and traditions. Despite the fact that the Romanies are recognised as one of Germany and Austria's autochthonous minorities, almost no effort has been made to provide tuition in the Romani language. There have been sporadic attempts to standardise the written form of the language, all centred round activity in the former West Germany rather than in the GDR or Austria, but with limited success. It was only in the 1980s that writing about and by the Romani community began to reach a wider audience. *Da wollten wir frei sein!* (1983), the account of the experiences of four generations of a Sinti family over the course of the twentieth century, was recorded and edited by Michail Krausnick. The autobiographical work *Wir leben im Verborgenen* (1988) by Austrian writer and singer Ceija Stojka was the first to depict the Romani experience of the Holocaust. Other examples of the culture of the Romanies are to be seen in the Yugoslav Romani writer and activist Rajko Djurić's dual language German/Romani edition of his poems, and in the work of the *Pralipe* theatre group in the Ruhr, which performs plays in the Romani language. Originally set up in Skopje in Yugoslavia, the group first came to Mülheim an der Ruhr in 1986 and has become internationally renowned for its breathtaking adaptations of the classics of world theatre.[19] Thus in terms of language, literature and theatre the German and Austrian cultures are being enriched by contributions from the Romani minority.

It is the promotion of the concept of the diversity of the Romanies which marks the 1980s, immediately prior to the fall of the Wall. Significantly, there was more awareness of the Romanies (including those of Eastern European origin) within the Western capitalist world than in the GDR, despite its geographical and political closeness to Eastern Europe. It was in the former FRG that the civil rights activism gained momentum, whereas in the GDR no such movement emerged.

### No more frontiers, no more walls?

Have the dramatic events of 1989 and the unification of Germany in 1990 radically altered the position of the Romanies in Germany and Austria? The most obvious consequences were the removal of political frontiers and the freedom of Eastern European Romanies to travel to the West, accompanied by positive initiatives at government level. Yet these tangible signs of a new dawn, a new framework, were overshadowed for many Romanies by the resurgence of virulent anti-Gypsyism in Germany and Austria. Before exploring the work of Romanies in the fields of civil rights, education and culture I would like to outline both the new official initiatives and the worrying evidence of hostility to Romanies.

Among the positive initiatives was the declaration on 29 June 1990 by the Conference on Security and Co-operation in Europe (CSCE, later OSCE) rejecting totalitarianism, racism, anti-Semitism and discrimination on racial grounds. A key document was the European Charter of Regional and Minority Languages of 5 November 1992, which included languages that were not geographically limited to a particular territorial area, where Romani was specifically cited. In February 1993 the Council of Europe recognised the contribution made by the Romani culture to cultural diversity in Europe and acknowledged the need to involve representatives of the Sinti and Roma community in issues affecting them. The pivotal demands were that 'Gypsies' be referred to correctly as 'Romanies', that prejudice against the ethnic group be eliminated, and that housing and social conditions be improved. The European Framework Convention for the Protection of National Minorities was agreed on 10 November 1994 and may be seen as a step forward but it does not define exactly what it understood by a 'minority'. In these changed conditions the ability of Romani activists to promote their cause is directly related to the strength of the lobby nationally and internationally. Even at the start of the new millennium the Danish minority in Germany, for example, has far more official recognition and support than that afforded to the Romanies.

Despite these official moves towards strengthening the rights of the Romanies, the fall of Communism did not signal the beginning of a new, more enlightened era. At the start of the 1990s attacks on Romanies in Rostock, in the former GDR, and in Austria bore witness to the fierceness of the antipathy to this group. While there were no recorded incidents of hostility to Romanies in the GDR during the period of Communist rule, and although the official 'anti-fascist' position promoted international solidarity with workers from other socialist countries round the globe, those foreigners living in the GDR, whether recruited workers or asylum-seekers, whether Romani or non-Romani, were by no means treated as equals. Just as attacks in the former GDR exposed racist undercurrents, these also emerged in Austria, a country which had not experienced the restrictions of a state socialist regime. In February 1995 a sign erected in Oberwart in Burgenland advocating that the Roma return to India was symptomatic of the xenophobic attitudes held by many Austrians. The verbal racism which led to the murder of four Romanies in Oberwart in 1995[20] showed all too clearly the consequences of the new Austrian laws relating to legal residence and asylum which were ratified between 1991 and 1993. These were the Asylum Law of 1 July 1992, the *Fremdengesetz* (Law on Aliens) of 1 January 1993 and the Residence Law of 1 July 1993. Indeed, in 1995 the hostile view of Romanies was reflected in an Austrian Gallup Institute poll, which revealed that 42 per cent of Austrians did not want a 'Gypsy' as a neighbour (Cahn1996: 10).

Laws may not always work in the interests of the intended beneficiaries. Cahn argues that 'the ground was prepared for the systematic exclusion of Roma in Austria through the recognition of a narrow and unrepresentative group of Roma as an Austrian "ethnic group"'(Cahn 1996: 7). Although the European Roma Rights Centre has reason to believe that there are significant numbers of Roma among Bosnian, Romanian, Macedonian and Turkish refugees in Austria, no case was recorded where an asylum-seeker actually sought asylum on the grounds of Romani ethnicity. However, many refugees ended up in *Schubhaft* (protective detention) and were then expelled to the East, 'recreating and reinforcing the already drastic geographic division of wealth, and saddling other, poorer states with aggravated social conditions caused by the surprise influx of populations over a short period of time' (Cahn 1996: 55).

The position after unification in the new FRG was very similar: concern was expressed about what was perceived as an undesirable influx of *Zigeuner* (Gypsies).[21] Disregard for basic human rights in the town of Stade provides an example. The positioning of signs in pub windows advertising horse-meat sausages might seem innocuous, but this was a thinly disguised strategy to dissuade Romanies from entering, since the horse is considered a sacred animal within Romani culture.[22] Following media outcry and public outrage the signs were removed but the question is whether the underlying wish to keep the Romanies out of the four walls of the pub had in fact disappeared with the signs. Had the walls of prejudice been removed from the minds of the people?

Whether in the former East or West of Germany or in Austria, the Romani civil rights movement clearly has to contend with a high degree of unpopularity. Yet at the same time there is a growing awareness of the importance of promoting minority cultures within the European Union. Subsidies and grants are increasingly available but these tend to perpetuate the existing power relationships and favour the longer established groups with middle-class support. Rather than rely on the framework of legislation and action taken by supra-national institutions such as the United Nations and the European Council, Romani bodies are beginning to demand greater representation, to speak for themselves rather than be spoken for. The long-standing debates between groups such as the *Zentralrat Deutscher Sinti und Roma* (Central Council of German Sinti and Roma) based in Heidelberg and other

Romani rights organisations in Germany have continued. Were the interests of the indigenous group more important than those of the Roma newly arrived from Eastern Europe? Should the organisations offer support to Romanies from Eastern Europe or allow the German government to provide money for the repatriation of Roma from Yugoslavia, where they would face conditions beyond description? In 1992, for example, approximately one quarter of the 438,191 refugees seeking asylum in Germany were from Romania, and of these some 100,000 were Romanies. In that same year an agreement with Bucharest was signed by the German Secretary of State. As a result between November 1992 and February 1993 over 150 Romanian Romanies seeking protection from persecution were sent back from Germany to Romania (Köpf 1994: 80–1).

Meanwhile, attention was gradually turning from domestic issues in Germany and Austria to debates with an international dimension. Writing of the constitutional and ideological debates from the 1980s onwards, Matras argues:

> As alliances were formed between Romani refugees from various countries and tribes, veteran immigrants, and German nationals among the Roma, the ideological common denominator became a pan-European Romani nationalism which crossed the traditional boundaries of clan-structure, tribal affiliation, and country of origin. This movement now sought outside intervention on the part of European, American, and Israeli politicians, international human rights organisations and multilateral institutions such as the Council of Europe and the United Nations, defining itself in opposition to state policy and even to some key constitutional concepts in Germany, such as the coupling of nationhood, citizenship and ethnicity, and breaking off from the inner-German conciliatory tone which had dominated Zentralrat activities so far.
>
> (Matras 1998: 58)

The need to improve the educational and career opportunities for Romanies, regardless of their country of origin, has been recognised by Romani and non-Romani activists alike. Nowadays the percentage of Romanies in Germany and Austria who travel as nomads is negligible,[23] but even so it is hard to encourage the Romanies to attend school on a regular basis. Like many other groups where the parents do not have German as a mother tongue, the Romanies are rarely in the mainstream grammar schools but tend to attend the *Hauptschule* or its Austrian counterpart (the equivalent of the former UK secondary modern school). Despite the desire by both Romanies and non-Romanies to promote knowledge of the Romani language there is a lack of qualified teachers and there are no textbooks available. In neither Germany nor Austria are there nationwide programmes to support Romanies similar to those operating in the United Kingdom through the Traveller Education Service. Goals for the future include producing teaching materials in the Romani language and training Romanies to work in bilingual classes in kindergarten, giving talks in schools and running vocational training courses, particularly using new technology. *Romano Centro* in Vienna helps children of Romani families who are in danger of ending up in special schools since their parents are often not able to read and write well.

In turn, inadequacies in the education system have repercussions for the labour market. Renata Erich from *Romano Centro* argues that the new laws which regulate foreigners working in Austria (the Residence Law, Asylum Law and Law on Aliens) have the effect that seasonal workers find it hard to acquire and keep a valid work permit, have limited access to accommodation and often end up working illegally. Consequently, they are liable to be charged with violating labour laws with the risk of deportation (Cahn 1996: 20–30).

Education does not only mean educating the Romanies. There is also a pressing need to educate the non-Romanies about their Romani neighbours. Institutions such as the Fritz Bauer Institut in Frankfurt or *Romano Centro* in Vienna[24] worked closely with schools, political parties, the church and the media. They encouraged individual Romanies to talk to schoolchildren and invite non-Romanies into their homes, seeking to challenge widely held views about the lifestyle of the Romanies and allow more interchange between the Romani and non-Romani population. Initiatives such as that in the town of Hamm in Westphalia are still few and far between. Here the Romanies hold an annual gala where their music and food are enjoyed by Gadje and Romanies alike.[25] Younger members of the Romani community are taught their own traditional music by Romani musicians who also joined forces with an existing local folk group. Together they produced a CD of Romani and Jewish music entitled *Lieder der Verfolgten* (Songs of the Persecuted), giving a voice to those who traditionally have none.

After the Romanies were officially recognised as an Austrian minority in 1993, the situation should, in theory, have improved. However, Cahn argues that no more than 5,000 Romanies received political and social rights through this recognition while some 20,000–30,000 were excluded (Cahn 1996:16). Not long after, on 5 September 1995, the *Roma Beirat* (Romani Advisory Group) was set up with Rudolf Sarközi, as chairman, (a survivor of the war time 'Gypsy Camp' at Lackenbach), consisting of four representatives from the Romani organisations, one representative of the Roman Catholic church and three members of the strongest parliamentary parties. The aim of the group was to help young people, the long-term unemployed and socially dis-advantaged Romanies, such as drug-addicts, the homeless and ex-convicts. Yet such advisory groups have few real powers.

Official groups can, however, be instrumental in bringing about changes in the attitudes of the majority population. One of the most significant steps forward for the Romani community since the fall of Communism is the increased recognition of the Romani victims of the Holocaust. The erection of memorial centres, monuments and plaques to Romani victims of the Holocaust increases the outward visibility of the group and the potential for recognition on the part of non-Romanies of their suffering.[26] Whereas there have been numerous media accounts and films of the suffering of the Jews, few of those which portray the fate of the Romanies have caught the public imagination. This makes it harder for those seeking compensation for suffering under the Nazis to convince those allocating funds. (In 1988 a law passed in Austria recognised the time spent in the so-called 'Gypsy Camp' in Lackenbach as comparable to time in a concentration camp.) As the survivors die, it is important that their experiences are preserved for posterity and in this respect the work of the *Zentralrat Deutscher Sinti und Roma* (Central Council of German Sinti and Roma) is of great importance. Yet is the setting up of monuments any guarantee of a change in attitudes?

A more personal approach to the dissemination of information is apparent in a number of autobiographical accounts by Holocaust survivors. Ceija Stojka (1992) *Reisende auf dieser Welt* (Traveller in this World)[27] and Philomena Franz (1992) offer the woman's perspective. Alfred Lessing (1993) offers insights into the life of a Sinti musician who actually ended up playing in front of the Nazis in a concentration camp. Karl Stojka (1994), Otto Rosenberg (1998), Lolo Reinhardt (1999)[28] and Walter Stanoski Winter (1999) all give highly individual accounts of their experiences of the Holocaust.

Cultural identity may be expressed not only in literature but also in pictures. There have been many works of art depicting 'Gypsies' over the centuries painted by non-Romanies but Austrian Holocaust survivor Karl Stojka is one of the very first Romanies to depict his own ethnic group. In his representation of experiences of concentration camps and the marginalisation and persecution of the Romanies, he creates startling, dramatic, challenging images that are highly politicised and leave the viewer in no doubt about the inhumanity of the Nazi regime.[29] He has exhibited his works in Austria and abroad, in the US, Germany, Poland, France, Holland, Japan and Hungary. Ceija, his sister, has also held many successful exhibitions of her art. Both artists wished to emphasise that although over half a century has passed since the end of the war, the events did actually take place and should never be forgotten. Ceija prefaces the catalogue of her paintings with the words, 'I'm afraid that Auschwitz might just be sleeping'.[30]

It is not only in the field of literature and art that the Romanies have been making their mark. Public visibility is important. Whereas other ethnic minority groups within Germany or Austria, such as the Turks or Italians, have access to newspapers, magazines and television programmes from Turkey or Italy, this option is not available to Romanies. Efforts to ensure that the language is preserved are thus crucial. Since many families no longer speak Romani, various Romani organisations attempt to teach them the language and are trying to put together a basic grammar book. In 1996 the ABC book *Amen Roman Pisinas* was published and in the same year a comic-strip version came out which is being used in schools on a trial basis. A computer game has been devised in Romani and the newspapers *Romano Kipo* and *Romano Centro* are published by *Romano Centro*. In 1996 the *ROMA-Dokumentations- und Informationszentrum* (Roma Documentation and Information Centre) was opened in Vienna, supported financially by the Austrian state and its federal states. Its work complements that done by the Central Council for German Sinti and Roma in Heidelberg which has a permanent exhibition about the genocide of the Sinti and Roma[31] as well as hosting a whole range of cultural events that aim to break down the boundaries between Romanies and non-Romanies.

## Challenging the virtual boundaries

At a time when the old boundaries have seemingly been lifted and free travel across Europe may seem almost guaranteed,[32] the equality of all citizens has not been achieved. Discrimination is still evident in the fields of education, employment and housing. To what extent can the new initiatives by the Romani organisations alter this?

Arguably the fate of the Romanies in Germany and Austria has not changed greatly since the fall of Communism. In my view this is due to the fact that the virtual walls, the deep-rooted attitudes, are harder to dislodge than any political or actual wall or boundary. There is a clear continuity of anti-Gypsyism after the demise of the Hitler regime, and government commitment to a true implementation of policies on minority groups and equal opportunities is often only skin-deep.

Discrimination may be stamped out when it occurs in a public, blatant form, such as in the erection of the horse-meat sausage signs in the German town of Stade, but the reaction to more substantial issues such as the bomb attack on the Burgenland Romanies in Austria has been muted, indeed hypocritical. After the initial display of media sympathy and shock the citizens of Jörg Haider and his right wing Freedom Movement have settled back into a state verging on indifference, but characterised by an unwillingness to take positive action to facilitate the integration of the Romanies into Austrian society on an equal footing.

After the fall of Communism the arrival of Eastern European Romanies brought to the surface much of the anti-Gypsyism latent in Germany and Austria, provoking angry attacks on their right to seek refuge there, but also stirring up resentment in some Romani quarters that the indigenous Romanies were being erroneously associated with the newcomers. Yet again walls are being erected, this time not only in the minds of the non-Romanies, but also in those of fellow Romanies.

It is thus essential that there be government recognition of the problems facing asylum seekers, that educational initiatives become more widespread and that the cultural achievements of the Romanies be given greater prominence within German and Austrian society. The history of the interrelationship between the Romanies and Germany and Austria has been complex in the post-Communist period. As the Romani civil rights movement gains strength internationally it is important that Romanies present a united front within Germany and Austria. As Romani Rose, the Chairman of the Central Council of German Sinti and Roma, said in a recent interview: 'Die Bilder im Kopf sind sehr, sehr fest.' (The images [of Romanies] in people's minds are very, very firmly established.)[33] The external walls have fallen, but many of the virtual walls have yet to be toppled.

## References

Awosusi, A. (ed.) (1996) 'Die ungarische Zigeunermusik', *Die Musik der Sinti und Roma* 1, Heidelberg: Dokumentations- und Kulturzentrum Deutscher Sinti und Roma.

Awosusi, A. (1997) 'Der Sinti-Jazz', *Die Musik der Sinti und Roma* 2, Heidelberg: Dokumentations- und Kulturzentrum Deutscher Sinti und Roma.

Bamberger, E. and Ehmann, A. (eds) (1995) *Kinder und Jugendliche als Opfer des Holocaust*, Heidelberg: Dokumentationszentrum Deutscher Sinti und Roma.

Brand, M. and Reinhard, R. (1995) *Wenn Strunzi einen Wunsch freigehabt hätte*, Hamm: Arbeitsgruppe am Schüttenort e.V.

Cahn, C. (1996) *Divide and Deport: Roma and Sinti in Austria*, Budapest: European Roma Rights Center.

Clark, C. (1997) '"New Age" Travellers: identity, sedentarism and social security', in T. Acton (ed.) *Gypsy Politics and Traveller Identity*, Hatfield: University of Hertfordshire Press, 125–41.

Dlugoborski, W. (ed.) (1998) *Sinti und Roma im KL Auschwitz-Birkenau 1943–44 vor dem Hintergrund ihrer Verfolgung unter der Naziherrschaft*, Auschwitz: Staatliches Museum Auschwitz-Birkenau.

Dokumentations- und Kulturzentrum Deutscher Sinti und Roma (1994) *Auf Wiedersehen im Himmel!: Die Sinti-Kinder von der St. Josefspflege*, Nuremberg: Medienwerkstatt Franken e.V.

Djurić, R. (1989) *Zigeunerische Elegien: Gedichte in Romani und Deutsch*, Hamburg: Buske.

Eiber, L. (1993) *'Ich wußte, es wird schlimm': Die Verfolgung der Sinti und Roma in München 1933–1945*, Munich: Buchendorfer.

Engbring-Romang, U. (1998) *Marburg. Auschwitz: Zur Verfolgung der Sinti in Marburg und Umgebung*, Frankfurt am Main: Brandes und Apsel.

Fings, K. and Sparing, F. (1992) *'Z. Zt. Zigeunerlager': Die Verfolgung der Düsseldorfer Sinti und Roma im Nationalsozialismus*, Cologne: Volksblatt.

Franz, P. (1992) *Zwischen Liebe und Haß: Ein Zigeunerleben*, Freiburg, Basle and Vienna: Herder.

Fraser, A. (1995) *The Gypsies*, 2nd edn, Oxford: Blackwell.

Gilsenbach, R. (1993) *Oh Django, sing deinen Zorn!*, Berlin: BasisDruck.

Heinschink, M. S. and Hemetek, U. (eds) (1994) *Roma: Das unbekannte Volk; Schicksal und Kultur*, Cologne and Weimar: Böhlau.

Heuß, H. (1995) *Darmstadt. Auschwitz: Die Verfolgung der Sinti in Darmstadt*, Darmstadt: Landesverband Hessen.

Heuß, H. (1996) *Die Verfolgung der Sinti in Mainz und Rheinhessen 1933–1945*, Landau: Verband Deutscher Sinti, Landesverband Rheinland-Pfalz.

Hundsalz, A. (1982) *Soziale Situation der Sinti in der Bundesrepublik Deutschland*, Stuttgart *et al.*: Kohlhammer.

Klopcic, V. and Polzer, M. (eds) (1999) *Wege zu Verbesserung der Lage der Roma in Mittel- und Osteuropa*, Vienna: Braumüller.

Köpf, P. (1994) *Stichwort: Sinti und Roma*, Munich: Heyne.

Jelinek, E. (1997) *Stecken, Stab und Stangl*, Reinbek bei Hamburg: Rowohlt.

Krausnick, M. (ed.) (1983) *'Da wollten wir frei sein!': Eine Sinti-Familie erzählt*, Weinheim and Basle: Beltz and Gelberg.

Lessing, A. (1993) *Mein Leben im Versteck: Wie ein deutscher Sinti den Holocaust überlebte*, Düsseldorf: Zebulon.

Liégeois, J.-P. and Gheorghe, N. (1995) *Roma/Gypsies: A European Minority*, London: Minority Rights Group.

Lindemann, F. (1991) *Die Sinti aus dem Ummenwinkel: Ein sozialer Brennpunkt erholt sich*, Weinheim and Basle: Beltz.

Matras, Y. (1998) 'The development of the Romani civil rights movement in Germany 1945–1996', in S. Tebbutt (ed.) *Sinti and Roma*, 49–63.

Mehr, M. (1987) *Kinder der Landstrasse: Ein Hilfswerk ein Theater und die Folgen*, Berne: Zytglogge.

Meister, J. (1987) 'Die "Zigeunerkinder" von der St. Josefspflege in Mulfingen', *1999: Zeitschrift für Sozialgeschichte des 20. und 21. Jahrhunderts, 2*.

Milton, S. (1998) 'Persecuting the survivors: the continuity of "anti-Gypsyism" in post-war Germany and Austria', in S. Tebbutt (ed.) *Sinti and Roma*, 35–47.

Puvogel, U. and Stankowski, M. (with Graf, U.) (1995) *Gedenkstätten für die Opfer des Nationalsozialismus: Eine Dokumentation*, 2nd rev. edn, Bonn: Bundeszentrale für politische Bildung.

Reinhardt, L. (1999) *Überwintern: Jugenderinnerungen eines schwäbischen Zigeuners*, Gerlingen: Bleicher.

Riechert, H. (1995) *Im Schatten von Auschwitz: Die nationalsozialistische Sterilisationspolitik gegenüber Sinti und Roma*, Münster and New York: Waxmann.

Rinser, L. (1985) *Wer wirft den Stein?: Zigeuner sein in Deutschland; Eine Anklage*, Stuttgart: Weitbrecht.

Rose, R. (ed.) (1999) *'Den Rauch hatten wir täglich vor Augen': Der nationalsozialistische Völkermord an den Sinti und Roma*, Heidelberg: Wunderhorn.

Rosenberg, O. (1998) *Das Brennglas*, Berlin: Eichborn.

Sandner, P. (1998) *Frankfurt. Auschwitz*: Die nationalsozialistische Verfolgung der Sinti und Roma in Frankfurt am Main, Frankfurt am Main: Brandes und Apsel.

Stojka, C. (1988) *Wir leben im Verborgenen: Erinnerungen einer Rom-Zigeunerin*, ed. K. Berger, Vienna: Picus.

Stojka, C. (1992) *Reisende auf dieser Welt: Aus dem Leben einer Rom-Zigeunerin*, ed. K. Berger, Vienna: Picus.

Stojka, C. (1995) *Bilder und Texte 1989–1995*, ed. P. Meier-Rogan, Vienna: Graphische Kunstanstalt Otto Sares.

Stojka, K. (1996) *Gas*, Vienna: Karl Stojka.

Stojka, K. and Pohanka, R. (1994) *Auf der ganzen Welt zu Haus: Das Leben und Wandern des Zigeuners Karl Stojka*, Vienna: Picus.

Tebbutt, S. (1998) 'Marginalisation and memories: Ceija Stojka's autobiographical writing', in A. Fiddler (ed.) *'Other' Austrians: Post-1945 Austrian Women's Writing*, Berne: Peter Lang.

Tebbutt, S. (2000) 'From Carmen to coppersmith?', in B. Axford, D. Berghahn, and N. Hewlett (eds) *Unity and Diversity in the New Europe*, Oxford *et al.*: Peter Lang, 213–28.

Tebbutt, S. (ed.) (1998) *Sinti and Roma: Gypsies in German-speaking Society and Literature*, New York, Oxford: Berghahn.

Winter, W. S. (1999) *WinterZeit: Erinnerung eines deutschen Sinto, der Auschwitz überlebt hat*, T. W. Neuman and M. Zimmermann (eds), Hamburg: Eregebnisse.

Wippermann, W. (1997) *Wie die Zigeuner: Antisemitismus und Antiziganismus im Vergleich*, Berlin: Elefanten Press.

Zimmermann, M. (1996) *Rassenutopie und Genozid: Die nationalsozialistische 'Lösung der Zigeunerfrage'*, Hamburg: Christians.

## Notes

1    Cahn (1996: 7) refers to the Roma and Sinti in Austria as an 'exceedingly diverse group of people'. The term 'Roma' is somewhat confusing, in that it is both a collective term for all Romanies and the term used specifically to refer to those Romanies of Eastern European origin, although rejected by some of these. In this chapter 'Romanies' is preferred in order to include equally both Roma and Sinti.

2    In the English-speaking world the terms 'Gypsy' and 'Traveller' are frequently used to refer both to members of an ethnic group and those who choose a particular lifestyle, including 'New Age Travellers', hippies and itinerant fairground workers (some of whom may incidentally be of Romani origin). Both groups suffer similar discrimination. See Colin Clark's account of the politics of prejudice in Acton (1997: 125–41). In the case of Germany and Austria the term 'Roma' (Romanies) is used only for members of the ethnic group.

3    Opinions differ about the exact number of Romanies who perished. One of the many difficulties in compiling statistics lies in the fact that when asked about their ethnicity some people may give a nationality (say Hungarian or Austrian) rather than declaring their Romani origins. See Dlugoborski (1998) for analyses of the persecution of Sinti and Roma in the Third Reich, in the occupied countries and in Auschwitz and other concentration camps, and for articles addressing the issue of compensation claims made by Sinti and Roma.

4   Very little has been written about the Romanies in East Germany, one of the few exceptions being Reimar Gilsenbach (1993) *Oh Django, sing deinen Zorn* (Oh Django, sing about your anger), but even here most of the articles are about the period before 1945.

5   It is important to note that the official name of the *new* Germany (after unification), the Federal Republic of Germany (FRG), is the same as that of the *former* West Germany, whose official name was also the Federal Republic of Germany.

6   See Fraser (1995) for the most comprehensive account in English of the history of different groups of Romanies (Gypsies) in Europe.

7   See Wippermann (1997) for an exploration of the parallels between the ideologies of Anti-semitism and Anti-Gypsyism and their consequences for the Jews and the Romanies.

8   The practice of removing Romani children from their natural parents continued right into the late twentieth century. The charitable organisation Pro Juventute in Switzerland did not discontinue this practice until 1973. See the work of Jenisch writer Mariella Mehr's *Die Kinder der Landstrasse* (1987) for reflections on the physical and psychological suffering which this caused.

9   Approximately 11,000 Romanies were living in Austria, the great majority in Burgenland.

10  See Fings and Sparing (1992), Eiber (1993), Heuß (1995 and 1996), Sandner (1998) and Engbring-Romang (1998) for detailed accounts of the persecution and deportation of Romanies from specific German towns.

11  See Zimmermann (1996: 101–5) for an overview of the position of the Burgenland Roma-nies in Austria and their defamatory presentation in local media. After 13 March 1938 the right to vote was taken away from the Burgenland Roma, they were forbidden from making music in public and banned from marrying Germans.

12  See Meister (1987) for an account of the fate of these orphans. Of the thirty-seven children deported, only four survived. After the end of the war compensation was finally paid in only fourteen of the cases. A film was later produced in 1994 by Romani Rose and Michail Krausnick with the title *Auf Wiedersehen im Himmel* (Until we meet again in heaven), which uses archive film footage and interviews with the survivors. See also Bamberger and Ehmann (1995) for some eleven articles presenting a critical examination of the use of the term 'Holocaust' and insights into the many ways in which children became the innocent victims of the Holocaust.

13  See Riechert (1995) for a wide-reaching account of the complexities of the Nazis' sterilisa-tion policy regarding the Romanies whether deported to Auschwitz or other concentration camps or not. Riechert also explores the derisory treatment after the war of Romanies claiming compensation on account of having been subjected to compulsory sterilisation.

14  It is paradoxical that despite the fact that the Romanies as a group were considered alien, a danger to the German race, a number of them did fight for their country in the First and later the Second World War.

15  See Sybil Milton's article (in Tebbutt 1998) for an in-depth analysis.

16  Their vans had been burnt by the Nazis when the Romanies were herded into labour or con-centration camps and deported. Nevertheless, many Romanies did return by choice to the town in which they had previously lived.

17  The emphasis was on the pre-school experience. At the start of the twenty-first century such projects still remain the exception, whereas in Great Britain there is now a well-established (although constantly threatened by government cuts) Traveller Education Service which helps Gypsies and Travellers to try to realise their true potential within the state education system.

18  See Yaron Matras' article (in Tebbutt 1998) on the civil rights movement in West Germany.

19  It is a tribute to the international reputation of the Pralipe Theatre that it was invited to

perform the play *Kosovo mon amour*, a play about Romanies, in October 2000 at the German pavillion at the Hanover Expo 2000. See also Tebbutt (2000) on the interconnections between cultural identity, Orientalism and Anti-Gypsyism.

20 The dramatisation by Elfriede Jelinek of the murder of four Romanies, *Stecken, Stab und Stangl* (1996), was named as play of the year in 1996 by the periodical *Theater heute*.

21 The cover picture of weekly news magazine *Der Spiegel* 36/1990 has the heading 'Asyl in Deutschland? Die Zigeuner' (Asylum in Germany? The Gypsies) above a mass of faces staring out at the reader.

22 The article in *Der Spiegel* 39/1997 points out that this subterfuge is to discourage unwanted guests.

23 Indeed since the end of the nineteenth century less than 10 per cent of the Romany population have travelled other than in the annual holiday. See Luise Rinser (1985) for an interesting deconstruction of commonly held prejudices about the Gypsies. Rinser argues that crime, for example, is no more prevalent in the Romany community than it is among the majority population of Germany.

24 The first Romani organisation to be set up in Austria was the *Verein Roma*, set up in Oberwart in 1989 with the aim of improving the life of Romanies in Austria. Other organisations set up in Austria include the *Kulturverein Österreichischer Roma* and the *Verein Österreichischer Sinti* which was set up in Villach.

25 See Brand and Reinhard (1995) for a version of the Hamm project produced for children.

26 See Puvogel *et al.* (1995) for the first volume of a vast project to document all sites in memory of the victims of National Socialism. The indexing makes it easy to identify all sites relating to Romani victims.

27 This was the sequel to her earlier work *Wir leben im Verborgenen* (1988) and concentrated much more on her work promoting Romani music, culture and traditions.

28 The fact that Reinhardt is writing in a dialect of German, Swabian, is interesting, since it highlights the fact that members of one minority group (here Romanies) may also be members of a further minority group, in this case that of the speakers of Swabian. The highly successful writer and singer José F. Oliver is similar in this respect in that he is of Spanish descent but grew up in Swabia and describes himself as an Andalusian Alemannic. Both he and Reinhardt have more than one cultural affiliation and highlight the hybridity of culture.

29 See Stojka's autobiography (1994) and the catalogue (1996) produced with the support of the Austrian Federal Ministry of Foreign Affairs.

30 See *Bilder und Texte*, a catalogue (1995) which includes reproductions of some of her many paintings, accompanied by some of her poems.

31 See Rose (1999) for an outstanding volume containing photographs, documents, articles and eye-witness reports by Romanies.

32 Although not for asylum seekers among whom number many Romanies.

33 Romani Rose was interviewed by the newspaper published by the main teachers' trade union in Germany, *Erziehung und Wissenschaft*, 1/2005, 34–5.

## CHAPTER THIRTEEN

# The Czech lands and Slovakia: Another false dawn?

## *Will Guy*

ROMANI BROTHERS AND SISTERS!
*Wake up! Let's wake up one another! The day our ancestors have awaited for many years has arrived. For the first time Roma who live in this land can take their fate into their own hands. Now it is up to us to decide how we are going to support each other and what we are going to do for our children.*

(quoted Davidová 1995: 220)

The ringing words of this early 1990 pamphlet, printed in Romani, Czech and Slovak, rallied Roma throughout Czechoslovakia to support their own all-Roma political party, Romani Civic Initiative (ROI), in the first free elections after the 'Velvet Revolution' had overthrown Communist power. The leadership of this fledgling party, drawn from the small but significant Romani intelligentsia, felt they had good reason for their optimism as, compared with their fellows elsewhere in Central and Eastern Europe, Roma in Czechoslovakia were perhaps the most integrated into wider society.

Ever since the ending of the Second World War the Czechoslovak industrial economy, more developed than its agricultural neighbours, had swiftly drawn Roma into mainstream employment and, although utilising them almost entirely as unskilled labourers, had provided many with reasonable wages and the chance to improve their living conditions. Also, a brief window of opportunity from 1969–73 had permitted Roma to form their own cultural and economic associations, in some ways the precursors of the Romani organisations of the 1990s.

But, at the same time, widespread repression had accompanied these undeniable benefits. State policy had breached the constitution and led to frequent denials of Romani human rights as freedom of movement was curtailed, women were coerced into sterilisation and children were increasingly consigned to special schools for the intellectually impaired. In spite of progress in their material circumstances many Roma were still condemned to ill-health and an early death. In 1989, shortly before the collapse of Communism, the journal *Demografie* noted that, during the decade 1970–80, Romani life expectancy at birth was 55.3 years for men and 59.5 years for women. These low levels were described as similar to those of 'developing countries' and equivalent to Czechoslovak life expectancies 'in the thirties' (Kalibová 1989: 250). It was little wonder, then, that the new Romani politicians were bitterly critical of previous policy towards Roma.

A decade later, the initial eager anticipation of the post–Communist world had been bitterly disappointed as the successor governments in both parts of the now divided state proved unable to protect their Romani citizens from savage, racist attacks or provide them with employment. Staring into a future without hope, large numbers of despairing Roma had turned their backs on their homelands and taken the extreme path of seeking asylum elsewhere in Europe and beyond. It could be argued that only the threat this flight posed to early entry into the European Union (EU) prompted Czech and Slovak political leaders to begin to take seriously, at long last, the desperate situation of their Roma fellow citizens.

This extended chapter covers what are now two separate countries. The justification is that not only were these combined in a unitary state for most of the twentieth century until 1993 but also that almost all the present-day Roma of the Czech Republic have their origins in Slovakia and often maintain extended family connections. This chapter explores parallels and differences between Communist and post-Communist experience and suggests that the inability, or reluctance, of central governments to impose their political will on local authorities might continue to frustrate attempts to improve the situation of Roma, just as it had in Communist times. While such an outcome would probably not prevent the entry of the Czech Republic and Slovakia to the EU, it would undoubtedly lead to further intensification of inter-ethnic pressures.

## Roma in Slovakia and the Czech lands before Communism

Shortly after the first recorded appearance in 1399 of Roma in the Czech lands a large band managed to obtain letters of safe conduct in 1423 from the Holy Roman Emperor Sigismund at Spiš castle in eastern Slovakia (Horváthová 1964: 37, Fraser 1992: 76). They did not remain long in Slovakia but travelled on. Around this time similar groups arriving from the east aroused great interest throughout Western Europe, and can perhaps be regarded as the precursors of the 'western pattern' of Roma development. There, Roma have made a living by skilfully utilising niches that generally required nomadism within developed capitalist economies. To the east, in less advanced economic conditions, Roma were needed for their labour power and were often encouraged or forced to settle from an early date (Guy 1975a: 204

and 2001, Mirga and Gheorghe 1997: 5). The territory of the former Czecho-slovakia straddles this developmental divide.

As early as the fifteenth century many Roma apparently settled soon after arrival in Slovakia, frequently in the vicinity of feudal castles such as Spiš, where the men found employment as grooms, smiths, musicians – and frequently as soldiers – while the women worked mainly as domestic servants and washerwomen. However, they remained distinct from the local peasantry, differentiated by their dark skin, language and customs. This separation was heightened by the fact that their arrival coincided with incursions by the Turks. Roma, in both the Czech lands and Slovakia, were frequently accused of acting as spies and incendiaries for these feared invaders. For long periods, as in the troubled aftermath of the Thirty Years' War (1618–48), they received savage treatment including execution and mutilation to deter further incursions but in Slovakia they were generally dealt with more leniently (Horváthová 1964: 97, Guy 1975a: 208–9, Jamnická-Šmerglová: 44–51).

In the Czech lands Roma remained nomadic, pursuing 'traditional' occupations such as horse-dealing, fortune-telling, dispensing folk medicine, begging and petty thieving, but in Slovakia nomads had dwindled to a small minority by the end of the nineteenth century. A census in 1893 recorded around 36,000 Roma in Slovakia of whom 2,000 were categorised as 'semi-nomadic' – with a winter base of a hut or tent – and only 600 (less than 2 per cent) as 'nomadic' (Horváthová 1964: 138).

The pace of sedentarisation had probably been accelerated by a sustained thirty-year assimilation campaign during the eighteenth century. The Habsburg monarchs, Maria Theresa and her successor Joseph II, attempted to turn all Roma on their lands into productive workers and raise taxes from them as part of an overall plan to transform their realm into a rational, centralised state (Willems 1997: 31–4). Their measures went far beyond settling those who were still nomadic and banning occupations such as horse-dealing. The aim was to integrate all Roma by housing them in serfs' villages and setting them to work as labourers on projects such as road-building or ditching, if they were not already engaged in craft work. In order to hasten their assimilation into the peasantry, Roma were forbidden to use their own Romani language, wear 'outlandish' clothes or 'waste time on music'. Most draconian of all, their children were to be forcibly removed and brought up by non-Roma. To signal the disappearance of this group as a distinct minority and the effective abolition of their identity the Roma were renamed *Neubauern* (new farmers) or *Ujmagyar* (new Hungarians) (Horváthová 1964: 113–36, Guy 1975b, Fraser 1992: 157–61).

How Roma were viewed in the first Czechoslovak Republic (1918–38), which united the Czech lands with Slovakia, is evident less from their formal status than from their treatment. Although they were recognised as a separate nationality in the 1921 constitution, in the same year the government circulated copies of the 1888 Austrian regulations on registering nomads. These repressive rules were to form the basis of Law 117 directed against 'nomadic gypsies' in 1927 (Horváthová 1964: 155, 161–2, Nečas 1995: 31–3, Guy 1975a: 211).

Such legislative changes were of less relevance to the settled Roma of Slovakia than their widespread destitution in the depressed economic conditions after the First World War and in the 1930s, which proved fertile ground for the rise of political extremism. The Slovak Peasants' Union complained bitterly that 'since they have nothing, the gypsies either beg or steal and as poverty cases are a burden on the peasantry' (quoted Horváthová 1964: 154). Others took more direct action, launching pogroms in reprisal for crop pilfering in which Roma were murdered and their huts razed to the ground. Even though young children were among the fatalities, the national daily *Slovák* condoned one attack as 'a [democratic] citizens' revolt against gypsy life', adding '[t]he gypsy element, such as it is today, is really an ulcer on the body of our social life which must be cured in a radical way' (Nováček 1968: 25–6). Meanwhile, mounting feeling against the Roma led to their exclusion from larger towns, particularly those with spas and a tourist trade (Horváthová 1964: 167). Yet not all Czechs and Slovaks shared this hostility for some remarkable, if isolated, attempts were made to improve the situation of Roma, particularly in the field of education.[1]

During the rise of fascism, pogroms against Roma also occurred in neighbouring Austria and Germany (Nováček 1968: 87) – precursors of the Holocaust to come during the Second World War when up to half a million of the region's Roma perished alongside the Jews.[2] At this time the two parts of the dismembered Republic came to exemplify the most extreme versions of the western and eastern 'solutions' to the 'gypsy problem'. In what had become the Czech Protectorate, all but a few hundred out of 6,500 Roma[3] were annihilated in the concentration camps, while in Slovakia, although many men served in forced labour camps, most of the estimated 100,000 Roma survived the war (Jamnická-Šmerglová 1955: 80–6, Horváthová 1964: 173, Daniel 1994: 125–35). Those in Slovakia owed their survival to the Nazi 'divide and rule' policy, for the eventual planned extermination of all Roma was delayed in the puppet state of the fascist Slovak Hlinka Party.

The extent of Czech and Slovak complicity in the 'final solution' of the 'gypsy problem' is unclear. It is undisputed that Slovak Hlinka guards carried out a series of bloody pogroms, burning Roma alive in their huts and machine-gunning those who tried to escape but only recently have investigations been published on Czech involvement in operating concentration camps for Roma in Lety and Hodonín (Nečas 1994, Pape 1997). However, there is evidence that some Slovaks and Czechs tried to protect their local Roma. Likewise, Roma sheltered and fought alongside Slovak partisans and were decorated for their heroism (Kenrick and Puxon 1972: 135–9).

288

## The Communist period – material progress and assimilation

The creation of the first Czechoslovak Republic in 1918 had juxtaposed, for the first time within a modern state, 'eastern' Roma in Slovakia with 'western' industrialisation in the Czech lands, but it was only after 1945 that an expanding peacetime economy needed to draw on this potential workforce. Post-war Czechoslovakia, the most industrialised state in the region and where wartime damage had been minimal, experienced a labour shortage that was particularly acute in areas of heavy industry. This was largely the consequence of the violent expulsion, in 1945, of the three million-strong German minority in retribution for its part in dismantling the inter-war republic (Plichtová 1993: 14). The immediate solution lay to hand in the Roma of Slovakia.

> Gypsies were moved from Slovakia to Czech industrial centres ... [near] the Czech-German border where they were employed, housed primarily in camps, and paid meagre wages. Their labour served, in part, to put the Czechoslovak economy back on its feet.
>
> (Kostelancik 1989: 309)

Far from all the new Roma workers were supplied by these enforced relocations, eventually discontinued in 1947, for thousands more followed them voluntarily (Grulich and Haišman 1986, Hübschmannová 1999: 126–7).[4] Whole families abandoned their huts in the segregated, shanty-town settlements of rural Slovakia, which had been the characteristic abode of most Roma for centuries, and flooded westwards in search of work. Soon these new arrivals had more than replaced the former Romani inhabitants of the Czech lands – but with the crucial difference that they were not nomads but rural-to-urban migrant workers.[5] As with migrant labour in Western economies, these newcomers were assigned the least desirable and most arduous work – men generally as heavy labourers in road-building and the construction industry but also as miners and factory workers; women mainly as cleaners, street-sweepers and dish-washers but sometimes as factory workers too (Lacková 2000: 172–9). For the first time in history Roma were entering the general labour market on a large scale and these migrants became the most proletarianised and urbanised of all European Roma.

On arrival from Slovakia, Roma were generally assigned to dilapidated inner-city housing as more suitable for them.[6] Romani families soon became concentrated in the decayed urban cores of Czech industrial areas during the 1950s, prompting the authorities to note with alarm that these migrants were not vanishing amongst other town-dwellers. With their distinctively dark skin and expressive behaviour they remained highly visible and separate communities in what had become virtually minor ghettos. Meanwhile, in Slovakia, the

289

isolated Romani settlements continued to be overcrowded and dangerously insanitary in spite of heavy out-migration. After years of concern the government eventually took action and in 1958 launched an ambitious campaign to turn the Roma into model socialist citizens by integrating them fully into the workforce and the community (Haišman 1999, Jurová 1993, Guy 1977). The timing was partly, although not entirely, a response to the lead given in 1956 by the USSR in banning nomadism, also followed in Hungary, Poland and Bulgaria (Lemon 2001, Kovats 2001, Mróz 2001, Marushiakova and Popov 2001).[7]

As with the Habsburgs,[8] wasted productive potential was a fundamental issue for the Communist state and consequently its first priority was to ensure that every adult Rom was drawn into permanent employment. The handbook to guide the practice of local authorities explained that:

> Heavy losses to the national economy ... are caused by this labour reserve of tens of thousands of predominantly young gypsies who either do not work at all or else whose work output is very low.
>
> (Czechoslovak Socialist Government 1959: 7–8)

Apart from its economic motivation the Communist assimilation campaign most closely resembled its Habsburg predecessor in the all-embracing scope of its attack on Romani identity for the Communists believed that integration could be successfully achieved only by the complete assimilation of all Roma. Accordingly, they denied any validity for Romani identity on the grounds that oppression under previous social orders had irreparably damaged Romani culture. Although Roma were not renamed 'new Czechs' or 'new Slovaks', as formerly, the formulation 'citizen of gypsy origin' was introduced to indicate that distinct Romani identity was a relic of the past.

> Experience shows that all measures which revive gypsy national [sic] consciousness, and their own special organisation and autonomy, preserve the present isolation and separation of gypsies from the remainder of the population, prevent the penetration of everything progressive from our environment ... and help conserve the old, primitive gypsy way of life with all its bad habits.
>
> (Czechoslovak Socialist Government 1959: 28)

The ideological rationale was the questionable claim that Roma failed to meet Marxist-Leninist criteria for national minority status (Sus 1961), but such an intransigent stance was characteristic of a period when the Party was consolidating its position by centralising power and curtailing any minority aspirations. At this time even Slovak Communists, seeking greater autonomy within the republic, were imprisoned on charges of bourgeois nationalism, while a leading Romani activist who sought permission to establish a cultural organisation for Roma was threatened with the same fate (Hübschmannová 1968: 37).[9]

A strategy of population dispersal was adopted at the outset but for it to be effective there had to be some means of administratively controlling the location of Roma. Law 74/1958 'on the permanent settlement of nomads', with sanctions of up to three years imprisonment, formally deprived an estimated 20,000–27,000 Roma of their right to freedom of movement and was potentially applicable to the remainder. But while the travels of the estimated 6,000 nomadic Vlach Roma were brought to a sudden end, the main apparent target – the 150,000 or more sedentary Slovak Roma – were left for the most part unscathed (Guy 1975a: 214–5). Seven years later, in an attempt to accelerate assimilation, Government Decree 502/1965 introduced a planned programme for transferring Roma from overcrowded settlements in Slovakia and dispersing them to suitable locations in the Czech lands. A maximum permissible proportion of Roma per community was set at 5 per cent (Guy 1975a: 219–20, Hübschmannová 1968: 39). As a Romani spokesman sardonically commented: 'They planned the numbers for each village – horses, cows and Gypsies' (Hübschmannová 1968: 37).

Within three years these unrealistic plans were frustrated, mainly by the refusal of Czech local authorities to accept shipments of Roma from Slovakia, and the co-ordinating government committee was dissolved in acknowledgement of its failure (Guy 1977: 249–342). Soon after, in 1968, federalisation of the republic allowed the Czechs to distance themselves still further from what the Slovaks vehemently insisted was a problem of whole-state dimensions. Apprehensively, they interpreted this move as an ominous statement of intent by the Czechs to refuse equal responsibility in any future solution (Guy 1998: 50–1).

> [These changes] ... perhaps suit the Czech regions where there are about 40,000 gypsies. In Slovakia, where today we have 170,000 (of which perhaps 100,000 live in quite inhuman conditions), the latest administrative structure for solving the gypsy question is utterly unsuitable.
>
> (Slovak Socialist Government 1968)

While federalisation had negative consequences for Roma – and undoubtedly prepared the ground for their problems following the 1993 break-up of the republic – it stemmed from a more tolerant approach to minorities during the brief period of political liberalisation known as the 'Prague Spring' of 1968. The collapse of the 'transfer and dispersal' programme coincided with this breathing-space, allowing Roma activists to gain permission, in both the Czech lands and Slovakia, to establish their own cultural and economic organisations, the Association of Gypsies-Roma (*Svaz Cikánů-Romů* in Czech). Lack of a credible alternative official policy allowed this experiment to continue for a few short years during the repressive period of 'normalisation' when the other reforms of the Dubček regime were reversed. A delegation[10] from the Czech branch took part in the historic, first World Romani

Congress in London in 1971 and later, Czechoslovak Roma in exile continued to play an important part in the development of the International Romani Union (Acton and Klímová 2001).[11]

Eventually, these associations were unceremoniously swept aside in 1973, partly on the grounds that they had failed in the tasks in which the Party had made it impossible for them to succeed but also because of fears of renewed demands for national minority status (Davidová 1995: 208–9). However, the Slovak Government had not even waited for the abolition of its Romani association before adopting a declared approach of 'acculturation' in 1972 (Jurová 1993: 93). Essentially a reversion to the earlier one-sided view that problems stemmed entirely from the 'cultural backwardness of Gypsies', this implied stripping Roma of their culture and re-educating them (Davidová 1995: 208–9). The language of policy-makers in the Czech lands was more temperate but, there too, Romani initiatives were ruled out in spite of frequent repetition of the mantra 'social integration'.

Six years after the suppression of the short-lived Romani associations, a dissident group, Charter 77[12], published a caustic report on Communist policy towards Roma listing specific human rights abuses (Charter 77 1979). This maintained that the denial of national minority status to Roma, which underpinned the rationale of the policy, 'was dictated by the desire of the ruling powers to reduce the size of the minority problem' (Charter 77 1979). Population control took a specific form in the case of Roma. Some of the fiercest condemnation in the report was of the practice of sterilising Romani women, either under duress and bribed by financial inducements, or without their knowledge at childbirth or during other operations (Charter 77 1979b: 22, Tritt 1992: 19–35, Pellar and Andrs 1990).[13]

Another main target of criticism was the planned segregation of Roma, which occurred in both halves of the Republic, in dedicated blocks of flats in towns where they were most numerous, a reversal of the earlier policy of dispersal and amounting to municipally-sponsored ghettos (Tritt: 56–8).[14] Meanwhile, in rural Slovakia, settlement sizes were growing as Roma were often blocked from buying or building houses in 'white' villages, perpetuating apartheid-style segregation (Guy 1975b, Lacková 2000: 183–4).

At the same time, the physical segregation of Romani dwellings was complemented by a matching educational ghetto as growing numbers of Romani children were unjustifiably consigned to special schools for those with learning disabilities (Tritt 1992: 37–9). The Charter 77 report denounced this practice, as did a much later ERRC investigation which reported that '[c]omprehensive statistical evidence [reveals that] ... from the early 1970s until 1990 ... there was a dramatic increase of Roma in special schools. By the mid-1980s almost every second Romani child attended a special school' (ERRC 1999a: 16).

Most of the measures condemned by the report were not new but rather a continuation of long-established practices. The use of the 1958 law on nomadism to control the movement of Roma, 'who, while not nomads, are forced to migrate on account of living conditions not of their own making', was branded as 'racist repression' (Charter 77 1979a: 7). In practice, this law had failed to stem the continuing migratory tide[15] and of more concern to Roma was the frequent and illegal refusal by local authorities, mainly Czech, to register them as residents – even if they already had found jobs (Charter 77 1979a: 7–8, Guy 1975b).[16] As a result, newcomers were excluded from the housing list and forced either to crowd in with relatives or squat in near-derelict buildings. A bleak alternative was to live in basic barracks near their workplace, commuting home to their families only at weekends. In many ways their situation was akin to that of migrant workers in the West, needed for their labour power but undesired as citizens – with the major difference that this was their own country (Guy 1975b).

The employment level for male Roma of productive age had reached the national average by 1970 in the Czech lands and was not far behind in Slovakia. Employment rates for Romani women were lower, particularly in Slovakia, but these showed a steady increase (MPSV 1971: Table III). Nevertheless, the claim to have integrated Roma into the labour force was sharply challenged in the Charter 77 report by the accusation that the Communist administration was deliberately perpetuating the disadvantaged situation of Roma in order to keep them as a flexible and compliant reserve pool of unskilled labour. A perceptive warning emphasised the acute vulnerability of Roma workers should the economy modernise in the future.

> The demand for unskilled labour will then fall, threatening the Roma with massive unemployment which will expose this ruthlessly urbanised minority to extreme pressures, and fuse their social ostracism and material oppression with a new ethnic consciousness, all the stronger the more cruelly it is today suppressed.
>
> (Charter 77 1979b: 7)

Exactly a decade later this chilling prophecy was to be fulfilled.

## Another false dawn?
## The first decade of post-Communism

The 1989 Velvet Revolution brought liberation from Communist rule to the Czech and Slovak peoples – including the half million or more Roma.[17] The dramatic change offered hope of greater Romani integration into public life and first omens seemed promising as formal political gains were accompanied by a flowering of Romani culture.[18]

The charismatic new president, Václav Havel, had been the leading figure in the Charter 77 dissident movement, championing the Romani cause.

Consequently, the newly-formed Romani Civic Initiative (ROI) was included as a partner in the coalition parties which swept to victory in the first post-Communist elections – Civic Forum (OF) in the Czech lands and Public against Violence (VPN) in Slovakia.[19] Matching their new political representation the formal status of Roma was reconsidered and in April 1991 the Slovak Government resolved 'to acknowledge the Roma to be a nationality in the contemporary terminology and to guarantee their political and legal equality of rights' (Tritt 1992: 14–16). The Federal and Czech governments soon followed suit. At the same time Roma of Czechoslovakia sought to re-establish links with broader Romani political movements and at the fourth World Romani Congress, held in Warsaw in 1990, the leader of ROI, Dr Emil Ščuka, was elected secretary general to the International Romani Union (Davidová 1995: 222, Acton and Klímová 2001).

During the last decade of Communism Havel had been regarded as the conscience of the Czechoslovak peoples but now his compassion for Roma was deeply unpopular. Opinion polls soon confirmed extremely high levels of hostility towards Roma (e.g. Times Mirror 1991), which found public expression in many ways as Roma were increasingly excluded from public space (Tritt 1992: 111–6). A report on the Czech lands noted that 'Roma are often denied access to pubs, discos, restaurants, swimming pools and other public establishments run by private individuals or the state' (Human Rights Watch 1996: 14), while the Slovak town of Spišské Podhradie imposed a night-time curfew on local Roma (ERRC 1997a: 47–8).[20]

An uncertain legal interregnum encouraged the emergence of neo-fascist groups that had more direct ways of expressing their feelings. These ranged from skinhead gangs to a Ku Klux Klan and a 'White League' (*Bílá liga*) (Tritt 1992: 2–3).[21] In the period between the fall of Communism in 1989 and May 1995 an estimated twenty-seven Roma died as a result of racial violence in the Czech lands alone (Human Rights Watch 1996: 6, 2). Similar attacks, sometimes leading to fatalities, also occurred in Slovakia (ERRC 1997a). The victims were killed in various ways – by beating, knifing, drowning, shooting, burning, bombing and by garrotting in the case of 'a six year-old Romany boy ... strangled in a playground by a skinhead using a cable' (ČTK 1995).[22]

Similar attacks were reported from neighbouring countries, yet governments did little to protect their Romani citizens other than occasionally tinker with the laws (Barany 1998: 319–23). In 1995, a brutal and highly publicised murder did prompt the Czech government to introduce longer sentences for 'racially-motivated attacks' (*Lidové noviny* 1995b, Guy 1998: 63–4) but such measures were largely ineffectual. Not only were those found guilty generally given suspended sentences or imprisonment shorter than one year (Czech Government 1999a: 8), often on the grounds of youth, but the failure of the law to define racist crime encouraged authorities not to identify assaults as such.[23]

Figures for racist crimes underestimated the extent of the problem since Roma were usually afraid to report incidents to the police (Czech Government 1999a: 8).[24] Many Roma reported that officers often looked on as disinterested bystanders when demonstrations or attacks took place (Tritt 1992: 93–109), while some had experienced 'witnessing or being a victim of police violence' (Human Rights Watch 1996: 6). This testimony was endorsed by official reports that law enforcement agencies often shared the views of those perpetrating such attacks. In the Czech lands 'an internal study by the Interior Ministry conducted in 1995 determined that racism was a serious problem within the police force' (Human Rights Watch 1996: 7–8),[25] while two years later it was conceded that 'there are ... sympathisers, even members, of the skinhead movement among the police' (Czech Government 1997b: I, 23, Jakl 1998). In Slovakia, however, there were reports of a more systematised violence (ERRC 1998), as in 1995 when over a hundred armed and masked police, allegedly in search of stolen property, made a planned raid on the largest Romani settlement in the country (Jarovnice), attacking the inhabitants with batons, knives, chemical sprays and electric cattle prods (ERRC 1997a: 36–44).[26]

Apart from racist attacks the most direct and widespread result of post-Communism for Roma was unemployment. Of all ethnic groups, Romani workers were undoubtedly the worst affected by economic restructuring (Human Rights Watch 1996: 4). Both unskilled and skilled workers in the inefficient, labour-hungry, smokestack industries of the command economy were the first to be shed (Premusová and Sirovátka 1996). However, other sectors previously employing large numbers of Roma actually expanded, like construction. However, such Roma workers often suffered a similar fate, being replaced by imported Ukrainian labouring gangs paid at much lower rates. The Ukrainians were often mafia-organised, operating outside of Czechoslovak labour law (Siderenko 1995, Wallace *et al.* 1996: 272–7). Meanwhile, Romani agricultural labourers, particularly in Slovakia, were thrown out of work as the fields of former collective and co-operative farms were either returned to their previous owners or privatised. Consequently, the little work that remained was usually casual and seasonal rather than permanent.

As well as suffering as the first to be dismissed and from privatisation, Roma were also victims of a relaxation of legal restrictions on employers (Lemon 1996: 28–30, Weinerová 1994). This discrimination was routinely institutionalised in both the Czech lands and Slovakia, where 'official lists of available jobs [in municipal labour exchanges] often .... note that the particular employer does not accept Roma' (Czech Government 1997b: I, 18,Tritt 1992: 76–90, Vašečka 1999: 2, Guy 1998: 58).

Reliable figures for Roma unemployment rates are unobtainable but a 1997 Czech Government report estimated these at around 70 per cent, rising to 90 per cent in some places, at a time when the national average was 5 per cent (Czech Government 1997b: I, 17). The situation was even starker in Slovakia with a national unemployment rate of around 15 per cent (Tritt 1992: 77–85, Plichtová 1993: 18). In contrast, a few Roma managed to benefit from the new opportunities. During the Communist era there had been a small number of Roma operating as illegal traders in Western consumer goods and as currency changers and, just as for their more numerous non-Romani counterparts, these activities 'translat[ed] into entrepreneurship' in the 1990s (Lemon 1996: 29). They were joined by others and, by 1997, there were an estimated 9,000 Roma officially licensed as traders in the Czech Republic (Czech Government 1997b: I, 17).

The limited research undertaken suggests that the very high levels of Romani unemployment were largely due to restructuring and deregulation of the labour market, and compounded by discriminatory practice (Premusová and Sirovátka 1996, Weinerová 1994). Nevertheless, the popular belief was widespread that unemployment among Roma is self chosen and 'that once [C]ommunism stopped forcing Roma to work they quit their jobs – that they refuse to work or live "honestly"' (Lemon 1996: 28).[27] A main reason why Roma were thought to be unwilling to work was that the low pay on offer for unskilled labour could not match the alternative income available from social support for those with children.[28] This belief was reminiscent of the Communist accusation that generous child benefits, designed to boost Czechoslovakia's dwindling population, were supposedly encouraging Roma to abandon wage labour for childbearing as a profession (Tritt 1992: 20).

An immediate consequence of pandemic unemployment among Roma was that growing numbers were driven into semi-legal or illegal activities. For children, mostly without qualifications, prospects were even bleaker. On the basis of highly contentious police statistics of dubious legality, it was claimed that Roma accounted for 20 per cent of all crime in the Czech Republic, although they formed less than 3 per cent of the population. Allegedly, their share of robbery and theft amounted to half or more of reported cases (Powell 1994).[29] Types of criminal activity most commonly mentioned by police and media were 'property crimes, receiving stolen goods and prostitution' (Czech Government 1997b: I, 22).[30] Meanwhile, in rural Slovakia, Roma were reduced to scavenging crops from the fields (Scheffel 1999: 45). These depredations infuriated the newly privatised farmers and in a nightmarish echo of the pre-war pogroms, these incidents sometimes triggered violent fights between Roma and Slovak villagers (*Lidové noviny* 1996).

NGOs, as well as Romani spokespersons, linked the apparent increase in criminality among Roma to their recent unemployment and hopeless prospects (*Romano kurko* 2000:7). Others offered different explanations in terms of 'innate tendencies and ... sometimes even genetic predisposition' (Czech Government 1997b: I, 22). While the 1997 Czech report rejected these widely-held views as 'openly racist', the inherent nature of such criminality was a central plank in the vehemently anti-Roma electoral platform of the far-right Republican Party, which won an increased share of the vote in the 1996 Czech elections.[31] And, in spite of official condemnations of extremism, doubts were raised about the administration's conception of Romani criminality by the controversial Czech citizenship law.

Romani experience throughout the 1990s was uniformly bleak as their always low social status went into free fall.[32] Racist attacks and vilification, unemployment and impoverishment, increasing residential, social and educational segregation were met with official inaction[33] in both the Czech lands and Slovakia, at least until the mid-1998 change of government in both countries seemed to offer some hope of change. But in this depressing decade two landmarks stand out for their powerful symbolic significance: the 1993 Czech citizenship law and the waves of emigrants seeking asylum, starting in the summer of 1997.

Three short years after the fall of Communism, the federal republic was divided in what was dubbed the 'Velvet Divorce' after the governing Czech party had seen a threat to its radical economic reforms in populist Slovak nationalism (Kavan 1996: 38). On 1 January 1993 Slovakia became an independent, sovereign state for the first time in its history, leaving Roma in the Czech lands as possibly the largest, though evidently unwelcome, minority. In fact, up to 80 per cent of Roma did not appear as such in the 1991 Census but camouflaging themselves on the census form as ethnic Czechs, Slovaks and Magyars was to prove of little help to Roma in the Czech lands.[34]

While Slovakia offered citizenship to any citizen of the former Czechoslovakia who wanted it, the new Czech Republic required anyone other than a previous Czech citizen to make a special application and meet stringent conditions in order to gain citizenship. These included proof of permanent residence in the Czech lands for at least two years and no criminal record for the previous five years. Most Roma living in the Czech lands were deemed to be Slovak citizens, because of their origins in Slovakia and the circumstances of federalisation in 1968, even though by the early 1990s Roma had been established in the Czech lands for over forty years and perhaps as many as two-thirds had been born there (Gross 1994: vi).

Many adult Roma, estimated as up to 50 per cent, were ineligible for Czech citizenship on the grounds they had convictions – though mostly for minor offences such as pilfering state property (Gross 1993).[35] Likewise, often because of bureaucratic resistance to registering them, many failed to meet the residence criterion, even though they had lived in the Czech lands for longer than the required period (Tolerance Foundation 1994: 17). Wildly conflicting claims were made by NGOs and the Czech government about numbers affected,[36] including deportees to Slovakia.[37] Undoubtedly some Roma were made stateless and there is ample evidence that some Slovak local authorities refused to register those either expelled from the Czech lands or driven by desperation to return to their former settlements.[38] But the vast majority of Roma in the Czech Republic simply remained there, irrespective of legal status, though some suffered the loss of their rights as 'foreigners in their own land'.[39]

International criticism, drawing on Romani and other NGO reports, was scornfully dismissed by Premier Klaus as 'insignificant' and even Havel, now re-elected as Czech President, publicly defended the new law (Gross 1994).[40] Continuing condemnation from the UNHCR and the Council of Europe, among others,[41] eventually led the Czech government to modify this law in April 1996, although the amendments were dismissed as little more than cosmetic changes to placate international opinion (O'Nions 1996: 8–10, Schlager 1998b: 32). Only after large numbers of Roma began to flee the republic as refugees, attracting embarrassing media attention, did the Czech government finally bow to the inevitable and on 9 July 1999 parliamentary deputies voted to make a significant amendment to this peculiarly pointless and vindictive law (*Lidové noviny* 10 July 1999, RFE/RL 1999).[42]

So much has already been written about the disputed citizenship law that, at this stage, it would be more helpful to reflect on its purpose and conse-quences. Of these, the outcomes are more evident.

One of the two main effects of the law was to bring misery to many Roma, who were given the stark news that they were now unwelcome in the country they regarded as home.[34] Even worse, Roma were threatened with the sudden removal of many of their basic rights. Shortly after the new law was enacted, the same blunt message – that Roma were a target of ethnic cleans-ing – was proclaimed on national TV to public applause. A Czech beauty queen from North Bohemia declared: 'I want to become a public prosecutor … so I can clean our town of its dark-skinned inhabitants' (Stewart 1997: 2).

The other effect was to bring unprecedented, international opprobrium on the new state for violating international law and breaching human rights. For the Czech Republic the citizenship law was an unprecedented public relations disaster which achieved nothing except to convince Roma they no longer had a future in their homeland. Such exclusion, even if formally successful, was never likely to result in a mass exodus of Roma to Slovakia. Instead, it drove many into exile in the West, precipitating an even worse international crisis for the state.

As regards the purpose of the legislation, Czech officials were unwilling to adopt the same open approach as the Slovaks because they hoped the impending split of the Czechoslovak Republic might give them a unique opportunity of ridding themselves of their now redundant Romani and for-eign workers.[44] An internal government document, leaked to the press, spelt out Czech intentions all too clearly:

We should use the process [of the division of the republic] for the purpose of departure of not-needed persons from factories, especially for the reasons of structural changes, and for the departure of people of Roma nationality to the Slovak Republic.

(Prostor 21 July 1992 quoted Human Rights Watch 1996: 19)

Viewed in this light the citizenship law was a direct continuation of the much earlier attempt by the Czech Republic to minimise its responsibility for Roma citizens. Federalisation in 1968, therefore, was a precursor not just of the break-up of Czechoslovakia but of the abandonment of a joint approach to Roma. The fundamental difference was that previously Romani workers were still needed in Czech industries; after 1989 they had become superfluous, thus fulfilling the first part of the Charter 77 prophecy. Even if documentary evidence is doubted, there is no other plausible explanation for the introduction of this tortuous law.[45]

For Roma in Slovakia, too, the break-up of the federal Republic led to an immediate deterioration of their position. Although not threatened with a loss of citizenship, Roma now found themselves the target of more explicitly racist abuse from politicians.[46] Ján Slota's policy recommendation for their treatment was 'a small yard and a long whip'. While similar views expressed by the Czech Republican Party might be dismissed as extremist rantings, Slota was leader of a party in the governing coalition. In particular, independence focused attention on the new state's fastest growing minority and fear of being dispossessed became a recurrent theme. As recently as 1999 a leading Slovak daily reported with alarm that 'if present demographic trends continue, one million ... Roma will live in Slovakia in ten years time and will make up the majority of the population by 2060' (*Pravda* 1 August 1999).[47]

In September 1993, the Slovak premier, Vladimír Mečiar, suggested that family allowances of Roma should be reduced to help cut 'extended reproduction of the socially unadaptable and mentally backward population'.[48] Official policy statements were hardly more reassuring. In spite of early formal recognition of Roma as a national minority in Slovakia, a 1996 blueprint for policy until the year 2002 revealed a familiar, denigratory view of these people as backward and primitive, needing social re-education to fit them for the modern world (Slovak Government 1996, ERRC 1997a: 69–71). The post of Government Commissioner for Citizens in Need of Special Care was created but no mention was made of action to combat ethnic discrimination (Vermeersch 2000: 6–7). The overriding emphasis on the need for 'acculturation' in the policy outline on 'activities and measures in order to solve the problems of citizens in need of special care' was very reminiscent of the earlier Communist approach.[49] Indeed, insistence that the situation of Roma should be treated as a complex of social problems of 'citizens with special needs' could be seen as extending the conceptual model used in education for segregating Romani children to almost the entire minority (PER 1992: 7–8).

As well as confining increasing numbers of children to special schools, another disturbing echo of Communist practice, in both Slovakia and the Czech Republic, was the intensification of the post-1960s policy of residential segregation. A council plan in Košice, the capital of East Slovakia, to move the city's entire Romani population to the Lunik IX district, was condemned as 'creating a 25,000–30,000 person ghetto' akin to a reservation (ERRC 1997a: 57). In the Czech lands it was eventually conceded that the growing practice of forcibly evicting Romani rent defaulters and relocating them to purpose-built, 'so-called "bare flats" [with only basic facilities], concentrated on the outskirts of towns, ... evoke[d] fears in the entire Romani community that this [wa]s a certain kind of "ethnic cleansing"' (Czech Government 1997b: I, 20). Similar fears were provoked by the later attempt of a local council in the North Bohemian town of Ústí nad Labem to wall off a block of flats, inhabited mostly by Romani families, providing a powerful symbol of the segregated ghetto.[50] Further wartime memories were evoked by controversy over the site of the former concentration camp at Lety, where Czechs had stood guard over Roma.[51]

Romani experience of post-Communist life, both before and after the division of the federal republic, left them in despair and with no tangible hope of improvement. Consequently, it was hardly surprising that a short series of TV documentaries, offering the mirage of life abroad without discrimination, should have sparked off a dramatic reaction which shocked the complacency of the Czech and Slovak Governments.[52]

The exodus started in August 1997 when around 1,500 Roma boarded flights to Canada, where they immediately requested asylum (Lee 2000: 54–5).[53] This soon led to the imposition of visa restrictions for all Czech citizens in October (Legge 1998a). Although most journeys were self-financed,[54] a mayor in the industrial city of Ostrava used municipal funds to subsidise some tickets on condition that the recipients gave up their state flats and right to return to them, even though there was no guarantee that they would be granted asylum.[55] She described this action as 'friendly gesture' (ERRC 1997b).[56]

Later waves of Roma migrants to Britain in mid-1997 and 1998[57] were stemmed in October 1998 when the British government imposed visa restrictions on Slovak citizens.[58] In Canada, asylum was eventually granted to over three-quarters of petitioners, on the grounds that their own state offered them no protection against racist attacks, but the British government took a quite different approach, treating the 'invaders' as economic migrants and granting asylum in only a few token cases (Lee 2000: 61, Legge 1998b, Travis 1998).[59]

What was to become the standard European response to subsequent attempts by Czech and Slovak Roma to flee their homelands revealed no small measure of hypocrisy. On the one hand, the Czech and Slovak Governments were condemned for violating their citizens' human rights but as soon as the victims arrived in EU countries, claiming human rights abuses, these same people – now refugees – were unequivocally branded as economic migrants and expelled as soon as possible (Cahn and Vermeersch 2000: 78–9).[60]

## The beginnings of a new approach?

Almost five years after the controversial citizenship law had been introduced the Czech government at last began to admit that international and NGO condemnation of this particular law and of general government inaction in alleviating the plight of Roma might be well founded. At the end of October 1997, it eventually accepted the *Report on the Situation of the Romani Community in the Czech Republic* by Pavel Bratinka, Minister without Portfolio and Chairman of the Government Council on Nationalities (Czech Government 1997b).[61]

This was a landmark in official Czech assessment of the situation of its Roma minority, drawing on a wide range of evidence including a sociological survey among local authority officials and Romani representatives as well as a study of media treatment of Romani issues.[62] Commissioned in January 1997, the report frankly admitted the continuing high levels of hostility towards Roma and that it was 'the fact that society is not willing to accept them, despite their efforts to integrate', that had driven many Roma to emigrate (Czech Government 1997b: I, 2–3).[63]

More importantly, for the first time, an official report conceded that in major respects the government had simply failed the Roma and that, in the light of 'practical experience and the actual situation, … it must be conceded that overall the criticisms are substantiated' (Czech Government 1997b: I, 2). A month earlier, the government had taken another important step in establishing an Interdepartmental (aka Interministerial) Commission for Romani Community Affairs as an 'advisory, initiating and co-ordinating body' (Czech Government 1997a), as the report had recommended.

A few days after the Czech government had eventually accepted the report, the centre-right ODS party of Václav Klaus, in control since the early 1990s, fell from power to be replaced for the first time by a new Social Democrat-led coalition, following the elections of June 1998. Meanwhile, in Slovakia the long domination of Mečiar's HDZS party was overturned in the September 1998 elections, bringing hopes of a more democratic approach to the plight of the Roma population in both countries.

At this time both the Czech and Slovak Republics, under their new governments, were eager to become members of the European Union. One of the criteria for entry was that candidate countries should have established institutions 'guaranteeing democracy, the rule of law, human rights and respect for and protection of democracy' (European Commission 1999: 4). Concern had already been expressed by the European Commission about the situation of Roma in July 1997 and the annual Regular Reports on progress of individual countries of November 1998 and October 1999 were even more critical. These reports included both the Czech and Slovak Republics among those applicants where 'Roma still suffer discrimination and social exclusion' (European Commission 1999: 4).

Continuing anxiety about EU entry stimulated renewed efforts in both countries to devise new policy initiatives. In the month following the elections, the ill-fated attempt to exclude Roma from the Czech state was finally abandoned when deputies drastically amended the citizenship law (RFE/RL 1999). Meanwhile the keystone of the Communist attempt to control Roma migration, the 1958 Law 74 on 'nomadism', had been quietly rescinded in March 1998 after forty years on the statute books and almost a decade after the ending of Communism (ČTK 1998).

Eighteen months after the reluctant acceptance of the Bratinka report and a few days after the Framework Convention (setting fuller criteria for EU entry)[64] had come into force on 1 April 1999, the new Czech Government approved a radical document outlining a draft conception of long-term policy toward Roma (Czech Government 1999b). In the same month, another report (Czech Government 1999a) on compliance with the Framework Convention (Council of Europe 1994) acknowledged the numbers involved by accepting that Roma had not declared themselves as such at the 1991 census out of fear.[65] At the same time, the draft conception flatly stated that the overall situation was no better than formerly, for '[d]iscrimination against Roma on the labour market [and elsewhere] ... has not abated' and 'there has been no marked improvement in the protection of Roma against racialist acts of criminal violence' (Czech Government 1999b: 11).[66] In the same spirit, the Czech Minister of the Interior agreed that Roma refugees 'were right when justifying applications for asylum abroad by saying they are persecuted by skinheads' (Grohová 1999). The draft conception concluded with a specially commissioned study, which offered a blunt warning 'of the likely development of the Romani community if the government adopts a wait-and-see policy', as it had hitherto. For the very first time the government was confronted with a cold, hard look into the future, which offered an apocalyptic vision (Socioklub 1999).[67]

It took another fifteen months until the final draft was approved in June 2000, putting forward a long-term plan from 2001 until 2020. The concept of assimilation was explicitly and unequivocally rejected in this conception for '[m]inority integration worthy of the name cannot amount to assimilation'.[68] Instead, Romani identity was to be reinforced and celebrated as the key to their integration as equals in what was now embraced as a 'multicultural society', for 'the more Roma will feel like being Roma, the more emancipated and responsible citizens they will be' (Czech Government 2000a: 1).

The main aim of the conception was stated to be 'the achievement of conflict-free co-existence of the Roma community with the remainder of society', which would depend on attaining a number of goals over the coming two decades. First among these was 'ensuring the safety of Roma' and others included 'the removal of all forms of discrimination', as well as 'improving the social situation of the Roma community, above all by lowering unemployment and raising their housing standards and associated levels of health' (Czech Government 2000a: 1).

However, as well as altruism, the motivation was also openly political, as the final paragraph of the conclusion made crystal clear:

> The way in which this conception is accepted ... and its goals realised ... will have a significant influence on the assessment of the EU Committee for the Czech Republic. In its last appraisal report this Committee was critical about the current manner of co-existence between the majority and Roma. The report to be made in autumn 2000 will be crucial for the entry of the Czech Republic to the EU. In this sense the government solution of the integration of Roma into society will influence the integration of the Czech Republic into Europe.
>
> (Czech Government 2000a: 24)

The policy implications of the conception were wide-ranging. Some appeared simply to extend and strengthen previous provisions, although on closer examination, these were more innovatory than they seemed.[69] Others, however, were radical new departures from previous practice. Measures to promote what amounted to affirmative action (literally 'equalising measures') were to be introduced in the areas of employment, improving qualifications and housing, although quotas were explicitly ruled out.[70] In an unusually frank admission the earlier draft of the conception had justified such a course of action as essential for 'without active government intervention the actual condition and present-day situation of the Romani community are hopeless' (Czech Government 1999b: 5).

Apart from extensive discussion of measures to raise employment levels, for example by tax incentives to employers, the most dramatic initiative was a commitment to abolish the consignment of normal Romani children to special schools for those with learning difficulties.[71] By 1999, the proportion of all Romani children in such 'ESN' [sic] (educationally sub-normal) schools had increased to 'roughly three-quarters' and this was 'subject to growing criticism from abroad where such schools are seen as tools of enforced segregation and ominous signs of a slide to apartheid' (Czech Government 1999b: 7,8).[72] Nevertheless, this declaration in the draft conception had not deflected a group of Romani parents from Ostrava, with the support of the European Roma Rights Center (ERRC), from challenging this practice in court in June 1999 (ERRC 1999b) nor the ERRC from releasing a critical report on special schools on the same day (ERRC 1999a).[73] In general, the conception envisaged that the same buildings were to be used but former special schools were to be converted to a mainstream curriculum (Czech Government 2000a: 12–16), which might be regarded either as a pragmatic use of existing resources or, alternatively, as cosmetic re-labelling.

Reading through the impressive range of structures to be established in order to supervise and carry out the numerous tasks described in the conception, the nagging doubt remains that the Habsburg and Communist schemes, too, had been planned in exhaustive detail but ultimately had foundered in their implementation at local level.[74] This was also a concern of the November 2000 Regular Report for the Czech Republic and particularly that for Slovakia (European Commission 2000a, 2000b).[75] At this point it is worth reflecting that a fifth of Czech officials in the 1997 survey ruled out any hope of successful integration. They believed that 'any attempts to solve the problem are useless, because their source and substance – the completely different Romani mentality – cannot be changed'. Most of these officials thought that 'Roma should live, as much as possible, in selected parts of towns (municipalities) where they could receive greater attention' (Czech Government 1997b: II, 3–4).

However, following acceptance of the conception in mid-2000, a lengthy report was produced listing progress made by the end of the year on 121 tasks undertaken (Czech Government 2000b). Therefore, in this light, perhaps hopes should be pinned, in contrast, on officials like the narrow majority of respondents in the 1997 survey who thought that 'Roma should live in ways which suit them, like any other citizens' (Czech Government 1997b: II, 4).

Meanwhile, following the 1998 elections in Slovakia, the previous Government Commissioner for Citizens in Need of Special Care had been replaced by one for the Solution of the Problems of the Roma Minority. The new commissioner was himself a Rom and in June 1999 his office produced a new policy paper, which was 'concerned with including the minority voice in the design and implementation of Roma-related policies' (Vermeersch 2000: 8).[76] This was adopted by government in September of that year (Slovak Government 1999c).[77]

Hopes were raised still further by the first foreign visit of the newly confirmed Slovak president, Rudolf Schuster, to Prague. Heading his agenda in the meeting with his Czech counterpart, Václav Havel, was a proposal to develop a joint programme for 'solving the Roma question', an offer which was readily accepted (Carolina 1999, Naegele 1999). It was no surprise that this problem was viewed as urgent, since only the day before the visit Finland had suspended visa-free entry for Slovak citizens in response to the latest wave of Roma asylum seekers.[78] Only a week earlier, on the assumption of the rotating EU presidency, the Finnish prime minister had bluntly warned

Slovakia that 'it is out of the question that countries where conditions are not in order should join the European Union'.[79]

Grounds for optimism were undermined later that same year when a derogatory document, distributed by the Slovak Presidential Office to the 'Meeting of Presidents of the Visegrad Four Countries',[80] suggested that prejudice was still firmly entrenched and that old attitudes had not really changed.[81] The following year Róbert Fico, charismatic leader of the newly-formed *Smer* (Direction) political party, heightened tension by claiming gynaecological evidence indicated that by 2010 there would be 1,200,000 Roma in Slovakia and that in East Slovakia their numbers would equal those of Slovaks in the region. For good measure, he predicted that up to 800,000 Roma would be dependent on benefits and this would overwhelm Slovakia's system of social support (SITA 9 June, quoted *Romano nevo lil'* 2000: 2).[82]

The more favourable political climate of the late 1990s presented sharp, new dilemmas for Roma political organisations. The initial optimism of the early 1990s had quickly subsided, accompanying the fall in levels of Romani political representation,[83] a phenomenon repeated elsewhere in the region.[84] But from the mid-1990s new groupings emerged, spurred into action by racist attacks and the emigration waves. Also, population growth began to translate into voting power, at least at local level in parts of Slovakia, where in the '1998 local council elections six mayors and eighty-six council members were elected from Roma political parties' (Vermeersch 2000: 10). However, the emotive issue of emigration proved divisive for Romani organisations.

Some, such as the Roma Intelligentsia for Co-existence (RIS) in Slovakia and Fund for Understanding and Hope in the Czech lands, were inclined to blame the emigration on the discrimination suffered by Roma (Vermeersch 2000: 10). Others, like the long-established ROI, feared that highlighting the issue would provoke even more resentment and further attacks against Roma. The emigrants were blamed by the public, politicians and media in Slovakia for the imposition of visas by Western states and in both Republics for endangering their counties' chances of admission to the EU.[85] In the view of ROI, a more prudent strategy was to seek accommodation with the state and negotiate favourable concessions in the manner of Romani Rose, leader of the long-established Sinti association in Germany, rather than challenge it. This stance helps explain why ROI tended to be critical rather than supportive of Roma emigrants.

This dispute was elevated to an even higher level with the prominence of the ROI leader, Emil Ščuka, as secretary general of the International Romani Union (since 1990) and his subsequent election in July 2000 as president at the Fifth World Romani Congress in Prague. In response to the passionate defence of asylum seekers by Western Roma representatives, the ROI strategy of accommodation was generalised as IRU support for a regional policy of 'stabilisation' for Roma, by which was meant their improved social integration, material conditions and legal safeguards in their homelands (Acton and Klímová 2001, Guy 2001).

This standpoint neatly fitted the requirement of the Czech government, in particular, for an amenable negotiating partner and supporter in its EU entry procedures. Also, far from posing a threat to the authority and cohesion of the centralised state as the Communists had feared, the current form of Roma nationalism – the call for Roma to be recognised as 'a nation without territory' – corresponded to the government's desire to 'internationalise' the whole question and in the process share the burden of its responsibilities.[86]

## Visions of the future

There is no doubt that considerable efforts have been made in recent years by both Czech and Slovak Governments to carry out a range of Roma-related activities, and to demonstrate this to the European Union (e.g. Czech Government 2000b, Slovak Government 2000). Such activities include what are generally small-scale projects, undertaken by Roma and pro-Roma NGOs and often funded through the EU's PHARE programme. In spite of such endeavours, most ordinary Roma have yet to see any significant change in their circumstances (Holomek 2000: 3). Given the late start and apparent slow rate of progress it seems unlikely that significant equalisation of Roma with other citizens will have occurred by the anticipated EU entry date of around 2005. In the event of failure to produce considerable improvements, those Romani organisations which have staked their future on the success of integration or 'stabilisation' policies may be in danger of forfeiting their support and of being replaced by more radical and militant leaders.

It remains to be seen, therefore, whether time will run out for the Czech and Slovak Republics and, by the same token, for their Romani citizens. In many ways the governments of both states wasted the 1990s for, in spite of certain positive measures, they were completely unable to prevent mass unemployment of Roma and their subsequent dependency on social support. Inevitably, this led to the catastrophic collapse of their never-high social status. Meanwhile, tacit public support grew for widespread attacks on Roma, who were left unprotected by the state. Roma with most to lose – by a tragic irony the most integrated – seized the remote hope of asylum abroad. Those unable, or unwilling, to take the option of flight increasingly began to stand their ground and fight, thus fulfilling the second part of the grim Charter 77 prophecy.[87] A Czech Rom stated the dilemma facing his people in stark terms: 'The question before us is this: Do we follow the path of Martin Luther King – or Malcolm X?' (Schlager 1998a: 28).

The choice will depend largely on whether the Czech and Slovak Governments, with the help of Roma and pro-Roma organisations and NGOs,[88] can successfully implement their policies at local level and ultimately on the response of the Czech and Slovak peoples to new government initiatives. One of the most depressing findings of the sociological survey, carried out in the spring of 1997 *before* the migratory waves, was that '[a]lmost two-thirds of all respondents ... think that ... problems with co-existence will continue to increase, regardless of the efforts devoted to preventing and solving them ... [since] the Romani population is growing faster than its ability to integrate'. It is to be hoped that the optimism expressed by more than four-fifths of representatives of Roma and pro-Roma initiatives, who disagreed with this view, is well founded (Czech Government 1997b: II, 4).

# References

Acton, T. and Klímová, I. (2001) 'The International Romani Union – An East European answer to West European questions?: Shifts in the focus of World Romani Congresses, 1971–2000', in W. Guy (ed.) (2001).

Barany, Z. D. (1998) 'Ethnic mobilisation and the state: the Roma in Eastern Europe', *Ethnic and Racial Studies* 21, 2: 308–27, March.

Braham, M. and Braham, M. (2000) 'Romani migrations and EU enlargement', *Cambridge Review of International Affairs* XIII, 2, spring-summer, 97–114.

Cahn, C. (1999) 'ERRC hosts family meeting in Ostrava, Czech Republic', *Roma Rights* 1.

Cahn, C. and Vermeersch, P. (2000) 'The group expulsion of Slovak Roma by the Belgian government: a case study of the treatment of Romani refugees in western countries', *Cambridge Review of International Affairs* XIII, 2: 71–82, spring-summer.

Carolina (1996) 'Czech Republican Party Chairman Miroslav Sladek spews anti-Rroma racism' (report of parliamentary session of 25 July), *Carolina* 212, (electronic newsletter of Charles University students), Prague, 2 August.

Carolina (1999) 'News in brief', *Carolina* 340, 30 June – 14 July.

Charter 77 (1979) 'Dokument 23 o situace Cikánů v Československu', *Listy* 2, 47, Prague: Charter 77 (*Charta 77*).

Charter 77 (1979a) 'Document 23 about the situation of Gypsies in Czechoslovakia – Part I', trans. M. Jackson, *Labour Focus*, March-April.

Charter 77 (1979b) 'Document 23 about the situation of Gypsies in Czechoslovakia – Part II', trans. M. Jackson, *Labour Focus*, May-June.

Council of Europe (1994) *Framework Convention for the Protection of National Minorities*, Strasbourg: Council of Europe, 10 November.

Council of Europe (1996) *Report of the Experts of the Council of Europe on the Citizenship Laws of the Czech Republic and Slovakia and their Implementation and Replies of the Governments of the Czech Republic and Slovakia*, DIR/JUR (96) 4, Strasbourg: Council of Europe, 2 April.

Czech Government (1997a) *Interdepartmental* (aka Interministerial) *Commission for Romani Community Affairs* (Meziresortní komise pro záležitosti romské komunity), Resolution 581, Prague: Government of Czech Republic, 17 September.

Czech Government (1997b) *Report on the Situation of the Romani Community and on the Present-day Situation in the Romani Community* (Zpráva o situaci romské komunity a k současné situaci v romské komunitě), (known as the Bratinka Report), Resolution 686, Prague: Office of Minister without Portfolio, accepted 29 October.

Czech Government (1999a) *Information about Compliance with Principles set forth in the Framework Convention for the Protection of National Minorities according to Article 25, Paragraph 1 of this Convention*, Prague: Government of the Czech Republic, April.

Czech Government (1999b) *[Draft] Conception of Government Policy towards Members of the Romani Community Designed to Facilitate their Social Integration* (Koncepce politiky vlády vůči příslušníkům romské komunity, napomáhající jejich integraci do společnosti), Decision 279, Prague: Government of Czech Republic, draft approved 7 April.

Czech Government (1999c) *Additional Information about Compliance with Principles set forth in the Framework Convention for the Protection of National Minorities under Article 25 of the Convention*, Prague: Government of the Czech Republic, December.

Czech Government (2000a) *Conception of Government Policy towards Members of the Romani Community Designed to Facilitate their Social Integration*, (Koncepce politiky vlády vůči příslušníkům romské komunity, napomáhající jejich integraci do společnosti), Decision 599, Prague: Government of Czech Republic, approved 14 June.

Czech Government (2000b) *Information about Carrying out the Government Decision Concerning the Integration of Romani Communities and the Progress of the State Administration in Realising Measures Arising from this Decision up to 31 December 2000* (Informace o plnění usnesení vlády týkajících se integrace romských komunit a aktivního postupu státní správy při uskutečňování opatření přijatých těmito usneseními ke dni 31. prosince 2000), Government of Czech Republic, December.

Czechoslovak Socialist Government (1959) *Práce mezi cikánským obyvatelstvem* (Work among the gypsy population), Handbook for local authorities – '*for official use only*' (emphasis in original), Edice časopisu Národní výbory, Prague: Úřad předsednictva vlády.

ČTK (1995) 'Racism in Czech Republic: profile', *ČTK News Archive*, backgrounder 64, Czech News Agency Internet posting, 18 May.

ČTK (1998) 'Bill lifting ban on nomadic life gets through Senate', *ČTK Press Statement*, 4 March.

Daniel, B. (1994) *Dějiny Romů: Vybrané kapitoly z dějin Romů v západní Evropě, v Českých zemích a na Slovensku*, Olomouc: Univerzita Palackého.

Davidová, E. (1965) *Běz kolíb a šiatrov*, Košice: Východoslovenské vydavateľstvo.

Davidová, E. (1970) 'The Gypsies in Czechoslovakia I: Main characteristics and brief historical development', (trans. [W]. Guy), *Journal of the Gypsy Lore Society* 3, 69, 3–4, July-October.

Davidová, E. (1995) *Romano Drom/Cesty Romů 1945–1990*, Olomouc: Univerzita

Palackého.

Davidová, E. and Guy, [W]. (1972) 'Czechoslovakia solves its Gypsy problem', *Race Today* 4, 3, March, 82–4.

Dženo Foundation (1997) *Status Report on the Romani Minority in the Czech Republic during 1995–6*, Prague: Dženo Foundation.

European Commission (1999) *Enlargement Briefing: EU Support for Roma Communities in Central and Eastern Europe*, Brussels: European Commission, December.

European Commission (2000a) *Regular Report on the Czech Republic's Progress towards Accession*, Brussels: European Commission, 8 November.

European Commission (2000b) *Regular Report on Slovakia's Progress towards Accession*, Brussels: European Commission, 8 November.

ERRC (1997a) *Time of the Skinheads: Denial and Exclusion of Roma in Slovakia*, European Roma Rights Center, Country Reports Series 3, Budapest: ERRC, January.

ERRC (1997b) *ERRC Press Statement – Czech Republic*, Budapest: ERRC, 15 August.

ERRC (1998) 'Police raid in Rudňany, central [sic] Slovakia', *Roma Rights*, Budapest: ERRC, summer. [Rudňany is in East Slovakia.]

ERRC (1999a) *A Special Remedy: Roma and Schools for the Mentally Handicapped in the Czech Republic*, Country Report, Budapest: ERRC, 15 June.

ERRC (1999b) 'Lawsuits filed by Roma challenge racial segregation in Czech schools', *ERRC Press Statement*, Budapest: ERRC, 15 June.

Fenyvesi, C. (1999) 'The Romani flight to Helsinki – neither the first nor the last', *RFE/RL Watchlist* 1, 26, 15 July.

Fraser, A. (1992) *The Gypsies*, Oxford: Blackwell.

Greenberg, S. (1993) 'Mečiar turns on the media', *The Guardian*, 27 September.

Grohová, J. (1999) 'Stále více lidi sympatizuje s extremisty', *Mladá fronta dnes*, 15 July.

Gross, T. (1993) 'The world overlooks Czech bigotry', *Prague Post*, 27 October.

Gross, T. (1994) 'A blot on the conscience: Czech attitudes on citizenship for gypsies come under fire', *Financial Times*, Supplement on Czech Republic, 19 December.

Grulich, T. and Haišman, T. (1986) 'Institutionální zájem o cikánské obyvatelstvo v Československu v letech 1945–1958', *Český Lid* 73, 2: 72–85.

Guy, W. (1975a) 'Ways of looking at Roma: the case of Czechoslovakia', in F. Rehfisch (ed.) *Gypsies, Tinkers and Other Travellers*, London: Academic Press (reprinted in D. Tong (ed.) (1998), 13–48).

Guy, W. (1975b) Historical text (no pagination), in J. Koudelka *Gypsies*, New York: Aperture.

Guy, W. (1977) *The Attempt of Socialist Czechoslovakia to Assimilate its Gypsy Population*, unpublished PhD thesis, Bristol: University of Bristol.

Guy, W. (1998) 'Afterword 1996' (to 'Ways of looking at Roma: the case of Czechoslovakia'), in D. Tong (ed.) (1998), 48–68.

Guy, W. (2001) 'Romani identity and post-Communist policy', in W. Guy (ed.) (2001).

Guy, W. (ed.) (2001) *Between Past and Future: the Roma of Central and Eastern Europe*, Hatfield: University of Hertfordshire Press.

Haišman, T. (1999) 'Romové v Československu v letech 1945–1967: Vývoj institutionálního zájmu a jeho dopady', in H. Lisá (ed.) (1999), 137–83.

Holomek, K. (2000) 'Jak omezit emigraci Romů', *Romano hangos* (Romani voice) 2, 8, 6 June.

Horváthová, E. (1964) *Cigáni na Slovensku*, Bratislava: Vydavateľstvo Slovenskej akadémie vied.

Hübschmannová, M. (1968) 'cikáni = Cikáni?', *Reportérova ročenka 1968*, Prague: Reportér, 32–9.

Hübschmannová, M. (1994) *Šaj pes dovakeras – Můžeme se domluvit*, Olomouc: Univerzita Palackého.

Hübschmannová, M. (1999) 'Od etnické kasty ke strukturovanému etnickému společenství', in H. Lisá (ed.) (1999), 115–36.

Human Rights Watch (1996) *Roma in the Czech Republic: Foreigners in their Own Land*, Human Rights Watch/Helsinki Report, 8, 11(D), NewYork: Human Rights Watch.

Jakl, R. (1998) 'Police struggle with own racial prejudice', *Prague Post on-line*, 4 March.

Jamnická-Šmerglová, Z. (1955) *Dějiny našich cikánů*, Prague: Orbis.

Jurová, A. (1992) 'Riešenie rómskej problematiky na Slovensku po druhej svetovej vojne', in A. B. Mann (ed.) *Neznámi Rómovia*, Bratislava: Ister Science Press.

Jurová, A. (1993) *Vývoj romské problematiky na Slovensku po roku 1945*, Spoločenskovedný ústav SAV n Košiciach, Bratislava: Goldpress.

Kalibová, K. (1989) 'Charakteristika úmrtnostních poměrů romské populace v ČSSR', *Demografie* 31: 239–50.

Kalibová, K. (1999) 'Romové z pohledu statistiky a demografie', in H. Lisá (ed.) (1999), 91–114.

Kavan, Z. (1996) 'Democracy and nationalism in Czechoslovakia', in B. Einhorn, M. Kaldor and Z. Kavan (eds) *Citizenship and Democratic Control in Contemporary Europe*, Cheltenham: Edward Elgar.

Kawczynski, R. (1998) 'Rudko Kawczynski briefs commission staff', *CSCE Digest* 21, 10, October.

Kenrick, D. and Puxon, G. (1972) *The Destiny of Europe's Gypsies*, London: Chatto Heinemann.

Kohn, M. (1995) *The Race Gallery*, London: Jonathan Cape.

Kostelancik, D. J. (1989) 'The Gypsies of Czechoslovakia: political and ideological considerations in the development of policy', *Studies in Comparative Communism* XXII, 4: 307–21, winter.

Kovats, M. (2001) 'Hungary: Politics, difference and equality', in W. Guy (ed.) (2001).

Kymlicka, W. (2000) 'Nation-building and minority rights: comparing West and East', *Journal of Ethnic and Migration Studies* 26, 2:183–212, April.

Lacková, I. (1999) *A False Dawn: My Life as a Gypsy Woman in Slovakia*, Hatfield: University of Hertfordshire Press/Centre de recherches tsiganes.

Laubeová, L. (1999) 'Multicultural? Here?', *The New Presence* 5, May.

Lee, R. (2000) 'Post-Communist migration to Canada', *Cambridge Review of Interna tional Affairs* XIII, 2: 51–70, spring-summer.

Legge, M. (1997) 'Expert: Government ducks blame on Romanies', *Prague Post on-line*, 17 September.

Legge, M. (1998a) 'Canadian asylum for Czech Romanies: immigration board decision criticises discrimination and alleges persecution', *Prague Post on-line*, 22 April.

Legge, M. (1998b) 'Romanies flee again', *Prague Post on-line*, 9 September.

Lemon, A. (1996) 'No land, no contracts for Romani workers', *Transition* 2, 13, 28 June.

Lemon, A. (2001) 'Russia: politics of performance', in W. Guy (ed.) (2001).

Lidové noviny (1995a) 'Prostitutky se stěhují na Plzeňsko', *Lidové noviny*, 2 March.

Lidové noviny (1995b) 'Czechs alarmed by rise in racially motivated murders', *Lidové noviny*, reprinted in *The Guardian*, 31 May.

Lidové noviny (1996) 'Bude multinárodní Spiš patřit Romům?', *Lidové noviny*, special supplement: 2, 27 September.

Lidové noviny (1999a) 'Rasových trestných činů ubylo, počet skinheadů naopak vrostl', *Lidové noviny*, 15 July.

Lidové noviny (1999b) 'Nad Českém se stále vnasi hrozba viz do Británie', *Lidové noviny*, 3 August.

Liégeois, J.-P. and Gheorghe, N. (1995) *Roma/Gypsies: A European Minority*, Minority Rights Group International Report 95/4, London: MRG.

Lisá, H. (ed.) *Romové v České republice 1945–1998*, Prague: Socioklub.

Marushiakova, E. and Popov, V. (2001) 'Bulgaria: Ethnic diversity – a common struggle for equality', in W. Guy (ed.) (2001).

Mirga, A. and Gheorghe, N. (1997) *The Roma in the Twenty-First Century: A Policy Paper*, Project on Ethnic Relations policy paper, Princeton: PER.

Mladá fronta dnes (1999) 'Za rasové motivované činy bývají často nízké tresty', 15 July.

MPSV (1971) *Zpráva o současném stavu řešení otázek cikánského obyvatelstva* (Report on the current state of solving questions of the gypsy population), Prague: Federal Ministry of Labour and Social Affairs, 24 November.

Mróz, L. (2001) 'Poland: The clash of tradition and modernity', in W. Guy (ed.) (2001).

Naegele, J. (1999) 'Slovak authorities suspect "plot" behind Romany exodus to Finland', *Radio Free Europe*, 14 July.

Nečas, C. (1994) *Nemůžeme zapomenout/Našt'i bisteras*, Olomouc: Univerzita Palackého.

Nečas, C. (1995) *Romové v České republice včera a dnes*, Olomouc: Univerzita Palackého.

Nováček, J. (1968) *Cikáni včera, dnes a zítra*, Prague: Socialistická akademie.

Office of the President of Slovakia (1999) *Meeting of the Presidents of the Visegrad Four Countries: Working Dokument [sic] on the Roma Issue in the V4 Countries*, High Tatras, 3 December, Bratislava: Office of the President of Slovakia, (quoted Cahn and Vermeersch 2000: 76–7).

O'Nions, H. (1996) 'Czech law developments', paper given at *Romani Studies and*

*Work with Travellers Conference*, University of Greenwich, July.

Pape, M. (1997) *A nikdo Vám nebude věřit: dokument o koncentračním táboře Lety u Písku*, Prague: GplusG.

Pellar, R. and Andrs, Z. (1990) 'Statistical evaluation of Roma women in East Slovakia', Appendix in P. Ofner and B. de Rooij *Het Afkopen van Vruchtbaarheid: Een Onderzoek naar Sterilisatiepraktijecten ten aanzien van Romavrouwen in Tsejchoslowakije*, Amsterdam: Lau Mazeril Foundation.

PER (1992) *The Romanies in Central and Eastern Europe: Illusions and Reality*, Project on Ethnic Relations (PER) report on roundtable discussions in Stupava, Slovakia (April 30-May 2), Princeton: PER.

Plichtová, J. (1993) 'Czechoslovakia as a multi-cultural state in the context of the region: 1918–92', in *Minorities in Central and Eastern Europe*, Minority Rights Group International Report 93/1, London: MRG.

Powell, C. (1994) 'Time for another immoral panic?: the case of the Czechoslovak Gypsies', *International Journal of Sociology and Law* 22, 2: 105–21.

Premusová, J. and Sirovátka, T. (1996) 'On the formation of long-term unemployment in the Czech Republic: an evaluation of the results of a comparative study of three localities' (in Czech), *Sociologický časopis* 32, 1, 39–50.

Radio Prague (1998) 'Romanies come home', *Radio Prague*, 15 June.

RFE/RL (1999) 'Czechs pass law enabling Roma to get citizenship', *RFE/RL Watchlist* 1, 26, 15 July.

Romano kurko (2000) 'Děti ulice', *Romano kurko* (Romani week) 10, 7, 13 July.

Romano nevo l'il (2000) *Romano nevo l'il* (Romani new letter) 10, 435–47, 13 May – 13 August.

Scheffel, D. Z. (1999) 'The untouchables of Svinia', *Human Organisation* 58, 1: 44–53.

Schlager, E. (1998a) 'Roma in the Czech Republic: the path of Martin Luther King or Malcolm X?', *CSCE Digest* 21, 4, April.

Schlager, E. (1998b) 'Czech citizenship law remains lightning rod for international criticism', *CSCE Digest* 21, 5, May.

Schön, J. T. (2000) 'Vlachiko Rómovia v SR', *Romano nevo l'il* 10, 424–434, 28 February – 14 May.

Siderenko, E. (1995) 'Gender, migration and the formation of ethnic niches in the labour market: the case of Ukrainians in the Czech Republic', paper for ESRC seminar series *Gender and Ethnicity in New Market Economies*, University of London.

Silverman, C. (1995) 'Persecution and politicisation: Roma (Gypsies) of Eastern Europe', *Cultural Survival Quarterly*, summer.

Slovak Government (1996) *Proposal of Activities and Measures in order to Solve the Problems of Citizens in Need of Special Care* (Návrh úloh a opatrení na riešenie problémov občanov, ktorí potrebujú osobitnú pomoc), Resolution 310/96, Bratislava: Government of Slovak Republic, 30 April.

Slovak Government (1999a) *Report Submitted by the Slovak Republic Pursuant to Article 25, Paragraph 1 of the Framework Convention for the Protection of National Minorities*, Bratislava: Government of Slovak Republic.

Slovak Government (1999b) *Information about the Activities of the Slovak Government in Regard to Solving the Problems of the Roma National Minority in the Slovak Republic* (Informačný materiál o aktivitách vlády Slovenskej republiky v oblasti riešenia problémov rómskej národnostnej menšiny v Slovenskej republike), Bratislava: Government of Slovak Republic, 15 September.

Slovak Government (1999c) *Strategy for the Solution of the Problems of the Roma National Minority and Set of Measures for its Implementation – Stage I*, (Stratégie na riešenie problémov romskej národnostnej menšiny a súbor opatrení na jej realizáciu – I. etapa), Resolution 821/99, Bratislava: Government of Slovak Republic, adopted 27 September.

Slovak Government (2000) *Elaboration of the Government Strategy for Addressing Problems of the Romani National Minority into a Package of Concrete Measures for year 2000 – Stage II* (Rozpracovaná stratégia vlády SR na riešenie problémov rómskej národnostnej menšiny do súboru konkrétnych opatrení na rok 2000 – II. etapa), Resolution 294/00, Bratislava: Government of Slovak Republic, adopted 3 May.

Slovak Socialist Government (1968) *Plnení harmonogramu práce ... za I–III štvrt'rok 1968 a návrh plánu na 1969* (Fulfilling the programme of work ... 1st to 3rd quarters 1968 and proposed plan for 1969), November.

Sme (1999) 'Visas halt Slovak Gypsies' [sic] exodus to Finland', *Sme*, 10 July.

Socioklub (1999) *Problems of Co-existence between the Romani Community and the Majority Population in a Socio-political Context*, study by Socioklub, Prague: MPSV (Ministry of Labour and Social Affairs).

Stewart, M. (1997) *The Time of the Gypsies*, Boulder Co.: Westview Press.

Sus, J. (1961) *Cikánská otázka v ČSSR*, Prague: Státní nakladatelství politické literatury.

Šiklová, J. (1999) 'Romové a nevládní, neziskové romské a proromské občanské organizace přispívající k integraci tohoto etnika', in H. Lisá (ed.) (1999), 271–89.

Šiklová, J. and Miklušáková, M. (1998) 'Law as an instrument of discrimination: Denying citizenship to the Czech Roma', *East European Constitutional Review* 7, 2, spring.

Times Mirror (1991) Times Mirror Survey, Washington DC: Times Mirror Center, quoted in *The Guardian*, 4 October.

Tolerance Foundation (1994) *Report on the Czech Citizenship Law*, Prague: Tolerance Foundation, 25 May.

Tong, D. (ed.) (1998) *Gypsies: An Interdisciplinary Reader*, New York: Garland.

Travis, A. (1998) 'Slovaks now required to have visa on entering UK', *The Guardian*, 8 October.

Trehan, N. (2001) 'In the name of the Roma? The role of private foundations and NGOs', in W. Guy (ed.) (2001).

Tritt, R. (1992) *Struggling for Ethnic Identity: Czechoslovakia's Endangered Gypsies*, Helsinki Watch report, New York: Human Rights Watch.

Vašečka, M. (1999) 'Put down in the under-class', *The New Presence* 10, October.

Vašečka, M. (2001) 'Roma', in G. Mesežnikov, M. Kollár and T. Nicholson (eds)

*Slovakia 2000: A Global Report on the State of Society*, Bratislava: Institute for Public Affairs, 169–99

Vermeersch, P. (2000) 'Minority rights for the Roma and political conditionality of European Union accession: the case of Slovakia', unpublished paper for *Conference 2000: New Directions in Roma Studies*, University of Greenwich/University of Birmingham, 28 June – 1 July.

Vermeersch, P. (2001) 'Roma identity and ethnic mobilisation in Central European politics', unpublished paper for *European Consortium for Political Research*, Grenoble, 6–11 April.

Víšek, P. (1999) 'Program integrace – řešení problematiky romských obyvatel v období 1970 až 1989', in H. Lisá (ed.) (1999), 184–218.

Wallace, C., Chmouliar, O., and Siderenko, E. (1996) 'The eastern frontier of Western Europe: Mobility in the buffer zone', *New Community* 22, 2: 259–86.

Weinerová, R. (1994) 'Romanies – in search of lost security? An ethnological probe in Prague 5', *Prague Occasional Papers in Ethnology* 3, Prague: Institute of Ethnology ČAV/Český lid.

Willems, W. (1997) *In Search of the True Gypsy: From Enlightenment to Final Solution*, London: Cass.

# Notes

1  After 1925 several schools for Roma were established in Ruthenia (now Trans-Carpathian Ukraine) and East Slovakia and in 1929 a group of East Slovak doctors founded the Society for the Study and Solution of the Gypsy Problem (Horváthová 1964: 168). The society published books and articles but also organised theatrical and musical performances in principal regional theatres and established a flourishing football team, named Roma, which even toured abroad (Davidová 1965: 26).

2  Kenrick and Puxon originally gave what they regarded as a conservative estimate of a quarter of a million deaths (Kenrick and Puxon 1972: 183–4). The IRU now claims that 'over half a million persons were exterminated' (Acton and Klímová 2001: Appendix 3).

3  Jamnická-Šmerglová quotes 1948 police records for a 1940 census of Roma showing 6,500 in the Czech lands and 60,000 in Slovakia. Kenrick and Puxon, also referring to police archives, cite a 1939 estimate of 13,000 in the Czech lands and explain the discrepancy by stating that 'several thousand managed to escape to Slovakia before deportations began' (Kenrick and Puxon 1972: 135). Horváthová's estimate of 100,000 Roma in Slovakia during the wartime period is an extrapolation from the census figures of 1927 and 1952.

4  At this time 40,000 ethnic Hungarians were forcibly relocated to the Czech lands while, like the Roma, many impoverished Slovaks also migrated westwards voluntarily in search of work (Plichtová 1993: 15).

5  This went unacknowledged in the description of a 1947 police census of 'wandering Gypsies and other work-shy vagabonds' which revealed that only two years after the end of the war there were 16,752 Roma in the Czech lands, over 16 per cent of a total 101,200 in the whole republic (Kostelancik 1989: 310, Jamnická-Šmerglová 1955: 86, Haišman 1999: 145). A decade later, in 1958, although no precise figures are available, the Romani population was estimated at between 120,000 and 150,000 of which perhaps a quarter were in the Czech lands.

6  '[The urban local authorities] practically ceased to house gypsies in decent flats in accept-

314

able residential districts. Instead, as a matter of standard practice, all new arrivals were allocated flats that were either cramped, dirty and mouldering or else cold and cavernous, located in houses long-destined for demolition and which stood in shattered, depopulated back-streets' (Jamnická-Šmerglová 1955: 89).

7    It was also in preparation for the transition from a People's Republic to the more elevated status of Socialist Republic, declared in 1960 (Guy 1975a: 214).

8    Economic considerations had been a major factor in the earlier assimilation attempt. Eighteenth century Hungary, of which Slovakia was then a part, had been severely depopulated in the wake of the conflict between Habsburgs and Turks and consequently labour power was at a premium (Fraser 1992: 157).

9    This followed earlier attempts in 1948 by Roma in Slovakia to set up a socio-cultural organisation, which was not allowed for similar reasons (Jurová 1992: 92).

10   This delegation was accompanied by the author and his ethnologist colleague and friend, Dr Eva Davidová.

11   The first president of the International Romani Union was Dr Jan Cibula, a Romani doctor from Slovakia.

12   Charter 77 (*Charta 77*) was established in 1977 to bear witness to violations of human rights safeguarded by the 1975 Helsinki Accords to which Czechoslovakia was a signatory. Václav Havel, now president of the Czech Republic, was a founder member and spokesperson.

13   A 1972 Decree on Sterilisation, issued by the Ministries of Health of the Czech and Slovak Socialist Republics, was careful not to mention Roma by name but other evidence makes it clear that this ethnic group was a prime target. A 1977 briefing paper for a Slovak Government commission referred to what it called the 'high unhealthy' level of the Roma population and urged increased grants for sterilisation to counterbalance the income from child benefits, since 'even a backward Gypsy woman is able to calculate that, from an economic point of view, it is more advantageous for her to give birth every year' (quoted Tritt 1992: 20).

14   The most notorious of such housing projects were Chanov in Most (Northern Bohemia), Lunik IX in Košice (Eastern Slovakia), and Dúžavská Cesta (also called 'Black City') in Rimavská Sobota (Central Slovakia) (Tritt 1992: 56–8, Hübschmannová 1994).

15   An internal government report revealed that a subsequent attempt to strengthen the law had been abandoned because 'the proposed solution of restricting the movement of the gypsy population in fact limits their freedom of residence and therefore is not in harmony with Article 31 of the constitution' (quoted Davidová and Guy 1972: 84).

16   The government committee, as the co-ordinating body charged with overseeing policy implementation, was quite clear about the illegality of local authority practice but appeared powerless to do anything other than complain – in strictly internal reports: '[L]ocal authorities protect themselves ... by refusing to register these citizens [i.e. Roma migrants] as permanent residents. However the Ministry of the Interior directive on Law 54/1949 Sb. about population registration specifically states that registration as a permanent resident may not be dependent on any other conditions, especially accommodation, economic, financial, etc.' (quoted Guy 1975a: 220).

17   According to administrative records, based on decisions by local authority social work departments about non-assimilated Roma, 'in 1989 there were approximately 400,000 –500,000 Roma in Czechoslovakia' (Plichtová 1993: 42), of which 145,738 were in the Czech lands forming 1.41 per cent of the total population there (Kalibová 1999: 99). Two years later the 1991 census, when Roma had the right to declare themselves as such for the first time in sixty years, showed there were 32,903 Roma in the Czech Republic and 75,802 in Slovakia, forming 0.32 per cent and 1.4 per cent respectively of the total population

(Kalibová 1999: 96–7). Plichtová tried to explain the huge discrepancy in the numbers as partly due to 'a low level of ethnic awareness' among Roma but also suggested 'fear of possible discrimination' might have been a factor (Plichtová 1993: 17, 42). This far more plausible explanation was eventually accepted by the Czech government in 1999 (Czech Government 1999a: 33). The estimated numbers accepted by European institutions are based on the opinion of researchers and, with allowance for demographic growth, correspond more closely to earlier administrative figures compiled by Communist officials, which are generally regarded as the most reliable source. These indicate that there are between 250,000 and 300,000 Roma in the Czech Republic and between 480,000 and 520,000 in Slovakia (Liégeois and Gheorghe 1995: 7). In 1999 the Czech Government accepted lower 'qualified estimates' of 200,000 for the Czech lands, 'divided into several ethnic groups' [sic] – 170,000 Slovak Roma (85 per cent), 18,000 Olah or Vlachiko Roma (9 per cent), 15,000 Hungarian-speaking Roma (7.7 per cent) and 'only about 100' Sinti, the original Roma inhabitants of the Czech lands (Czech Government 1999b: 6–7). Slovakia contains the same groups although numbers are larger but here, too, it is recognised that declared ethnicity greatly underestimates those who would normally acknowledge Romani identity and is no help at all in differentiating between sub-groups (Slovak Government 1999a). In 2000, the leader of a Vlachiko organisation made the unsubstantiated claim that there were 100,000 Vlachiko Roma in Slovakia, amounting to a third of all Roma living there (Schön 2000: 8). According to a leading Czech demographer, projections made on the basis of 1980s data would indicate a total population of 'almost half a million' on the territory of the former Czechoslovakia by the year 2005, with rather more than a third (200,000) living in the Czech Republic (Kalibová 1999: 107).

18   Meanwhile, newspapers and magazines in the Romani language sprang up and over thirty cultural organisations applied for official registration throughout the republic. A museum of Romani culture was founded in Brno, while in East Slovakia a Romani theatre opened its doors in Prešov and a innovatory department of Romani music was established as part of the existing conservatory in Košice. Many of these cultural and political activities were launched and sustained with financial support from the state. Likewise educational experiments using teaching materials in the Romani language were introduced. In July 1990, this new beginning was celebrated in Brno by the first World Romani Festival, with President Havel as guest of honour (Davidová 1995: 222–7).

19   In June 1990, six Romani deputies gained seats in the Czech parliament, of which five were OF candidates and one seat was gained (VNP) in Slovakia (Vermeersch 2001: 3).

20   Around ten other villages and towns in the Spiš region adopted similar measures which, after protests from Roma and NGOs, were dropped a month later 'when the Slovak Parliament declared them unconstitutional on July 15, 1993' (ERRC 1997a: 48).

21   The vast majority of the attacks were carried out by groups of skinheads, revealed by research to be mainly immature, aggressive juveniles aged under twenty, though some were under fifteen, the age of criminal responsibility. They were predominantly from blue-collar backgrounds with only elementary school education or apprenticeships (Czech Government 1997b: I, 22). While the 1997 research reported they came from 'non-problematic families', a later view talked of 'social difficulties faced by these young people who are easily manipulated' (Czech Government 1999a: 9).

22   The victims were not exclusively Roma, for Vietnamese migrant workers and African and Arab students also suffered (Tritt 1992: 2, footnote 2), but 'the overwhelming majority of ... [attacks] were directed against Romanies (Gypsies) or people mistaken for Romanies' (ČTK 1995). The first recorded death in 1990 may have been such a case, where a Turkish national was knifed by a skinhead gang in Plzeň.

23    In one bizarre ruling a district court decided an attack could not be racist since 'the injured Roma are of the same Indo-European race as the perpetrators' (Czech Government 1999b: 4). A Slovak court in Banská Bystrica made a similar ruling in May 1999 (Fenyvesi 1999).

24    Since the fall of Communism in 1989 and May 1995 an estimated twenty-seven Roma died as a result of racial violence in the Czech lands while 181 racist attacks were reported for 1995 alone (Human Rights Watch 1996: 2). Not much had changed by late 1997 with 'over 150 such cases' that year, although in 1998 the number decreased to 138, including two deaths. However, a spokesperson for HOST stated that the number of racist crimes registered by this NGO was 40 per cent higher (*Lidové noviny* 1999a, *Mladá fronta dnes* 1999).

25    This charge was met with a flat denial by a police spokesperson who did not even feel the need to resort to the familiar 'just a few rotten apples' defence: 'There is no racism in the police. It's just a matter of their [police officers'] personal experiences. And a lot of them have had bad experiences with Roma. And someone dealing with them on a day by day basis could even say that every Roma is a thief. It's an individual matter' (Human Rights Watch 1996: 7–8).

26    The 1993 Minority Rights Group report, *Minorities in Central and Eastern Europe*, seemed unaware of any irony in its cover picture, captioned: 'Local police protect Roma community in Slovakia'. In spite of providing the main image, the Roma are dealt with in a single paragraph in the chapter on 'Czechoslovakia as a multi-cultural state ...' (Plichtová 1993). The author was Slovak.

27    In 1997, sociological research in the Czech Republic revealed that 89 per cent of labour office representatives from all localities with a substantial Romani community thought that a significant cause of their unemployment was 'the Roma's unwillingness to work regularly, long term, systematically', whereas '68 per cent of Roma[ni representatives from the same localities] disagreed that they [i.e. Roma] do not work because they are unwilling to' (Czech Government 1997b: II, 17).

28    A mid-1997 comparison showed that a family with three children was entitled to monthly support of approximately 11,600 Czech crowns (ČZK), compared to an average wage of around 10,000 ČZK, 'which is not achievable in the job market for Roma – usually unskilled labour – [so] they often prefer to receive welfare benefits' (Czech Government 1997b: I, 17). In 1995–6, of those Roma still with jobs in the Czech lands, 90 per cent of men worked as manual labourers, mainly in construction, while women most commonly had jobs as cleaners. Their average wages were 6,000 ČZK for men and 2,500 ČZK for women (Dženo Foundation cited Czech Government 1997b: I, 17).

29    In similar vein, police in the Czech town of Teplice estimated that although Roma were only 7 per cent of the population, they accounted for 60 per cent of all crime and up to 80 per cent of assaults (Czech Government 1997b: I, 22). However, other evidence challenged the reliability of such typical estimates. A 1995 survey-based study, using international comparisons, claimed that when socio-economic conditions were taken into account, 'rates of crime in poor Romani neighbourhoods [in Eastern Europe] ... [were] no higher than in poor non-Romani neighbourhoods'. Also, contrary to popular stereotypes, 'rates for violent crime such as murder and rape ... [were] far lower among Roma than the national averages' (Silverman quoted Lemon 1996: 29).

30    Romani women joined the mushrooming growth in prostitution as previous legal restraints were removed and the economic situation deteriorated. In this they were by no means alone for a police spokesman from Plzeň reported that, while a fifth of prostitutes on the city streets were Romani, the great majority (70 per cent) were Czech. The remainder were from Slovakia, Ukraine or Belarus (*Lidové noviny* 1995a).

31    In his inaugural speech to the Czech parliament, Republican leader Miroslav Sladek

317

proposed that 'for Gypsies the age of criminal responsibility should be from the moment of birth because being born is, in fact, their biggest crime' (Carolina 1996). The Republicans' support unexpectedly halved in the following elections, in 1998, when they failed to reach the 5 per cent threshold and so lost their representation in parliament. Once more, the Republican campaign was anti-Roma with billboard posters attacking their dependence on social support.

32  90 per cent of Romani representatives in the 1997 survey saw their 'minority's social and educational decline' as a 'very important' factor in their 'different [lowered] status in society' (Czech Government 1997b: II, 2–3).

33  The exception was governmental willingness to support Romani culture in the form of publications in Romani, language courses for teachers, music and dance and the Museum of Romani Culture. Also, both Czech and Slovak Governments sponsored conferences on the situation of Roma. For example, in 1992 the Federal, Czech and Slovak Governments sought the help of a US-based conflict resolution agency, Project on Ethnic Relations (PER), to organise a roundtable meeting of 125 participants from all over Central and Eastern Europe, which brought together leaders of Romani communities, government officials and academic experts (PER 1992: 1).

34  On occasions, the 'official' census figures for Roma have been presented by the Czech Government in negotiations to minimise the size of the problem arising from the 1993 citizenship law. This subterfuge was sharply rejected by the Council of Europe as 'unsatisfactory … when at the same time the authorities of Ostrava admit that in that [city] … alone the Roma population amounts to at least the same figure' [as that suggested for the whole of the country] (Council of Europe 1996: 18).

35  By refusing citizenship on these grounds the Czech authorities were adding an extra penalty, *ex post facto*, to those who had already been punished for their crimes and in many cases this was a far severer sentence than was possible for the offence in question. This amounted to a violation of Article 15 of the International Covenant on Civil and Political Rights which the Czech government had adopted (Council of Europe 1996: 25, Human Rights Watch 1996: 21–2, O'Nions 1996).

36  Romani activists and NGOs estimated, on the basis of survey research, that between 10,000 and 25,000 long-term or life-long residents of the Czech Republic remained without Czech citizenship, while in response the Czech Ministry of the Interior claimed that by the end of 1995 only 200 former Czechoslovak citizens had been actually denied Czech citizenship.

37  In 1994, 154 Slovak citizens were expelled from the Czech Republic (Council of Europe 1996: 31) and 244 the following year and 'there is reason to believe that many of those deported to Slovakia were Roma who, for one reason or another, were denied Czech citizenship despite having genuine links to the Czech Republic' (Human Rights Watch 1996: 28).

38  A mayor from East Slovakia reported that of about one hundred Roma who had come to his town from the Czech lands in the two years since the division of Czechoslovakia only two had been granted residency permits (Human Rights Watch 1996: 29). A major national daily reported a similar situation elsewhere in the same region, where those refused residency had remained as 'illegal' immigrants (*Lidové noviny* 1996). Yet Slovak local authorities were well aware that it was *they* who were acting illegally (Vašečka 1999: 2). Vašečka gives a stark account of the deteriorating conditions in such settlements during the 1990s (Vašečka 2001: 192–3)

39  In spite of governmental assurances to the contrary (Council of Europe 1996: 28–31), various local authorities throughout the Czech Republic told human rights lawyers that Roma without Czech citizenship 'would be treated like foreigners in future and would lose their benefits under the law' (Gross 1993). This could mean loss of unemployment, health, wel-

fare and insurance benefits as well as of the right to free education, to vote and to pass-ports. A later report showed such instances had occurred (Gross 1994: vi).

40    Although the Council of Europe set no conditions on minority rights for admitting the Czech Republic as a member in June 1993, this lenient stance changed as criticism of the citizenship law steadily grew. The CSCE High Commissioner on National Minorities 'strongly urged that such legislation be changed' and US Congress members asked Premier Klaus to alter what they described as 'the most extensive revocation of citizenship since the end of the Second World War' (Gross 1994).

41    An international NGO condemned official evasiveness: 'Czech officials have refused to pro-vide credible and consistent documentation on the question of numbers' (Human Rights Watch 1996: 18, 26), while a Council of Europe report drew attention to poor official record keeping and confusion, commenting tartly that 'the Czech authorities are *today faced with the uncertainties of their own administrative expediency*' (Council of Europe 1996: 18, emphasis in original).

42    Although only those with permanent residency were eligible and formal application was still necessary, this step still represented a policy reversal of major symbolic importance.

43    '[T]he Czech law was designed to make it uncomfortable for Roma to remain in the Czech Republic' (Schlager 1998b: 32).

44    Šiklová and Miklušáková suggest that 'an exodus of Roma from Slovakia was anticipated' but note that '[t]hough officials now deny it, the Czech government must have been aware of the exclusionary potential of the new law', citing an April 1993 report which states: 'It can be expected that … at the beginning of 1994, a number of Roma will find themselves in the position of foreigners living in the Czech Republic, without any legal basis' (Šiklová and Miklušáková 1998: 4).

45    Suspicions that the implicit desire was to confirm the new Czech Republic as a homogenous 'ethnic' state, after a lengthy process since 1945 of progressively shedding non-Czech peo-ples, are strengthened by the special treatment of the Volhyn Czechs. Legal obstacles bar-ring citizenship to this returning émigré group of ethnic Czechs from the former USSR were promptly amended in 1994, suggesting a merging of the concepts of ethnicity and citi-zenship in a manner characteristic of German practice (Schlager 1998b: 32).

46    In general, Slovak politicians and media were far less inhibited than their more wary Czech counterparts. Stefan Pauliny, Slovak ambassador to the Netherlands, described Roma in 1994 as persons who 'prefer to avoid working, are engaged in criminality rather than seek-ing jobs, are molesting their surroundings and disregarding the rule of law' (*Romnews* 13 December 1994).

47    A Czech daily headed a special report on an area of East Slovakia with large numbers of Romani inhabitants: 'Will the multi-ethnic Spiš [region] come to belong to the Roma?' (*Lidové noviny* 1996).

48    In response to international condemnation, Mečiar threatened the Czech journalist report-ing him with prosecution for defamation of the state, punishable by up to two years impris-onment, and accused him of complicity in an international plot to bring about the 'disintegration' of Slovakia (Greenberg 1993). He also claimed he had been misquoted, but a verbatim transcript of his speech revealed his remark was really an expression of fear about the consequences to the ethnic balance in Slovakia of the high birthrate of Roma in comparison with that of 'whites'. '"So the prospect is that this [population] ratio will be changing to the benefit of Romanies" he observed. "That is why if we did not deal with them now, then they would deal with us in time …" A matter of us or them. What "deal" might mean in this context was left to hang in the air, loose talk often being the safest for the speaker and the most threatening for its target' (Kohn 1995: 179).

49 Both the tone ('socially unadaptable', 'negative social behaviour', 'bad way of life', etc.) and the tortuous circumlocutions – in the title and paragraph headings – to avoid naming Roma as the real subject of the report are characteristic of the 1959 government documents, advising local authorities how to implement the assimilation campaign, as well as the 1972 Slovak Government policy of 'acculturation'.

50 Although this wall was eventually demolished following government intervention, the Czech central authorities declared their impotence over the actions of the town council, pleading that 'Article 8 of the Constitution [guaranteed] the principle of self-government of territorial administrative units' (Czech Government 1999c: 1, Guy 2001).

51 The camp at Lety became the subject of heated disputes due to the apparent reluctance of the Czech authorities to relocate the pig farm, which currently occupies the site, and construct an appropriate memorial. This was interpreted as epitomising official indifference to Czech crimes against Roma and to the suffering inflicted at the camp.

52 The series, called *Na vlastní oči* (In your own eyes), was shown by the popular independent TV station Nova.

53 By June the following year, 600 of the original 1,500 had returned to the Czech Republic (Radio Prague 1998). Smaller numbers of Roma refugees also arrived in Canada from Slovakia (Braham and Braham 2000: 98) and later from Hungary (Lee 2000: 61–4).

54 Romani spokespersons characterised many emigrants as not the poor but 'upper-class' or 'young [and better] educated ... [who] don't see any ... future ... for their children' (Legge 1998a).

55 In the meantime, the president of the Ostrava branch of ROI unsuccessfully requested collective asylum from the US embassy for all Czech Roma (Naegele 1999).

56 Her reported justification for paying two-thirds of the ticket costs was astonishingly blunt – that 'in Ostrava there are two groups – "Roma" and "whites" – who cannot live together and ... the local administration should not refrain from helping one group – Roma – find a solution' (ERRC 1997b).

57 Around 1,500 arrived in 1997, mainly from the Czech Republic, while the following year Roma came predominantly from Slovakia – 1,256 in the first half of 1998 (*The Guardian* 8 October 1998, Legge 1998a, Vašečka 1999: 3). However, the flow from the Czech Republic resumed in the summer of 1999, peaking in June when 143 families sought asylum (ČTK 29 July 1999).

58 EU members imposing visa restrictions on Slovakia at various times included the UK, Ireland, Belgium, Denmark, Norway and Finland (Cahn and Vermeersch 2000: 78). Only Canada has treated the Czech Republic in the same way.

59 Of over 3,000 Roma refugees to the UK in 1997 and 1998, only five from Slovakia and one family of three from the Czech Republic were successful in gaining asylum (*Lidové noviny* 1999b).

60 Some Slovak Roma initially denied asylum in the UK had actually appealed successfully but the Home Office had immediately lodged counter-appeals ('Gypsy rulings put pressure on ministers', *The Guardian*, 1 December 1998). Eventually, the test case of Milan Horváth, from a village near Michalovce in East Slovakia, was dismissed in an appeal to the House of Lords on the grounds that, even though he might well have a well-founded fear of persecution, 'the authorities in Slovakia are willing and able to provide protection to the required standard, and Gypsies [sic] as a class are not exempt from that protection' ('Lords dismiss Roma asylum test case', *The Guardian*, 7 July 2000).

61 The report's outspoken criticism of previous Czech policy had led to its earlier rejection by the cabinet, which required a redraft to include 'concrete examples and concrete solutions'. Bratinka himself revealed that, '[a]ccording to the cabinet, the report was written from the

other side of the river. ... [It] was not pleased by the negative tone and non-standard style of the report, which drew information from non-governmental sources'. His deputy, the author of the report, was far more outspoken, even threatening resignation: 'Screw the government. ... I tried very hard to point out what positive steps the government had taken. But I found out that previous obligations [aimed at improving Romani conditions] were not fulfilled. I am afraid the government doesn't really want to solve this issue' (Legge 1997).

62    Material from this report has been drawn on extensively in this chapter.

63    Mass asylum seeking by Roma is linked to three factors, which explains why the largest waves came from the Czech Republic, Slovakia and, to a lesser extent, Hungary. These are: no visa restrictions on travel, the financial means to buy tickets, and, most importantly as with much migration, the level of consciousness and expectation among would-be emigrants. 'The critical measure is not so much how badly off the Roma are in a country ... but what the gap is between ever-increasing Roma expectations and government measures to address their concerns. In Romania the Roma have been conditioned to suffer and accept mistreatment that Roma in [the Czech Republic, Slovakia,] Hungary and Poland would not tolerate' (Schlager quoted Fenyvesi 1999).

64    The Framework Convention required EU candidates 'to promote, in all areas of economic, social, political and cultural life, full and effective equality between persons belonging to a national minority and those belonging to the majority' (Council of Europe 1995: Article 4, Paragraph 2). See Braham and Braham (2000) and Guy (2001) for fuller discussion.

65    The report openly stated: 'The reason for the low number of persons who declared "romipen" (Romani national identity) is fear of possible consequences. Information collected in a 1930 public census, when all citizens were required to state national identity in a non-anonymous manner, was used in 1939 and thereafter to send Romanies into concentration camps and later to death transports. Due to the aversion of the majority towards Romanies, declaration of ... Romani national identity, albeit anonymous, demands a certain amount of bravery' (Czech Government 1999a: 33). In fact, a similar undercount occurred in the 1930 census (Davidová 1970: 94).

66    A slightly later Czech government report of July 14 1999 actually recorded an annual decrease of over 10 per cent in racially motivated crimes from the previous year but at the same time the estimated number of 'extremists' almost doubled (*Lidové noviny* 1999a).

67    The bleak and menacing conclusions of this independent study read like no other government report: 'Beside bringing international dishonour upon the country for failure to uphold human rights, and consequently non-admission to the European Union, ... [a wait-and-see] approach and/or inadequate solution would lead – as it is already leading now – to a growing lack of understanding, tension and emigration of the most integrated Roma. ... It would gradually preclude co-existence and lead up to physical separation (walls, objectively arisen ghettos for non-payers of rents, and ultimately to intentional evacuation). ... This kind of approach would lead to hostile self-defence, radicalisation, Black Panthers, Palestinisation, potential political misuse, destabilisation of regions and the state, an untenable process of lapsing into conflicts with ultimate segregation or bilaterally welcomed exodus' (Czech Government 1999b: 12).

68    Although assimilation was still accepted as a solution for individuals, if freely chosen, any future assimilation of all Roma was now seen as 'very regrettable', and not only just for themselves. 'The denationalising of Roma, their cultural and linguistic Czechification, would be a cultural loss for the whole of Czech society' (Czech Government 2000a: 1).

69    These included the safeguarding of Roma minority rights, improving their democratic representation, strengthening anti-discrimination laws, retraining of those involved in criminal proceedings, appointing Romani counsellors to act as mediators, recruiting more Romani

assistants in schools, protecting Romani culture including language, supporting civic associations promoting co-existence, establishing citizens' advice bureaux and commissioning of further research.

70  In fact, those eligible for 'equalising measures' (*vyrovnávací akce*) were 'persons in a disadvantaged situation as a result of social – and even ethnic – reasons, and by this definition are not limited only to members of the Romani community'. This rather tortuous formulation might seem reminiscent of the patronising Slovak circumlocution 'citizens in need of special care' but the purpose was different. The 1996 policy in Slovakia was in direct descent from the earlier 1972 'acculturation' approach but the aim of the Czech conception was to provide direct and additional help to Roma, as Roma, but without it appearing as such. The 1997 Bratinka Report had been very critical of 'affirmative action', not least because of the dangers of backlash from excluded members of the majority, who would resent Roma once more appearing to benefit undeservedly from state handouts (Czech Government 1997b: I, 30–31). Here it is worth pointing out that Kymlicka is sceptical about affirmative action for Roma: 'Given that these policies have not been very successful so far in improving the situation of blacks, it is not clear how much we should expect from them in the case of the Roma' (Kymlicka 2000: 204).

71  Many NGOs, e.g. *Nová škola* (New School), had long opposed such segregation and had been active in developing alternative educational strategies, such as the recruitment of Roma teaching assistants, which 'was initiated and conceptualised wholly by non-governmental organisations' (Laubeová 1999). This initiative was eventually adopted by the Czech Ministry of Education and is proving one of the most promising innovations.

72  The idea of teaching Roma in smaller classes had already been floated the previous year in *Učitelské noviny*, the main Czech journal on educational issues, and in early 1999 was being piloted in ten schools (Czech Government 1999a: 25). Likewise, there were 23 Roma teaching assistants in action by June 1998. Nevertheless, the ERRC accused the new strategy of failing to 'address … the issue of discrimination in the school system' (Cahn 1999).

73  Ultimately this case was taken to the European Court of Human Rights.

74  For a comprehensive denunciation of the Communist regime's failure to implement its programmes effectively beyond the sphere of central government planning, see Víšek (1999: 184–218).

75  For the Czech Republic it noted that '[t]he inter-Ministerial Roma Commission still has no budget to implement policies, no executive power and few permanent staff' (European Commission 2000a: 26). This was precisely the predicament of the co-ordinating government committee in the mid-1960s, which failed to implement the programme of transferring and dispersing Roma throughout the federal republic!

76  However, Vermeersch noted that there was no clear structure allowing Romani organisations to participate and that the Commissioner, an appointee rather than elected officer, had lost credibility among many Roma because of his support for the government view that refugees from Slovakia were simply economic migrants (Vermeersch 2000: 8).

77  In the meantime, the 1996 policy document had been updated slightly in November 1997 by Resolution 796/97 of the Slovak Government.

78  By mid-July 1999 over 1,000 Roma were reported to have requested asylum in Finland in that year 'with the bulk of them arriving in the [l]ast few weeks' (*Sme* 1999, Fenyvesi 1999).

79  The Finnish prime minister reiterated and broadened this message shortly afterwards declaring: 'It is up to the governments [of Central and East European countries] to take the issue seriously and stop the discrimination of Roma' [sic].

80  The 'Visegrad Four' countries, regarded as among the front-runners for EU entry, are the Central European states of the Czech and Slovak Republics, Hungary and Poland.

81   The following passage does not quite reach the depths of a Jan Slota utterance: 'The lifestyle of many of them is oriented towards consumption and they live from hand to mouth. Because of their lower educational standard, the philosophy of some of them is simply to survive from one day to the next. If we add their increased propensity to alcohol abuse, absence of an at least minimum degree of planning, and low concern for developing normal habits including the feeling of responsibility, hygienic habits and ethics, this philosophy is changing today to that of living "from one benefit to the next"' (Office of the President of Slovakia 1999: 7, quoted Cahn and Vermeersch 2000: 76–7).

82   These claims were ridiculed as wild, unsubstantiated exaggerations in the Romani press, which cited demographic and ethnographic experts in their rebuttal (*Romano nevo lil'* 2000: 3).

83   In the 1998 elections there was only one Romani deputy, Monika Horáková, elected to the Czech Parliament – and not for a Romani party.

84   Even where not weakened by factionalism, Roma organisations had little power to achieve much. For example, '[r]elative cohesiveness among the Slovak Roma ha[d] not yielded benefits for the collective, mainly because a number of successive Slovak governments ha[d] neglected the Roma and their problems' (Barany 1998: 320).

85   The daily *Pravda* headlined its front page story 'Organised Exodus' (*Pravda* 6 July 1999), while President Schuster believed the migration was a plot, insisting that 'time will confirm how these Roma were organised, in what manner, and why they were chosen' (Naegele 1999). The 2000 Regular Report on Slovakia noted that '[s]ome political representatives have blamed the situation on the Roma themselves or attributed it to organised gangs' but added: 'The underlying social and economic roots can nevertheless not be ignored' (European Commission 2000b).

86   This strategy was taken a step further in April 2001 by an agreement between the Czech Foriegn Ministry and the IRU (see Acton and Klímová 2001). Likewise, on 27 July 1999 the Slovak Ministry of Foreign Affairs insisted, in response to the refugee crisis, that 'the problem of Roma is not only a specifically Slovak problem … but has Europe-wide dimensions and for this reason, too, it will need to be solved on a Europe-wide basis' (Slovak Government 1999b: 4).

87   '[W]here Roma face severe violence and discrimination … young, disaffected Roma are increasingly reacting to their abuse with aggression – potentially setting the stage for violent inter-ethnic conflict. Young Roma in the Czech Republic, Slovakia, Bulgaria, and Macedonia are among the most radicalised' (Kawczynski 1998: 98).

88   Such as *Vzájemné soužití* (Mutual co-existence) in Ostrava, headed by a charismatic development worker from India, Kumar Vishwanathan, which brought Romani and Czech communities together in the wake of the devastating floods of 1997. However NGOs can have their own problems of impermanence, limited resources and disorganisation (see Trehan 2001, Šiklová 1999).

As elsewhere in rural Hungary, the Romungro Roma of Heves slaughter pigs they have reared in preparation for the Christmas festivities (Rolf Bauerdick).

The Kedves Haz Kollegium in Nyirtelek, Eastern Hungary forms part of an innovative educational programme which directly challenges the widespread prejudice that Roma children are educationally inferior and need to be segregated from non-Roma children in the school system (Jason Orton).

Kalderash woman with characteristic dress and ornaments at annual Kalderash celebration in Horezu, Valcea county, Romania, 2000.

Kalderash artisan, Caldarar Ioan, making a copper can, the traditional craft of this community in Bratei, Sibiu county, Transylvania.

Large family house of wealthy *Calderari* Roma in Ciurea, Iaşi county, Romania, August-September 1997. The village of Ciurea in north-eastern Romania has 5,000 inhabitants of which 1,000 are Roma. Rich and poor Roma co-exist in Romania, sometimes even in the same village or in neighbouring villages (Christina McDonald).

House interior of wealthy *Calderari* Roma in Buzescu, Teleorman county, Romania, 1997. A main livelihood of this community in southern Romania is dealing in non-ferrous metals (Monica Serban).

Waste recycling amidst the smog of burning refuse. Built on the municipal rubbish dump of Oradea in western Romania, the settlement of Episcopia Bihor is home to 150 Roma, too poor to afford alternative accommodation (Rolf Bauerdick).

The small Romani settlement of Pata Rât on the outskirts of Cluj-Napoca in Transylvania, Romania has about 130 inhabitants.

For generations Roma have made charcoal by traditional methods in the wooded, mountainous areas of Bulgaria. Their customers are Greek dealers for whom it is cheaper to buy charcoal in low-wage Bulgaria than produce it in Greece (Rolf Bauerdick).

Ursari Roma (bear keepers) living in the Bulgarian woods near Sosopo on the shore of the Black Sea, where their bears perform for tourists on the beaches. In neighbouring countries Ursari often lost their livelihood after protests about cruelty to animals led to prohibition of their trade (Rolf Bauerdick).

Shakir Pashov (centre) among participants at a conference of the All-Gypsies' Organisation against Fascism and Racism and for the Promotion of the Cultural Development of the Gypsy Minority in Bulgaria', March 12–13 1949.

Founding congress of National Euro-Roma Association, led by the ethnic Bulgarian Tsvetelin Kuntchev (holding flag). Sofia, 12 December 1998.

Founding of Free Bulgaria Party in Plovdiv, 8 April 1999. Initiator was Kiril Rashkov (centre – seated next to his wife). Also present was celebrated Romani poet Sali Ibrahim (far left).

Old couple (Mechkara or Mećàr group) at home in Baltez, near Fieri, western Albania, 1999.

Wedding party (Mechkara or Mećàr group) in front of groom's house in Baltez, Albania, 1999.

Afternoon school in Roma quarter of Baltez, Albania, 1999

Playing cards in the Albanian town of Lezha

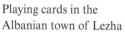

Stefano Montesi

Stefano Montesi

Romani quarter of Mali Mokrilug, Belgrade, inhabited by 6,000 Roma. November 2000.

Romani mahala (quarter) in Peć (Kosovo), where a group calling themselves 'Egyptians' live.

Funeral of four Ashkali (Albanian-speaking) Roma, killed after returning to their village to repair their damaged houses in Kosovo Polje (Kosovo), 15 November 2000.

Burnt-out Romani houses in Pejá, Kosovo. After Serbia was defeated by NATO bombing in 1999, Roma in Kosovo were accused by their ethnic Albanian neighbours of collaborating with the Serbs. In savage reprisals Roma were attacked, killed and driven out while their houses were set on fire (Rolf Bauerdick).

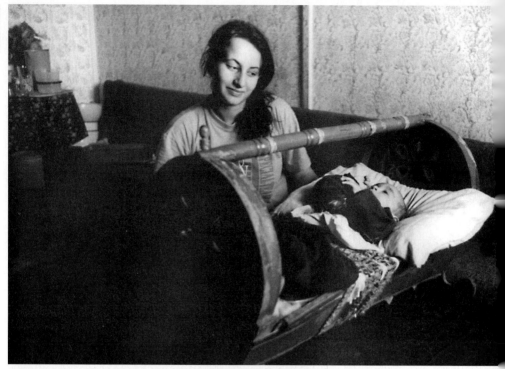

Hairie, married with one child, lives in a refugee camp near Sarajevo but came to Konik refugee camp in Podgorica in search of her mother. Podgorica, Montenegro, November 2000 (Stefan Montesi).

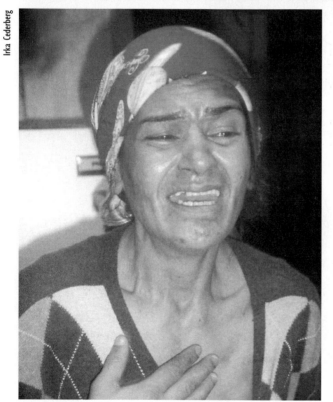

Many Roma from Albania and Kosovo have attempted the perilous crossing to Italy, often dying in the attempt. Bina Ajeti, a refugee from Priština, Kosovo, lost thirteen of her loved ones on an ill-fated voyage in 1999 on which 103 Roma drowned. She now lives in an Italian refugee camp outside Florence. (Irka Cederberg)

## CHAPTER FOURTEEN

# Hungary: politics, difference and equality

*Martin Kovats*

The study of Roma politics is still in its infancy, not least because of the relatively recent emergence of such activity.[1] This chapter focuses on Hungary, the country which has done most to encourage an explicit political dimension to Roma identity through state support for self-organised groups, the inclusion of Roma in Europe's most comprehensive minority rights legislation (Law on the Rights of National and Ethnic Minorities (1993), hereafter Minorities Law) and the creation of a nationwide network of representative Roma institutions (the minority self-government system).

Politics is fundamentally about relationships of power, ranging from the local to the global level, and, as such, is a strange (and distorting) medium full of ambiguities and contradictions. Though the further evolution of Roma politics is inevitable, it cannot be assumed that the process will necessarily bring benefits to Roma individuals and populations as a whole. Each Roma population politicises in its own time and in its own way in accordance with local conditions. Nevertheless, by analysing the Roma political experience in Hungary, it is possible not only to identify the factors determining behaviour and outcomes within that country, but also to establish parameters for the ongoing debate about the role of Roma politics, as well as identify points of reference with which to evaluate the political activity of Roma populations in other states.

## The incorporation of the Roma into the Hungarian state and society

### Feudal flexibility

A date for the arrival of a significant number of Roma into Hungary is still unresolved.[2] It has been argued that the existence of a number of settlements from the early fourteenth century with versions of *cigány* (the Hungarian for Gypsy) in their name (Cigánd, Cigányegyhaza) indicates a relatively early presence. However, this view is dismissed by the historian, Pál Nagy, whose most recent contribution to the debate identifies the first record of Roma settlement from the 1450s (Nagy 1998: 31–3, 66–7).

More research is needed to identify precisely the political/legal status of Roma during this early period and we must be conscious of the fact that contemporary notions of citizenship did not apply in the feudal world where status and rights were often related to ethnicity (and position within the division of labour). From (and even prior to) the foundation of the Hungarian state in 1000, the ruling élite sought to attract foreigners (non-Magyars) in order to bring skills and labour power into the country.[3] The newcomers 'obtained the privileges of choosing their own justices, living according to their own customs, and paying taxes in money based on holdings of land instead of a poll-tax' (Pamlényi 1975: 63). The situation of the Roma is more complicated because they did not arrive by invitation. Based on detailed archival research, Nagy argues that there is no evidence of Roma, as a population, being provided with any collective privilege (Nagy 1998: 125), though certain itinerant groups received a kind of privilege in the form of letters of safe conduct (Fraser 1992: 76). It appears that local Roma groups were attached to town or castle authorities who determined their place of settlement, employment and wages. These arrangements were often subsequently confirmed by royal decree. What proportion of the Roma population was covered by such arrangements is hard to quantify because there is inevitably less documentary evidence regarding those who lived a less regulated existence.

In addition to such ethnic diversity, the early Roma settlers benefited from the tripartite division of the country for most of the sixteenth and seventeenth centuries which precluded the establishment of centralised government.[4] Roma could provide support for the various armies on the ever-shifting frontline between Muslim and Christian empires (skilled and unskilled labour, information). Roma also filled a variety of occupations including public executioner, market inspector, doctor, international wine merchant. The absence of persecution is also demonstrated by the establishment of a Gypsy Quarter (*cigányváros*) in the capital, Buda, during the sixteenth century (Mészáros: 1976: 483).

## *Habsburg rule and the emergence of Gypsy policy*

Towards the end of the seventeenth century, the victory of the Habsburgs, and their absolutist pretensions, led to a decline in local autonomy and in the application of feudal privileges. It also affected the ethnic mix and demographic structure of the country with the arrival of many new landlords and the importation of immigrant labour to fill depopulated areas. The first half of the eighteenth century was also a time of economic stagnation and the rapid growth in the numbers of landless and dispossessed people. Against this background Roma policy first emerged in the sense of regulations explicitly targeting the Roma population as a whole. Roma were required to settle under the authority of landlords, whom a decree of 1725 also obliged to pursue and expel itinerants from their areas. By the 1760s resistance to serfdom led to a deepening of state involvement and produced the now well-known regulations and policy of assimilation of Empress Maria Theresa. In 1767 all Roma were made subject to the jurisdiction of the local courts, in effect completing the legal integration of the Roma into the state and society.[5]

The consequences of eighteenth century policies of persecution and violent assimilation were profound, most notably in producing the economic and social marginalisation of Roma individuals, communities and identity. The consistent failure of policies to achieve their stated aim (the peaceful absorption of Roma into the ranks of the serfs) also created a culture of antipathy between the authorities and Roma, with the former identifying the cause of this failure with the lack of 'civilisation' of the Roma themselves. However, in order to identify the factors determining the contemporary circumstances of the Hungarian Roma and of state-Roma relations, we need to move forward to the next critical period. The late nineteenth and early twentieth centuries saw the emergence of new factors, most notably the social, economic and political effects of agricultural recession and early industrialisation, as well as the evolution of Magyar national identity.

## Roma and the emerging nation-state

With the decline of serfdom from the mid-nineteenth century Roma had to shift for themselves within the new economic environment. Inevitably, without land (only 3.4 per cent of the Roma population was identified as working their own land at the end of the century), capital or developed economic and social relations, most were confined to occupations offering little security or possibility of development. An extensive register in 1893 found that 40 per cent of Roma worked as agricultural day labourers, one quarter were involved in metal work, carpentry or construction while a further 10 per cent lived through providing entertainment (Pomogyi 1995: 17). Agricultural depression from the end of the nineteenth century led to a fall in wages and in demand for casual farm labour. Roma artisans were also hit hard by the development of manufacturing industries which priced them out of the markets for metal and wooden utensils. The majority of the Roma in Hungary entered the twentieth century facing declining economic opportunity and rising poverty which persisted until the 1960s (Csalog 1993: 29–33).

Roma were not the only people to suffer economic distress during this period which saw mass emigration, numerous outbreaks of rural militancy, the formation of trade unions and revolution. However, the fate of Roma was also marked by the deepening perception, particularly on the part of state authorities, of their being 'alien' to the Hungarian nation, despite the fact that Roma fought alongside Magyars in 1848–9 (during the failed liberation struggle against the Habsburgs) and increasingly adopted the Hungarian language.[6] This perception was created in part by the arrival, in increasing numbers from the 1860s, of Roma liberated from slavery in neighbouring Romania. The poverty and cultural isolation of the newcomers presented a challenge to the authorities with which they singularly failed to cope. The lessons of previous centuries had not been learned, and expelling itinerants from one locality to another simply served to breed fear and resentment while failing to solve the 'problem'.

However, the fundamental cause of tension lay in the increasing exclusivity of Magyar national identity. To secure popular support for the anti-Habsburg struggle, the leaders of the 1848–9 Revolution mobilised the Magyar population with passionate nationalist rhetoric. Initially, this process did not adversely affect the Roma but was targeted against rival 'nationalities', primarily northern (Slovak) and southern (Croat) Slavs. Following the *Ausgleich,* the new ruling élite introduced the policy of magyarisation to secure their status and powers within the Empire.[7] The arrival and persistence of Romanian Roma, who did not assimilate either socially or economically, led to Roma identity becoming part of defining what was not Magyar (in both ethnographic and moral terms) which also adversely affected the long-established Hungarian Roma population. In 1920 Hungary regained independent statehood, though, as a war loser, at the price of losing two-thirds of its territory and millions of Magyars who became subjects of 'alien' nations (Slovakia, Romania and Yugoslavia). The politics of the inter-war Horthy regime was based on revising the country's borders and Magyar chauvinism.[8] Whereas Maria-Theresa had offered Roma the economic security of serfdom in exchange for cultural assimilation, during the first decades of the twentieth century the Hungarian state gave only unemployment and an ideology of cultural exclusion, a combination which led inexorably, through increasing pogroms, towards the mass murder of the Holocaust during World War Two.[9]

## The first Cultural Alliance

The post-war Hungarian state[10] paid practically no attention to the Roma who were defined (in the census) as those whose mother-tongue was Romani. This census produced conveniently low figures of 21,387 (1949) and 25,633 (1960), i.e. less than 0.3 per cent of the total population (Crowe 1991: 119–20). The 'uprising' of 1956 profoundly affected the Hungarian state and society and contributed to a revision of official attitudes towards the Roma. In part, this was due to the dedication and hard work of a Romani journalist, Mária László, who in 1957 persuaded the authorities to allow the establishment of the Cultural Alliance of Hungarian Gypsies (*Magyarországi Cigányok Kulturális Szövetsége*). The constitution of the Alliance emphasised the need for the state and Roma (representatives) to develop policies to improve opportunities for and the living conditions of Roma people. Nevertheless, initial plans emphasised the promotion of Roma languages and culture, leading Sághy to conclude that the aim was 'unambiguously to create the basis for achieving nationality status' (Sághy 1999: 24).

The Alliance coincided with (and possibly even initiated) a revival of state interest in the Roma. To understand the context to this development it should be recognised that state socialism explicitly sought the transformation and modernisation of the economy and society (as distinct from social and economic evolution based upon competition between interests within civil society). Furthermore, the Roma population was in a profoundly disadvantaged condition having suffered decades of poverty and discrimination and having received practically no support to recover from the trauma of the war. In 1957 the Ministry of Labour commissioned a survey of the employment, housing, health and cultural[11] circumstances of the Roma population, the findings of which provided the basis for the watershed politburo decree of 1961 on Tasks in Relation to Improving the Circumstances of the Gypsy Population.

## Ideology of assimilation

Before looking at the effect of Communist policy on the living conditions of Roma people, it is necessary to examine the position adopted by the state towards Roma identity. Despite praise for its work, the 1961 decree abolished the Alliance declaring it 'unsuitable' for the tasks ahead. The Alliance's demise reflected the conscious decision on the part of the state authorities to strive for the full assimilation (cultural, as well as social and economic) of the Roma. To what extent this approach represented a racist contempt for all things Roma is hard to gauge, though contemporary documents indicate that this was a minor factor, particularly at the higher levels of the policy making process. Instead, Communist ideologues saw Roma culture as 'introspective', 'conservative' and 'backward', defined by centuries of persecution and discrimination and perpetuated by racism, unemployment, unhygienic ghettos and illiteracy. Its abolition would liberate Roma people, allowing them to take their place alongside all other citizens and to enjoy the benefits of modernisation (Turóczi 1962: 74–5).

In fact, Roma culture was attributed far less influence in the perpetuation of Roma disadvantage than that of prejudice on the part of society as a whole. The chauvinism of previous regimes was responsible for widespread prejudice and discrimination against the Roma, even on the part of state and Party organs. Supporting Roma identity would simply retard progress because it was irredeemably linked to negative attitudes. In effect, the Kádár government sought to cure racism by abolishing that which 'provoked' it. Assimilation was also justified by an interpretation of Roma history which emphasised the steady disintegration of the Roma 'nation' from a supposed unified origin into the spatial, linguistic, cultural and occupational diversity evident both within Hungary and abroad (Turóczi 1962: 79).

## Integration policies

The Communists' unambiguous emphasis on (material) equality over (cultural) difference defined policy for the next twenty years. Probably the single most important factor in this approach was the desire to incorporate into the socialist system of extensive economic development the Roma who represented one of the few remaining untapped pools of labour in the country. The 1957 survey had found that only around 30 per cent of Roma were in regular employment, another 30 per cent worked occasionally while 40 per cent were effectively unemployed (Faludi 1963: 8–11). By the mid-1980s Roma employment levels (85 per cent men, 53 per cent women), closely conformed to the national average. However, Roma were not evenly distributed throughout the economy and their late arrival into the industrial labour force, the persistence of prejudice and the retarding effects of other aspects of disadvantage (relatively lower levels of educational attainment, the quality and location of housing, poorer health, etc.) meant that they were heavily over-represented amongst unskilled workers (Mezey 1986: 275–87).

In addition to employment, which was encouraged through the growth in the number of jobs, wage subsidies to encourage enterprises to take on and keep staff, as well as campaigning against discriminatory practices, policy also focused on housing and education. This effectively complemented the employment strategy by improving access to Roma labour and its quality. In the early 1960s most Roma lived in over 2,000 'Gypsy settlements' (*cigánytelep*), isolated communities with little to no infrastructure and in accommodation often deemed unfit for human habitation. A slum clearance programme, combined with regular wages, access to public housing and to low-cost building loans, enabled Roma to enjoy more comfortable and healthy housing, though even by the mid-1980s Roma tended to occupy smaller and poorer quality accommodation than the national average (Havas *et al.* 1995: 77). Rehousing also led to significant change in the geographic distribution of the Roma population. Tens of thousands of Roma moved into urban areas and, in the countryside (where most Roma still lived), there was a general movement closer to the centre of villages (Kocsis and Kovács 1999: 13–20).

Important, if slow, progress was made in education. In 1961 only 2–3 per cent of Roma children completed eighth grade (usually completed at age fourteen and representing the most basic educational qualification required for employment). Twenty-five years later this figure was approaching 40 per cent with over 4,000 Roma participating in secondary education. Improvements were largely due to greater accessibility of schooling and better living conditions combined with campaigning amongst Roma (and non-Roma parents) and the educational authorities. The effectiveness of the policy was limited by the low base of the starting point (one-third of Roma adults were illiterate in 1960) (Faludi 1963: 11), and prejudice remained a significant obstacle to the progress of many children. Antipathy towards Roma school attendance on the part of schools was identified early on but, despite formal calls to end segregation within classes and the creation of 'Gypsy' schools, these were not eradicated and the appearance of increasing numbers of Roma within the educational system led to growth in the number of segregated classes (Kemény 1999b: 245). Though many Roma were able to enjoy vocational secondary education, the numbers in grammar schools and of those going on to tertiary education remained very low.

If Communist integration policies failed to achieve equality for Roma people, they at least allowed the Roma, both individually and collectively, to participate in and benefit from the increase in wealth and improvement in public services during the 'golden age' of state socialism. Failure was due, in part, to the extent of the disadvantages of the Roma population and an insufficiency of time (only twenty-five years) in which they could catch-up. The gains of the Roma in absolute terms, while important, were also offset by improvements throughout society. Disadvantage was not so much abolished as reconstructed.

## The failure of assimilation

Integration policies were also undermined by the regime's inevitable failure to eliminate public perception of Roma identity. As noted, anti-Roma prejudice was perceived by policy makers as being a major factor in creating and perpetuating Roma disadvantage. However, as Michael Stewart observed, the state was not able to compel local authorities in particular, and the wider public in general, to end discriminatory behaviour. Whereas Habsburg assimilation policies foundered on poor communications, Communist policy failed primarily because of a lack of political will to take the necessary steps to eliminate prejudice which would have proved highly unpopular in many quarters. In addition, 'assimilation' (in the sense of the total loss of identity) prevented the development of a formal Roma 'voice' that could provide alternative explanations for the tensions inherent in the integration process. Consequently, a tendency developed, throughout society, to blame the Roma themselves for these, leading to a revitalisation of prejudice rather than its reduction.[12]

Other factors also contributed to the growing realisation that Roma identity was not likely to disappear. A consequence of developing programmes for and monitoring their effects upon Roma, was to stimulate research into the nature and scope of Roma 'difference'. In 1971 a national Roma survey was commissioned which found that non-native speakers of Hungarian (Romani and Beash speakers) suffered particular disadvantage in school because of their limited knowledge of Hungarian and the failure of the school system to compensate for this (Kemény 1974: 63–72). Improving Roma access to education also enabled some Roma to articulate their feelings about their culture and identity in a manner more accessible to mainstream society.[13]

By the end of the 1970s, despite the significant social and economic advances made by the Roma population as whole, it was becoming increasingly obvious that Roma identity had not been eliminated. Indeed, Kemény's research had proved that, far from disappearing through assimilation, the number of officially identified Roma had actually increased by over 150 per cent in a decade and was continuing to grow rapidly (Kemény 1974: 64). In addition, the establishment of the first World Romany Congress (1971), Hungary's formal acceptance of the minority rights provisions of the Helsinki Accords (1975) and the work of a small, but growing, number of Roma intellectuals, such as Ágnes Daróczi, committed to developing Romani culture and achieving nationality status, meant that the official position of refusing to acknowledge Roma identity became increasingly untenable. In 1979 the Roma were recognised as an ethnic group, a novel status falling short of 'nationality' with its associated right to self-organisation. However, this was only a partial retreat as ethnic status was conceived as a temporary measure necessary to facilitate full 'assimilation'.[14]

## The 'new consensus'

Real change in Roma policy occurred in the early 1980s following a severe currency crisis which also heralded the start of the country's long transition to a market economy and a pluralist political system. In 1984 the Patriotic People's Front, (*Hazafias Népfront*), the umbrella organisation for state socialist civil society, published a report which concluded that 'integration [of the Gypsies] is restricted by our difficult economic situation ... a consequence of which is that we must now consider the Gypsy population as playing an important role in the construction of a new consensus' (Blaha *et al.* 1995: 27). The basis of this 'new consensus' was that the costs of achieving equality for Roma citizens, in respect of living conditions and opportunities, were now considered prohibitive. Consequently, 'integration' was to be replaced by negotiating a cheaper relationship between the state and society with representatives of the Roma as a distinct, culturally based population, i.e. the struggle for equality was to be subordinated to the promotion of 'difference'.

The institutional arrangements of the new policy were soon put in place. In 1985 national and county-level Gypsy Councils were set up and, in the following year, the Cultural Alliance of Hungarian Gypsies (*Magyarországi Cigányok Kulturális Szövetsége*) was established (not to be confused with the organisation bearing the same name formed on the initiative of Mária László in 1957). The Gypsy Councils were political bodies but they had no budget and their members were selected by national or local officials and did not enjoy any popular mandate. The imminent dissolution of the one-party system prevented the Gypsy Councils from developing a significant role or identity. The Cultural Alliance, on the other hand, enjoyed considerable public funding which it used to promote Roma cultural organisations and events. This discrepancy in state support between 'political' and 'cultural' activities characterises the emphasis the new policy approach placed on culture. This is not surprising as, coincidental with these developments, the mid-1980s saw the re-emergence of Roma unemployment and, by 1990, around 40 per cent of Roma workers had lost their jobs (Havas *et al.* 1995: 75).

## The promotion of identity and declining living standards

In Hungary the transition to a multi-party system and the end of Communist rule was more gradual than in any other state of the Soviet bloc. Consequently, the continuation of this shift in policy is less strange than might first appear. Indeed, the fundamental change of direction was developed further and accelerated by a new Minorities Law in 1993. This aimed at reviving national identities (alongside the development of civic identities) to fill the ideological vacuum left by the abandonment of state socialism. For the minorities, the state pledged to 'to halt the process of assimilation' (Tabajdi 1997: 10) and to facilitate their cultural and educational autonomy.

Inclusion in the Minorities Law (as an 'ethnic' minority enjoying the same rights as other, 'national', minorities) symbolised the incorporation of Roma policy into this wider political process of reviving national identities. In addition to setting up almost 300 self-organised groups, Roma embraced the minority self-government system, established by the Minorities Law as the institutional means for exercising collective minority rights, and formed almost 500 groups in 1994–5 and over 700 in 1998. Hundreds of Romani cultural events were organised during the 1990s, often with state or NGO support. Also numerous Roma journals were established and Roma programmes were broadcast on television and radio. A number of schools and other educational initiatives targeting Roma were created and Roma studies were included in the curricula of many teacher training institutions. 'Positive discrimination' became an integral part of policy towards the Roma.[15]

Such initiatives appear a step forward from the Kádárist definition of the Roma as a 'disadvantaged social layer'. However, they need to be examined within the context of another characteristic feature of the Roma during the 1990s, the mass impoverishment of the population, growing inequality and an increase in prejudice and discrimination. Unemployment continued to rise and by 1994 only one quarter of healthy Roma of working age had regular work (MTA Szociológiai Intézete 1994: 25). While prejudice may have played a part, the main reason for such high Roma unemployment was that the economy no longer had need of their labour. Structural unemployment was exacerbated by the demographic spread of the population, concentrated in the countryside and in the least developed counties of northern and eastern Hungary, leading the Ministry of Labour to conclude that 'in these surroundings they are no longer semi-skilled or unskilled workers any more, but are Gypsies plain and simple' (Ágoston 1994: 2). By the mid-1990s 'official' Roma unemployment was five times the national average and over 70 per cent of Roma lived below the poverty line compared with only 15 per cent of the total Hungarian population (*Népszabadság*, 13 May 1995).

Some Roma survived 'transition' relatively unscathed and a number flourished by exploiting new economic opportunities, primarily in the service sector. The majority of Roma, made dependent on an undeveloped welfare system and facing rising prices and declining public services, were exposed to the multiple disadvantages associated with impoverishment. Difficulties in covering loan repayments, rent or utility bills led many to be threatened with eviction or to seek cheaper, less desirable accommodation. Freeing up the property market increased inequalities and resulted in the (re)formation of ghettos, as well as a number of high profile attempts by local authorities to rid their areas of some Roma residents.[16] Roma suffered higher rates of child mortality and chronic illness and had a life expectancy on average ten years lower than the already low national average (Puporka and Zádori 1999: 11–20). Disadvantage within the educational system was exacerbated by declining access to nursery education and an increasing tendency to place Roma in so-called 'remedial' classes or special schools (Szilágyi and Heizer 1996: 22, A Kisebbségi Ombudsman 1998: 17). Educational attainment was also undermined by the probable over-representation of Roma amongst the 150,000 children officially recognised as suffering from malnourishment (*Népszabadság*, 28 October 1998). In the 1990s the chances of Roma going on to higher education were fifty times lower than for non-Roma pupils (*Népszabadság*, 5 February 1998). Despite Roma being the main victims of racially motivated crime, Roma were highly over-represented amongst the prison population (*Népszabadság*, 21 November 1998).

## The rise of Roma politics

The greater availability of public funds to promote Roma civil society from 1991 meant that the third characteristic feature of the Roma's experience of post-Communism has been the unprecedented expansion of Roma political activity. By 1998 there were over 1,000 registered Roma organisations (self-governments and self-organised groups) most of which undertook some form of interest representation, as well as enabling several thousand Roma individuals to enjoy an income from public activities. Theoretically, such a growth in lobbying capacity should have increased concessions from government to the Roma population. However, the decline in the economic and social circumstances of most Roma indicates that Roma politics was ineffective in representing the interests of its constituency. We should not be surprised at the limitations of Roma political activity. In addition to the numerous structural factors undermining the creation of an effective political movement (poverty, geographic dispersion, cultural and linguistic diversity, lack of experience and a long-standing tradition of avoiding conflict), it must be remembered that the formal expression of Roma interest representation was created in 1985 precisely to *reduce* the obligations owed by the state towards its Roma citizens. This role for Roma politics was merely extended in the 1990s as the inherent weakness of the Roma as a political community meant that it was relatively easy for the state to manage its development (Kovats 1997: 70–1).

Political realignment and the desire for change at the fall of Communism enabled liberal Roma activists, many of whom had been excluded from the 'official' Communist Roma bodies, to take the initiative in Roma politics. This took the form of preventing the creation of a new monopoly body for national Roma representation in the form of the Democratic Alliance of Hungarian Gypsies (*Magyarországi Cigányok Demokratikus Szövetsége*). This group had coalesced during the struggles against the ailing Communist regime and produced the organisation *Phralipe*, founded in early 1989. Out of this *Phralipe* movement, in 1991, emerged the Roma Parliament which sought to act as a collective forum, independent from the state, to which the rapidly growing number of self-organised Roma groups could attach themselves. The Minorities Law (1993) effectively squashed this development by imposing a legislatively defined mechanism for Roma interest representation (the minority self-government system) and restricting the Roma political agenda to one based on minority rights rather than demands for material and social equality (Kovats 1998). Power within Roma politics was returned to the hands of activists willing to accommodate to the state's conception of appropriate Roma political activity. These took control of the National Gypsy Minority Self-government in 1995 and secured re-election in 1999 under the leadership of Flórián Farkas.

## The contradiction of Roma policy

The predominant emphasis on Roma identity in post-Communist policy was also reflected by the limited ambition of programmes to support Roma participation in the mainstream economy and society. The dramatic rise in Roma unemployment produced no coherent response in policy which, in the early 1990s, evolved no further than by crisis management. The coming to power in 1994 of the socialist-liberal coalition, which lasted until 1998, led to a degree of stabilisation and the construction of a Medium Term Action Plan. This was reissued in a similar, if vaguer form by the Young Democrat-Smallholders coalition government in 1999. Though containing a variety of initiatives, the main employment strategies in these plans focused on including Roma in public work schemes and in encouraging subsistence farming. While each of these undoubtedly assists the individuals and families involved, neither provide any long-term solution as public work schemes are designed less to get the unemployed back to work but to enable them to re-qualify for unemployment benefit. Turning Roma into smallholders or peasants does not enable them to acquire the skills or income necessary to compete with other sections of society in an increasingly technology-based economy. A review of the subsistence programs supported by the Public Foundation for Gypsies (*Cigányokért Közalapítvány*) showed an average investment of 1 million forints (£3,000) for twenty-four families producing a monthly return (in either cash or kind) of 2,000–10,000 forints (£5–30), i.e. still substantially below the poverty line. This indicates that policy was still based on limiting costs to the state.[17]

Education is almost universally seen as the long-term solution to Roma disadvantage and significant progress was made in supporting educational initiatives such as the Gandhi Grammar School, Roma '*Esély*' Vocational School, a nationwide network of hostels to support Roma in secondary education and in making available a variety of grants and scholarships. Such initiatives aim to create an educated Roma middle class but this raises the question of the fate of the mass of Roma, who are not included in this social experiment. During the 1990s, the issue of the over-representation of Roma classed as 'backward' has not been addressed and a tendency was identified towards 'spontaneous' segregation (Vég 1995: 9). Rather than facilitating equal opportunities, guidelines for promoting minority education focused, for the Roma and only the Roma, on overcoming their educational 'difficulties'. In 1998 the Parliamentary Commissioner for Minority Rights, Jenő Kaltenberg, expressed concern that this policy implies that the Roma collectively experience problems, rather than individual Roma pupils (A Kisebbségi Ombudsman 1998: 22). Governments consistently rejected calls for an anti-discrimination law which would co-ordinate existing provisions, define discrimination and provide appropriate and accessible remedies. Over half the provisions of the two action plans for 'Improving the Circumstances of the Gypsy Population' involved commissioning further research and neither contained targets for measuring the success of policies. This meant that, despite the rhetoric, it remained unclear quite what level of improvement might be expected and by when. The kind of timetable to which the plans are working was indicated, in 1996, when the government expressed the view that 'it will take twenty years for the Roma to reach the level of [social and economic] integration achieved during the 1980s' (Szilágyi and Heizer 1996: 20).

It is insufficient to explain away the inadequacies of the action plans as a temporary problem of 'transition'. Instead, we must look at the more profound obstacles to the development of policies to ensure Roma obtain material and social equality with other citizens. The first of these is the cost, complexity and perceived unpopularity of government providing 'too much' support for Roma. The free-market ideology of the post-Communist era does not encourage job creation for a large number of superfluous workers, support for whom would also inevitably mean depriving other interests of resources. Furthermore, as the Kádár regime experienced, even if resources are available it is very difficult to ensure that they are used effectively and desired outcomes are achieved. The low social status of Roma, their lack of voting power and of influential allies, mean that politicians see the Roma as a contentious issue and a vote loser. Nevertheless, Hungary has good grounds for arguing that it needs the support of outside agencies, particularly European institutions, in managing a serious situation inherited from previous eras. Furthermore, it is becoming increasingly obvious that 'Europe' will have to devote more attention and resources to the Central and Eastern European Roma if the process of enlarging the European Union is to be successful. However, it is unlikely that Hungary will be willing to draw attention to such a serious economic, social and political situation while its application for EU membership is still under review. Once a full EU member Hungary could lobby hard for support for its Roma population but it may be many years before such political security is achieved.

Finally, and probably most intractably, the fate of the Roma is inextricably linked to the problematic of Magyar identity. The philosopher, Miklós Tamás Gáspár, has pointed out the unresolved tension between viewing Magyar identity as representing a distinct ethnic group or as an essentially linguistically defined group including all who live and participate in Hungarian society and its culture (Gáspár 1998: 28). It could be argued that minority rights create the possibility of an inclusive civic identity acknowledging non-Magyar identities and culture as integral to and contributing to a broader Hungarian identity and culture.[18] However, this view appears hard to sustain when the promotion of Roma identity is viewed alongside the dis-integration of most Roma from mainstream society. In practice the embrace of minority rights is very much part of a process of reviving links with Magyar communities abroad in anticipation of their 'return' to the nation within a common European home.[19] As János Kenedi observed as early as 1986, 'Hungarian ethnic consciousness regains self awareness by differentiating itself from the Gypsies' (Kenedi 1986: 13).

## Conclusion

During the second half of the twentieth century, tension between the existence of distinct Roma identities and culture, and the role of Roma as citizens of the state remained unresolved. The Kádár regime unambiguously promoted the establishment of equality at the expense of identity. Industrialisation led to significant improvement in the living conditions of Roma people. Meanwhile, instead of eliminating Roma identity, such development increased the size and significance of the Roma population, while also providing the material and intellectual basis for an unprecedented representation and expression of Roma identity. However, as a result of national economic crises, the policy of assimilation was abandoned in the mid-1980s. Since then the pendulum has swung far in the other direction with policy focused on promoting Roma 'difference' at the expense of supporting living standards and opportunities.

By the end of the 1990s Hungary had got itself into a very strange political situation. On the one hand, the state encouraged Roma political activity within the context of the 'new consensus' and the wider policy of reasserting national identities. Yet, at the same time, government was concerned to prevent Roma politics making demands, based upon the needs of Roma people, which it was unable or unwilling to accede to. Therefore, a political mechanism was put in place to reduce pressure upon the state – the minority self-government system. As a result, because pressure was reduced, the state was able to limit its investment in the Roma, thus perpetuating disadvantage and inequality. The situation is stable for as long as Roma expectations and lobbying capacity remain at a level low enough for the state to satisfy its limited demands. However, there are grounds to be doubtful on this matter, not least because the problems governments have faced in constructing an effective Roma policy over the centuries have been fundamentally due to the state's failure to recognise the aspirations and capabilities of Roma people. The growing political significance of the Roma in Hungary means that, if the country is to avoid a political crisis, steps need to be taken soon which will effectively and significantly reduce the disadvantage and discrimination from which Roma have increasingly suffered since the ending of Communist rule.

# References

A Kisebbségi Ombudsman (1998) *A Kisebbségi Ombudsman Jelentése a Kisebbségek Oktatásának Átfogó Vizsgálatáról*, Office of the Parliamentary Commissioner for Minority Rights.

Ágoston, E. (1994) *Hungary – The State of Crisis-Management in the Social Stratum of the Unemployed Gypsies*, (unpublished), Budapest: Ministry of Labour.

Barany, G. (1994) 'Hungary – from aristocratic to proletarian nationalism', in P. Sugar and I. Lederer (eds) *Nationalism in Eastern Europe*, Washington: University of Washington Press, 269–79.

Blaha, M., Havas, G., and Révész, L. (1995) 'Nyerőviszonyok', *Beszélő* 6, 19: 17–30.

Crowe, D. (1991) 'The Gypsies in Hungary', in D. Crowe and J. Kolsti (eds) *The Gypsies of Eastern Europe*, Armonk: ME Sharpe, 117–32.

Crowe, D. (1995) *The Gypsies of Eastern Europe and Russia*, London: IB Taurus.

Csalog, Zs. (1993) 'A cigányság a Magyar munkaerőpiacon', *Szociológiai Szemle* 3, 1: 29–33.

Faludi, A. (1963) *Cigányok*, Budapest: Kossuth.

Fraser, A. (1992) *The Gypsies*, Oxford: Blackwell.

Gáspár, M. (1998) 'Trianon árvái', *Népszabadság*, 28–9.

Havas, G., Kertesi, G. and Kemény, I. (1995) 'The statistics of deprivation', *The Hungarian Quarterly* 36, summer, 63–85.

Karsai, L. (1992) *Út a Holocausthoz: a Cigánykérdés Magyarországon 1919–1945*, Budapest: Cserepfalvi.

Kemény, I. (1974) 'A magyarországi cigány lakosság', *Valóság* 1: 63–72.

Kemény, I. (1999a) 'A magyarországi cigányság szerkezete a nyelvi változások tükrében', *Regio* 1: 3–13.

Kemény, I. (1999b) 'Tennivalók a cigányok/romák ügyében', in F. Glatz (ed.) *A Cigányok Magyarországon*, Budapest: MTA, 229–56.

Kenedi, J. (1986) 'Why is the Gypsy the scapegoat and not the Jew?', *East European Reporter* 2, 1: 11–14.

Kenrick, D. and Puxon, G. (1972) *The Destiny of Europe's Gypsies*, London : Chatto-Heinemann.

Kocsis, K. and Kovács, Z. (1999) 'A cigány népesség társadalomföldrajza', in F. Glatz (ed.) *A Cigányok Magyarországon*, Budapest: MTA, 13–20.

Kovats, M. (1997) 'The good, the bad and the ugly: three faces of 'dialogue' – The Roma in Hungary', *Contemporary Politics* 3, 1: 55–71.

Kovats, M. (1998) 'Minority rights and Roma politics' in K. Cordell (ed.) *Ethnicity and Democracy in the New Europe*, London: Routledge.

Mészáros, L. (1976) 'A hódoltsági latinok, görögök és cigányok történetéhez', *Századok* 110, 3: 474–89.

Mezey, B. (1986) *A Magyarországi Cigánykérdés Dokumentumokban 1422–1985*, Budapest: Kossuth.

MTA Szociológiai Intézete (1994) *Beszámoló a magyarországi roma (cigány) helyzetével foglalkozó 1993 októbere és 1994 februárja között végzett kutatásról*, (unpublished), Budapest: MTA Szociológiai Intézete.

Nagy, P. (1998) *A Magyarországi Cigányok Története a Rendi Társadalom Korában,* Kaposvár: Csokonai Vitéz Mihály Tanitóképző Főiskola Kiadója.

Pamlényi, E. (ed.) (1975) *A History of Hungary,* London: Collets.

Pártos, F. (1980) 'A cigány és nem cigány lakosság véleménye a főbb társadalompolitikai céltűzésekről', *Szociológia* 1: 1–17.

Pomogyi, L. (1995) *Cigánykérdés és Cigányügyi Igazgatás a Polgári Magyarországon,* Budapest: Osiris-Századvég.

Puporka, L. and Zádori, Zs. (1999) *The Health Status of the Romanies in Hungary,* Budapest: Roma Press Centre.

Sághy, E. (1999) 'Cigánypolitika Magyarországon 1945–64', *Regio* 1: 16–35.

Stewart, M. (1997) *The Time of the Gypsies,* Oxford: Westview Press.

Szigethy, G. (ed.) (1982) *István Király Intelmei,* Budapest: Magvető.

Szijjártó, A. (ed.) (1998) *A Cigányság Megélhetését Támogató Mezőgazdasági Programok Hatásvizsgálatának Néhány Eredménye,* (unpublished), Agrárgazdasági Kutató és Informatikai Intézet.

Szilágyi, Zs. and Heizer, A. (1996) *Report on the Situation of the Gypsy Community in Hungary,* Budapest: Office for National and Ethnic Minorities.

Tabajdi, Cs. (1997) *Kisebbségi Érdekérvényesítés, Önkormányzatiság, Autonómiaformák,* Budapest: Osiris.

Turóczi, K. (1962) 'A cigányság társadalmi beilleszkedéséről', *Valóság* 6: 72–80.

Vég, K. (1995) 'Cigány Útvesztők', *Amaro Drom* 1: 6–10.

# Notes

1    There are a number of earlier examples of formal Roma/Gypsy political activity such as in Bulgaria during the nineteenth century and that of the Kweik family in Poland in the 1930s. Initiatives in Western Europe date from the late 1960s and the emergence of international Roma organisations starting with the meeting of the first World Romany Congress in 1971. However, we are now living in a qualitatively new historical period, particularly with regard to Central and Eastern Europe, where three-quarters of the European Roma/Gypsy population lives. This new situation was created by the growth of Roma populations, in both absolute and relative terms, and the effect of communist industrialisation, which led to an unprecedented level of dependency for Roma people on extra-communal bodies. These factors have made survival strategies based on isolation and avoiding conflict increasingly obsolete by requiring ever more engagement with mainstream authorities (banks, employers, welfare agencies, hospitals, local authorities, schools, the legal system, NGOs, sponsors of cultural activities, etc.).

2    Over the last 1,000 years, the territory nominally attributed to the Hungarian Crown has varied dramatically. The borders of today (imposed by the Treaty of Trianon in 1920) represent an historical low point for a country which, for many centuries, also included Transylvania, Slovakia, Croatia and northern Serbia. In this chapter, Hungary should be taken to refer to the kingdom/state as it existed at the time under discussion.

3    The early Hungarian policy of 'multiculturalism' is illustrated by the advice to his son of the founder of the Hungarian state, King István, that 'a country which has only one language and one set of customs is weak and bound to fall' (Szigethy 1982: 17).

4    Transylvania was ruled by Magyar aristocrats under Ottoman supervision; central Hungary

was occupied by the Turks, though local administration remained in the hands of the native élites; Royal (western) Hungary was under Habsburg control.

5   For a detailed discussion of assimilation policies, see Crowe (1995: 73–7). For the full text (in Hungarian) of the 1767 decree see Nagy (1998: 45).

6   Census returns from the late nineteenth and early twentieth centuries showed a rapid decline in those registering Romani as their mother tongue. The process of exchanging Romani (and to a lesser extent Beash) for Hungarian continues with almost 90 per cent of Roma surveyed in 1993–4 claiming Hungarian as their mother tongue. It can be hypothesised that the formation of the Romungro (literally Hungarian Roma) identity is related to the adoption of Hungarian (Pomogyi 1995: 7, Kemény 1999a: 8–9).

7   *Ausgleich* is the term given to the Compromise between the Habsburg monarchy and the Hungarian Diet in 1867 which gave Hungary autonomy over its internal affairs. Despite the passage of a Nationalities Act in 1868, which 'guaranteed' non-Magyars (around 50 per cent of the total population) civil equality and free use of their languages, in 1870 the policy of 'magyarisation' was adopted which made Hungarian the language of the civil service, courts and the educational system (Barany 1994: 269–79).

8   Admiral Miklós Horthy came to power by overthrowing the Hungarian Soviet Republic of Béla Kun and instigating the White Terror which targeted Communists and Jews and led to the loss of over 5,000 lives. In the 1920s a series of laws were passed restricting access of Jews to higher education and to the professions (*numerus clausus*). Hungary became an ally of Nazi Germany, with whose help it temporarily recovered part of the territory lost in 1920 (Pamlényi 1975: 454–7 and 472–3).

9   The scale of Roma losses during World War Two is still hotly debated with estimates ranging from 28,000 to 'a few hundred' (Kenrick and Puxon 1972: 125, Karsai 1992: 144).

10  In 1945 elections produced a parliamentary majority for the Smallholders Party but a coalition government was formed with socialists and Communists. The latter secured supreme power in 1949.

11  The research did not consider culture as folklore but as referring to matters such as radio and television ownership, cinema visits, consumption of newspapers, etc.

12  Ferenc Pártos' research in 1979 showed significant levels of antagonism towards Roma, especially in areas where there had previously been little to no Roma presence (Pártos 1980: 12–16).

13  From the late 1960s poetry and prose works by Roma writers began to be published in Hungary including, Károly Bari's *Holtak Arcok Fölé* (1969) and Menyhért Lakatos *Füstölt Arcok* (1972).

14  The 1979 Decree clearly illustrated this compromise, stating that the 'Gypsy population cannot be seen as a nationality, but as an ethnic group which is gradually integrating, rather assimilating, into society' (Mezey 1986: 274).

15  Positive discrimination was included in the 1997 Medium Term Action Plan for Improving the Circumstances of the Gypsy Population and again in 1999 (see section on the Action Plans).

16  Such as at Székesfehervár and Zámoly. For a full account of the attempt by Székesfehervár Town Council's attempt to expel a number of Roma families, see *Phralipe*, January 1998 (special edition).

17  The Public Foundation for Gypsies is a government-funded body and the primary mechanism for financing explicit Roma projects. It was created in 1995, initially with a budget of 150 million forints, rising to 250 million in 1998. Its main tasks were to support Roma pupils through grants, encourage Roma entrepreneurs and to invest in subsistence farming projects (Szijjártó 1998: 33–4).

18    In English, it is easy to distinguish between Hungarian (someone/something from Hungary) and Magyar. This is not the case in the Hungarian language where the word 'Magyar' is the ubiquitous adjective for both (for example, the country is *Magyarország*, 'Magyar Country'). Therefore, it is important that Hungarian Roma identity is not considered as representing an exclusive ethnic identity distinct from (ethnic) Magyar identity, but that Hungarian Roma can continue to maintain a Magyar Roma identity. Put another way, 'Magyar' needs to be understood in a way which also includes Roma identity. If this seems a difficult concept to express, it can begin to be appreciated just how much more difficult it is to put into practice, as well as the problem of a minority rights discourse that promotes a world based on emphasising ethnic 'difference'.

19    The preamble to the Minorities Law reveals its role within the context of the decline of nation-state and European enlargement in stating that the Law is 'guided by the aim of creating Europe without borders'.

## CHAPTER FIFTEEN

# Romania: representations, public policies and political projects[1]

*László Fosztó and*
*Marian-Viorel Anăstăsoaie*

Two senior officers from the Republic of Moldova, guerrilla warfare specialists who formerly served in Afghanistan and Chechnya, were hired by the municipal office in Piatra Neamţ, to safeguard public order in several blocks of flats in the Dărmăneşti neighbourhood, where Roma live. The mayor plans to rehabilitate the D2 and D3 blocks in this area and has recruited the two officers in order to evict the inhabitants, who have resisted this measure for some time.

(Curierul National, 20 October 1999)

T his report was published in a newspaper with a wide circulation and although this example could be considered extreme, it is not exceptional in public discussion about Roma in Romania. Journalists interested in sensational news often focus on the 'Roma issue' but rarely with the intention of understanding the sources of tensions. On the other hand, since 1989 human rights activists and Roma and non-Roma political leaders have presented alternative views in statements about the situation of Roma in Romania. In most cases, conflicts between Roma and the majority society are headline news (as in the quotation above), but with few exceptions the means of representation and access to decision-making are entirely in the hands of the majority.

Although there has been much discussion about issues and problems relating to Roma in Romania it is no easy task to present an overall account of the topic. The complexity of the situation is partly due to historical differences between regions, language and cultural diversity among groups and more recently to different directions taken in pursuing political strategies and action. However, problems such as increasing poverty and unemployment among Roma and violent attacks by the local majority (both Romanian and Hungarian) are related to the emergence of a market economy and transformation of the political system, which are ongoing processes of the Romanian 'transition'.

Successive waves of westward migration since 1989 have made Roma from Romania the centre of attention in Western European countries too.

In the West interest has focused more on understanding the situation of Roma in Romania and has been reinforced by fears of an invasion that are regularly invoked by the press. However, little empirically-based research is available on the Roma in Romania. The fact that Romania has the largest Roma population in Europe is widely quoted, although the figures are highly contested. The last national census in January 1992 recorded 409,723 Roma. However, various researchers and activists estimate the true figure to be much larger, ranging from one million to three and a half million with the estimated proportion of Roma in the total population (22,760,449 in 1992) consequently varying from 2 to 15 per cent. Indeed, given their demographic structure, Roma in Romania may well play an important role in future social developments and political projects that will concern not only Romania but other countries as well.

This chapter does not aim to summarise previous research in order to make general statements about the Roma population in Romania. Instead, we propose to look at specific situations through which the reader can gain an insight into the processes by which images and representations are produced by and about the Roma in Romania. We argue that these representations have their roots in the social realities of the subjects who sustain and promote them. At the same time the development of public policy is dependent on the perception and identification of the nature of problems, mediated through such images and representations.

The structure of the chapter is as follows. After a short discussion of the main theoretical concepts, we briefly summarise the historical experience of Roma in Romania. Then we focus on various educational, employment and cultural policies and programmes concerning Roma which were carried out by state and non-governmental organisations after 1989. We also look at ways in which Roma have begun to enter political life in Romania.

Drawing on the insights of anthropology, we argue for a perspective that takes account of how national politics and policies are seen and experienced at local level. Using the case of the multi-ethnic Transylvanian region, we illustrate the dynamics of local, inter-group power relations within the framework of changing economic and political conditions. This approach emphasises the ability of members of local communities to use, transform and/or manipulate the categories and measures of both local and central administration. Placing local settings within the national and even international context in this way provides a far more comprehensive picture of the social location of Roma in Romania.

The second case study, an analysis of a talk-show with two Roma leaders in the autumn of 1999, concentrates on issues such as types of policies designed to address the situation of Roma, political legitimacy and (non) authentic auto-representations, as they are used in the arguments of the two leaders.

To conclude, we try to summarise the experience of the Roma in the 1990s in terms of the dynamics between politics and representations. We also try to indicate some possible lines of future evolution as regards Roma in Romania.

## Representations

The study of representations has a long and distinguished tradition in the history of social science. Here we limit ourselves to a brief summary of the concepts used in this chapter. Following the distinctions made by Agnes Heller (1996) we can identify two semantic areas associated with this concept – on the one hand, representation meaning a creative process of building up the image of an object; on the other hand, in a political context, as being the representative of a larger group. These two aspects, even if separable analytically, are interdependent in social situations. The activities of categorising the social world and creating images of it are interwoven with similar problems to those arising from the political activity of speaking and acting on behalf of others.

We also distinguish between auto-representation (or self-representation) and hetero-representation (or representation by others), depending on the subject making the representation. Strictly speaking, most instances of representation are of hetero-representation, the only exceptions being self-portraits and confessions. But, in a wider sense, members of a group could be elected as representatives of that group, or could claim they were representing them, in this way constituting auto-representation by the community.

In the case of the Roma these processes could involve contests for the support of group members, raising the problem of the authenticity of auto-representation. In so far as we do not accept a primordial definition of group membership, a contest involving rival claims to authenticity can be seen as a fight for the position of being the acknowledged representative and over the political legitimacy of the representation. Therefore such auto-representation also depends on the power of would-be representatives to mobilise the group, in order to legitimate their representation.

On the other hand, hetero-representations have political implications too, for governmental and non-governmental bodies at various levels frequently develop their perceptions of Roma without reference to auto-representations. The assumptions underlying the programmes and policies promoted by these official institutions can often be found in the hetero-representations constructed by various outsiders. In this way, non-Roma politicians could appeal for and indeed count on the support of the Roma population in their campaigns. Naturally, this kind of hetero-representation fuels the criticism of many Roma, who are insiders claiming authentic auto-representation for themselves.

These considerations are also relevant in the field of political action, including scientific discourse, for the adoption of the radical position that only auto-representation is legitimate could rule out any attempt to develop an outsider's view of the social reality of Romani life. Both authors of this chapter are gadje[2] (non-Roma) and have no political ambitions in presenting this account, although they are aware that publication of their views may have unforeseen consequences.

## Representing the historical experience of the Roma

The present situation of Roma in Romania is extremely varied as regards regional differences, historical experience, socio-occupational structure and cultural background making it hard, though not impossible, to sketch a historical narrative of the group from their 'arrival' to the present[3]. However, the historical account in this chapter concentrates on the period from the First World War onwards, since unification in 1918 brought Roma from the previously separate political region of Transylvania and the Romanian principalities of Moldavia and Wallachia under the same rule. Slavery of Roma in the Romanian principalities and the assimilationist policy of the Habsburg Empire in Transylvania were important, formative historical experiences, relevant to the current social-political status of Roma in present-day Romania.

Viorel Achim (1998) published the most recent historical study of Roma in Romania, based on research carried out between 1993 and 1995. Achim dated the emergence of historical and ethnographical interest in Roma living in the territories of the Romanian principalities from around the 1840s onwards.[4] This interest was stimulated by the intellectual debates surrounding emancipation of the Roma from slavery. The abolitionist arguments of enlightened intellectuals proved successful and Roma were legally freed from slavery in the mid-nineteenth century. However, emphasis on this period in historical accounts of Roma remained long lasting.[5]

The period of slavery gives rise to speculation about whether the Roma became enslaved after their arrival in the area or were brought as slaves to the Romanian principalities by thirteenth century Tartar invaders. The latter theory was refuted as both historically false and racially and ethnically prejudiced by Nicolae Gheorghe (1983: 15). He argued instead that the process of enslavement should be understood as embedded in the political, social and economical processes of the feudal principalities. This argument suggested new perspectives for studying different degrees and types of enslavement.

Slavery eventually ended in both principalities after a series of abolition laws, the last of which was passed in 1855–6. These legislative measures prompted what almost amounted to an exodus. Freed groups travelled westwards to neighbouring countries, even to Western Europe, and then remained in their new surroundings for various lengths of time. This mass movement at

the end of the nineteenth and beginning of the twentieth century is sometimes referred as the second migration of the Roma. Another important legal
measure in the territories of the Romanian principalities was the land reform
of 1864. As a result of this reform some groups of Roma settled near existing
villages and towns while some Roma even established new villages of their
own (Achim 1998: 103).

After the unification of 1918, Roma with their varying legal and social
status from different regions were brought under the uniform jurisdiction of
the modern Romanian state. In 1930, in the first census after unification,
262,501 persons declared themselves as *ţigani*, which represented around 1.5
per cent of the population. The 1920s and 30s saw the emergence of formal
political activity by Roma in Romania. Organisations were created, newspapers published and this developing Roma mobilisation in Romania can be
seen as an important moment in the context of the international Romani
movement (Achim 1998: 132).

At the same time there was increasing interest in the history and social
conditions of Roma. Gheorghe Porta's (1939) book is considered by Achim
as the first reliable account of this topic. The socio-economic situation of the
rural Roma population was documented in a series of studies in ethnography
and rural sociology, carried out under the auspices of the Romanian Social
Institute (*Institutul Social Român*) led by Dimitrie Gusti.[6] Although characteristic of the period these investigations were stimulated by interest in rural
development and the integration of Roma into Romanian society and the
wider economy.

In contrast to these developments, the Second World War was a tragic
time for the Roma in Romania. The regime of Marshal Ion Antonescu[7] pursued anti-Gypsy policies and many Roma were deported and died in
Transnistria. Although these years are very important for Romani history few
studies have been carried out in Romania, although Western scholars such as
Kenrick and Puxon (1995: 108–112) and more recently Kelso (1999) have
researched and written on this period. Achim (1998: 133–52) included a
chapter based on archival research, but nevertheless the history of these years
remains largely unwritten, even though there are many documents available in
the archives. As a result public discussion on the fate of the Roma under the
Antonescu regime is non-existent.

There is also no adequate account of the period of Communist rule,
although this can be partly blamed on the nature of Romanian state socialism. Official documents were not published and even today the archives are
difficult for researchers to access (Achim 1998: 153). There are no reliable
statistical data and it was nearly impossible to carry out field research during
the years of Communist rule. However, an alternative source lies in personal
memories and life stories which could still be explored to develop an oral
history of these years. The fruitfulness of this approach is demonstrated by

Sam Beck's (1993) dialogue with Nicolae Gheorghe.

Broadly, the Communist era in Romania can be divided into two major periods. The first started with the ending of the Second World War and lasted until 1965 when Nicolae Ceaușescu came to power. During these years the Roma organisations founded before the war were dissolved, as were many other civil organisations that were regarded as incompatible with the new system. In addition, Roma were excluded from the list of 'cohabiting nationalities' and this denial of their separate ethnicity was combined with official neglect of the social problems of the Roma. Although collectivisation of agriculture in the 1950s represented an attack on economic inequality in rural areas, this left the marginality of the Roma unchanged. However, collective farms did create new job opportunities for many Roma living in the countryside, mostly in places where others were unwilling to live.

After 1965, however, it increasingly became obligatory to accept jobs offered by the state socialist economy as part of the drive to achieve the target of 'full employment' for all those of working age. Decree no. 153, issued in 1970, punished 'social parasitism', 'anarchism' and deviance from the 'socialist way of life' with jail or hard labour. Although the decree made no special mention of ethnicity it affected a large part of the Roma population who did not conform to the norms of the regime. Another decree, passed in 1966, banned abortions for women under forty-five who had not given birth to four children. This law brought about considerable demographic changes and led to increased numbers of children being abandoned by their desperate parents in orphanages and special schools (școală ajutătoare), including children of Roma origin (Crowe 1999: 62–3).

The only published document on official policy towards Roma was a 1983 report by the Propaganda Section of the Central Committee of the Romanian Communist Party (Human Rights Watch 1991: 108–16). This was an evaluation of a 1977 Central Committee programme to integrate the Roma population. The report's substantive findings, discernible in spite of the inevitable propaganda gloss, reflected some of the main problems among the Roma population, in particular the high rate of unemployment – especially among women at 48 per cent – and inadequate housing conditions. As well as discussing social problems the report criticised Roma for maintaining their non-socialist attitudes, such as 'social parasitism', the nomadic way of life of some and avoidance of registering with state institutions (Achim 1998: 159–60).

As for the opinion of Roma about state policies concerning them, we have the letters of Alexandru Danciu and Cosmina Cosmin that were sent to Radio Free Europe in 1982. Cosmina (probably an assumed name), a Romani woman, denounced the ignorance displayed by state policies in disregarding the discrimination against Roma in everyday situations. Developing her theme she compared the possibilities for cultural affirmation, offered by the 'cohabiting nationality' status (even if this was limited and used for propaganda purposes) to Hungarians, Germans and even smaller groups like Tartars and Armenians, with the 'pseudo-ignorance' shown towards Roma. She termed official practice 'pseudo-ignorance' because in spite of Roma being denied a separate ethnic identity, this did not prevent the police from maintaining special records and statistics for 'Gypsy criminals' (Cosmin 1983: 34).

At this time only a few public affirmations of their identity were made by Roma in Romania including a Romani Cultural Festival organised on 8 September 1984 at Bistritza cloister in Vîlcea county, the site of an annual pilgrimage. This pilgrimage had long served as a meeting point for the *Kalderash* as in 1978 when Ion Cioaba had been elected as *bulibasa* (leader) for the whole *neam* (kinship group). The 1984 festival was planned by *Kalderash* Roma from the city of Sibiu, and was organised with the assistance of local Romanian officials from Vîlcea country. Large numbers of Roma and non-Roma attended the festival where Romani folklore was presented on stage for the first time (Gheorghe 1985). The following year the central government prevented the festival being repeated (Pons 1999: 32), an act characteristic of this severely repressive regime that left little room for public affirmation of Romani culture.

From the 1970s onwards Romania slid into a deepening economic crisis but the regime seemed incapable of internal reform. For, while signs of economic and cultural change could be seen in neighbouring countries, the Ceauşescu regime adhered firmly to a nationalistic version of Stalinism.

The forced industrialisation of towns had led some Roma to take up unskilled work in factories but after 1989, such workers were the first to become unemployed, sharing the fate of farm workers – including Roma – who lost their jobs after de-collectivisation. Partly in view of these developments Achim stated in a recent article that 'it is evident to us that the present-day Roma "problem" derives from the "problem" of the 1970s and 80s. In our case the Roma "problem" is a heritage of Ceauşescu's socialism' (Achim 1999). After the fall of Communism the only sociological research carried out on a national scale was apparently based on similar presuppositions. According to the conclusions of this research, sponsored by the Institute for Life Quality Research, the problem of the Roma is not primarily an ethnic problem and therefore one of discrimination. 'The ethnic problem cannot be disregarded, but this is a secondary problem sustained mainly by social and economic problems' (Zamfir and Zamfir 1993: 156). These accounts (or representations) locate the 'Roma problem' in an economic and social context, suggesting policies to deal with hardships experienced in these areas. Without denying the importance of economic and social factors we would like to reframe the situation of Roma in Romania in more political and cultural terms.

## Post-communist representations

After the fall of Communism new types of social conflict emerged both within the new democracies and between former Communist countries and Western European states. The intensification of nationalist feeling led to internal tensions and several waves of international migration in which Central and Eastern European Roma played a prominent part. Westward migration from Romania – especially of Roma – stimulated new interest in the circumstances of the Roma in Romania. We argue that this situation should be understood on at least two distinct levels: firstly, on the level of public institutions and legislation and, secondly, on the level of social life, ranging from media discourses to the politics of everyday life.

In the 1991 Romanian Constitution Roma were recognised as a national minority, a situation without precedent in Romanian political life. Now, just like Hungarians and other minorities in Romania, Roma could organise political parties on an ethnic basis and participate in politics as a formally acknowledged group for the first time. However, legal recognition alone was not able to solve many of the problems Roma communities faced in their everyday lives. Indeed, in many respects, the extent of continuity between the Communist and post-Communist periods is more significant than any changes that have occurred.

In spite of the public attention paid to them Roma were in no position to make use of the new media to promote their interests or foster better under-standing between Roma and the majority community. Looking back, many non-Roma perceived the Communist period as one where Roma were given undeserved advantages, in spite of the evident drawbacks described above. In this atmosphere of mutual mistrust several violent conflicts erupted in settle-ments throughout the country during the first half of the 1990s.

After 1989, attacks targeting Roma frequently made the headlines in the mass media.[8] There is not space here to comment in more depth on the aggression displayed in Romanian public life immediately after 1990 but nevertheless, without diminishing their seriousness, incidents involving Roma must be seen within the broader context of other violent events. These include the *Mineriade*, when miners from the Jiu valley savagely attacked anti-Iliescu demonstrators in Bucharest, and the bloody confrontation between ethnic Romanians and Hungarians in the Transylvanian town of Tîrgu-Mureş. For Roma the worst years were 1990 and 1991 when most outbursts of violence against them took place in rural areas, often following a typical scenario.[9]

Usually the spark was an argument or fight between Roma and non-Roma, provoking a violent reaction from non-Roma. Also characteristic, at least for the earlier incidents, was the non-involvement of the police or their lack of effective response in failing to stop the violence. In some cases they stood by as Roma houses were set on fire or simply watched without intervening while Roma were beaten by non-Roma. In fact, in one instance in Comaneşti, police officers themselves were directly involved in an attack in which two Roma were killed. In addition, subsequent administrative processes at local or national level were prolonged and generally the judicial process of investigating and prosecuting those accused of these offences was extremely slow and inefficient.[10] Such delays only strengthened the conviction among Roma that attacks against them were not treated seriously by the authorities and would not result in adequate sentences for those found guilty. Consequently Roma victims were left unsupported and the whole community became increasingly mistrustful of the capacity or resolve of the state to protect them.

However, it should be mentioned that these kinds of violent incidents have not occurred in recent years. One factor explaining this change might be the growing awareness of the non-Roma population of the possible consequences of being convicted. Organisations such as Human Rights Watch or the European Roma Rights Center have played an important part in lobbying and publicising the judicial proceedings of cases like that of Hădăreni. Another factor is the greater readiness of Roma leaders to react promptly to the occurrence of anti-Roma incidents. Moreover, the management of conflict between Roma and non-Roma seemed to become more effective in the second half of the decade.

A wide variety of organisations need to be taken into account when considering the formal structures which have created a new context for issues of concern to Roma. At national and sub-national level the state is represented by the government, ministries and regional and local administration. In addition, other types of participant appeared on the scene and have been increasingly influential during the second half of the decade. These include supra-national organisations such as the United Nations and its agencies (e.g. UNESCO, UNCHR), the Organisation for Security and Co-operation in Europe (OSCE), the Council of Europe and European Union, as well as the specialised committees on migration, minorities and human rights, etc.). Other types of institutions engaged in dealing with Roma-related issues are the many and varied NGOs, amongst which the most active and significant in terms of resources are the Open Society Institute (OSI) and the Project on Ethnic Relations (PER).

It is not possible to deal with all these levels and organisations here, partly because of the complexity of the processes and partly because the outcomes are not yet evident. Nevertheless, it is possible to make at least a preliminary assessment of results. Since 1996 several governmental offices and commissions have been established in order to deal with the problems of national minorities. In 1997 the Department for the Protection of Minorities and the Office for Roma were created and a Minister for the Protection of Minorities was attached to the prime minister's office. The following year an

Inter-ministerial Commission for Minorities was set up (with the participation of seventeen ministries and departments) and within it an Inter-ministerial Commission for Roma (eight representatives). Some ministries have their own special programmes addressing Roma-related issues: the Ministry of National Education has a programme for education in Romani, the Ministry of Culture supports initiatives regarding Romani culture and even the justifiably much-criticised Ministry of the Interior is trying to change its attitude.

In the sphere of civil society the Civic Assembly of Roma Associations in Romania was convened in January 1998 and the Working Group of Romani Associations (GLAR) created, with representatives of Roma associations, in order to collaborate with governmental structures. GLAR assists in carrying out a PHARE-funded programme of the European Union, Improving the Situation of the Roma in Romania (1999–2000), which aims to plan a strategy for the protection of the Roma minority for the Romanian government. These institutional developments reflect changes in the official position and policy towards Roma in Romania. The inclusion of ordinary Roma in joint ventures promises a more sensible approach in helping Roma and better feedback of results.

## Case studies

In politics, both local and national Roma political organisations make their presence felt at various levels and in different locations. The following case studies provide an insight into the complex processes at work.

### Roma in local communities in Transylvania

Hungarians are the largest ethnic group in eastern Transylvania and study of group relations in local communities provides a basis for understanding the interaction between groups and competing representations. In this multi-ethnic region both traditional and new patterns of ethnic relations can be seen operating in competition with each other. Here, the changing economic, legal and political contexts generate instant responses to new conditions. The following interpretation of the behaviour of local Roma, based on field research and the findings of previous case studies (Fosztó 1998a, 1998b), cannot be assumed to be typical of Roma elsewhere in Romania but can be seen as variants arising from local conditions. One can learn from these but should not draw general conclusions.

Eastern Transylvania is largely rural but with some medium size towns that experienced intensive development and industrialisation in past decades which resulted in considerable change in local ethnic balances. The workforce for the new industries was imported partly from neighbouring villages but also from other regions, mainly from distant areas with an overwhelmingly

Romanian population. In spite of these changes Hungarians remained in the majority followed by Romanians and then by considerable numbers of Roma. Roma communities are divided by self-identification, occupation and language. The languages spoken by Roma here are mainly Romanian and Hungarian with only a small proportion speaking Romani. This division provides an opportunity for categorising Roma along national lines into 'Romanian Gypsies' and 'Hungarian Gypsies'. This classification is made by non-Roma, but Roma also distinguish themselves according to their mother tongue, although some of the 'Romanian Gypsies' identify themselves as Boyas (*Baiesi*).[11] However, the majority of Romanian speakers and also those who speak Hungarian assert they themselves are not 'real Gypsies'.[12]

The representation of Roma by outsiders is significant since it defines Roma identity in terms of the wider context of ethno-national competition, specifically the continuing contest between Hungarians and Romanians.[13] Therefore, depending on which side is doing the categorising, in addition to the national classification a distinction is drawn between 'allied Gypsies' and 'non-allied Gypsies'. Such a possibility arises because of the absence of a powerful third party claiming to define Roma as a distinct category. This situation is specific to this region alone and perhaps to some other places in Transylvania, but the interpretation suggested here is more general. In spite of the legal recognition of Roma as a national minority only a low profile of self-representation, as such, can be observed.

This lack of self-representation (or under-representation) can be attributed partly to the marginalisation and stigmatisation of Roma but also to the different strategies adopted by particular Roma communities. In the following two cases the local politics of non-Roma authorities and the response of Roma meet/avoid each other in different ways. In the first case, a village where Hungarians and Romanian-speaking Roma live together, Roma inhabitants decided to avoid the national classification by using an entirely different representation – the alternative offered by Pentecostalism. This strategy aimed at social integration for these Roma at a quite different level. The second case, of a town in the region, exemplifies the relationship between Hungarian-speaking Roma and local Romanians and Hungarians. This case reveals some characteristic features of the relationship between Roma and local authorities and the role of Roma middlemen in the relationship but also uncovers some contradictions in the representation of these Roma as 'allied Gypsies'.

The first case of Romanian-speaking Roma in a Hungarian village could be an example of Hungarians using the representation of them as 'non-allied Gypsies', although in reality the situation is more complex. For a long time the Hungarians ignored the problems of their Roma fellow-villagers – poverty, bad housing conditions and unemployment that worsened after 1989. However, their attitude towards Roma gradually changed as they began to notice a considerable increase in the Roma population, related to their differing age structure, so that there are now roughly equal numbers of Roma and Hungarians in the village. A feeling of anxiety replaced the previous disregard and some Hungarians began to speak about a deliberate state policy behind the growth in Roma numbers. A member of the local council is elected from among Roma but in spite of this limited political representation the problems of their community remain largely unresolved. Meanwhile the growing influence of the Pentecostal church is perceived by Hungarians as a kind of institutional support offered by outsiders to the local Roma community. Here we will focus on one important element of the relationship between these two groups, language use in different social contexts.

The language spoken by village Roma is actually a dialect of Romanian, but Hungarians do not distinguish between the local dialect and the official language of the state.[14] For them, Romanian is the language of power, which they speak mainly in formal situations when dealing with the state administration and yet many of them are far from fluent in this language. Therefore, communication in Romanian implies for them the inferior role in an asymmetric relationship. Roma speak Hungarian too, as a second language, and likewise communication in Hungarian implies for them a similarly disempowered position in many situations as speaking Romanian does for Hungarians – but for different reasons. The fact that Hungarians form the majority in the region and the economic marginality of Roma both contribute to this perception. Therefore, in inter-ethnic encounters Hungarians prefer to speak Hungarian rather than Romanian to Roma in order to maintain their instinctive feeling of superiority.

The growing importance of Pentecostalism in the local Roma community in recent decades has also influenced language usage. Roma use official Romanian in church services and bibles are also printed in this language. Pentecostal services are attended almost exclusively by Roma, Hungarians being largely Calvinists, and the few Hungarians sometimes present adapt to the situation. The Pentecostal service is an important formal setting where Roma can define the rules of interaction. In this church interpersonal relations are expressed in universalistic religious terms, taking no account of ethnic or national divisions, but the fact that the service is held in Romanian ensures the relative superiority of Roma. A growing awareness of their linguistic advantage can be observed inside the Roma community. Institutionally, the network of Pentecostal communities provides an alternative space for social organisation that avoids the domination of non-Roma representatives and offers Roma a way to escape their stigma and subordination at local level. In a wider sense these developments have stimulated the Roma community to seek resources other than those provided and regulated by the local authorities.

In some respects the second case illustrates the opposite of the above process since the situation of Hungarian-speaking Roma in a town inhabited by a Hungarian majority and a Romanian minority (around 25 per cent) yields insights into the function of 'allied Gypsies' being represented by Hungarians. The proportion of Roma in this town is about the same as that of Hungarians in Romania (roughly 7 per cent). In spite of the urban setting a considerable number of the Roma inhabitants live in a fairly traditional 'Gypsy settlement'. Communication between municipal institutions and the Roma community is carried out through a set of well-established 'channels'.

These channels are mainly maintained by mediators or middlemen among the Roma, who developed their special function to fill an important gap. On the one hand they meet the need of the administration to communicate and control, while on the other the need of Roma community members for some access to municipal institutions. To some extent these mediators can be considered as representatives of Roma in the institutional environment but they also serve as the informal representatives of municipal institutions in the Romani world. In order to illuminate these processes and their implications for local and low-level policy making we consider the case of the town council.

In 1992 a Roma councillor was elected to the local council on the list of the Democratic Alliance of Hungarians in Romania (DAHR). Other political parties also tried to persuade the Roma community to support them but none could gain their trust. A sense of historic affinity and the common language both favoured the Hungarian organisation. But the decisive factor was the role of the person who agreed to be the Roma representative. Men from his family had traditionally assumed the role of middleman in communication with municipal institutions.

In the subsequent elections of 1996, however, he was unsuccessful due to his low ranking on the DAHR list[15] but instead was appointed to the post of permanent consultant. With good reason he saw this change as a worsening of his position, brought about by DAHR scheming, but he did not give up his role as a mediator. For not only did his position, both inside and outside the Roma community, largely depend on performing this role but in any case the long established channel, kept open by middlemen, was needed by both sides to maintain successful communication between them.

To conclude that in this case the local DAHR was discriminating against the Roma population would be misleading. Focusing on the local situation and its context, a structural explanation would appear more plausible. As described above, the role of the mediator is crucial in the interaction between Roma and the local administration. Consequently this role requires a person with the ability to assess situations shrewdly and to communicate effectively, and moreover who can sustain relationships in both worlds. However, the rewards offered by the mediator role are more symbolic than material and, in so far as the prestige of the mediator within the Roma community depends on performing the middleman role, his capacity for autonomous policy making is correspondingly reduced.

## *Media case study*

Anybody interested in researching hetero-representations of Roma would find rich materials in the Romanian press. These representations are invariably sketchy and constructed around common stereotypes of *ţigani* as thieves, who are also dirty and make disastrous ambassadors for the image of Romania abroad. There are cases, however, when Roma have had the chance to represent themselves in the media or to respond to gadje interlocutors. We chose one of these situations when two important Roma leaders debated for more than an hour on a very popular Romanian talk-show.[16]

The Tuca show (named after its moderator) featured two Roma leaders – King Cioaba and Mădălin Voicu MP, a deputy representing Roma in the Romanian parliament. The debate was an interesting performance focusing on who was a 'real Rom' and who had the better claim to legitimacy in representing Roma in Romania. Marius Tuca 'moderated' the discussion in a fairly aggressive and provocative manner, trying to reveal conflicts between the two leaders. In fact, at the time of the discussion, there was a dispute between the leadership of the Roma Party (*Partida Romilor*) and the organisations of King Cioaba. One of the reasons for the split was the decision of the Roma Party (RP) to lend its support in the coming elections to the party of Ion Iliescu, which was in the lead at that time in the opinion polls.

Other disagreements lay in differing perspectives about ways in which Roma should become involved in politics and also about what kind of claims should be made on the state. At the 1996 elections Voicu was elected to a legally guaranteed place for Roma on the RP list. At that time the RP was a coalition of fourteen smaller organisations and parties including those of Cioba, who had also been elected to the county council in his native town of Sibiu on the list of the same coalition. However, because Cioba rejected the agreement made with Iliescu, the RP had retaliated by declaring it would withdraw its support from him.

Part of the discussion revolved around how party support could be withdrawn from Cioba, as an RP member and leader of two smaller organisations in the coalition, with Cioba naturally arguing that this action made no sense. However, expulsion could have adverse consequences for him, since the RP as a parliamentary party was entitled to state funding, enabling it to build an infrastructure and thus increase its power to mobilise. The problem of funding was touched on once during the discussions but did not become an issue. Instead, the question was raised whether the RP was seeking hegemony over the entire Roma movement in Romania.

Cioba accused Voicu of trying to monopolise the representation of Roma or at least attempting to subordinate other parts of the Roma movement to the RP. In making this charge Cioba used the metaphor of the 'chamber orchestra', mocking Voicu as its 'conductor'. This allusion to the occupation of Mădălin Voicu, a professional musician, stemmed from the underlying provocative strategy of the moderator, Tuca, in trying to show that there were serious contradictions and animosity between Roma groups. In fact, apart from this allusion, there were no hostile exchanges between the two leaders that derived specifically from their origin in different groups.

The question of authenticity took the form of a discussion about miscegenation. Cioba was strongly against intermarriage between Roma and gadje and maintained his position both against Tuca, who accused him of being against love between a man and a woman, and Voicu, who criticised this endogamy as discriminatory. Voicu, from a mixed marriage himself, felt excluded by Cioba's position but at the same time stated that he himself was a Romanian. He modified this claim (to half-Romanian) only after being challenged by Cioba, who demanded what he was doing in a discussion which was supposed to be for Roma leaders. Voicu saw himself as a representative of the Roma, serving this ethnic group, and so he was indignant that his authenticity should be contested: 'The fact that I represent you, for better or worse as I am doing now, should be respected. You shouldn't ask: "What is that Romanian or gadjo doing there?" You should say instead: "Here is a guy who has put his heart and soul and everything into serving an ethnic group which is very hard to unite."'[17]

As well as ethnic endogamy, the maintenance of the Romani language and cultural traditions were elements in Cioba's strategy for Roma to make progress in Romania. In his view the Pentecostal religion, of which he was a follower, could produce satisfactory changes in the way of life of the Roma without leading to assimilation. Voicu, in contrast, proposed orthodoxy (the faith of the majority) as an alternative option.

For his part, Voicu derided the institution of the 'king' as feudal backwardness, while Cioba interpreted his title as a truly contemporary European tradition, citing the examples of England and Spain. By these attacks on Cioba's title, Voicu tried to undermine the legitimacy of the traditional type of Roma leadership as anachronistic. He proposed instead his 'republicanism' and displayed openly assimilationist tendencies. He also labelled himself a social democrat in order to make the RP agreement with Iliescu's party more plausible. In his defence Cioba argued that his title was not in contradiction with the Romanian Constitution; he had inherited it from his father, and it was functional within the ethnic community. However, as a would-be modern representative of Roma, Voicu proved relatively uniformed about Romani democratic institutions, knowing hardly anything about the Working Group of Romani Associations (GLAR).

In this heated debate[18] it was clear to viewers that behind the personal conflicts real political alternatives were at stake. Divergent approaches to politics and competing mobilisation strategies were advocated by the two leaders. While Voicu adopted a more centralist and inclusive line and followed the policy of the RP – to ally itself with a powerful gadje party, Cioba opted for a more devolved system, favouring 'independent politics' or the 'politics of minorities'. This provoked Voicu into distancing himself from allegedly 'anti-national actions' for which Hungarians and the DAHR were often blamed. Pursuing this theme he criticised Cioba for promoting federalism and accused him of wanting to split the Romanian state in order to create a divided Transylvania. In these arguments the security concerns of the unitary Romanian state were clearly evident as the backdrop to what might otherwise have been naively regarded as purely Roma politics.

## Conclusion

In this chapter we proposed to consider the changing representations of the Roma in Romania. Our presumption was that in looking at the processes by which these representations are produced and maintained we could understand something about the social situation of the participants involved. Furthermore, the representations through which social reality is perceived significantly influence political actions. At the outset we distinguished between two basic categories: auto-representations and hetero-representations. Consequently, part of the chapter addressed hetero-representations, such as historical accounts, ethnographic and sociological studies, reports by human rights organisations, etc. Although some of these were written by Roma, we addressed the problem of auto-representation in a separate case study, drawing attention to the more political sense of the concept *representation.*

As elsewhere, hetero-representations have a long pedigree in Romania. Interest in the situation of Roma began in the 1830s, stimulated by the debate on the abolition of slavery. It was renewed at the end of the First World War, when unification created the modern Romanian state. The third period of heightened interest followed the fall of the Communist regime in Romania. These events brought to the attention of the general public a series of problems which had been ignored, hidden or considered non-existent beforehand. Roma were brought to the attention of the public partly by the overwhelmingly negative, stereotypical images in the media but also by news reports about the violent attacks on Roma communities.

These alarming accounts later became the main mobilising factor at national and international level in offering protection to the victims and prompting legal action against the perpetrators. Such violent conflicts have not recurred in more recent years. In this respect the pressure from locally-based and international civil society was crucial. This could be seen as the start of a trend which could continue in the future: the increasing impact of Roma and non-Roma NGOs on more conventional political processes.

Roma were acknowledged as a national minority for the first time in the history of Romania in 1991. This completely new situation offered Roma communities the possibility of articulating their positions and representing themselves in the political life of the country. As a result recognition marked the beginning of a new period for Romani politics in Romania. Initiatives making use of the political space offered by minority status are clearly visible today and probably will intensify in the near future. At the same time embryonic regional co-operation will be crucial in developing and co-ordinating strategies with other Roma organisations in neighbouring states.

However, another new factor in the post-Communist situation is international involvement in the problems of Roma in Romania. Indeed, many of the domestic changes have been driven by the influence of supranational organisations. Their involvement is expected to remain constant or even to increase in order to deal with problems that are too broad to be considered as limited to a single state.

## References

Achim, V. (1998) *Ţigani din istoria României*, Bucharest: Editura Enciclopedica.

Achim, V. (1999) 'Cit de veche este le noi "problema" tiganilor (romilor)?' *Dilema* 314: 12–18, February.

Beck, S. (1993) 'Racism and the formation of a Romani ethnic leader', in G. E. Marcus (ed.) *Perilous States: Conversation on Culture, Politics, and Nation*, Chicago: University of Chicago Press, 165–86.

Boia, A. (1938) 'Intergrarea ţiganilor din Şanţ (Năsăud) in communitatea românească a satului', *Sociologie Românească* III, 7–9: 351–65.

Chelcea, I. (1944) *Ţigani din România, Monografie etnografică*, Bucharest: Editura Institului Central de Statistica.

Cosmin, C. (1983) 'Roumanie: crise et répression', *L'Alternative*, 20 January, 32–5.

Crowe, D. (1999) 'The Gypsies of Romania since 1990', *Nationalities Papers* 27, 1: 57–67.

Fosztó, L. (1998a) 'Cigány-magyar egymás mellett élés Székelyszáldoboson', in K. Bari (ed.) *Tanulmányok a cigányságról és hagyományos kultúrájáról*, Petőfi Sándor Művelődési Központ Gödöllő, 93–110.

Fosztó, L. (1998b) *Cigánytelep a gettóvá válás útján*, unpublished manuscript.

Gheorghe, N. (1983) 'Origins of Roma slavery in the Romanian principalities', *Roma* 7, 1, January.

Gheorghe, N. (1985) 'Roma cultural festival in Romania', *Roma* 9, 2, July.

Heller, A. (1996) 'Önreprezentáció és mások reprezentációja', *Kritika* 12: 4–8.

Human Rights Watch (1991) *Destroying Ethnic Identity: The Persecution of Gypsies* in

*Romania*, Helsinki Watch Report, New York: Human Rights Watch, September.

Human Rights Watch (1994) *Lynch law: Violence against Roma in Romania*, Helsinki Watch Report 6, 17, November.

Kelso, M. (1999) 'Gypsy deportations from Romania to Transnistria 1942–44', in D. Kenrick (ed.) *In the Shadow of the Swastika: The Gypsies during the Second World War*, Paris and Hatfield: Centre de Recherches Tsiganes/University of Hertfordshire Press, 95–130.

Kenrick, D. and Puxon, G. (1995 [72]) *Gypsies under the Swastika*, (reprint of The Destiny of Europe's Gypsies), Hatfield: University of Hertfordshire Press.

Kogălniceanu, M. (1837) *Esquisse sur l'histoire, les moeurs at la langue des Cigains connus en France sous le nom de Bohémiens*, Berlin.

Păun, D. I. (1932) 'Ţiganii în viaţa satului Cornova', *Archiva pentru Ştiiţa şi Reforma Socială* X, 1–4: 351–65.

Pavel, D. (1998) 'Wanderers: Romania's hidden victims (1991)', in D. Tong (ed.) *Gypsies: An Interdisciplinary Reader*, New York: Garland Publishing Inc.

Pons, E. (1999) *Ţiganii din România o minoritate în tranziţie*, Compania.

Porta, G. (1939) *Contribuţiuni la istoricul ţiganilor din România*, Bucharest.

von Wlislocki, H. (1890) *Von wandernden Zigeunervolke: Bilder aus dem Leben der Siebenbürger Zigeuner – Geschichtliches, Etnologisches, Sprache und Poesie*, Hamburg. [(2000) Despre poporul nomad al rromilor. Imagine din viaţa rromilor din Transilvania, Bucharest: Editor Atlas – (recent Romanian translation)].

Zamfir, E. and Zamfir, C. (1993) *Ţigani intre ignorare şi îngrijorare*, Bucharest: Editura Alternative.

# Notes

1   The authors wish to express their gratitude to Michael Stewart and Will Guy without whose encouragement and comments this chapter could not have been written.

2   Viorel is Romanian while László is an ethnic Hungarian from Romania.

3   Traditional historical accounts agree that Roma reached the territory of present-day Romania around the mid-fourteenth century. However, an alternative hypothesis places their arrival as early as the twelfth century (Crowe 1999:57). The first documents mentioning Roma in Romanian territories date from 1385 (Wallachia) and 1428 (Moldavia). See also Achim (1998: 21–2).

4   Achim (1998: 10) considers Mihail Kogălniceanu's study (1837) the first major contribution to the history of Roma in Romania, describing their situation in Moldavia and Wallachia on the eve of emancipation. An early account of the Roma in Transylvania was published by Heinrich von Wlislocki (1890).

5   Achim (1998) devotes about half of his book (87 pages) to the period of slavery and emancipation with many references, while periods like the Antonescu regime and the deportation of Roma during World War Two are restricted to 20 pages (based mostly on archival research) and the Communist regime to only 10 pages (with very little data).

6   For example: Păun (1932), Boia (1938) and especially Chelcea (1944). See also Achim (1998: 122–7).

7   Antonescu came to the power after King Carol II abdicated on 6 September 1940.

8  According to Human Rights Watch (1994) up till 1994 there had been twenty such incidents where Roma were victims.

9  Pavel (1998) points out an important exception: the attacks on Roma in Bucharest neighbourhoods during the events of 14–15 June 1990, when the miners from the Jiu valley went there in order to 'restore the peace'.

10  In the case of the Hădăreni events, the subsequent legal proceedings were extremely complicated. Indeed, before 1996 was difficult to obtain any convictions (Haller Istvan, personal communication).

11  Elsewhere referred to as Beash-speaking.

12  The terms in quotation marks are those used in practice by Roma. We distinguish between the categories used by social participants themselves and those used by us for analytical purposes.

13  We characterise this relationship as competitive although a closer look at relations between Romanians and Hungarians living alongside each other reveals non-competitive aspects as well. Nevertheless, the maintenance of the symbolic boundary between the two is a powerful factor indicating group mobilisation on both sides, which is quite different from the normal presumption of individual competition.

14  The linguistic situation of the Roma can be described as diglossia where the local Romanian dialect is the familiar language variant they use in everyday communication and the literary Romanian is the language they use mainly for church services and in other formal situations.

15  The local council consists of twenty-four members of which six are usually Romanian councillors, depending on the ethnic population proportions in the town. Therefore, the first eighteen nominated on the DAHR list are virtually safe seats. He was put in nineteenth place on the list.

16  The transcript of the discussion is more than 30 pages long, therefore it would be impossible to review all the topics covered.

17  'Faptul că eu vă reprezint în forma proastă, bună cum o fii ea în momentul de faţă, ar trebui să vă onoreze, n-ar trebui să vă pună problema că ce caută românul ăla sau gajiul ăla. Ci uită domnule, un băiat care şi-a pus şi sufletul şi obrazul şi tot în slujba unei etnii, care e foarte greu de unit.'

18  Tuca with his inadequate questions and comments usually supported Voicu's position, but his main contribution was simply to add heat to the discussions.

## CHAPTER SIXTEEN

# Bulgaria: ethnic diversity – a common struggle for equality

*Elena Marushiakova and*
*Vesselin Popov*

E ven the most superficial acquaintance with Gypsies[1] in Bulgaria gives some idea of the great variety of its Gypsy communities, not all of which acknowledge a Roma identity. These include traditional communities (both nomadic and sedentary), plying their customary trades and retaining their language and distinctive ethnic and cultural traits, as well as communities who have integrated with the surrounding non-Gypsy population and are relatively well-educated and involved in wider society. For a better understanding of the present day situation of the Gypsy minority in Bulgaria we have to consider the fundamental ethnic and social parameters that affect them, to take into account their specific ethnic and cultural features, as well as to view their place in society from a historical perspective (Marushiakova and Popov 1997b). Only then do the current problems of Bulgarian Gypsies and the main trends in their development within the broader Gypsy community become more comprehensible.

## Typology (and early settlement)

Bulgaria was populated by Gypsies mainly as a result of the influx of three migratory waves. The first wave resulting in large-scale settlement can be traced back to the period between the twelfth and fourteenth centuries, but it is possible that there were prior contacts, perhaps even as early as the ninth century in the opinion of some scholars. From the fifteenth to nineteenth centuries, many Gypsies settled in towns and villages throughout the Ottoman Empire, while others continued living as nomads and retained their traditional trades. Meanwhile a new type of semi-nomadic lifestyle emerged, where some Gypsies took shelter in a winter residence but travelled within regional boundaries for the remainder of the year.

In the second wave, during the seventeenth and eighteenth centuries, large numbers of Gypsies entered the Bulgarian part of the Ottoman Empire from the Danubian principalities of Wallachia and Moldavia. The third great wave came from the same region during the second half of the nineteenth century and beginning of the twentieth, following the ending of Gypsy slavery in these principalities. Immigration of Gypsies from neighbouring countries, mainly Romania and Greece, continued during the twentieth century and was usually related to changing state borders as a result of war – namely the Balkan wars of 1912–13 and the two world wars which followed.

The Bulgarian Gypsies, like Gypsies everywhere, are not a homogeneous community. They are divided by many internal differences into separate meta-groups, subgroups and yet further subdivisions. Nevertheless, all Gypsies in Bulgaria belong to the Roma stream and can be classified on the basis of language (or dialect), lifestyle, boundaries of endogamy, occupational specialisation, length of settlement in Bulgaria, etc. These classifications are related to structures of perceived identity and result in a complete picture of the state of the Gypsy 'ethnos'. This picture is by no means static or inflexible; it has changed in the post and in the future is liable to alter yet again. However, this chapter is concerned with the position today.

The metagroup community of settled Gypsies or *Yerlia* is the largest and most varied. These Gypsies are the descendants of the first migratory wave, who speak different dialects of the Balkan group of *Romanes*. Significant numbers had already settled in Balkan town or village *mahalas* (Gypsy quarters) during the period of the Ottoman Empire. The *Yerlia* community is divided into two main subdivisions: *Dasikane* Roma or 'Bulgarian Gypsies' (Christians) and *Xoraxane* Roma or 'Turkish Gypsies' (Muslims). Within these subdivisions there are some more or less endogamous groups, which have retained their traditional functions and occupations as well as an awareness of their identity as a distinct group.[2]

At the same time there are sizeable communities who remember their respective group divisions and previous occupations but no longer practice them. Here the boundaries between groups have been largely obliterated and the sense of belonging has shifted from a more localised identity to the frame of the wider community of *Dasikane* Roma or *Xoraxane* Roma, with 'Bulgarian Gypsies' living mostly in West Bulgaria and 'Turkish Gypsies' in East Bulgaria. These coalescing processes are mainly found in big city *mahalas*, where memories of old group divisions are weak. In some cases, especially after a number of changes of name and religion, such as those in Sofia, community awareness can be at a more general level (only as *Yerlia* or settled Gypsies). Here, as in the above example, the ethnic identification is as members of the metagroup.

Another large group, almost entirely within the *Yerlia* nowadays, is the community of *Vlaxichki* (Wallachian) Gypsies (an appellation used in Western Bulgaria) or *Laxo* (*Laxoria*, *Vlaxoria* as used in Eastern Bulgaria). These Gypsies use dialects of *Romanes* which belong to the Old Vlax dialect group and their ancestors arrived from Wallachia in the second wave of migration.

Formerly they were nomads, subdivided into *Sitaria* (sieve-makers), *Reshetaria* (colander-makers), *Zagundzhia,* etc., but during the 1920s and 30s, or even later, they began to settle, mostly in urban Gypsy *mahalas*. Here, they gradually joined the existing metagroup communities of *Dasikane* Roma and *Xoraxane* Roma and in the process some changed their religion so that those in Eastern Bulgaria are now Muslims. Today there is widespread co-existence between *Yerlia* and *Vlaxichki* Gypsies (*Laxo*) and intermarriage is common, but the different group origin of the latter is still remembered. *Vlaxichki* Gypsies sometimes differ in appearance and possess some cultural and behavioural traits, which give them a special place in the general metagroup frames of the communities they have entered.

Some members of these communities gradually become differentiated on the basis of their preferred ethnic identity, for example some 'Muslim/Turkish Gypsies' who have lost most of their group characteristics and are often bilingual (speaking Turkish and *Romanes*) or entirely monolingual (speaking only Turkish). They live primarily in East Bulgaria and prefer to introduce themselves as Turks or only as *milliet* (i.e. a nation or people). Other examples are the *Dzhorevtsi* (mules) who prefer to identify themselves as Bulgarian, and the *Agupti* in the Rhodope mountains who stand apart from other Gypsies and have almost blended in with the local Turks and Bulgarian Muslims (often referred to as 'Pomaks').

A second major and very distinct metagroup among Bulgarian Gypsies is that of the *Kaldarasha/Kardarasha* community, descendants from the third wave of migration. These were nomads until 1958 and are now scattered all over the country, living mostly in villages and small towns rather than in larger towns. They speak the New Vlax dialect of *Romanes* and are internally divided into further subgroups.[3] All *Kardarasha* are strictly endogamous within the wider boundaries of the community as a whole.

The Thracean *Kalaydzhia* (tinsmiths) are clearly distinguishable from the two major metagroups of *Yerlia* and *Kardarasha*. Their semi-nomadic lifestyle, strong endogamy within the boundaries of their community, primary role of group identity, etc., is similar to that of the *Kardarasha* but their language belongs to the group of Old Vlax dialects. Nowadays they live mostly in villages scattered throughout the Thracean plain and keep their distance from the other subdivisions of the Gypsy community.[4]

The third major and distinctive metagroup is the *Rudara* community who are called *Vlax* (Wallachian) Gypsies or *Vlaxs* by the Bulgarians. Its members speak a dialect of Romanian and have a preferred *Vlax* or 'old Romanian' ethnic identity. Until recently *Rudara* were nomads who had spread around the world during the 'great *Kelderara* invasion'. This community consists of two main subdivisions of *Lingurara* (spoon-makers), who make wooden goods, and *Ursara* (bear and monkey trainers) and is internally divided into regional sub-divisions.[5] The boundary of endogamy is within the greater

*Rudara* community. *Rudara* live all over the country, mostly in villages and small towns in their own *mahalas*.

Estimates of the number of Gypsies inhabiting Bulgarian lands in different periods differ. Official population censuses vary widely and by a margin of at least two or three times as is apparent from comparisons with data from other censuses carried out for administrative purposes. One such census of the Ministry of Internal Affairs in 1989 registered 576,927 Gypsies, while the National Census of Population and Housing Stock on 4 December 1992 registered 313,396 people who had declared themselves as Gypsies, of whom 310,425 people said that the Gypsy language (*Romanes*) was their mother tongue (Rezultati 1994). We estimate the number of people of Gypsy origin in Bulgaria as being approximately 700,000-800,000. One also needs to consider how many of them would want to declare themselves as Gypsies.

Unfortunately, we have to admit that there is no information on the population of the various Gypsy groups and their major subdivisions. We can only make a rough estimate. There is no doubt that more than half of the Bulgarian Gypsies belong to the *Yerlia* community (including the *Laxoria* who have joined it). *Xoraxane* Roma are more numerous than *Dasikane* Roma. As far as the other communities are concerned, we believe that *Rudara* are slightly more numerous than *Kardarasha*.

## History

It is hardly surprising that centuries of co-existence between Gypsies and the surrounding population have led to cultural borrowings by Gypsies of certain patterns of social organisation from the wider macrosociety.

Gypsies in the Ottoman period had a special place in the overall social and administrative organisation of the Empire. Despite the division of the population into two main categories – the faithful (*Moslim*) and the gentiles (*Raya*) – Gypsies had their own, specific dual status outside these two categories. They were categorised on the basis of ethnicity, something quite unusual for the Ottoman Empire, with no clear distinction between Muslim and Christian Gypsies. All were tax-paying subjects of the Empire, included in its legislation and with a specific place in its social structures. On the whole, the situation of Gypsies was similar to that of the subordinated local population, with the exception of some minor privileges for Muslim Gypsies (Marushiakova and Popov 2001).

During the period of the Ottoman Empire, from as early as the Middle Ages, the Gypsies gradually became an integral part of society in spite of their lower social status and the attitude of the population towards them. There was a widespread sedentarisation of Gypsies in the towns, where they provided unskilled labour or worked as craftsmen, and in the villages, where they often made their living from farm work. During the first half of the

373

nineteenth century when the first Bulgarian textile factories were established in Sliven, most of the workers were Gypsies who played an active part in the syndicalist and other political struggles of the time. In Bulgaria, nomadic Gypsies (or rather semi-nomads) were far fewer than sedentary Gypsies; but they, too, had a fixed residence and civic duties. All these factors contributed to the social integration of the Gypsies and it is no accident that the first timid efforts to seek civil emancipation for the Gypsy community date from Ottoman times. One such attempt in 1867 was the appeal for the establishment of an independent Gypsy church made by Ilia Naumchev following the model of the struggle for emancipation of all Balkan nations at that time (Marushiakova and Popov 1995: 39–45).

After the independent Bulgarian state had been established in 1878, the Gypsies began to search for their own place in its social and political structure. On 31 May 1901 an amendment to the Election Law was passed almost unanimously, suspending the right to vote of both the Muslim Gypsies (the majority) and the nomads, thus violating the constitutional principle of equal voting rights for all Bulgarian citizens. The ethnic Turkish and Bulgarian Muslim members of Parliament voted for this amendment to exclude their fellow Muslims. In response, the first Gypsy conference was convened in Vidin in 1901 and the decision was taken to start a campaign to revoke this unconstitutional change in the law. The Bulgarian lawyer, Marko Markov JD, and the '*tzari-bashi* of Bulgarian Gypsies', Ramadan Ali, drafted an elaborate petition, insisting that the Gypsies in Bulgaria should have the same rights as the rest of the population. This petition was submitted to the National Assembly on 1 June 1905. The lack of reaction led to the convocation of the first Gypsy congress in Sofia on 19 December 1905, where a new petition making the same demands was approved and brought once again to the attention of the National Assembly. Eventually, the National Assembly passed a new electoral law, where the restrictions on the voting rights of these Gypsies were dropped.

A new stage in the Gypsy movement for civil equality began after the end of World War One with the establishment in Sofia of the 'Egypt' organisation, headed by Shakir Pashov. This organisation was outlawed in 1925 but was later re-established under the name of *Istikbal* (Future). In 1931 the Gypsy 'Mohammedan Cultural Organisation for National Education' began publication of the newspaper *Terbie* (Education), with Shakir Pashov as editor-in-chief. The following year the Mezdra conference attempted to broaden the national influence of this organisation but after a *coup d' état* on 19 May 1934 overthrew the elected government, the organisation was dissolved and its newspaper suppressed.

During World War Two the Gypsies in Bulgaria were not sent to concentration camps or subjected to mass annihilation, as happened elsewhere in Europe, nor are there any documents providing evidence of such intentions

(Kenrick 1999: 89–94). The Gypsies were not mentioned explicitly in the anti-Jewish *Law for the Protection of the Nation* and the only reference to them in the official legislature of that time was Decree 4567 of the Council of Ministers, which declared:

> Jews are prohibited ... from having marital or sexual relations with people of Bulgarian or similar origin, such marriages concluded after this law is enacted will be considered invalid. Note: The regulation also refers to the marriages of Gypsies to people of Bulgarian or similar origin.
>
> State Gazette, 29 August 1942

There is no information on how this part of the regulation was observed in respect of Gypsies or if it was ever applied. During the war many Gypsies were rounded up for compulsory labour, mainly harvesting or work on roads, railways and other public utilities. Meanwhile their free movement in towns was restricted with the excuse that they were spreading contagious diseases. A number of Gypsies joined the anti-fascist struggle and a few died as partisans or in helping them. Gypsies in the town of Sliven were particularly active, continuing their former radical tradition. The number of Gypsies who participated directly in the anti-fascist movement in Bulgaria was relatively small but this was clearly a reflection of their place in society at that time.

## Gypsies during the so-called 'epoch of socialism'

Following the Communist take-over, on 9 September 1944, the policy of the incoming government was to involve the Gypsies in actively 'building a new life' as an ethnic community with their own identity and equal rights. However, this policy, supposedly based on the Soviet model, was only to last from the late 1940s until the early 1950s.

On 6 March 1945 an 'All-Gypsies' Organisation against Fascism and Racism and for the Promotion of the Cultural Development of the Gypsy Minority in Bulgaria' was established, once more headed by Shakir Pashov. The following year the newspaper *Romano Essi* (Gypsy voice) made its appearance and in 1947 the Gypsy theatre 'Roma' was founded in Sofia. On the political front local branches of the Gypsy organisation, with equal rights to other non-Gypsy branches, were formed as sections of the Fatherland Front – a mass umbrella organisation for civil societies under the guidance of the Bulgarian Communist Party (BCP). A National Conference of Gypsies in Bulgaria, held on 2 May 1948, confirmed its commitment to the policy of the new Communist government.

However, this policy of engagement with the Gypsy community proved short-lived. In the 1950s the independent Gypsy organisations were abolished and popular Gypsy leaders were isolated and excluded from public life. This marked the shift to a new policy towards Gypsies, the final goal of which was their complete assimilation into the 'Bulgarian socialist nation'. A number of measures were taken in order to achieve this aim:

- restricted and decreasing reference to Gypsies in official documents and the mass media, starting with a terminological shift when 'gypsies' suddenly became 'citizens of gypsy origin'. Later, all explicit use of the term 'gypsies' vanished and was replaced by various euphemisms such as 'dark skinned citizens', 'children who don't speak Bulgarian', etc.
- no more state support for the development of Gypsy culture
- termination of the processes of 'Turkisation' of the Gypsies through the obliteration of Islamic elements in their culture – primarily by 'renaming' Muslim Gypsies, i.e. substituting Bulgarian names for their original Turkish-Arabic ones.[6]
- provision of permanent residence and regular occupations for all Gypsies. The first step in this direction was the ban on nomadic lifestyle with Decree no. 258 of 17 October 1958, whereby 'vagrancy and panhandling' were prohibited and citizens were obliged 'to undertake labour beneficial to society and to work according to their strength and abilities'.

At the end of the 1970s, following consultations with other socialist countries, Decree no. 1360 of the Secretariat of the Central Committee of the BCP of 9 October 1978 specified the general directions of the new Gypsy policy:

> The emphasis should be placed on their involvement in labour which benefits society, on progress in their education, on improvement in their living standards, on an increase in their consciousness and self-confidence as fully-fledged citizens of socialist Bulgaria, on their growing participation in building a developed socialist society.
>
> Decree no. 1360

This decree also specified some concrete measures (although in practice little was done to implement them) which sometimes achieved the opposite of what was intended, in spite of excessive requirements for formal reporting. For example, the segregated Gypsy *mahalas* were supposed to be abolished and their inhabitants rehoused in districts where they would be surrounded by Bulgarian neighbours, but only thirty-six out of the 547 mainly urban *mahalas* were 'closed' and some of these reappeared a few years later. Even though the Decree explicitly stated that 'segregated schools should not be allowed' for Gypsies, schools of this kind not only survived but even acquired legal status, concealed by the euphemism 'schools for children with low standards of living and culture'. The limited aims of such schools were to teach 'elementary literacy and some professional skills and discipline'.

The last phase in the government's special policy towards Gypsies coincided with the 'Process of Revival' of 1984–5, the goal of which was the

376

assimilation of Bulgarian Turks by means of 'scientific proof' of their Bulgarian origin and compulsion to change their names. As it proved impossible to apply this approach to the Gypsies, the official position was to deny their very existence in Bulgaria. The authorities considered Gypsies officially non-existent – all mention of them in public life and the media vanished, and in some places the Gypsy *mahalas* were hidden behind high concrete walls.

Naturally, such an absurd policy yielded no results – the Gypsies did not cease to exist. Yet, at the same time efforts were made to improve the living conditions and raise the educational standards of Gypsies in order to make them equal citizens, even if the practical implementation of these measures was inadequate and hampered by superfluous paper-work. If we are to be objective, it must be acknowledged that overall social development during the state socialist era brought certain positive benefits for the Gypsies. Even the ban on the nomadic lifestyle was perceived in a very positive light by Gypsies at the time, especially from a present-day perspective, since the nomads were given the opportunity to receive favourable credits, to settle permanently and build their own houses, etc. The standard of living and civil status of the Gypsy community improved rapidly and significantly compared to the previous period. The Gypsies had permanent employment, since unemployment was virtually unknown during state socialism, thus improving their living conditions. With active support from the state many Gypsies succeeded in obtaining a relatively good education, including higher education, and for a time some sections of the Gypsy community were able to play an active part in the social and political life of the country. However, these positive trends were accompanied by a multitude of unsolved problems. As regards the contemporary situation, it is far more important to recognise the actual impact of this policy on the Gypsy community than to consider the often unrealistic, strategic goals of the Communist government.

From a historical perspective there are no essential differences in the attitude of the Bulgarian state towards the Gypsies during the two major periods of policy development (1878–1944 and 1944–1989). Indeed, the basic approach of all Balkan nations to the Gypsies was not one of confrontation but was rather a condescending attitude adopted towards a community of a lower status whose members did not deserve special attention, provided 'they knew their place' and did not create problems. This explains why, for long periods, the Gypsies were not the focus of any special state policy and also why, whenever such a policy was introduced, it was inconsistent, out of touch and produced no tangible results. In fact, whenever the Gypsies became the focus of state policy, they were always the secondary and additional target of political decisions aimed at some other minority, other social structures or society as a whole. For example, the ban on Gypsy organisations in 1925 was enforced by a law intended to eradicate the political power of the Left. Likewise, the ban on their organisations in 1934 was a by-product of the attempt to put a stop to the activities of Turkish minority organisations. Similarly, restrictions on Gypsies during World War Two were applied in the context of anti-Jewish legislation. Even the ban on the nomadic lifestyle was a result of similar bans imposed on nomad shepherds (Karakachans and Aromanians) and followed from the adoption of the principle of a sedentary life for all citizens of the country. Finally, all further actions taken by the state in the 1960s, 70s and 80s were a part of an attempt to assimilate members of the Turkish (and, more broadly, Muslim) population or alternatively to force them to emigrate.

This general pattern in the approach of the state towards the Gypsies, which has endured throughout the centuries, helps to explain the processes taking place after the change of regime in 1989 until the present day.

## Post-communism

In Bulgaria the collapse of the Eastern European state socialist system in 1989 was followed by a long transition period, which is still continuing, accompanied by permanent social, economic and political crises. This general state of crisis strongly affected many aspects of the Gypsies' situation in Bulgarian society. In the economic restructuring after 1989 the Gypsies were the first to suffer since most were soon thrown out of work – in the cities after factories were closed and in the villages after the demise of co-operative farms. Unemployment and the lack of social support completely changed their way of life. Gypsies adapted relatively quickly to the new situation by taking refuge in the 'black' (or shadow) economy, which is a significant force in Bulgaria. This fact needs to be emphasised because, according to official statistics and representative sociological data, there appears to be no way Gypsies in Bulgaria could be able to live since almost all are unemployed, with no registered income, and only a few receiving occasional social support.

The Gypsies have adopted various economic strategies. Many, mostly in towns, have taken up peddling, not only at home but often abroad as well – mostly in Turkey and Yugoslavia. Others rely on being hired for occasional unskilled work, e.g. in construction. Some Gypsies, mostly living in villages, make a livelihood by seasonal agricultural work and by gathering wild herbs and mushrooms. Yet others have gone back to their old traditional crafts, although sometimes in modified form, such as different kinds of blacksmith's or tinsmith's work, weaving straw mats and basket-making among others. Some of these crafts involve a nomadic lifestyle. There are frequent transborder labour migrations, especially of the *Rudara*, who are employed illegally as agricultural workers on farms in Greece, Italy and Spain. Some Gypsies, mainly *Kardarasha*, have secured relatively good positions in the black economy (manufacturing alcoholic beverages, undertaking building projects, buying and selling metals or agricultural produce). The overall picture is very varied and is related to a number of factors, including the internal differentiation among the Gypsy community itself.

Considerable changes have also taken place in social relations. The economic crisis and political struggles created social tensions which, in turn, often led to escalating problems in relations between ethnic groups. At the start of the transition period the Gypsies were inevitable scapegoats in the popular search for those to blame for the social crisis. This victimisation often went as far as pogroms, murders of Gypsies by skinheads and police violence (Bulgarian Helsinki Committee 1994–9, Human Rights Project 1994–9, Zang 1991). Gradually, however, the situation became calmer and these relationships gradually resumed their former customary pattern. The Gypsies are still discriminated against and remain victims of violence, at an inter-personal level and in certain everyday situations, as well as at the hands of state institutions – mainly the police. However, the predominant pattern is once more for Bulgarians to despise Gypsies as an inferior people who have to know their place and problems usually arise when Gypsies are no longer willing to remain in this allotted place. Due to their raised consciousness of civil rights Gypsies now seem to have become more sensitive to discriminatory attitudes. Meanwhile small, unorganised groups of Bulgarian young men proclaim themselves as skinheads in imitation of similar movements in the West. However, attempts to create a popular movement based on racist ideology and directed against the Gypsies amount to little more than media sensations and have no real potential to develop further in Bulgaria.

The Gypsy policy of state institutions and local authorities since 1989 can be summed up as abdication of real political action and, instead, simulation of action, although the form this takes differs over the years. In 1991 a new constitution was adopted based on the premise of individual civil rights. The most frequently cited Gypsy-related excerpt from this constitution is Art. 6, para. 2, which does not allow for 'any limitations of the rights or privileges based on ... ethnic belonging ...'. Consequently, when the problems of minorities are raised, the typical reply is that according to the constitution all Bulgarian citizens are equal, and no special privileges can be granted. However, in November 1992 the Constitutional Court gave an interpretation of the above text, which allowed for 'certain socially justified privileges' for 'groups of citizens' in 'an unfavourable social situation'. This at least served as a basis for encouraging a more positive state policy towards Gypsies, although mostly confined to improving their socio-economic position.

Executive government's method for dealing with this policy area remained almost unaltered in spite of changes of government and cabinet personnel. There were discussions about creating a special body, attached to the Council of Ministers and including representatives of various ministries, which would introduce a co-ordinated state policy for Gypsies. Finally, in 1994 an Inter-departmental Council on Ethnic Problems was organised.

In 1995, with the coming to power of the Bulgarian Socialist Party (BSP), this council was transformed into the Inter-administrative Council on Social and Demographic Issues but it remained completely inactive.

At the start of 1997 the new government of the Union of Democratic Forces (UDF) established the National Council on Ethnic and Demographic Issues at the Council of Ministers but this council was very inactive and this lethargic attitude of the state forced Roma organisations to take the lead themselves. The Human Rights Project initiated and organised the preparation by Roma leaders and independent experts of a Framework Programme – *For Equal Participation of Roma in the Public Life of Bulgaria* (Programme 1998). This Programme turned its back on cheap speculation about specific social and economic problems and instead paid particular attention to their major cause, the unequal position of the Gypsies in Bulgarian society. It outlined the main course of action the state had to follow in order to implement its Gypsy policy: establishment of a state body to fight discrimination, desegregation of 'Gypsy schools', legalisation of existing Gypsy neighbourhoods, provision of access to the national media and so on.

The Framework Programme was discussed in detail, supplemented and approved by all Roma organisations in the country at a National Round Table in October 1998 and was proposed to the government as a basis for its future work. In response to this initiative of the Roma organisations and in view of the then approaching local elections, the government adopted the slogan of integration of the Gypsies through their participation in local authorities. The government, with the collaboration of a well-known international NGO, also tried to impose its own programme, prepared by Spanish experts from the Council of Europe. However, the Roma leaders rejected the government proposal and after long negotiations an agreement was signed between the Roma organisations and the Council of Ministers on 7 April 1999. The Council of Ministers discussed and approved the Programme proposed by the Roma in a special decision at its session of 22 April 1999. To this day, however, the Bulgarian government has limited itself to appointing a single Gypsy, Yosif Nunev, to the National Council as an expert and to making a number of statements in the media and at international forums, without implementing any specific activities for the accomplishment of the programme goals.

The Gypsy policy of the state can be characterised as a lack of any real desire to change the existing situation. On occasions when, for one reason or another, the Bulgarian state needs to have a position on specific problems related to Gypsies (such as participation in certain programmes of European institutions), it still prefers to simulate activity instead of making use of the existing potential for change. This situation is not affected by differences between political parties because the attitude of the state towards the Gypsy issue has been predetermined by underlying stereotypes and prejudice towards Gypsies in Bulgarian society.

Since 1989 a new and important factor influencing the development of the Gypsy community has been the rapidly developing non-governmental sector (Marushiakova and Popov 1997b: 37–56). In Central and Eastern Europe non-governmental organisations (NGOs) were created after the regime changes in 1989 and exist thanks solely to the financial support of programmes and foundations abroad. The number and activities of NGOs in Bulgaria expanded rapidly and these now form one of the few successful business sectors, following a Western, mostly US-inspired, pattern of development. The non-governmental sector firmly believes that the problems of the Gypsies are the main priority of their sponsors and that is why they include them among their own priorities. According to the Association of Bulgarian Foundations and Societies, there were 1,200 organisations aiming to work with minorities (mainly Gypsies) in 1997.

However, one should not be misled by such statistics for neither Bulgarian society as a whole nor the Gypsies themselves have a clear idea about the number of people and organisations 'taking care' of them. Most of these organisations deliberately remain only semi-legal. They are registered officially and report their 'activity' to sponsors from abroad, while rigorously avoiding any mention of their activities in Bulgaria. The numerous larger-scale projects on civic education, conflict resolution, 'open education', sexual literacy, family planning, protection of Gypsy women from violence and others belong to this type of activity. They usually take the guise of endless courses and seminars, which have led to the formation of a small and self-closed stratum of paid 'professionals in the NGO sector' and a small circle of Gypsies, who have become professional 'seminar attenders'. The activities of NGOs have often been used by the state to distance itself from the problems of Gypsies and transfer its own responsibilities to the non-governmental sector, for example, in the case of homeless children. It is extremely dangerous that the non-governmental sector frequently not only does not urge the state to perform its functions, but on the contrary has provided it with an excuse to ignore the problem.

We can see with increasing clarity a merging of NGO models of working with those of state institutions. Indeed, these are often partners in various European programmes and their interests coincide to the detriment of the Gypsies. A single example is enough. In the spring of 1998 a seminar was held in the town of Lom, where representatives of government, local authorities and the organisers (a well-known international NGO) proclaimed their success in establishing a model of collaboration for solving the social and economic problems of Gypsies. Only few weeks later Roma from this same town, who had not receive their social support payments for over a year, tried to set fire to themselves in public (PER 1998).

In other cases there is a direct clash of interest between the NGO sector and the Gypsy community, as in the case of segregated Gypsy schools. Several NGOs are carrying out a number of educational projects involving Gypsy children which would no longer be required if these schools cease to exist.

Nevertheless, in spite of the emergence of a parasitic 'Gypsy industry', the non-governmental sector and especially the Romani NGOs have still made contributions to positive change in Bulgarian society.

### Roma organisations and their political activity

After 1989 Gypsies were free to proclaim their identity and organise their own unions and consequently organisations gradually began to emerge, influenced by the surrounding social and political environment. However, as elsewhere, whatever potential existed for formal political mobilisation has as yet remained largely unfulfilled, although it must be acknowledged that in reality these possibilities were severely limited.

Between 1989 and 1997 many new political organisations were formed to represent Gypsies, all of them claiming to be 'national' and to have clear-cut political aims. These were invariably closely associated with their leaders: Confederacy of Roma in Bulgaria (Peter Georgiev), United Romani Union (Vassil Chaprazov), Democratic Union Roma (Manush Romanov), Federation of the United Romani Communities (Vassil Danev), Romani Union for Social Democracy (Milcho Russinov), Independent Democratic Union Roma (Assen Hristov), Club 'Union' (Toma Tomov), Roma Public Council 'Kupate' (Agreement), established in 1997 as a satellite organisation of the UDF and led by Zlatko Mladenov and Simeon Blagoev. These so-called 'national' organisations consisted mainly of their own leaders and an insignificant number of activists; they had almost no organisational activities and no effective political lobby. Unsurprisingly, their popularity among the wider Gypsy population in Bulgaria remains insignificant. Fuller details of Gypsy political mobilisation are given in the appendix.

Disappointment in the 'political road to development' gave a powerful impetus to the growth of the Gypsy NGO sector and led to its rapid expansion. More than 150 Gypsy NGOs have already been registered and are now functioning. They carry out their projects with financial assistance from various sources, often with salaries that are many times higher than the average Bulgarian income. The few attempts to unite and co-ordinate the activities of all Gypsy NGOs have been unsuccessful and the optimistically named Association of Roma NGOs, established by Peter Kostov and headed by Toma Tomov, has turned out to be an NGO without the participation of any members from already existing organisations.

A much more promising approach has been that of the Human Rights Project, a Bulgarian Gypsy human rights organisation established in 1992, which co-operates actively with other organisations in Bulgaria and abroad. It has ceased to be a typical human rights organisation and is really working for the development of the Gypsy community instead of merely servicing what might be termed the 'Gypsy industry'. In the process of preparing and approving the Framework Programme, the Human Rights Project succeeded in achieving an informal association of Gypsy organisations, which in spite of their many differences have united behind common principles and positions that they have had to defend before the Bulgarian government.

Here we should question the extent to which these attempts at formal political mobilisation have affected the life of most Gypsies in Bulgaria. We can say with certainty that at present they involve only a small part of the Gypsy population in certain areas. Large parts of the community remain virtually unaffected by Gypsy politics, for example the *Rudara*, most Turkish-speaking Gypsies and many traditional Gypsy groups, etc.

## The involvement of Kardarasha in politics

Initially the *Kardarasha*, too, kept their distance from these post-Communist mobilisation processes. *Kardarasha* Gypsies maintain strong ethnic and cultural traditions including internal self-government (the *Meshariava* or Gypsy court) and strong endogamy. Yet, although 'traditional' in some respects, *Kardarasha* are also innovative and are always seeking new economical niches and, compared with other Gypsies, their community is relatively well off. It was therefore an entirely rational idea for them to turn to these new social activities, since they saw in them a way of partially legalising their businesses and also involving them with public procurement, the most profitable type of business at present.

Consequently they soon sent their representatives, for example Vassil Danev, Toma Tomov, Zlatko Mladenov and Alexander Philipov, to participate in the new system of Gypsy NGOs, and to the Rroma Soros Foundation and the Roma Program of the Open Society Fund. They also pursued a parallel strategy with the help of the media, presenting a more familiar style of leadership by 'Gypsy kings' (such as Kiril Rashkov '*Tzar* Kiro'). Meanwhile, they experimented with a transformation of the traditional form of internal self-government by creating a 'Supreme *Meshare*' headed by Zlatko Mladenov.

The *Kardarasha* community recently became the basis for a new stage in the development of the Gypsy community through the activities of the Euro-Roma organisation. This was inspired by Tsvetelin Kanchev, an ethnic Bulgarian who has been adopted into the *Kardarasha* community. Kanchev is a rich businessman and has been a member of parliament since the autumn of 1997, originally aligned to the Bulgarian Business Block but later as a member of the Bulgarian Euro-Left. After lengthy preparation, the founding congress of the National Euro-Roma Association was held in Sofia in

December 1998 and was attended by 3,386 delegates from 205 municipal organisations from every region of the country. This was the largest public event of its type to be staged in Bulgaria and, equally importantly, it was the first time in modern Gypsy history when subdivisions co-operated as independent participants in the political life of the country. The establishment of this new Euro-Roma organisation was proof that Gypsies did not need the shelter of others' political umbrellas but could rely on their own power. The current constitutional ban on ethnically-based parties was no real limitation since it had proved ineffective and could be ignored with ease. Euro-Roma was very active in 1999 in preparation for the coming local elections as were other Gypsy political parties.[7]

Such intensive mobilisation by Gypsy parties alarmed the government, which retaliated in the summer of 1999 – just before the local elections – by striking against the most popular organisation, Euro-Roma, by depriving Kanchev of his parliamentary immunity. He was detained on criminal charges, although public opinion did not regard these as genuine. This government action was reminiscent of the similar case of Kiril Rashkov, who was detained for several months on speculative charges which were not proven. However, the arrest of Kanchev was a severe setback for Gypsy hopes of achieving economic power and political influence through their own political representation.

The gap left by the attack on Euro-Roma was partially filled by the Free Bulgaria party, whose election campaign relied on the principle of people supporting those in their own ethnic group, with Roma voting for Roma and *milliets* voting for *milliets*.[8] The results of these local elections, in October 1999, were a great shock for Bulgarian society. The Free Bulgaria party received 52,300 votes and eighty-one municipal councillors, which ranked it among the top ten political groupings. Euro-Roma itself had fifty-six municipal councillors but over the whole country Gypsy parties, separately or in various local coalitions, received about 2 per cent of the votes and about 200 municipal councillors. In addition, they gained key positions in a number of municipal councils, as well as the office of mayor in several of the larger villages. In this way the Gypsies and their parties have become an important factor in Bulgaria's modern political progress and only the future will reveal how these processes will develop.[9]

## *The influence of the evangelical movement*

A different path in the search for community development is demonstrated by the growth in influence of various Evangelical churches among the Bulgarian Gypsies. The first Evangelical churches were built in Gypsy neighbourhoods between the two World Wars and although limited in numbers, their work never stopped. After 1989, they were joined by a number of new churches, whose activity was directed mainly toward Gypsies. These Gypsy church communities gradually became differentiated on an ethnic basis: they elected their own pastors, began to build their own churches in Gypsy neighbourhoods and are now only formally related to the broader church organisations. Recently many Bulgarian Gypsies have been attracted to these 'new churches', while a wholly independent Roma Church is currently being registered.[10]

Conversion to a different religion is often seen as a method for seeking an altered place in society, a way of adjusting to new conditions and as a means of escaping from the crisis in one's own ethnic community. In Balkan conditions, where ethnic and religious identities are often confused, this could lead to changes in ethnic affiliation.

## Conclusion

It is not easy to summarise the development trends among Bulgarian Gypsies. Current approaches have proved disappointing and bitter experience has convinced Gypsies that these do not have the potential to ensure any real improvement for their community. The paternalistic approach of the 'benevolent white brothers', all too evident in the activities of political parties, the state and NGO sector, has placed Gypsies in the position of being forever taught and protected. Yet, at the same time, it has destroyed the adaptive mechanisms of the Gypsy community and in the long run will hinder their potential for natural development. This is demonstrated by the fact that whenever there has been an opportunity for independent Gypsy action or initiatives, such as Euro-Roma or the Framework Programme, the state and NGOs – with a few exceptions – have used lame excuses to unite and unanimously oppose the Gypsies (or refuse to support them). The political parties (and the governments that are based on them) need the Gypsies as voters, while the NGOs (including those based outside Bulgaria) need a community with problems in order to protect, care for and defend its rights, etc. However, these bodies do not see themselves as benefiting from the development of a community able to solve (or try to solve) its problems independently.

It has become clear that international institutions cannot solve the problems of Gypsies in individual countries, and the many examples of the 'Gypsy industry' sector at various levels (both state and NGO) only serve to confirm this belief. Moreover, the models proposed by the West are often inadequate or lead to results that are the opposite of those intended (as in Bosnia and Kosovo). Meanwhile, the abolition of restrictions on international contacts by Gypsies shows that all-Gypsy unity is still only an ideal which will take a long time to achieve and will become successful only if it is based on what Gypsies have achieved in each particular country.

In conclusion it is not easy to say whether the Bulgarian Gypsies will have the strength to take their destiny into their own hands, either through NGOs or through political movements, but it is evident that this goal is clearly perceived and despite inevitable disappointments is hardly likely to be forgotten.

# Appendix
## Attempts at Gypsy political mobilisation in Bulgaria – 1989–99

At a founding conference on 17 March 1990 the decision was taken to establish a Democratic Union Roma, whose chair became Manush Romanov. The initiative for this union came from the Bulgarian Socialist Party (BSP) but as a consequence of acute political conflict during what was called a round table meeting, Manush Romanov steered this union towards the rival UDF party. Shortly before the elections in the spring of 1990 and prompted by the BSP, alternative local Gypsy organisations began to emerge all over the country, such as the Movement for the Social and Cultural Development of the Gypsies, Organisation for the Social Development of Gypsies – Ascent, Cultural and Educational Society of Gypsies, Unity, Club of Gypsy Intellectuals and others. The majority of these associations had an uncertain status and most of them ceased to function after the parliamentary elections.

For a time the activities of these organisations were limited, even though there were three Gypsy members in Parliament: Manush Romanov (UDF), Sabi Golemanov and Peter Alexandrov (BSP). Only in the summer of 1991, when political conflicts in the country were on the rise and new elections were approaching, did these Gypsy organisations reactivate themselves. Manush Romanov failed completely in his attempt to transform the Democratic Union Roma into a political power. In the autumn of 1991 he left the UDF, where he had the undefined status of 'observer', because he was ignored in the pre-election coalition.

In early 1992 there was a move towards unity among the existing Gypsy organisations, irrespective of their political views. After a number of preliminary meetings the United Roma Union was created, with Vassil Chaprazov as its chair, at what was called the Uniting Conference in Sofia on 17 October 1992. However, supporters of the confederate model refused to join the new leadership and declared that they would not dissolve their own organisations. At the same time other Gypsy leaders boycotted the conference (Marushiakova 1992: 51–62, Popov 1992: 41–50).

At the start of 1993 the leaders of some Gypsy organisations proposed a new union whose individual organisations would preserve their independence and on 8 May 1993 this new organisation was officially named the Confederacy of the Roma in Bulgaria, led by Peter Georgiev. The goal of the Confederacy was to work for the unity and ethnic emancipation of Gypsies in

Bulgaria and to 'enter the corridors of power' as a self-declared 'non-political organisation'.

These Gypsy organisations were relatively inactive until the parliamentary elections in the autumn of 1994. After long pre-election negotiations, some Gypsy leaders were included in the electoral lists of various political parties and unions. However, their low placing in these lists made their chance of being elected almost negligible. The pre-election agreement of Georgi Parushev with the Movement of Rights and Freedoms (MRF), the party of the Turkish minority, is especially interesting. It gave Gypsies the right to participate in the elections as MRF members in more than one third of the electoral districts (where there was no Turkish population and the MFR received no votes). However, this did not result in a Gypsy presence in Bulgarian political life after the elections. Only one Gypsy was elected as a member of the new parliament – Peter Georgiev from the BSP. Somewhat later, in 1996, Dimitar Dimitrov from Vidin also entered Parliament as a member of the BSP and a substituting deputy.

The political crisis in late 1996 and early 1997, as well as the elections in the spring of 1997 galvanised the Gypsy organisations into action once more. They had several meetings in order to prepare a joint policy and action plan and joint candidates for parliament, but no agreement was reached. Although some Gypsy leaders were included in the electoral lists of some parties, these were once more in places where the chance of being elected was almost non-existent. Others ran for parliament as 'independent' candidates, but on the whole Gypsies did not obtain any political representation in these elections. Subsequently, Assen Hristov (substituting deputy) became a member of parliament as a representative of the UDF in 1998.

## References

Bulgarian Helsinki Committee (1994–1999) *Human Rights in Bulgaria in 1993(-1998) Annual Report*, Sofia: BHC.

Human Rights Project (1994–1999) *Annual Report for 1993(–1998)*, Sofia: HRP.

Kenrick, D. (ed.) (1999) *In the Shadow of the Swastika: the Gypsies during the Second World War*, 2, Interface Collection, Hatfield: University of Hertfordshire Press.

Marushiakova, E. (1992) 'Gruppi ed organizzazioni zingare in Bulgaria e il loro atteggiamento verso l' impegno politico', *Lacio Drom* 28, 1–2: 51–62.

Marushiakova, E. and Popov, V. (1997a) *Gypsies (Roma) in Bulgaria*, Frankfurt am Main: Peter Lang Verlag.

Marushiakova, E. and Popov, V. (1997b) 'The Gypsy minority in Bulgaria – literacy, policy and community development (1985–1995)', *Alpha 97*, Toronto and Hamburg: Culture Concepts Publishers/UNESCO Institute for Education.

Marushiakova, E. and Popov, V. (2001) *Gypsies in the Ottoman Empire*, Interface Collection, Hatfield: University of Hertfordshire Press.

Marushiakova, E. and Popov, V. (eds) (1995) *Studii Romani* 2, Sofia: Club '90.

PER (1998) *The Roma in Bulgaria: Collaborative Efforts Between Local Authorities and Nongovernmental Organisations*, Princeton: Project on Ethnic Relations (PER).

Popov, V. (1992) 'Il problemo zingaro in Bulgaria nel contesto attuale', *Lacio Drom* 28, 1–2: 41–50.

Programme (1998) 'For equal participation of Roma in the public life of Bulgaria', *Roma Rights in Focus*, Newsletter of Human Rights Project 10, (special edition).

Rezultati (1994) *Rezultati ot prebroyavaneto na naselenieto, Tom I - Demografski charakteristiki,* (The results from the census of population, 1 – demographic characteristics), Sofia: Natsionalen statisticheski institut.

Zang, T. (1991) 'Destroying ethnic identity: The Gypsies of Bulgaria', *Helsinki Watch Report*, New York: Human Rights Watch.

# Notes

1   The term 'Gypsies' is preferred to Roma because of the variety of Romani groupings, not all of whom consider themselves to be Roma.

2   For example, among *Dasikane* Roma such groups are: *Kalaydzhia* (tinsmiths); *Burgudzhia* (gimlet-makers), *Koshnicharia* (basket-makers), *Dzhambazia* (cattle dealers) etc.; among *Xoraxane* Roma there are: *Muzikantia* (musicians), *Fichiria, Futadzhia, Koshnicharia* (basket-makers), *Dzhambazia* (cattle dealers), *Zvancharia* (bell-makers), etc.

3   Such as *Zlataria* (*Grastaria, Nitsuleshi, Serbian Gypsies*), *Dodolania, Tasmanaria, Zhaplesh, Layashi/Laynesh, Nyamtsuria* (German or Austrian Gypsies), etc.

4   The Thracean *Kalaydzhia* are divided into two subgroups – the *Wlaxorya* and *Salatsi.*

5   Such as *Monteni, Thracieni, Zagoriani*, etc.

6   This process took place in several stages, beginning in 1962 (after the special Decision A101 of the Political Bureau of the Central Committee of the BCP, whose purpose was 'to curb the negative tendencies … among Bulgarian Muslims, Gypsies and Tartars to identify with the Turks … and to enhance patriotic education') and ending in 1984-5.

7   These included the Democratic Congress Party (led by Ramadan Rashid), the Union for Democratic Development (Ivan Kirov), the Bulgarian Party 'Future' (led by Russi Golemanov), the 'Free Bulgaria' Party (led by Angel Rashkov, the son of '*Tzar* Kiro') and the small *Rudara* Party 'Political Party Democratic Movement *Rodoliubie*' (recently created and led by Ivan Kostov – a member of *Rudara* community).

8   A *milliet* (millet) was a faith community (religion), which broadly denoted a people ('nation') and was used as the basis for community self-regulation during the Ottoman Empire.

9   The chapter includes the period up to the end of 2000.

10  This church is led by Boris Borisov from the town of Lom.

## CHAPTER SEVENTEEN

# Albania: awakening from a long sleep

*Tracy Koci*

U ntil recently Albania was considered to be a land of mystery and has been described as one of the 'least known and least accessible countries of the world' (Blejer *et al.* 1992: 1). This image is the result of almost fifty years of isolation when Albanians lived under an authoritarian regime with a Marxist ideology and Stalinist practices (Blejer *et al.* 1992: 1). Years of suffering and hardship, however, did little to dampen the Albanian people's strong sense of national pride. This is evident from the place of legendary military heroes such as Enver Hoxha and Skenderberg in the history of Albania, where they are seen as defending Albania's national sovereignty in the face of invasion, occupation and war.

Albanian people's pride in their heritage conflicts with their regret over the many years of isolation. Albanians now feel a need to modernise in order to 'catch up' with the rest of the world. The lifestyles of others, as seen on television programmes broadcast from their closest neighbours, Greece, Macedonia and Italy, present them with images of a preferred 'European' way of living, featuring large homes, electrical appliances and fashionable clothes. The Albanian Roma are no different from the rest of the Albanian population in this respect. Whilst they often do not accept certain European values, such as equal rights for women, they usually aspire to the same material goods, representing modernisation and prosperity.

The effects of modernisation and change on Albanian Roma are analysed here in contrasting images derived from the past. These fall into three groups: the changes in Roma lifestyle during and after Communism, the growing sense of identity among Roma as opposed to images imposed upon them by others, and the emerging concept of 'difference' as a social construct in Albanian society which, in turn, influences the development of a political identity for Roma.

Albania is a country of contrasts where the beauty of the landscape is typified by sandy white beaches, pine forests and quaint medieval mountain villages. These picture-postcard images clash with the reality of modernisation: the decaying, abandoned factories, huge rubbish dumps, polluted shanty towns and half-finished concrete monstrosities that surround Albania's city centres. In Tirana, Albania's capital, the most obvious gulf is between rich and poor. Government officials and the new breed of criminal élite hurtle around Tirana sounding the horns of their Mercedes cars, flashing expensive watches, blasting out loud 'modern' music and speaking intensely into their mobile phones. In contrast, the local working people struggle daily into Tirana by dilapidated horse and cart, heading for the bazaar or city centre where they offer their wares on small roadside stalls.

The Roma are part of the local working population, visible everywhere in Albania but especially in the cities. They sell second-hand clothes, work on small street stands trading in everything from cigarettes to music cassettes, barbecue corn-cobs as snacks and occasionally beg for money.

### Minorities in Albania

In 1986 the total population of Albania was declared to be 3.4 million people (Pettifer 1996: 5). The ethnic mix is mainly Albanian with some Greeks, Serbs, Montenegrins, Macedonians, Roma, Vlachs, and Jev. The Vlachs and the Jev are the groups most often mentioned in literature relating to the Albanian Roma. These accounts are usually written by non-Roma who tend to confuse the three groups.

The Roma population of Albania is officially considered to be 1,261. However, since there is no category in the census which identifies Roma, this figure appears to have no reliable basis. The Albanian Roma organisation, *Amaro Drom*, gives the widely divergent figure of 100,000 Roma in Albania (*Zëri i Popullit*, 9 July 1989), which closely corresponds to the estimate accepted by the European Union (Liégeois and Gheorghe 1995: 7).

The Vlachs, numbering 50,000–100,000, are a mainly nomadic people, living predominantly in the Korca region. They are not considered to be Roma, neither by themselves nor by the Roma, and they speak a Latin-based language similar to modern Romanian. The Vlachs maintain a traditional culture as pastoralists with herds of sheep and goats (Pettifer 1996: 79, Winnifrith 1987). Crowe (1995: 199), however, suggests that the Vlachs are 'white Gypsies' who denied their Gypsy origins and began to intermarry with the non-Gypsy population, although other experts strongly disagree.[1]

The Jevgit or Jev are also confused with the Roma. They are thought by some to be the first Roma to arrive in Albania who eventually lost most of their Romani language. It is also suggested that during the Communist period they declared Egypt to be their country of origin in an attempt to gain some political leverage. However, unlike the speculation about the Vlachs, there does appear to be some historical evidence supporting their claim (Poulton 1995: 141–2).

Jevgit are variously described as a people descended from Coptic migrants who came to Albania from Egypt in the fourth century; as disguised Turks; or as assimilated, 'non-nomadic' Roma. Some Romani activists claim that Enver Hoxha 'invented' the category. A 1938 article by Margaret Hasluck in the *Journal of The Gypsy Lore Society* notices a number of different sub-groupings, but only one large 'Gypsy' minority divided into 'sedentaries' (i.e. Jevgit) and 'nomads' (Roma).

(Fortuna and Cortiade 1997)

The Jev, however, strongly deny that they are Roma and affirm their Egyptian origin. Likewise Albanian Roma consider the Jev to be 'different' from themselves, even though they occasionally intermarry.[2] Both groups identify themselves as 'brown' and when necessary tend to align with each other politically.[3] Roma history in Albania is closely linked with that of the Jev hence confusion between the two groups by non-Roma is a recurring theme in historical literature.

There are four main groups of Roma in Albania, the *Mećkàră*, the *Kallbuxhi*, the *Ćergàră* or *Škodràră* and the *Kurtòfă* (Kurtiade 1995: 10). There are differences between these groups and a variety of spellings for group names. For example, the two largest groups, the *Mećkàră* and the *Kallbuxhi*, differ in several ways. The *Mećkàră* are involved in agriculture, metalwork, storytelling and music. They are considered to be more stable because they rarely travel and tend to dress more conservatively. The *Kallbuxhi* by comparison dress more flamboyantly and are often nomadic or semi-nomadic. Neither group considers the other to be more or less Romani for Roma do not consider nomadism to be an essential characteristic for Romani identity but rather a stereotype imposed by the non-Roma. Nevertheless, these groups sometimes express negative views of each other, focusing on the 'essence of difference' (Anthias and Yuval-Davis 1992: 15). The *Mećkàră*, for example, are quick to point out that the *Kallbuxhi* are 'less modern', 'less intelligent' and 'darker' than themselves. The *Kallbuxhi* insult the *Mećkàră* in similar ways. However, neither group, considers this rivalry to be serious and there are no problems of tension or conflict between these groups. The Roma in Albania live and work together, intermarry, use a similar language and share the same political aspirations for equality. The 'inclusionary and exclusionary' boundaries (Anthias and Yuval-Davis 1992: 31), which preserve group identity, have little significance within the Roma community as a whole but on occasions they can be useful to persuade outsiders of the superiority of the speaker's group.

The Roma in Albania have no political concept of themselves as 'black' (Roma) as opposed to 'white' (Albanians). Nor does the general Albanian population polarise the two groups in this way. The unusual absence of what Kurtiade (1995) termed an 'enemy image' in this public perception of Roma is attributed to the efforts to banish all reference to ethnicity and difference during the long period of Enver Hoxha's rule. Racism undoubtedly exists in Albania but, until quite recently, in a less obvious way than in other countries of Central and Eastern Europe.

Roma often comment that the Albanians cannot and do not want to understand what it means to be a Rom. This lack of interest in Romani identity and culture is demonstrated in the under-representation of this group in the media and politics. Roma, who rarely intermarry with ethnic Albanians, speak openly about Roma skin colour which ranges from very dark to fair. Indian films are popular amongst the young Roma, who not only enjoy the romance and music but also identify with the characters' ' brown skin'. Yet, from a political perspective, 'blacks as victims and whites as perpetrators of racism' does not appear to exist in the consciousness of the Roma people of Albania (Anthias and Yuval-Davies 1992: 15–35).

Similarly, the position of the non-Roma population in Albania is one of embracing everything modern and European rather than thinking of themselves as a multicultural community. Even after the ending of Communist rule, concerns of class and 'common cultural need' (Brah 1992: 129) rather than colour, appear to be far more prominent in the political discourse of Albania.

## Pre-Communist history

As elsewhere in the region, undertaking historical, social and anthropological research is difficult as Albanian Roma express little interest in their past in spite of an amazing repertoire of folk tales, passed down from generation to generation, which may contain clues to their origins and subsequent experience.

Nevertheless, there are historical references to Roma from the Middle Ages onwards and Kolsti (1991: 51) suggests that Roma have been in Albania for 600 years. The earliest mention of Roma in the Balkans was in Macedonia in 1289 (Crowe 1995: 195) and shortly after a fourteenth-century Bulgarian text, the *Life of Saint Barbarus*, described Egyptians 'living in large numbers' along the Albanian coast (Crowe 1995: 2), although this could have indicated either Roma or Jev. There are references to levies collected from Muslim and Christian Gypsies in Albania and western Greece in 1605 and again at the end of the seventeenth century (Crowe 1995: 198–9). One writer suggested that Ottoman taxes were deliberately increased for Roma in order to 'tax them out of existence' (Crowe 1995: 199).

The long years of Ottoman rule in Albania had a lasting effect on the culture of present-day Albania, influencing its religion, language, customs and architecture. After the break-up of the Empire and in the aftermath of the Balkan wars, Albania was eventually declared an independent sovereign state in July 1913. In the process, however, parts of the territory largely inhabited by ethnic Albanians were given to neighbouring Serbia, Montenegro and Greece, leaving half of the Albanian population outside the new state of Albania (Pettifer 1996: 33–4). This continuing mismatch of borders and population distribution provides the context for the recent conflict in Kosovo and Macedonia and should also be borne in mind when discussing Roma in Albania. However, this chapter mainly concerns only those Roma who were able to remain within the national borders of Albania.

Following independence, Albania was caught up in a series of wars and during hostilities between Albania and Serbia from 1917 to the 1920s, atrocities committed against the Albanian population in Kosovo were also extended to the Roma, causing many Kosovar Roma to flee to Albania. There appears to be little evidence of violent attacks on Roma by Albanians, although Crowe gives examples of some hostility. In 1920 the Albanian government attempted to stop Roma from dancing in public for money and Muslim Roma were described as not 'appreciated' in mosques or burial grounds. 'Consequently, in 1923, the Rom in Durazzo built their own mosque' (Crowe 1995: 214–5).

A 'British Albanophile', Joseph Swire (1937), gave an impression of the life of settled Roma in Albania during the interwar period, describing their occupations as 'blacksmiths or executioners or scavengers', refuse collectors and drowners of dogs. At the same time, however, he noted that many Roma men worked at the ports as 'stevedores and boatmen and porters', while the women – described as 'stocky and hardworking' and 'keep[ing] their houses much cleaner than the lowland Albanians' – were 'often employed for servants'. He also described tent-dwelling nomadic Roma, the men 'mak[ing] baskets and ropes and deal[ing] in horses' and the women 'practis[ing] fortune telling and … most lascivious' (Crowe 1995: 215).

Swire's often stereotypical comments can be compared with accounts from Albanian Roma who describe their occupations during the interwar years as being those of metal, craft and agricultural workers, potters and musicians – particularly in demand at Albanian wedding feasts. Indeed, Roma often recall the period before the Second World War with fondness. Elderly Roma reminisce about the abundance of food during these years, about living well and being able to receive a basic education.

In November 1926 King Zog was crowned King of the Albanians and immediately pledged allegiance to Italy, opening the way for Italy to gain control of the state in 1938. Shortly after, following Mussolini's invasion and Zog's flight into exile, Albania became an Italian province. During these years the Italians unsuccessfully attempted to eradicate Albanian culture and language but took little interest in the Roma, who were seen as an 'insignificant part' of the total population (Kenrick and Puxon 1995: 108). The Italian collapse in September 1943 resulted in a German invasion but persecution of 'tinguish them from Turks and Vlachs. During the war some Roma were sent to camps in Yugoslavia, some collaborated with the Nazis against the Serbs while others joined the Communist partisan forces (Kolsti 1991: 51, Kenrick and Puxon 1995: 108). Most Romani villages can identify at least one or more members of their community who fought with the partisans.

## The Communist period: the denial of 'difference'

In late 1944, the most renowned partisan in Albanian history, Enver Hoxha, and his Party of Labour assumed power. The new Communist government subjected the Albanian people to the strictest controls and gradually isolated them from contact with the rest of Europe and the world. Naturally shunning Western states, Albania broke off relations with Yugoslavia in 1948, the Soviet Union in 1961 and the Republic of China in 1978, leaving this small country in complete isolation (Pettifer 1996: 41, Blejer *et al.* 1992).

Under this severe regime landowners were dispossessed of their lands and all religious institutions were closed down. The pro-atheism campaigns of 1967–76 included the burning of religious books, historical texts and libraries as well as the imprisonment of priests and imams (Pettifer 1996: 75). Albanians became afraid to speak out, afraid of being different and afraid of expressing opinions that differed from Party policy. Meanwhile, Enver Hoxha was revered as the protector and father of the people, an image that persists even today amongst older people who hold him in high esteem. For many, the legends and exploits of Enver Hoxha still occupy an important place in Albanian history. Stories continue to be told such as the one suggesting that as a baby he was breastfed by a 'Gypsy' (Champseix and Champseix 1992: 136).

Although Romani cultural traditions were not openly repressed under Communism, discrimination took other forms (Pettifer 1996: 80). Ethnic groups were not encouraged to express their own distinct cultural identities but instead the image was promoted of a homogenised society where everyone was equal. This approach was not without its advantages for Roma children were encouraged to go to school with others and Roma women worked on co-operative farms alongside non-Roma Albanians.

In a country where communications were poor and telecommunications virtually non-existent, power was devolved for practical purposes to regional level. In the provinces, for example, the lives of local people were controlled by brigadiers, part of whose function was spying for the Communist Party. Favouritism was commonly practised, both by Roma and non-Roma brigadiers, as they had the authority to decide who had the best jobs and housing. In the case of Roma families this was usually determined by the social standing of particular families in the local community.

Cultural assimilation was a clear policy goal during the Hoxha regime. However, no formal legislation or practical measures were introduced to force nomadic Roma to settle and nor were there any policies to prevent Roma from using their own language. Roma continued to hold feasts and to celebrate special Romani feast days such as *Xerdelezi*. Even though Communist propaganda sought to exert a strong influence over literature, theatre and art, Roma artists and musicians were able to articulate Romani culture in their work. The only real limitation on the arts was the requirement that forms of artistic expression should not be influenced by the West or appear to derive inspiration from this tainted source. Rather than seeking a target in the Roma, the 'enemy image' was instead attached to the evils of the West and all forms of organised religion.

Albanian Roma people often talk nostalgically about life under Communism. They particularly praise the sense of security, the lack of crime and the simplicity of life. Especially valued is the stronger sense of communal life of those times. Travelling picture shows, amateur theatre performances and feasts were occasions where communities came together to celebrate. This happens less often today due to the profound influence of television on family life. Cusack, an Australian writer, visited Albania prior to the pro-atheism campaigns. Her impressions of the Roma are of 'gaily dressed gipsies peddling home-made tin ware', 'tambourines and strainers and the other oddments that are the speciality of the nomad gipsies who followed the spring from the south' (Cusack 1966: 10, 57). She also mentions Roma who were mechanics and hospital workers and recounts meeting a 'gipsy orchestra' (1966: 9, 115, 156, 198). In her portrayal of the Bairam Muslim Festival in Tirana she describes 'a group of gipsies' in 'festive array, with white sequinned scarves' (1966: 116). Although a vivid sense of romanticism and idealism pervades this author's narrative, her account does provide a rare example of an outsider's view of the life of Albanian Roma under Communism. Her comments contrast dramatically with the negative imagery of Swire (1937) from thirty years earlier.

## Post-Communism: the emergence of 'difference'

Following the death of Enver Hoxha in 1985 his successor, Ramiz Alia, introduced a programme of slow and cautious reform but a few years later, aware of recent events elsewhere, Albanians were overwhelmed by the desire for rapid and revolutionary change. In 1990–1 mass demonstrations destroyed symbols of Communism such as the bronze statue of Enver Hoxha in central Tirana. This turbulent time was marked by widespread protests, looting and rioting, and while foreign embassies were swamped with would-be emigrants, others took matters into their own hands and poured onto overflowing boats for the short but hazardous voyage to Italy.

Albanian Roma describe the emergence from Communism as like 'waking from a long sleep' as they, together with other Albanians, at last

became aware of the outside world again from uncensored television programmes, telephone calls from those who had escaped earlier and contact
with foreign visitors. Yet for Roma and non-Roma alike their new life was not
to be as they imagined and all were soon desperate to escape the chaos and
the uncertainty that confronted them.

Democratic elections took place in 1991 resulting in a new government
the following year, led by Sali Berisha. However, in spite of what appeared
positive steps towards democratisation – such as the division of co-operative
land between communities, the renewed possibility of free enterprise and the
resumption of foreign trade with Turkey, Italy and Greece – popular frustration increased. This was because of the slow pace of change, the perceived
lack of interest and assistance from the outside world and the worsening
economic hardship suffered by the vast majority of Albanians.

The whole economy was in a critical state but in 1997 the situation
became even more desperate following the collapse of pyramid investment
schemes. Although these scams were by no means unique to Albania, the
unfamiliarity of Western-type business practices led far more people than
elsewhere to invest their entire savings, many even selling their houses to raise
funds in order to participate. These pyramid schemes sought to lure investors
with promises of impossibly generous interest rates but were bound to
become insolvent when the 'flow of new investors dried up' (Krusheinycky
1997: 2). The image of Roma was not helped when the press accused 'Sudja
the Gypsy' of running one of the failed schemes, although in fact he was a
Jev.[4] The inevitable collapse of these schemes meant ruin to their investors
and led to the fall of the government amid accusations of corruption. In the
aftermath the whole country descended into lawlessness and anarchy, particularly in southern Albania where weapons and ammunition were looted and
many were injured as fighting broke out between rival criminal gangs
(Robertson 1997: 1, Tihon 1997: 4). Once more many swarmed to the ports,
desperate to leave Albania.

Over the last ten years the collapse of the Albanian economy and consequent lack of industry have resulted in crippling unemployment, fuelling
mass emigration in search of work. These pressures have also affected Roma,
who compare it with their previous situation under Communism when all
Roma went to school and occasionally university, followed by a secure job or
employment on a co-operative farm. However, Roma are often disadvantaged
in making these desperate and mostly illegal journeys abroad. Due to their
relatively greater poverty they rarely have the money to bribe border guards
and are often brutally beaten or even killed when crossing borders (ERRC
1997: 73). Roma have told me that when they are captured in Greece they are
sometimes incarcerated in large numbers for several days, in tiny prison cells,
where they are given very little food or water. Accounts of trips to Greece
suggest that Greek soldiers have raped women and children and beaten Roma

men so that they are never able to walk again.

Albanian immigrant workers in Italy suffer similar police brutality. However, the most tragic aspect of illegal migration to Italy is that of young women and underage girls who are sent to Italy for prostitution. Roma are often the victims of such trafficking. Coerced or brainwashed into believing that their daughters will have a better life in Italy, parents give their daughters to mafia groups or marry them to pimps. Such decisions are powerfully motivated by desperate poverty and the desire to improve the living conditions of the family as a whole. When questioned, most of these parents appear to have little knowledge of what will be expected of their daughters in Italy. The few Roma women who have returned from Italy are usually ostracised by the community and are considered to be unmarriageable.

In many respects non-Roma and Roma face similar problems in present-day Albania. Both groups struggle to find work in a ruined economy. Both suffer from a loss of security and protection, which leaves them exposed to the corruption of police and government officials as well as the threats of criminal gangs. Both, too, are victims of Albania's infrastructure problems – the limited availability of water, electricity, health facilities, welfare, employment, education and decent housing. In an economic environment where all are endeavouring to gain access to scarce resources, 'difference' has now become an issue. The former idealised equality and lack of reference to difference has been replaced in political discourse by an identification of difference and an emphasis on what that difference means in relation to obtaining resources. This altered situation has forced Albanian Roma to mobilise in a way they never thought was important or necessary under Enver Hoxha's regime.

Mobilising politically is a challenge for Albanian Roma. Unlike France and Spain, where the Christian faith has played an important part in Romani culture, religion does not unify the Roma in Albania. The many years of anti-religious Communism have eroded many of the beliefs and customs attached to the Muslim faith. Some researchers conclude that at present religion is neither 'a comfort' nor 'a base for a new militant mass' (Anthias and Yuval-Davis: 1992: 36). Others, like Pettifer, are more cautious, remarking that it is 'difficult to evaluate how far traditional allegiances have survived the fifty years of Communist oppression of religion' (Pettifer 1996: 75).

Though 'race' and colour were acknowledged as differences, these had not seemed a viable basis for Romani mobilisation in the past. However, a 1997 report by the European Roma Rights Center (ERRC 1997), which focused on persecution of Roma – particularly by the police and government officials – strongly suggested that racism is now a problem in present-day Albania. It is unclear whether discrimination existed as a hidden and unrecorded feature in the past or is a consequence of the emerging competitive environment in Albania which has fostered a change in attitude towards the Roma. It is also difficult to determine the relevance of class or level of poverty. Incidents recorded in this report fall into three categories: revenge killings, acts of police corruption and brutality, and events linked to race or skin colour.

In 1997 a particularly savage revenge killing took place in the town of Levan, home to one of the largest Roma communities in Albania, and featured in international news reports. In Levan Roma are frequently terrorised and raided by armed mafia but attempts at self-defence only provoke further attacks in reprisal. Roma from this town told how Roma villagers killed two armed mafia men who had attacked their homes. The police, who were powerless to help the Roma, feared a revenge killing and asked the Roma to arm themselves and patrol the village. Five months later, in retribution, four children were covered with petrol and burnt to death by Albanian mafia gunmen.

> Albania is known throughout the world as the pre-eminent country of *revenge* with the *blood feud* a factor in the social life of the many remote mountain communities. The Albanian character is seen as a product of this world, with immense emphasis being put on personal loyalty and bravery, but with a common disregard for the requirements of the state legal system.
>
> (Pettifer 1996: 83)

Roma in general do not become involved in these 'revenge cycles' which are said to characterise Albanian communities in the north. They generally keep to themselves and if revenge killings do occur it is within the confines of their own communities. In the above example from Levan, the lack of police protection left the Roma with no choice but to defend themselves. However, as elsewhere in Central and Eastern Europe, there is evidence that police themselves are sometimes the perpetrators of crime.

In April 1996 Levan had been the location of another attack on Roma but on this occasion carried out by twenty police officers (ERRC 1997: 34). On the pretext of searching for two thieves the police had raided a Roma village, shooting in the air and forcibly entering people's houses, where Roma were kicked and beaten. As the two alleged thieves were not at home, one of their brothers was taken instead.

Of all crime experienced by Albanian Roma in recent years the most tragic and painful is the theft of their children by mafia gangs. Hivzi Bushati, chief of the Berat police department, reported that 'girls or young women' were stolen to be 'forced into prostitution in Italy' and that 'children of both sexes' were taken 'for the theft and use of their internal organs' (ERRC 1997: 38). These stolen children are rarely found by the police. One family told me of a thirteen-year-old Roma bride who had been abducted by a mafia gang and taken to Italy. The distraught family went to the police station where it was suggested that if they paid 1,000 US dollars the crime would be 'investigated'. Since they were unable to pay the bribe the family was then accused of 'giving' their daughter to the mafia and wasting police time. The father was subsequently beaten up by the police.

Albanian Roma also suffer abuse when in police custody and in prison as the testimony of a victim makes clear.

> We were put in separate cells next to each other. The seat in my cell was made of concrete. They made me sit handcuffed with my hands behind my back. Eight police officers came in and started beating me all over my body. The three policemen from the bar were the worst. They beat me with chair legs and kicked me all over. They broke my eardrums so that blood started pouring out of my ears and they broke my ribs. Over my own screams I could hear my brother screaming through the walls.
>
> (ERRC 1997: 39)

Albanian Roma say that they are treated differently by the police from non-Roma Albanians, except for the very poor. However, they explain this conduct not as discrimination but due to the fact that non-Roma Albanians usually have family connections, which means that any ill-treatment would have adverse consequences for the police. The Roma, by comparison, are less likely to have family members in positions of power in the government, in mafia gangs or in the police force. Not all Albanian Roma, however, are victims. In Tirana, for example, there are some Roma who have achieved wealth and influence since the end of Communist rule by establishing their own criminal connections.

Under the Communist regime it would have been impossible for armed gangs to terrorise families for personal gain but in present-day Albania Roma are ideal targets for such exploitation because, in a situation of scarce resources, they are less likely to receive police protection than other members of the community. Albanian Roma cannot rely on the police to follow up crimes or apprehend criminals since they see the police, with justification, as disorganised and powerless to control mafia gangs. The ERRC report concluded that, in comparison with non-Roma, Albanian Roma suffer more police abuse, pay larger bribes and suffer more when kept in detention.

There is an element of racial abuse in some incidents, suggesting that Roma are targeted because they are Roma. For example, one Rom commented: 'The police always say things like, "Don't say you don't have money! You *gabel*[5] are all bosses. You can buy the whole country"' (ERRC 1997: 24). Albanian Roma are now reluctant to send their sons to enlist for national service and suggest that there has been a dramatic increase in racism in the armed forces since the end of Communism, as is suggested by the following testimony:

> Out of 600 soldiers, we were the only Roma. It was very bad in the army. The soldiers in our unit beat us and called us 'niggers' and 'dirty Gypsies'. Every day

at meals, the others spat in our food and forced us to eat it. We had to sleep in separate rooms and we always had to do all the dirty jobs. It is not that we worked separately, but the others always ordered us to do their work too. If we refused they would beat us.

(ERRC 1997: 62)

Education, too, is an area where the young have become vulnerable to physical and verbal abuse and many Roma families are no longer sending their children to school, particularly their daughters. Parents also view the influence of Western values as harmful, threatening and at odds with the future most aspire to for their daughters – a life that revolves around husband and family.

When Communism ended, young Roma girls and women were no longer required to attend school or to work on co-operative farms. Consequently they now marry young, usually at the age of thirteen. There is virtually no access to contraceptives in Albania and little pre- or post-natal care available, hence the burden on all women is enormous. Women are seen as entirely responsible for child care and housework as well as expected to work in the family business or on their plot of land. A report compiled by an Albanian women's group 'confirmed a high rate of violence against women' (*The European* 1996: 2). Of the 849 women who filled out the questionnaire, 64 per cent had experienced domestic violence in the previous year.

How many of these women, if any, were Roma is unknown. However, comments from Roma women suggest that domestic violence is on the increase. This is largely due to the frustration many men feel as a result of unemployment and lack of income. At the same time many men are wary of their wives' efforts to adapt and modernise as this is perceived as a threat to family stability and the traditional Romani way of life.

This brief account of the social problems faced by Albanian Roma demonstrates the chaos and lack of security associated with adapting to a post-Communist society. The last ten years have been extremely difficult for Roma and non-Roma alike. However, the struggle has been even harder for the Roma because of their greater poverty, their relative lack of power and influence either at local or national level and, also because of the challenge that modernisation has posed for traditional Romani culture.

## Romani mobilisation in Albania

Albanian Roma are responding to the challenge of changing circumstances by developing new forms of organisation and activities. By promoting their distinctive culture, they are emphasising the positive aspects of their difference to counter negative stereotypes of Roma identity. The basis of their current mobilisation is the Bill of Rights, adopted by the Albanian Government in 1993, which guarantees civil and political rights. This legislation represents a safeguard and guarantee for all Albanian Roma groups since it provides a framework for organisations such as *Rromani Baxt* and *Amaro Drom* in their task of challenging abuses of human rights. Within this context *Amaro Drom*, the group with which I am most familiar, has worked hard to gain recognition from government, NGOs and local authorities.

*Amaro Drom* was founded in Tirana in May 1991 by its director, Skender Veliu, with the aims of supporting Roma equal rights, language and culture. Since then it has networked with other Roma organisations throughout the world. *Amaro Drom* also liases with non-Roma groups such as the Jevgit, Vlach and Greek minority associations. Recent activities of *Amaro Drom* include helping a police investigation into the disappearance of children in Levan, and organising a project to supply water to Roma communities in the same town.

*Amaro Drom* is currently working together with the education ministry in promoting school places for Roma children and in preserving the Romani language. Since funding for Roma organisations in Albania is poor, *Amaro Drom's* monthly newspaper, *Ylli Karvanit*, ceased publication and one of the first Roma schools in Tirana was compelled to close.

In contrast, a successful project supported by *Amaro Drom* has been the establishment by Latif Kazanxhiu of the Vakthi Scheme Roma School in Baltez. This school teaches children about their Romani language and culture and enables young Roma girls to be educated in a safe, community-centred environment with which their parents feel comfortable. Although it has been in operation for two years the school struggles to survive with few resources and little support for its teachers but nevertheless remains a symbol of hope for the whole community of Baltez (Smith 1999).

This school and the two Roma organisations are examples of the efforts Roma are now making to protect and support their people and to improve their image in the eyes of non-Roma Albanians. Despite the ten years of political turmoil and chaos in Albania these organisations have survived by uniting in response to a common political and cultural need.

## Conclusion

Albania's history provides a kaleidoscope of contrasting images and among the sharpest of these contrasts is that between the situation of Albanian Roma during the periods of Communism and post-Communism. Within a few years they were plunged from relative security and integration to a precarious existence near the margins of society.

A country once torn by war, invasions and occupations eventually awoke from the 'long sleep' under Enver Hoxha's rule to a new unpredictable world fraught with chaos and insecurity. The initial frustration of the Albanian population, arising from an inability to participate immediately in Western society, swiftly turned to anger – a clamouring to embrace the material benefits of Western culture and an identification of difference as a criterion for the right to these resources. In this turbulent and more starkly differentiated Albania, the position of Roma suddenly shifted from a lower yet accepted stratum of society – a reflection of their previous place in the Ottoman world – to the position of least deserving in the desperate queue to claim scarce assets.

Previously there seemed little need for the Roma of Albania to affirm their difference or mobilise on this basis but now in the changed circumstances, when branded as different from other ethnic groups in Albania, they cling to their traditions as a positive way of preserving their identity.

> Ethnicity is a resource that Albanian Roma have yet to exploit fully as a means of gaining access to funding and support. Yet it should be recognised that, in following this path, ethnicity is not ... merely a counter resource to some other basis of power chances; it is deeply embedded in the overall power relations of the society[.]
>
> (Mason 1986: 9)

So, although 'exclusions and subordination' undoubtedly characterise class and ethnic relations in Albania (Anthias and Yuval-Davies, 1992: 18), these should not be seen as the only determinants for the future of Albanian Roma. The future for the Roma of Albania must involve a strategy which avoids an 'enemy image' and a focus on racism to the exclusion of other concerns. Pettman's comments about Australia are equally applicable to Albania.

> ... While racism is much deeper and larger and wider (and more personal, cultural and political) than many of us imagined – it isn't everything. There is a danger, having discovered the ramifications of racism in Australia, of assuming that every social problem is due to colour or culture.
>
> (Pettman 1986: 9)

In this respect, a deeper analysis of the history of the Roma, in both pre- and post-Communist Albania, reveals that

> [t]he reality is the interrelationship of the different forms of inequality, and the dynamics which generate them, are the key to understanding oppression and exploitation in individuals' lives.
>
> (Pettman 1988: 16)

In their endeavour to strengthen Romani identity the continuing difficulty faced by Roma organisations is that of encouraging young Roma to be proud of their culture, heritage and language in a difficult and often hostile environment. To do this they are constructing their own responses to change through the development of Roma organisations. There are also other aspects of present-day Romani life which demonstrate the positive steps Albanian Roma are taking towards self-determination. However, these activities have a significance that extends beyond the immediate goal of reinforcing their own community since Albanian Roma have a vital role to play in building an Albania which recognises difference as valuable, rather than viewing it as a drawback to progress.

## References

Anthias, F. and Yuval-Davis, N. (1992) *Racialized Boundaries: Race, Nation, Gender, Colour and Class and the Anti-Racist Struggle*, London: Routledge.

Blejer, M. I., Melange, M., Sashay, R., Hides, R. *et al.* (1992) 'Albania: From Isolation Toward Reform', *Occasional Paper* 98, International Monetary Fund, Washington DC: IMF, September.

Brah, A. (1992) 'Difference, diversity and differentiation', in J. Donald and A. Rattansi (eds) *'Race' Cultural Difference*, London: Sage/Open University Press, 126–45.

Champseix, E. and Champseix J.-P. (1992) *L'Albanie ou la logique de désespoir*, Paris: Editions la Découverte.

Crowe, D. M. (1995) *A History of the Gypsies of Eastern Europe and Russia*, New York: St. Martin's Press.

Cusack, D. (1966) *Illyria Reborn,* London: Heinemann.

Elezovski, A. (1999a) *'Last information from Kosovo'*, paper supplied by Roma community center 'DROM', Kumanovo (Macedonia), Kumanovo: DROM.

Eleszovski, A. (1999b) *'Situation of Roma in Europe and Balkans'*, paper supplied by Roma community center 'DROM', Kumanovo (Macedonia), Kumanovo: DROM.

ERRC (1997) *No Record of the Case: Roma in Albania*, European Roma Rights Center, Country reports series, 5 June, Budapest: ERRC.

Fortuna, P. and Cortiade, M. (1997) *Rromani Baxt* to *Le Monde*, January 2, unpublished, quoted in ERRC 1997: 11.

Hasluck, M. (1938) 'The Gypsies of Albania', *The Journal of the Gypsy Lore Society*, XVII, 2: 49–61, April.

Kenrick, D. and Puxon, G. (1995) *Gypsies under the Swastika*, Hatfield: University of Hertfordshire Press.

Kolsti, J. (1991) 'Albanian Gypsies: The silent survivors', in D. Crowe and J. Kolsti (eds) *The Gypsies of Eastern Europe*, Armonk, New York: M. E. Sharpe.

Krusheinycky, A. (1997) 'Berisha rallies support as turmoil spreads', *The European*, 20–26 February.

Kurtiade, M. (1995) 'Between conviviality and antagonism: The ambiguous position of the Romanies in Albania', *Patrin* 3.

Liégeois J.-P. and Gheorghe, N. (1995) *Roma/Gypsies: a European Minority*, London: Minority Rights Group.

Mason, D. (1986) 'Introduction' in J. Rex and D. Mason (eds) *Theories of Race and Ethnic Relations*, Cambridge: Cambridge University Press.

Pettifer, J. (1996) *Blue Guide Albania*, second edn, London: A. and C. Black.

Pettman, J. (1986) 'What is Racism?' in B. Chambers and J. Pettman (eds) *Anti-Racism: a Handbook for Adult Educators*, Canberra: Australian Government Publishing Service, 3–10.

Pettman, J. (1988) 'Whose country is it anyway? Cultural politics, racism and the construction of being Australian', in *Journal of Intercultural Studies* 9, 1: 1–24.

Poulton, H. (1995) *Who are the Macedonians?* London: C. Hurst and Co.

Robertson, J. (1997) 'Albania declares emergency', *The Guardian,* 3 March.

Smith, T. (1999) *Power, Politics and Conflict: A Critical Reflection on the Establishment of the Rom Gypsy School, Baltez, Albania*, unpublished paper, 1–21[6].

Swire, J. (1937) *King Zog's Albania*, New York: Liverith.

*The European* (1996) Untitled,1–7 February.

Tihon, F. (1997) '"What are we doing here?" ask saviours of Albania', *The European,* 19–25 June

Winnifrith, T. J. (1987) *The Vlachs: The History of a Balkan People*, New York: St. Martin's Press.

Zëri i Popullit (1989) quoted in D. Hall (1994) *Albanian and the Albanians*, Pinter Reference, London: Pinter, 25.

## Notes

1   Conversations I have had with Dr Tom Winnifrith, formerly of Warwick University in the UK and an expert on the Vlachs, suggest otherwise. He has spent a lifetime studying the Vlach people of Albania and has yet to find any connection between the Roma of Albania and the Vlachs (personal communication).

2   This is reflected in comments made to me by Roma about the Jev such as: 'they have a different mentality for life', 'they are more educated', 'they dress differently and trim their moustaches differently', 'they do not speak Romani' and 'the Jev are darker, have fuller lips and more prominent cheek bones'.

3   'Ultimately, both Jevgit and Roma live beyond the colour line in Albania and are regarded as similar by the majority' (ERRC 1997: 12).

4   Albanians often translate 'Jev' as 'Gypsy' (ERRC 1997: 19).

5   Pejorative term for Gypsies (Roma) in Albanian (ERRC 1997: 19).

6   This paper was written by the author of this chapter.

## CHAPTER EIGHTEEN

# Former Yugoslavia:
# A patchwork of destinies

*Donald Kenrick*

The date of arrival of the Roma in the lands that were to become Yugoslavia is not documented but there are references to individuals from 1289 onwards and it is likely that several hundred had arrived in the years before the Ottoman conquests in the fifteenth century, when they were joined by larger numbers accompanying the victorious Turks. The Romani population in this region during the Ottoman hegemony comprised nomads, as well as sedentaries working in agriculture or as miners and traders (Marushiakova and Popov 2000). Nowadays the Roma in these lands can be classified by religion or language. They may be Orthodox, Catholic or Muslim and speak Arlia, the speech of long-settled urban populations, or a range of dialects used by previously nomadic groups, such as the *Gurbet*.

As a country Yugoslavia exists only from 1918, the name itself from 1921. During the Second World War it was conquered by Nazi Germany and divided by the occupiers into several administrative regions and various parts were occupied by Hungarians, Bulgarians and Hitler's Italian allies. Although a puppet government was established in Serbia, for practical purposes it was under German military rule. In this wartime period many Roma were arrested, alongside Jews, to be shot as 'hostages' by German soldiers in revenge for attacks by partisans. Concentration camps were also set up near Belgrade and Niš. In Croatia power was in the hands of the fascist Ustashi party and some 28,000 Roma were murdered in the extermination camp at Jasenovac. However, there was no systematic attempt to wipe out the Roma elsewhere in occupied Yugoslavia (Kenrick and Puxon 1995).

After liberation in 1944 Yugoslavia was re-established as a republic and under the leadership of Tito (Prime Minister 1946–53 and President 1953-80) became a federation of states, each with an ethnic majority. Each state decided whether its Roma should be classed as a minority or an ethnic group, while the rights and privileges varied from state to state according to this designation. The 1971 census recorded 78,485 Roma for the whole of Yugoslavia, an unbelievably low figure, even allowing for the losses during the Nazi period. As their confidence increased more Roma acknowledged their ethnicity in 1981 (168,127) but there was a slight drop in recorded numbers in 1991.[1]

Some 2,000 Roma belonged to the League of Communists (Report on Serbia 1998), the single party permitted under Tito, but this was not the limit of their political activity. In contrast to some other Eastern European countries, in Tito's Yugoslavia the Roma were free to organise – at least on a cultural plane. One of the first Romani organisations to be established was the Cultural Society Rom founded in Belgrade in 1969 and its formation was followed by the emergence of many local organisations.[2] Five years later the Federation of Rom Societies of Serbia was founded, uniting some forty local Romani organisations. In spite of inter-ethnic and political tensions following the death of Tito in 1980, the first Roma had been elected to town councils and Sait Balić from Niš became a member of the Serbian National Parliament. Four years later there were already fifty-three elected Romani members of town or provincial councils in addition to the one seat in the Serbian Parliament (Report on Serbia 1998). In 1981 the first bilingual radio programme in Romani and Serbian had been broadcast from Belgrade, entitled *Ašunen romalen* (Listen, Roma) and the series continued until 1987.[3]

From the late 1960s onwards, in parallel with this domestic mobilisation, Yugoslav Roma played an important part in the activities of the International Romani Union. At the first World Romani Congress, held near London in 1971, the Belgrade poet Slobodan Berberski was elected president. After a decade in office he was replaced by Balić at the Third Congress in Göttingen (1981), while the writer and journalist Rajko Djurić was chosen as the secretary. The Fourth Congress in Warsaw (1990) saw Djurić promoted to president, with the secretaryship going to a Czech Rom, Emil Ščuka. Even after being forced to quit Yugoslavia because of his opposition to the Bosnian war, Djurić remained president until 1999 when he resigned because of ill health. He did however attend the Fifth Congress in Prague in 2000 where he was replaced by Emil Ščuka (see Acton and Klímová 2001).

The political problems following Tito's death came to a head as Communist Party rule collapsed throughout Central and Eastern Europe in 1989 and in the following year the Yugoslav Federation began to break up. By 1996 only Serbia (including the previously autonomous provinces of Voivodina and Kosovo) and Montenegro remained in the smaller Federation. However, one cannot talk about Roma 'after the end of Communism' in the ever-shrinking Yugoslav state, for the government in Belgrade under the leadership of Milosević[4] was still following centralist Communist principles, although the name of the ruling party had changed to the Socialist Party. However, a multi-party system had been permitted, providing the opportunity for some Romani ethnic political parties to emerge. The first was the Romani Social Democratic Party founded in Leskovac in April 1990, with Djurić as its president. In the 1990 parliamentary elections, however, this party did not manage to win any seats. In September of that same year the Democratic Party of the Roma of Serbia and Yugoslavia was founded in Kragujevac, with Miroslav Jovanović as its president (Report on Serbia 1998).

As the Federation disintegrated Roma were wooed by rival factions and in particular by the Serbian and Macedonian governments. During the ensuing conflicts they were conscripted into the armies of the new states that had been created around them and as a result Roma often found themselves facing each another at the front line.

The sections below deal with the states emerging from the break-up of Yugoslavia in the order of their formation, leaving the rump Yugoslav Republic to the end. A central place in this account is given to the bitter experience of the Roma of Kosovo, where the Romani minority was squeezed between larger and more powerful ethnic groups, being opportunistically recruited to their neighbours' cause when convenient and cynically discarded or expelled when their usefulness had passed. Nowhere is there a better illustration of the tragic yet historically familiar role of the Roma as political pawns in power games beyond their control.

## Slovenia

Slovenia became an independent state in 1991 after a brief skirmish with the Yugoslav Federation. It had been the most homogeneous of the former Yugoslav republics but this raised questions about the status of minority populations within the new republic. Speaking of Roma, Article 65 of the constitution of the new republic runs: 'The legal situation and particular rights of the Romani population living in Slovenia will be settled by the law'. This vague statement has never been fully defined.

The 1971 Yugoslav census had recorded 977 Roma while in the 1991 census (the last in the Federation) 2,293 had declared themselves as Roma and, inexplicably, a larger number – 2,847 – said Romani was their mother tongue. A recent, semi-official figure is 7,000,[5] while in reality the population is probably nearer to 10,000.

Roma have been living since the seventeenth century in three regions of present-day Slovenia: Prekmurje and the borders of Austria and Hungary, Dolenjska (south-east of Ljubljana), and a smaller number – largely *Sinti* – in Gorenjska-Alta Carniola near Bled. Although the indigenous Roma have escaped the miseries of war their situation is unenviable. Most live in segregated settlements, are unemployed and subsist on welfare payments,[6] while the percentage in prison is much higher than for the Slovenian population as a whole.[7]

It is never been clarified what precisely the 'particular rights' enshrined in the new constitution comprise. In practice, the Roma appear to have fewer rights than the Hungarian and (smaller) Italian minorities as regards the use of their own Romani language in schools, the media and dealings with officials. The national law on local self-government stipulates that in areas where minorities live they should have members on councils but in 1998 there was only one such representative.[8]

As elsewhere, the Roma in Slovenia suffer discrimination and prejudice.[9] Many reside in separate settlements, sometimes in poor conditions on the edge of villages. Nearly all live in temporary dwellings such as huts or even containers. There are also new Romani immigrants from other parts of war-torn Yugoslavia living on the edge of many large urban areas. Housing and work remain the prime problems for the Roma of Slovenia.[10] There have been some examples of extreme prejudice in housing as in 1997, when the Slovene inhabitants of Malina prevented a Romani family from moving into a house in their village – a move designed as part of an integration programme.[11] Local authorities refuse planning permission for Roma to build houses, refuse to find accommodation for them and then blame them for building houses illegally or for living in poor conditions (*Delo*, 4 April 1998).

The central government of Slovenia has set up an Inter-departmental Commission for Roma Matters which, apart from representatives of ministries, also has members of the local authorities in areas where Roma live and from Romani organisations. In 1995 the government started a programme to improve the lot of the Roma. Its aims included improving the living conditions in Romani settlements and increasing the educational opportunities for Romani children from nursery school to university.[12] However, such official initiatives for Roma depend on local goodwill to carry them out. The Roma in Prekmurje are the best organised and generally co-operate with the authorities. But, in 1998 they organised a demonstration – blocking a highway – to press for the building of a road to the Romani village of Beltinci.[13]

Roma children, as elsewhere in Central and Eastern Europe, have problems when they come to school because they do not know the majority language and lack social skills, while many schools try to avoid registering Romani children.[14] Their lack of education leads the majority of Roma to depend on unskilled work and they are the first to go when factory personnel are shed. Such employment as there is includes cleaning, farmwork, road construction, stonemasonry and dealing in horses.[15] Even qualified Roma find it difficult to get work because of discrimination.[16]

In the first seven years of the new state seven Romani organisations were founded[17] and they have now come together in one union, *Zveza Romskih društev Slovenije* (The Association of Romani Organisations in Slovenia), whose president is the author Jožek Horvat-Muc. These organisations are involved in the fields of culture, education, information and sport but not politics.[18] Radio broadcasts in Romani come from Murska Sobota and Novo Mesto. In Murska Sobota there is also a theatre group which has been functioning since 1992.[19] A magazine, *Romano Them* (Romani World), is published by a non-governmental organisation, while the Romani organisation in Murska Sobota produces its own bilingual paper, *Romske novice*.

## Croatia

Croatia declared its independence from the Yugoslav Federation in 1991 but, partly due to the presence of Serbian population enclaves, this led to a bitter and protracted war. Fighting against the Serbian-dominated Yugoslav army continued until 1995 and Roma were among the civilian victims, although the number of casualties is difficult to estimate. Many Roma who did not escape from Baranja (in western Slavonia) were killed by the Serbian occupiers.[20] On 31 November 1991, Serbian irregular units burnt down the Romani quarter of the village of Torjanici and killed the remaining eleven inhabitants. Because the Roma were Catholics like the Croats, they were accused of collaborating with them. In another incident, in 1993, Roma were driven out of Dubac, a suburb of Zagreb, by Croats returning from fighting the Serbs and have had to resettle elsewhere in Croatia.[21]

Official census figures had recorded 313 Roma in 1961, rising to 1,257 in 1971, 3,858 in 1981 and 6,695 in 1991 (the last count before independence). Various sources give totals ranging from 35,000 to 150,000 and around 80,000 would be a reasonable estimate.[22] The Romani population of Croatia consists of several different clans: *Koritari* (speaking a Carpathian dialect of Romani); *Kalderash* and *Lovari*; *Arlije*, *Gurbet* and other recent immigrants from Macedonia as well as from the conflicts in Bosnia and Kosovo.[23] All still face discrimination and harassment.[24]

The Romani Society (*Ćidinipe Romano*) in Croatia was founded in 1991 with its headquarters in Virovitica. In 1994 activists started publishing the bulletin *Romano Akharipe /Glas Roma* (Romani Voice) and this was followed by *Romengo Cacipe* in 1997, the organ of the first Romani political party, *Stranka Roma Hrvatske* (the Croatian Romani Party). In 1997 this party elected Cana Kasum as its president, replacing Vid Bogdan, and Kasum stood unsuccessfully for election to parliament.[25]

Meanwhile important initiatives were taken in the field of education. In 1994, the first summer school was organised in Zagreb for thirty-eight Romani children (Kranzelić 1995) and in 1998 a youth organisation was established, *Udruga mladezi Roma Hrvatske*. Broadcasts in Romani are transmitted from Pula and Beli Manastir.

## Bosnia-Herzegovina

In the federal state of Yugoslavia as re-established after 1945, the Roma were recognised as a national minority in the Republic of Bosnia and Herzegovina.

They were allowed to run their own organisations and use the Romani language which gave a great impetus to activism. In this area the majority of Roma speak the Arlia or Gurbet dialects. In 1986 Sarajevo hosted a seminar which was a landmark in the development of Romani culture, not only in Yugoslavia but for the whole of Europe. Delegates came from many countries – though not from the local Roma community – and Romani was used by many of the speakers as well as in the final conference report (Šipka 1989).

The 1991 census recorded only 7,251 Roma but the probable Romani population before the recent conflict was circa 80,000.[26] Since 1992 an unknown number of Bosnian Roma have sought refuge in other countries.

During the armed conflict in Bosnia, which lasted from 1992 to 1995, Roma found themselves conscripted into all the three warring armies (Bosnian, Croatian and Yugoslav/Serb) (Latham 1999: 213). After the establishment in 1995 of the Bosnia-Herzegovina Republic (Muslim-Croat Bosnian Federation), Romani populations were found to have survived the fighting in Tuzla, Sarajevo and other towns, though many had fled during the war to Western Europe. The Romani population of Sarajevo is now between 1,000 and 2,000, some 350 of whom live in the previously Serbian district of Ilidza.[27]

There was, unsurprisingly, no functioning Romani organisation in Bosnia during the war period except in Sarajevo but some six active organisations now operate in the state. *Braca Romi* (Romani Brethren), founded in 1993, continues to function locally in Sarajevo,[28] while the German-based *Gesellschaft für Bedrohte Völker* helped set up an All-Bosnian Roma Union which held its first conference in 1997.

Several deputations visiting Tuzla and other towns since the end of the conflict have found that the Roma are at the bottom of the list for receiving humanitarian help from outside agencies. At the time of writing several thousand Romani refugees from Bosnia are still in Germany and smaller numbers live in other Western countries. Some are being sent back to Bosnia, though there are some doubts whether the new constitution will allow all the Roma who once lived in Bosnia to become citizens of the new federation as they may not all be able to establish residence. This is because they were born in or spent long periods in other republics of the former Yugoslavia. A fact-finding mission under the auspices of the Council of Europe visited Bosnia in May 1996 and recommended that both parts of the Republic, Bosnia-Croatia and Republika Srpska (see below), recognise Roma as a nationality (Latham 1999: 217).

## Republika Srpska

When Bosnia was partitioned, the political entity known as Republika Srpska was set up which is *de facto* under Serb rule. The current total Romani population figure is unknown but there are 200 living in the area of Banja Luka and a similar number in Bijeljina. The Romani population is small because during the three years of fighting those Roma who were Muslims – the majority – were expelled from this area. Roma expelled from Bratunac, for example, now live in Virovitica in Croatia. Almost the entire pre-war populations of Banja Luka and Bijeljina, both numbered in thousands, have left. The Roma in Bijeljina were told: 'Either leave or be killed' and the majority fled. The Romani settlements of Jasenje and Staro Selo have been destroyed. In 1994 the 200 Roma in the village of Klasnice in northern Bosnia, in Republika Srpska, asked the UN High Commissioner for Refugees to arrange their evacuation.[29] Several thousand Roma who formerly lived in the area now under Serb control are living as refugees in Western Europe, in particular Germany, Italy and the United Kingdom, and they, too, like those from Bosnia proper, are unlikely to be accepted as citizens if they return.

## Macedonia

Macedonia became independent through a peaceful process in 1992. The estimated Romani population is at least 200,000, although the 1994 census listed only 42,707, a decrease on the 55,575 recorded in 1991. This was in spite of the availability of census forms in the Romani language. Many Macedonian Roma joined the partisans during the Second World War and survivors believe that Tito promised them their own state after the war. This promise, if it had been made, was not carried out as the Yugoslav government would have seen a smaller sovereign Macedonia as prey for Greek and Bulgarian expansionist ambitions.

On 1 September 1990, the leaders of the Macedonian Romani community called on all Roma to stop identifying themselves as Albanians simply on the basis of a common religion, Islam, and declared 11 October 1990 (already a Macedonian public holiday) to be a day to celebrate the cultural achievements of Roma in the country (Poulton 1993a, 1993b). When, in 1993, Macedonia became *de jure* a new state, Roma from all over the country joined in the celebrations. President Kiro Gligorov publicly acknowledged the Roma as 'equal citizens of the Macedonian state'. They were recognised as a nationality in the preamble to the new constitution, while Romani language television programmes are broadcast from Skopje and several local radio stations have followed the early example of Tetovo.[30]

The Romani intelligentsia took advantage of the new political freedom to form political parties, the main one being PSERM (Party for the Complete Emancipation of Roma in Macedonia), claiming at one time a membership of 36,000 (Poulton 1993b). Its president, Faik Abdi, was also at one time a member of the Macedonian parliament, representing Shuto Orizari (see below). PSERM has been the prime mover in securing Romani rights. After a split a second party emerged, the Alliance of Roma in Macedonia, led by Amdi Bajram, who was re-elected as an MP in 1998. Yet a third party, the Democratic Progressive Party of the Roma in Macedonia, now controls Shuto Orizari through the mayor, Nezdat Mustafa.

The association of Romani women known as *Daja* (Mothers) has its headquarters in Kumanova and branches elsewhere. It was set up with a grant from the Soros Open Society Institute but is still financially weak. Amongst the many other Romani non-governmental organisations should be mentioned *Mesecina* in Gostivar, which played an important role in helping Romani refugees from Kosovo.

In spite of the central government's encouragement of the political and cultural advancement of the Roma, there is much unemployment and poor housing. Some inter-ethnic conflict, mainly between Albanians and Roma, has been reported (ERRC 1998),[31] as well as police brutality, often directed against street traders.[32]

Shuto Orizari is perhaps the only town in Europe with a Romani majority. Shutka, as it is popularly known, is a satellite town outside Skopje in Macedonia which grew rapidly after the Skopje earthquake of 1963 when large numbers of Roma from the town were resettled there in houses donated by foreign governments. It grew further as the result of a voluntary decision by the inhabitants of the old Romani quarter of Topana in Skopje to leave and move into the new town. By the mid-1970s Shutka had its own district council offices, a cinema and a football ground. Some 5,000 more houses were subsequently built, assisted by the granting of free building land and flexible town planning regulations. The estimated population in 1977 was already 40,000. However, facilities in Shutka are poor. There is only one ambulance and specialist medical care is lacking while the standard of education in the two primary schools is low.[33]

A special educational programme for the Romani language in schools throughout the state began in principle in September 1993, consisting of language classes for grades 1–8. As part of this programme a 40,000 word Macedonian-Romani dictionary is in preparation, as well as other teaching material. Here the main dialects are Arlia (Erlia), the most widely spoken and the mother tongue of an estimated 80 per cent of Macedonia's Roma, together with Burgudji, Djambazi and Gurbet. It has been agreed to use the Arlia dialect – the speech of the long-settled urban populations in the Balkans – as the basis for a standard language for educational purposes, using the Latin alphabet (Friedman 1995).[34] In addition to the teaching of Romani in primary education classes, there are proposals for Skopje University to inaugurate a Department of Romani Studies for the study of, and research into, language, history and culture. Some hundred potential teachers of Romani attended a seminar convened by the Ministry of Education at Skopje

University in October 1993 but the full implementation of the Romani language programme has been held up by the lack of materials and qualified teachers. The situation may improve after the graduation of more than fifty Romani students, currently attending various full-time courses at the university.

Looking at the fragmented former Yugoslavia it can be said that, in spite of some discrimination and harassment, it is in Macedonia that Romani culture is most alive, both in the home and beyond with regular radio and TV broadcasts.[35]

# Kosovo

The southern province of Kosovo is currently still *de jure* part of Serbia and Yugoslavia, following the twelve-week war in 1999, waged by NATO against rump Yugoslavia to prevent the ethnic cleansing of the indigenous Albanian inhabitants. *De facto*, however, it is now controlled by Kosovar Albanians and the successors to their guerilla force, the Kosovo Liberation Army (KLA). This is in spite of, or because of, the presence of the NATO-supplied K-FOR military forces in the role of peacekeepers.[36]

Kosovo was a thriving centre for Romani culture in the years after 1945. A group of young poets received acclaim well beyond the province largely because of the efforts of Marcel Courthiade in getting their work published.[37] Until recently two magazines – *Rota* and *Ahimsa* – were being published in Priština. In 1983 radio broadcasts in Romani began in Priština, amongst the earliest in Europe, and these continued for many years, while weekly television broadcasts started in the same town three years later. Broadcasts have been resumed but not in Romani (OSCE 1999a). Formal education was rather less successful since although some schools introduced Romani in 1985, this was without a curriculum or any text books. In this region the Arlia and Gurbet dialects were widely spoken.

The 1971 census showed 14,493 Roma in Kosovo, while in 1991 a more realistic figure of 45,745 was recorded. The estimated Romani population before the recent conflict was, however, at least 100,000.[38] The majority were Muslim Roma but there were small minorities of Orthodox and Catholics. Although all official census figures of Roma populations in former Yugoslavia should be regarded as underestimates, there is particular justification for this in the case of Kosovo.

During the weeks preceding the 1971 and 1981 censuses both ethnic Albanians and Turks tried to persuade Roma to declare themselves as Albanians or Turks respectively while the Serbs encouraged them to register as Roma, in order to reduce the nominal percentage of Albanians in the country.[39] Later, a further complicating factor emerged when, following the example of some Roma in Macedonia, an Egyptians' Association was set up in Kosovo in 1990. This claimed that several thousand 'descendants of the Pharaohs' lived in the province. The question of 'Egyptians' is discussed in more detail at the end of this chapter.

Yet, in spite of pressure both from Serbs and ethnic Albanians on the Roma to align themselves with one of the larger groups, the Association of Roma People of Priština had a membership of more than 10,000. Its president, Baskim Redjepi, was a deputy in the Priština city council while the poet, Bairam Haliti, worked in the Centre for Minority Languages and Culture in Priština. Later, Haliti was to flee to Zemun in Serbia after being denounced as a collaborator and war criminal by the KLA.[40]

From 1981 the desire of many Kosovar Albanians for a fully independent Kosovo strengthened. Sometimes this turned to violence against Serbs but also against the Roma, whose leaders supported the Serbs. Such attacks only served to reinforce the alignment of the Roma with the dominant Serbs. When Yugoslav government tanks arrived in Priština prior to the autonomous status of Kosovo being revoked in 1990, the Romani population unwisely turned out to welcome them.[41]

Meanwhile, Albanian resistance continued and in 1998 the central government of Yugoslavia launched an offensive against the KLA, leading some 2,000 Roma to leave Kosovo for Voivodina in northern Serbia to flee the hostilities.[42] After Serbian troops recaptured Orahovac from the KLA and massacred some 200 civilians, Roma were used to load corpses onto lorries (*Sunday Times*, 26 July 1998). The use of Roma as gravediggers, reminiscent of how they were used by the Nazis in Yugoslavia to bury Jews, was to escalate during the period of the NATO raids the following year.

During the 1990s, as economic and social segregation intensified, Albanians voluntarily or unwillingly left their jobs under the Serbian-led administration and many Roma took over the vacant posts, a move that was not to endear them to the Albanians. In social life Serbs replaced Albanian musicians by Roma while the Albanians themselves employed Albanian musicians in preference to Roma.

At the end of the decade in a rapidly deteriorating situation, the Yugoslav delegation to the Paris peace talks on Kosovo in 1999 included Albanians and Turks, Kosovan Roma and the newly discovered minority of 'Egyptians', alongside a Serbian majority. Amid this claim of multi-culturalism, the delegation refused for several days to have direct talks with the KLA, whom they persisted in calling 'terrorists'. For the Romani and Egyptian delegates, Ljuan Koka and Cherim Abazi, their participation in the talks was to lead to their enforced flight to Serbia to escape Albanian hostility.

Then came the period in 1999 during which NATO carried out intensive bombing raids. We will not pre-empt history's judgement on whether Serbian atrocities against Albanians escalated during that time, although at the very least they continued. But it is important to examine the manipulation of the

Roma minority during this dramatic period when they were the victims of both warring groups. Roma were swiftly enrolled by the Serbs to help them terrorise the ethnic Albanians. Men of military age were forcibly recruited into the army and others were posted at the doors of food shops to keep the Albanians out.[43] In self-defence, interpreted as complicity by the Albanians, the Roma in several villages marked an R on their doors to distinguish them from the Albanian houses when the Serbian auxiliaries arrived to burn and kill (Murphy 1999).[44] Some Roma had work as gravediggers before the bombing started. Now their services were called upon by the Serbs to bury their Albanian victims. But the number of victims was such that extra hands were needed.[45]

Other Roma fled the country, either to escape NATO bombing raids or because – as Muslims – they, too, were being targeted by the Serbian auxiliaries. Some 2,000 fled to Macedonia where they were helped by Romani organisations and individual families in the face of discrimination by Macedonian agencies. Over 20,000 took refuge in Serbia, over 800 in Albania, 8,000 in Montenegro and a smaller number in Bosnia.

In June 1999, after Milosević agreed to peace terms, NATO forces entered the province as K-FOR peacekeepers. As the Serbian troops withdrew from Kosovo they looted the houses of Albanians who had fled during the period of the air strikes. The Serbs forced the Roma to load the most valuable items onto their lorries and then told the Roma to take what was left. Undoubtedly, some did so.[46]

The departure of the Serbian army and police was soon followed by a series of retaliatory attacks by Albanians from Kosovo and from Albania proper on both civilian Serbs and Roma. By 12 August 1999 UNHCR estimated that 170,000 Serbs had already fled in the days since K-FOR arrived, leaving only 30,000. The Roma were to follow.

Many of the Albanians who returned from refugee camps in Macedonia and Albania were to take revenge on the Romani community as a whole because of those members who had actively helped the Serbs. It is not yet clear how much of the ethnic cleansing of Roma that was to follow can be attributed to Kosovo Albanians and how much to intruders from Albania proper but that is beyond the scope of this chapter. Whoever the perpetrators were, the Roma were now to suffer what the Albanians had suffered from the Serbs.

Pogroms since the end of the conflict include the following. In June 1999 the Romani quarter in Mitrovica was burnt down and the inhabitants fled to Priština. Roma in Kosovo Polje (near Priština) also came under threat and 3,500 took refuge in a school. Roma and 'Egyptians' in Djakovica and elsewhere were told they would be killed if they stayed. On June 29 twelve houses were burnt down in Sitinica, a mixed village inhabited by Roma and ethnic Albanians. The Romani quarter of Dusanova in Prizren has also been burned down, as have many houses in Obilic and the quarter of Brekoc in Djakovica.[47]

German K-FOR troops discovered fifteen injured Roma in a police office that had been taken over and used by the KLA as a prison in Prizren. A sixteenth man had been beaten to death. It was alleged the victims had taken part in looting.[48] Romani victims of Albanian violence, however, have included many who could have taken no part in helping the Serbs. For example, a nine-year-old girl, J. Q., was beaten in the Fabricka Street quarter in Kosovska Mitrovica and in the same quarter three elderly Roma died in their houses when these were set on fire by Albanians.[49]

Shukrije Bajrami fled from the fighting to Vucitrn to the house of a relative with her four-year-old daughter. There the local Albanians told the Roma: 'Leave because we are going to kill you.' As she spoke to a reporter another Romani house went up in flames. A young man wearing a KLA beret watched the house burn (*Financial Review*, 25 June 1999). Many reports have also been filed of rapes of Romani women by men in KLA uniforms (*Financial Review*, 25 June 1999; *Daily Telegraph*, 22 July 1999).

In addition to the improvised refuge in Kosovo Polje, K-FOR built a camp housing 5,000 'internally displaced' Roma at Obilic (near Priština) in a pine forest and surrounded it with barbed wire covered with plastic sheeting. Albanians removed the protective sheeting so they could hurl insults and missiles at the Roma in the camp. In December 1999 the residents were moved to an army barracks in Plemetina. Roma elsewhere have complained that K-FOR does nothing. There are countless reports of Roma seeing their homes looted and burnt while British and other K-FOR troops stood by unable or unwilling to help.[50]

Although ethnic Serbian refugees from Kosovo were reluctantly accepted into Serbia proper, many Roma were stopped on the border and told to go back to their homes by the police (*The Guardian*, 23 June 1999).[51] Meanwhile, thousands of Roma from Kosovo have taken refuge in several countries. As attacks increased, over 2,000 Roma fled to Italy in June and July 1999,[52] but in August the Italian authorities said they would no longer accept refugees from Kosovo as the fighting was over. Nevertheless, Roma still attempt the sea crossing, sometimes with tragic results.[53]

An OSCE report suggested there were some 25,000 Roma of various clans still in the province, living in a 'precarious' state and the new millenium has seen further attacks (OSCE 1999b). Amongst the reports we read that seven Roma were murdered between February and May, an eleven-year-old boy was beaten and thrown into the river at Klina in March, while sixteen Roma families were forced out of Ogoste by ethnic Albanians displaced from an Albanian settlement on the other side of the Kosovan border in southern Serbia (UNHCR/OSCE 2000).

Most of the Roma intelligentsia have fled and, as at present in 2001, it seems that the conflicts in this region have extinguished what had once been an inspirational example to Roma elsewhere.

## Rump Yugoslavia

The 1991 census gave a figure of 70,126 Roma in Serbia (excluding Kosovo and Voivodina). The figures were rising steadily which reflected not merely the high birth rate of the population but also increasing self-confidence and willingness to be recognised as Roma at the start of the 1990s. However, there still remains some way to go before the recorded population reaches the estimated real figure of 600,000.[54] As noted above, Roma in Yugoslavia can be classified by religion (Orthodox, Catholic or Muslim) or language (Arlia, the speech of the long-settled urban populations, or a range of dialects used by previously nomadic groups, such as the *Gurbet*). This applies equally to Serbia.

Before the break up of the federal state the Roma in Serbia had made attempts to get their status raised to that of a national minority, a desire that was voiced at academic conferences in Belgrade in 1976 as well as Novi Sad (Voivodina) in 1990 and 1997 (Report on Serbia 1998). In the terms of the 1991 Constitution of Serbia, the Roma had the lowest status – the third rank, as an 'ethnic group'.

Faced with the disintegration of the federal republic, the Belgrade government made considerable efforts after 1993 to gain the support of its Romani population. The attendance of government officials at an official orthodox church service in Romani was heavily publicised and subsidies were given to Romani newspapers. The poet Trifun Dimić was able to publish the New Testament in Romani as well as a first reader for schools. However, a conflicting message was sent by the harassment of Rajko Djurić, journalist and poet as well as president of the International Romani Union, who was forced to flee the country because of his opposition to the government's support for the Bosnian Serbs during the conflict in Bosnia (Latham 1999: 209).

The Romani Congress Party (RKSD) was founded at a meeting in Belgrade in 1997 on the symbolic date of 8 April (declared as Romani National Day at the First World Romani Congress) and has a membership of some 2,000. One of its aims is for Roma to attain the status of a national minority. Its president, Dragoljub Acković, is editor of the magazine *Romano Lil* and of the revived Romani radio programmes.[55]

Yet, in spite of more overt Belgrade government support for Roma, police harassment is common and, as in Macedonia, street traders are a prime target.[56] There have been reports of isolated cases of racist attacks on Roma though Romani leaders have said they hear of such attacks in Belgrade every two or three days.[57] Skinheads are active and in one reported incident in September 1996, they assaulted Roma in Kraljevo. Mostly, the skinheads choose as their targets individual Roma in isolated streets. Graffiti saying 'Death to Roma' have appeared in Kragujevac, while houses have been set on fire in some places (Latham 1999: 209). Prejudice is widespread and some villages will not allow the Roma to bury their dead in Orthodox cemeteries while there have cases of been discrimination in bars in Raska. In October 1997 the Serbian daily *Nedeljini Telegraf* published an article entitled: 'We shall expel the Roma, Negroes, Gays and Junkies and create a Great White Serbia', quoting the words of skinheads from Novi Sad.

Even before the current economic depression, living conditions for Roma were inadequate and in some parts of Serbia Romani life expectancy for Roma is only 29–33 years. Unemployment is high and such work as the Roma have is usually of low status such as day labourers, herdsmen, skinners, street sweepers or as cemetery workers. Meat is rarely on the menu in the Romani home and clothing is poor. Child allowances have not always been paid to Roma and Albanians.[58]

The majority of Romani children do not complete primary education and even the cultural association, *Matica Romska*, accepts that more than 80 per cent of the Romani population is illiterate. One reason is that 30 per cent of Romani children arrive at primary school with no knowledge of Serbian because of the isolation of their communities, and there is little pre-school provision by which they could learn the language of the education system (Report on Serbia 1998). Less than one per cent of Roma have completed higher education.[59] There is, however, a Romani Cultural Federation, whose members must have at least a college degree. Members of the Federation were active in founding the Romani Congress Party (see above). As elsewhere in Eastern Europe a number of Romani children are placed in special schools, not because of lack of intelligence but after failing tests which are designed for those living in a different culture.[60]

Organisations having a brief other than culture and political activity are the [Romani] Committee for the Protection of Human Rights in Yugoslavia, founded in 1997 and based in Kragujevac, and the Society for the Improvement of Romani Settlements, established under the leadership of the architect Vladmir Macura and the sociologist Aleksandrea Mitrovic.

Yugoslavia still includes the republic of Montenegro and the previously autonomous region of Voivodina, both of which are discussed below.

## Montenegro

Montenegro was independent or semi-independent from 1389 to 1918, when it became part of Yugoslavia. At the time of writing, Montenegro is still part of the reduced Yugoslav state. The 1971 census recorded 396 Roma but the estimated population is 2,000, still low compared with other regions of Yugoslavia. Up to 1940 the Roma in Montenegro were almost entirely nomadic, unlike elsewhere in the Balkans, but the occupation of Yugoslavia by the Axis powers evidently put a stop to their wandering and few resumed the nomadic life after the liberation. Many Roma from Montenegro did, however, emigrate as workers to Western Europe in the 1970s.

Roma in Montenegro have not escaped prejudice – a pogrom in Danoilovgrad when the Gypsy quarter was burnt down being the most visible manifestation of this feeling.[61] The small Romani population has been expanded by refugees from Kosovo who may stay and bring their cultural heritage to build a larger and more vibrant community.

## Voivodina

Voivodina is a province of Serbia and the Yugoslav Republic. It remains part of Serbia, its autonomy having been suspended in 1990 at the same time as a similar proclamation in the province of Kosovo. During the Second World War it was occupied by Hungary which tried to deport many of the Romani population into Serbia proper. Nevertheless, many Roma remained there throughout the wartime period. When Voivodina was re-occupied by Yugoslav forces after the Second World War the population was manipulated in various ways until the ethnic Hungarian majority became a minority (Kabok 1994).

The official returns in the 1971 census showed 7,760 Roma but by 1991 the figure reached the more realistic total of 24,895.[62] The estimated Romani population was 55,000 before the recent immigration from Kosovo. A number of dialects are spoken, in particular Vlach Romani and Gurbet, though many Roma have Hungarian or Romanian as their mother tongue (Savic 1995). The frontier town of Sremska Mitrovica saw an influx of Muslim refugees from Bosnia after 1992 bringing its Romani population up to some 8,000 (Report on Serbia 1998). Further refugees have arrived from Kosovo in recent months.

In Voivodina, the Roma are not integrated and most still live in settlements on the outskirts of towns and villages. Anti-Roma graffiti have appeared here, too,[63] and instances of police brutality have been reported.[64] Educational levels for Roma are low, as elsewhere in Yugoslavia.[65] In 1996 the cultural organisation *Matrica Romska* was set up in Novi Sad but with a remit to cover all Serbia. Its first president was the writer Trifun Dimić.[66] The following year a round table on the Standardisation of the Romani Language in Yugoslavia was organised in Novi Sad by the *Matrica Romska* and the Voivodina Society for the Romani Language,[67] one of many attempts in recent years to standardise Romani. The organisation *Društvo Voivodina* (Voivodina Association) is also working for the advancement of the Romani language,[68] while recently, optional instruction in Romani was introduced in primary schools in Obrovac and Tovarisevo.[69]

## Egyptians

A number of groups in the Balkans, previously thought to be Roma but who no longer spoke the language, began some twenty years ago to claim that they were not Roma but descendants of Egyptian immigrants to Europe. They were followed in 1984 by some blacksmiths in Ulcinj (Montenegro) who wanted to declare themselves as a separate ethnic group to be known as *Kovaci* (Smiths) (Duijzings 1992: 6, Poulton 1993a: 91).[70] By 1990 the 'Egyptians' had grown to a sizeable movement and associations were founded in Ohrid (Macedonia) and Priština (Kosovo), with a total membership of some 10,000.[71] They asked to be recognised as an ethnic group for the Yugoslav, Serbian and Macedonian censuses of 1991 but no separate figures have been published listing them.

Persons calling themselves Egyptians now number many thousands and are also found in Albania, where they are known as Evgjit or Jevg. In that country, a non-Romani origin has been accepted for longer (ERRC 1997: 10–13). The Serbian-led government in Belgrade was pleased to welcome the emergence of the 'Egyptians' as they helped to diminish the percentage of Albanians in Kosovo and the ethnologist, Hadzi Ristić, stated that he had found traces of Egyptian presence in Macedonia (Duijzings 1992: 7). It seems likely that the 'Egyptians' emerged from the population of Albanian-speaking Roma who found, after 1990, that there was no advantage in being Albanian in either Kosovo or Macedonia. However, they had little inclination to call themselves Roma, because of the low social status of this group.

It is debatable as to whether there is any historical justification for an Egyptian population in Europe distinct from the Roma. According to legend, however, an Egyptian sailor, shipwrecked on the coast near Durres (Albania) around the year 825, was able to converse – in Coptic, presumably – with local 'Egyptians'. There are also the records of new arrivals in Western Europe in the fifteenth century claiming to have come from Little Egypt and, indeed, the first references to Roma in English law and literature use the term 'Egyptian'.[72] Most historians place this Little Egypt on Peloponnese (Greece) and few serious scholars accept the claims of the modern 'Egyptians' of the Balkans.

## Conclusion

On balance we can say that in spite of the new freedom to organise and publish, the Roma are worse off economically and socially in the newly independent states than they were in federal Yugoslavia. Everywhere, unemployment has risen and racial tensions have come to the surface. In four of the six republics Roma have not only experienced the common suffering of war but have been singled out for special discriminatory treatment. Worst of all, in the

420

extreme cases of Bosnia and Kosovo, there has been a massive displacement of Roma as Muslim Bosnians and Kosovar Albanians strive to create states where they will be the unchallenged majority.

## References

Acton, T. and Klímová, I. (2001) 'The International Romani Union: An East European answer to West European questions?', in W. Guy (ed.) *Between Past and Future: the Roma of Central and Eastern Europe*, Hatfield: University of Hertfordshire Press.

Berberski, S. (1984) *Naše Teme* 28, 7–8: 1344.

ERRC (1997) *No Record of the Case: Roma in Albania*, country report by European Roma Rights Center, Budapest: ERRC.

ERRC (1998) *A Pleasant Fiction: The Human Rights Situation of Roma in Macedonia*, country report by European Roma Rights Center, Budapest: ERRC.

Duijzings, G. (1992) 'The Egyptians in Kosovo and Macedonia', Dutch original in *Amsterdams Sociologisch Tijdschrift* 18: 24–38.

Friedman, V. (1995) 'Romani standardisation and status in the Republic of Macedonia', in Y. Matras (ed.) *Romani in Contact*, Amsterdam: John Benjamin.

Kabok, I. (1994) *Madjaroj (hungaroj) en Vojvodino*, Budapest: Sorabano.

Kenrick, D. and Puxon, G. (1995) *Gypsies under the Swastika*, 2nd edn, Hatfield: University of Hertfordshire Press.

Kranzelić, V. (1995) 'Organisation of teaching at the summer school for Roma children in Croatia', *Roma in Croatia*, Zagreb: Croatian Institute for Migrations and Nationalities.

Latham, J. (1999) 'Roma of the former Yugoslavia', *Nationalities Papers* 27, 2: 205-26.

Marushiakova, E. and Popov, V. (2000) *Tsiganite v Osmanskata Imperia*, Sofia: Litavra.

Murphy, B. (1999) 'Refugees! Cleansing came quickly', *Associated Press Online*, 4 November.

OSCE (1999a) *Report on the Joint OSCE/ODIHR-Council of Europe Field Mission on the Situation of the Roma in Kosovo*, August.

OSCE (1999b) *Kosovo/Kosova - As Seen, As Told*, II, Warsaw: OSCE, December.

Pleše, B. (1998) 'Community violence against Roma in Montenegro and the inactivity of the state', *Roma Rights*, Budapest: ERRC, Autumn, 46-8.

Poulton, H. (1993a) *The Balkans: Minorities and States in Conflict*, London: Minority Rights Group.

Poulton, H. (1993b) *The Roma in Macedonia: A Balkan Success Story?*, Radio Free Europe/Radio Liberty Research Report, 27 April.

Poulton, H. (1995) *Who are the Macedonians?*, London: Hurst.

Report on Serbia (1998) *Report on the State of the Romany National Minority in Serbia*, circulated on web.

Savic, S. (1995) 'From multilingual to monolingual Voivodina: the case of the Gypsies', *Grazer Linguistische Studien* 43: 195-203.

Šipka, M. (ed.) (1989) *I Romani Ćhib thaj Kultura* (Romani Language and Culture), Sarajevo: Institut za proučavanje nacionalnih odnosa.

Tebbutt, S. (2001) 'Germany and Austria: The "Mauer im Kopf" or virtual wall', in W. Guy (ed.) *Between Past and Future: the Roma of Central and Eastern Europe*, Hatfield: University of Hertfordshire Press.

UNCHR/OSCE (2000) *Update on the Situation of Ethnic Minorities in Kosovo*, 31 May.

## Notes

1   An alternative published figure for 1981 is slightly different: 168,197. The total for 1991 was 143,519.

2   Such as The Society Rom (1969) and the Rom Society in Niš (Report on Serbia 1998).

3   Other cultural initiatives included a bilingual children's paper – Ćhavrikano Lil – which appeared for a short time in 1985 and was revived in 1995.

4   Eventually voted out of office in the elections of September 2000.

5   Institute for Nationality Questions in Ljubljana.

6   Personal communication, Bojan Deklava, Department of Social Pedagogy, Ljubljuana.

7   Press release on the report made on behalf of the Slovene government to the UN Committee on Torture, 7 August 2000.

8   Janez Sarkez in Murska Sobota/Prekmurje (Fergus Smith, posting to Romnet, 20 October 1998).

9   During the 1990 referendum on independence the authorities in Dolenjska first tried to prevent Roma from voting and then set up a separate polling station because the gadje (non-Roma) refused to vote in the same place as the Roma (Fergus Smith, posting to Romnet, 5 April 1998).

10   Jožek Horvat-Muc, however, gives a brighter picture of the situation of the Roma in Slovenia in an interview with *Romani Patrin*, Oberwart, October 1999.

11   European Roma Rights Center (ERRC) letter to the Prime Minister of Slovenia, 7 November 1997 and ERRC Statement to OSCE, 19 November 1997. The following year farmers in Mlacevec, Dolenjska armed with pitchforks set up a 24-hour guard to stop Roma moving into their village (Fergus Smith, posting to Romnet, 20 October 1998).

12   In 1997 there was one school where Romani was taught.

13   Fergus Smith, posting to Romnet, 30 May 1998.

14   Only 25 per cent of the Romani children are at school.

15   The collection and sale of herbs is also a traditional activity.

16   One in four have only daily or seasonal employment, three in four depend upon welfare payments to survive.

17   These included associations in Novo Mesto, Murska Subota, Krsko, Puconci Srdica and Velenje.

18   They arrange annual events for International Romani Day (8 April) and in 1995 the first International Meeting took place in Murska Sobota. These meetings are devoted to culture, history, language and ethnology.

19   The group has written two of its own plays and performed in many towns in Slovenia and even in Hungary.

20   Personal communication, Sami Ališan.

21   Personal communication.

22  The Croatian Romani Party estimate is 40,000 (personal communication) but Mirjana Domini writes: 'the Gypsies state that there are 150,000 in Croatia' in her article 'Changes in the Republic of Croatia and the state of minorities', in *Nationen, Nationalitäten, Minderheiten* (Vienna: 1994).

23  There are also clans speaking Romani (*Bajash*) and Albanian (*Ashkalije*).

24  90 per cent are unemployed and 40 per cent live in poverty (personal communication, Kasim Cana). In spring 1999 one Rom was beaten up in Rijeka and another in Zagreb. The victim in Zagreb, Šemsa Sevčić, was twice sent home from hospital although he was later found to have two broken ribs. It has been said that because injuries that Roma receive are minor they do not report incidents to the police. A school in Medjimurje has a separate entrance for the Romani children.

25  Other Romani associations are in Rijeka, Zagreb (*Zajednica Roma Grada Zagreba* and *Ćidinipe Roma ani Zagreb*) and elsewhere. The organisations are keen on presenting a public image of the Romani population, its culture and history. For example, the Zagreb Association, led by Sami Ališan, organised a celebration of Romani International Day in 1993 in the Intercontinental Hotel, Zagreb, while in 1998 a memorial commemoration was held at the site of the Jasenovac concentration camp. Vid Bogdan is now president of an association representing the Romanian-speaking Roma.

26  *Pogrom*, Göttingen, March/April 1997, suggests 60,000. The 1991 figure is taken from Mönnesland's table included in a report from the Palme Center in Stockholm. His figures for some other republics differ slightly from those cited in this text.

27  Others have stayed on in Gorica. However, two Roma areas of Sarajevo were destroyed during the conflict (*Pogrom*, Göttingen, March/April 1997).

28  Other bodies are active in Kiseljak (*SAE Roma*), Visoko and Zenica.

29  For Klasnice, see *Washington Post*, 19 March 1994. See also *Pogrom*, Göttingen, March/April 1997.

30  A few bilingual (Macedonian and Romani) magazines have been published sporadically. The cinema in Shutka (see above in main text) often shows Indian films which have a special appeal to the Roma, and Indian videos sell well.

31  Attacks on Roma in spring 1999 were reported from the towns of Kočani and Vinica, where an eight-year-old Romani boy had been beaten by a teacher in late 1998. See also cases reported in the 1998 ERRC report.

32  One street trader, a woman, died while being arrested in Skopje in 1996 (ERRC statement to OSCE, 19 November 1997). Jasar Perusan's complaint that he had been twice beaten by the police in Stip in 1998 was dismissed by the court who refused to accept medical evidence and ruled that there was no evidence that his injuries had been inflicted by the police. On the day of his appeal to the civil court he was arrested early in the morning, beaten up again and prevented from attending the hearing (ERRC, letter to the Macedonian General Prosecutor, 31 March 1999).

33  According to the Romani economist Šenci Šajnov (Latham 1999: 219).

34  The language is currently taught in four primary schools in Skopje and one in Tetovo.

35  The *Phralipe* theatre group left Macedonia towards the end of 1990 when the Communist Party took over its premises and is now based in Germany (see *Frankfurter Rundschau*, 23 November 1990 and Tebbutt 2001).

36  K-FOR was the multi-national force replacing NATO after the cessation of hostilities in Kosovo.

37  Published in *Études Tsiganes* 28 (1982) and 29 (1983).

38  A figure of 600,000 cited by the Hamburg-based Roma National Congress seems exagger-

ated (e-mail to Romnet).

39  See Orhan Galjus article *Roma of Kosovo*, posted on the Web. Also Slobodan Berberski claimed that Roma had been threatened that unless they declared themselves as Albanians they would either be forced out of Kosovo or else Muslim imams would refuse to perform religious rituals, such as funerals, for them (Beberski 1984: 1344).

40  A poem by Haliti can be found in Hancock, I. *et al.* (eds) (1998) *Roads of the Roma*, Hatfield: University of Hertfordshire Press.

41  Personal communication, Imer Berisha.

42  Posting to bit.listserv.hungary, 31 July 1998.

43  Personal communication, Isuf Berisha.

44  Elaine Lafferty reported that Roma in Vucitrn had sprayed ROMI on their homes (Lafferty, E. (1999) *A Visit to a Devastated Land*, posted on Romnet, 19 June).

45  Ali and Shefki from Prizren had been street sweepers. On one occasion they were taken to Pusto Selo where they had to dig up ninety bodies which had been hastily buried in plastic and to load them onto lorries. They were made to work for five hours without a break until the job was finished. After the end of the air strikes the KLA told them they could stay in Prizren so that they could give evidence to the War Crimes Tribunal. Others were not to be so fortunate. For Gypsy gravediggers during the period of NATO hostilities, see also [London] *Standard*, 17 June 1999; *The Times*, 19 June 1999; *The Guardian*, 14 June 1999; *Daily Telegraph*, 22 June 1999.

46  Personal communication, Isuf Berisha.

47  'Sometimes entire Romani neighbourhoods have been burnt as was the case in Mitrovica' (OSCE 1999a); personal communication, Sevdiye Ahmeti.

48  *Infoblatt*, 9 August 1999.

49  J. Q., interviewed by ERRC, ERRC press statement, 9 July 1999.

50  Unarmed Albanian civilians openly looted Roma houses in the afternoon of 2 July in Moravska Street, Priština while four armed British K-FOR soldiers in a jeep watched from 50 metres away without intervening (interview with Kasum Cana, *Feral Tribune*, Split, 9 August 1999). British K-FOR soldiers are also reported to have ignored the expulsion of Roma and the burning of their homes in Graca (report of Theodor Fruendt for RomNews Network, 17 February 2000). Paul Polansky lists several similar incidents in a report by the *Gesellschaft für bedrohte Völker* organisation (see main text).

51  See also ERRC statement on Roma in Kosovo, 9 July 1999.

52  510 arrived in one boat on 29 June 1999 (*La Stampa*, 30 June 1999).

53  One hundred Roma drowned when a small fishing boat sank in August 1999 (*The Independent*, 27 August 1999).

54  This figure is based on estimates by *Matica Romska*, Alain Reyniers, Tatomir Vukadinović and Rade Uhlik (Report on Serbia 1998).

55  Report on Serbia (1998) and interview with Dragoljub Asković (Latham 1999: 205-26).

56  A report from Sabac in 1989 speaks of Romani street traders having their feet beaten by the police and then refused treatment by doctors. Other reports are witness to beatings and other mistreatment on the barest pretence.

57  For example, teenager Dušan Jovanović, who was beaten to death by skinheads in Belgrade in October 1997. A pregnant woman was earlier beaten up in Skadarska Street (ERRC statement to OSCE, 19 November 1997; *Globe and Mail*, 23 October 1997; *New York Times*, 22 October 1997). Dragoljub Acković's wife was twice attacked by skinheads in October 1999 (ERRC open letter to Minister of Internal Affairs of Serbia, 28 October 1999).

58  *Pogrom*, Göttingen, June/July 1993: 45.

59  This represents 0.2 per cent of those recorded as Roma in the 1981 census.

60 A day centre was set up in Kragujevac for children aged 3–7, funded by Open Society and a British organisation OKSOM, to teach the children Serbian and prepare them for primary school. The result was that these Romani children achieved very high results in the tests conducted prior to enrolment in primary school. We do not know of any other facility of this kind in Serbia (Report on Serbia 1998).

61 In April 1995, following an accusation that a young Montenegrin girl had been raped by a Romani youth, a mob burned down the houses in the Romani quarter of Danoilovgrad while the police looked on. As a result, Roma inhabitants were driven out of their homes and had to take refuge in a neighbouring town, Roma children lost their school places for lack of a permanent address, and Roma men were sacked for not reporting for work. Only one local person was charged in connection with the affair, for 'endangering public safety'. The charges against him were later dropped 'for lack of evidence' (Pleše 1998: 46-8).

62 The figure of 24,366 is found in some publications.

63 One instance of graffiti, saying 'Roma! Beat it from Serbia', stayed for almost a year on the wall of the National Bank of Yugoslavia in Novi Sad before it was removed.

64 Here, too, beatings by the police are alleged by Roma but official investigations are slow to start, long drawn-out and inconclusive.

65 In 1993 there were only forty-three Romani secondary school pupils and no Roma in higher education – this from a population estimated at well over 50,000.

66 Trifun Dimić is a leading figure in the cultural movement in Voivodina and Serbia. He has translated the New Testament, the Five Books of Moses and the Epic of Gilgamesh, apart from compiling a first reader in Romani *(Lil Ramosarimako)*.

67 The Voivodina Society for the Romani Language and Literature and Customs published a journal *Romologija* and a monthly magazine *Alav e Romengo*.

68 Classes are held for children and there are magazines and a TV programme which has been produced since 1992 in Novi Sad. The radio station there began Romani broadcasts in the same year and provision has grown to three hours on Saturday mornings.

69 The curriculum is based on that used for other minority languages such as Hungarian. Salaries of the teachers are paid by the government which co-financed the production of textbooks together with the municipality of Backa Palanjka.

70 Duijzings, English version (1992: 6, note 10).

71 For Ohrid, see *Tanjug*, 6 June 1990 and *BBC* SWB EE 0837 B/10, 8 August 1990.
   For the Egyptians generally, see Duijzings (1992) and Poulton (1995: 141–2).
   Mother Theresa was the most well-known of the Macedonian Egyptians.

72 The word 'Gypsy' itself (and its equivalents in other languages, such as *Gitan* and *gitano*) derive from 'Egyptian'.

# Brief notes on contributors

**Thomas Acton** is Professor of Romani Studies at the University of Greenwich. After running the first Gypsy Council caravan summer school near London in 1967 he completed a doctorate on Gypsy politics at the University of Oxford in 1973. He has subsequently published widely on Romani matters on which he is acknowledged as a leading international authority.

**Marian-Viorel Anăstăsoaie**, a sociology graduate of the University of Bucharest, gained an MA in History from the Central European University, Budapest. He is currently Fellow of the Civic Education Project, teaching anthropology and researching nationalism and ethnicity at the Faculty of European Studies, Babeş-Bolyai University, Cluj in Transylvania.

**Mít'a Castle-Kaněrová** was Senior Lecturer in Social Policy at the University of North London until 1999, when she left to work with Roma refugees returning to the Czech Republic as project manager with the International Organisation for Migration in Prague. Since 1998 she has been a Visiting Professor at Charles University in Prague.

**László Fosztó** is Fellow (Eastern Scholar) of the Civic Education Project, teaching anthropology in the Hungarian Language and Culture Department at Babeş-Bolyai University, Cluj in Romania, where he was born. Formerly he studied sociology at the Eötvös Loránd University, Budapest and holds an MA in Nationalism Studies from the Central European University, Budapest.

**Nicolae Gheorghe** is Advisor to the ODIHR Contact Point for Roma and Sinti Issues, part of the OSCE in Warsaw, and as such is the most senior Romani employee of any international organisation. Formerly he was researcher at the Institute of Sociology in Bucharest, Co-ordinator of the

Roma Center for Social Intervention and Studies (CRISS) in Romania and Vice-President of the International Romani Union.

**Will Guy** is Lecturer in Sociology at the University of Bristol, where he is a member of the Centre for the Study of Ethnicity and Citizenship. He has been actively involved with Czech and Slovak Roma since the early 1970s (see back cover).

**Ian Hancock** of the Romani Archives and Documentation Center is Professor of Linguistics at the University of Texas at Austin. He has been a prominent Romani scholar and activist for many years and was appointed by President Clinton to the US Holocaust Commission. Formerly he represented the International Romani Union at the United Nations.

**Valdemar Kalinin**, born in what is now Belarus, formerly served as a Soviet paratroop officer but now works as an Education Welfare Officer and interpreter with Roma refugees in London. He is a poet and translator, with Romani as his mother tongue, and recently translated gospels for Roma in Latvia, Lithuania, Belarus and Ukraine.

**Kristina Kalinina** is currently a student of theoretical physics at University College London. She also works with Roma children in the London Boroughs of Waltham Forest and Camden and, as a Romani speaker, interprets for refugee legal services as well as undertaking employment as a proof-reader.

**Donald Kenrick** is a writer, interpreter, occasional lecturer and consultant on Romani asylum seekers, following a long career in adult education. Formerly Secretary of the Gypsy Council, he is now an Honorary Vice-President of the Gypsy Council for Education. He holds a PhD for his study of a Romani dialect in Bulgaria, speaks Macedonian and Serbo-Croat and has travelled extensively in Yugoslavia, both before and after the recent turmoil.

**Ilona Klímová** is a PhD researcher at Trinity Hall, Cambridge, specialising in the Romani voice in world politics. She co-edited an influential Cambridge publication on Romani migration and has recently assisted the ODIHR Contact Point for Roma and Sinti Issues as well as contributing to a round-table on Romani migration at the Czech Academy of Sciences.

**Tracy Koci** is an Australian Rom, now living in London. After graduating from the University of South Australia she completed her MSc in Geelong,

427

Victoria. Together with her husband, the Albanian Romani artist Ferdinant Koci, she helped found the Vakthi Scheme Roma school in Baltez, Albania, and is now establishing a foundation to provide further village schools and a refuge in Tirana for Romani children.

**Martin Kovats** lived and worked in Hungary from 1991-93 before studying for an MA at the School of Slavonic and East European Studies (SSEES) in London. After completing his PhD in 1998 on Roma Politics in Hungary he undertook postdoctoral research on the Hungarian minority self-government system and most recently has been Research Fellow at the Centre for Russian and East European Studies at the University of Birmingham.

**Alaina Lemon** is Assistant Professor in Anthropology at the University of Michigan, having gained her PhD from the University of Chicago. Since 1988 she has conducted extensive archival and field research in Russia, amounting to four years in all, and in 1995–96 also worked in Prague for the Open Media Research Council as media analyst of Romani issues.

**Elena Marushiakova** and **Vesselin Popov** work at the Institute of Ethnography and Museum of the Bulgarian Academy of Sciences and founded the Society for Minority Studies *Studii Romani* after the events of 1989. They have written about Roma in Bulgaria and more recently in the Ottoman empire and are actively involved with a number of associations for Romani studies and various international research projects. In 1995 they created the Roma Heritage Museum Fund at the National Ethnographic Museum in Sofia, establishing the first museum-based exhibition on Gypsies in Bulgaria, and in 1998/1999 set up an exhibition in Budapest on Roma in Central and Eastern Europe.

**Lech Mroz** is Professor at Warsaw University, where he is Head of the Department of Ethnology and Cultural Anthropology. As well as publishing on Roma he also researches nomadic peoples in Siberia, India and elsewhere and lectures on ethnic relations in Europe and Asia. Since 1990 he has managed a research group studying Belarus, Lithuania, Ukraine and Siberia and acts as a consultant on Roma to institutions in Poland and abroad.

**Michael Stewart** spent 1984–5 in Hungary researching his PhD, including sixteen months living in a Romani settlement. Since then he has held teaching and research positions at Cambridge University, Nanterre, Paris, London School of Economics and University College London, where he is currently Lecturer in Anthropology. He teaches on Roma at the Central European

University in Budapest and in 1993 directed a BBC film about Czechoslovak Roma. At present he writing a book about the persecution of the Roma in the 1930s and 40s.

**Susan Tebbutt** is Senior Lecturer and Head of German at the University of Bradford. As well as publishing numerous articles on Roma and culture, she edited a 1998 volume *Sinti and Roma: Gypsies in German-speaking Society* and in 2000 was co-organiser of a conference on Roma. She has also written about aspects of German culture and society.

**Nidhi Trehan** is a PhD researcher at the London School of Economics examining the Romani civil rights movement. From 1996-97 she worked as a researcher and educational co-ordinator for the European Roma Rights Center (ERRC) in Budapest and previously undertook research on Romani children in the Hungarian educational system with a fellowship from the New York-based Institute for International Education.

**The University of Hertfordshire Press** is the only university press committed to developing a major publishing programme on social, cultural and political aspects of the Romani and other Gypsy people who migrated from north west India at the beginning of the last millennium and are now found on every continent. Recent titles include:

**A false dawn: my life as a Gypsy woman in Slovakia.**
*Ilona Lackova (Interface Collection, Volume 16)*
ISBN 1-902806-00-X.
The inspirational life story of a remarkable woman transcribed and edited from recordings in Romani. The author witnessed the destruction of the Romani culture, language and way of a life in the 'false dawn' of the post war Communist era.

**What is the Romani Language?**
*Peter Bakker et al (Interface Collection, Volume 21).*
ISBN 1 902806 06 9.

**The Roads of the Roma: the PEN Anthology of Gypsy writers**
*Edited by Ian Hancock, Siobhan Dowd and Rajko Djuric*
ISBN 0 900458 90 9,
Forty-three poems and prose extracts, most appearing in English for the first time, are arranged alongside an 800-year chronology of repression. What emerges is a portrait of a people struggling to preserve their identity in a hostile world.

**Gypsies under the Swastika**
*Donald Kenrick and Grattan Puxon (Interface Collection, Volume 8)*
ISBN 0 900458 65 8
The most comprehensive and up to date single volume account of the fate of the Gypsies in the Holocaus

**Gypsies in the Ottoman Empire; a contribution to the history of the Balkans**
*Elena Marushiakova and Vesselin Popov (Interface Collection, Volume 22)*
ISBN 1 902806 02 6.
The European part of the Ottoman Empire – the Balkans – has often been called the second mother
the Gypsies. From this region Gypsies moved westwards taking with them inherited Balkan cultural
and traditions.

**Moving On: The Gypsies and Travellers of Britain**
*Donald Kenrick and Colin Clark.*
ISBN 0 900458 99 2.
The only general introduction to the struggle of Gypsies to survive as a people in Britain today.

**Roma, Gypsies: Texts issued by International Institutions**
*Compiled by Marielle Danbakli (Interface Collection Volume 5).*
ISBN 1 902 806 15 8

For further details see: http://www.herts.ac.uk/UHPress/Gypsies.html

*Or request a copy of our catalogue from:*
University of Hertfordshire Press
Learning and Information Services
University of Hertfordshire
College Lane
Hatfield, AL10 9AB
Britain

Tel: +44 1707-284654
Fax: +44 1707-284666
E-mail: UHPress@herts.ac.uk